Chopin's Europe

Dedicated to the memory of
Pamela Załuski (1935–2003)

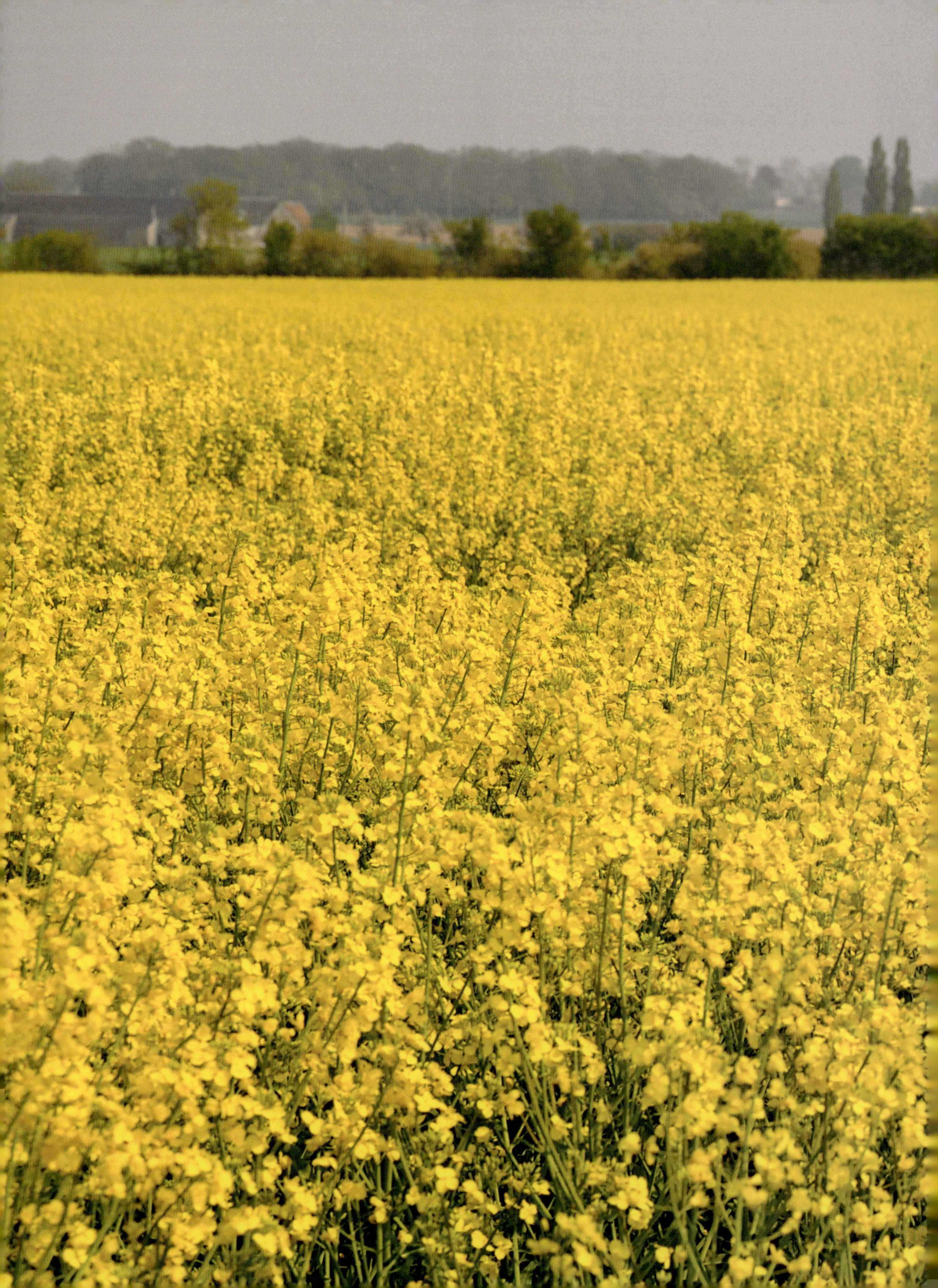

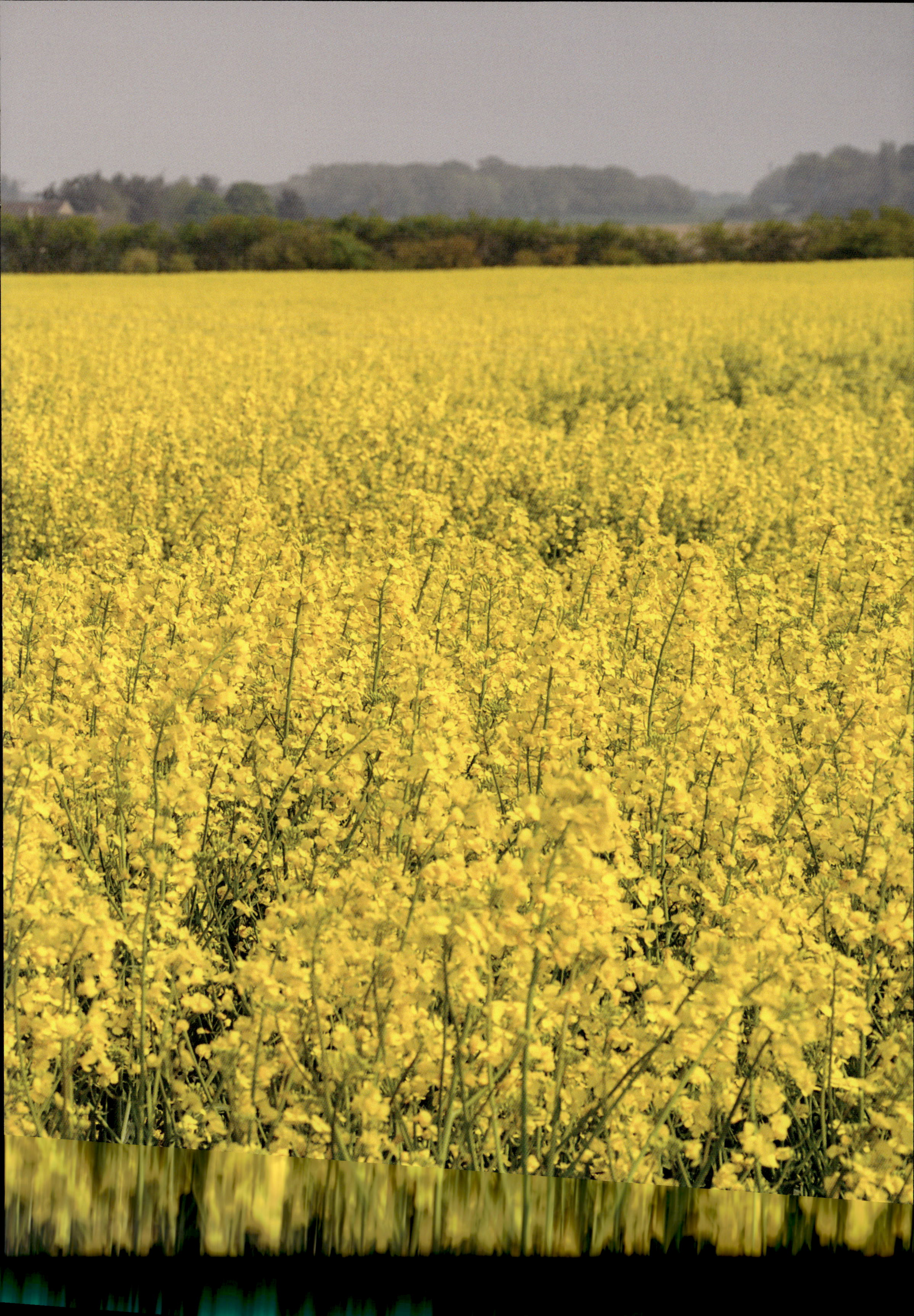

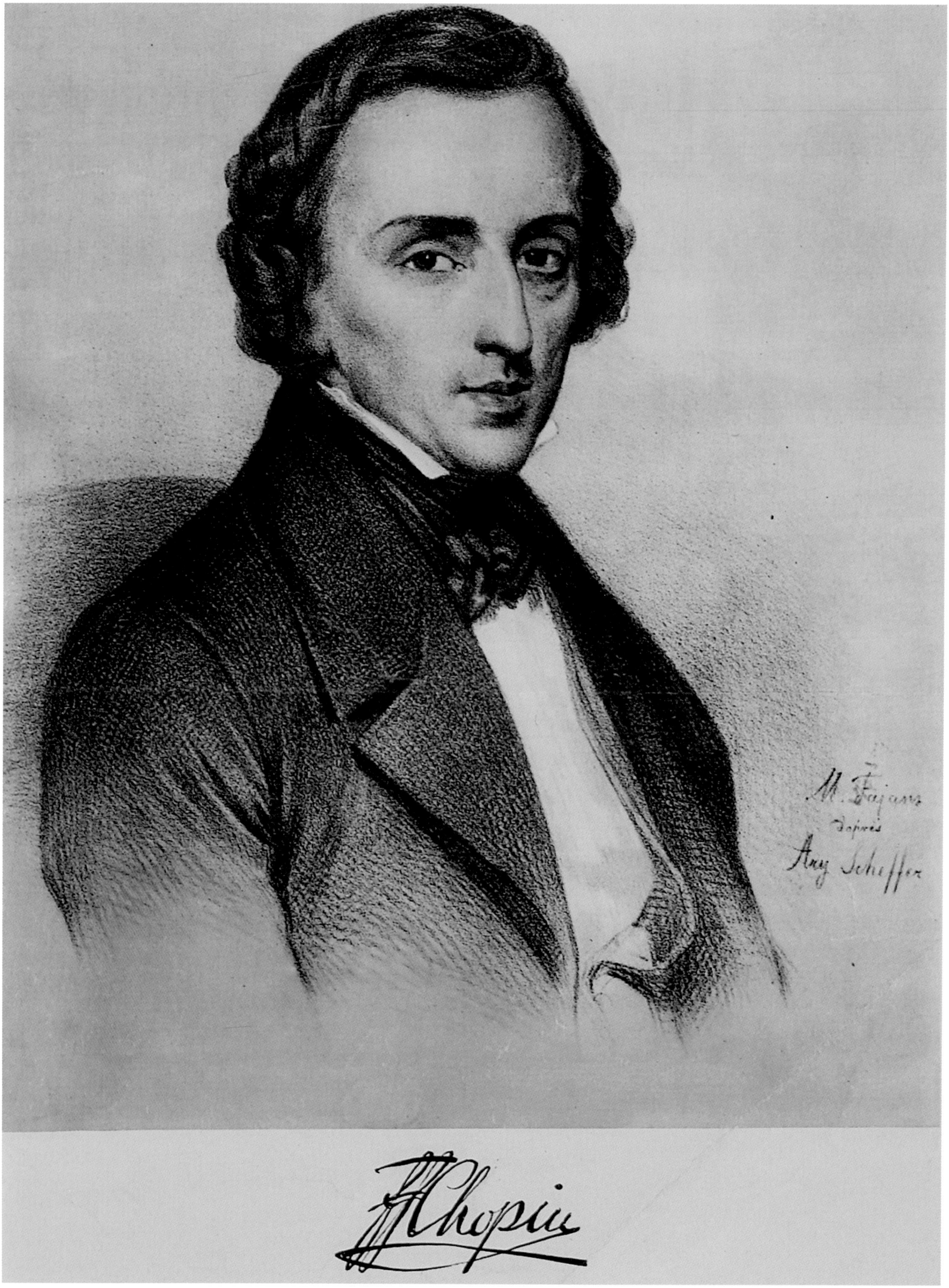
M. Fajans
d'après
Ary Scheffer
FChopin

Chopin's Europe

photographs
Hanna and Juliusz Komarnicki
text
Pamela and Iwo Załuski

Sport i Turystyka
MUZA SA

Cover design and graphic layout
Michał Piekarski

Editing
Barbara Czechowska

Proofreading
Jędrzej Burakiewicz, Paul Newbery

Photographs:
The Historical and Literary Society/Polish Library in Paris (Photo: Jean-Marc Moser)
[Towarzystwo Historyczno-Literackie/Biblioteka Polska w Paryżu]: p. 4, 268
LEEMAGE/EAST NEWS: p. 8
Jacek Tofil: p. 22
Janusz Leśniak: p. 49

The extracts of correspondence quoted in the book come from: *Chopin' Letters*, edited by Henryk Opieński, Dover Publications, New York 1988

Foreword by Martha Argerich translated by Hanna & Juliusz Komarnicki

The Authors, Photographers and Editors are most grateful to the Fryderyk Chopin Institute and the Fryderyk Chopin Society, Warsaw, The Historical and Literary Society/Polish Library in Paris [Towarzystwo Historyczno-Literackie/Biblioteka Polska w Paryżu], Chopin Museum, Marienbad, Regional Museum, Teplice, The Curator, Valldemosa Monastery, Majorca, Lady Margaret Torphichen, Calder House, Miss Jane Kellett, Edinburgh, Mr. Charles Maclean, Strachur House, Mrs.Valerie Mcintyre, White House of Milliken, Renfrewshire, Chaumet Jewellers, 12 place Vendôme, Paris, Sig. Carlo. Piccardi, Lugano, Sig. Dario Müller, Agno (Lugano), Mr. Michał Byczkowski, Warsaw, for their help and cooperation in making this book possible.

ISBN 978-83-7495-744-1

Sport i Turystyka – MUZA SA
Warsaw 2010

Contents

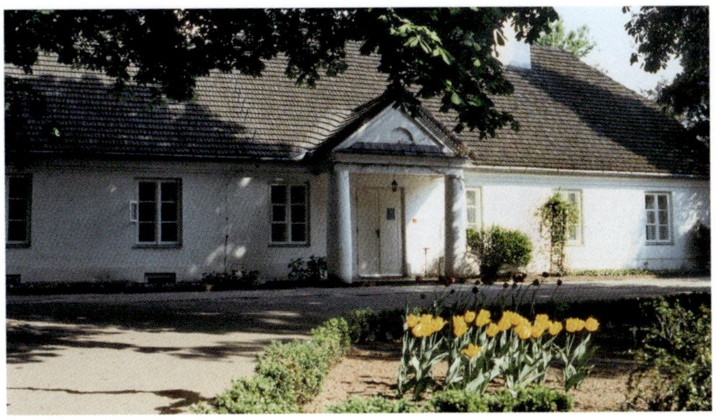
Poland 10

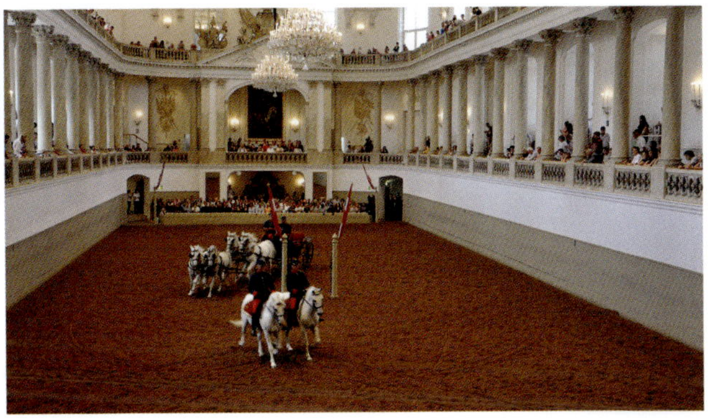
Vienna 52

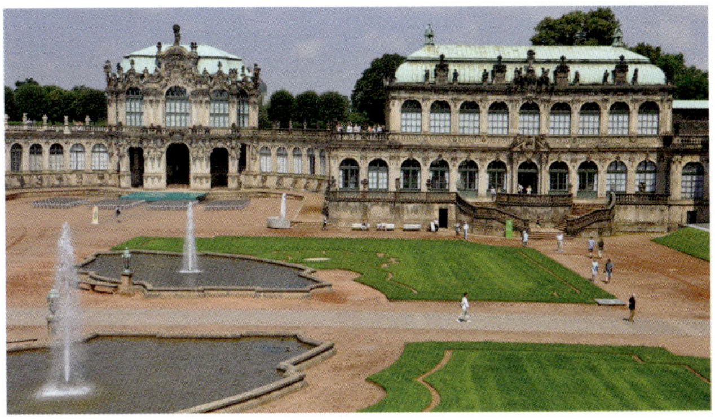
Bohemia & Saxony 76

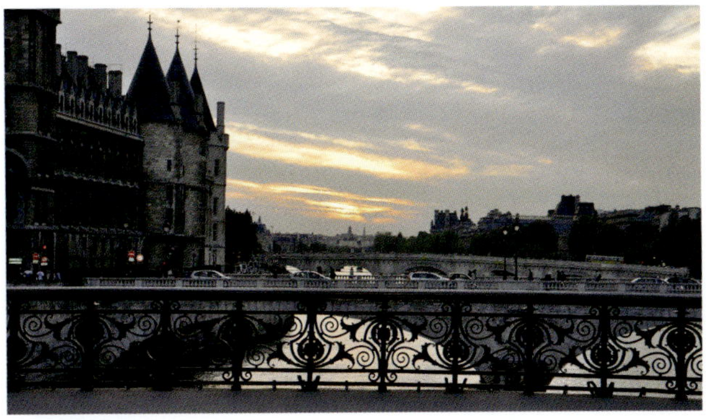
The Paris Years 122

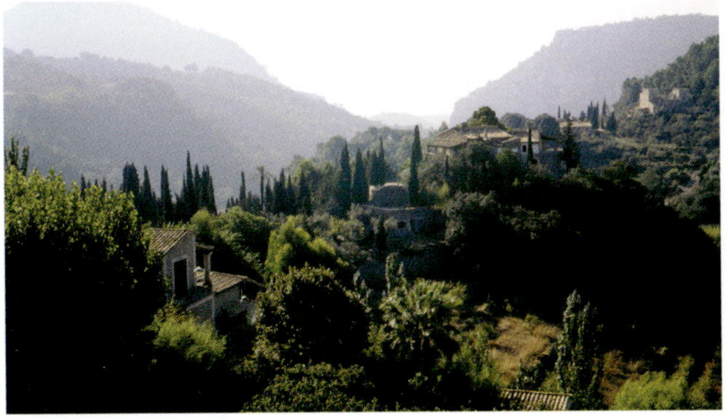
Majorca 162

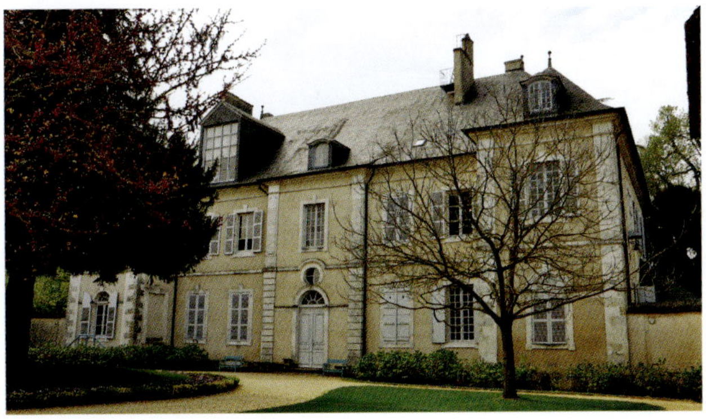
Nohant 186

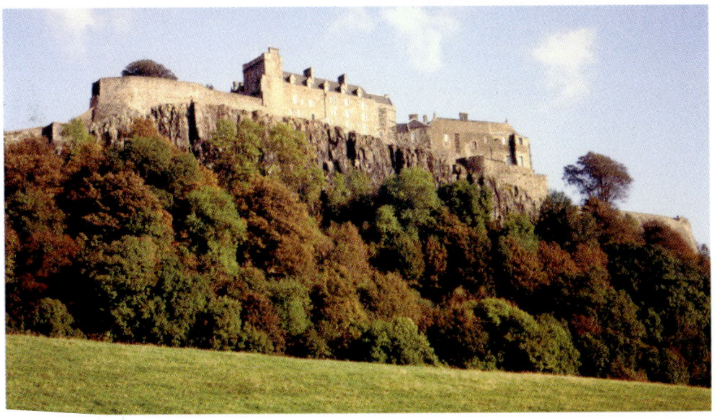

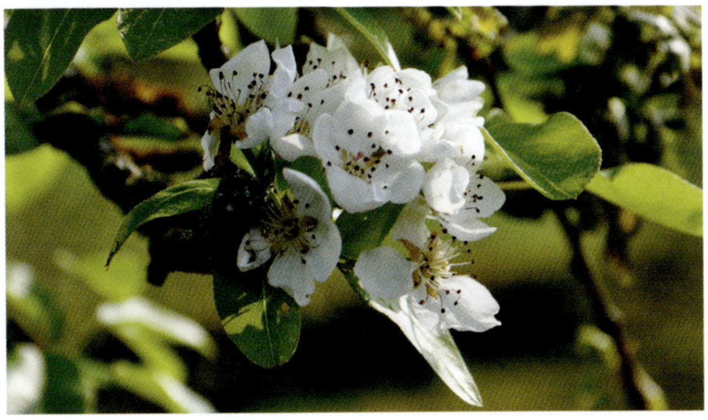
Epilogue 250

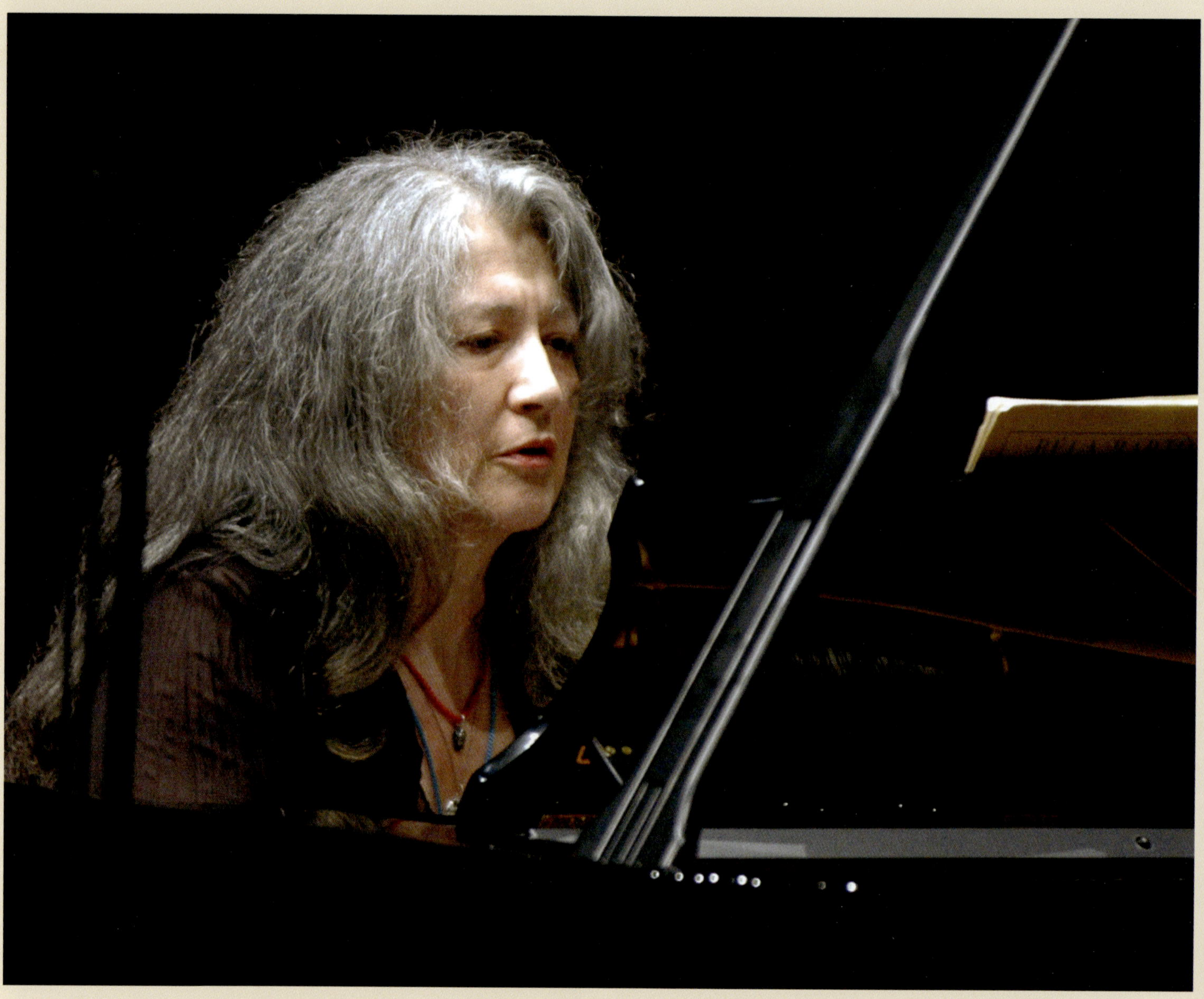

Connecting music with its place of creation can sometimes be evident, yet at other times it remains elusive.

This applies not only to composers but also to their interpreters.

The nomadic life of musicians, who often have to suffer many inconveniences and separations from their families, is also an opportunity for them to establish deep relationships with a disparate cross-section of people from a variety of countries, all of which leads to an enviable status of becoming true citizens of the world.

The authors and photographers of this book are to be congratulated for the excellent work, all of which adds a new dimension to our understanding of Chopin.

Martha Argerich

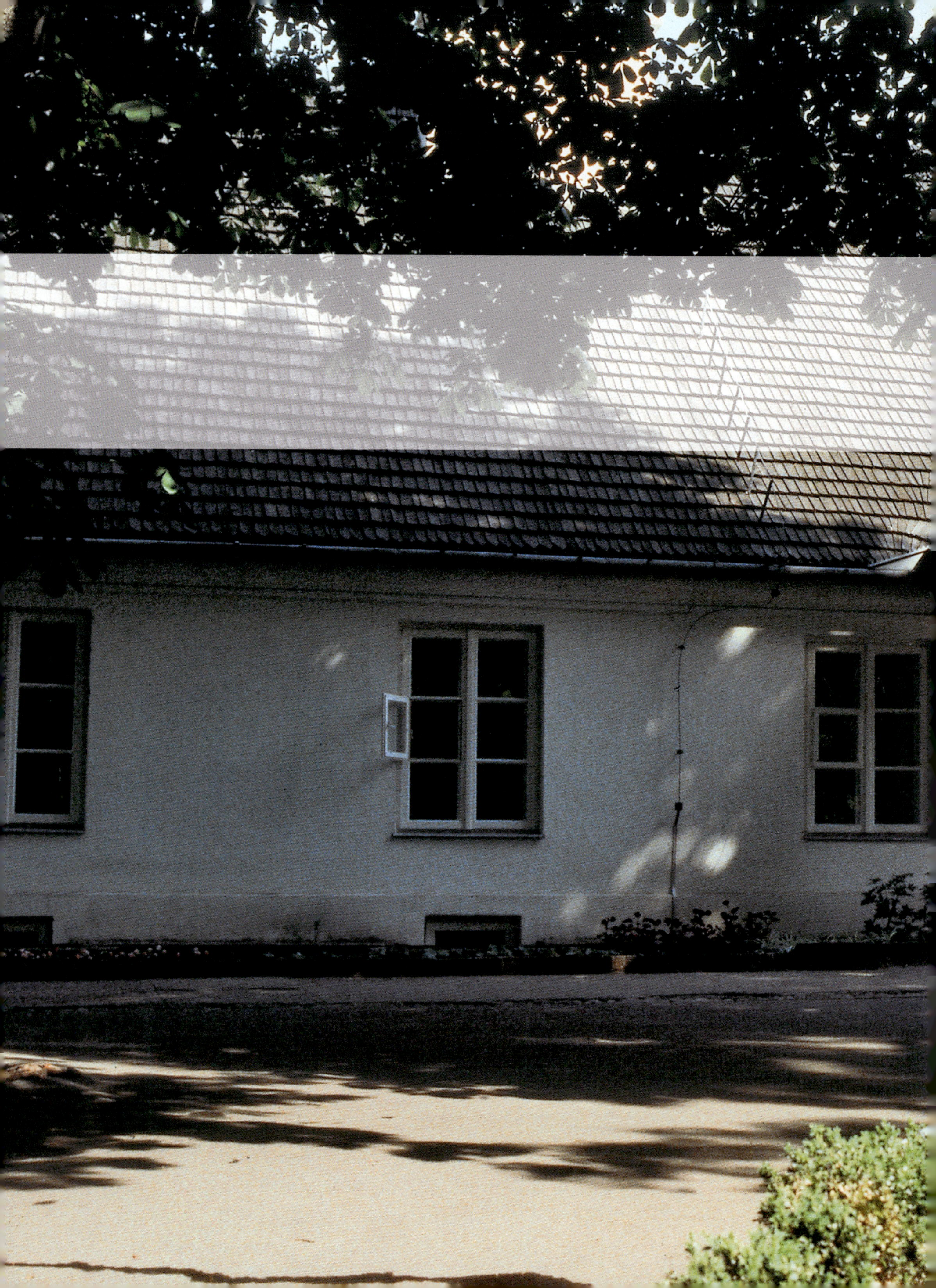

Poland

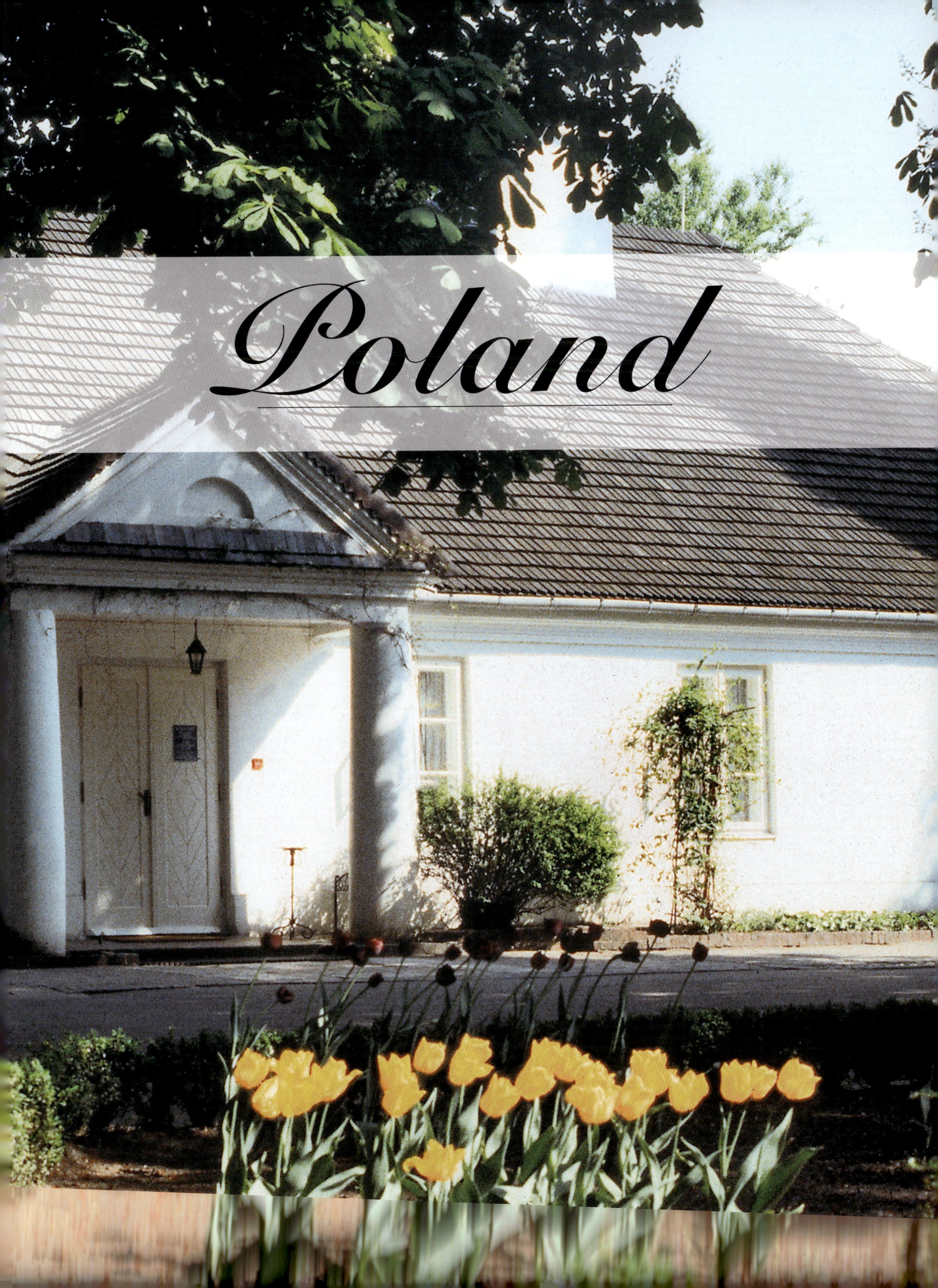

Fryderyk Franciszek Chopin was born in the Grand Duchy of Warsaw on 1 March (or 22 February) 1810. His parents were the French immigrant Nicolas Chopin and his Polish wife, Justyna Krzyżanowska, who were employed by Countess Ludwika Skarbek of Żelazowa Wola, to the west of Warsaw, as tutor to her three children and companion respectively. He was their second child, Ludwika being their first. On 23 April the baby was baptised at the church of St. Roch in Brochów. His godparents were Fryderyk and Anna (later Wiesiołowska) the two eldest of the Skarbek children.

That year Professor Samuel Linde, Rector of the Warsaw Lyceum, offered the post of French teacher to Nicolas Chopin, and in October the family moved to Warsaw. The Lyceum was housed in the Saxon Palace, off the Krakowskie Przedmieście, where an apartment went with the post. On 9 July 1811 the Chopins' third child, Izabela, was born, followed on 20 November 1812 by the sickly Emilia, who survived, despite expectations.

By the end of the year survivors from Napoleon's doomed Russian campaign appeared in Warsaw. In their wake came the Russians, and Tsar Alexander's brother, Grand Duke Constantine, was installed as Military Governor of Warsaw. In 1815 the Congress of Vienna created the Kingdom of Poland, with Tsar Alexander I as King. It was a period of stability; industry thrived, as did the arts, and piano factories and music shops appeared everywhere. The Chopins had a pianoforte, on which Justyna taught Ludwika, who in turn taught Fryderyk.

In 1817 the Lyceum was relocated to the Casimir Palace almost opposite, followed the following year by the University.

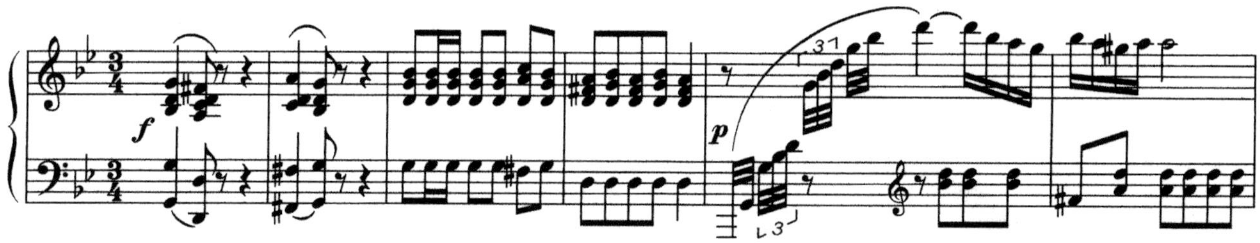

The Polonaise in G minor, Chopin's first published composition, written at the Casimir Palace when he was seven years old. He dedicated it to Wiktoria Skarbek, a cousin of Countess Ludwika Skarbek.

Brochów
The Parish Church of St. Roch (now St. John the Baptist) at Brochów where Nicolas Chopin and Justyna Krzyżanowska were married on 2 June 1806. The wedding was celebrated to the familiar sounds of the kujawiak and the oberek, the dances with which the region is particularly associated. On 23 April 1810 their only son and second child was baptised Fryderyk Franciszek in this same church.

← Żelazowa Wola
The west wing of the former Skarbeks' Manor at Żelazowa Wola, where Fryderyk Chopin was born on 1 March (or 22 February) 1810. The estate was a wedding present to the Chopins from Countess Ludwika Skarbek when Frycek's parents got married in 1806.

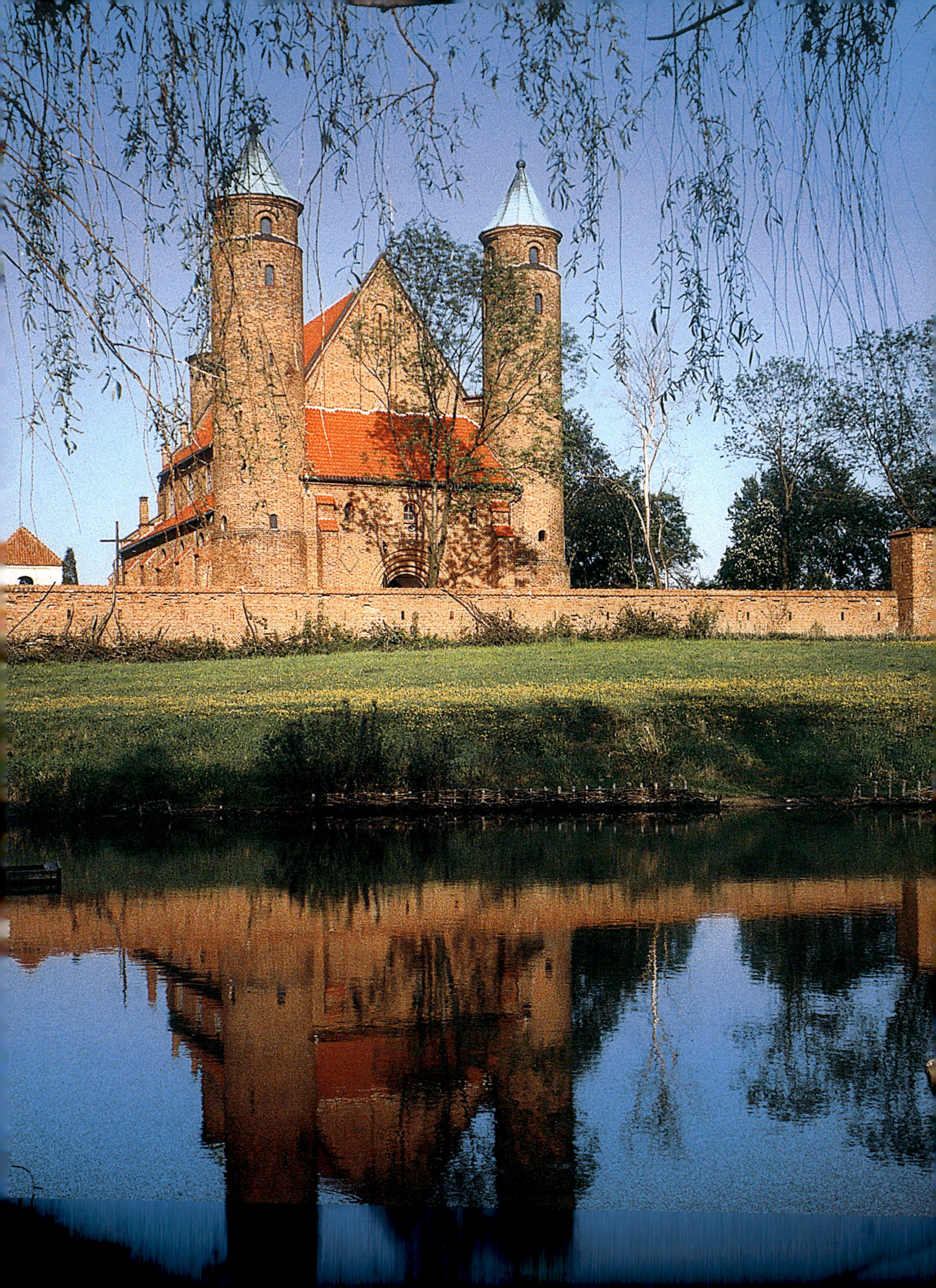

I could express my feelings more easily if they could be put into notes of music, but as the very best concert would not cover my affection for you, dear papa, I must use the simple words of my heart to lay before you my utmost gratitude and filial affection.

Fryderyk Chopin's name day card
to his father (6 December 1818)

Fryderyk was now also being taught the piano by his mother, and he particularly loved the Polonaises of Michał Kleofas Ogiński, the first ones composed to be listened to, rather than for dancing. Shortly afterwards, at the age of seven, he wrote the Polonaise in G minor (BI 1), his first privately published composition, in the same style.

Nicolas and Justyna then engaged Wojciech Żywny as piano teacher for Fryderyk, and very soon he was playing at soirées throughout Warsaw, and the word spread of a little "Polish Mozart" in the city. He played at Countess Zamoyska's at the Błękitny Palace, at the French Theatre in the Radziwiłłowski Palace, at the Benevolent Society Building in the Krakowskie Przedmieście, and at the residences of the cream of Polish aristocracy.

Grand Duke Constantine sent for Fryderyk to his residence at the Belweder Palace to practise French with his son, Paul; but hearing Fryderyk improvising at the piano, the Duke was so impressed that he gave him an open invitation to visit at any time and play with Paul and Alexandrine, the daughter of Paul's tutor, the Comte de Moriolles: Fryderyk, Paul and "Moriolka" were the same age. Fryderyk's very close friendship with Moriolka continued until well into his teens.

In 1821 Żywny admitted that he could teach Fryderyk no more and resigned, although he remained a close friend of the family. In April 1821 Fryderyk composed his Polonaise in A flat (BI 5) for his former teacher's sixty-sixth birthday.

At thirteen Fryderyk started at the Lyceum, where he made many friends, some of whom invited him to spend summer holidays at their homes. Among these was Dominik Dziewanowski, whose family estate was at Szafarnia, and Jan Białobłocki at Sokołowo. During his stays Fryderyk was introduced to the sound of the Mazurka on its home ground and picked up its subtle modal and harmonic nuances, which he later made his own. At Szafarnia, with Dominik's help, Fryderyk edited a whimsical local paper based on the format of the Warsaw Courier, which he then sent home as a newssheet. Four "editions" of the "Szafarnia Courier" were "published". As reporter "Mr Pichon" (an anagram of Chopin) Fryderyk reported anything that took his fancy with his customary sense of humour.

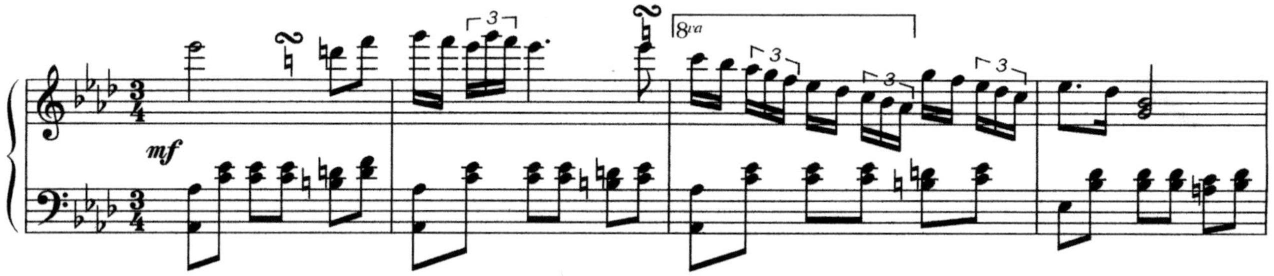

Eleven-year-old Chopin dedicated his Polonaise in A flat to his beloved teacher, Wojciech Żywny.

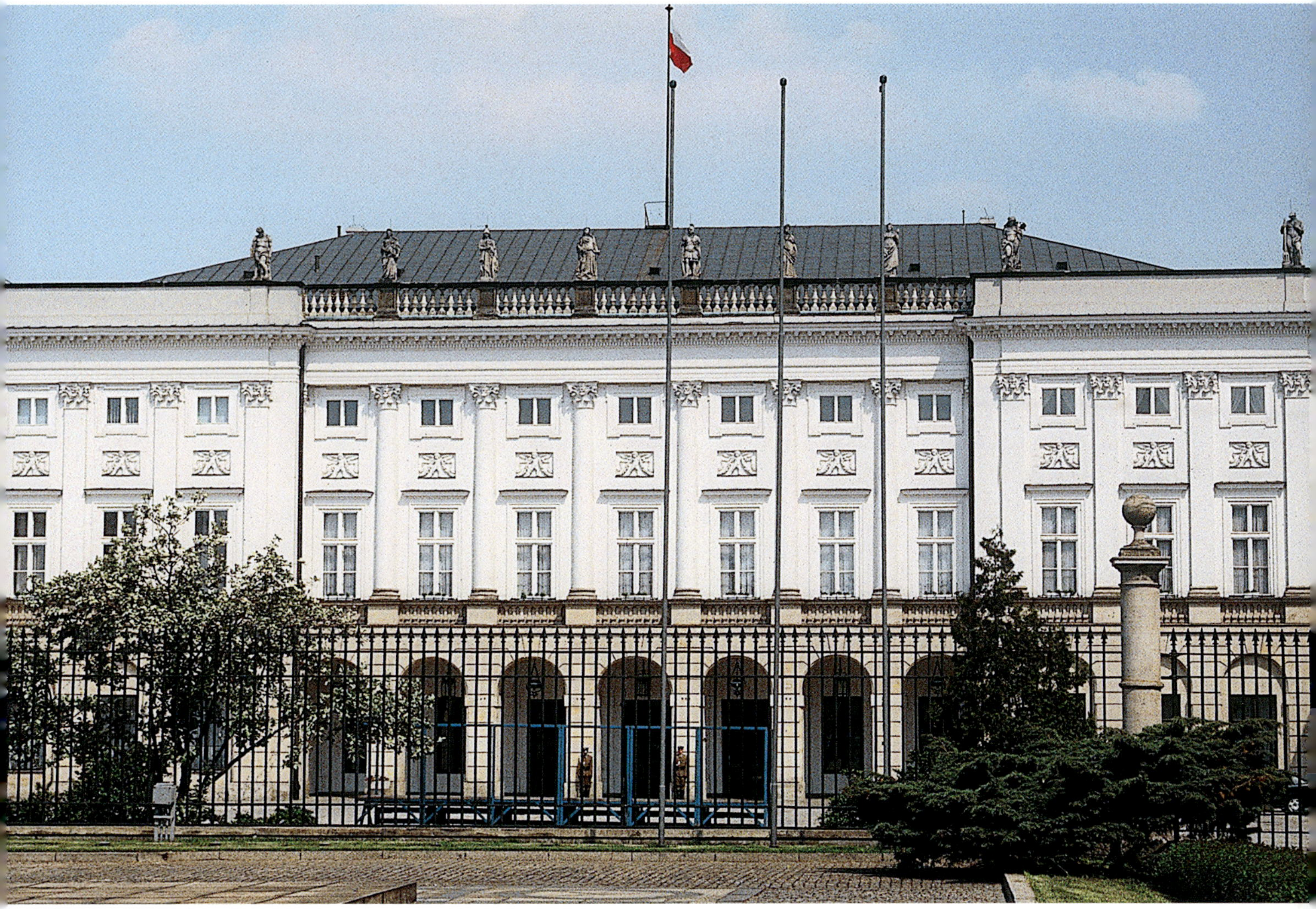

Warsaw
The Radziwiłłowski Palace, today the Presidential Residence, where eight-year-old Frycek Chopin gave his first public concert in what was then the French Theatre, with a performance of Gyrowetz's Piano Concerto in E minor.

On 15 August there was a musical gathering at Szafarnia of a score or so of miscellaneous persons. Mr Pichon figured in the programme with a piano concerto by Kalkbrenner. This did not have as much effect on the miscellaneous persons as the żydek performed by the same Mr Pichon.

"Szafarnia Courier" Issue No 2, 19 August 1824

Dominik's Aunt Ludwika took the boys on numerous outings, including at least two to Golub and Dobrzyń, where they visited the medieval Castle perched on its hill. The two towns were situated on either side of the River Drwęca, the former in Poland and the latter in Prussia. Fryderyk also visited Toruń, where he stayed at the Fenger Palace, the home of Jakub Fenger, Countess Ludwika Skarbek's father.

In 1825 Tsar Alexander came to Warsaw to open the Seym. He visited the Lyceum, where Fryderyk formally presented him with a set of dances – now lost – for the Tsarina. The Tsar also attended a concert at the Augsburg Evangelical Church of the Holy Trinity, off Królewska Street, at which Fryderyk improvised on the aeolomelodicon, a hybrid piano-harmonium invention, with various special effects and pedals, of the kind that were in fashion at that time. The delighted Tsar presented him, and the manufacturer, Brunner, with a diamond ring each. Fryderyk also regularly played the organ at the Church of the Visitation, next to the Casimir Palace, whenever the boys of the Lyceum attended Mass there.

I am appointed organist to the Lyceum... the most important person in the whole Lyceum after his reverence the priest. Every Sunday I play the organ for the Wizytki and the others sing.

Fryderyk Chopin to Jan Białobłocki
(Warsaw, November 1825)

Tuberculosis was one of the banes of nineteenth century Warsaw, and both Emilia and Fryderyk showed symptoms. Taking the waters was considered beneficial, so the Chopins and the Skarbeks decided to make up a party to spend the summer holidays of 1826 at the spa of Duszniki, travelling in three separate groups; Ludwika Chopin went with Fryderyk and Prakseda Skarbek and their seven-year-old son,

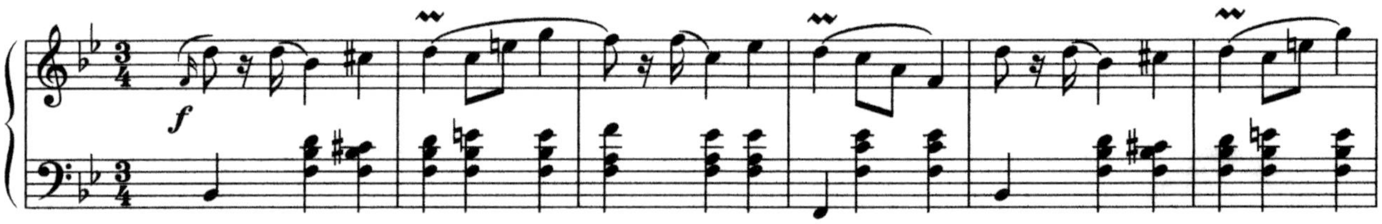

Chopin's Mazurka in B flat of 1825 was published without an opus number; it uses the Lydian mode, with the sharpened 4th, a common device in Mazovia.

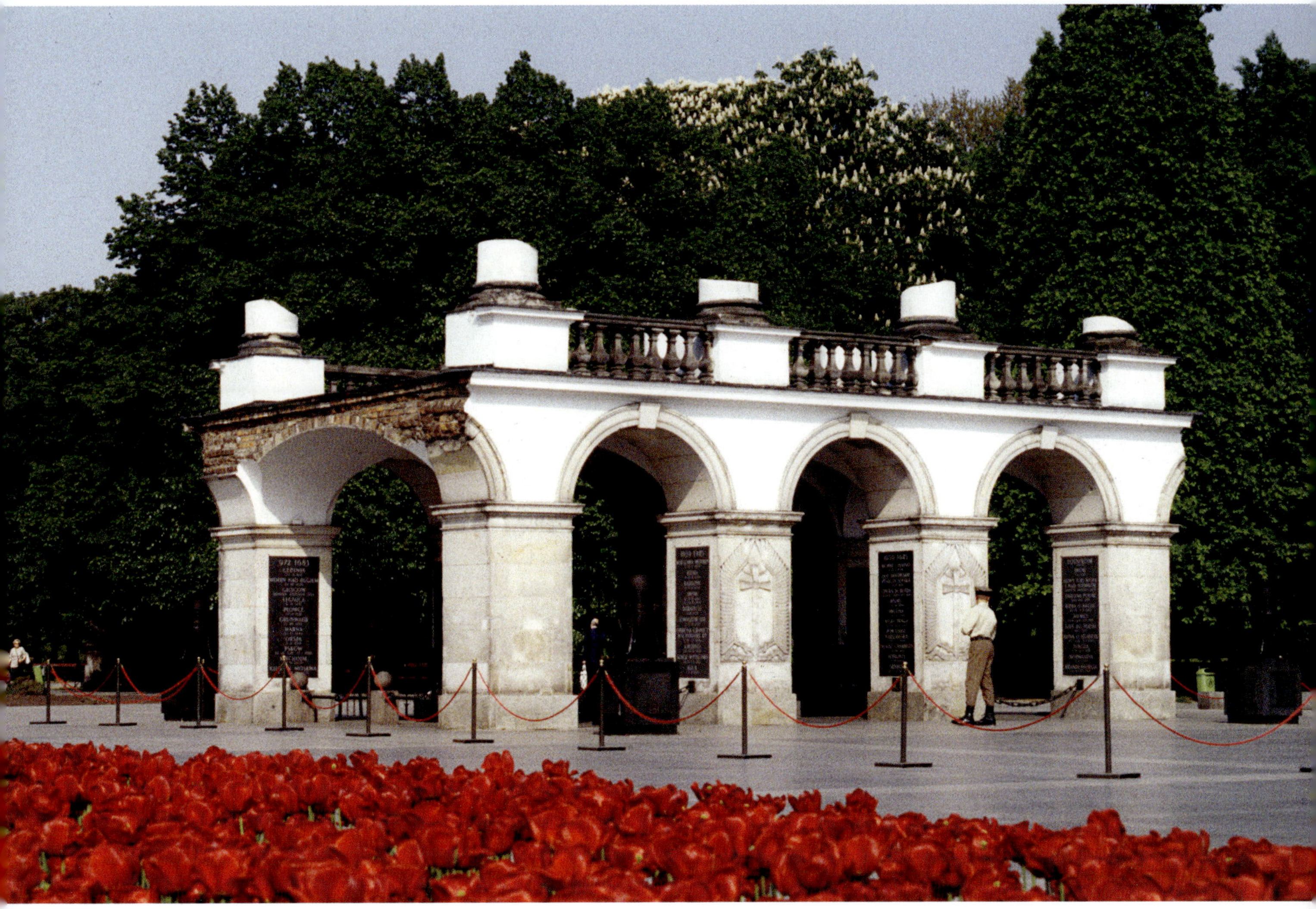

Warsaw

All that remains today of the Saxon Palace, Frycek's first home in Warsaw, is now the memorial to the Unknown Soldier. Nicolas Chopin accepted the offer to fill the temporarily vacant post as teacher of French at the Lyceum, which was housed there. An apartment on campus went with the post.

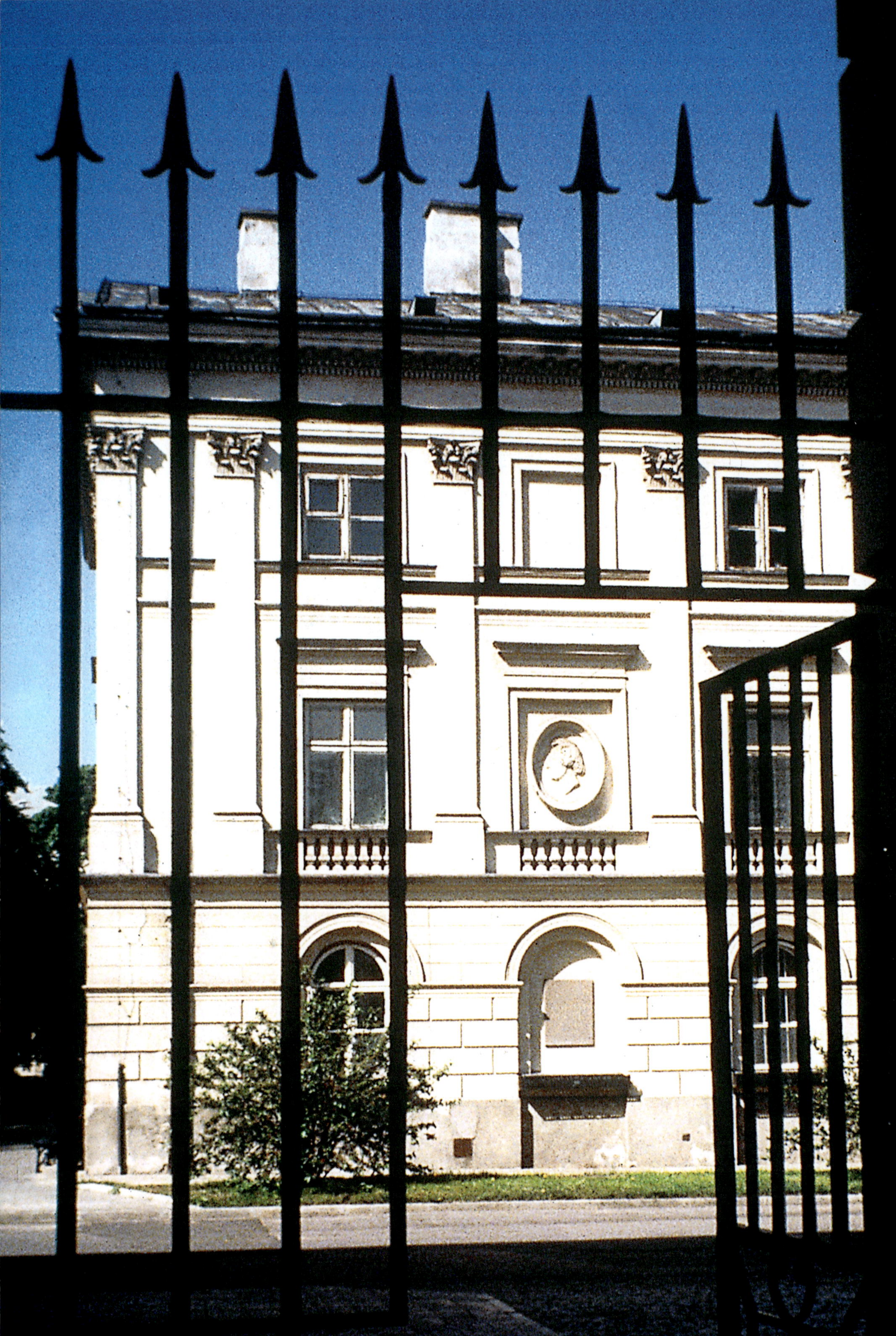

Józio, while Countess Ludwika Skarbek, also a tuberculosis sufferer, and Emilia, followed soon after.

Fryderyk had to wait until his final school examinations. The evening before his departure, he and his friend, Wilhelm Kolberg, attended Rossini's *The Thieving Magpie* at the opera, after which Fryderyk wrote his Polonaise in B flat minor as an "adieu" to his friend.

On 28 July Fryderyk and his mother set off by diligence from the Post Office in Kozia Street. They passed through Sochaczew, Łowicz and Kalisz, and crossed the border into Prussia at Biskupice – where there was an old timber church – and continued on to Wrocław, where they stayed at the *Golden Goose* in Olawska Street. They arrived at Duszniki on 3 August, and lodged at Burgels Hof. The spa was beautifully laid out, and criss-crossed with walkways lined with flowerbeds.

The days were spent walking and socialising to the accompaniment of the spa wind band, or taking refreshments at the popular Bear Inn. The waters were taken twice a day at the wells, where attendant girls waited on a podium with safety railings round it to scoop the water in a jug at the end of a pole from a deep hole in the ground, where the steaming water could be seen several feet down. For the more adventurous, there were walks in the hills or on the banks of the River Bystrzyca. The town boasted a paper mill, which was open to the public, and in the Strążyska Valley Mendelssohn's (an uncle of the composer) iron foundry spewed black smoke over the hills. Fryderyk also climbed the 150 steps up the Einsiedelei Hill to the Hermitage, which consisted of one room, a chapel and a small vegetable garden, occupied by a priest.

You go to the top of one of the highest hills near here, and climb about 150 steps in a straight line, cut out of the stone almost vertically, to the Hermitage, from where there is a splendid view.

Fryderyk Chopin to Wilhelm Kolberg
(Duszniki, 18 August 1826)

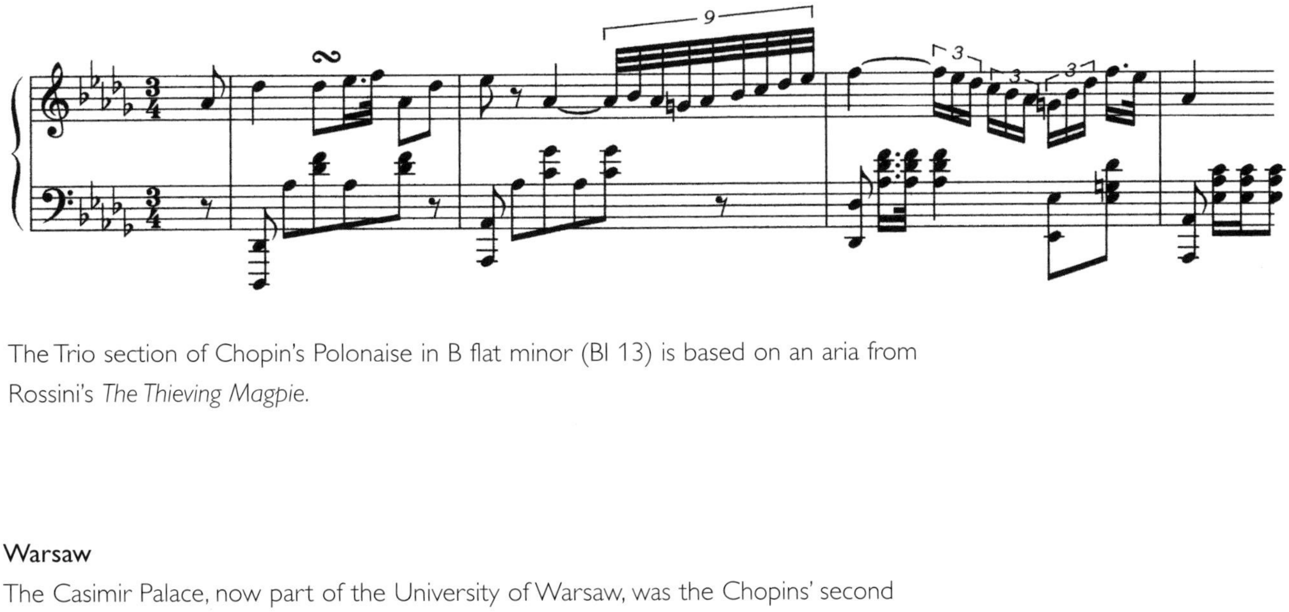

The Trio section of Chopin's Polonaise in B flat minor (BI 13) is based on an aria from Rossini's *The Thieving Magpie*.

Warsaw

The Casimir Palace, now part of the University of Warsaw, was the Chopins' second home in Warsaw. Their apartment was on the second floor of the south wing. The move took place in 1817 when Grand Duke Constantine took over the Saxon Palace for military purposes, and the Lyceum had to be relocated. In the centre of the picture can be seen the plaque commemorating Chopin's stay there.

Fryderyk's allocated well was the Lau-Brunn, where the attendant was a pretty Czech girl called Libusza. Her father worked at the foundry, her mother was dead, and she acted as housewife and mother to her four younger siblings. She was popular with everyone, including the starry-eyed Fryderyk, who called on her at home several times. One day there was an accident at the foundry, and Libusza's father was crushed to death by a roller, so Fryderyk arranged a concert for the orphans' benefit. The very successful event took place in the small manor in the centre of the spa on 11 August, with a repeat performance on 16 August. The children's plight was addressed: Libusza went to stay with an aunt in Prague, while the other children were taken into care by the council. Fryderyk's philanthropy was reported in the Warsaw press.

On 11 September Fryderyk and his mother set off for home. After a passing visit to his godmother Anna Wiesiołowska (née Skarbek) and her family at Strzyżewo, Fryderyk called on the cello-playing Prince Antoni Radziwiłł, his wife, Princess Ludwika, of the Prussian Royal family, and two of their daughters, Wanda and Eliza, the former a pianist and the latter an artist, whose famous sketch of Fryderyk at the piano was drawn on this occasion. Fryderyk had an open invitation to Antonin, the Prince's timber hunting lodge in the forests to the south of Poznań. After the Congress of Vienna, his father-in-law, King Friedrich Wilhelm III, appointed him Governor of the Duchy of Poznań.

That autumn Fryderyk enrolled at Józef Elsner's Warsaw Conservatory of Music. His circle of friends now included pianist Julian Fontana, Jan Matuszyński, Wilhelm Kolberg, who lived downstairs, Konstanty Pruszak, whom Fryderyk visited for a summer of fun and games with a crowd of young people at his parents' estate at Sanniki in 1828, and Tytus Woyciechowski, who had an estate at Poturzyń, which Fryderyk visited on one memorable occasion in 1830. They all patronised in equal measure the opera in Krasiński Square, or Warsaw's cafés; the Dziurka and the Honoratka in Miodowa Street, and the Mrs Brzezińska's in Kozia Street.

Fryderyk's girlfriend during his teenage years was Alexandrine "Moriolka" de Moriolles, with whom he used to play when they were children. One of their preferred meeting places was the Park behind the University, which had by this time become the Botanical Gardens.

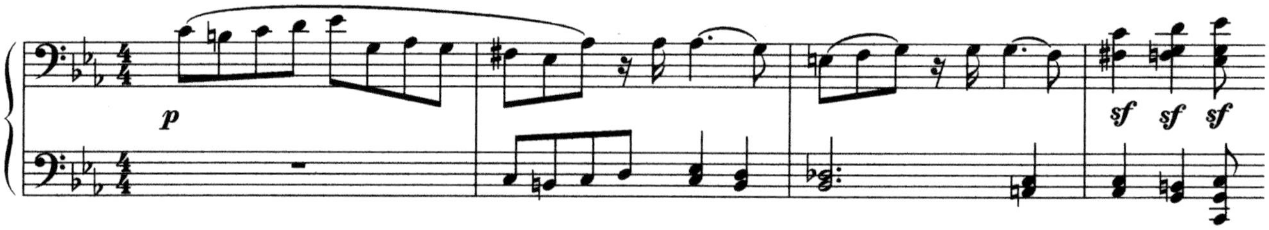

Chopin dedicated his first Piano Sonata to Elsner, but later withdrew this as he did not consider it to be good enough.

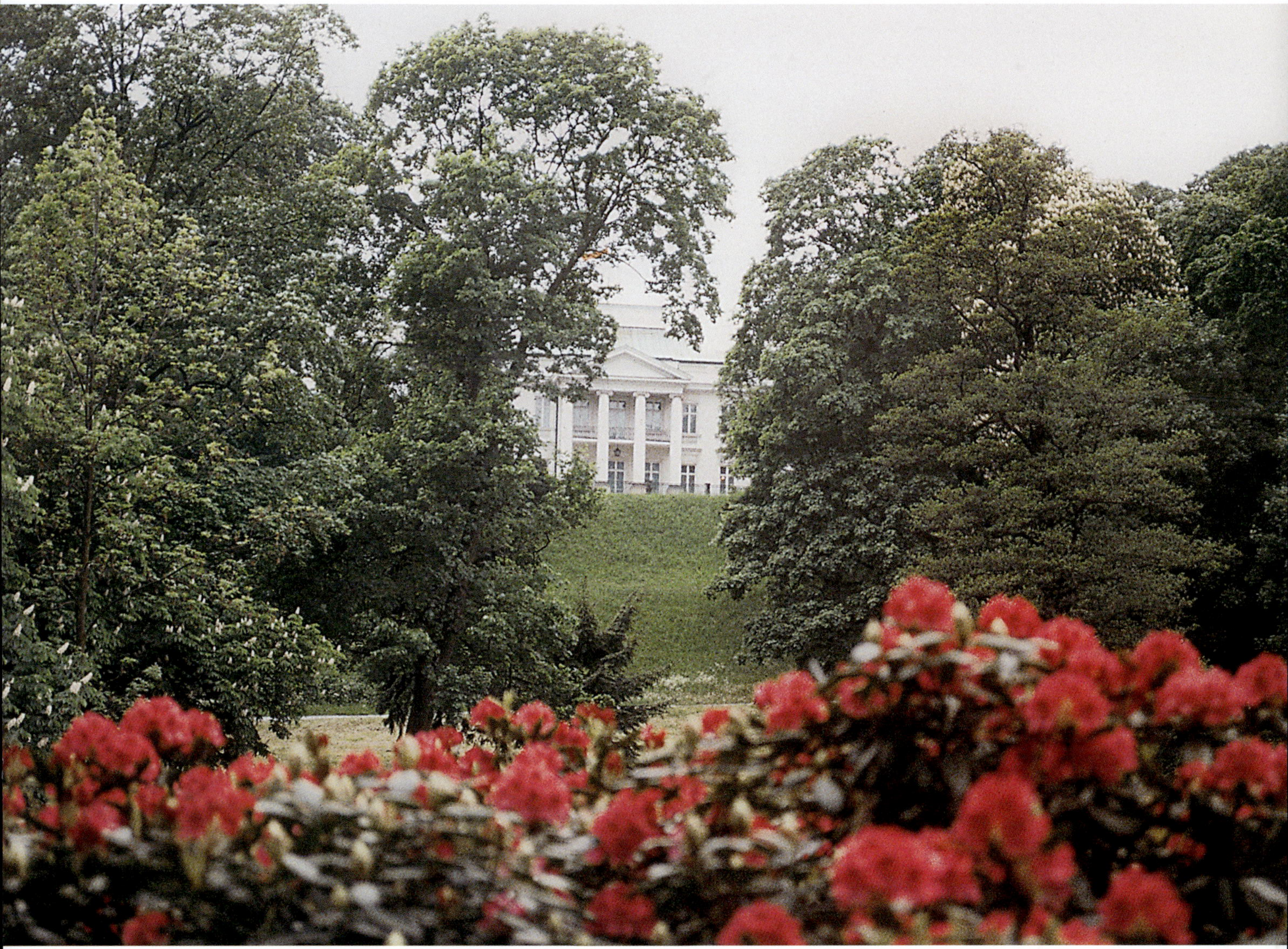

Warsaw

The Belvedere Palace, where Frycek often came as a child to play here for Grand Duke Constantine, who would send his carriage to fetch him to the Palace, initially to practise French with his son Paul. However, after having heard Fryderyk improvising at the piano, the Duke was overwhelmed, and his visits became a regular occurrence.

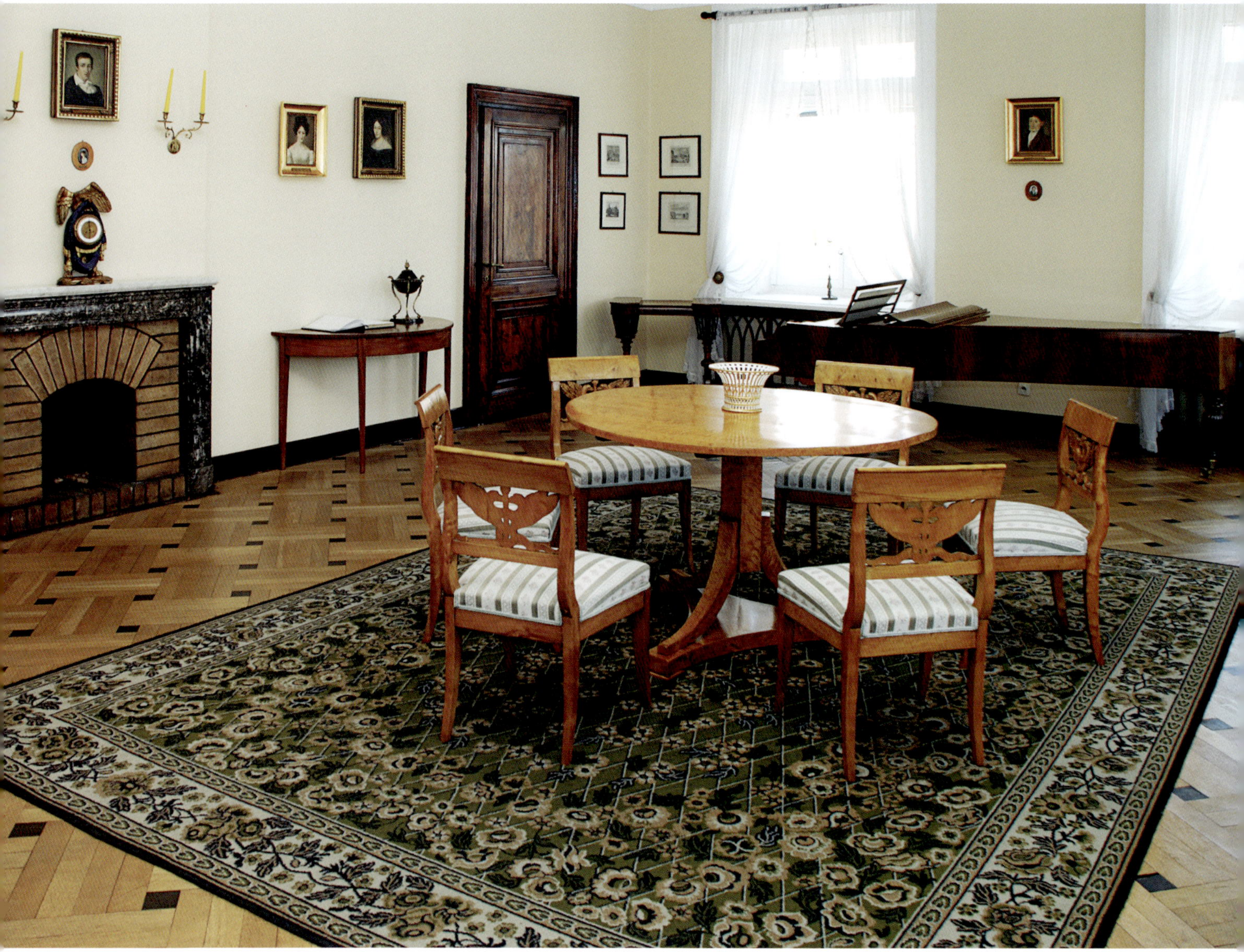

Warsaw

Shortly after the death of Fryderyk's 14-year-old sister Emilka in April 1827, the Chopin family moved to a much larger apartment on the second floor of the Krasiński Palace off the Krakowskie Przedmieście. This was to be Fryderyk's last home in Poland before his final departure in November 1830. Today the apartment has become one of Warsaw's Chopin museums.

If you knew what changes there are in our Botanical Garden; they have put such flower beds, paths, plantations, shrubs and so on that it's a pleasure to go in, especially as we have a key.

Fryderyk Chopin to Jan Białobłocki (Warsaw, June 1826)

In 1827 Emilia died of tuberculosis, aged 13, and the Chopins moved to a larger apartment in the Krasińki Palace. There Fryderyk wrote his Variations on Mozart's *Là ci darem la mano* for piano and orchestra, Op. 2 – his first attempt at scoring for orchestra. That same year Count Ksawery Zboiński, Emilia's godfather, proposed that Fryderyk should join him for a summer trip in his carriage to his extended family's estates in eastern Prussia. Another invitation to the region came from the violinist, composer and patron of music, Count Antoni Sierakowski to his estate at Waplewo, near Malbork. The round tour included Kowalewo, Płock on the River Vistula, Rościszewo, and Kikół Palace, with its lake. At the bridge over the River Drwęca at Lubicz, which was the Prussian border, they turned north to the Manor at Turzno, and on to Kozłowo, situated on the banks of the River Wda. On 9 August, after nearly a fortnight, the Zboiński carriage arrived in Gdańsk. The party put up at the *Drei Mohren hotel*, where they were met by Count Antoni Sierakowski, who had come over from Waplewo. After five days, during which they visited Count Antoni's father's house in Sopot, as well as all the sights of Gdańsk, Fryderyk went on to Waplewo for a stimulating week making and talking music with one of east Prussia's premier patrons of music. Fryderyk then spent a further five days in Gdańsk with Count Ksawery before returning to Warsaw.

In the autumn of 1828, Fryderyk accompanied Warsaw University Professor Feliks Jarocki to an international Congress of Naturalists in Berlin. Fryderyk found the Congress boring, but the Prussian capital's concerts and the opera gave him some relief. On the way back from Berlin the diligence passed through Sulechów, and stopped at the Post Stage in the Market Square. As there were no fresh horses available, the driver announced a delay. The postmaster invited the passengers to refreshments at his house, where there was a piano, at which Fryderyk, to kill time, sat down and improvised a medley of Polish airs for the benefit of the local Germans.

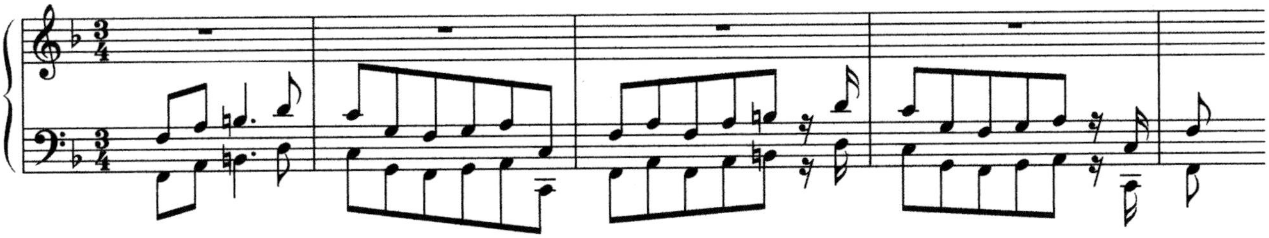

Chopin dedicated his *Rondo à la Mazur*, Op. 5 to Alexandrine de Moriolles, his girlfriend of his teenage years.

→ **Warsaw**

The Chopin Memorial in the Łazienki Gardens was created by the Polish sculptor and painter Wacław Szymanowski (1859–1930). It was erected in 1926, and destroyed by the occupying Germans in 1940. It was reconstructed in 1958.

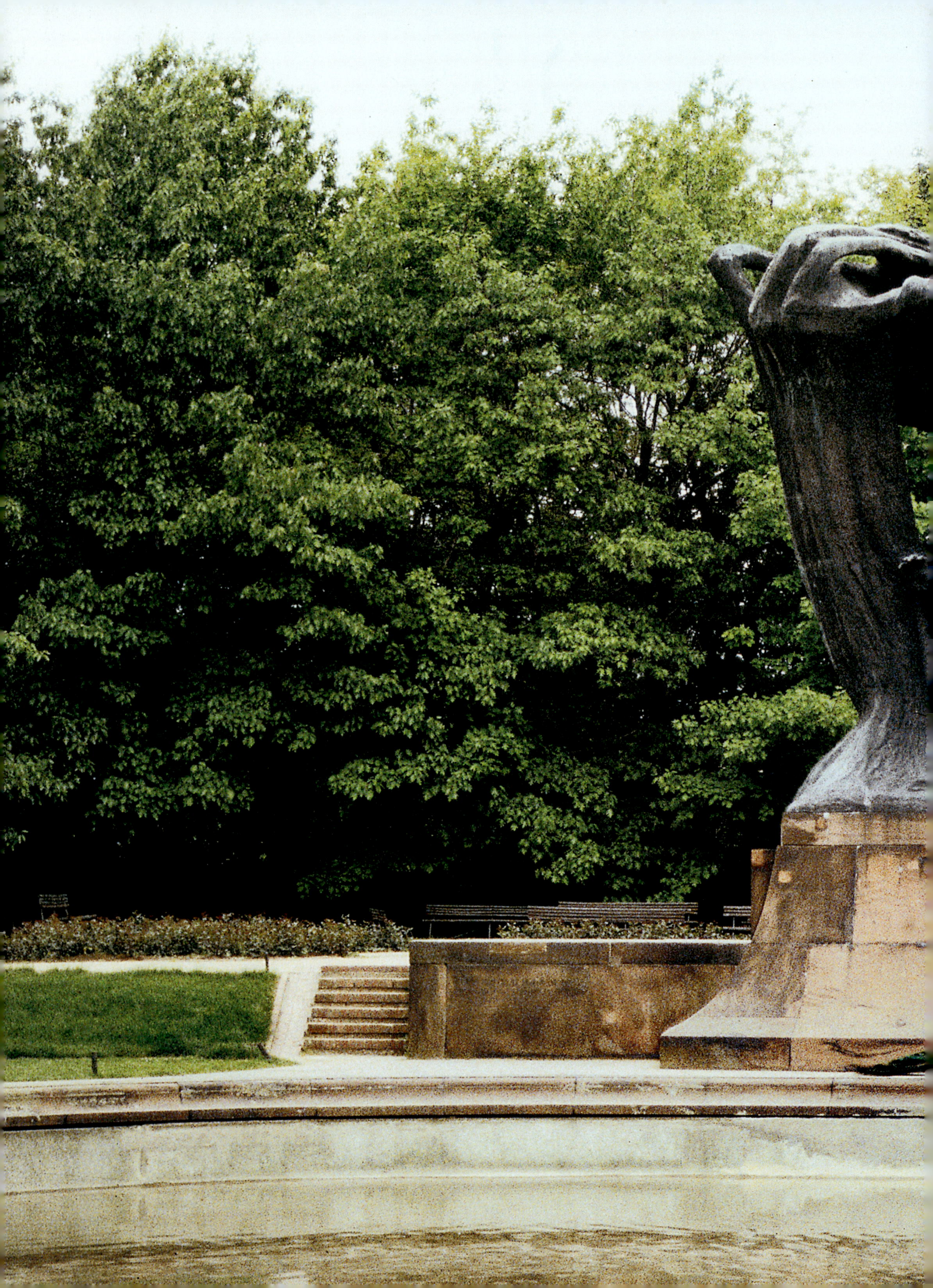

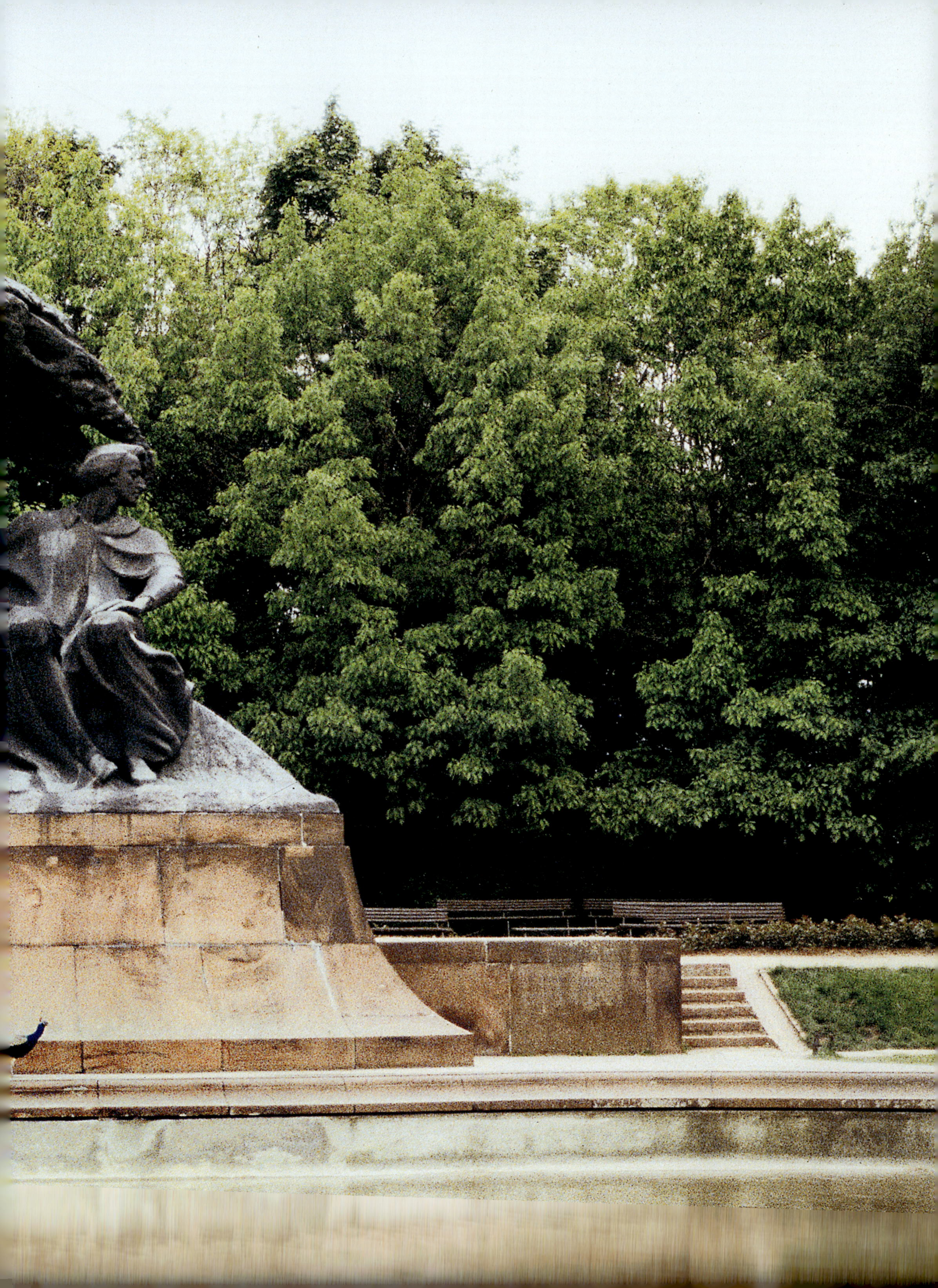

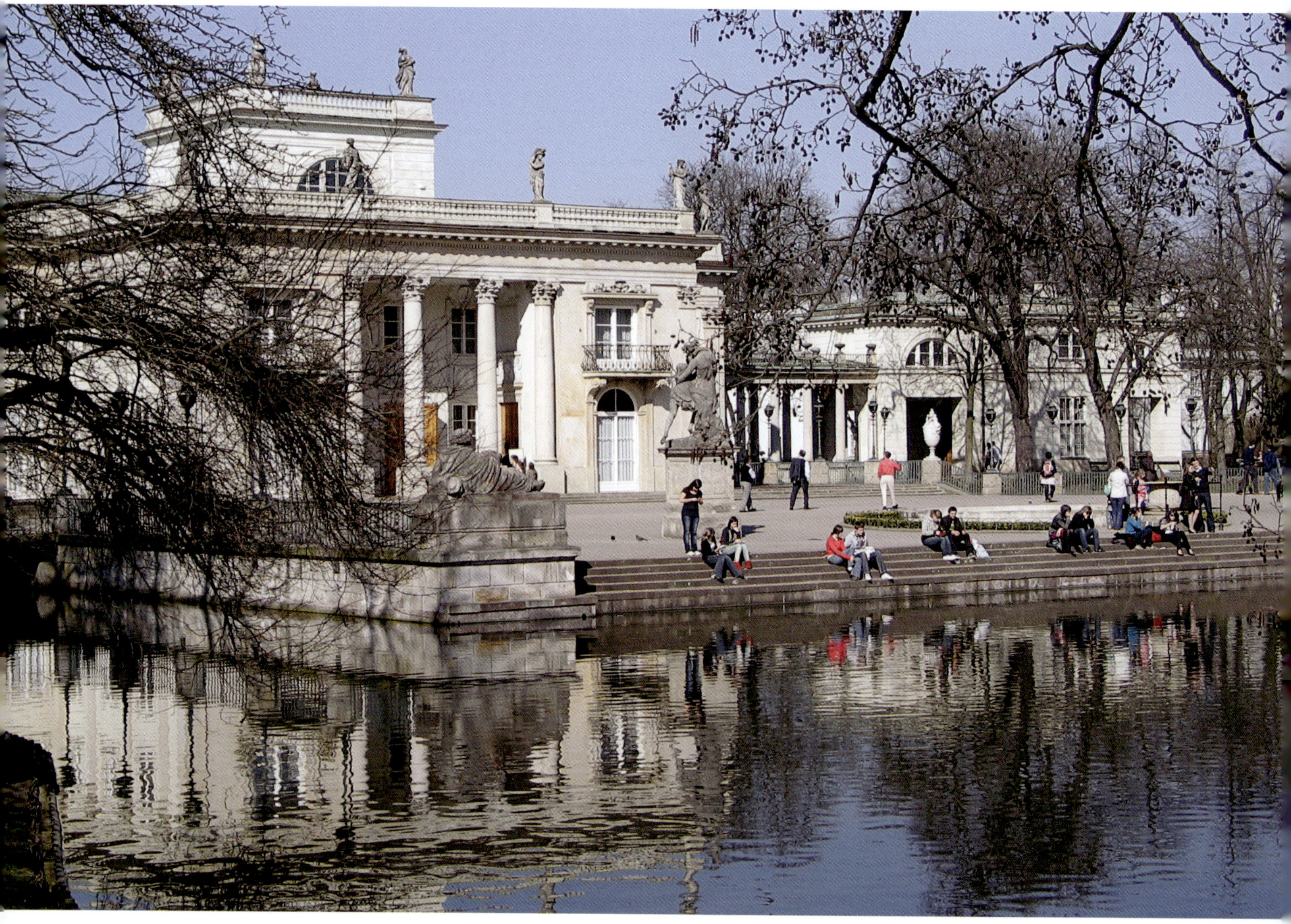

Warsaw

The Łazienki Gardens, where young Frycek, when not performing for the Duke, played with Paul and Alexandrine, the daughter of Paul's tutor, the Comte de Moriolles. Fryderyk, Paul and "Moriolka" (as she was affectionately called) were the same age, so adventures and pranks in the Łazienki Gardens were the order of the day. Chopin's close friendship – and later romance – with Moriolka continued until his final departure from Warsaw.

Everyone was delighted and impressed, especially Cantor Kahler, a local music teacher, who later recalled the occasion.

Young man, I'd have given ten years of my life to be able to play like you. If Mozart had heard you he'd have shaken your hand and cried Bravo!

Recollections of Cantor Kahler,
on hearing Chopin playing at the Postmaster's house

Eventually fresh horses were harnessed and the coach set off once more for the next stage back to Poznań.

After the Sulechów experience Fryderyk began to formulate in his mind a composition for piano and orchestra based on Polish folk songs. The idea eventually took shape as the *Grand Fantasia on Polish Airs*, Op. 13.

In Poznań Fryderyk and Professor Jarocki stayed with Archbishop Teofil Wolicki, a relative of the Chopins, at his Residence on the "holy island" of Ostrów Tumski. The next day Fryderyk called on Prince Antoni Radziwiłł at his official Governor's Residence, the former Jesuit College in the centre of the city. He was warmly welcomed by the Prince, who immediately arranged a concert for an invited gathering of Poznań society. The Prince gave musical soirées, and maintained a regular string quartet in which he himself played the cello.

Among the singing students of the Conservatory was Konstancja Gładkowska. Fryderyk often accompanied her during practices, and fell hopelessly in love with her. Being shy, he kept this love to himself, and confided only to Tytus Woyciechowski and Jan Matuszyński that he had found his "ideal". Exhortations to declare himself bore no fruit; Fryderyk seemed determined to keep her on a pedestal – an impossible, unattainable dream.

Szopen Friderik (special ability, musical genius, etc)

Elsner's typically terse final report
on Chopin's achievements showed him to be a man
of few words and restraint

In July 1829 Fryderyk Chopin graduated from the Conservatory and decided to go to Vienna. He set off with four travelling companions: university professor Romuald Hube, classics teacher Ignacy Maciejowski, and old school friends Marceli Celiński and Alfons Brandt.

The first stop was Kraków, where the party spent several days sightseeing, including Wawel the tombs of Prince Józef Poniatowski and Kościuszko, under whom his father had fought. There was also Kościuszko's newly completed 300-foot high Mound, made of soil from his battle sites, including Maciejowice, the Market Square with its Cloth Hall in the centre,

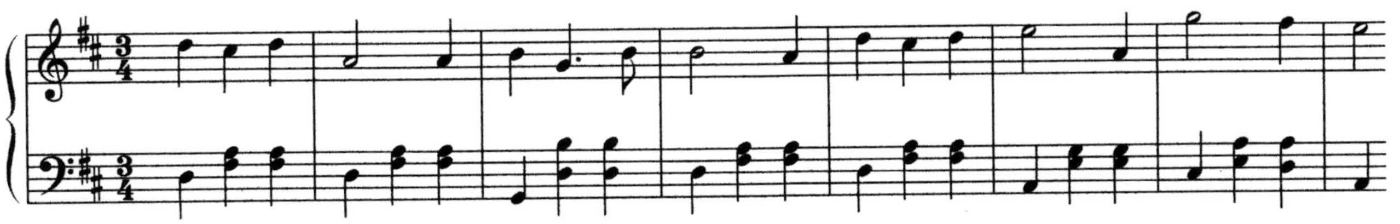

The folk melody, *Laura i Filon*, which Chopin used in his *Grand Fantasia on Polish Airs*, Op. 13.

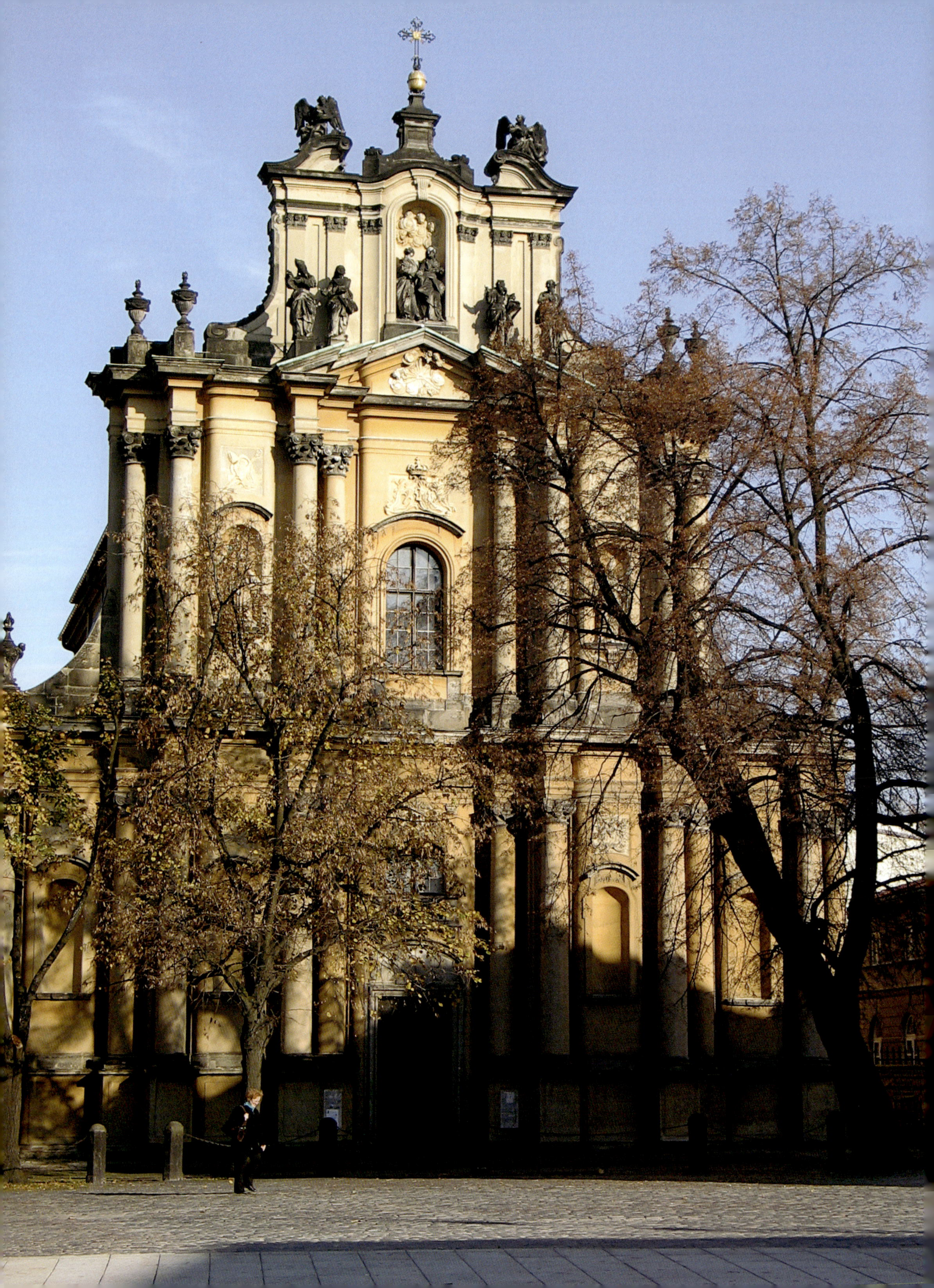

dominated by the unidentical twin spires of the Church of St. Mary; from the taller of the two, every hour, on the hour, a bugler sounded the *hejnał*, the aborted bugle call commemorating the bugler boy who had warned the inhabitants of a Tartar attack 600 years previously, and died as he played. Fryderyk was inspired by the local dance to write a miniature piano concerto, the *Rondo à la Krakowiak* Op. 14.

The companions visited Wieliczka, one of the oldest and biggest salt mine in the world, where he signed the Visitor's Book.

On 26 July the party hired a peasant and his cart to take them to the fourteenth-century Ojców Castle, in the valley of the River Prądnik to the north of Cracow. Once the residence of the Counts Załuski, by that time it was in the early stages of decline. They intended to stay the night at Mr Indyk's hostelry in the nearby village of Pieskowa Skała, but the driver got lost, was unable to cross the swiftly flowing, rock-strewn little river, and they all ended up stuck in the middle.

About 9 in the evening, when we were wandering about, not knowing what to do, we met two strangers, who took pity on us and undertook to guide us to Indyk. We had to go on foot for about 2 miles in the wet among a mass of rocks and sharp stones and to keep crossing the stream on round logs, and all this in the dark night.

Fryderyk Chopin to his family (Vienna, 1 August 1829)

They eventually arrived at Mr Indyk's, cold and soaked through, but Mrs Indykowa, a good fire, a jug of wine and a sense of humour all saved the day. The next day the five tourists returned to their lodgings in the city.

Just to the south west of Cracow at Bielsko-Biała, was the Austrian border. The party crossed Moravia and reached Vienna on 31 July.

After three weeks in the musical capital of Europe, Fryderyk returned to Poland by way of Prague, Dresden, Wrocław and Kalisz. There he stayed with his friend Dr Adam Helbich, with whom he attended a wedding at the Bronikowski Palace at Żychlin.

On his return, Fryderyk found Warsaw depressingly empty and provincial.

That autumn Fryderyk stayed once more with the Radziwiłłs, this time at Antonin. On this

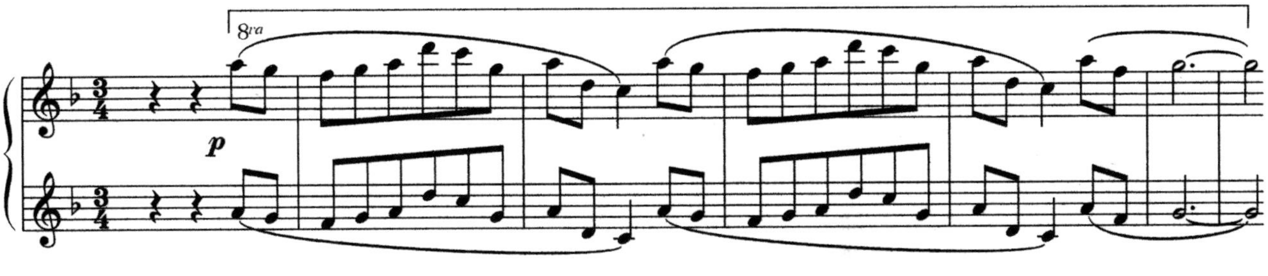

Chopin's *Rondo à la Krakowiak* is considered by many as his finest work for piano and orchestra.

Warsaw

The church of the Visitation in the Krakowskie Przedmieście still houses the organ, which Frycek regularly played when boys of the Lyceum attended Mass there. His knack of leading from hymns and responses into his own improvisations was legendary, and he sometimes became so carried away that he had to be restrained to enable the service to continue.

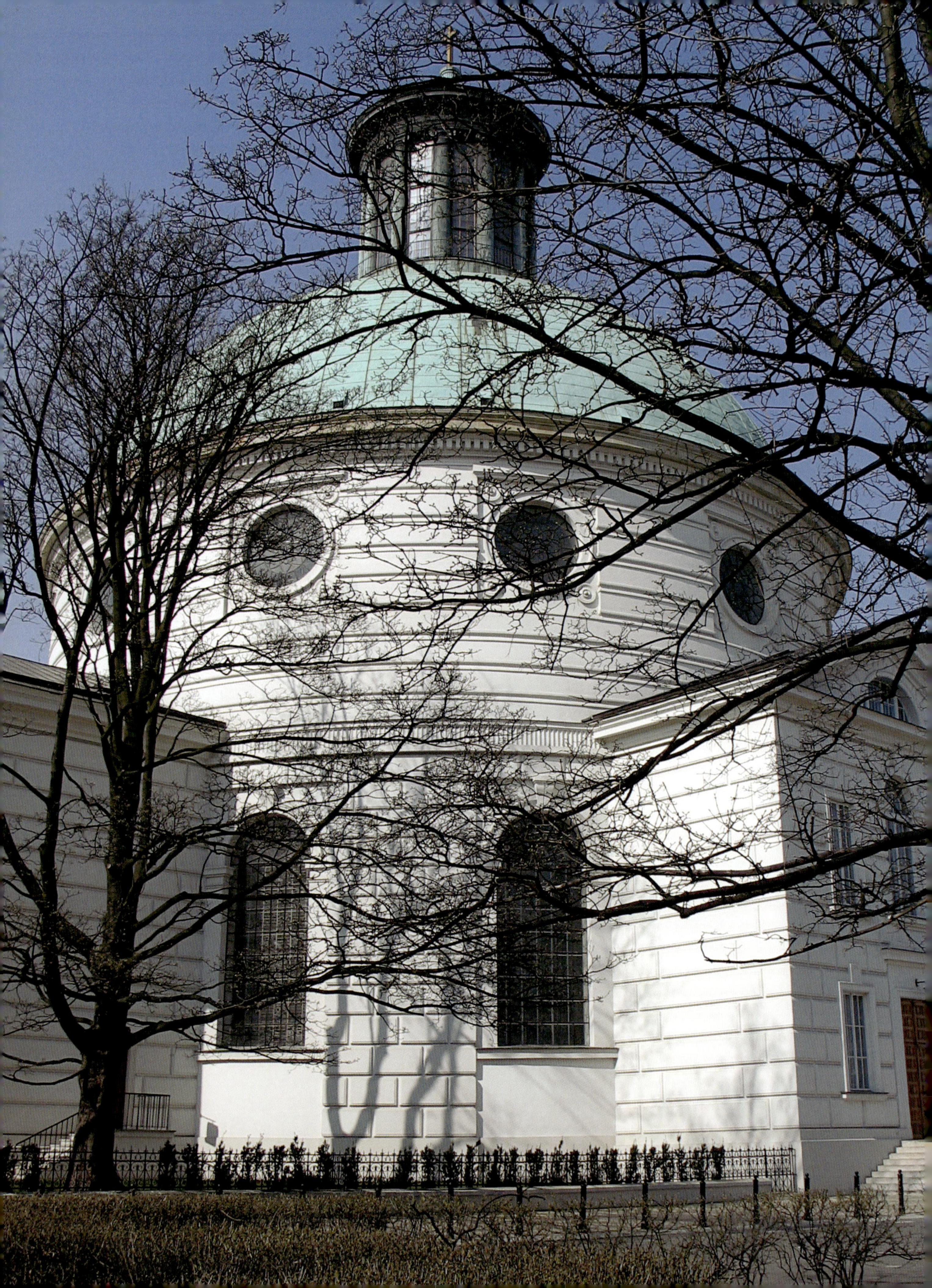

occasion everyone sat round the piano to sing and play their way through the Prince's recently completed opera, *Faust*. Fryderyk was full of admiration for the work, which was later premièred in Berlin, and continued to enjoy success for many years. He also gave piano lessons to Princess Wanda.

I have been giving Princess Wanda lessons. She is quite young, seventeen and pretty, really it was a joy to guide her little fingers.

Fryderyk Chopin to Tytus Woyciechowski
(Warsaw, 14 November 1829)

That same year, inspired by the Prince's cello technique, Fryderyk wrote a glitzy Polonaise in C for cello and piano, for the Prince to play with his daughter. While in chamber music mode, he also wrote his Piano Trio in G minor, which he dedicated to Prince Radziwiłł.

I gratefully accept the dedication of your Trio which you are kind enough to offer me. Accept, my dear Chopin, my renewed assurances of the interest which your talent arouses in me, and of the high esteem in which I hold you.

Prince Antoni Radziwiłł to Fryderyk Chopin
(Antonin, 4 November 1829)

On 19 December he gave a concert at the Merchants' Hall in Miodowa Street and returned to composition. He expressed his ongoing love for Konstancja with an Adagio, which became the slow movement of his Piano Concerto in F minor. This was premièred with a small ensemble on 3 March 1830 in the Chopins' apartment in front of a select gathering, and was followed by a full concert performance at the National Theatre on 17 March. But even then Fryderyk was already writing the slow movement of his E minor Concerto, again a poem of love to his "ideal".

He also stayed for three weeks at Żelazowa Wola, composing, and at the end of August he visited the music-loving, violin-playing General Piotr Szembek at his garrison at Sochaczew, situated on the eastern side of the River Bzura. Fryderyk was amazed by the military band.

It is all played on a type of bugle, and you would not believe how fast they can do chromatic scales, and diminuendo ascending...

Fryderyk Chopin to Tytus Woyciechowski
(Warsaw, 31 August 1820)

On 11 October Fryderyk's new E minor Piano Concerto was premièred, again at the National Theatre.

On 2 November 1830 Fryderyk again left Warsaw for another visit to Vienna, this time accompanied by Tytus Woyciechowski. He was not to know that his homeland was once again only days away from insurrection and war. He was not to know, at the border of Bielsko-Biała, that he would never see his homeland again.

Warsaw
The Augsburg Evangelical Church of the Holy Trinity where Frycek played the aeolomelodicon – a hybrid keyboard instrument of the kind that was popular at the time – for Tzar Alexander I in the spring of 1825. The delighted Tsar presented him, and the manufacturer, Brunner, each with a diamond ring.

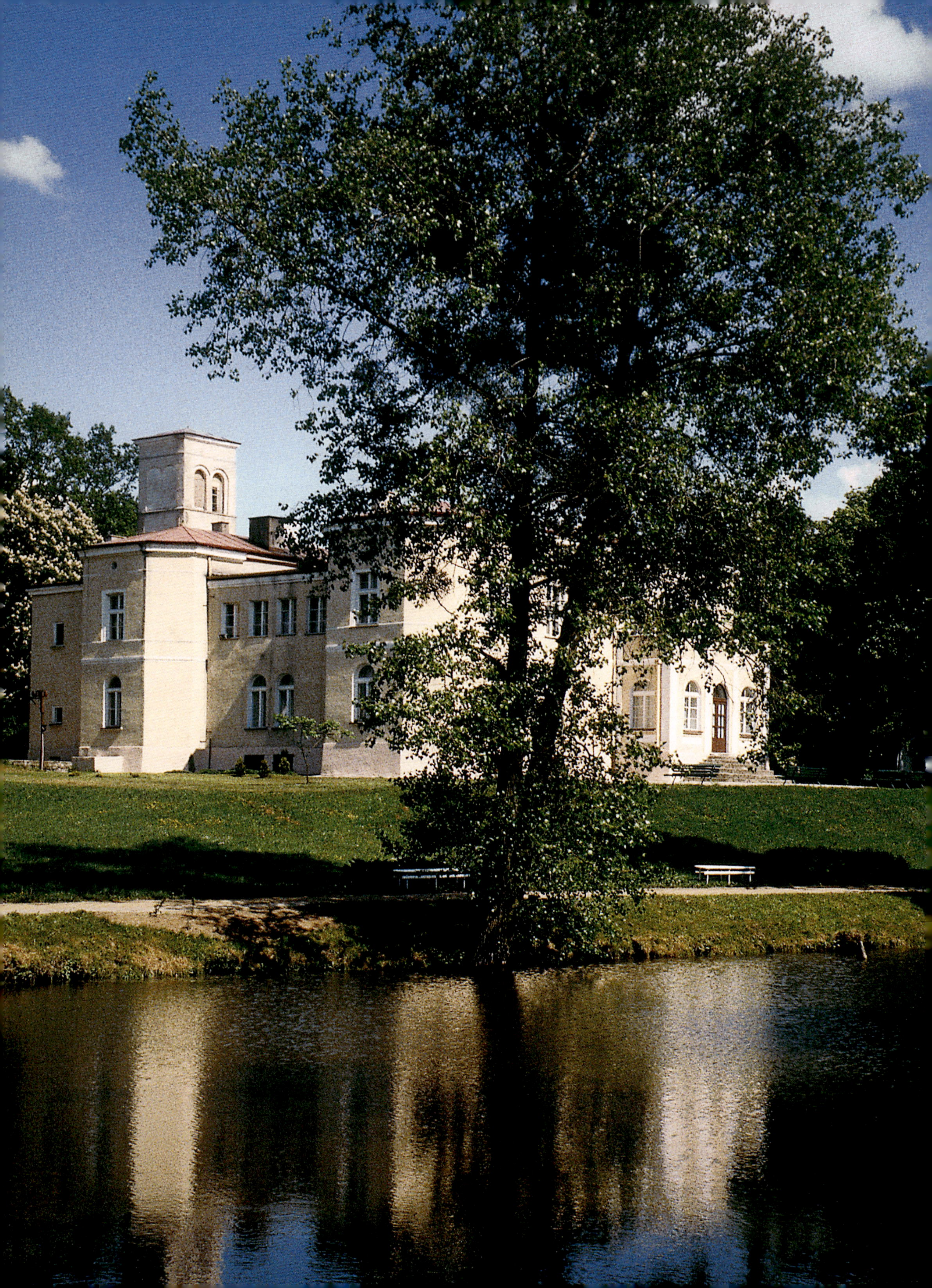

Żelazowa Wola is now the world's premier Chopin site, with the alcove where he was born preserved. The Church of St. Roch at Brochów are still there, now the Church of St. John the Baptist. The garrison at nearby Sochaczew is no longer there, although some ruins remain on the eastern banks of the River Bzura. Virtually all the Chopin sites in Warsaw are still in existence, although most of them have been rebuilt, notably in the years following World War 2. The exception is the Saxon Palace, of which only a column of arches remains, a guarded monument with an eternal flame burning to the Unknown Soldier in the Saxon Gardens. The Chopins' apartment at the Lyceum in the Kazimierz Palace is marked with a commemorative plaque. Today this houses the Oriental Institute of the University of Warsaw. The Radziwiłł Palace is now the residence of the President of the Polish Republic, and one room has been set aside in the Krasiński Palace, and furnished as the commemorative "Chopin Salonik." A post office in Kozia street marks the post stage in Chopin's time, from which diligences set off further afield, although Mrs Brzezińska's coffee house is long gone, as are the other coffee houses in Miodowa street. The Merchants' Hall is now the Belgian embassy. The Church of the Visitation and the Augsburg Evangelical Church of the Holy Trinity are still as they were in Chopin's day.

Most of the sites associated with Chopin's travel throughout Poland are still there, although Sokołowo is one of the few completely original buildings connected to Chopin still standing in Poland. Szafarnia and Sanniki are today Chopin sites where concerts and festivals are regularly held. Polish Golub and Prussian Dobrzyń, where the Castle is situated, are now a united town astride the River Drwęca. The historic centres of Płock, Gdańsk and Toruń are also largely unchanged, although the Sierakowski manor in Sopot has been rebuilt, and Waplewo has recently been restored to its former splendour.

Poznań's Ostrów Tumski and the Jesuit College, Prince Radziwiłł's Residence, are still there as is his hunting lodge to the south, Antonin, which is now a hotel and venue of concerts and festivals. The ancient timber church at the old border village of Biskupice has survived, as have both the Manor and the Evangelical church at Żychlin. The Postmaster's house in Sulechów was demolished shortly after the end of World War 2. The historic centre of Wrocław is largely unchanged, and the Merchants' Hall building is still there. At Duszniki the Hermitage, the Paper Mill and the small Manor are as they were in Chopin's time.

All the Kraków sites are unchanged, as well as the salt mine at Wieliczka, where Chopin's signature is still kept. Ojców Castle, dilapidated in Chopin's day, is now a historic ruin. Mr Indyk's hostelry in Pieskowa Skała is no longer there, but a new café-restaurant has recently been built on its site on the wooded hillside overlooking the car park.

The Woyciechowski manor at Poturzyń no longer exists, but the inter-connecting lakes are still there, as are the ruins of the stables, where Chopin reputedly stayed in the loft above during his visit.

Szafarnia

The country house of Frycek's school friend Dominik Dziewanowski, where Frycek spent the summer holidays of 1824 and 1825. Today it is the venue of Chopin concerts and festivals. Frycek was fascinated with the quirks of country life and sent home to his parents 4 editions of his home-made periodical, the "Szafarnia Courier" which throw considerable light on life at that time from the point of view of a teenaged city-dweller with a sense of humour.

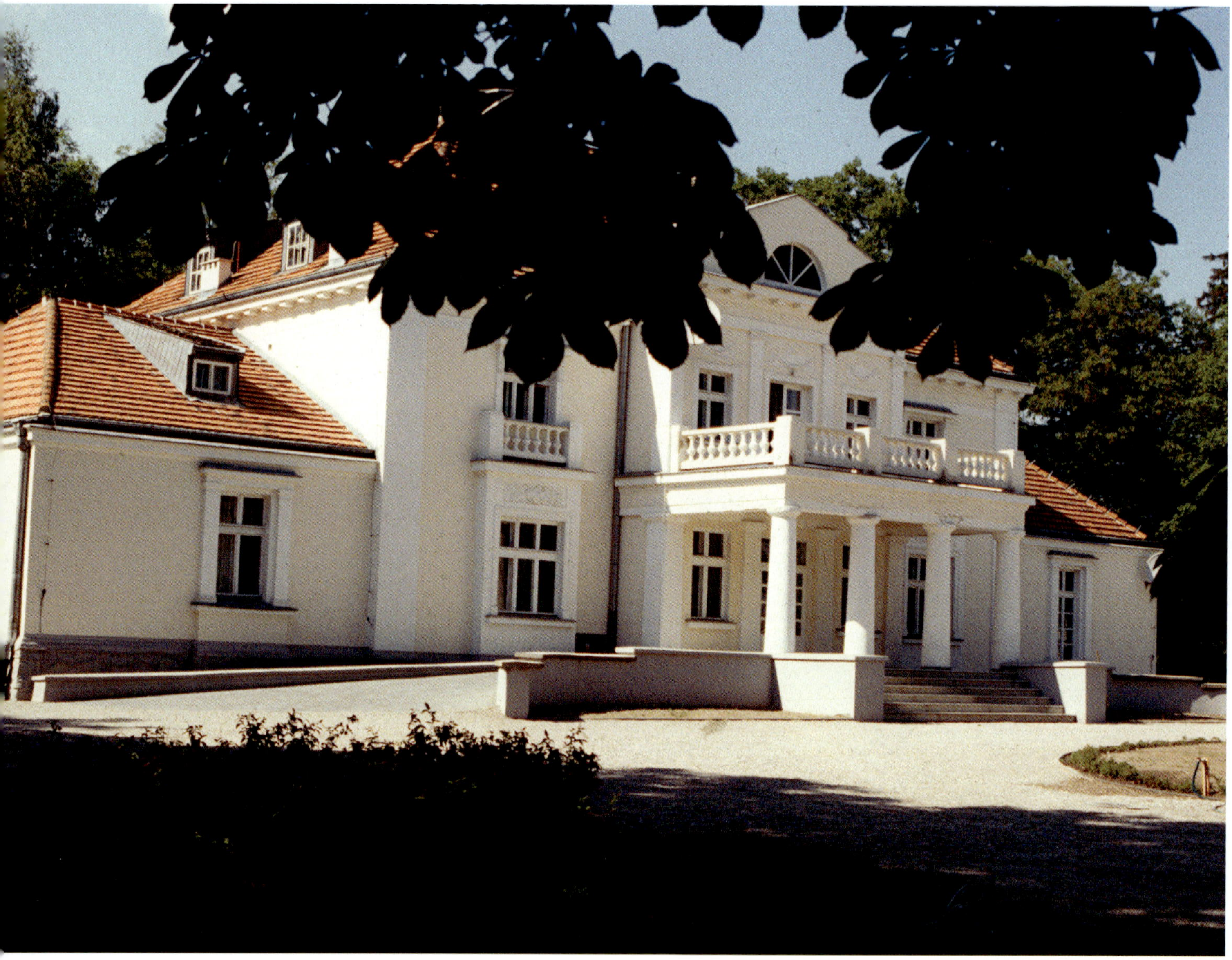

Sokołowo

The manor at Sokołowo, the home of Frycek's ill-fated school friend, Jan Białobłocki, whom Frycek visited in 1825. Jan, who was terminally ill with tuberculosis, lived there with his stepfather Antoni Wybraniecki. One memorable Sunday the two boys spent the day experimenting with the latest musical marvel the pantaleon, another hybrid keyboard instrument fashionable at the time, before going to the orchard to eat apples. The manor is one of the few original Chopin sites remaining in Poland.

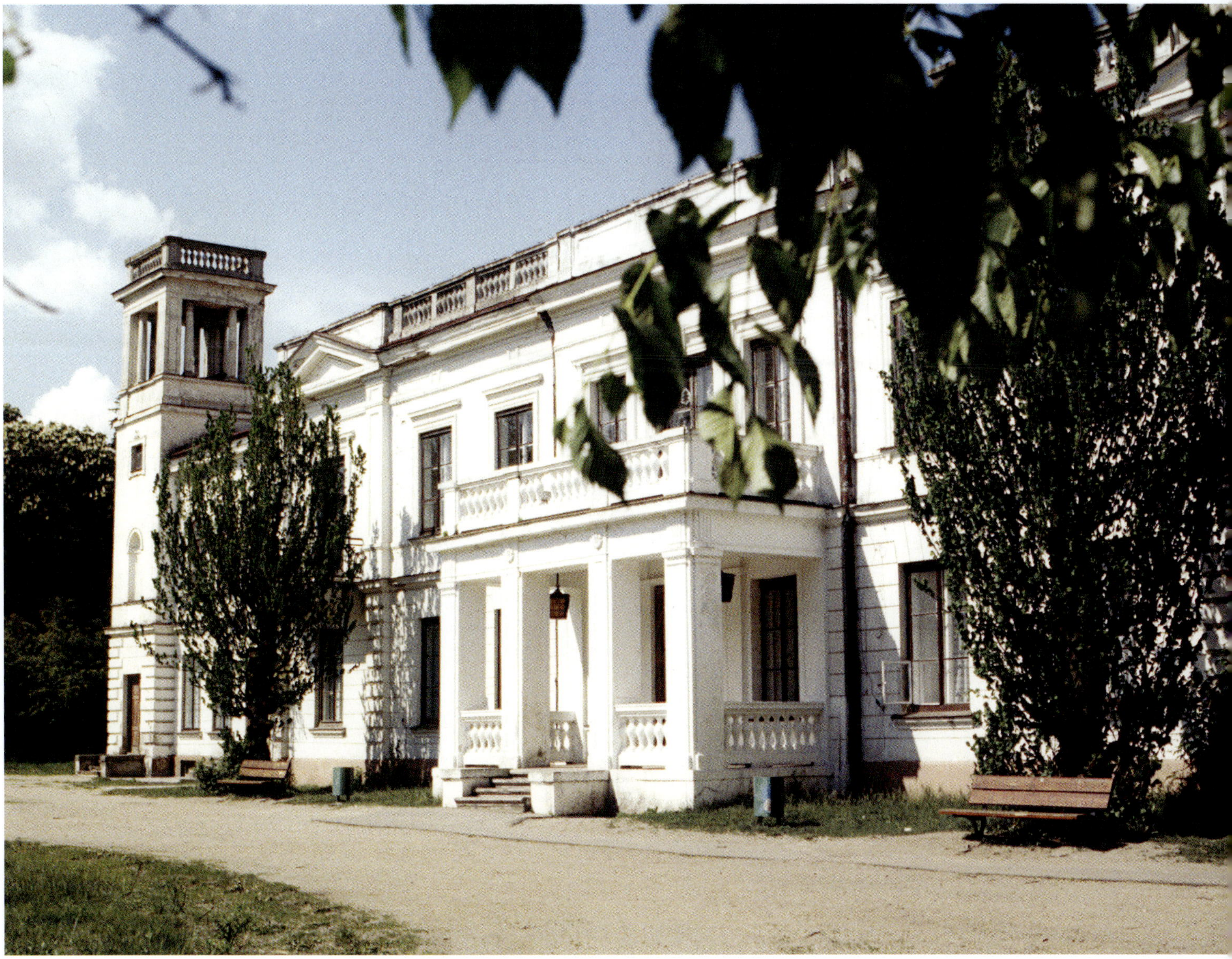

Sanniki

The manor where Frycek stayed with his school friend Konstanty Pruszak, in the summer of 1828. That summer Sanniki was full of young people enjoying open air charades and plays alternating with local dances, at which the swirl of the colourful local costumes complemented the sounds of the mazurka, the kujawiak and the oberek, as the youngsters danced and loved into the night.

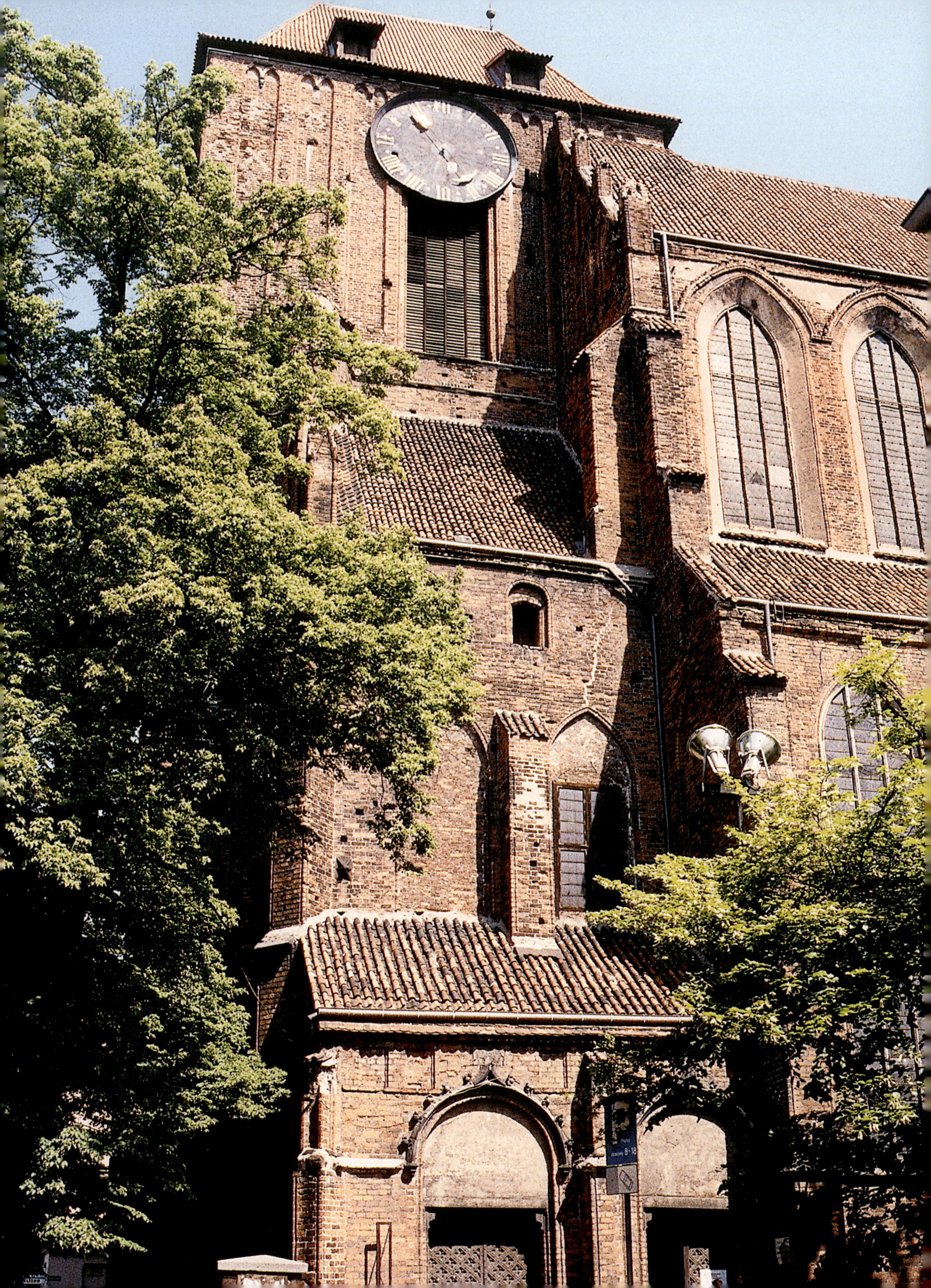

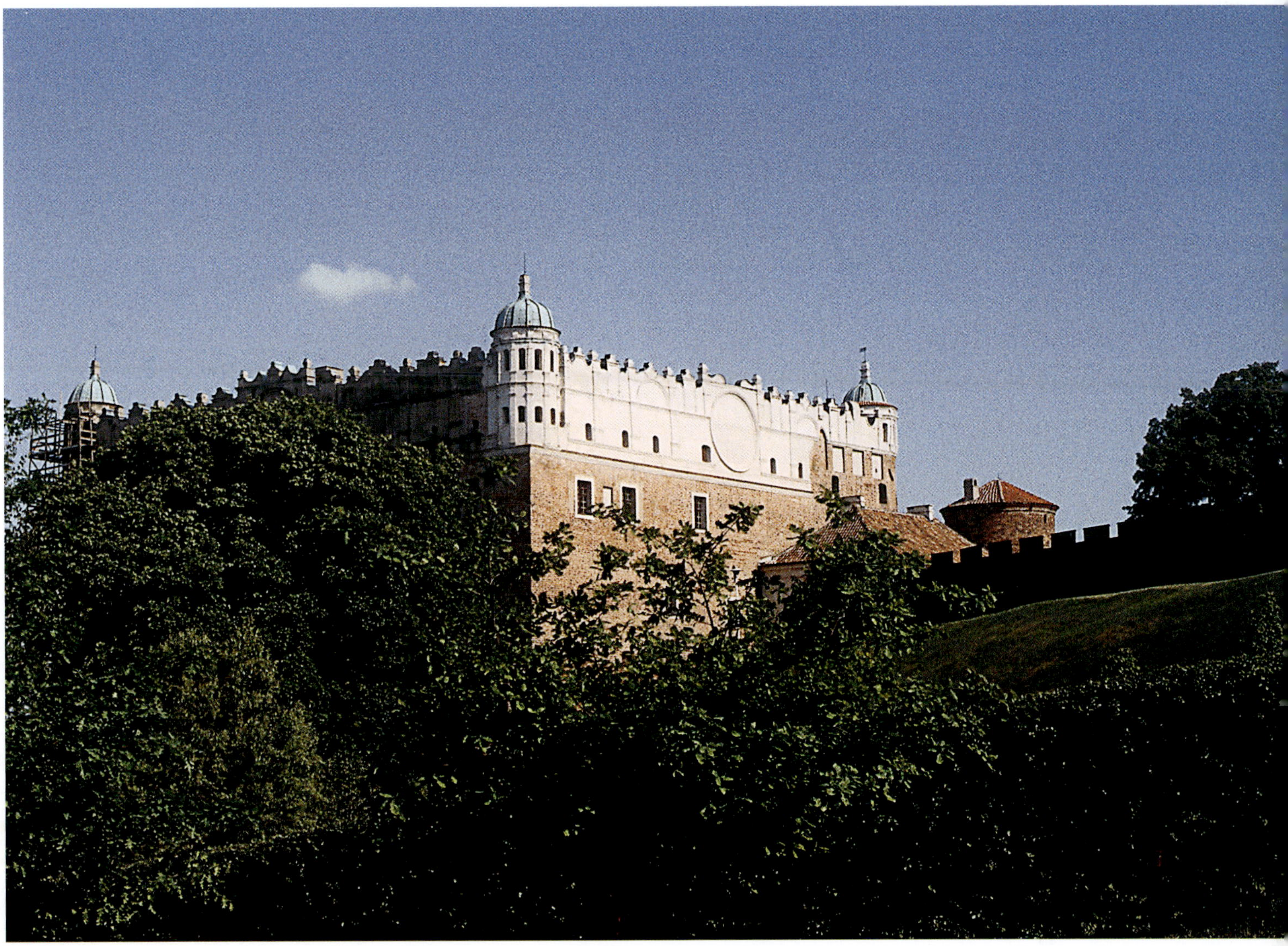

Golub-Dobrzyń

The castle, perched spectacularly on its hill, was originally built by the Teutonic Knights, and extensively restored in the seventeenth century. The courtyard was full of merchants, beggars, peasants, tourists and street entertainers. Frycek was particularly amused by a musician churning out a *staierek*, a type of German waltz, on his hurdy-gurdy.

← Toruń

The Church of St. John. While staying in Szafarnia in 1825 Frycek visited the medieval city of Thorn, today Toruń. He was singularly impressed with the magnificent buildings such as this church, as well as those of the Blessed Virgin and St. Jacob, the Town Hall and the Crooked Tower. But what the 15-year-old Frycek liked best were the *pierniki* – local gingerbread cakes which came in every shape from biscuit to sculpted coach and horse.

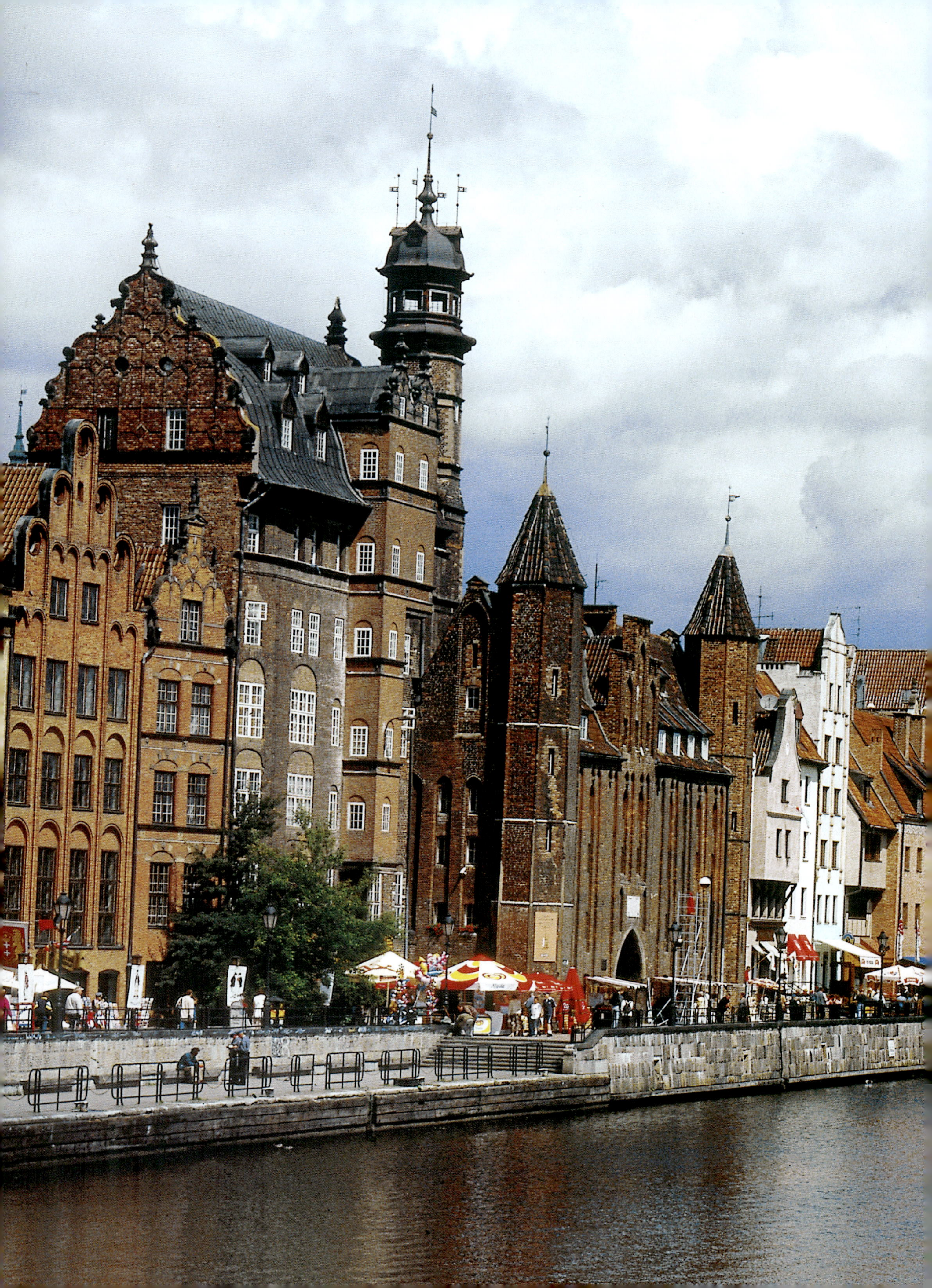

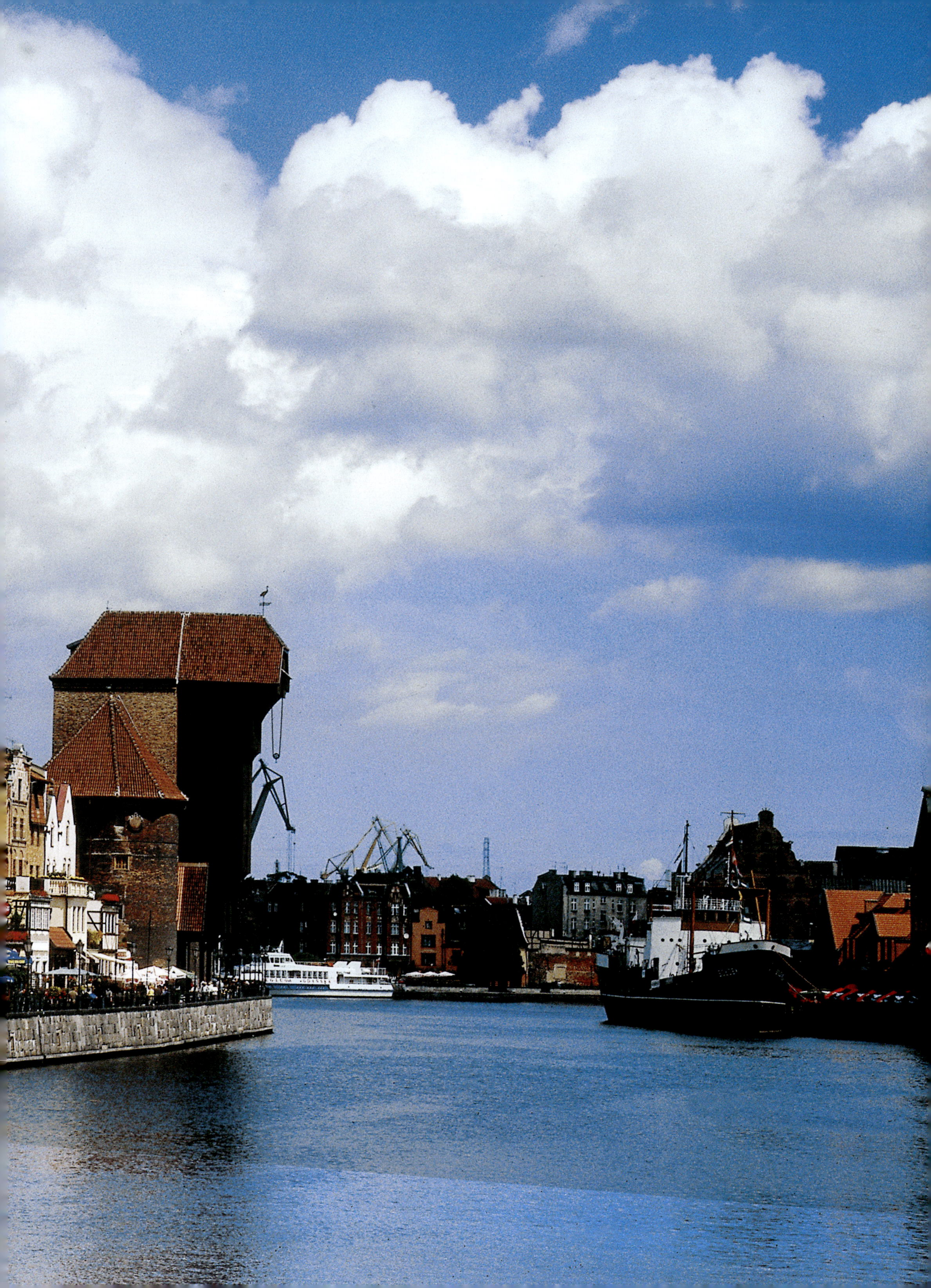

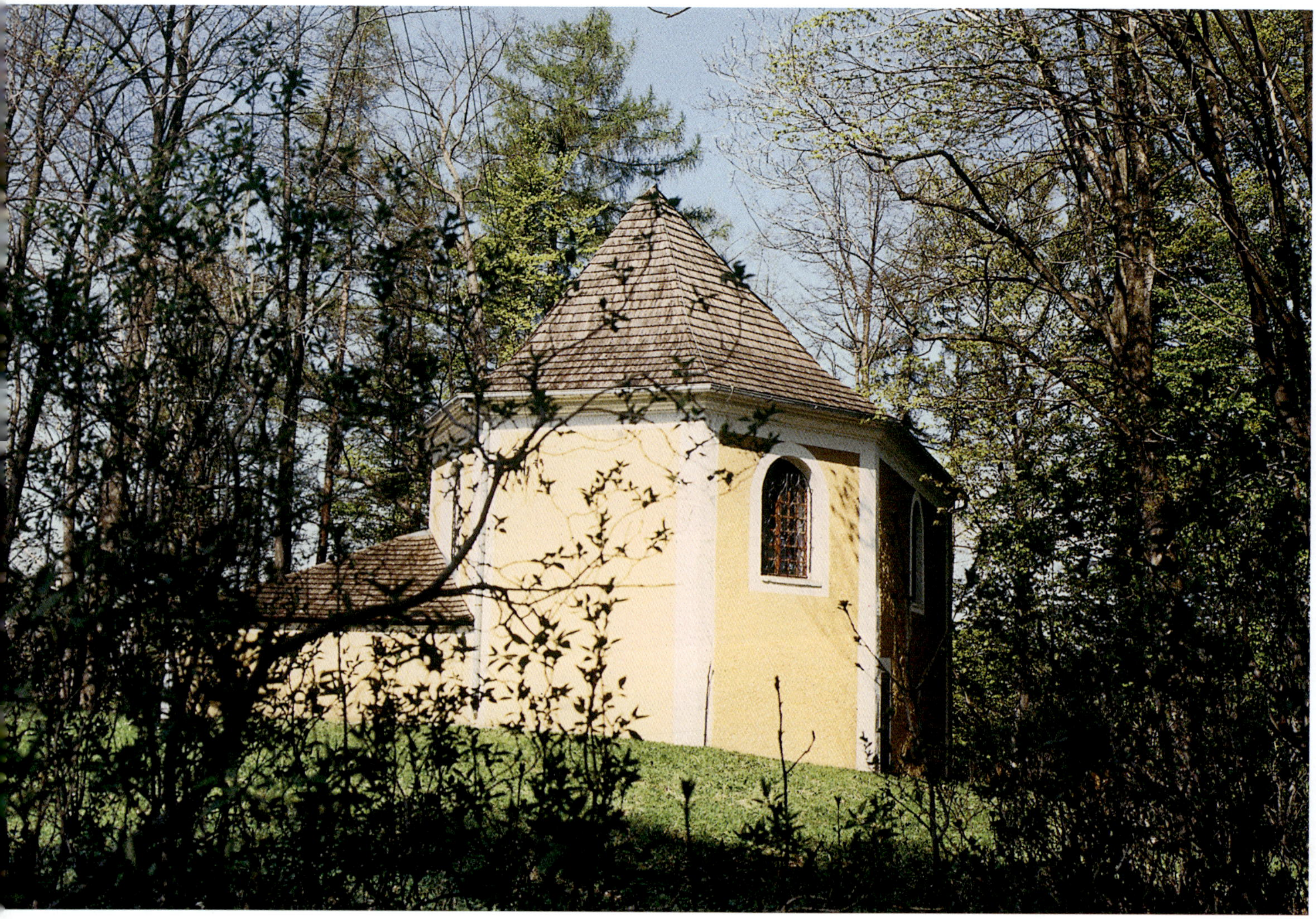

Duszniki-Zdrój

The Hermitage - formerly the Museum of the Chopin Festival. In the summer of 1826 the Chopin family came to the spa at Duszniki "to take the waters". Frycek climbed the 150 steps of the Einsiedelei Hill to the Hermitage which at his time was occupied by a solitary Catholic priest. According to a legend in 1698 the children of Duszniki climbed the hill knelt and prayed for deliverance from a plague that was ravaging the region. Duszniki was spared and the people built the Hermitage and installed a priest in thanks for their deliverance. The arrangement was still maintained in Chopin's day.

→ The manor where Frycek gave two charity concerts in August 1826. These concerts were for the benefit of a local young girl who was orphaned there during the Chopins' stay. Today it is the Concert Hall and venue of the annual Duszniki Chopin Festival.

← **Gdańsk**

The Waterfront, with its iconic view of the famous medieval crane, is one of the sights of this ancient Hanseatic city. Fryderyk came here with a party in August 1827 on his way to Waplewo to stay with music patron Count Antoni Sierakowski.

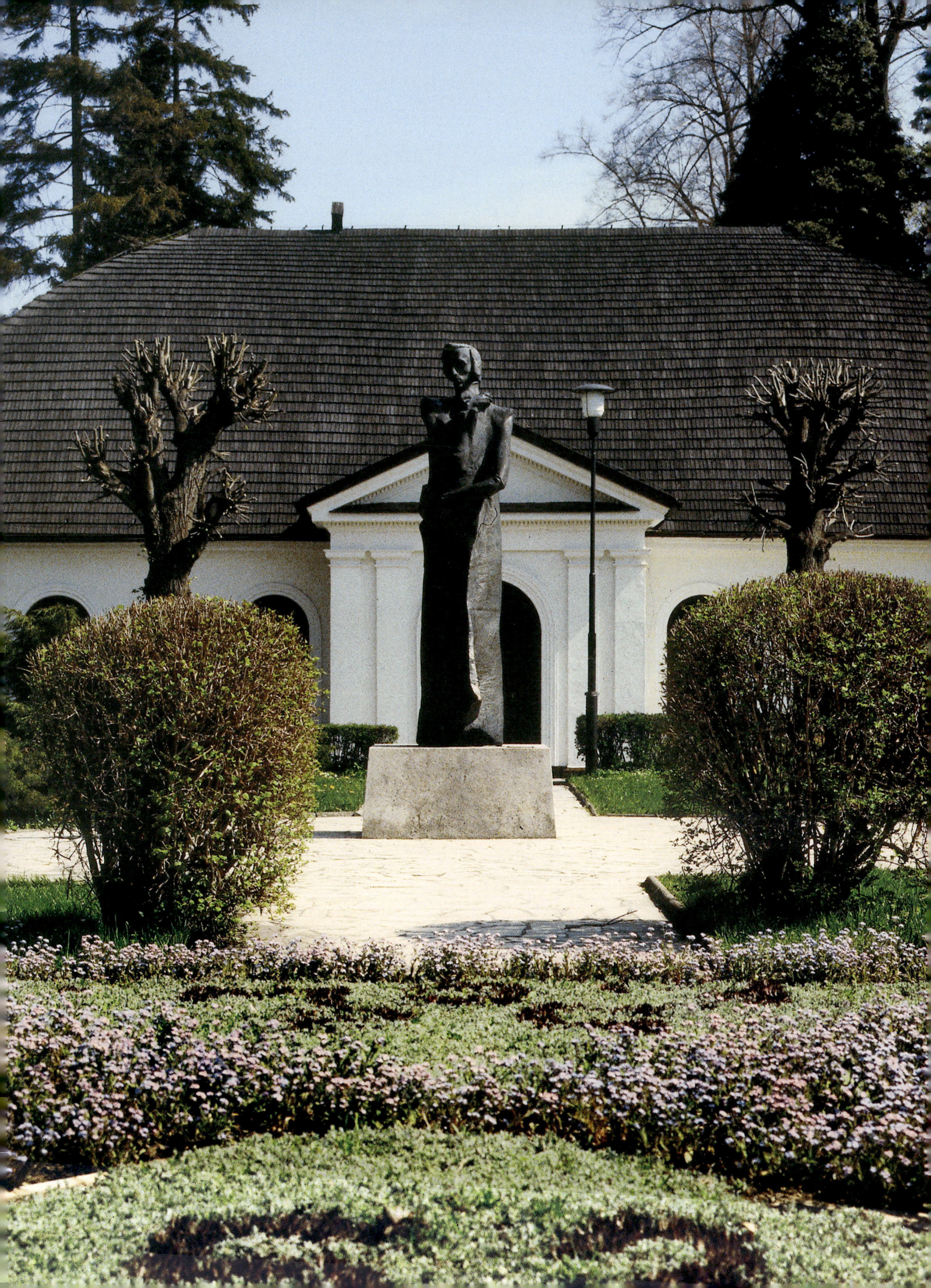

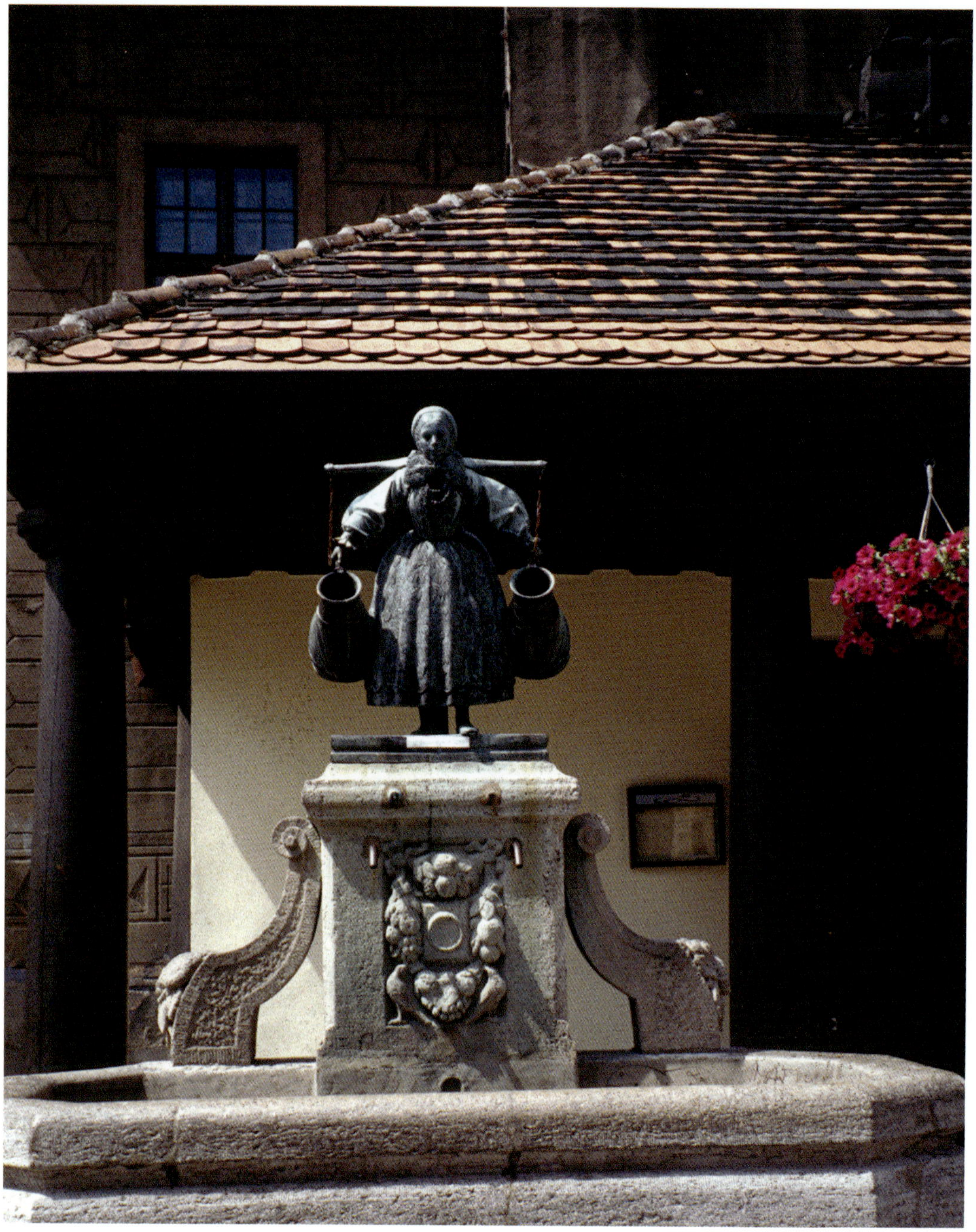

Poznań

The "Bamberka" well in the Old Town Square is a symbol of this great city, in which Frycek enjoyed the hospitality of Prince Antoni Radziwiłł, the Governor of Poznań, at his official residence in the autumn of 1828.

→ Antonin

The hunting lodge where Frycek was guest of Prince Antoni Radziwiłł on a number of occasions, the first being on his return from Duszniki in September 1826. His last visit was in the autumn of 1829, when he composed his Polonaise brillante in C for cello and piano for the cello-playing Prince to play with his daughter, Princess Wanda.

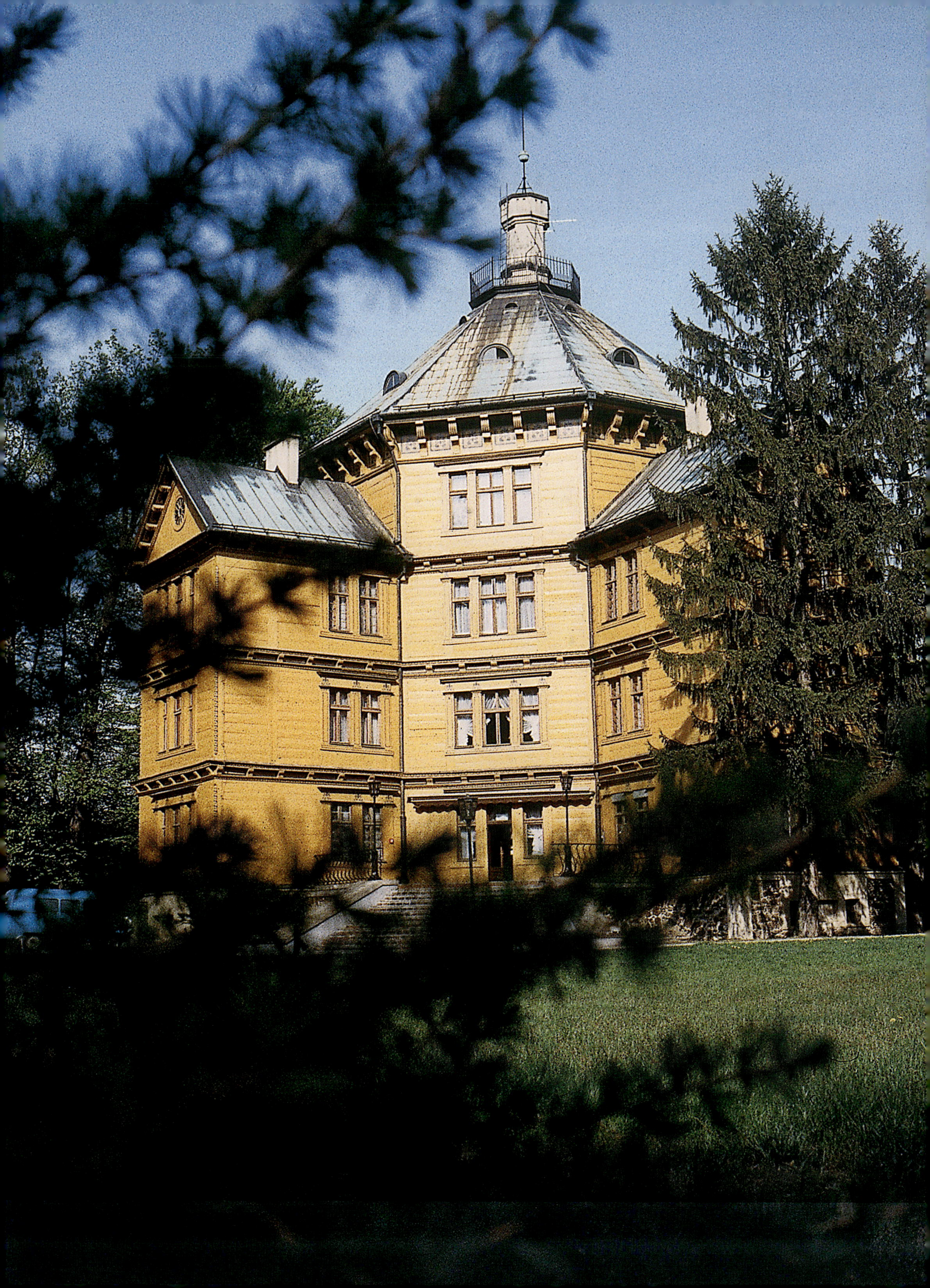

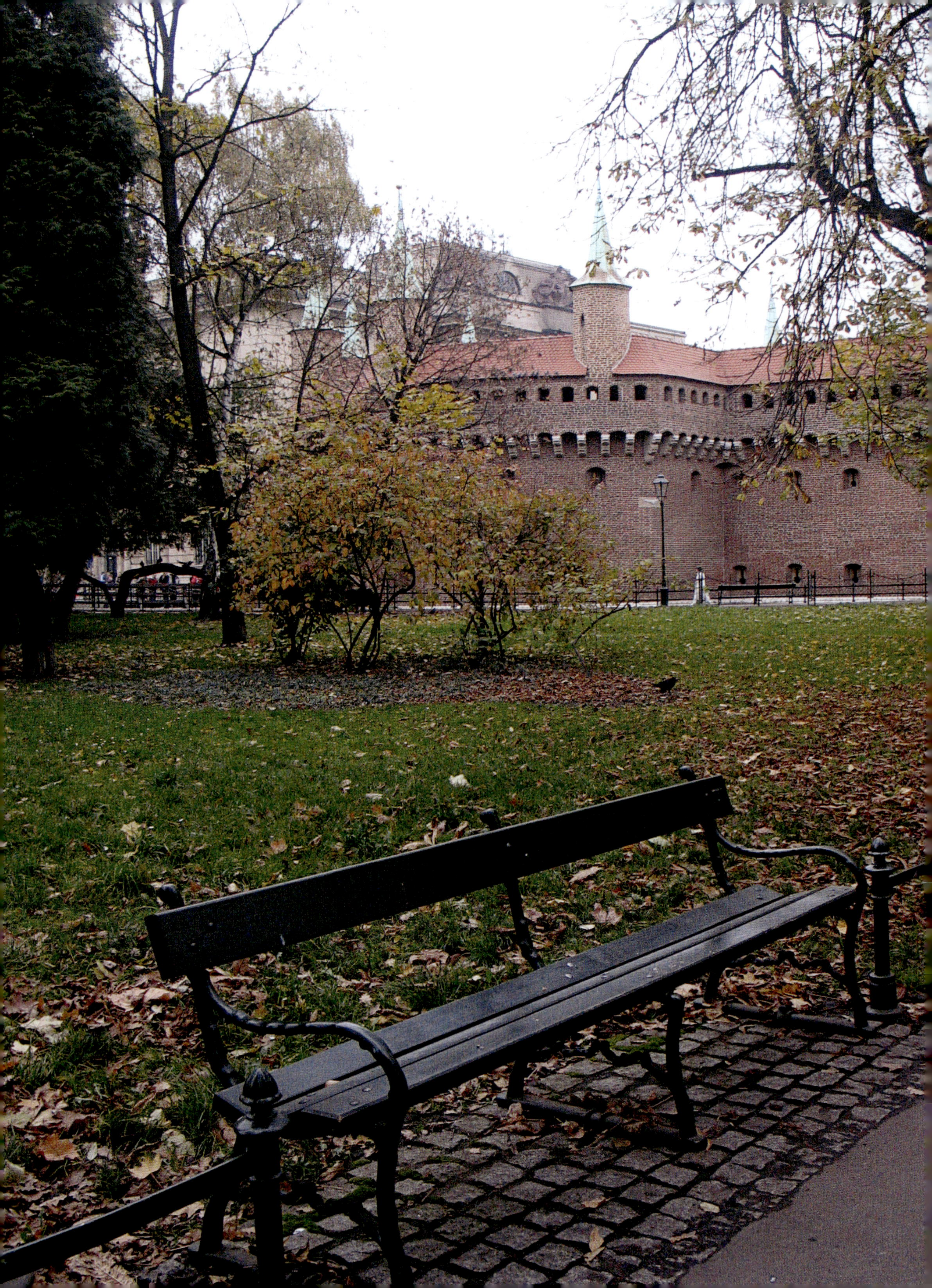

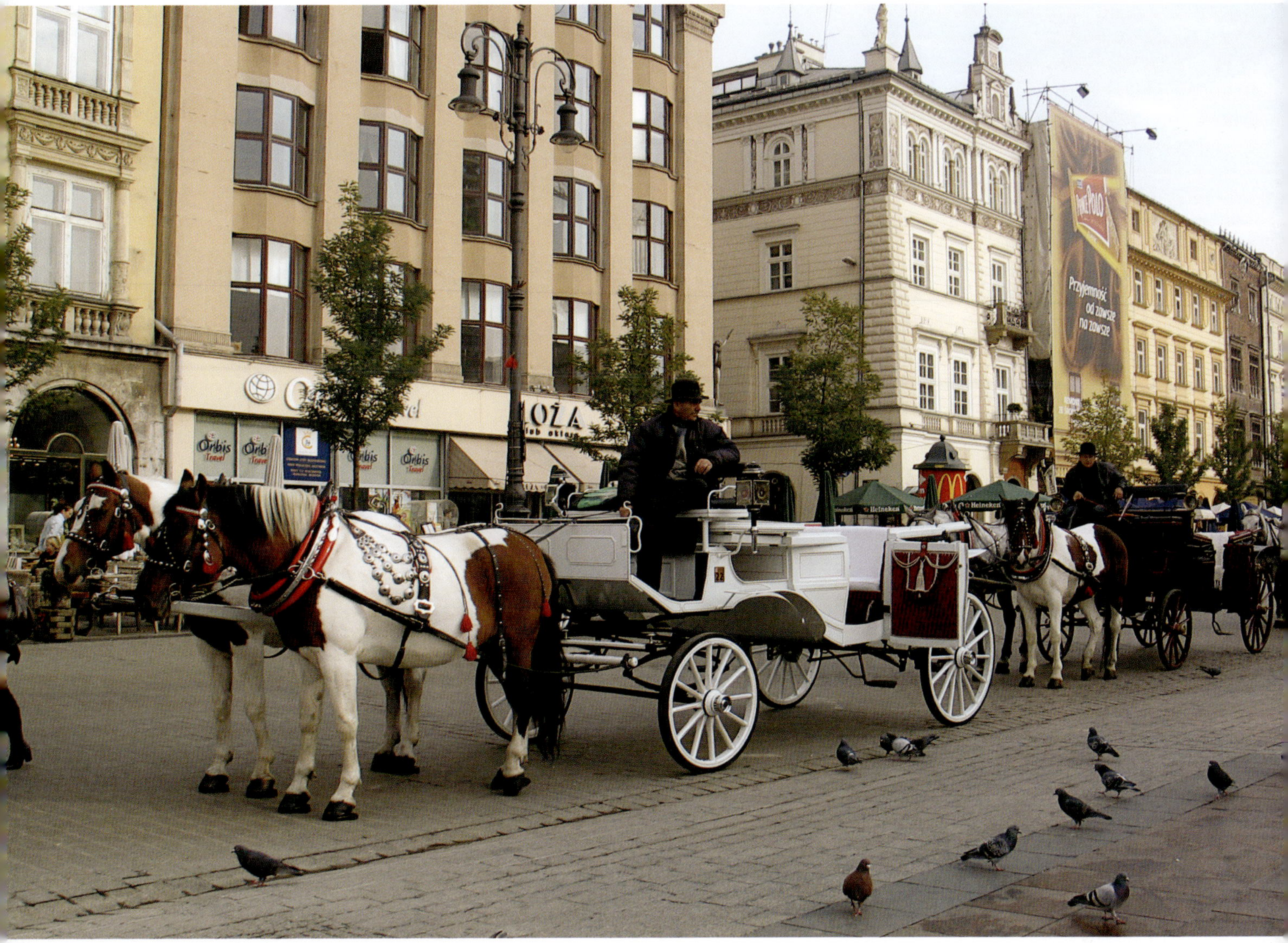

Cracow

Fryderyk and his four travelling friends visited Cracow in 1829 on their way to Vienna, and stayed for several days to see the historic sites of Poland's former capital. The most popular way to visit the city was, and still is, by horse-drawn carriage.

← Among Cracow's attractions was the Barbakan, once the gateway to the old walled city. The "Planty" Gardens are today situated where the walls once protected the city from invaders, and form a complete circle of greenery and walkways round the city centre.

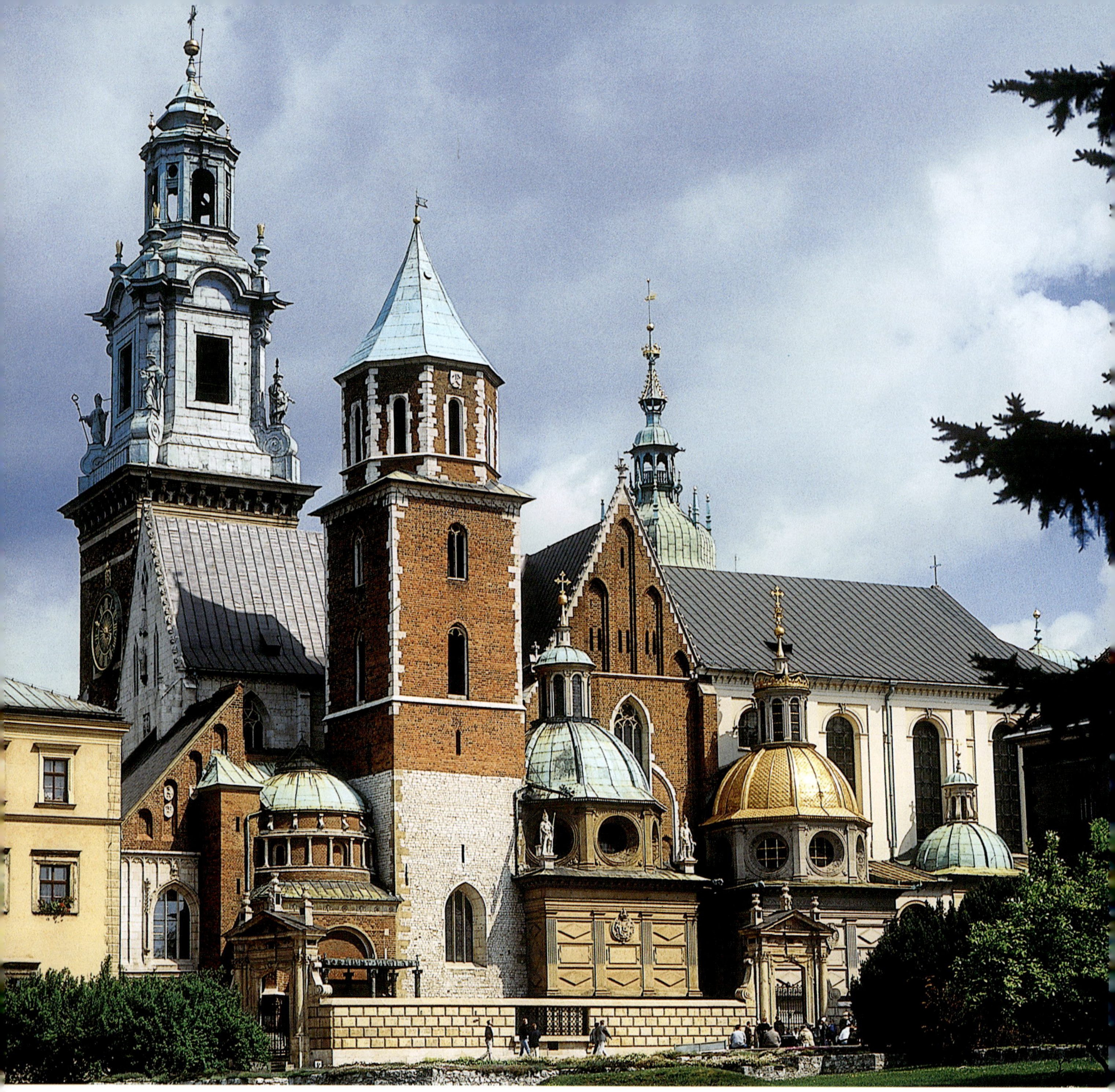

Cracow

The Wawel Castle complex was, at the time of Chopin's visit, a military barracks. In the Cathedral are the tombs of many former kings of Poland, famous citizens, including Prince Józef Poniatowski and Tadeusz Kościuszko. At the Congress of Vienna in 1815 Poland's ancient capital and its immediate surroundings were designated the Republic of Cracow.

→ The Rynek Główny, or Main Square, is one of the largest medieval town square of any European city. On the right the side entrance to the Renaissance cloth hall Sukiennice (currently housing gift shops, restaurants and merchant stalls) with the National Gallery of Art upstairs. It is flanked by the Town Hall Tower (*Wieża Ratuszowa*).

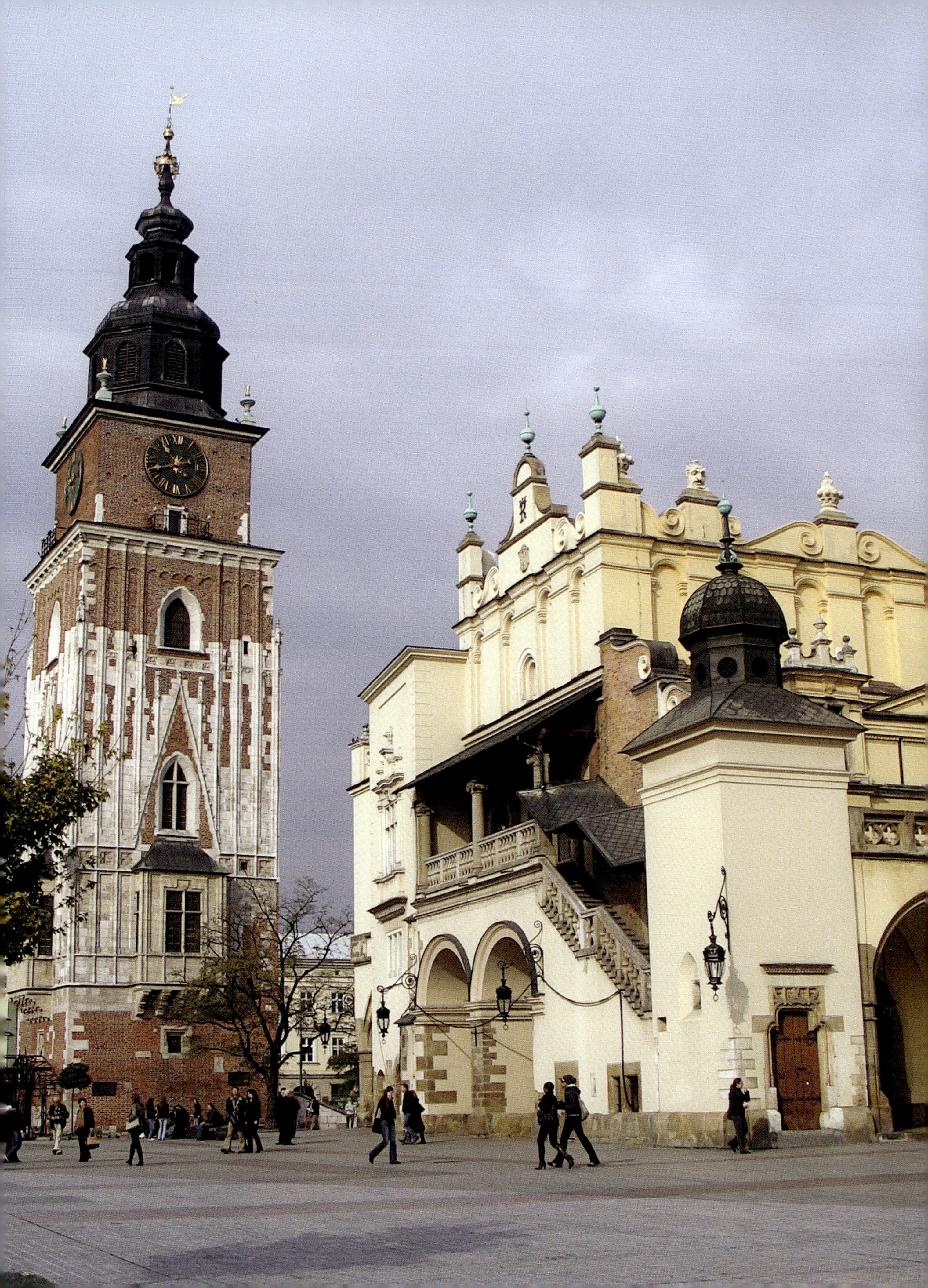

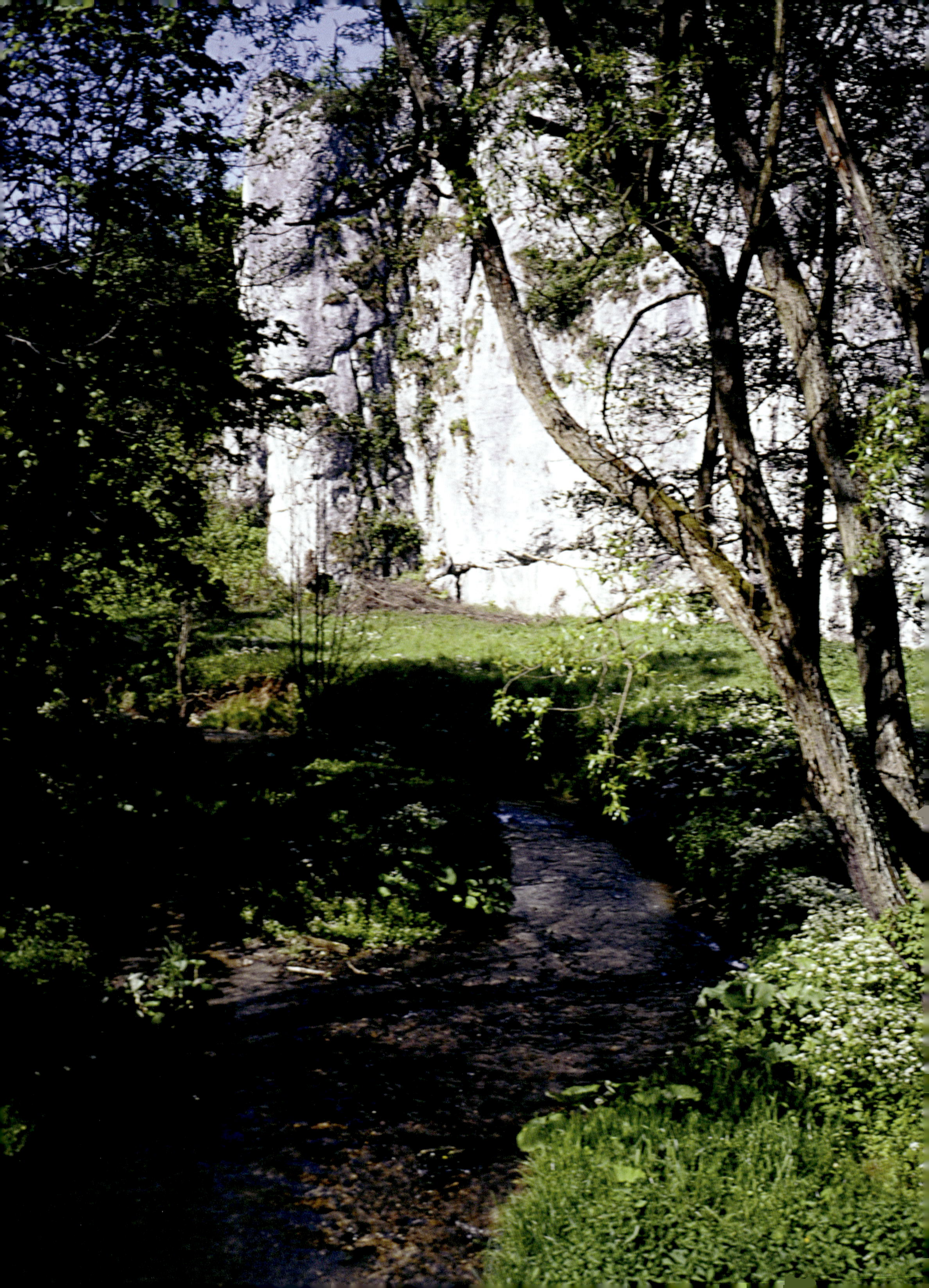

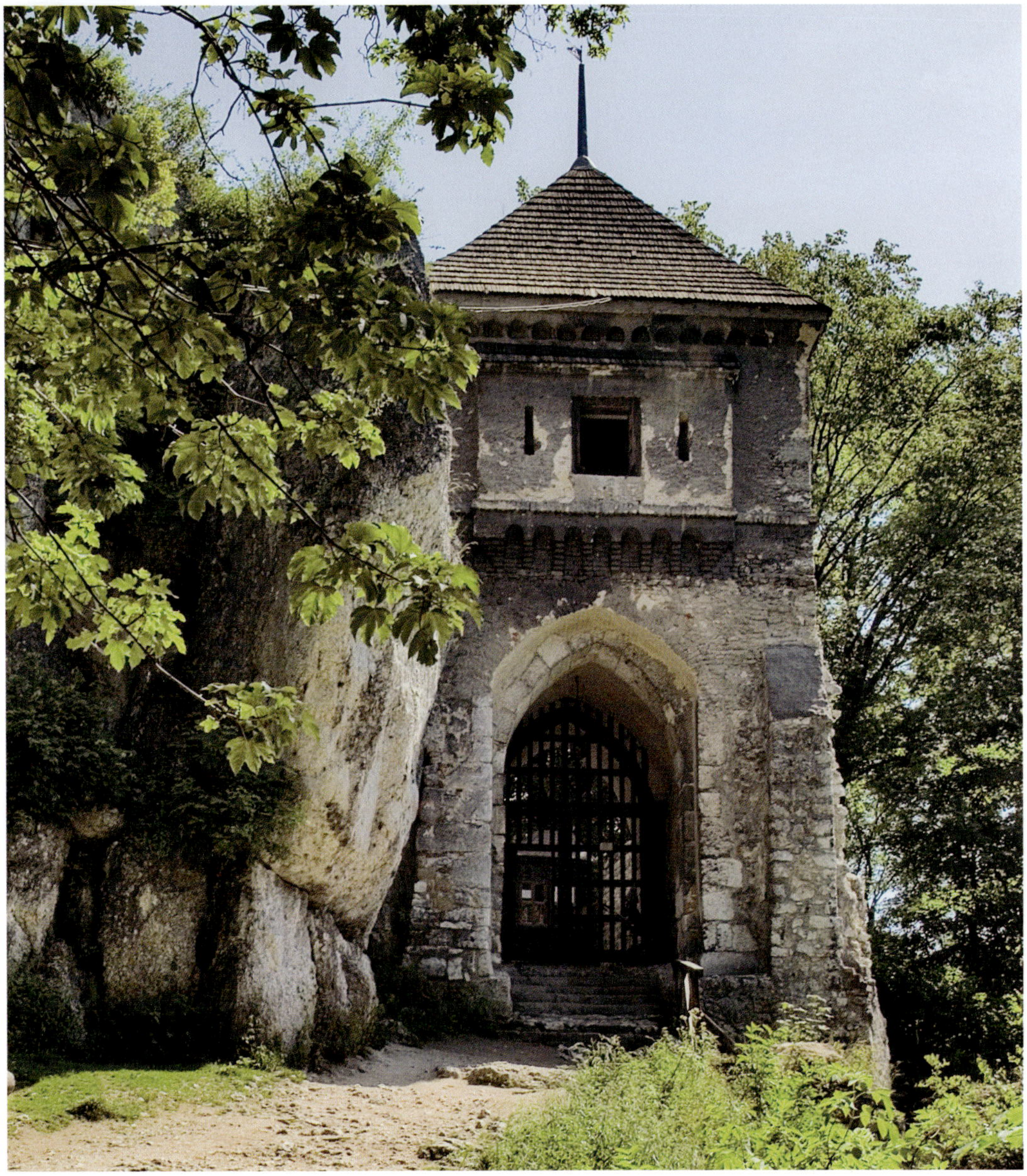

Photo: Janusz Leśniak

Ojców

The fourteenth century Ojców Castle, traditionally the retreat of artists and kings, perched spectacularly on a crag in the valley of the River Prądnik to the north-west of Cracow, had, 30 years previously, been the residence of the Counts Załuski.

← The Prądnik Valley

On July 26 Chopin's party hired the services of a peasant and his cart to take them to Ojców, intending to stay the night at the Hostelry of Mr. Indyk in the nearby village of Pieskowa Skała. The expedition went awry, the peasant got lost, was unable to cross the swiftly flowing, rock-strewn little River Prądnik, and they ended up stuck in the middle at nine o'clock in the evening. They eventually arrived at Mr. Indyk's, cold and soaked through, but Mrs. Indykowa, a good fire, a jug of wine and a sense of humour all saved the day.

→ Poppies are to be seen everywhere in Poland and were always very dear to Chopin.

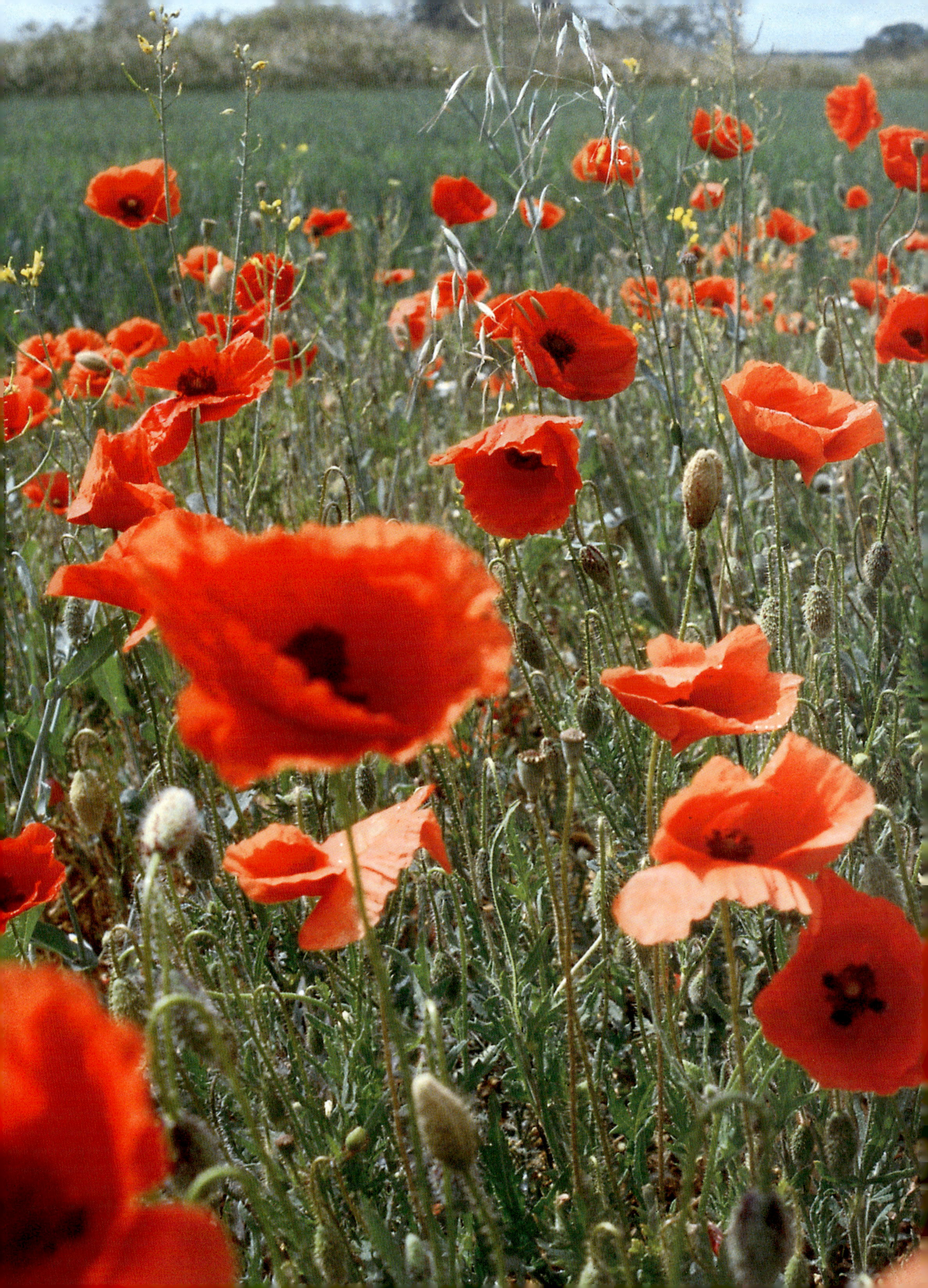

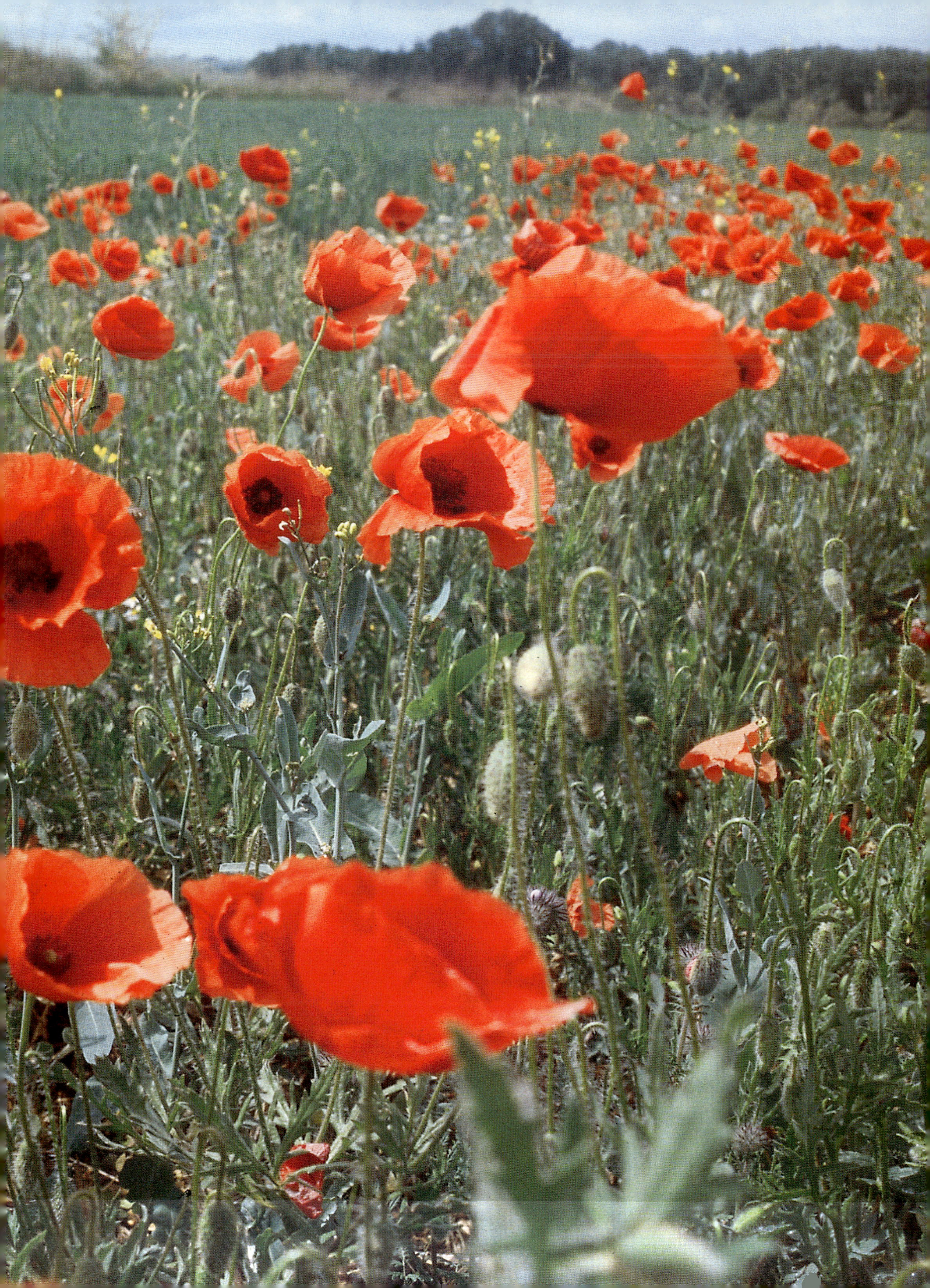

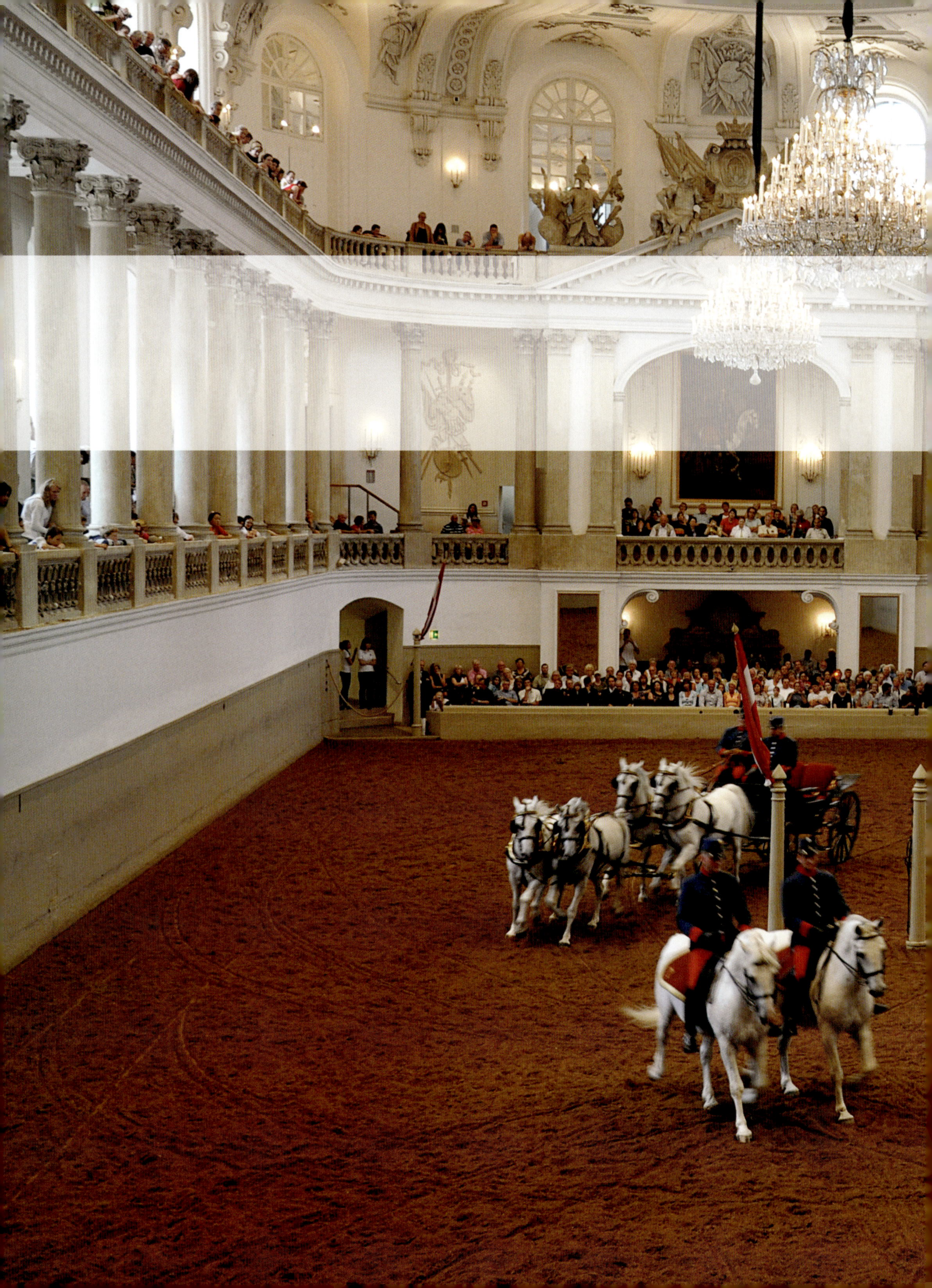

Vienna

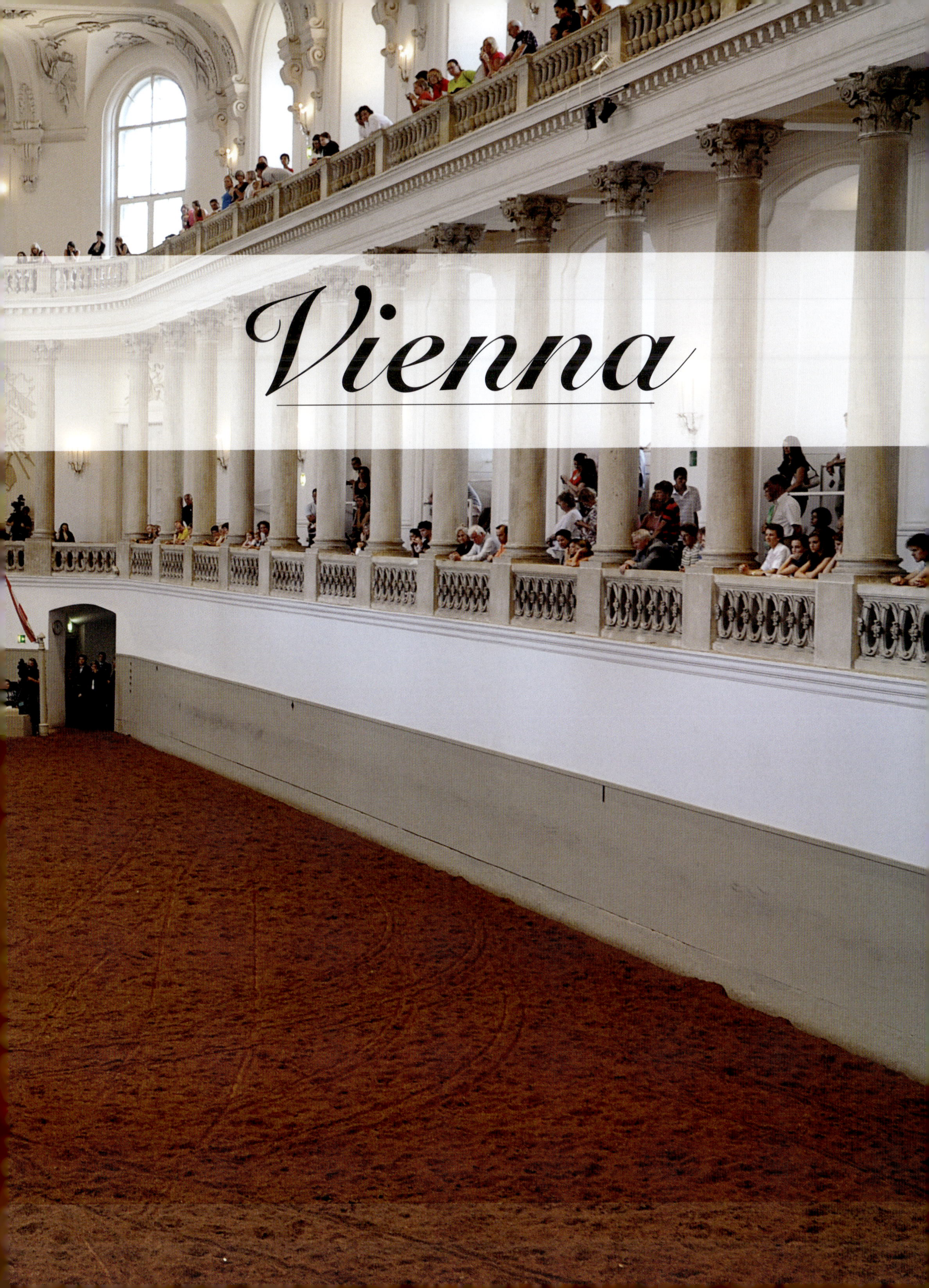

On 31 July 1829 Fryderyk Chopin and four friends, having satisfied the stringent customs regulations imposed on all visitors, entered Vienna. For Chopin the trip was a Mozart odyssey, even though Vienna's reputation as the musical capital of Europe was drawing to a close. Beethoven and Schubert had died within the past three years, and Mozart, considered unfashionable by a population demanding constant novelty, was all but forgotten. Musicians were increasingly looking to Paris as the hub of the musical world.

I am well and happy. I don't know why, but I appear to astonish the Germans, and I am astonished at their finding anything to be astonished at. Thanks to Elsner's letter, Haslinger doesn't know what to do with me.

Chopin to his family (Vienna, 8 August 1829)

Chopin's first visit was to publisher Tobias Haslinger, to whom he had sent his Variations on *Là ci darem la Mano* from Mozart's *Don Giovanni,* at his shop off the Graben. Haslinger wanted Chopin to perform his Variations to complement their scheduled publication that month, so he took him to see Wilhelm Würfel, whom Chopin remembered as the former professor of music at Warsaw University, and who was now a leading figure in Viennese musical circles. Würfel and Count Wenzel Gallenberg, the Director of the Kärntnertor Theatre, arranged two concerts, each the customary mix of orchestral and piano music interspersed with operatic arias. At the first, on 11 August 1829, a small but enthusiastic audience applauded Chopin the moment he appeared, and also after every Variation. He finished with an improvisation on themes from François-Adrien Boieldieu's *La Dame Blanche* and the Polish folk song, *Chmiel,* after which the audience refused to let him leave.

Chopin met various members of Vienna's musical establishment, including Count Moritz Dietrichstein, composer and father of budding piano virtuoso Sigismund Thalberg, who tried to persuade him to stay in Vienna; leading conductors Konradin Kreutzer and Ignaz von Seyfried; violinist Ignaz Schuppanzigh, leader of the most famous String Quartet of the time; and 60-year-old Adalbert Gyrowetz, whose Piano Concerto Chopin had played in Warsaw as an eight-year-old. He also met the father of modern pianism, Carl Czerny, a close associate of Beethoven, brilliant pianist, prolific composer, and Vienna's foremost piano teacher. Czerny went every day to Haslinger's to meet whoever was in town and invite them to his apartment in Krugerstrasse to talk and make

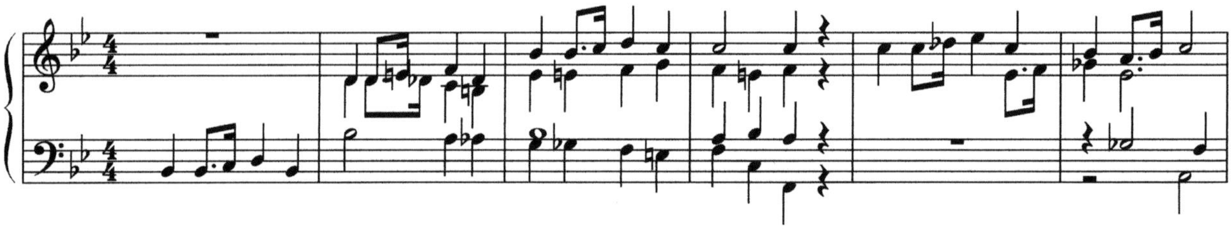

Chopin's *Là ci darem la mano* Variations were first heard in Vienna on 11 August 1829.

→ **The Graben**

Tobias Haslinger's music shop, where Vienna's musicians used to congregate, overlooked the Pestilence Memorial in the Graben.

← **The Spanish Riding School**

The Spanish Riding School and the Winter Manege is the home of the world famous Lipizzaner stallions. Situated almost opposite the Hofburg, it was only about 100 metres away from where Chopin had his apartment during his stay in Vienna.

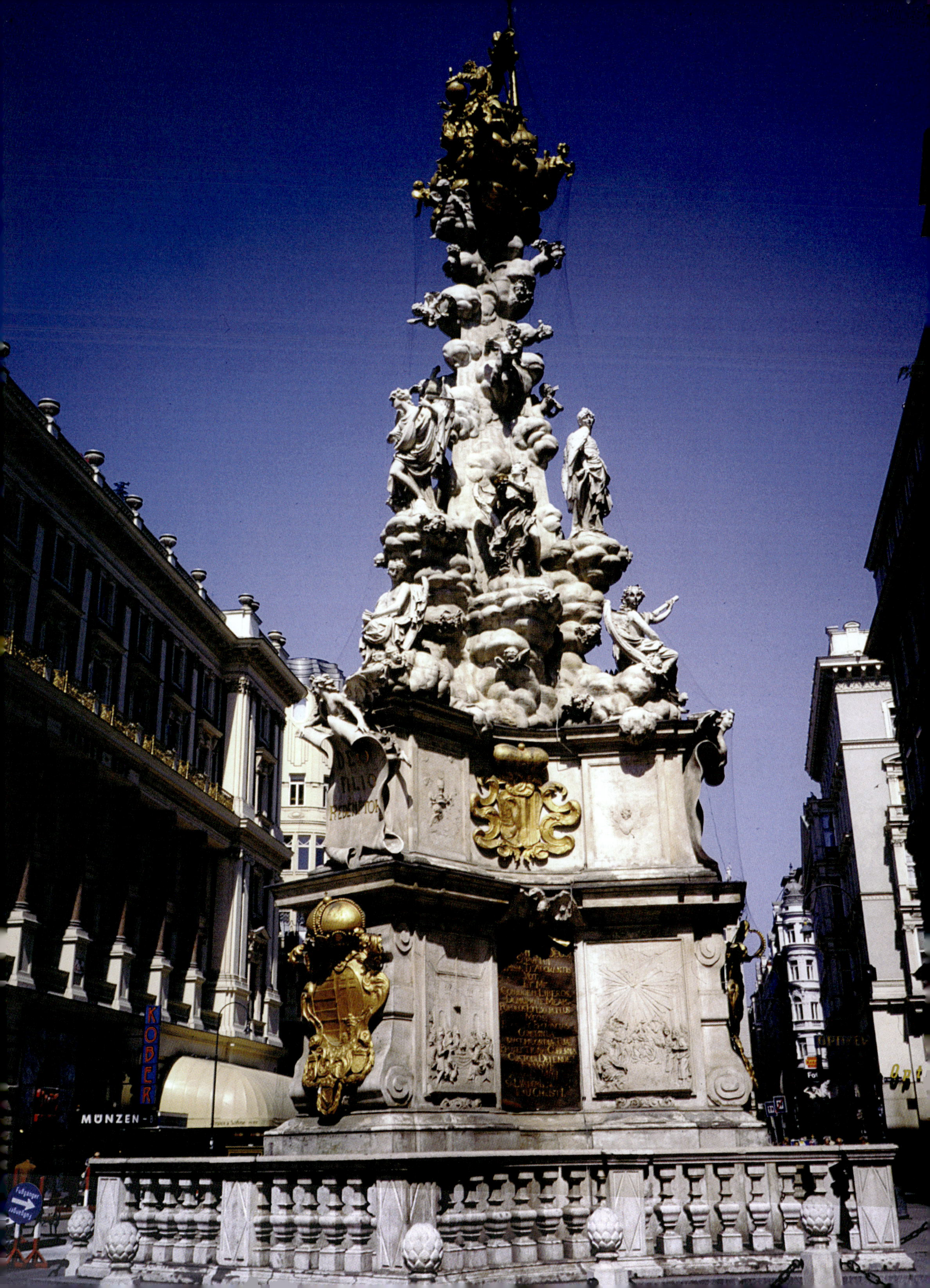

KODER
MÜNZEN

music. Chopin played duets with him, and found he liked the man but not his compositions.

Czerny has again arranged some overture for 8 pianos and 16 players, and is quite pleased. Otherwise I have not seen a single pianist here.

Chopin to his family (Vienna, 1 December 1830)

Chopin was later introduced to 18-year-old Leopoldine Blahetka, the city's leading female pianist, who, he wrote, *thumps frightfully*.

For the second concert, on 18 August, at which Chopin played the *Rondo à la Krakowiak* as well as the *Là ci darem la mano* Variations, the Kärntnertor Theatre was packed with a wildly applauding and cheering audience. Chopin had undoubtedly conquered Vienna, even though there were reservations about his soft touch, and the fact that he did not hit the keys hard enough – like Leopoldine Blahetka.

The day after the concert Chopin and his four travelling companions returned to Poland by way of Prague and Dresden.

Fifteen months later, on Tuesday 23 November 1830, Chopin was in Vienna once more, this time accompanied by his closest friend Tytus Woyciechowski. The two young men presented themselves once more to the uncompromising Viennese immigration machine before entering the city. They put up at the prestigious Hotel *Stadt London*, but moved to the cheaper hotel *zum goldenen Lamm* in Leopoldstadt, before finding a comfortable and less expensive apartment at 9 Kohlmarkt.

Chopin's hopes of further fame and fortune suffered a setback when news came from Poland of the storming of the Belvedere Palace by an insurgent group on 29 November 1830. Once again Poland was at war. Tytus decided to return immediately to take up arms, but persuaded Chopin to take his father's advice and stay – to fight for his country with his art. Chopin dithered, then decided to follow Tytus back to Poland; but after several stages he realised the futility of such a course of action, and returned to Vienna.

Chopin's second visit to Vienna had none of the urgency of the first, and he found himself in limbo. Haslinger was no longer interested in his compositions, Gallenberg had lost his post at the Kärntnertor Theatre, and Würfel was ill. In the minds of the fickle Viennese, he was now last year's pianist, and a Pole in a land fiercely opposed to the Polish Uprising. Vienna was only interested in Rossini operas and the Waltz.

Here waltzes are called works! And Strauss and Lanner, who play them for dancing, are called Kapellmeisters!

Chopin to Józef Elsner (Vienna, 26 January 1831)

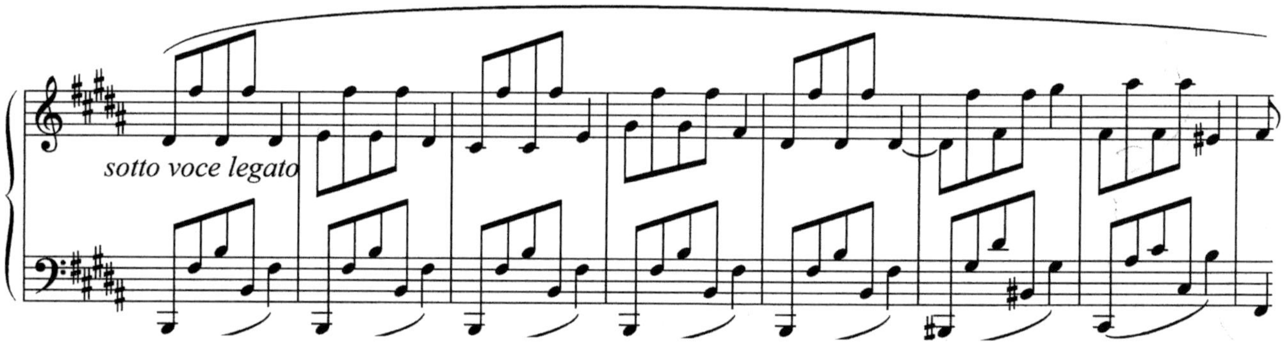

No one hearing Chopin playing his B minor Scherzo in Vienna imagined that it was only a matter of time before playing the trio section could lead to deportation to Siberia.

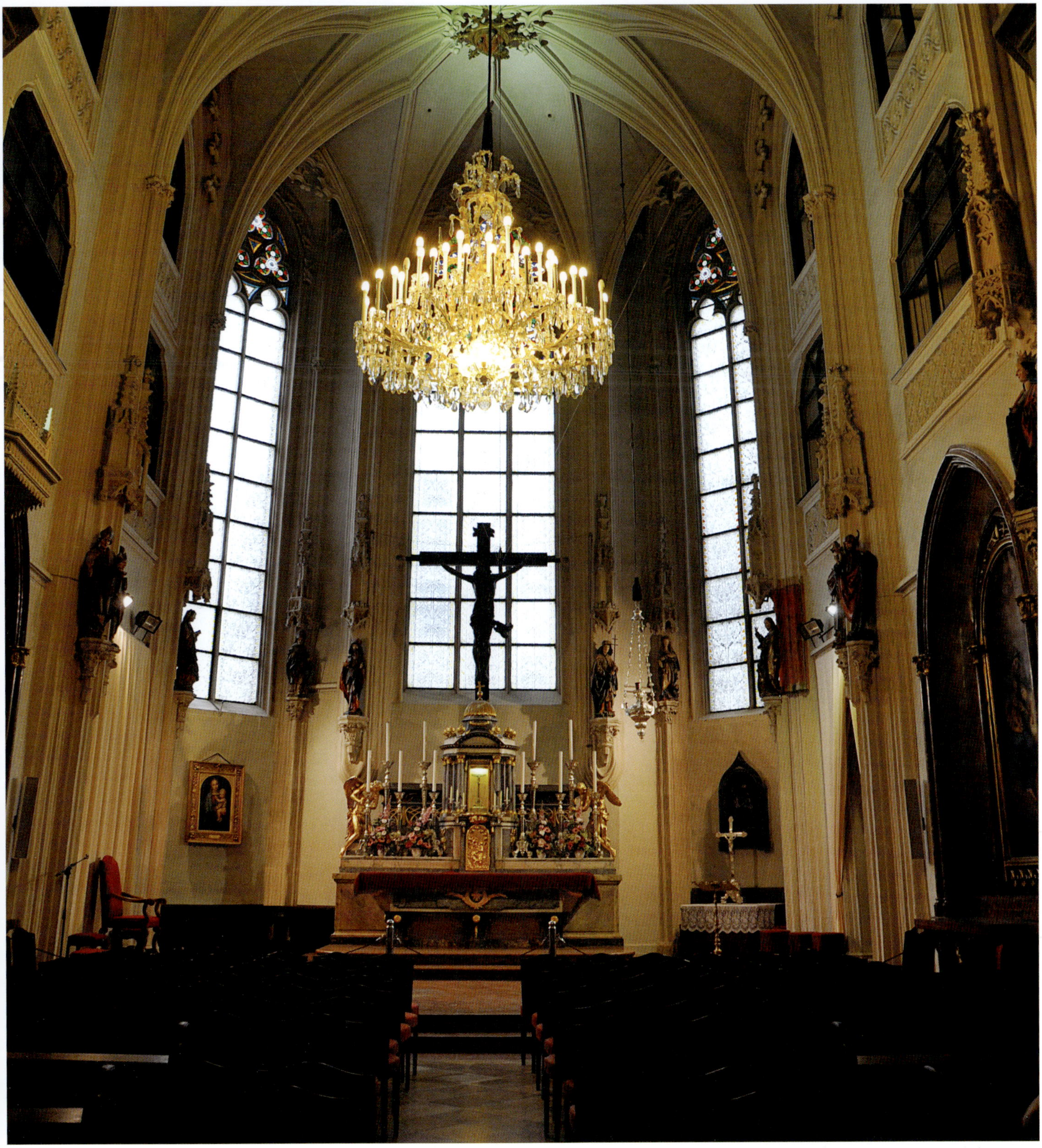

Hofburg
On Christmas Eve 1830 Chopin attended Midnight Mass at the Hofburg's Imperial Chapel, where his friend, violinist Josef Slawik, was playing in the orchestra.

Chopin idled the next four months away around Vienna, sightseeing, socialising and going to the opera. He spent Christmas Eve in St. Stephen's Cathedral, recalling Christmases past. He went to hear Midnight Mass at the Imperial Chapel, where his friend, violinist Józef Slawik, was playing in the orchestra.

At midnight I went into St. Stephen's, just to look at the huge building at that hour; I got into the darkest corner at the foot of a Gothic pillar. I can't describe the greatness, the magnificence of those huge arches. A mournful harmony all around, I never felt my loneliness so clearly.

Chopin to Jan Matuszyński (Vienna, 26 December 1830)

Chopin's Scherzo in B minor, Op. 20, with its trio section recalling the best-loved of all Polish Christmas carols, *Lulajże Jezuniu,* dates from these days of dark depression. It would one day, after his death, be banned as subversive: his fight against oppression had already begun.

Chopin remained on the peripheries of Vienna's musical life. He considered forming a trio with Slawik and cellist Josef Merk. Johann Nepomuk Hummel and his son Eugen, who painted his portrait, were frequent visitors to his rooms. He called on Abbé Maximilian Stadler, Mozart's friend and biographer, at his apartment in the former Rasumovsky Palace. Fryderyk went with Sigismund Thalberg, a pianist whose *donner und blitzen* style was diametrically opposite to his own, to an organ recital at the Evangelical church in Dorotheergasse. He continued to play duets with Czerny.

Try to defend Polish music, express any opinion about it, and you'll be taken for crazy; all the more as Czerny, Vienna's oracle in the manufacture of musical taste, has never yet used a Polish melody for variations.

Chopin to his family (Vienna, 28 May 1831)

In June 1831 Chopin went out into the countryside: once to the summer residence in the Wienerwaldt of Dr Johann Malfatti, whence there was a panoramic view of Vienna, and once to Leopoldsberg and Kahlenberg.

From the Leopoldsberg you can see all Vienna, Wagram, Aspern, Pressburg, the Neuburg Convent, the castle where Richard the Lion Heart was a prisoner, and all the upper reaches of the Danube. After lunch we went to

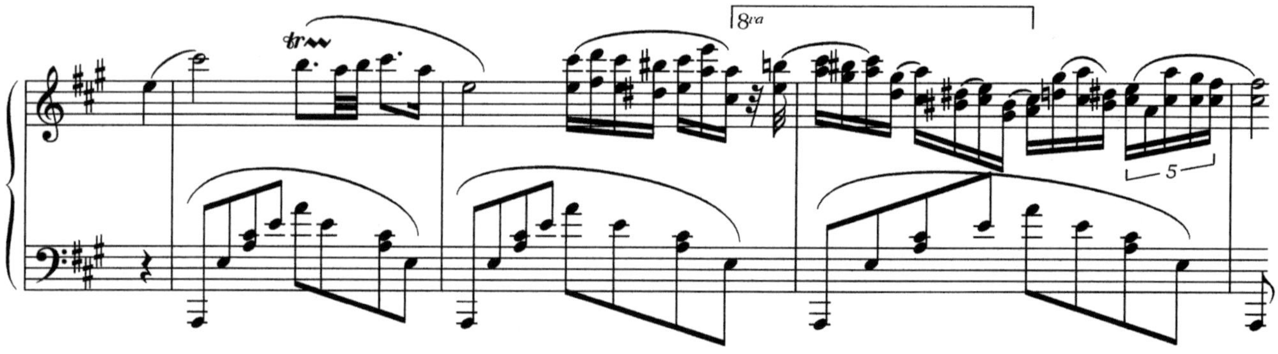

Chopin's *Fantasia on Polish Airs*, which he performed both in Munich and Vienna, is effectively a miniature piano concerto in one movement.

Kohlmarkt

Between November 1830 and July 1831 Chopin rented an apartment at Kohlmarkt 9, which today is a bookshop and map house.

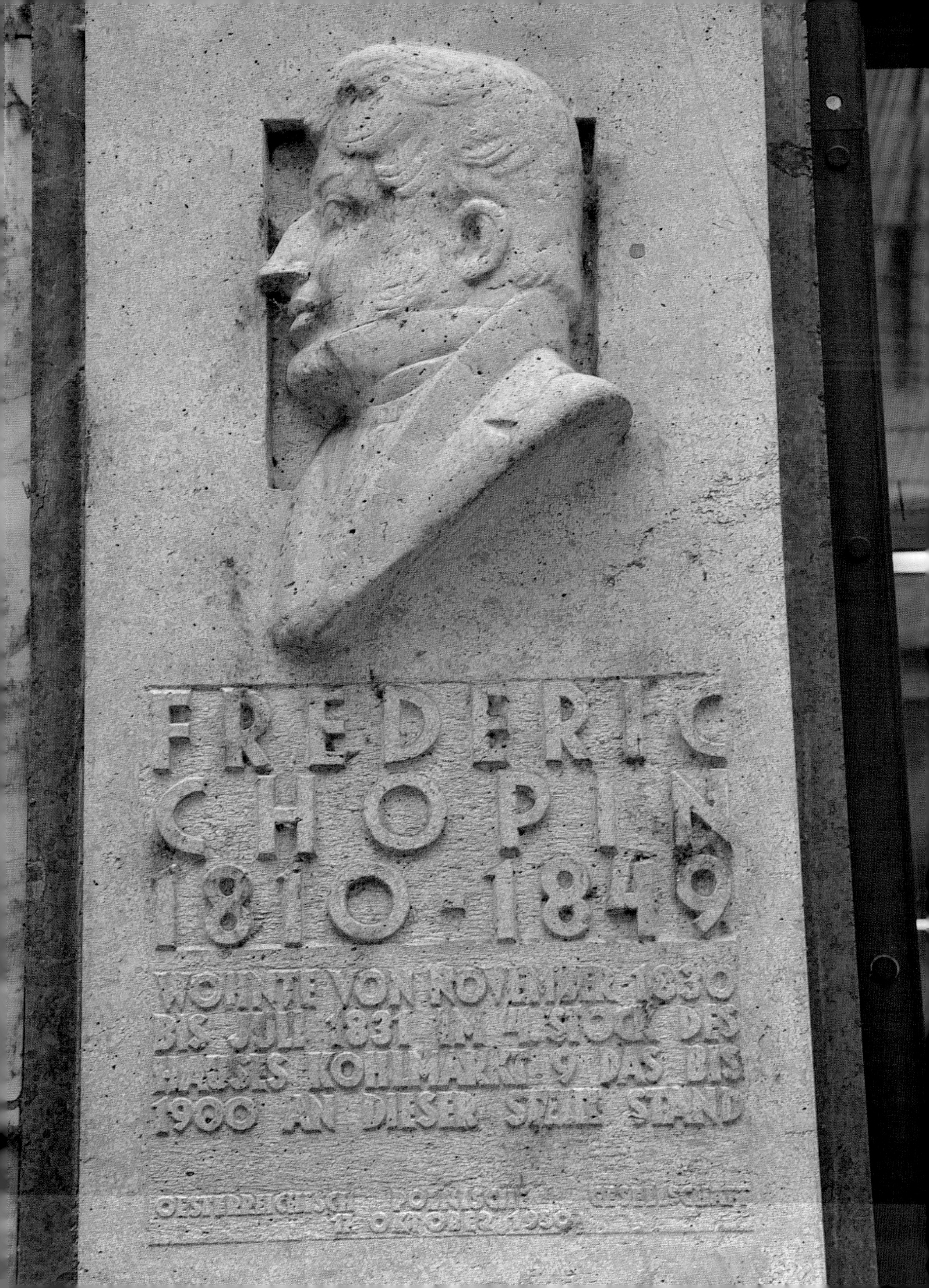
FREDERIC
CHOPIN
1810-1849
WOHNTE VON NOVEMBER 1830
BIS JULI 1831 IM 4. STOCK DES
HAUSES KOHLMARKT 9 DAS BIS
1900 AN DIESER STELLE STAND
OESTERREICHISCH POLNISCHE GESELLSCHAFT

the Kahlenberg, where King Sobieski had his camp. There's a church there in which he himself said mass before attacking the Turks.

Chopin to his Family (Vienna, 25 June 1831)

The Polish Uprising kept his thoughts on his family and friends in Poland, including Tytus Woyciechowski, and Jan Matuszyński, the go-between in his lingering love for Konstancja Gładkowska, the young singer who captured his heart and became his "ideal" before his departure from Poland, and a lock of whose hair he carried with him. He performed his E minor Concerto, the slow movement of which was an outpouring of his love for her, at the only two concerts in which he took part in the eight months that he spent in Vienna: one at the Redoutensaal on 4 April 1831, and one on 11 June at the Kärntnertor Theatre.

Chopin, his sights set on Paris, left Vienna on 20 July, initially for Munich, the capital of King Ludwig I's Bavaria. On 28 August he took part in a concert at the Philharmonic Society Hall, in the Wittelsbacherplatz, at which he played both the E minor Concerto and his *Fantasia on Polish Airs.*

Mr Chopin... showed an excellent virtuosity in the treatment of his instrument; besides a developed technique, one noticed especially a charming delicacy of execution, and a beautiful and characteristic rendering of the motives.

30 August 1831 issue of "Flora", on Chopin's Munich concert

Chopin arrived at Stuttgart, the capital of King Wilhelm I's Württemberg, on 8 September 1831, the day that Warsaw fell to the Russians, who exacted terrible retribution. He stayed with Peter Johann Pixis, the brother of the Kapellmeister at the National Theatre in Prague. There he poured out his soul at the dreadful news from Poland in his angry Etude in C minor, Op. 10 No 12, the so-called "Revolutionary".

The tower clocks of Stuttgart strike the night hours. Ah, how many corpses are being made in the world in this minute! Children have lost their mothers, mothers their children. How many plans have gone to waste, how much grief over the dead at this moment?

Chopin's notebook (Stuttgart, September 1831)

He only stayed in Stuttgart for two days before departing on the long, final stage, to a new life in his father's native land.

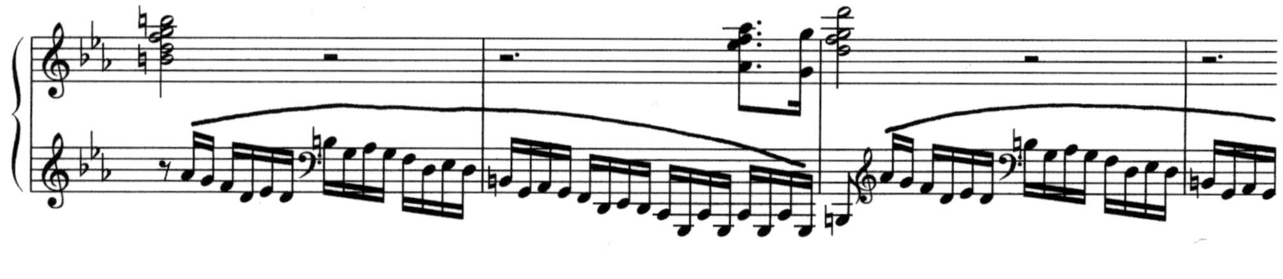

Chopin expressed his rage at the Russian invasion of Poland with his "Revolutionary" Etude in C minor, written in Stuttgart shortly after his departure from Vienna for Paris.

Hofburg
The back entrance, as seen from the Kohlmarkt, to the Imperial Palace of the Hofburg, where Chopin gave a concert in the Redoutensaal on 4 April 1831.

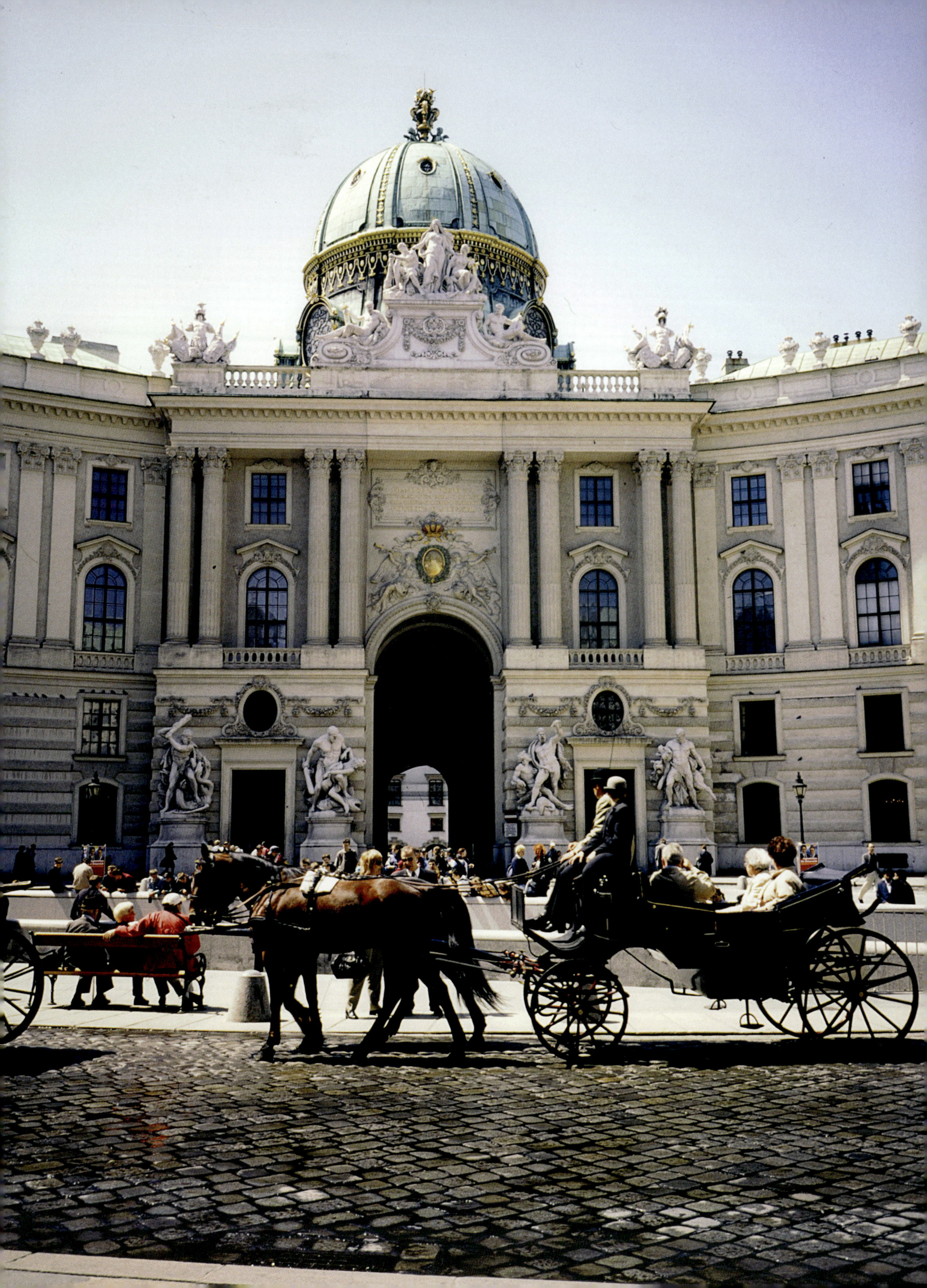

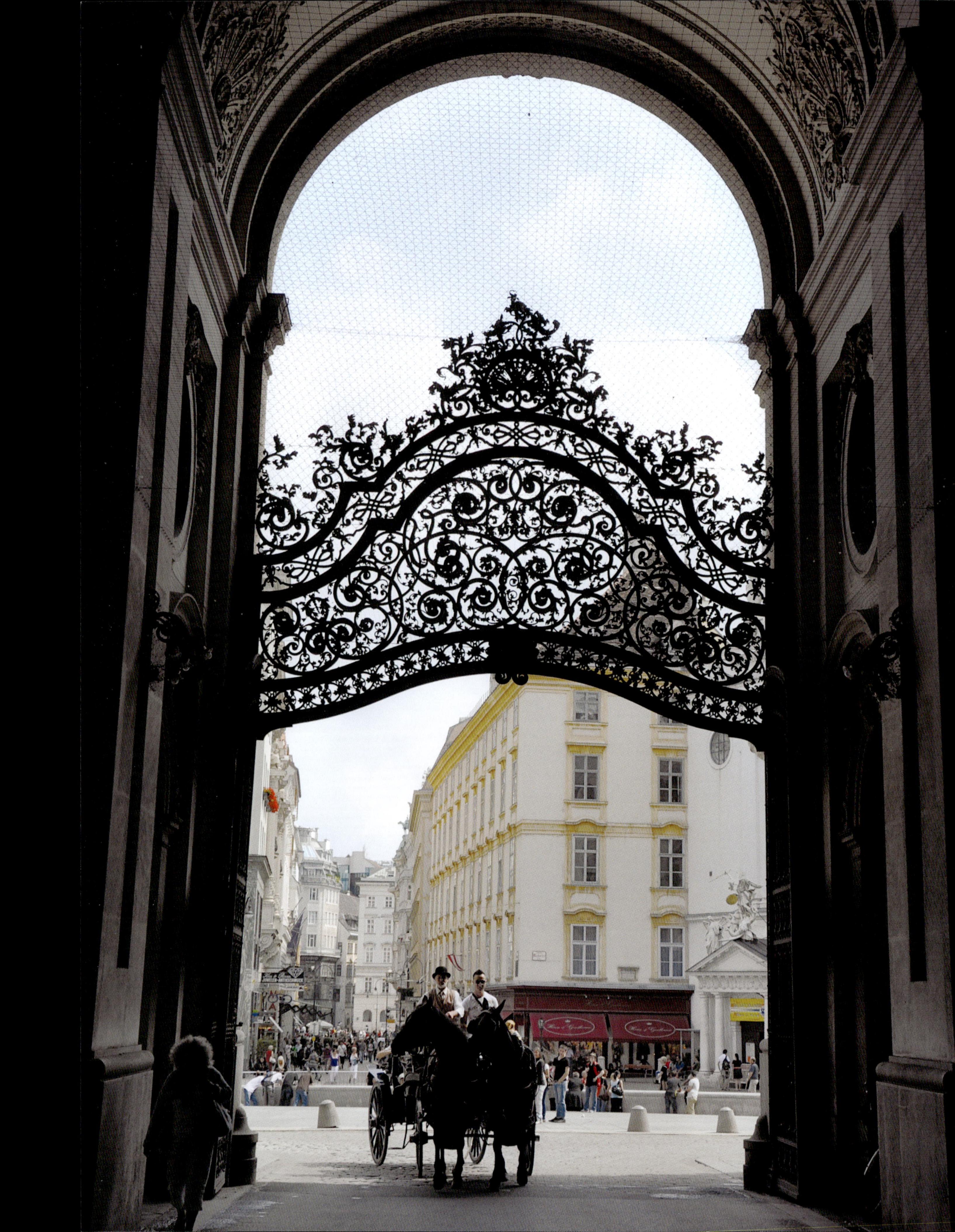

The major Chopin sites of Vienna, such as St. Stephen's Cathedral, the Prater, Leopoldsberg, the Church of St. Joseph at the Kahlenberg, the Imperial Chapel of the Hofburg, and the Evangelical church in Dorotheergasse, are still there; the Redoutensaal in the Hofburg is now a conference centre; the apartment in the Kohlmarkt, although rebuilt, bears a commemorative plaque. Sacher's confectionery establishment now stands on the site of the Kärntnertor Theatre, and Paternostergaschen, off the Graben, where Tobias Haslinger's shop was situated, no longer exists.

The Hotel *Stadt London* stood off the Postgasse near the Dominican church, and the Hotel *zum goldenen Lamm* stood by the Franzensbrücke in Leopoldstadt. Stadler's apartment in the former Rasumovsky Palace is now the Geological Museum in Rasumovsky Gasse. Czerny's apartment has been rebuilt, its site approximately at today's 3 Krugerstrasse.

The Munich Philharmonic Society's Hall is no longer in Wittelsbacherplatz, but Stuttgart's Stiftskirche, in the Schillerplatz, chimes today as it did in Chopin's time.

Hofburg
The wrought-iron entrance to the Hofburg, with its view onto the Kohlmarkt, is one of Vienna's landmarks.

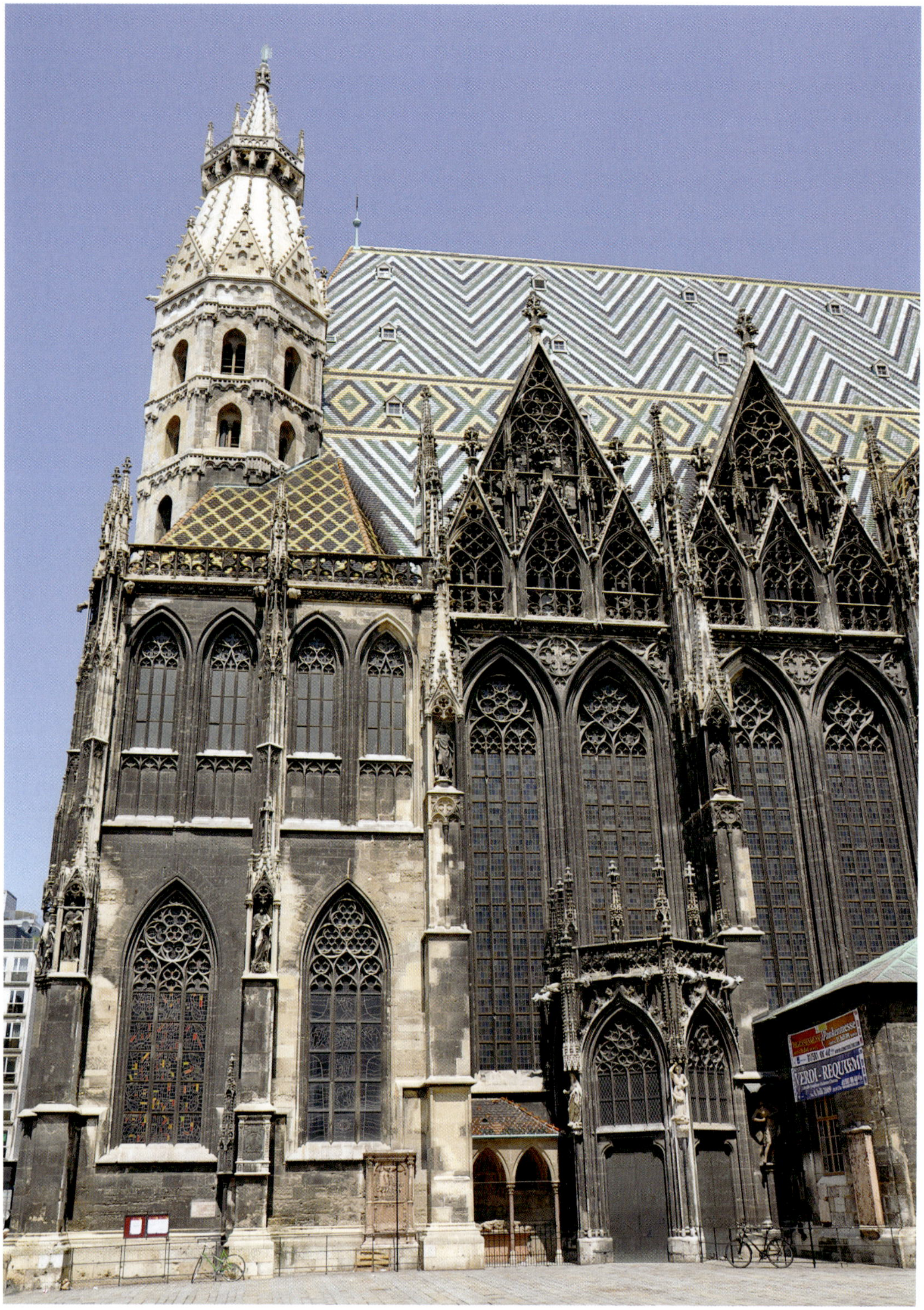

St. Stephen's Cathedral

St. Stephen's Cathedral is the mother church of the Archdiocese of Vienna and the seat of the Archbishop of Vienna. Its current Romanesque and Gothic form as seen today, was largely initiated by Rudolf IV in 1359 and stands on the ruins of two earlier churches, the first being a parish church consecrated in 1147. As the most important religious building in Austria's capital, the cathedral has born witness to many important events in that nation's history and has, with its multi-coloured tile roof, become one of the city's most recognizable symbols.

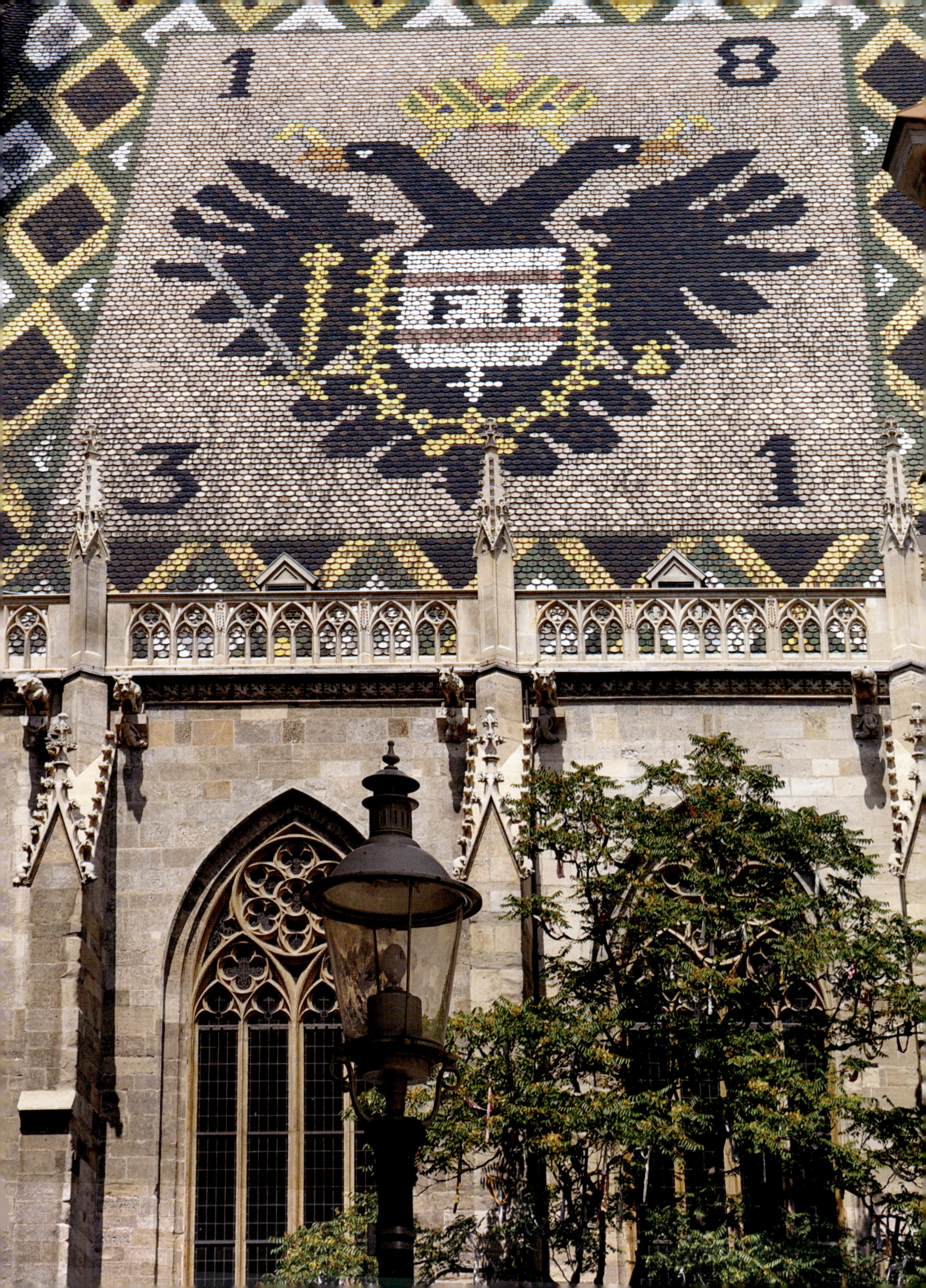

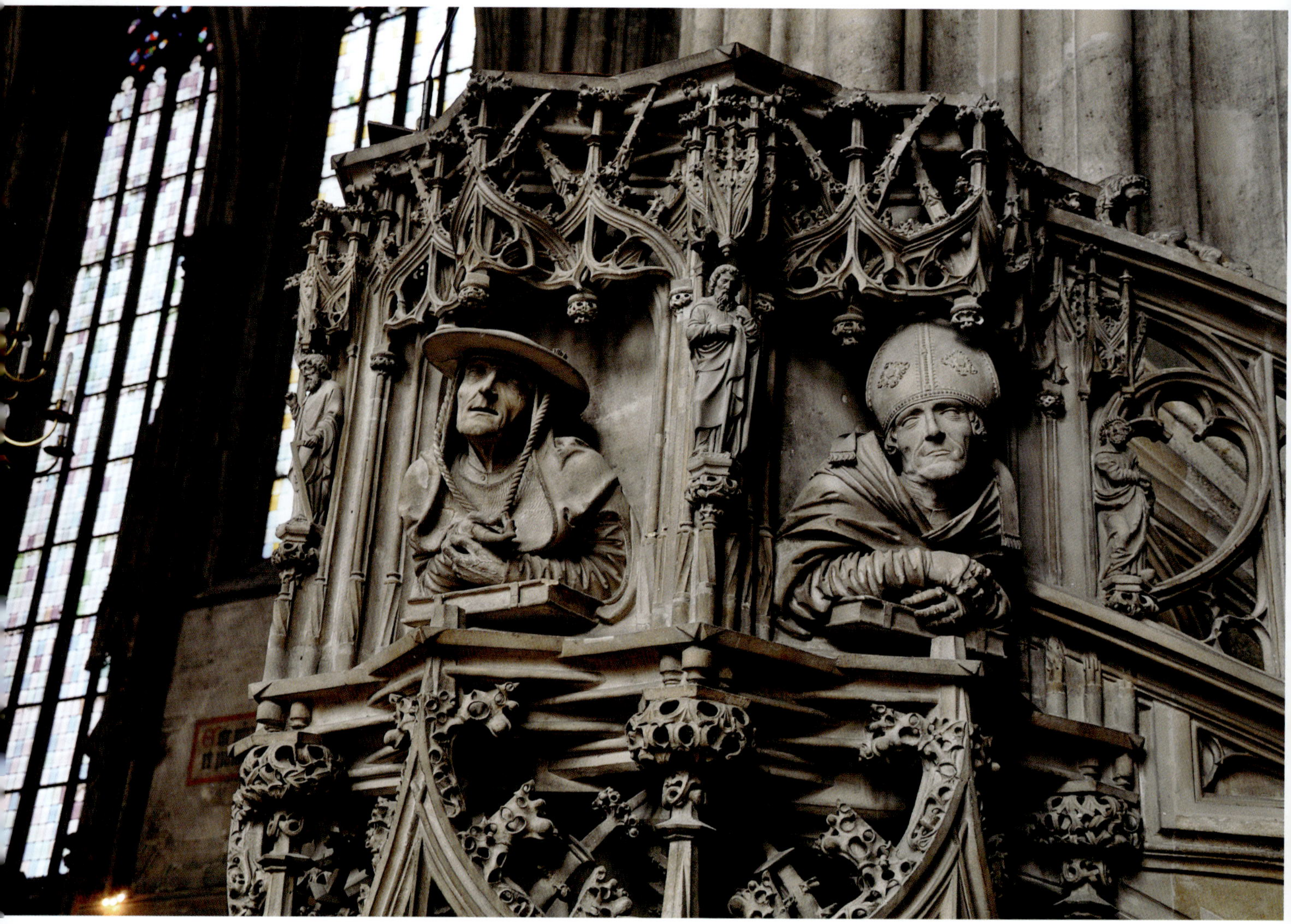

St. Stephen's Cathedral

Detail of the stone pulpit, a masterwork of late gothic sculpture now attributed to Niclaes Gerhaert van Leyden. The two relief portraits are of St. Jerome and St. Augustine of Hippo, two of the four original Doctors of the Church; the other two, St. Ambrose and St. Gregory the Great are on the other side of this pulpit.

→ During a quiet period on Christmas Eve 1830 Chopin went into St. Stephen's Cathedral, to meditate and admire its greatness and the magnificence of its huge arches.

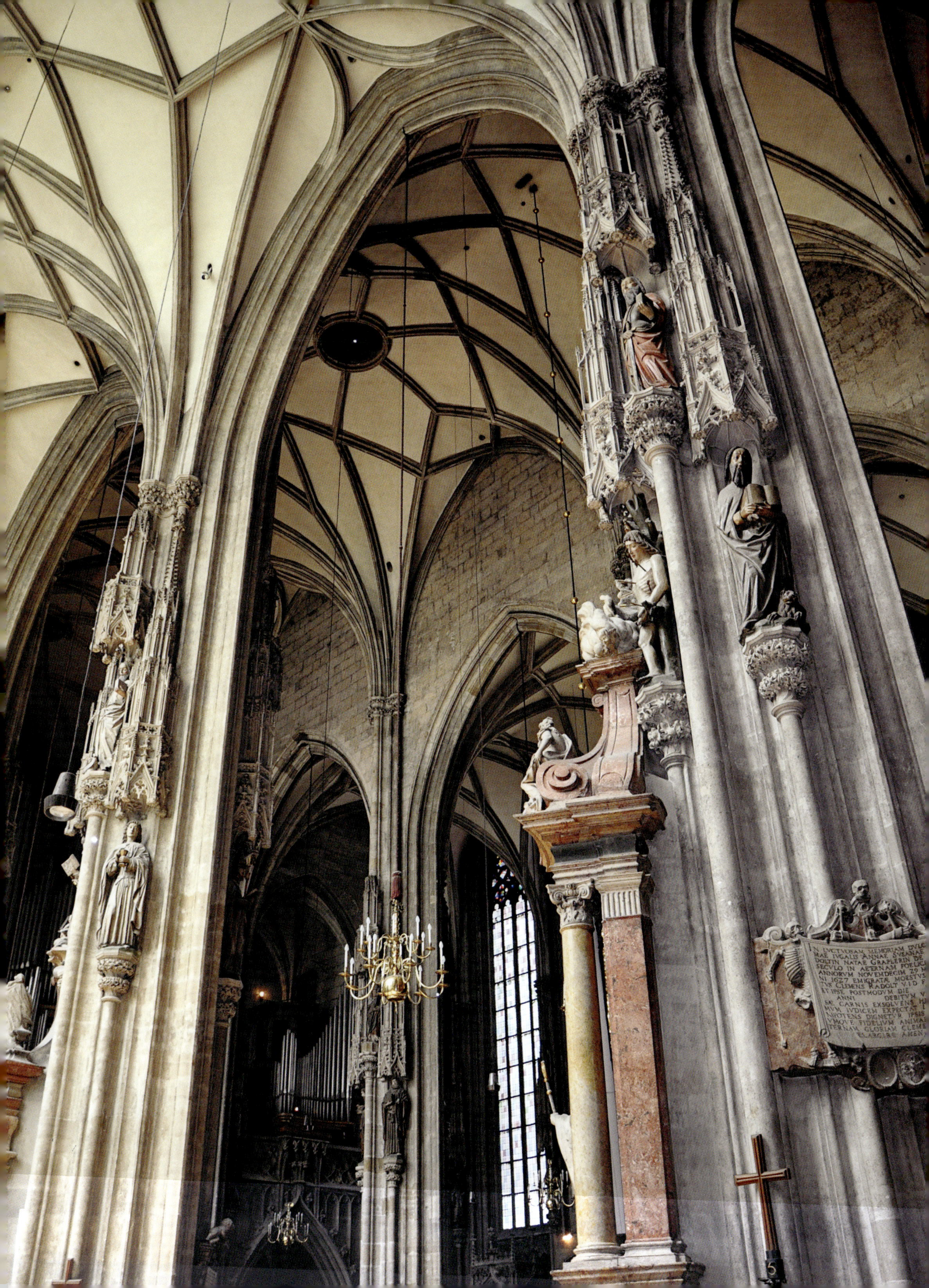

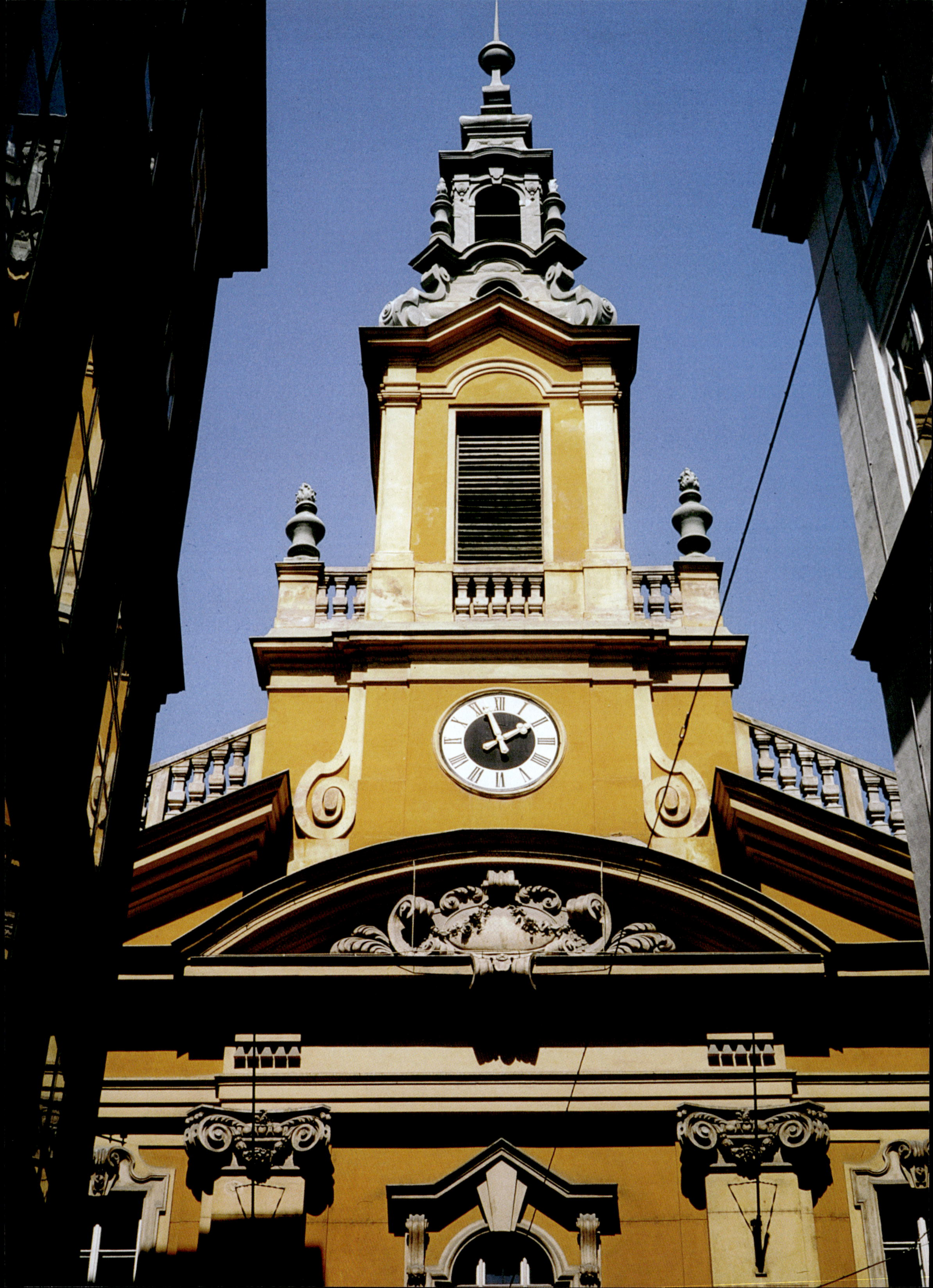

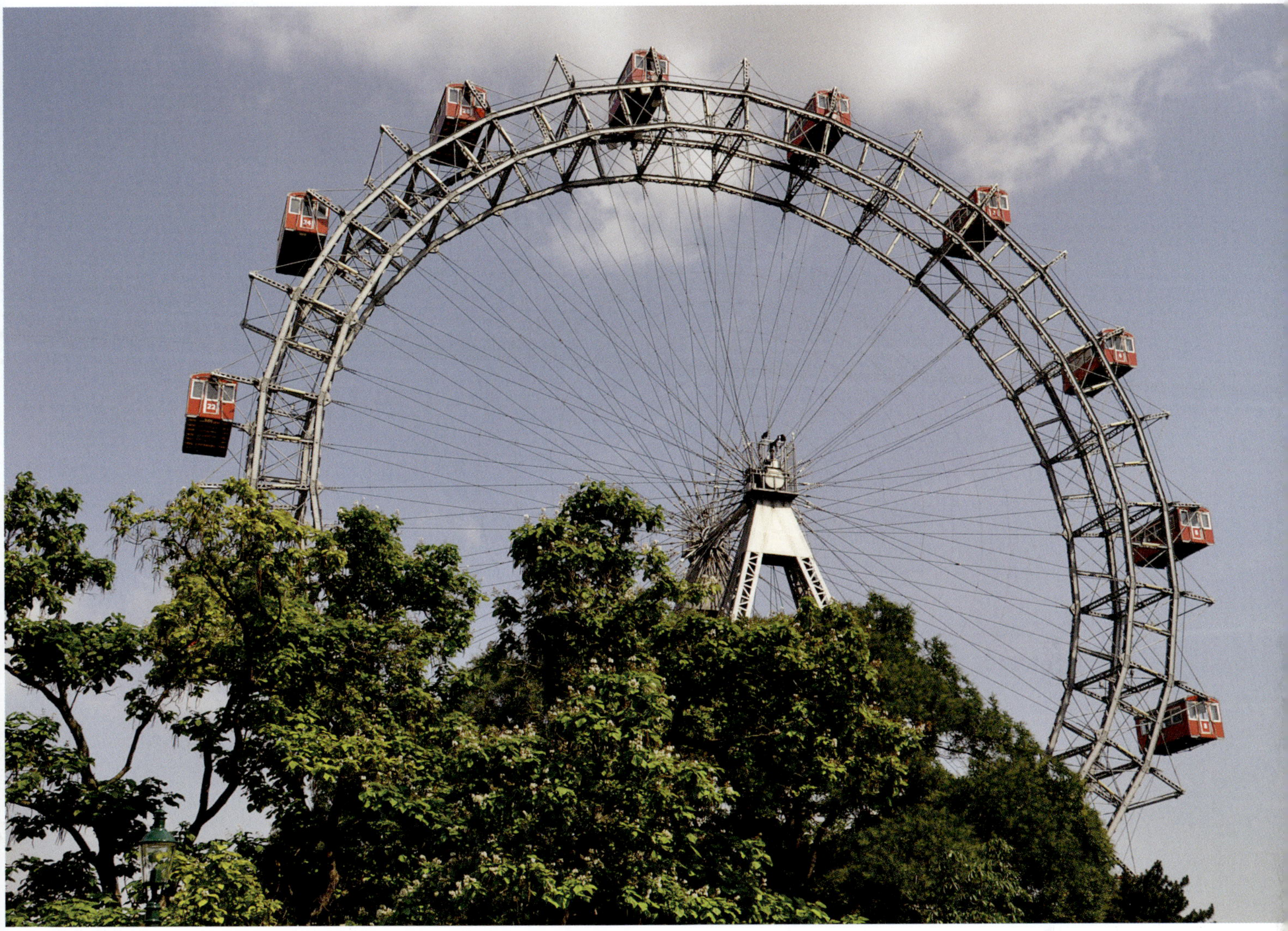

The Prater

Emperor Joseph II opened the Prater, Vienna's biggest public park, in 1766 for the purposes of free public enjoyment, and allowed the establishment of coffee-houses and places of entertainment. Known today as the Wurstelprater, it is an extensive fun-fair dominated by its famous landmark Ferris-wheel, or Riesenrad, built in 1897 for Vienna's World Exhibition.

←Dorotheergasse

The Evangelical church in Dorotheergasse where on 27 May 1831 Chopin attended an organ concert by Hesse with Sigismund Thalberg.

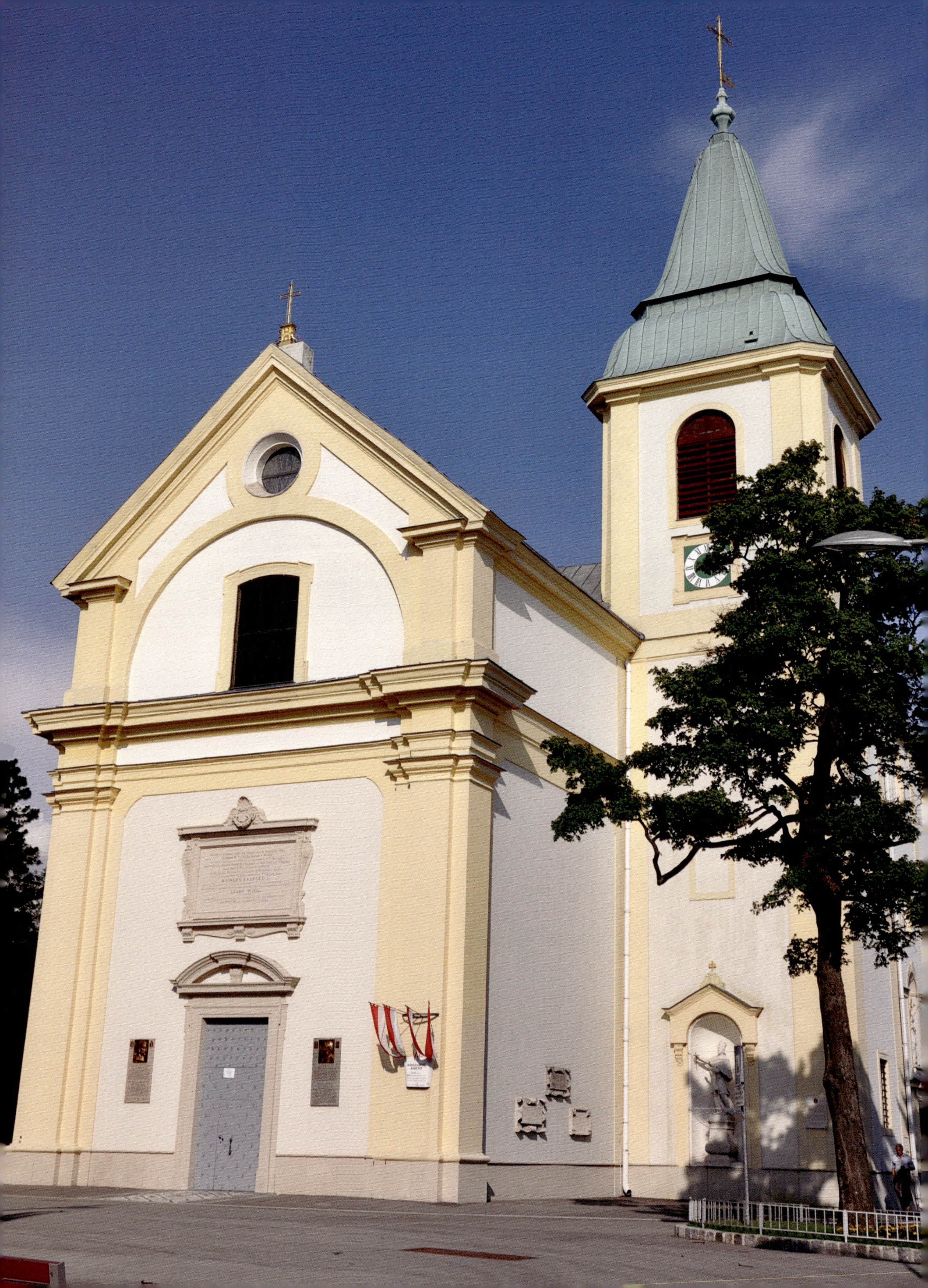

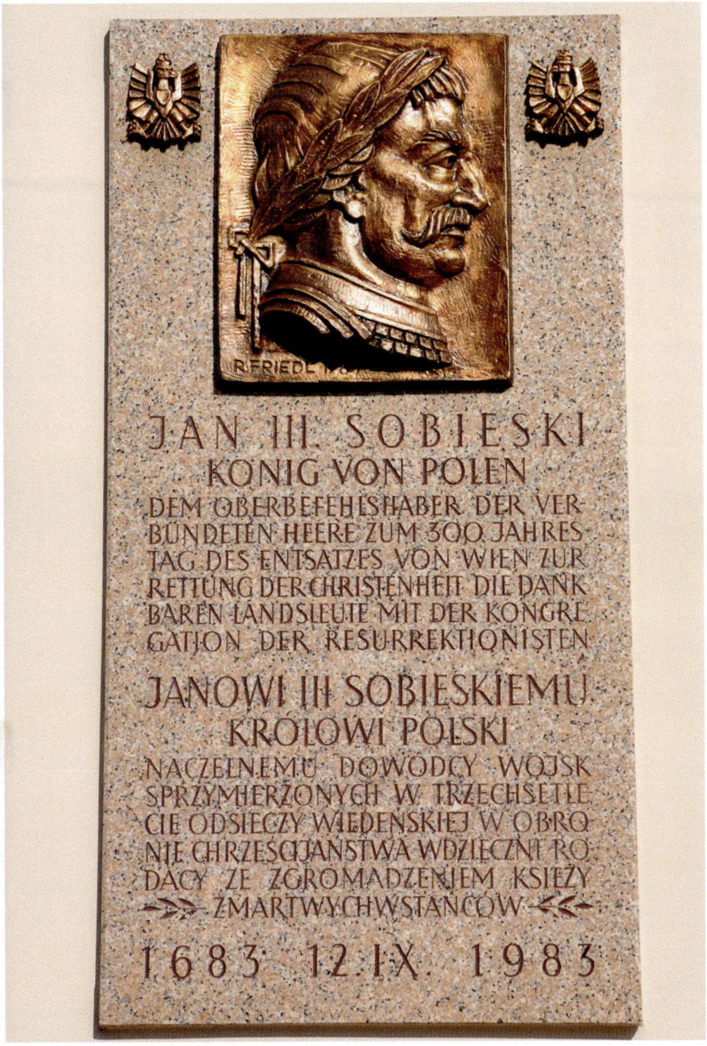

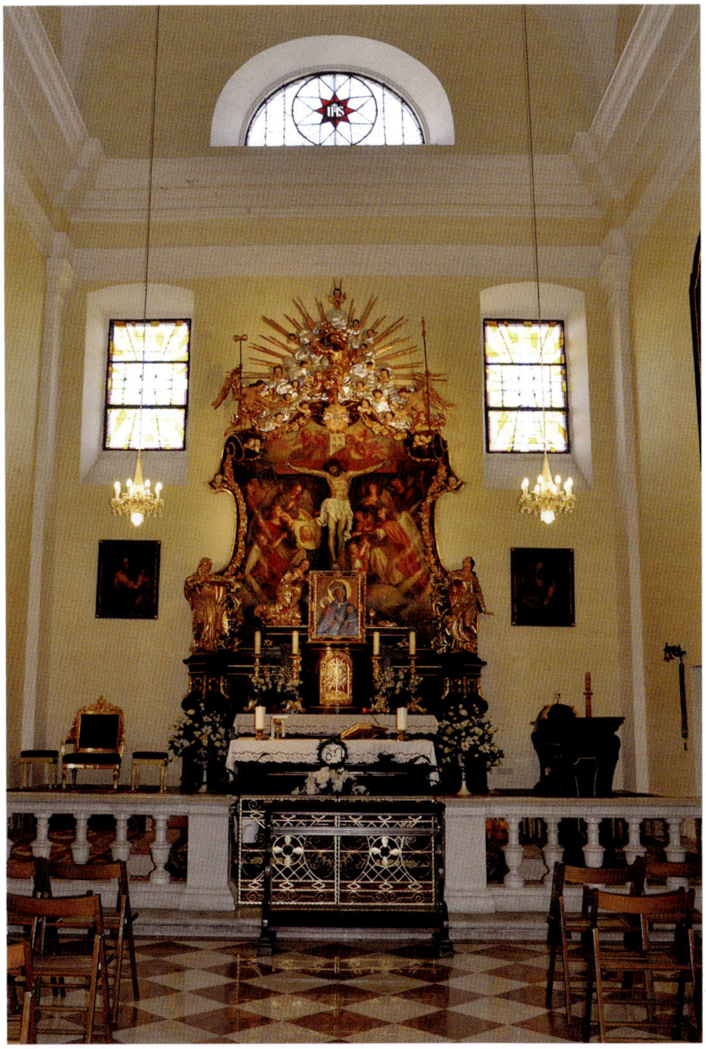

Kahlenberg

Chopin visited St. Joseph's church on the Kahlenberg, a few kilometres outside Vienna, in June 1831. It was here that Jan Sobieski, King of Poland, attended mass on the morning of 12 September 1683 before defeating the Turkish army, and ending the siege of Vienna.

A plaque at the church of St. Joseph commemorates Sobieski's victory.

The interior of St. Joseph's church, which is still a major place of pilgrimage, especially for Poles, and where Mass is said every afternoon.

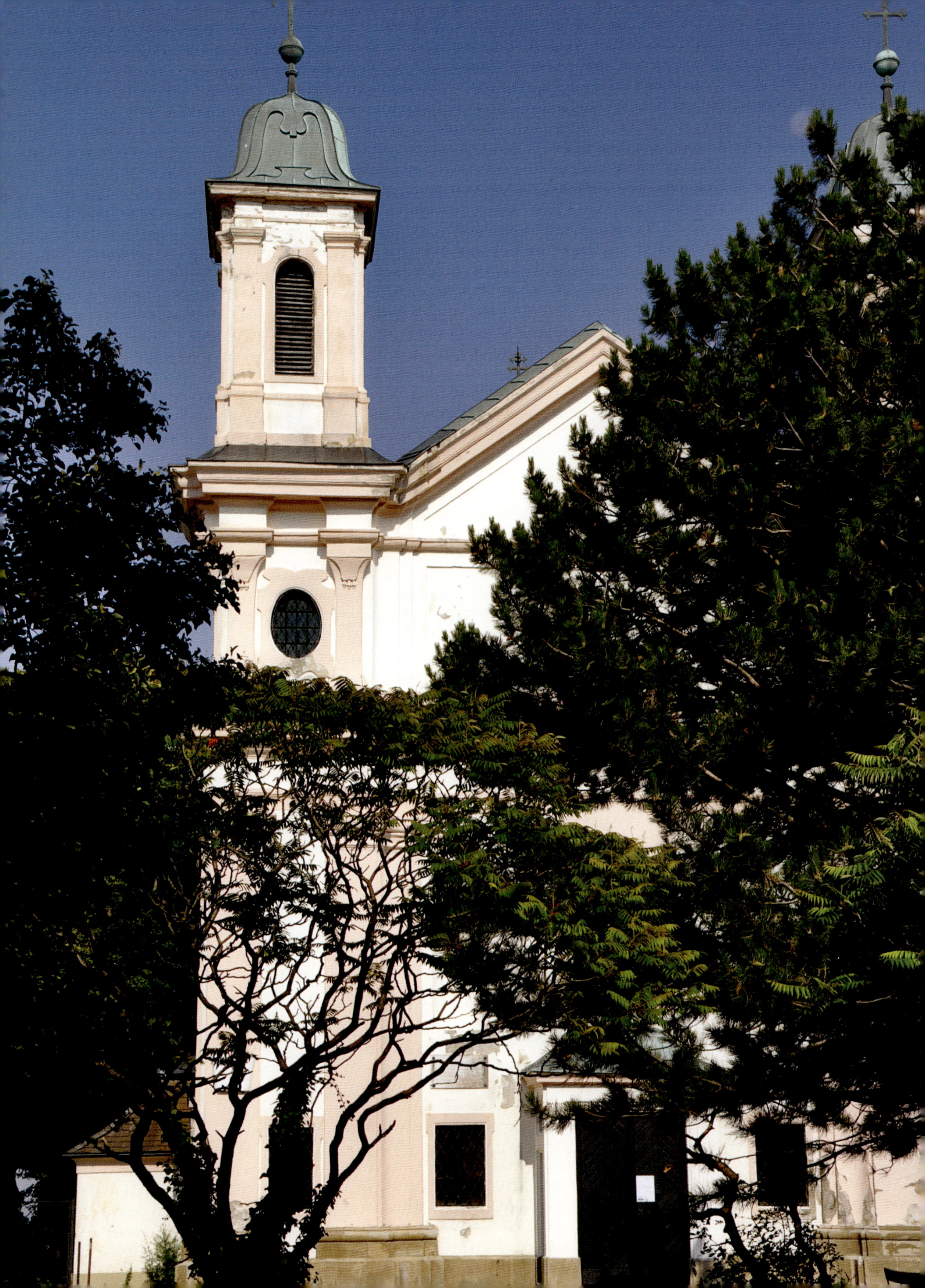

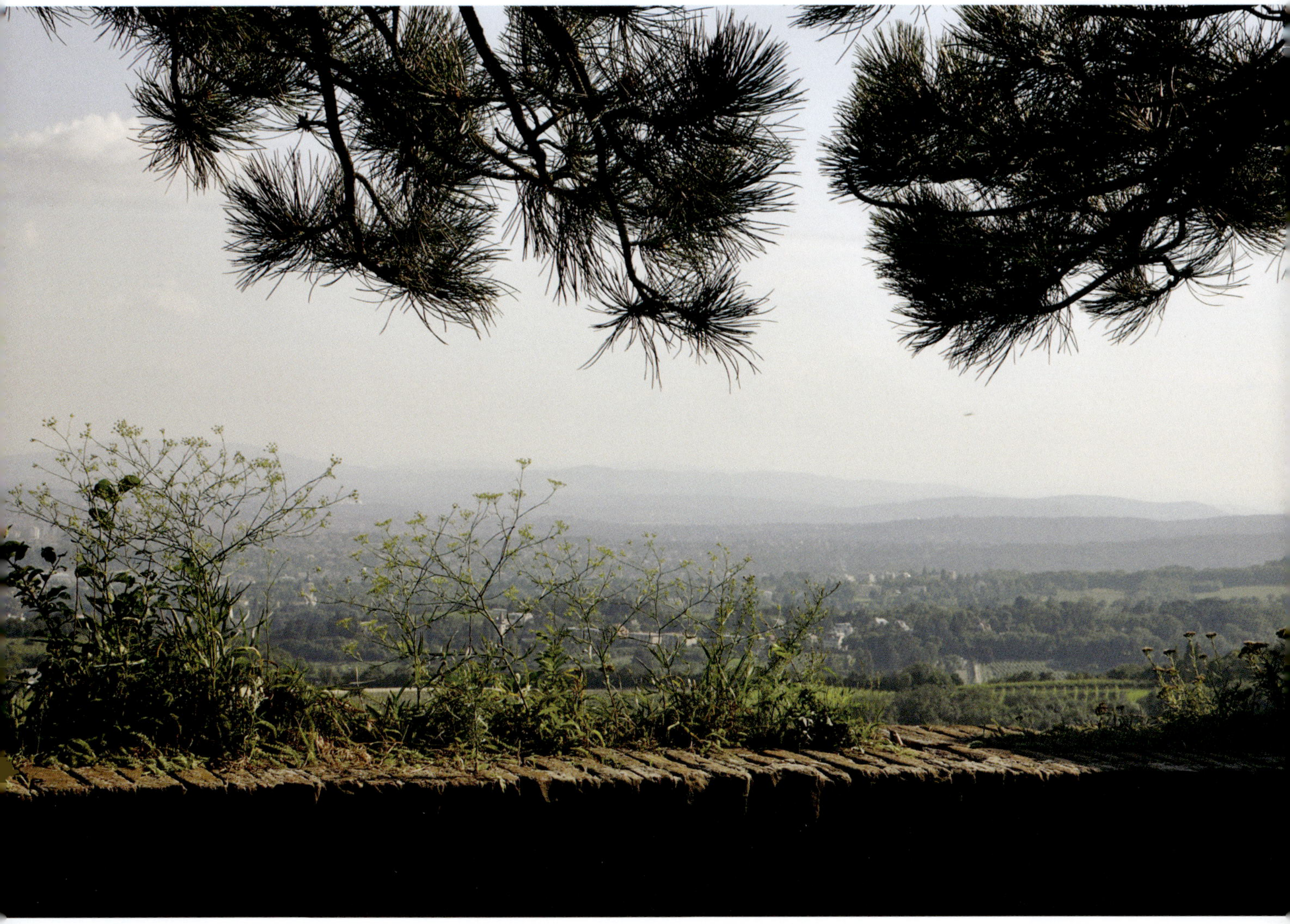

Leopoldsberg
In June 1831 Chopin paid a visit to St. Leopold's church, today a popular hilltop tourist attraction just outside Vienna.

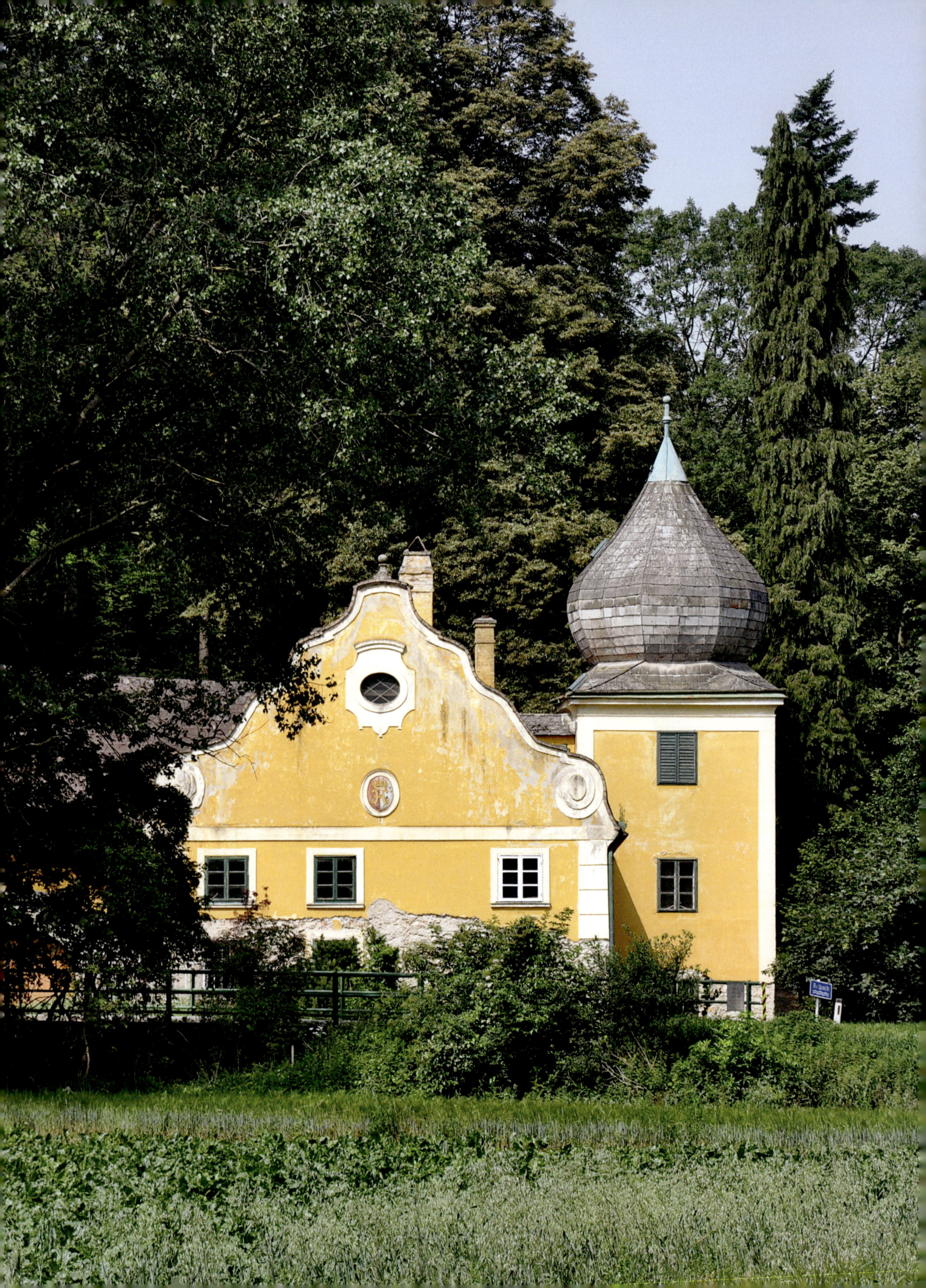

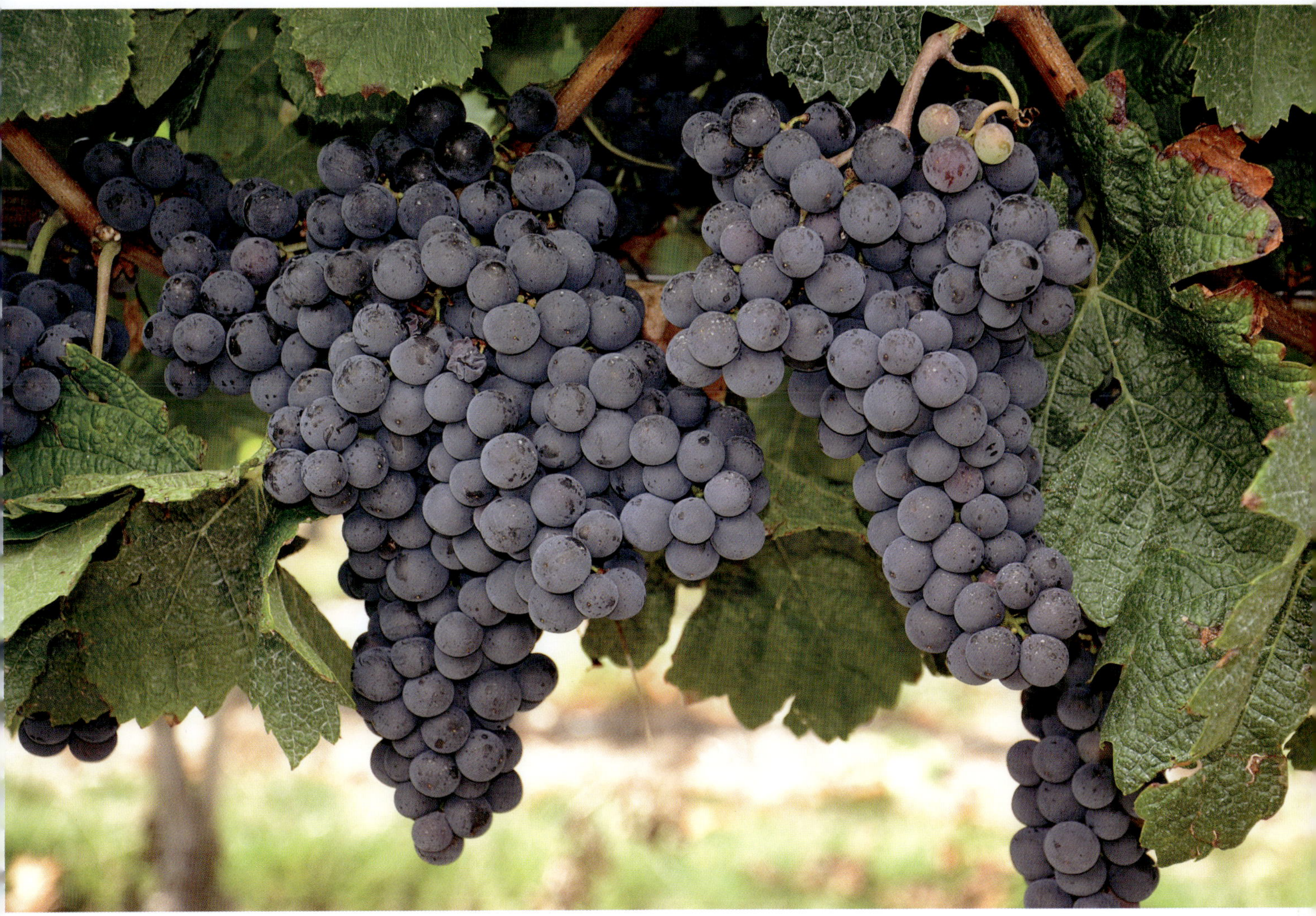

Vienna is known for its excellent wines and many vineyards can be found in the hills around Vienna which Chopin often used to visit.

← **Vienna Woods**
A typical old Austrian hunting lodge in the Vienna Woods.

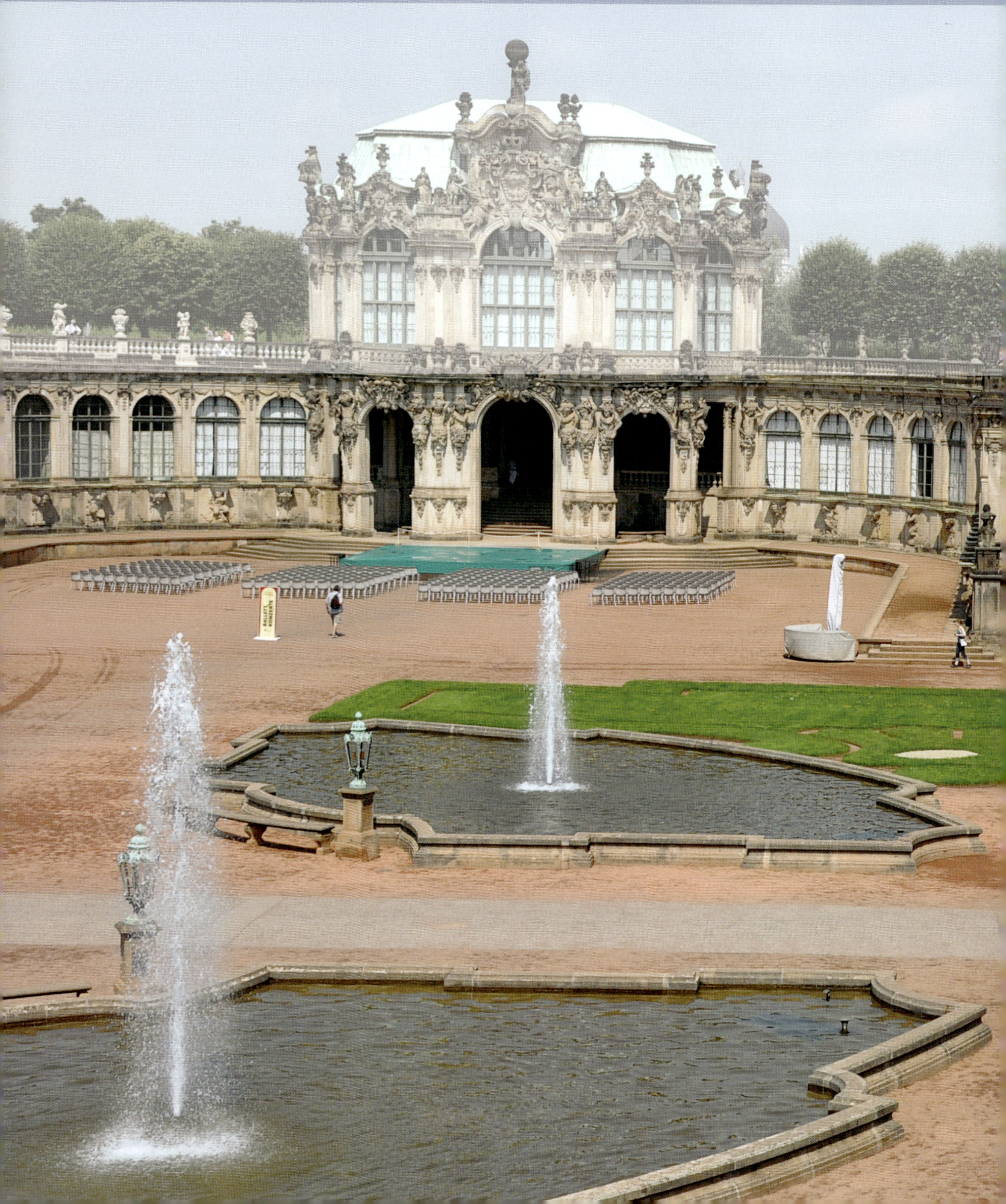

Bohemia & Saxony

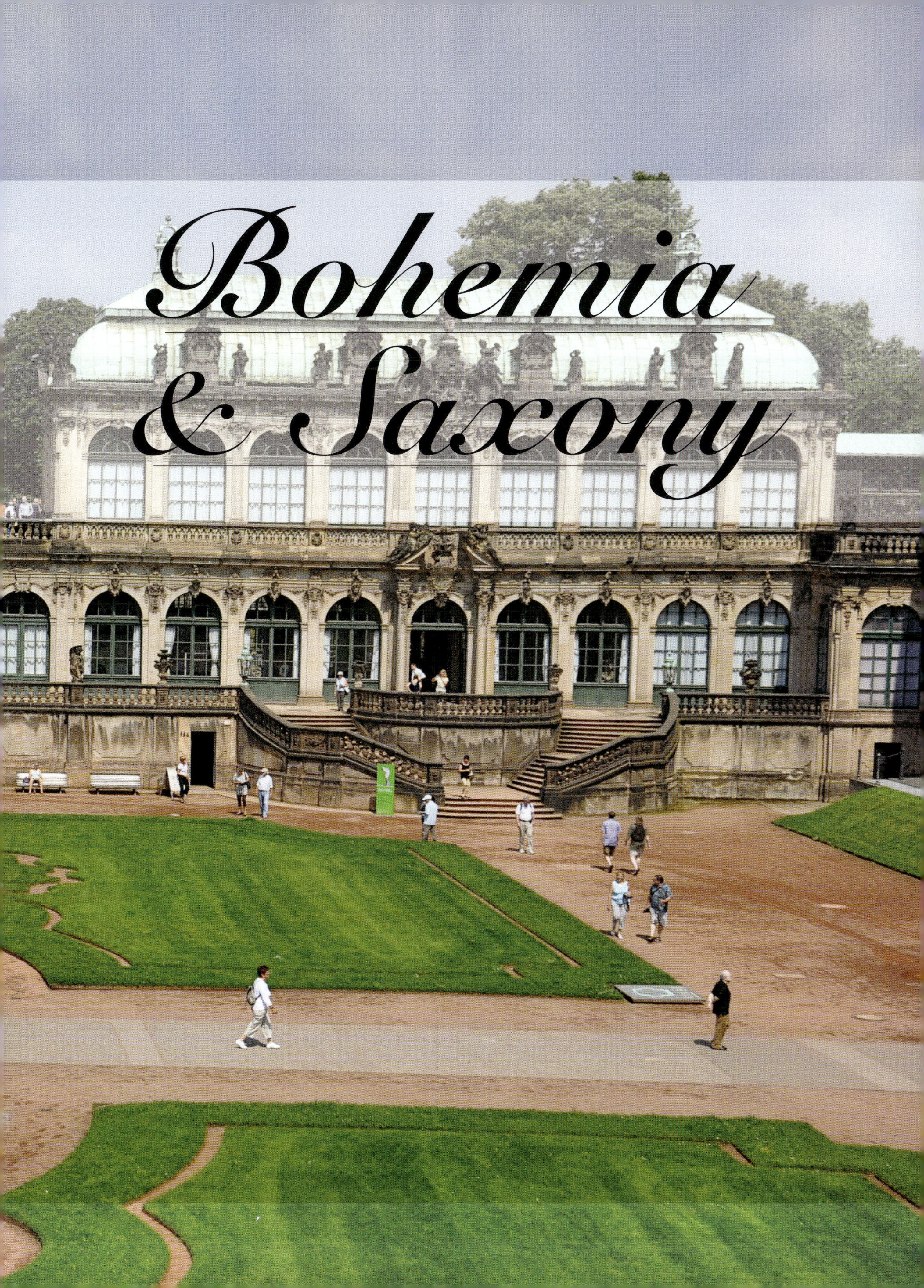

To the north of the beautiful, mountainous region of central Europe known as Saxon Switzerland lies the Kingdom of Saxony and its capital, Dresden, with Bohemia – part of the Austrian Empire – and its capital, Prague, to the south. Fryderyk Chopin visited the region on three occasions, the first of which was in the summer of 1829, during his return to Poland from his first trip to Vienna, accompanied by four friends.

Having set off from the Austrian capital on Wednesday 19 August, the five young men arrived in Prague at noon two days later, and put up at the Hotel *U Modre Hvezdy*, just off the Staromestke Namesti. The group spent the next two days sightseeing. They walked through the narrow streets of the Old Town, past the Klementinum – then the Music Conservatory – and over Charles Bridge on the River Vltava to climb the steep streets and stone steps of Castle Hill until they reached St. Vitus' Cathedral, the setting, nearly 40 years earlier, of Rosetti's Requiem on the death of Chopin's beloved Mozart.

The town is beautiful on the whole, when one sees it from the Castle Hill; large, ancient and once opulent.
Chopin to his family (Prague, 22 August 1829)

Chopin called at the National Theatre, where *Là ci darem la mano* was first sung at the première of Mozart's *Don Giovanni* in 1787. He presented letters of introduction to Director Stiepanek, and to his Kapellmeister, Friedrich Wilhelm Pixis. He also met, on the stairs, pianist and Dresden Cathedral organist August Klengel, who happened to be in Prague. They all went to Pixis' apartment in the Klementinum, where he taught, for a musical evening. Klengel, whom Chopin considered a very friendly and useful contact, gave Chopin an open invitation to visit him in Dresden.

On Sunday morning the group called on Vaclav Hanka, the curator of the National Museum. He entertained the visitors enthusiastically, and asked for a contribution to his visitors' book. One of the group, Ignacy Maciejowski, inscribed two four-line stanzas, to which Chopin added four bars of a Mazurka.

Maciejowski hit on the idea of writing a four-verse mazurka, so I added the music and inscribed myself together with my poet, as originally as possible. Hanka was pleased; it was a Mazur for him, celebrating his services to the Slavonic world
Chopin to his family (Dresden, 26 August 1829)

Prague
Prague's famous Astronomical clock, situated in the Staromestke Namesti, was not far from the Hotel *U Modre Hvezdy*.

← **Dresden**
The Zwinger Palace is one of Germany's major landmarks. The location was formerly part of the Dresden fortress of which the outer wall is conserved. The name derives from the German word Zwinger, meaning the outer ward of a concentric castle. It was designed by court architect Matthäus Daniel Pöppelmann and built in stages between 1710 and 1728 during the reign of Augustus the Strong, elector of Saxony and King of Poland.

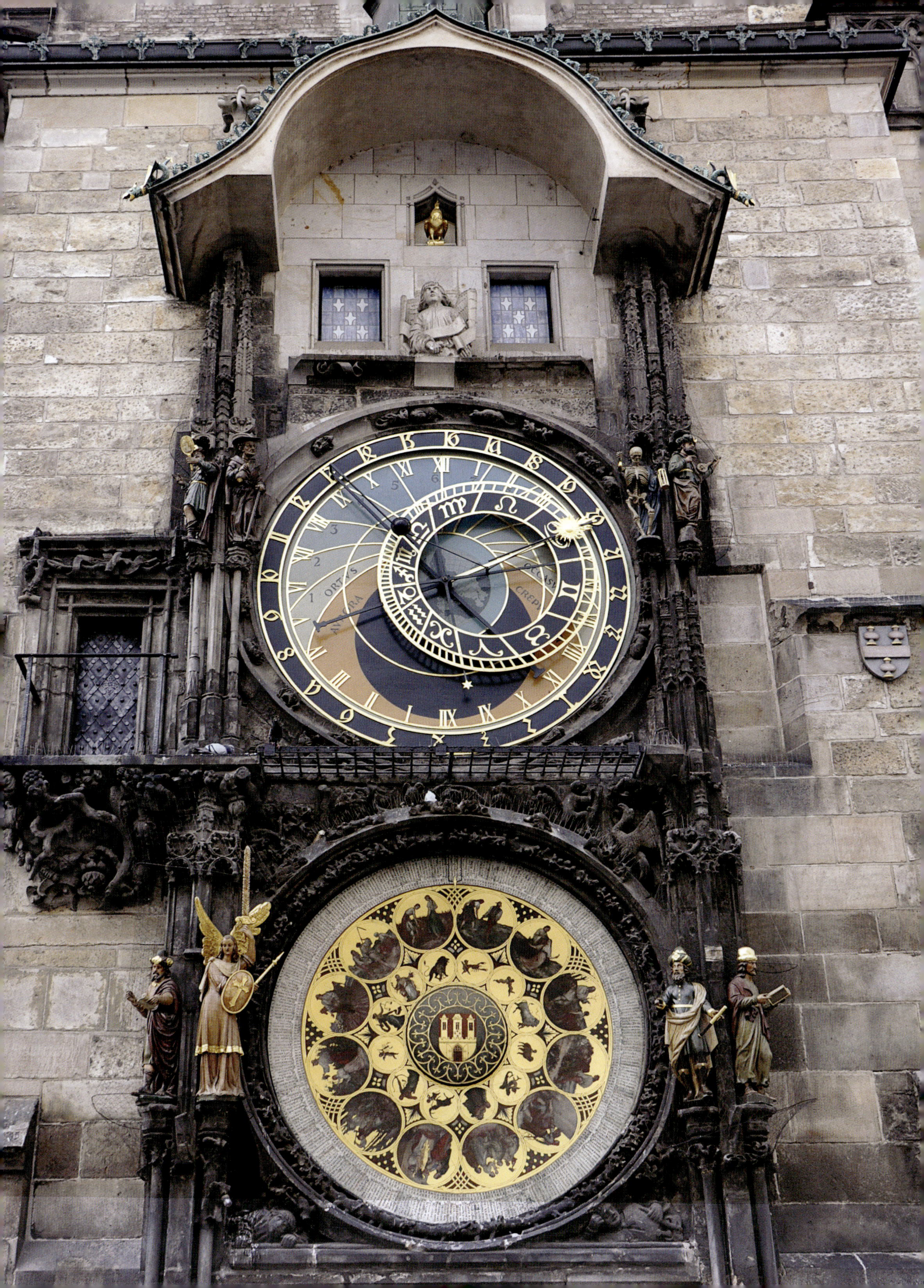

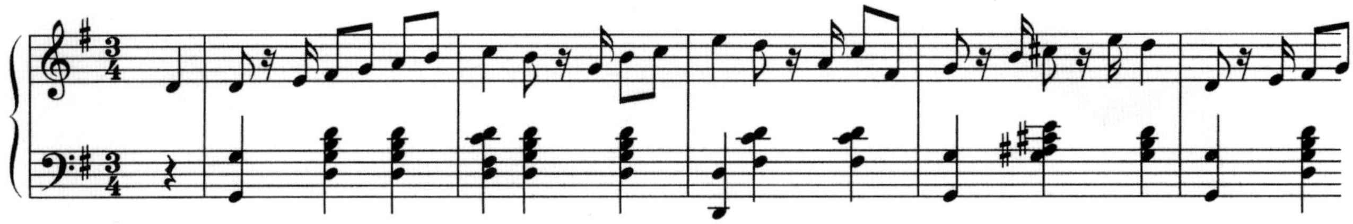

Chopin's Mazurka in G was written in 1826, and dedicated to Vaclav Hanka, the curator of the National Museum in Prague.

After that Hanka took the group to see more of the sights of Prague before they took the noon coach for Teplice.

The spa town of Teplice, situated in the foothills of the Erzgebirge Mountains, was a favourite watering place of the aristocracy. Among the names familiar to Chopin on the hotel guest list was that of Warsaw judge Ludwik Łempicki, who was overjoyed to see him. He took Chopin to a dinner party at Teplice Castle, opposite the hotel, the magnificent residence of Prince Karl Josef Clary, who virtually owned the whole town. After dinner, when asked to improvise, Chopin sat at the piano and asked for a theme. A popular aria from Rossini's *Mosè in Egitto* was proposed, upon which Chopin wove one of his legendary instant tone poems. He was recalled to play three more times by the adoring gathering – especially a group of ladies who, Chopin recorded, were lace-making, knitting and embroidering.

Teplitz is lovely; I was there one day, and spent the evening at Princess Clary's.

Chopin to Tytus Woyciechowski
(Warsaw, 12 September 1829)

The next day Łempicki showed Chopin the sights and the springs, and took him by carriage to see Wallenstein's Castle at nearby Duchcov. It was there in 1787 that Casanova, working as librarian to Count Waldstein, took time off from writing his memoirs to involve himself in Mozart's *Don Giovanni* – as advisor in matters of Love.

We went everywhere, including Wallenstein's palace at Duchcov. There was a fragment of the great soldier's skull, the halberd with which he was killed, and many other relics.

Chopin to his family (Dresden, 26 August 1829)

On Tuesday 25 August the group set off northwards through the mountains, and reached Dresden, where they put up at the Hotel *zur Stadt Berlin.*

Dresden was the capital of King Anton's Saxony, which had close historical associations with Poland, and boasted a large Polish community. Chopin spent four days sightseeing among the wide streets and magnificent buildings. He presented his letters of introduction, including one from Klengel to Francesco Morlacchi, the Director of Dresden's Orchestra, who took Chopin to hear a performance by Dresden's first pianist, Antonina Pechwell. He attended a performance at the Opera of Goethe's *Faust* to commemorate its author's 80th birthday. He also visited the magnificent Art Gallery, the Great Garden and the Grüne Gewölbe in Dresden Castle, where the crown jewels were kept.

Prague

The Tyn Cathedral dominates the Bohemian capital's Staromestke Namesti.

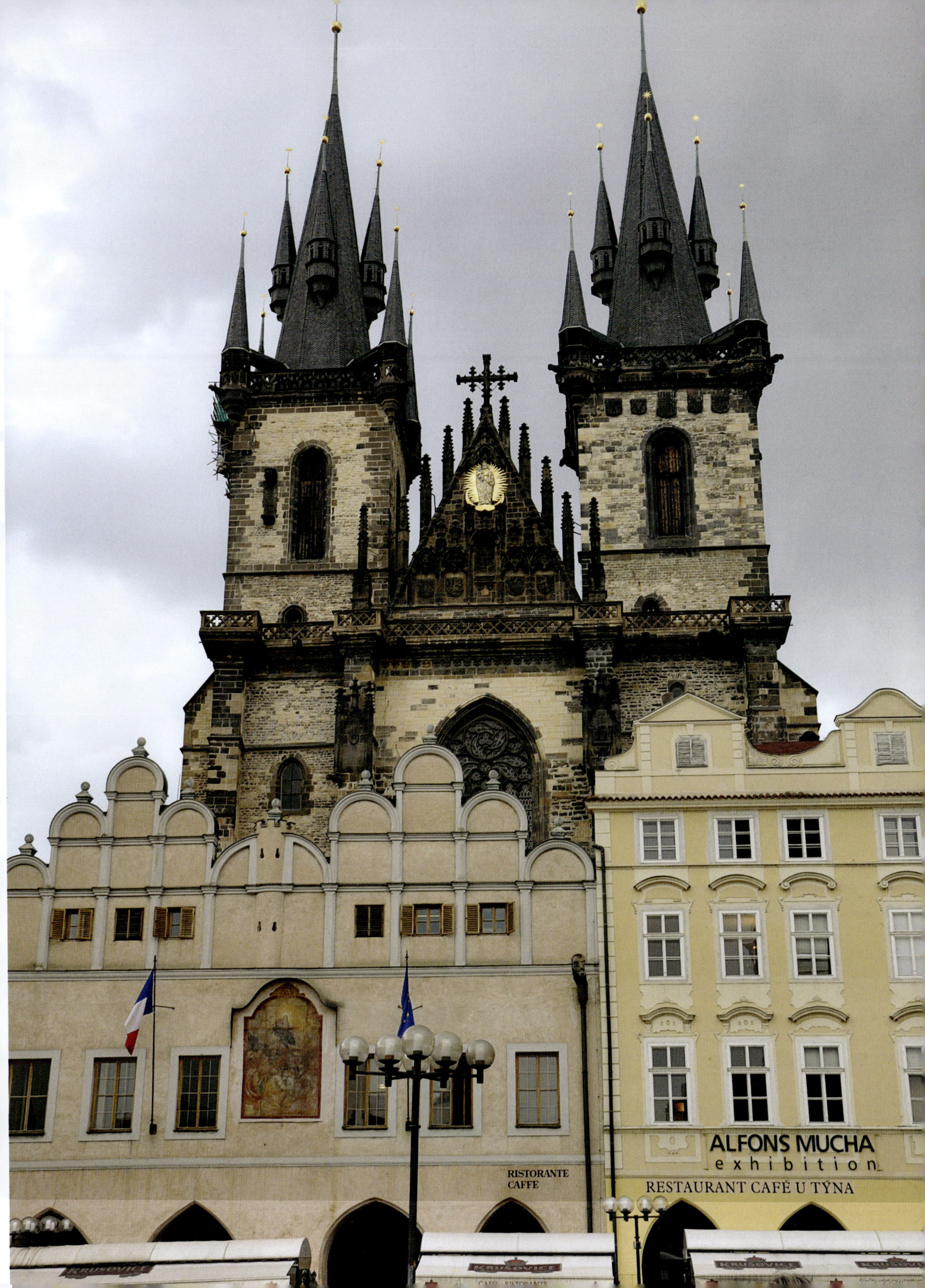
RISTORANTE
CAFFE
ALFONS MUCHA
exhibition
RESTAURANT CAFÉ U TÝNA

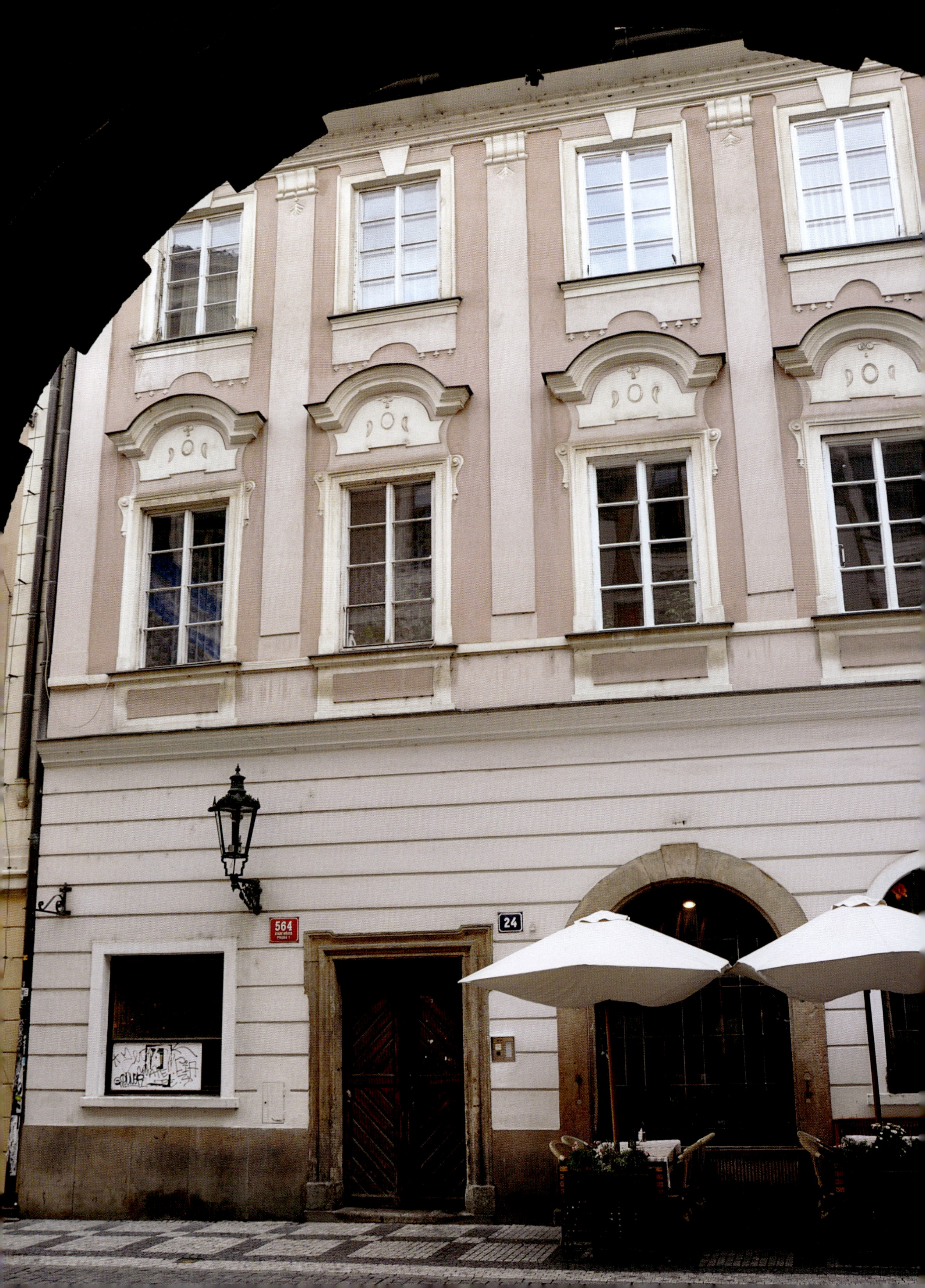
564
24

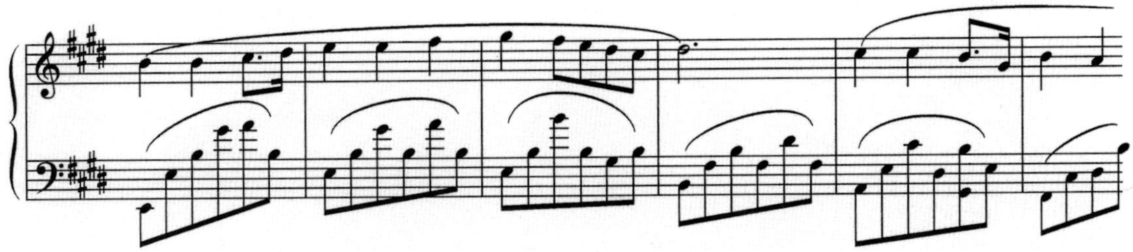

The lyrical second subject from the first movement of Chopin's Piano Concerto in E minor, which he eventually dedicated to Friedrich Kalkbrenner.

I have seen the picture gallery here, an exhibition of produce, the principal gardens; I have returned some calls, and am now going to the theatre; I hope that is enough for one day!

Chopin to his family (Dresden, 26 August 1829)

Chopin left Dresden for Poland on 29 August, and reached Warsaw on 12 September 1829.

However, he returned some 15 months later, en route for Vienna, travelling in the opposite direction with Tytus Woyciechowski. They arrived in Dresden on Friday 12 November 1830, and, forsaking the chance to see Auber's *La Muette de Portici* at the Opera, they went to hear a performance by Antonina Pechwell at the home of a certain Herr Kreissig. Then they left to catch the last act of Auber's opera. On Saturday Chopin visited Klengel, who was overjoyed to see him, and that evening Chopin and Tytus went to see Rossini's *Tancredi*, at which the King was present.

The week in Dresden went so fast that I could not keep track of it. Klengel, when I got to know him better, that is, when I played him my concerto, said it reminded him of Field's playing, that I have a rare touch.

Chopin to his family (Prague, 21 November 1830)

Chopin saw the King again at High Mass at the Cathedral on Sunday. The music was by local composer Baron Miltitz, and Klengel played the organ. Afterwards Chopin went to a dinner given by the local Polish community. Monday was again spent with Klengel, who showed Chopin the Silbermann organ at the Cathedral, and Chopin played him his new Piano Concerto in E minor, his current *pièce de resistance*. The Adagio was written with the image of singer Konstancja Gładkowska, Chopin's "ideal", in mind. Now only a lock of her hair remained to him, fashioned into a ring by his sister Ludwika before his departure from Poland.

Chopin and Tytus Woyciechowski left Dresden for Vienna, where they arrived on 22 November 1830.

Chopin's third visit to Bohemia and Saxony, at the instigation of the Wodziński family, was in 1835, when he had been settled in Paris for four years. He left Paris by diligence, and reached Karlsbad, or Karlovy Vary, as the town was called in Czech, on August 15 1835. He put up at the Hotel *zur goldenen Rose* in the Sprudelgasse, opposite the Church of St. Mary Magdalen, unaware that his parents had also booked in earlier that day. It was only the following

Prague

In the Old Town, at 24 Celetna Street, is the site of the Hotel *U Modre Hvezdy*, where, in 1829, Chopin and his friends stayed during the first of his three visits to the Bohemian capital.

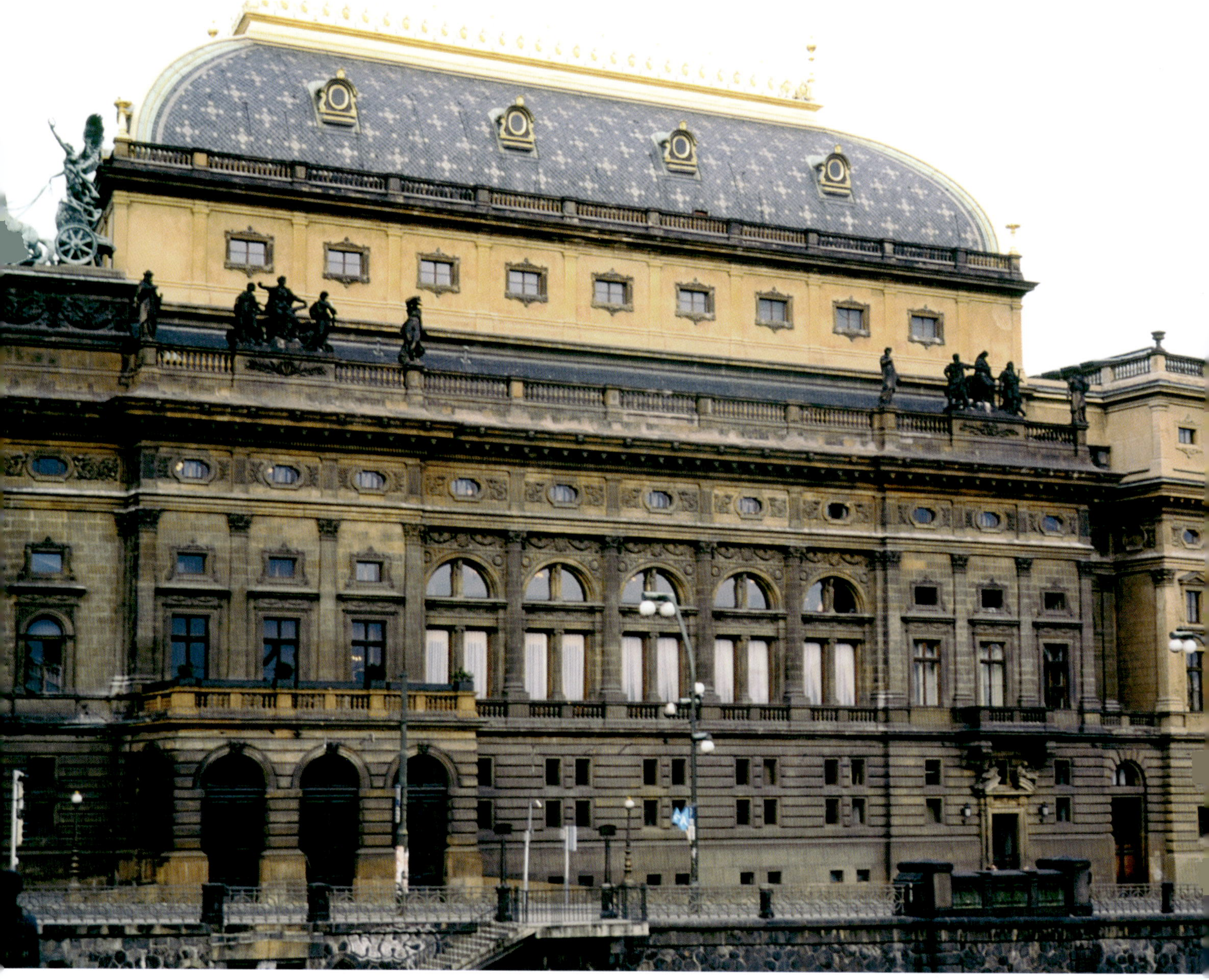

Prague

In August 1829 Chopin presented letters of introduction to Director Stiepanek of the National Theatre, and to his Kapellmeister, Friedrich Wilhelm Pixis. The theatre, today known as the Estates Theatre, was the venue of the première of Mozart's *Don Giovanni* in 1787.

morning that they finally met, amid scenes of great joy.

We are happier than we can describe. We hug one another, and then hug one another again. It's better not to try to think today, just to be happy.

Chopin to his sisters (Karlsbad, 16 August 1835)

The fashionable spa resort of Karlovy Vary, a great favourite with Europe's royalty and aristocracy, was beautifully set among the wooded hills of western Bohemia, which abounded in mineral-rich waters that gushed from the numerous springs in and around the town. Between the Hotel and the babbling little River Tepla opposite, there was a hot spring from which emanated a constant wisp of steam. Chopin accompanied his parents as they took the waters, ate with them, and walked with them, arm in arm, around the town and its environs, watching the yellowing approach of the central European autumn. He took part in the social and musical scene, and made music with Josef Dessauer and Adalbert Gyrowetz, both of whom were staying in Karlovy Vary. Chopin also met Count Franz-Anton Thun-Hohenstein, to whose children, including 20-year-old daughter Josephine, Chopin had given lessons the previous year.

On 6 September Chopin and his parents set off for home. Initially they travelled by way of Duchcov and Teplice to accept Count Thun-Hohenstein's invitation to spend a few days at Děčín. This imposing Castle was perched spectacularly on a lofty crag overlooking a young River Elbe, which at that point was about to flow through the beautiful, mountainous region known as Bohemian Switzerland. They stayed there for a few days, again enjoying the scenery by day and socialising and making music in the evenings with the young Thun-Hohensteins. Chopin wrote and dedicated the first version of the Waltz in A flat Op. 34 No 1, which he later revised, to Josephine.

On 19 September, five days after his parents continued their homeward journey to Warsaw, Chopin himself left for Leipzig. There he had arranged to meet Mendelssohn, who had been appointed director of the Gewandhaus Orchestra

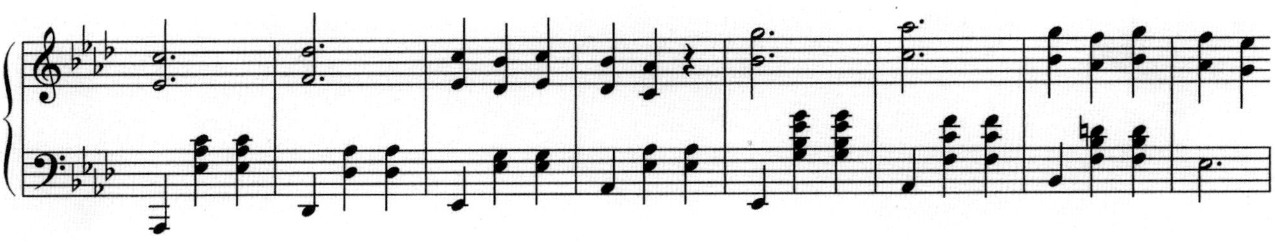

Chopin wrote the Waltz in A flat Op. 34 No 1, for Countess Josephine Thun-Hohenstein, at her home, Děčín Castle, in Bohemia.

earlier that year. The route took him through Dresden. The post-road led into the valley of the Elbe, with the now golden-clad Erzgebirge Mountains on either side. He crossed into Saxony's beautiful region known, on this side of the border, as Saxon Switzerland.

In Dresden Chopin by chance met his school friend Feliks Wodziński. He had known the Wodzińskis for most of his life. Feliks and his brother Antoni had been school boarders in the Chopins' Warsaw apartment, and Chopin used to give piano lessons to their sister Maria when she was nine years old. Feliks, who was passing through Dresden, asked Chopin to call on his mother, Countess Teresa Wodzińska, and his two sisters, Maria and Józefa. They were staying with their elderly uncle Maciej in his apartment in Rampischerstrasse, the historic centre of the Saxon capital.

Chopin saw again, after 7 years, the little girl to whom he used to give piano lessons. The sight of the dark, 16-year-old beauty put his plans for a swift return to Paris on hold, and he tarried in Dresden for two weeks, staying at the Hotel *Stadt Gotha*. He spent most of his time with Maria, under her knowing mother's approving eye, and found himself hopelessly in love. This was Chopin's third visit to Dresden, so he knew it well. The young sweethearts strolled together through the city's fine streets, along the green banks of the Elbe, and to the Great Garden, where the autumn colours were at their most glorious.

In the evenings they made music, and Chopin was proud to learn that his former pupil had become a very proficient pianist. He wrote her the Waltz in A flat, Op. 69 No 1, which he copied into her album.

Chopin left Dresden on 3 October, with very mixed feelings. Having fallen prey to his habitual shyness with girls, he had failed to summon up the courage to declare his love to Maria.

The next day he arrived in Leipzig, and booked in for two nights at the *Hotel de Saxe*. He then went straight to Mendelssohn's apartment at Königstrasse 3, where the two young men spent most of the day together, talking and making

Prague

The foyer of the Estates Theatre by night.

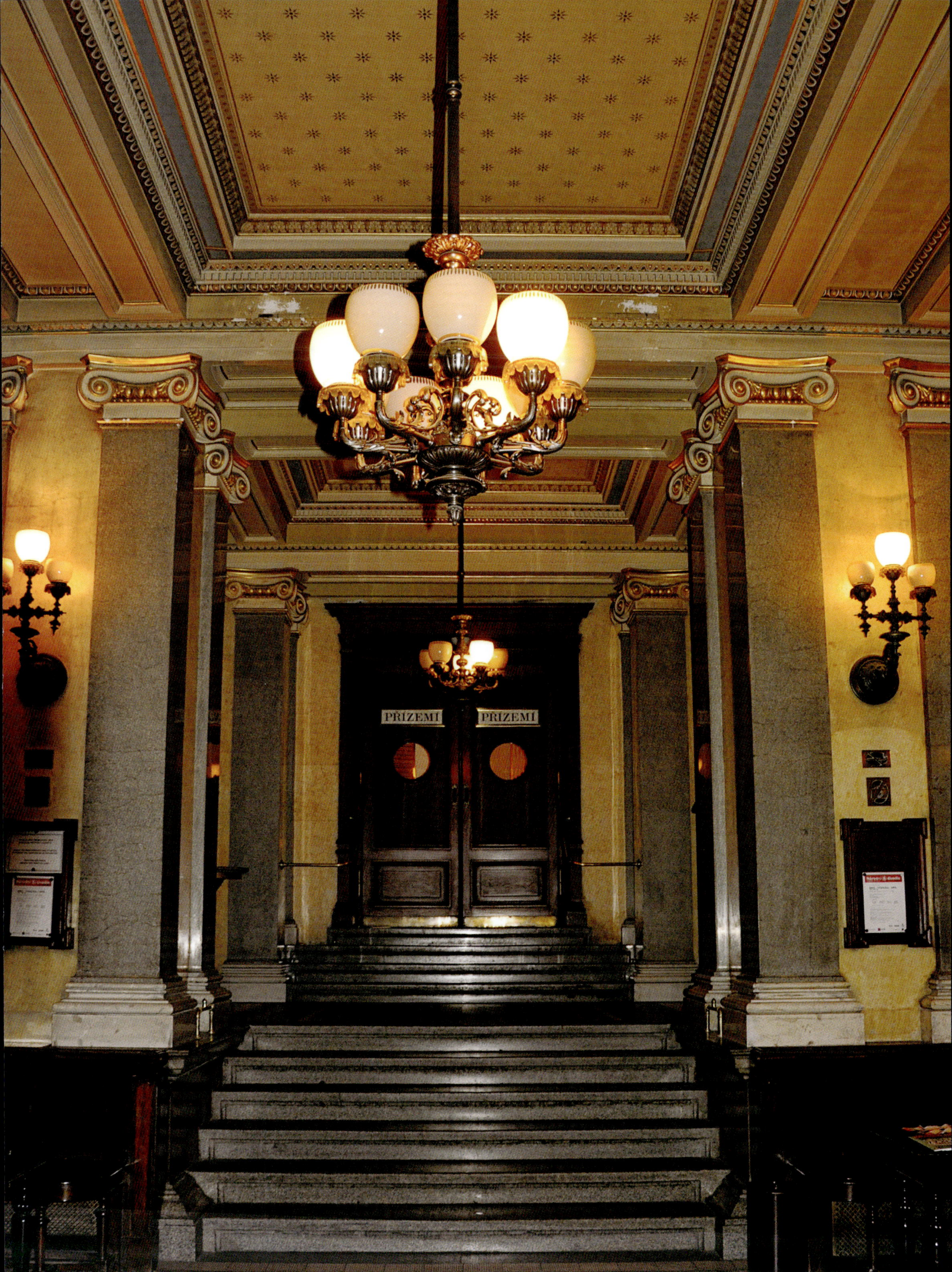
PŘÍZEMÍ
PŘÍZEMÍ

music, before going on to the home of Friedrich Wieck and his 16-year-old pianist daughter Clara, who lived at Grimmaischestrasse 36. Clara's future husband Robert Schumann was also there, anxious to meet the legendary Chopin in the flesh. For the rest of the day the four giants of Romantic pianism played for each other, and Chopin told a delighted Clara that she was the only woman in Germany who could play his compositions.

Hats off, gentlemen, a genius!

Robert Schumann,
writing on Chopin's *Là ci darem la Mano* Variations
in the "Allgemeine Musikalische Zeitung" 7 December 1831

The next day Chopin set off for the university city of Heidelberg, to stay with the family of his pupil and friend, Adolf Gutmann. The city, dominated by the ruins of the fourteenth century Castle standing sentinel on the hills above the vine-clad River Neckar, was in the full flush of autumn's golds and russets, but Chopin was in no position to appreciate the town's beauties as he fell seriously ill on arrival. He stayed laid up with a chest infection at the home of his friend and admirer Katherine Diller de Pereira and her sister for about three weeks. The two ladies spared no effort to nurse Chopin back to health.

What a blessing that Providence allowed you to fall in with two guardian angels who lavished their care on you, and still often enquire about your health.

Nicolas Chopin to his son, à propos the latter's stay in
Heidelberg, 9 January 1836

Fryderyk Chopin reached Paris at the end of October. The three-month trip had drained him, both emotionally and physically, and rumours abounded that he had died. These rumours reached Warsaw, where the Wodzińskis called on Chopin's frantic parents to ask if the rumours were true. In the end the Warsaw press had to issue an official statement that Chopin was alive, and back in Paris.

Chopin eventually recovered, but fell seriously ill once more during the spring of 1836. With the onset of summer his health improved somewhat, and when he heard that the Wodziński ladies would be spending August in Marienbad, he set off at the beginning of July once again for

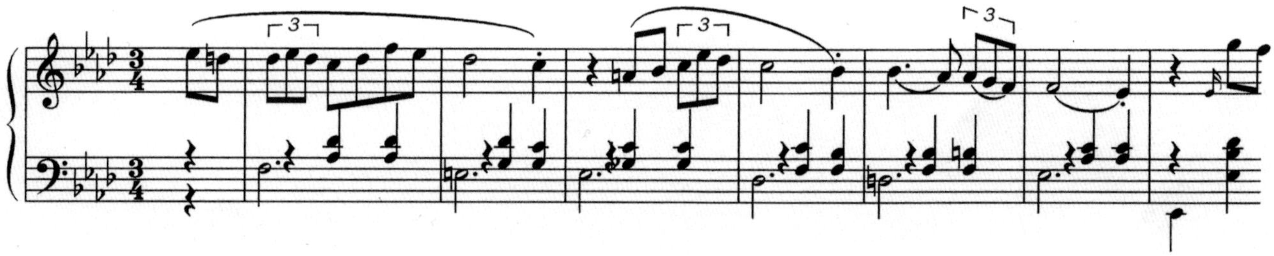

Chopin dedicated his Waltz in A flat, Op. 69 No 1, to Maria Wodzińska with the dedication: *Pour Mademoiselle Marie, Dresden, septembre 1835.*

Prague

The entrance to the Klementinum, which, at the time of Chopin's visit to Prague, served as the Music Conservatory, where Chopin and Stiepanek, Pixis and Dresden Cathedral organist, August Klengel, who happened to be in Prague at that time, all went to Pixis' apartment for a musical evening.

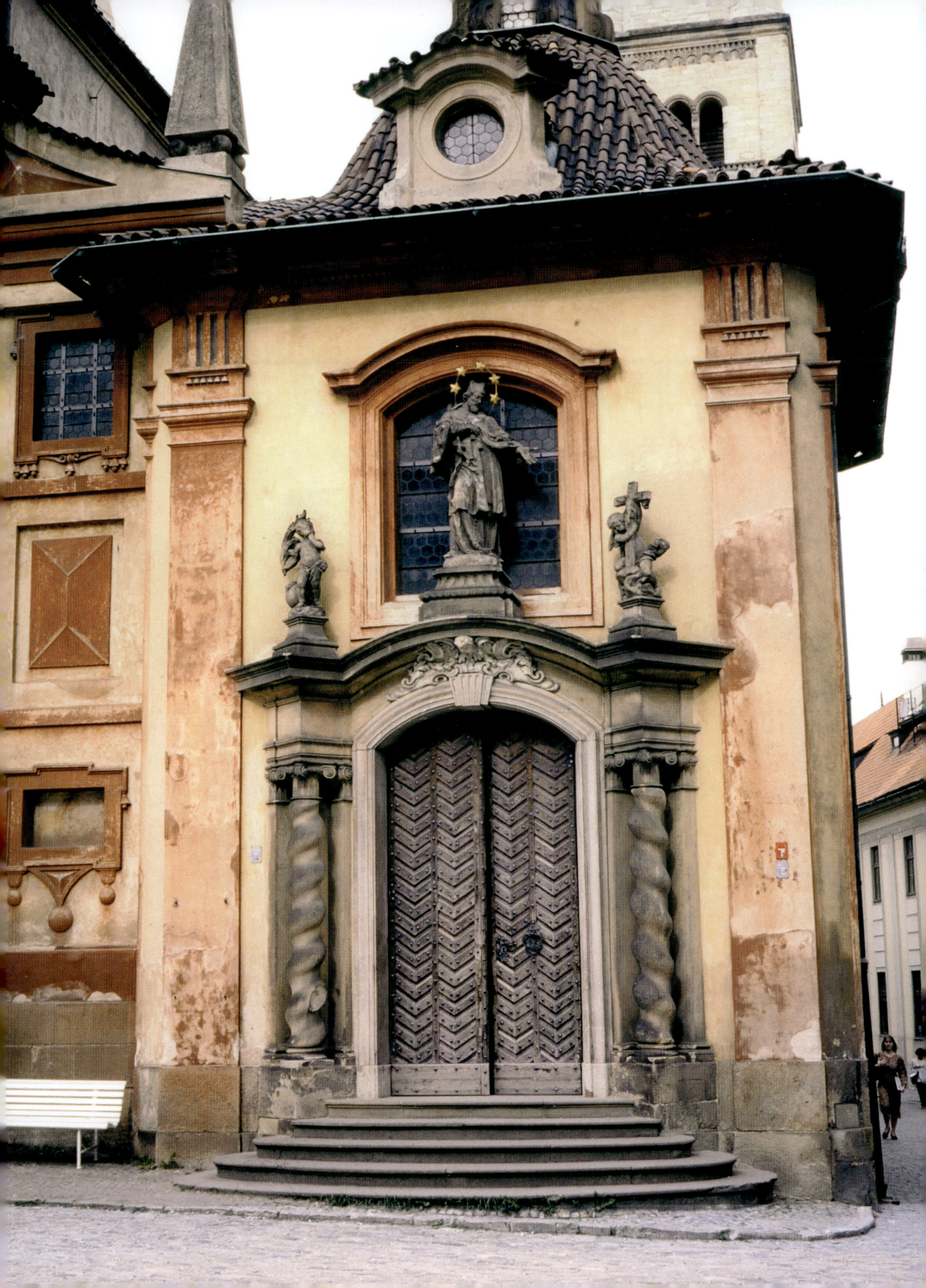

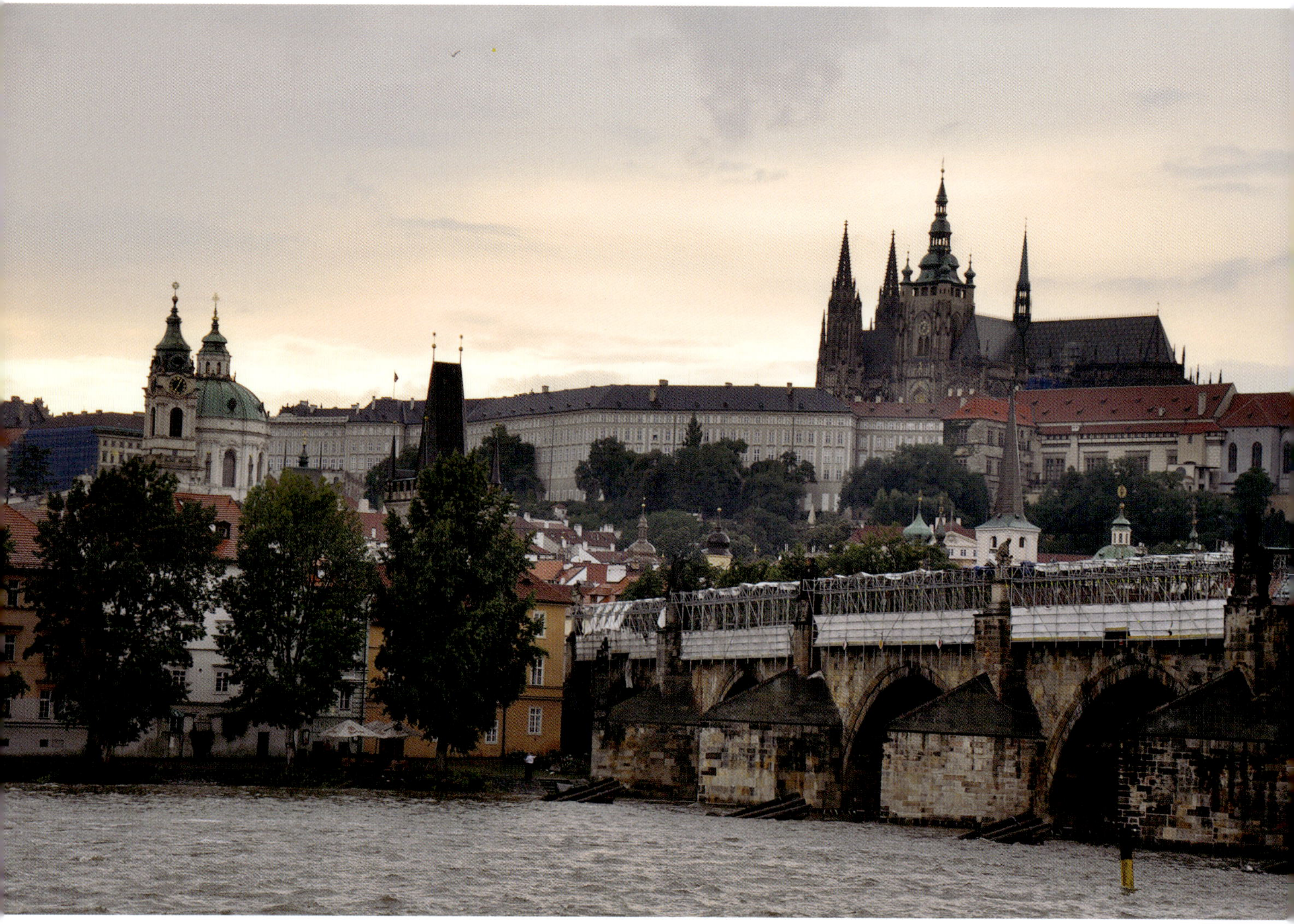

Prague

The view onto Castle Hill with St. Vitus' Cathedral, is among Prague's most spectacular. During his 1829 visit Chopin and his four friends crossed the Charles Bridge on the River Vltava to climb the steep streets and stone steps to the Cathedral, the setting, nearly 40 years previously, of Rosetti's *Requiem* on the death of Chopin's beloved Mozart. The Castle is reputed to be one of the biggest in the world. It was built in the French Gothic style and took many centuries to complete because of wars and insufficient funds.

Bohemia, on his fourth visit, looking forward to seeing Maria again. Countess Wodzińska had taken rooms at the Hotel *zum weissen Schwann*, while Chopin took rooms on the floor above.

Marienbad, or Mariánské Lázně, as the town was called in Czech, vied with its two main rivals, Karlovy Vary and Teplice, for the position of Bohemia's premier watering place. Of the three, Mariánské Lázně was the prettiest, even though it was generally high society's third choice. Developed in the heyday of the Hapsburg Empire, the town sat attractively among wooded hills surrounding the gushing springs of the valley. The wide streets, with their well-stocked shops, the beautifully laid-out gardens, the winding walkways that snaked past grand villas set in forest glades, as well as the springs, wells and drinking fountains, could not have been a more romantic backdrop to the love that blossomed that summer between Chopin and Maria. Every evening the sound of the piano wafted from Chopin's windows into the garden below.

Among the compositions that came to the fore at this time was the Ballade in G minor, first written in 1830, and now prepared for publication. He also taught Maria to play one of the 5 Etudes from Op. 25, that he had recently written, and he set Stefan Witwicki's poem, *Pierścień* (the Ring), to music for her. While Chopin played, Maria painted: among her works was the famous portrait of him, which is now in a private collection.

At the end of August the Wodzińskis set off for home by way of Dresden. Chopin, who intended to return again by way of Leipzig, accompanied them. On the eve of their parting, Chopin overcame his reticence and proposed to Maria, and was accepted. The following morning he asked her mother's permission; this was provisionally granted on the understanding that, firstly, the engagement should be kept secret for the moment, secondly, that Maria's father would be consulted, and thirdly, that Chopin should take greater care of himself, as his ill-health was likely to be an obstacle to acceptance.

Chopin left Dresden that afternoon for Leipzig with a light heart. There he again met the Wiecks and Schumann, to whom he played his new works, although Mendelssohn was away at the time.

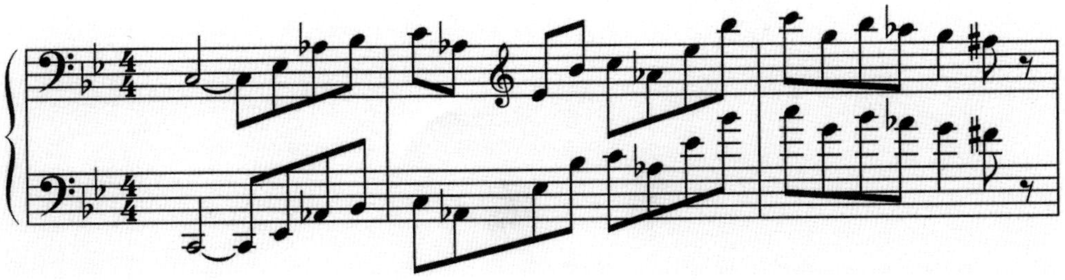

The dramatic opening bars of Chopin's Ballade in G minor Op. 23, first written in 1830, which he often played in Marienbad in the summer of 1836.

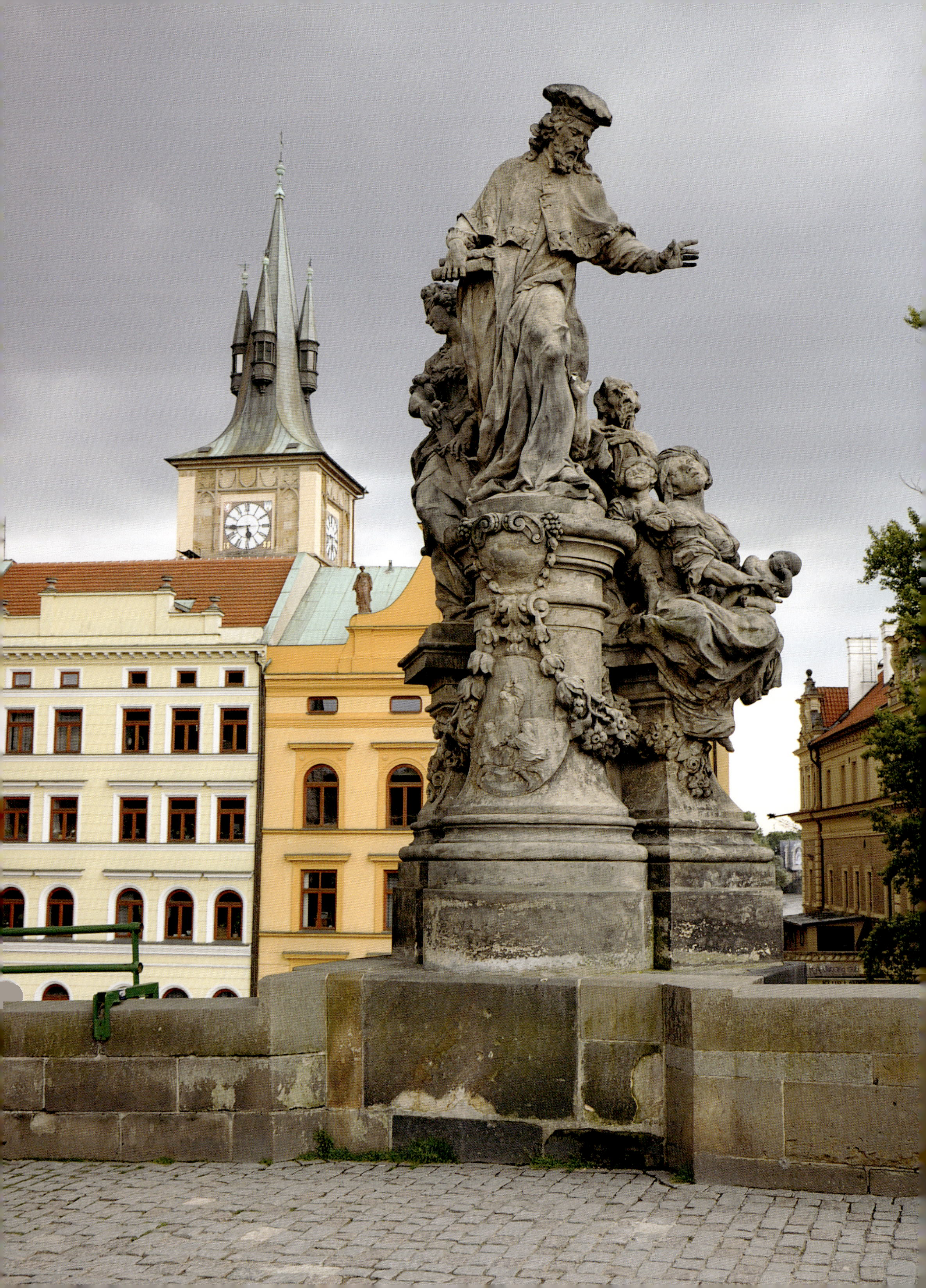

Chopin returned to Paris in the autumn. Meanwhile Maria's father, Count Wincenty Wodziński, decided against allowing the engagement to continue, and that Chopin should be discouraged from pursuing the idea. His ill-health was indeed a major factor, but because the Wodzińskis came of aristocratic stock, he decided that Maria should, after all, marry a titled person.

Chopin knew nothing of these deliberations, and continued to correspond with Maria and her mother. As the months went by the letters from Maria became lukewarm, sometimes even merely postscripts to those of her mother. Chopin, realising that he was being rejected in stages, fell into a deep depression. He placed Maria's letters, and a rose that she had given him in Dresden, in an envelope, and tied them up with a pink ribbon. On the outside he wrote the words *Moja bieda* (My misery).

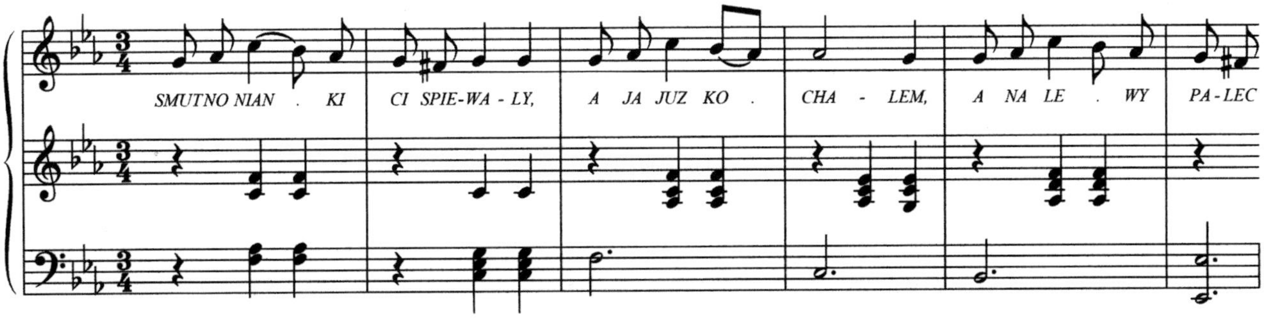

Chopin's song, "Pierścień" (the Ring), is a setting of a poem by Stefan Witwicki, and was written for Maria Wodzińska in Marienbad.

Prague

The Charles Bridge, with its famous sculptures, was constructed during the reign of the Holy Roman Emperor Charles IV in the fourteenth century, and only completed a hundred years later. At the time of Chopin's visit it was known as the Stone Bridge or the Prague Bridge, and was the only bridge over the river. It was not until 1871 when it came to be known as the Charles Bridge.

All the Bohemian Chopin sites remain intact, although some have been rebuilt, among them Prague's National Theatre, now the Estates Theatre in Ovocny Trh, and the National Museum, in Wenceslas Square, which still has Hanka's visitors' book. All the other sites, including that of the Hotel *U Modre Hvezdy* at 24 Celetna Street, are the original buildings, as are the Castle in Teplice and Wallenstein's Castle at Duchcov. The Sprudelgasse and the Hotel *zur goldenen Rose* in Karlovy Vary no longer exist. The hotel in Mariánské Lázně is today the Chopin House Museum in Trida Odboraru. Děčín Castle is still there, now restored to its former splendour.

Most of Dresden's original Chopin sites were destroyed in World War 2. The Cathedral still houses the Silbermann organ. The Gemaldgalerie Alte Meister is situated on the site of the original Art Gallery in the Zwinger complex, which also housed the Opera. The Grüne Gewölbe was in the Albertinum Museum complex, and the Great Garden is now the Volkspark. Only one section of the Rampischerstrasse has survived, and the Police Station occupies the site of Count Maciej Wodziński's apartment. In Leipzig no records of the *Hotel de Saxe* remain, although the Grimmaischerstrasse, now rebuilt, is still there. There is no known Chopin site in Heidelberg.

Teplice

Castle Square. A Pestilence memorial stands in the centre of Teplice, the fashionable spa town in northern Bohemia where Chopin and his travelling companions arrived on 23 August 1829. Beethoven spent several summers there and in 1812 put the final touches to his *Seventh Symphony*. There is a Beethoven memorial and museum in the town.

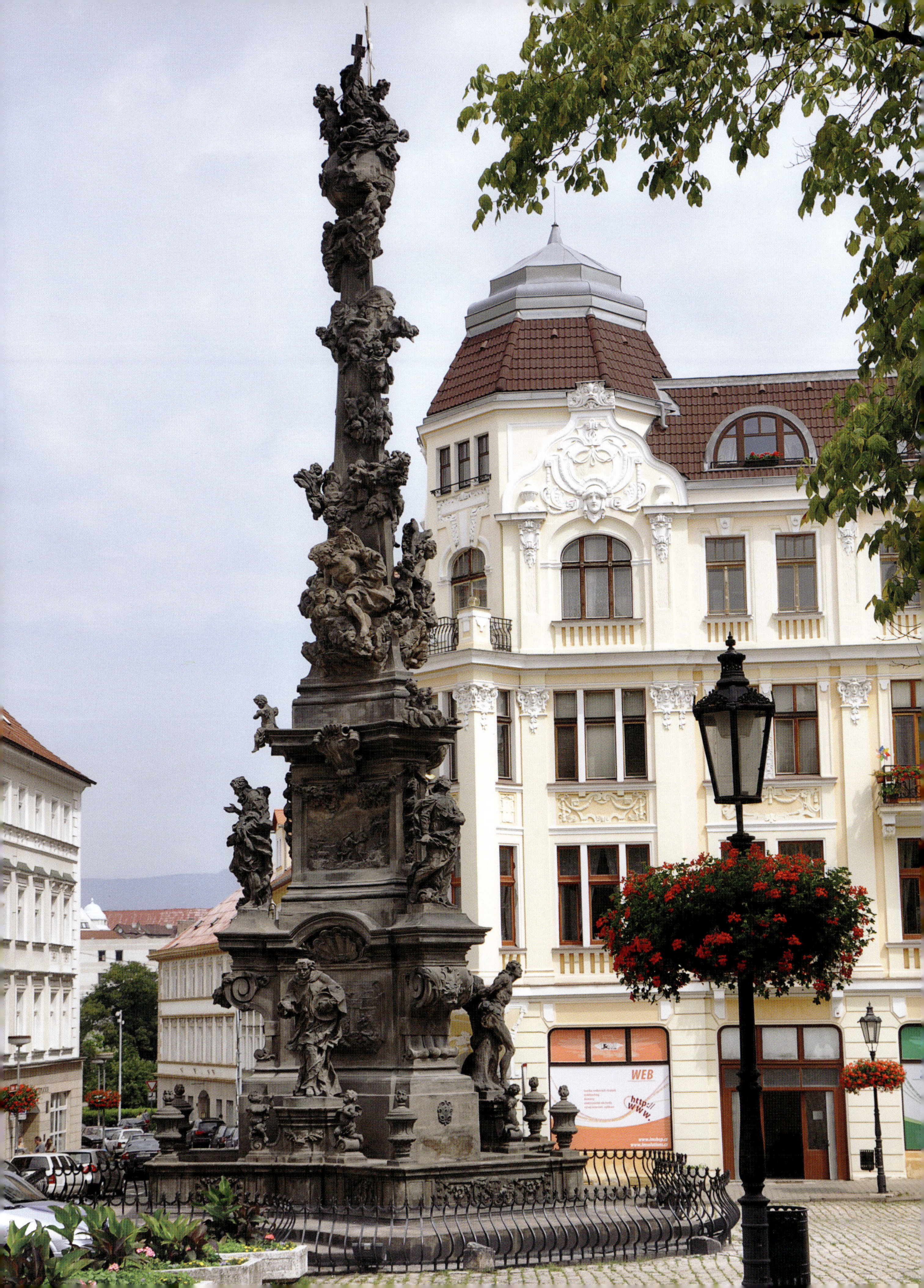
WEB

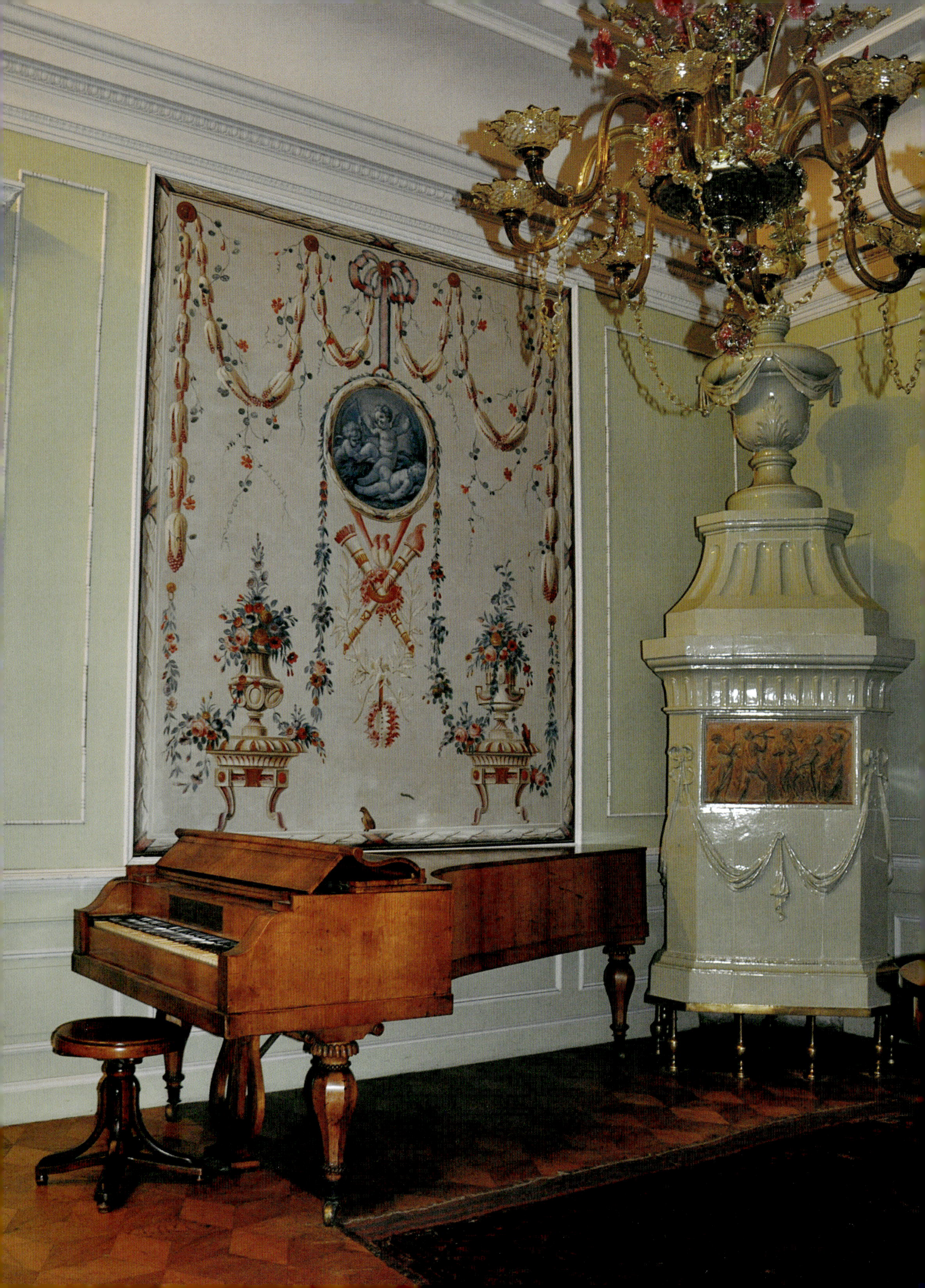

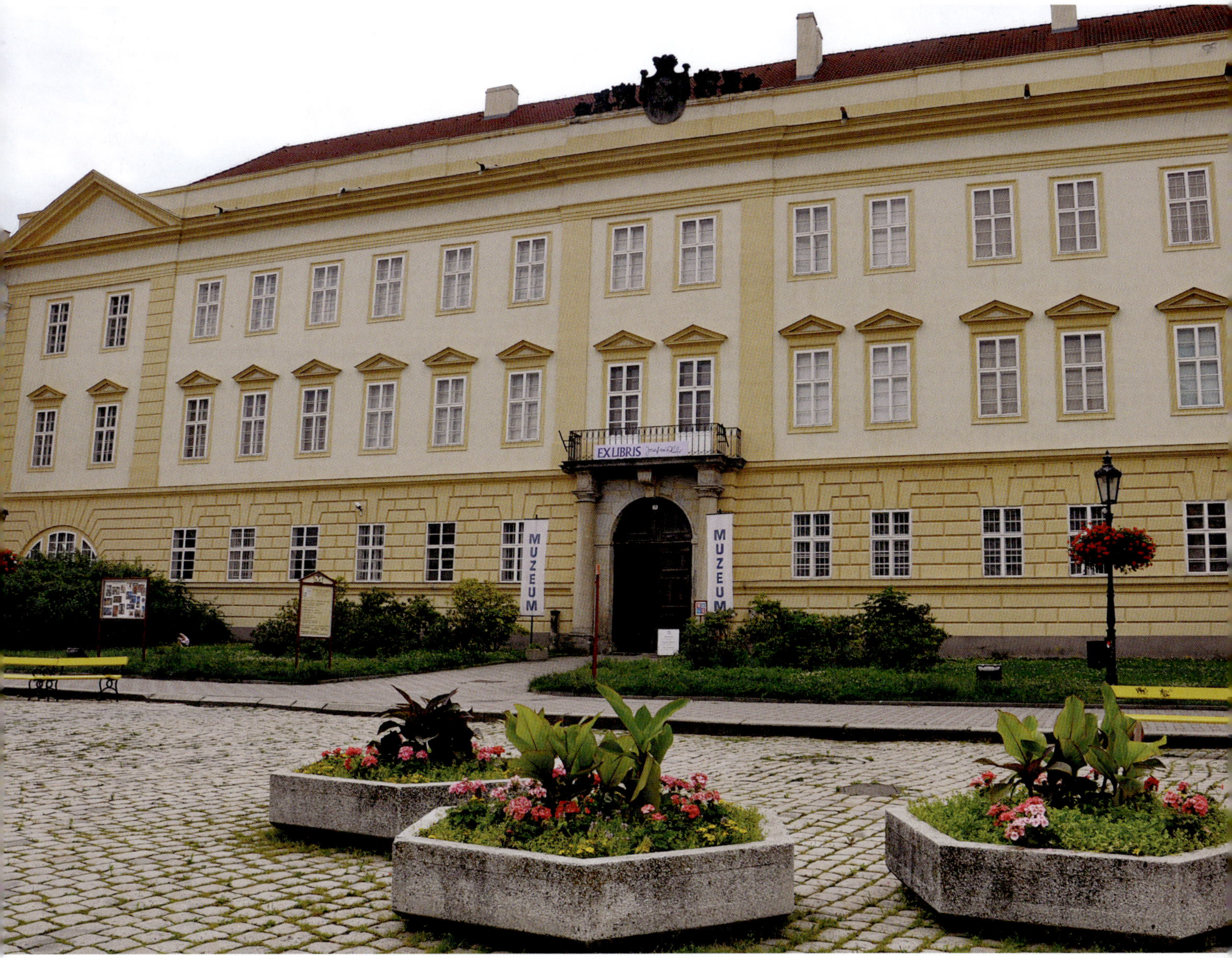

Teplice

On the evening of his arrival in Teplice Chopin attended a dinner party given by Prince Clary at the Castle, conveniently situated just opposite their hotel. Chopin returned to this town in 1835 and 1836 on his way to Karlsbad and Marienbad.

← The Bösendorfer fortepiano on which Chopin played in August 1829 after the dinner party given by Prince Clary, much to the delight of the other guests (*by kind permission of the Teplice Regional Museum*).

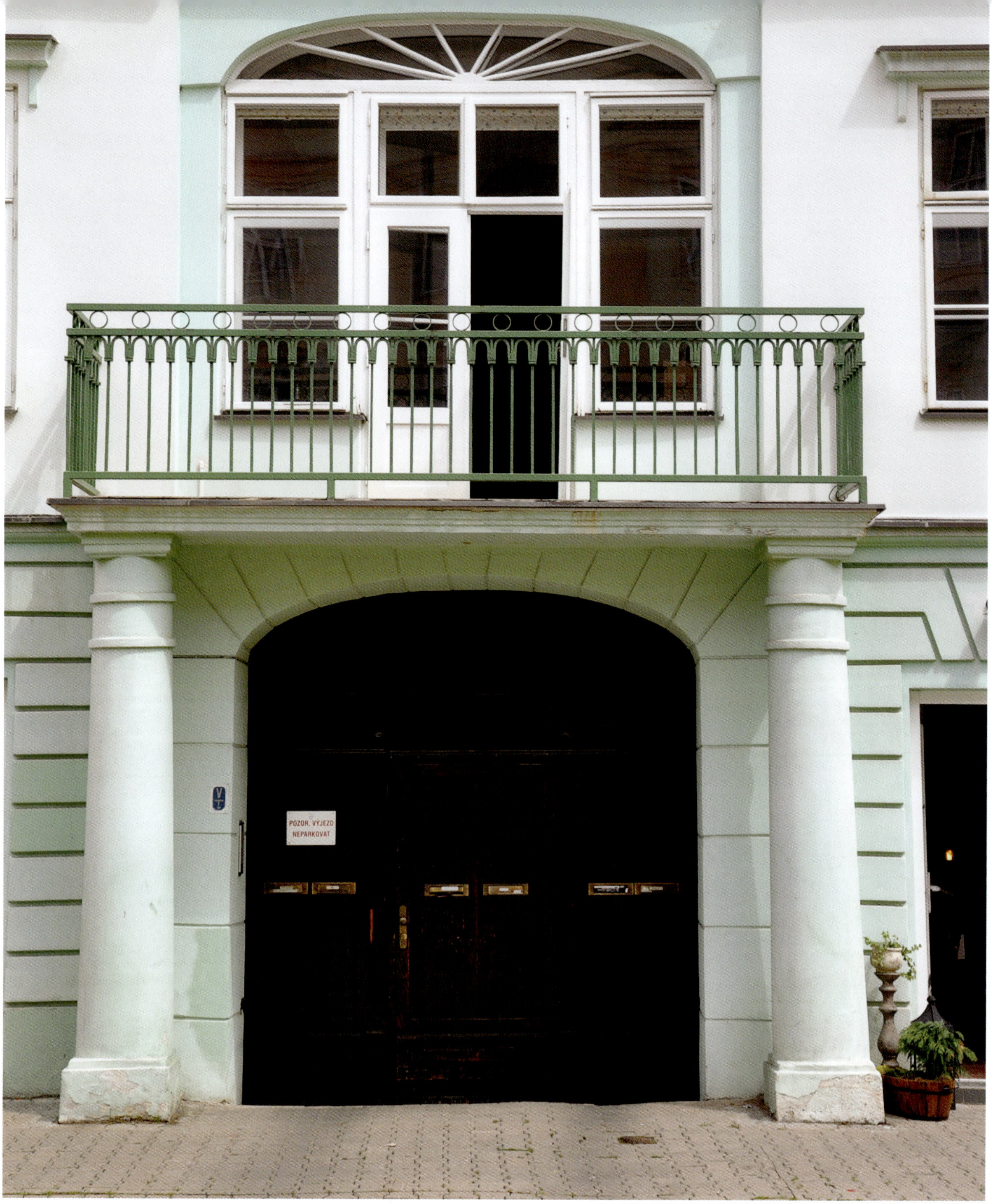

Teplice

Castle Square. Teplice owes its fame to the fact that in 1813 the monarchs of Russia, Prussia and Austria signed the Triple alliance there against Napoleon. The balcony from which they announced its signature is still there.

→ The building which was the hotel where Chopin stayed in Teplice with his travelling companions is still there, opposite Teplice Castle. The Hotel *Prince de Ligne* was originally built in 1824 under another name and was restored at the turn of the Millennium.

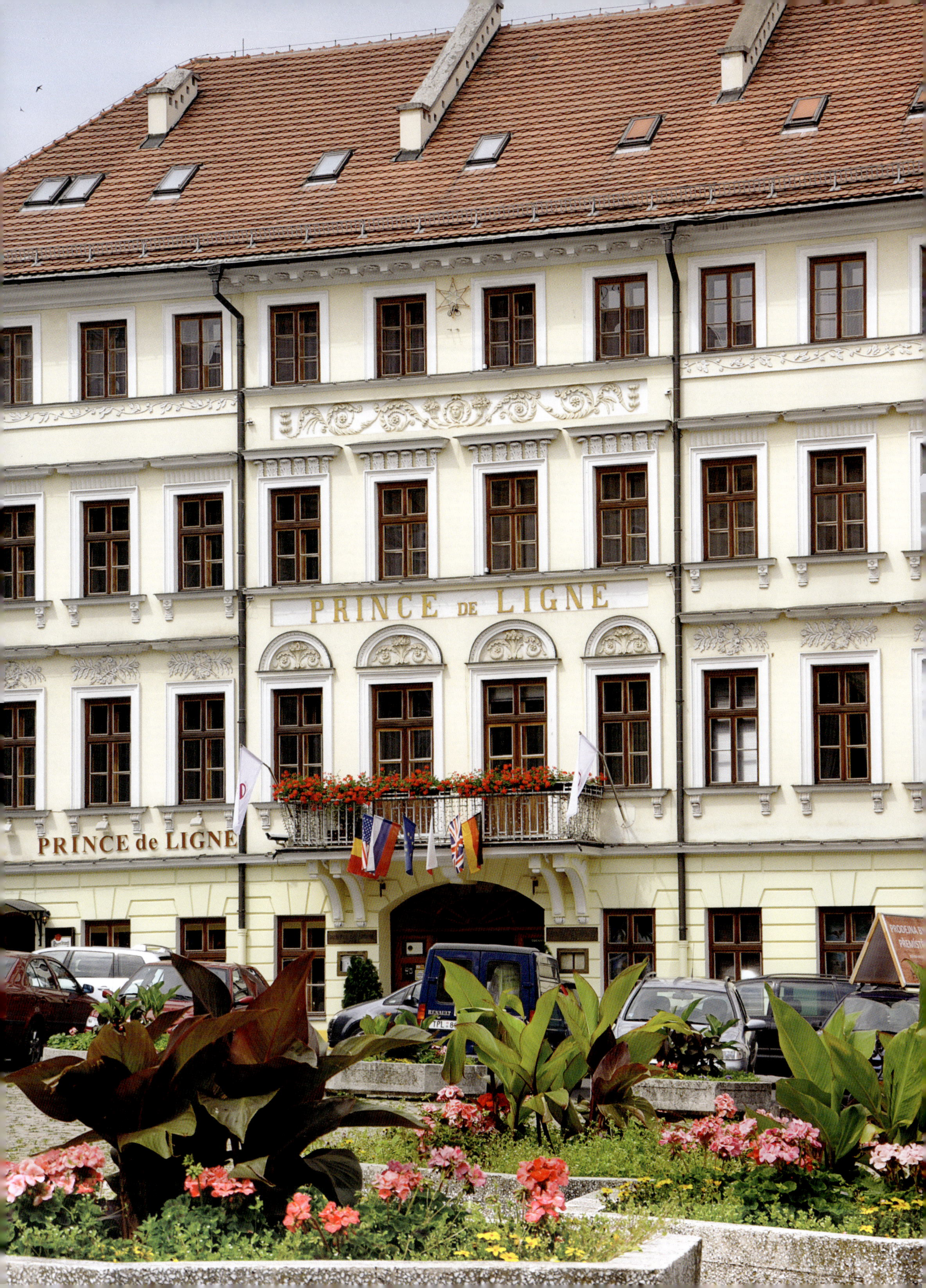
PRINCE de LIGNE
PRINCE de LIGNE

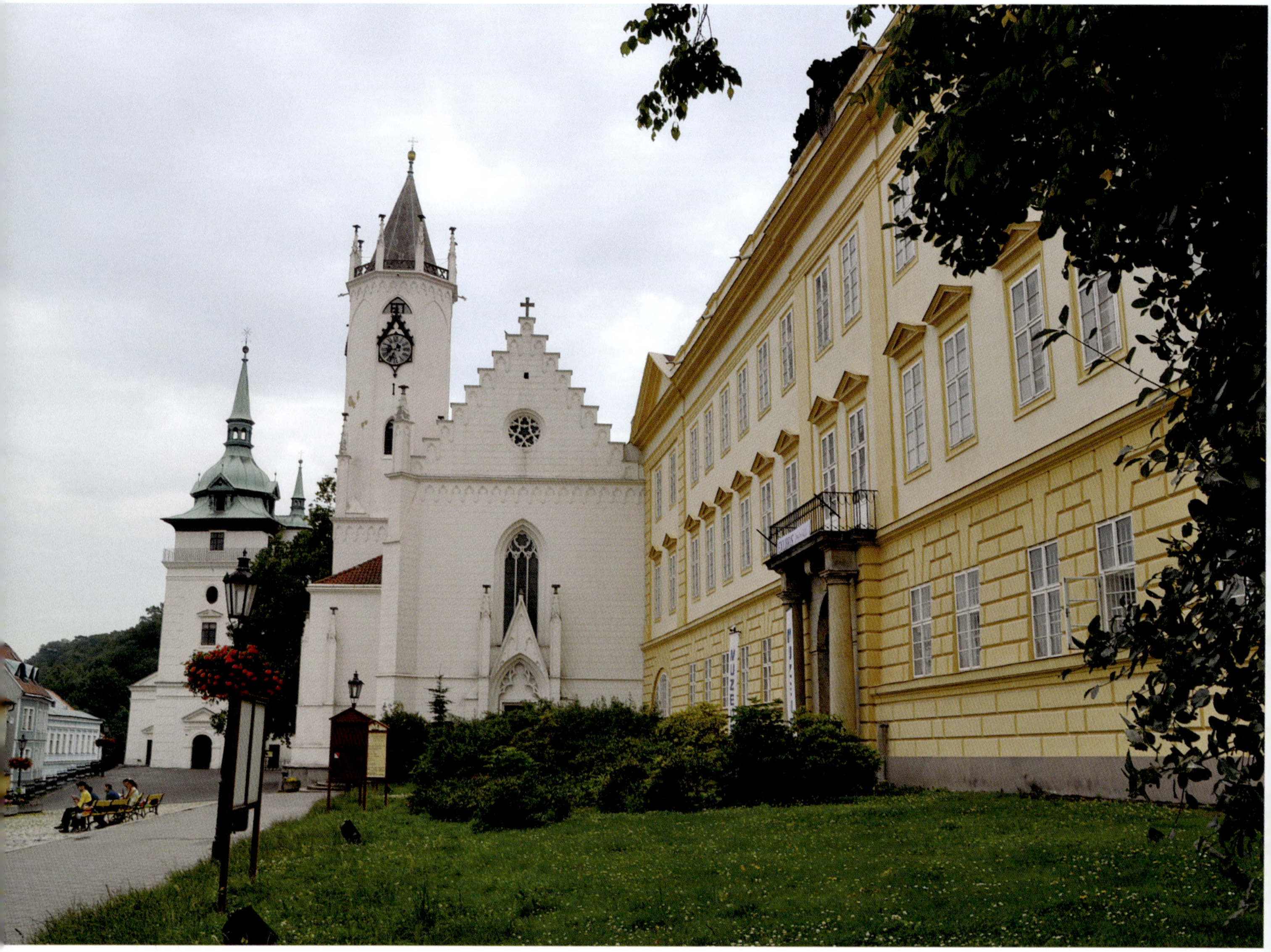

Teplice

The Church of the Elevation of the Holy Cross stands just beside the Castle. In the background stands the Russian Orthodox church.

→ Duchcov

Chopin visited Duchcov Castle, also known as Wallenstein's Castle, with his friend, Warsaw judge Ludwik Łempicki, on 24 August 1829. It was here, in 1787, that Casanova, working as librarian to Count Waldstein, took time off from writing his memoirs to involve himself in Mozart's *Don Giovanni* – as adviser in matters of love, which is why it has also been nicknamed Casanova's Castle.

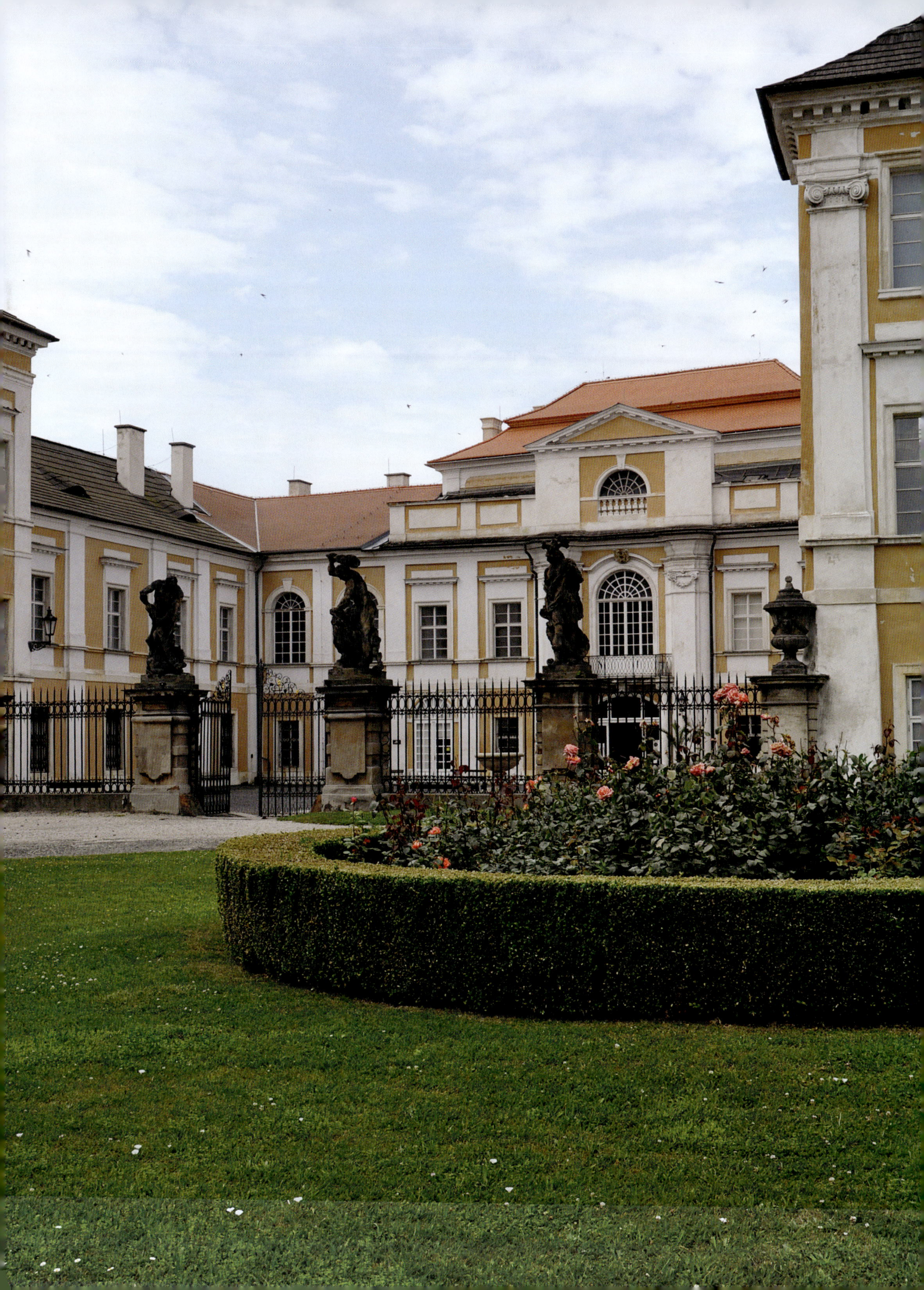

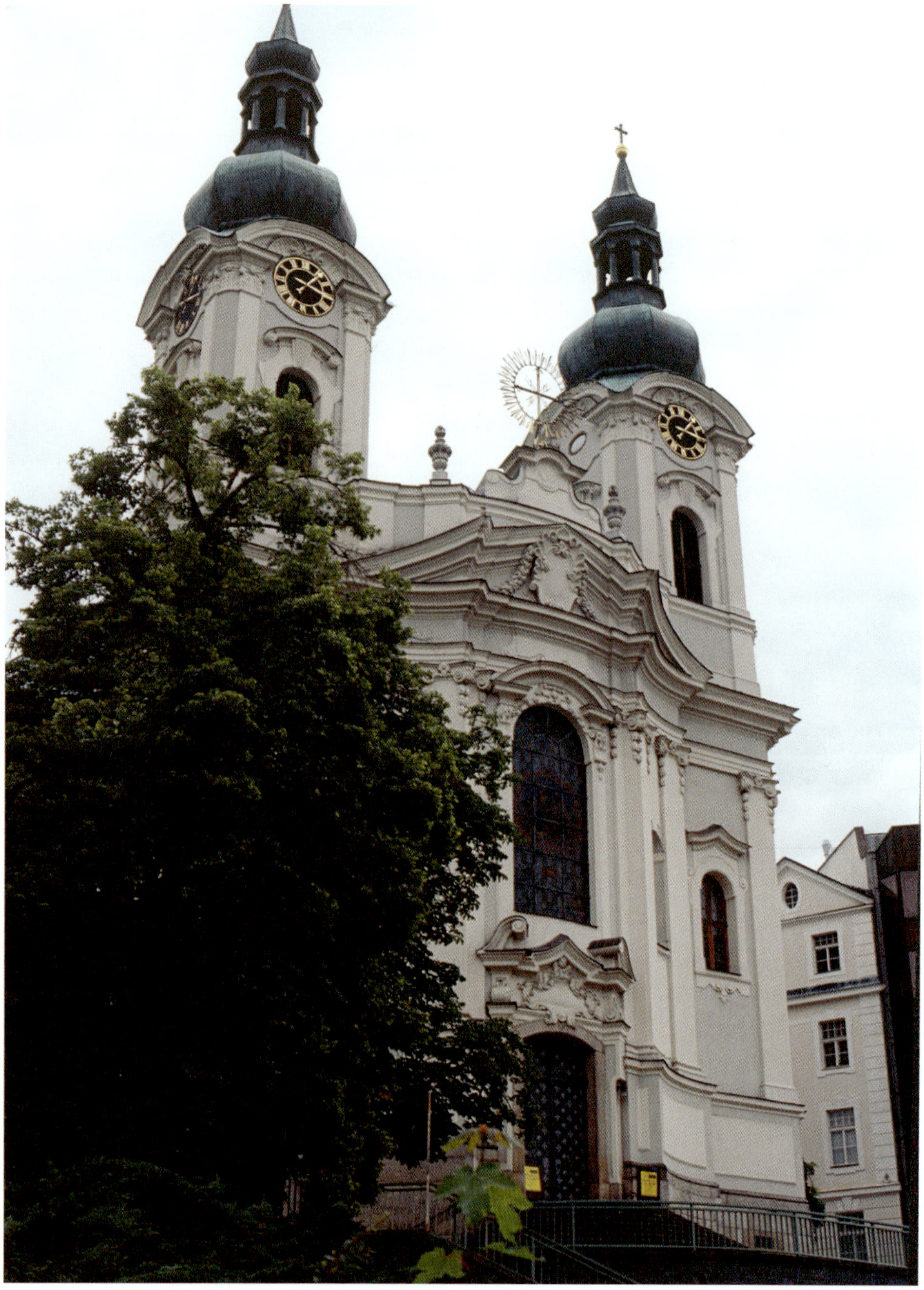

Karlsbad

The Church of St. Mary Magdalen stands opposite the Hotel *zur goldenen Rose,* in the Sprüdelgasse where Chopin stayed with his parents in 1835. This was the only time that Chopin met up with his parents after leaving Poland in 1830.

→ Děčín

Děčín Castle, overlooking the River Elbe, is where Chopin and his parents stayed in September 1835 as guests of the Thun-Hohenstein family. It was the last occasion that Chopin saw his parents, who left for Warsaw before their son checked out five days later to continue his journey on to Dresden – and into the Maria Wodzińska affair.

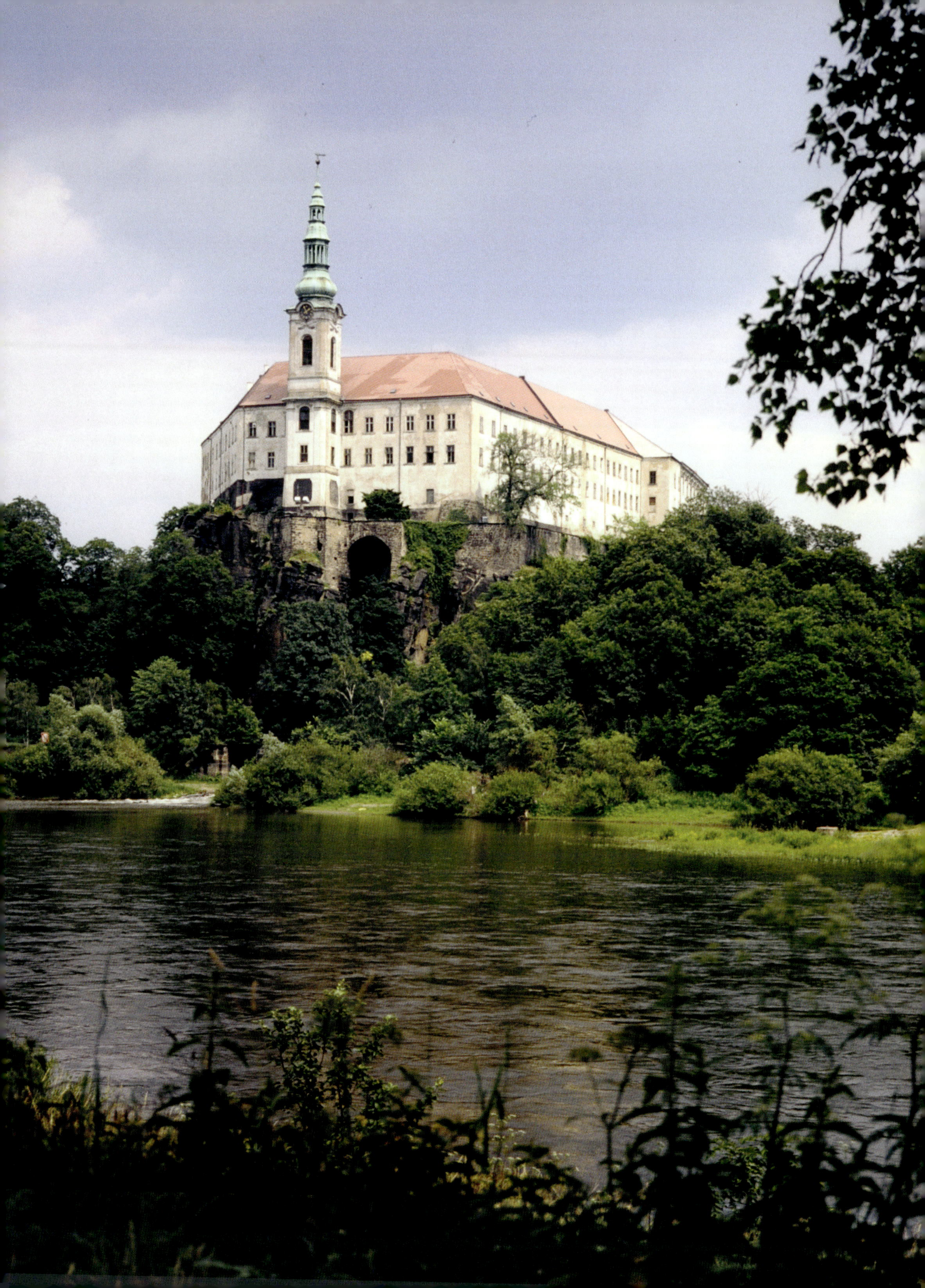

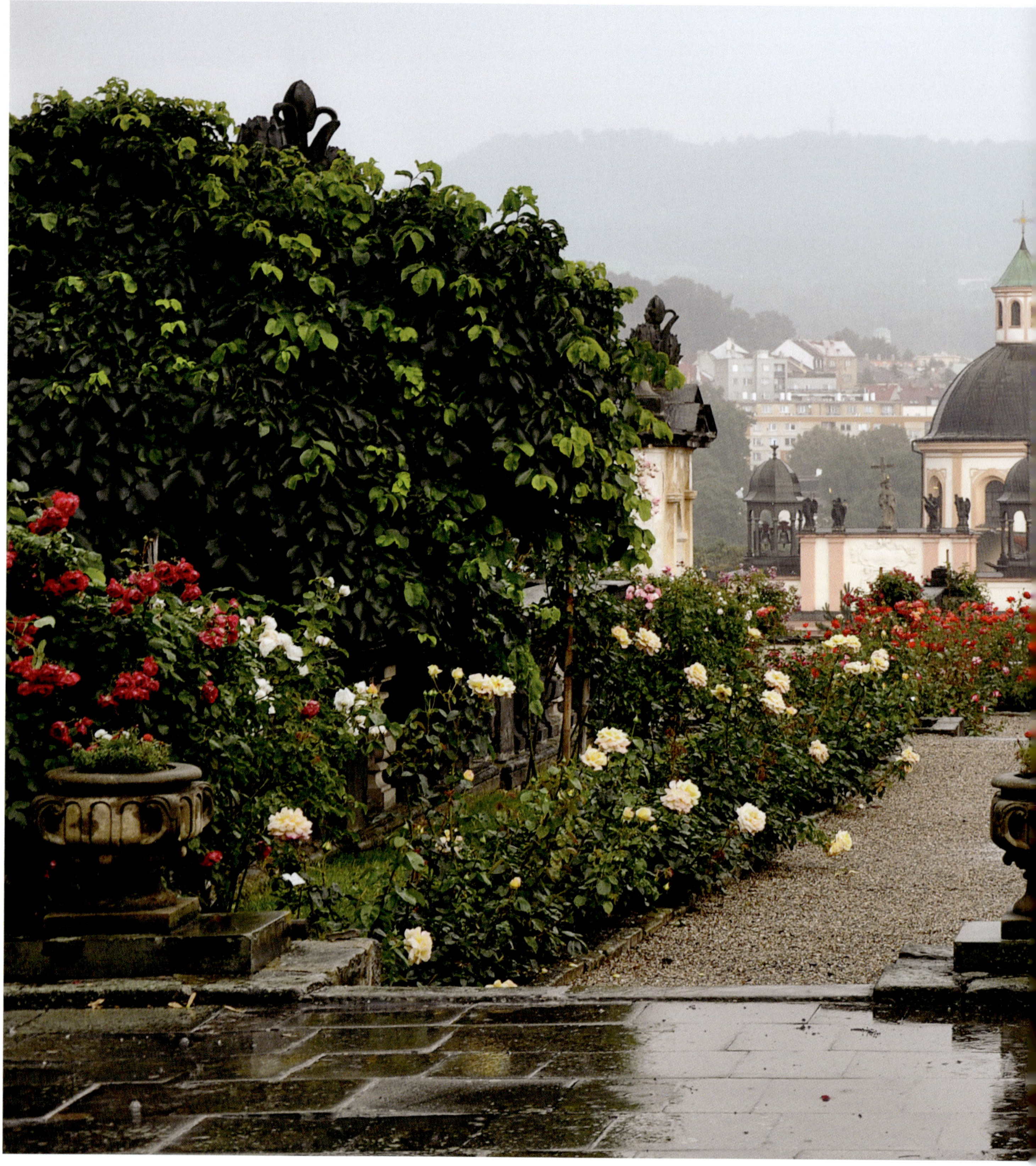

Děčín

The Rose Garden was established by Maximillian, Count of Thun-Hohenstein in the seventeenth century. The lofty two-storey gloriette, with its stairs and terraces, was only restored at the turn of the Millennium.

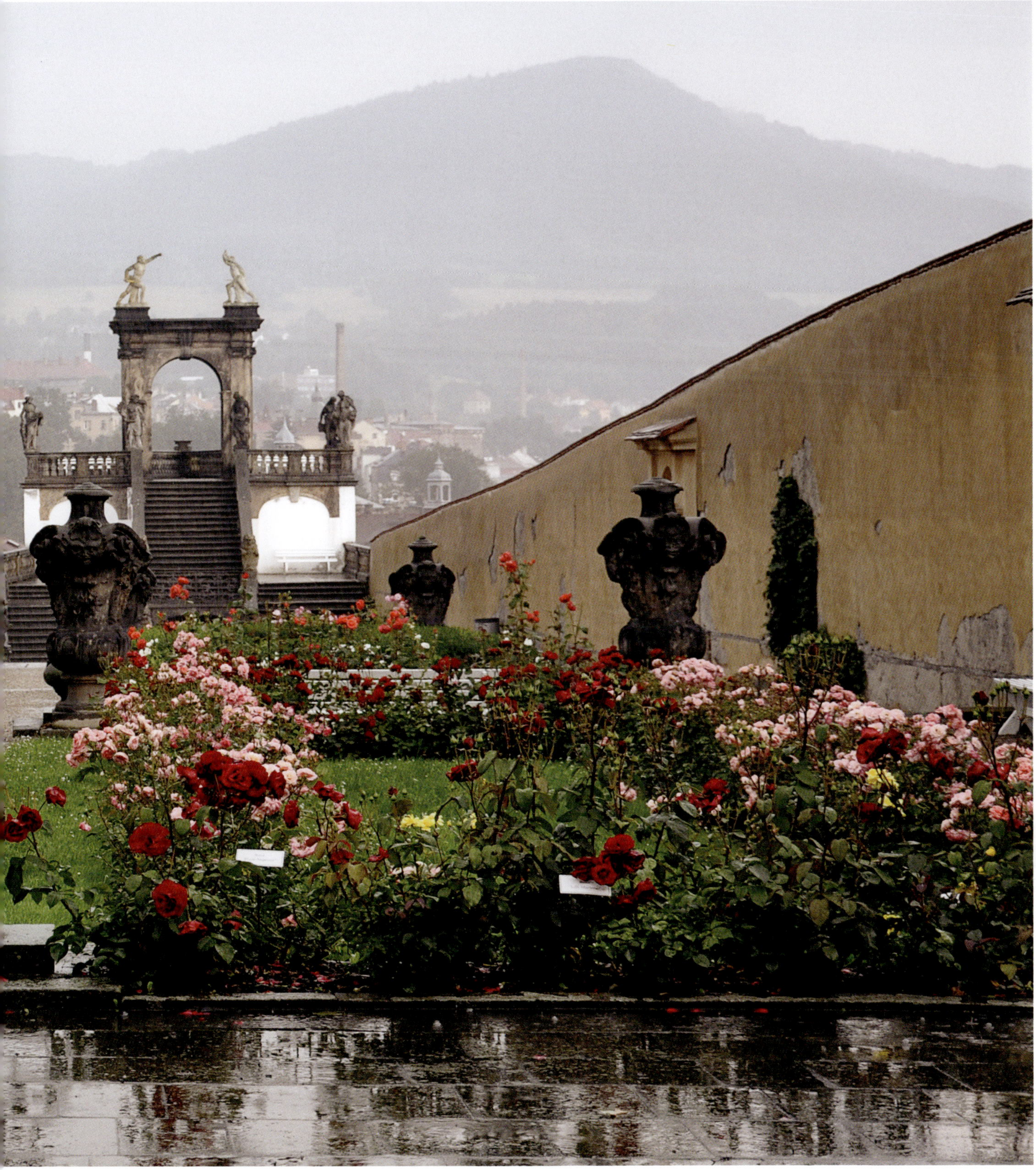

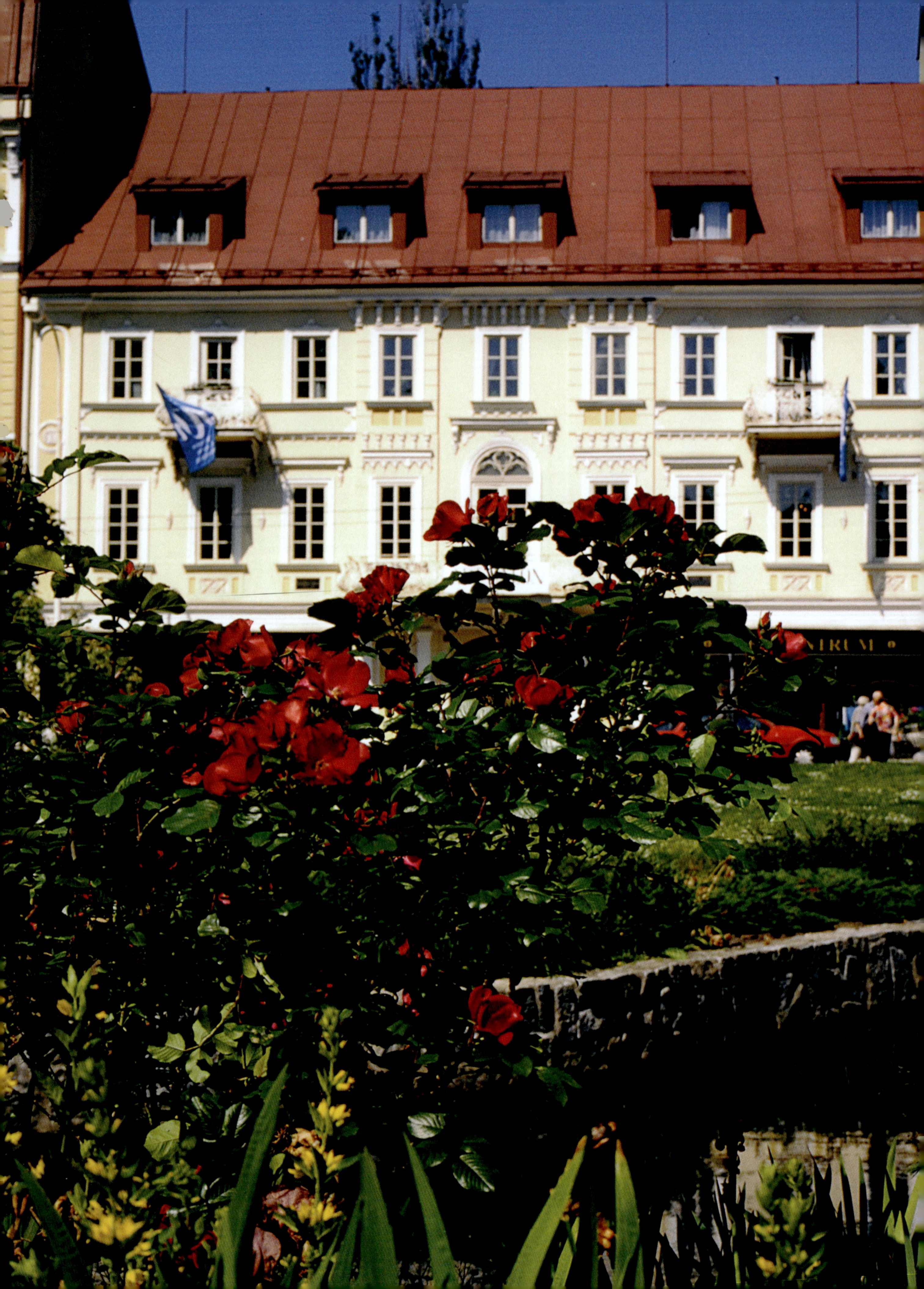

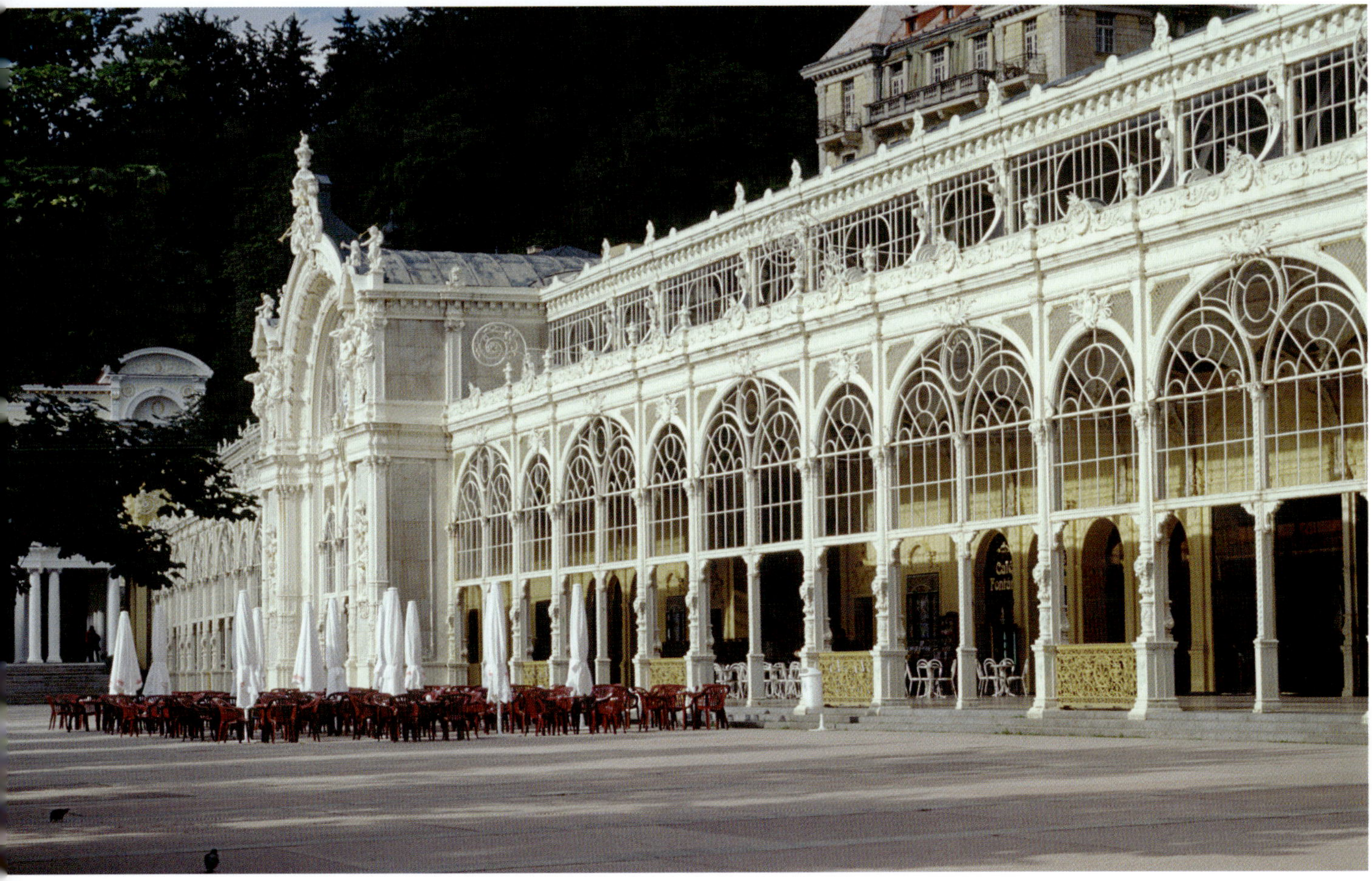

Marienbad

Marienbads iconic colonnade, immortalised in several films, is a masterpiece of 19th century architecture.

← The building in Marienbad that used to house the Hotel *zum weissen Schwann*, where Chopin stayed in the summer of 1836, is now the Chopin Museum, seen here from the park outside. When he heard that the Wodziński family would be spending the summer at this very fashionable spa, Chopin took rooms on the floor above them. His subsequent summer romance with Maria blossomed around the beautiful hills and gardens of this fine town during those idyllic August days.

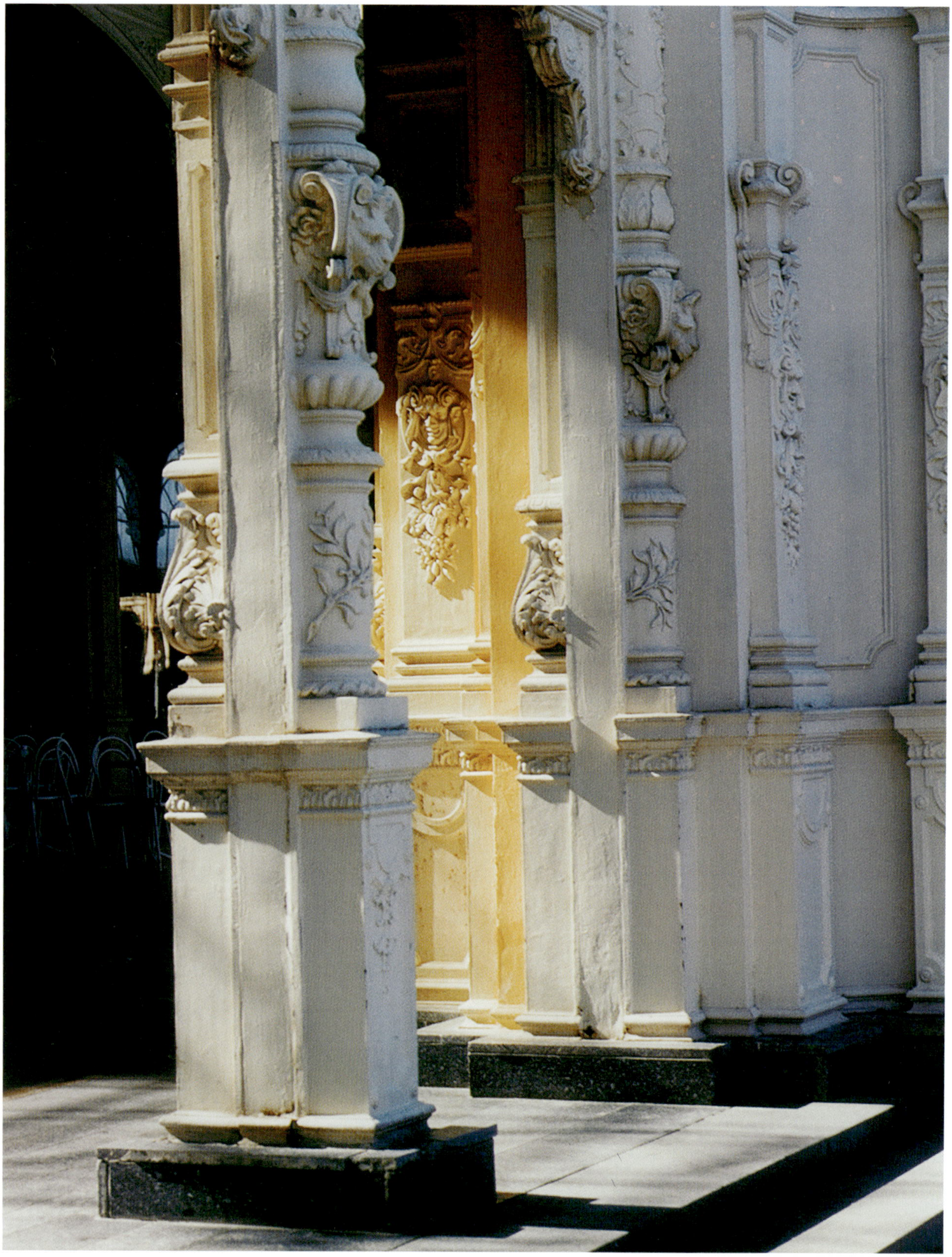

Marienbad
Details from Marienbad's Colonnade.

→ The Memorial in the park overlooked by the Chopin Museum commemorates the composer's visit to Marienbad in 1836.

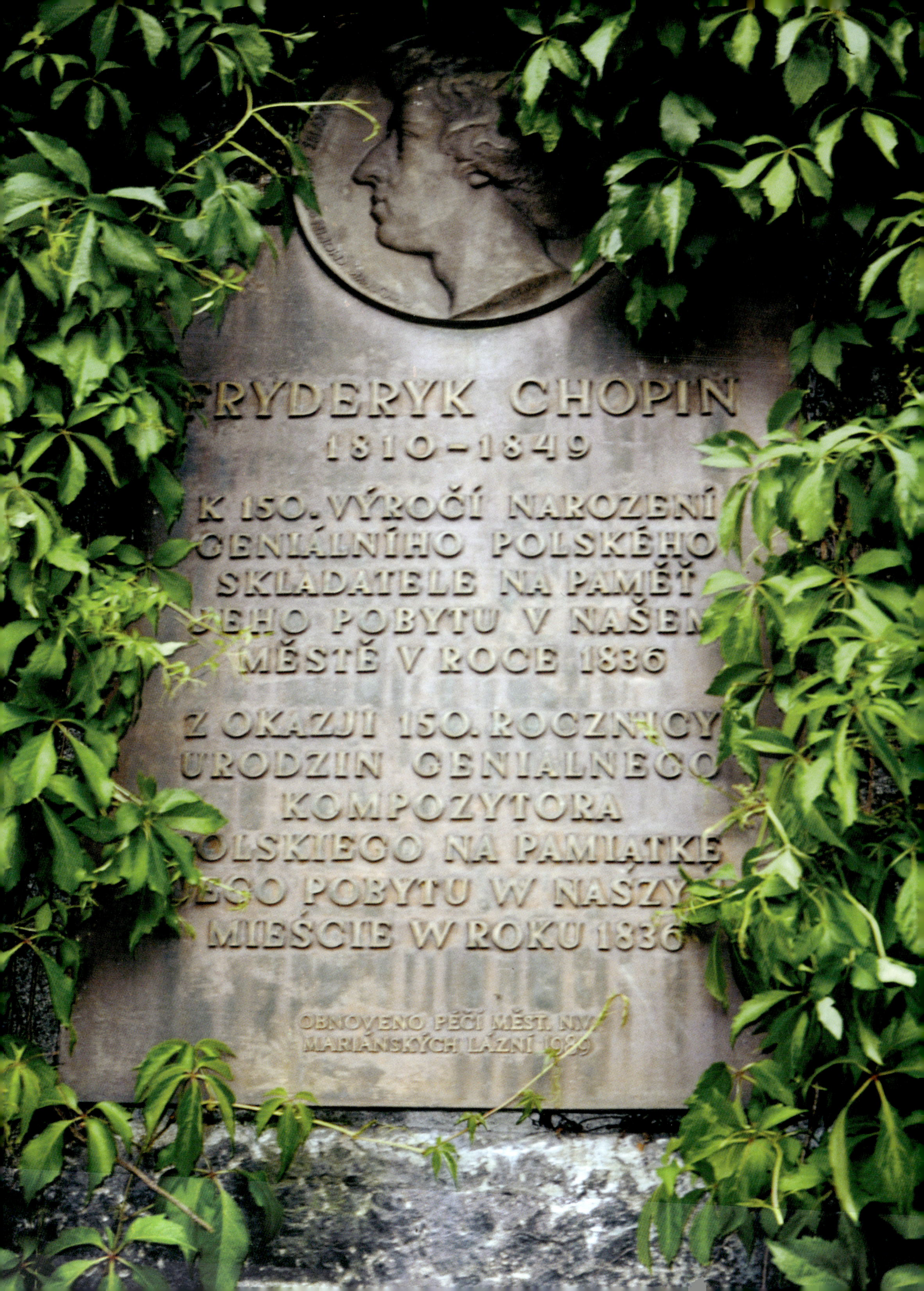
FRYDERYK CHOPIN
1810–1849
K 150. VÝROČÍ NAROZENÍ
GENIÁLNÍHO POLSKÉHO
SKLADATELE NA PAMĚŤ
EHO POBYTU V NAŠEM
MĚSTĚ V ROCE 1836
Z OKAZJI 150. ROCZNICY
URODZIN GENIALNEGO
KOMPOZYTORA
OLSKIEGO NA PAMIĄTKĘ
EGO POBYTU W NASZY
MIEŚCIE W ROKU 1836
OBNOVENO PÉČÍ MĚST. NV
MARIÁNSKÝCH LÁZNÍ 1989

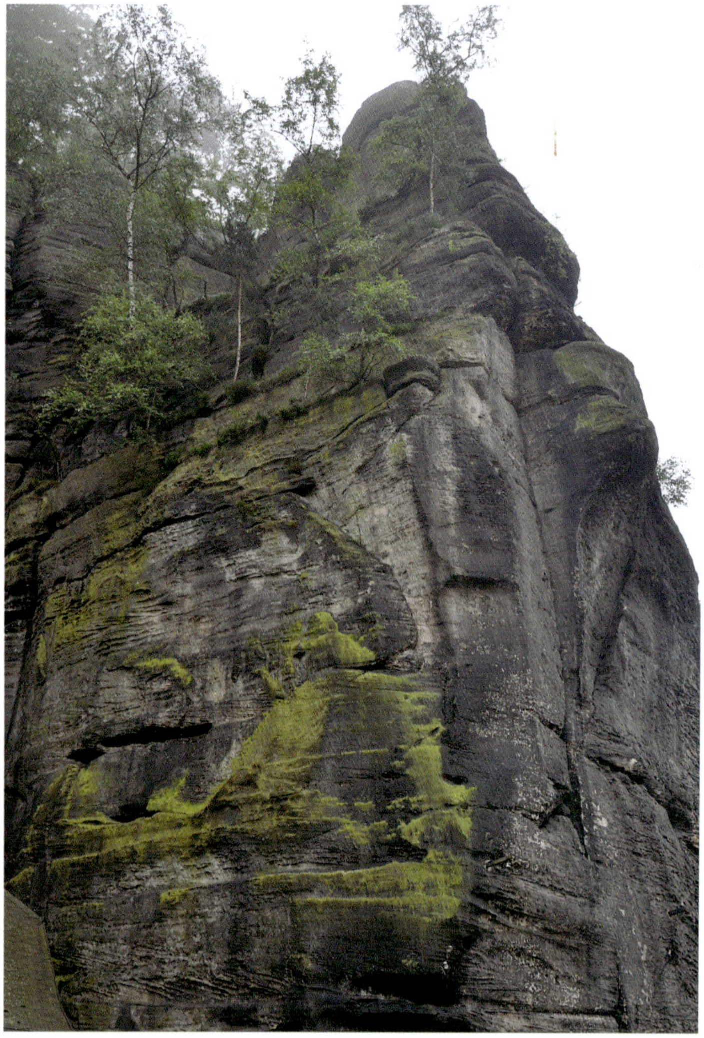

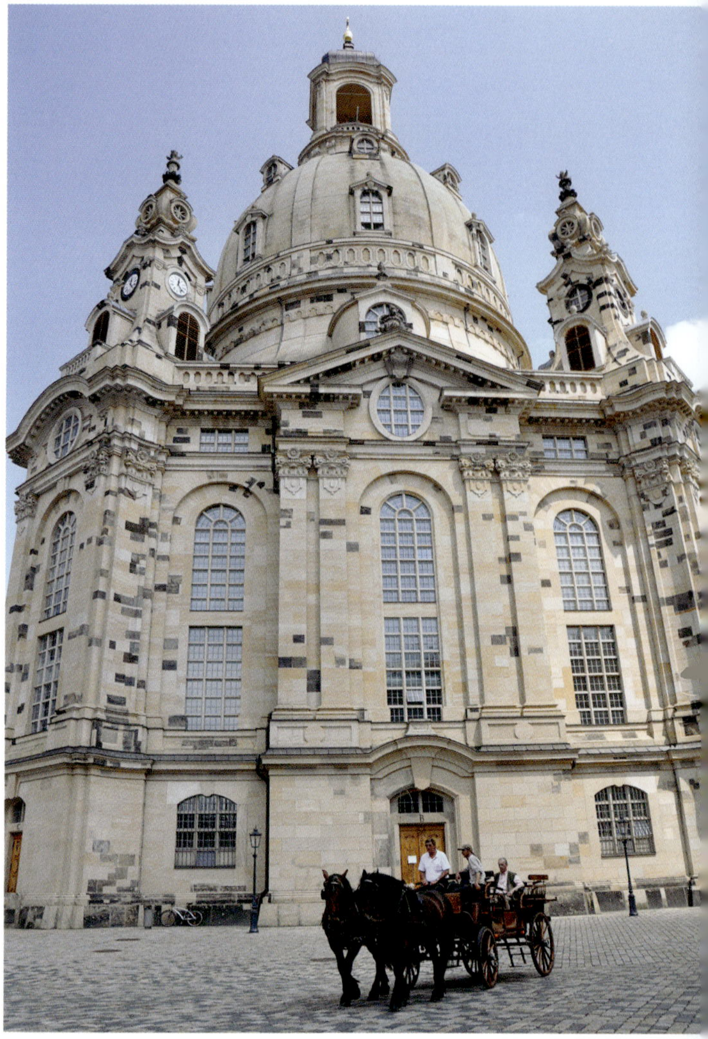

From Teplice to Dresden

The road goes through the picturesque region known as Bohemian – or Saxon – Switzerland. It follows the course of the young River Elbe, and is known for the curious basalt rock formations of its gorges and stunning views onto the river.

Dresden

The Frauenkirche, originally built between 1726 and 1743 by Saxony's Catholic Prince Elector, Friedrich August I, was completely destroyed by the Allied bombings in February 1945, but has been rebuilt to its former glory in 2005. It stands as one of the very rare examples of a Lutheran Baroque church.

→ The Silbermann organ in the Frauenkirche is modelled on the one in the Cathedral on which Chopin played his Piano Concerto in E Minor in 1830 for his friend Klengel who was the organist there at that time.

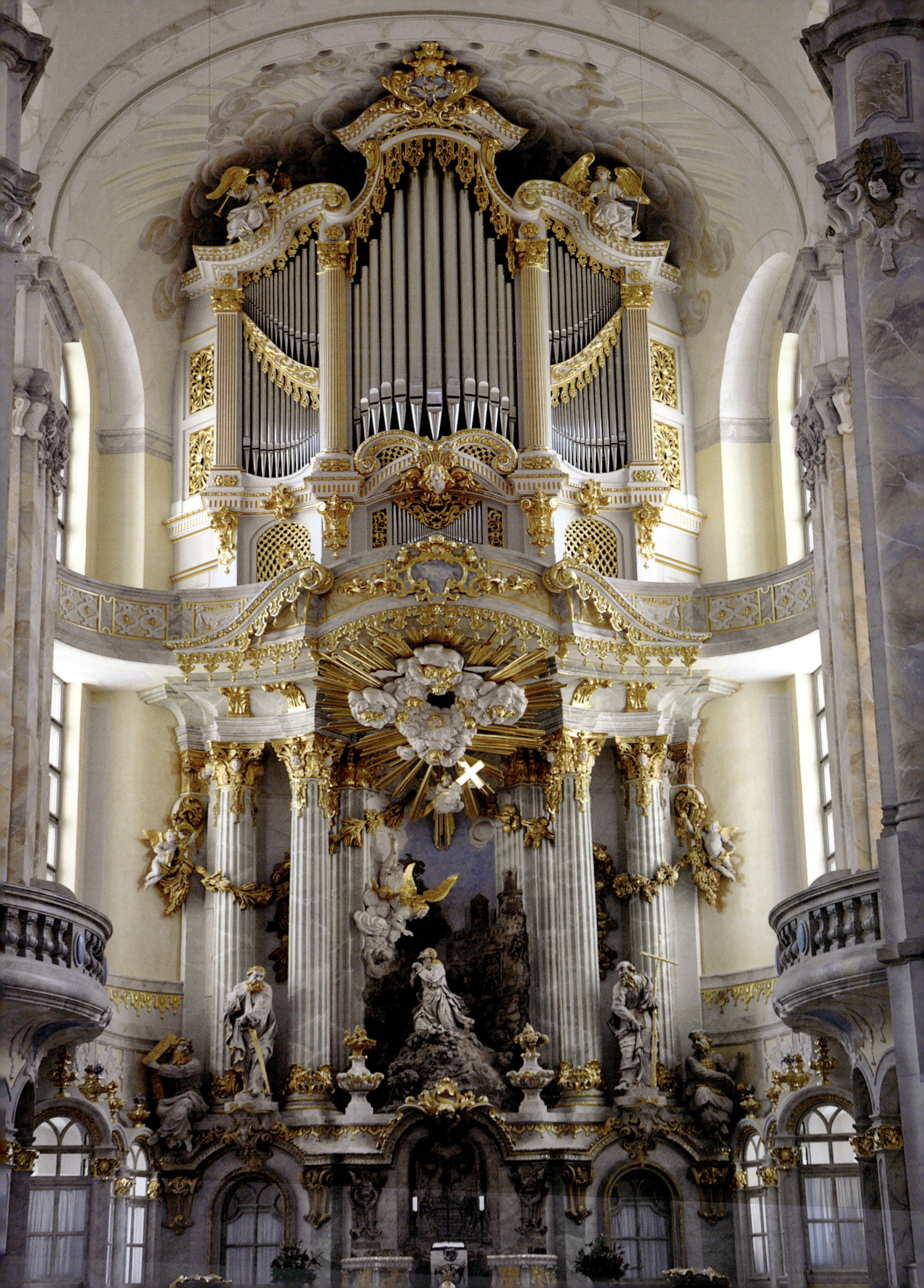

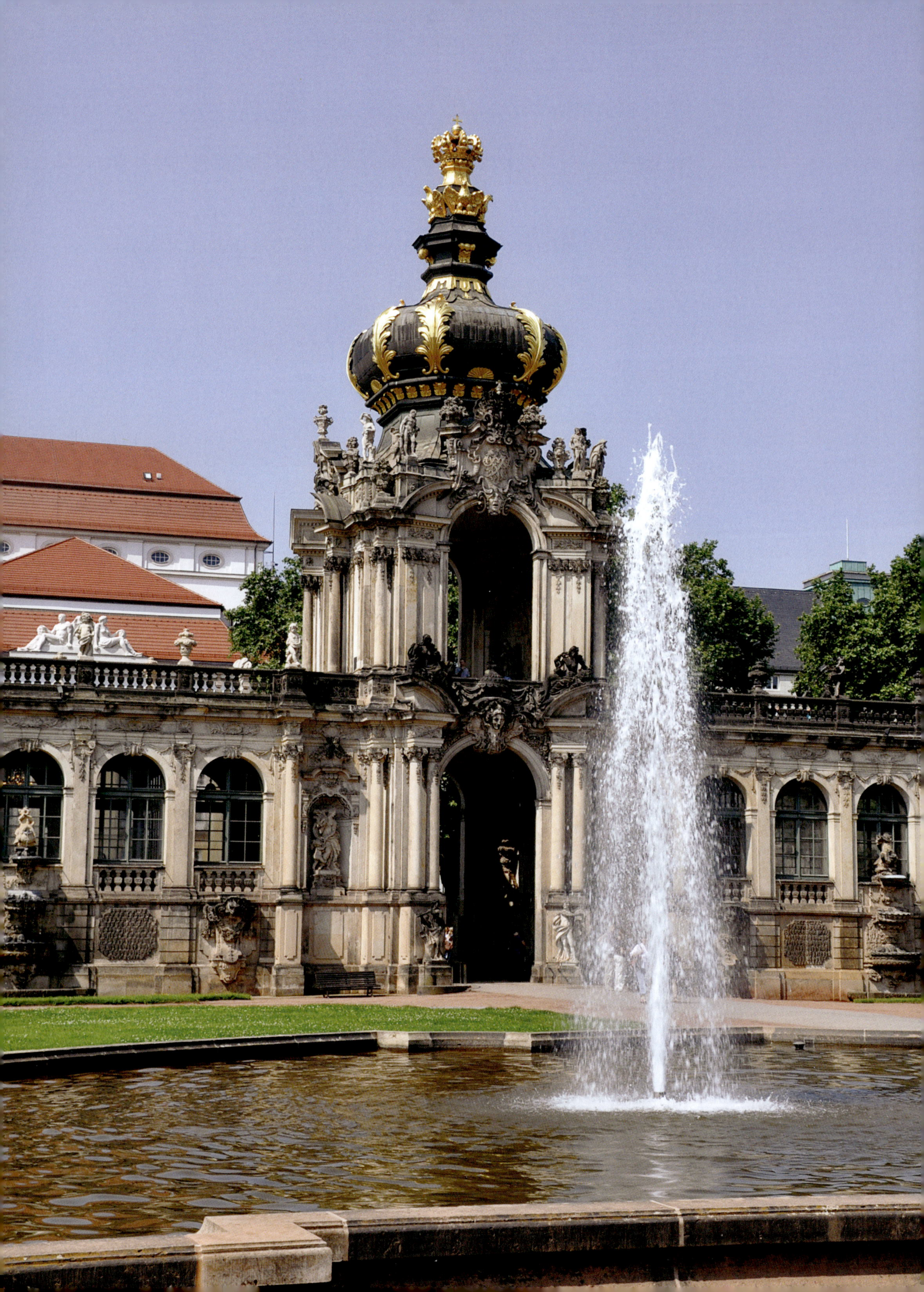

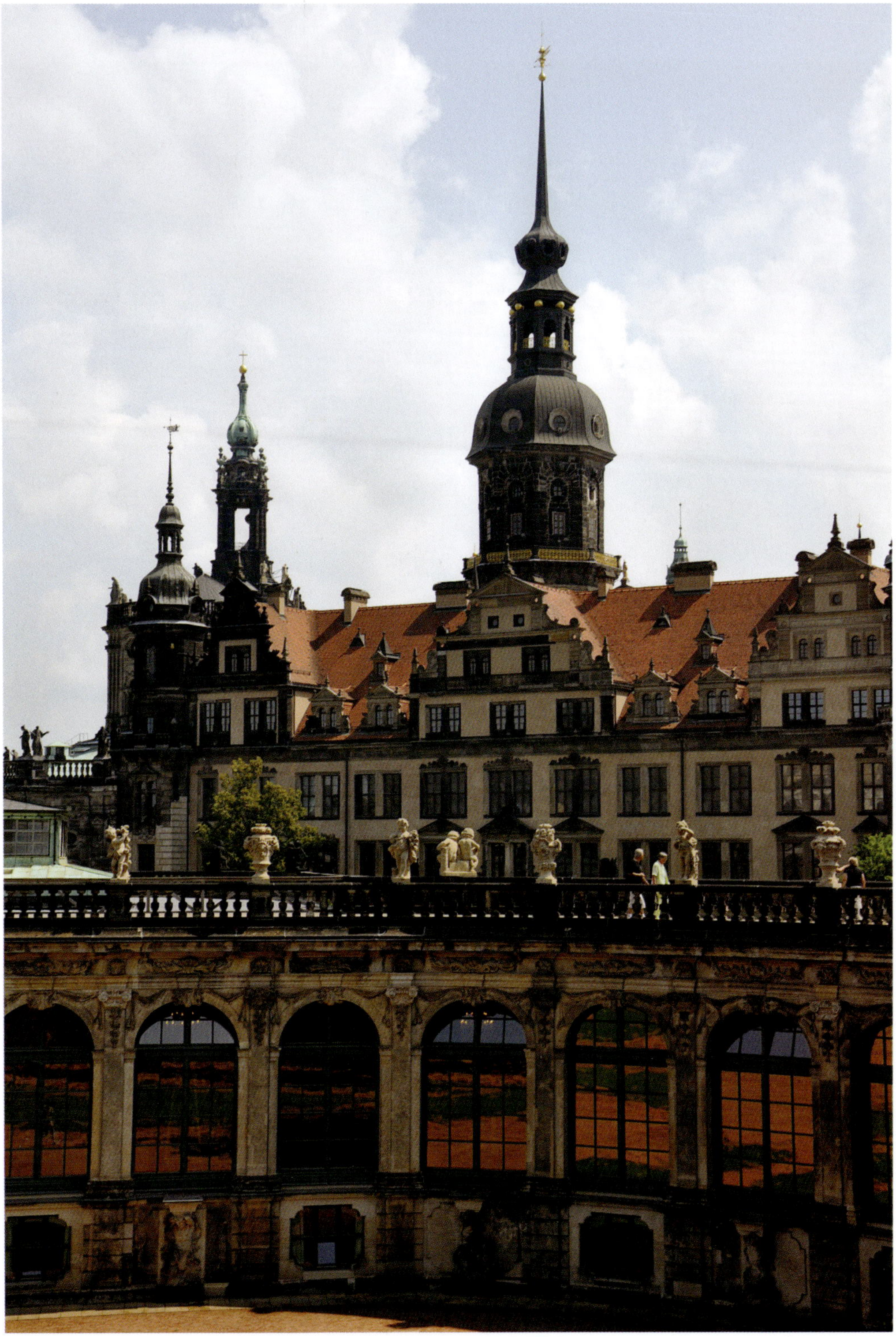

Dresden
View from the Zwinger Palace. On the left can be seen the spires of the Hochkirche, or Cathedral, where Chopin played on the organ.

← The Zwinger's famous "Crown-tower" illustrates the fact that this magnificent palace is considered to be one the major landmarks of German baroque architecture. Nearly completely destroyed by carpet bombing in 1945, it was rebuilt to its former splendour after the War.

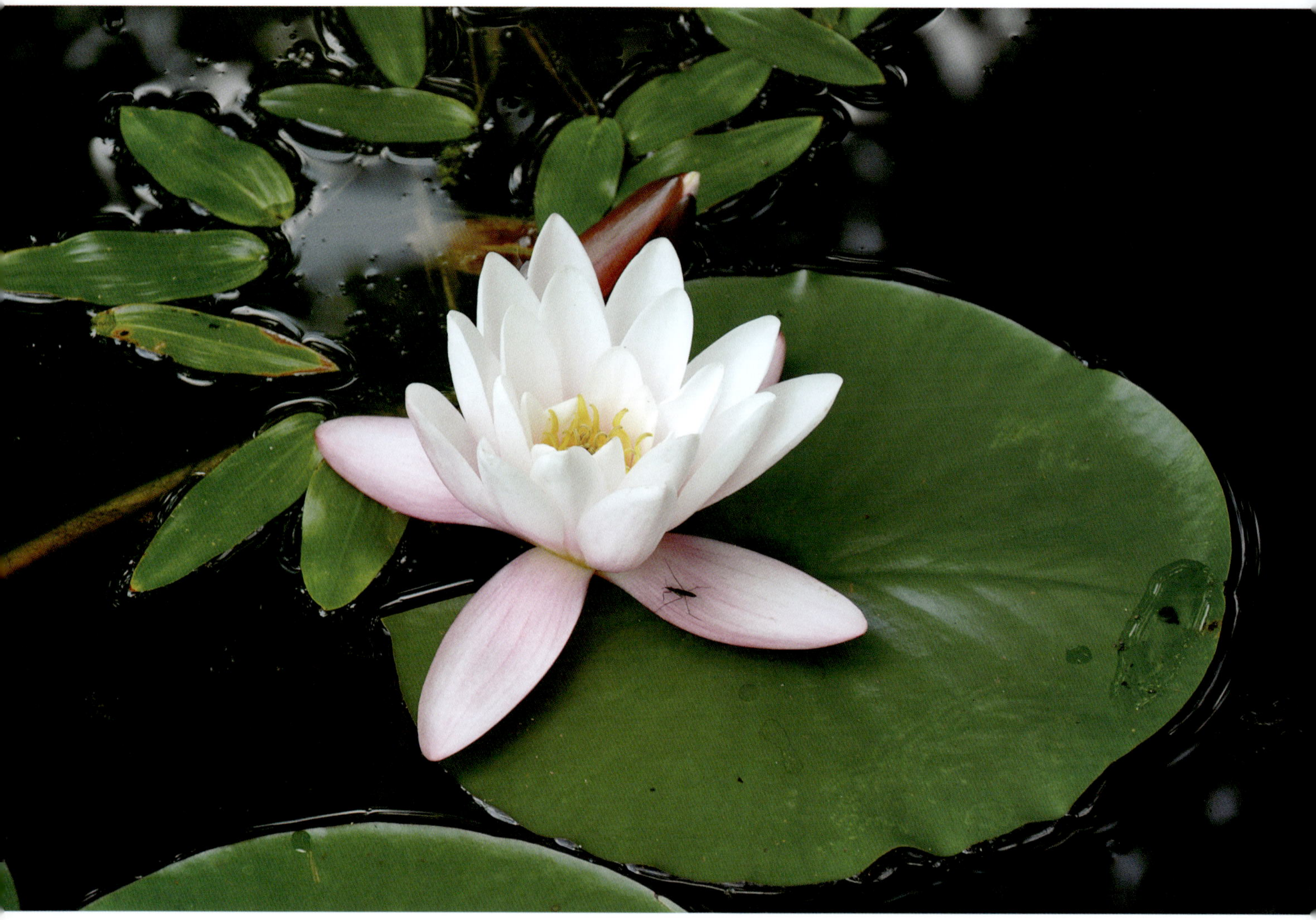

Dresden

Chopin and Maria Wodzińska often went for walks in the Great Garden during his heady summer of 1835. The Botanical Gardens is part of the Great Garden.

→ The entrance to the Gemäldegalerie Alte Meister, the Art Gallery in the Zwinger Palace visited by Chopin during his stay in the Saxon capital.

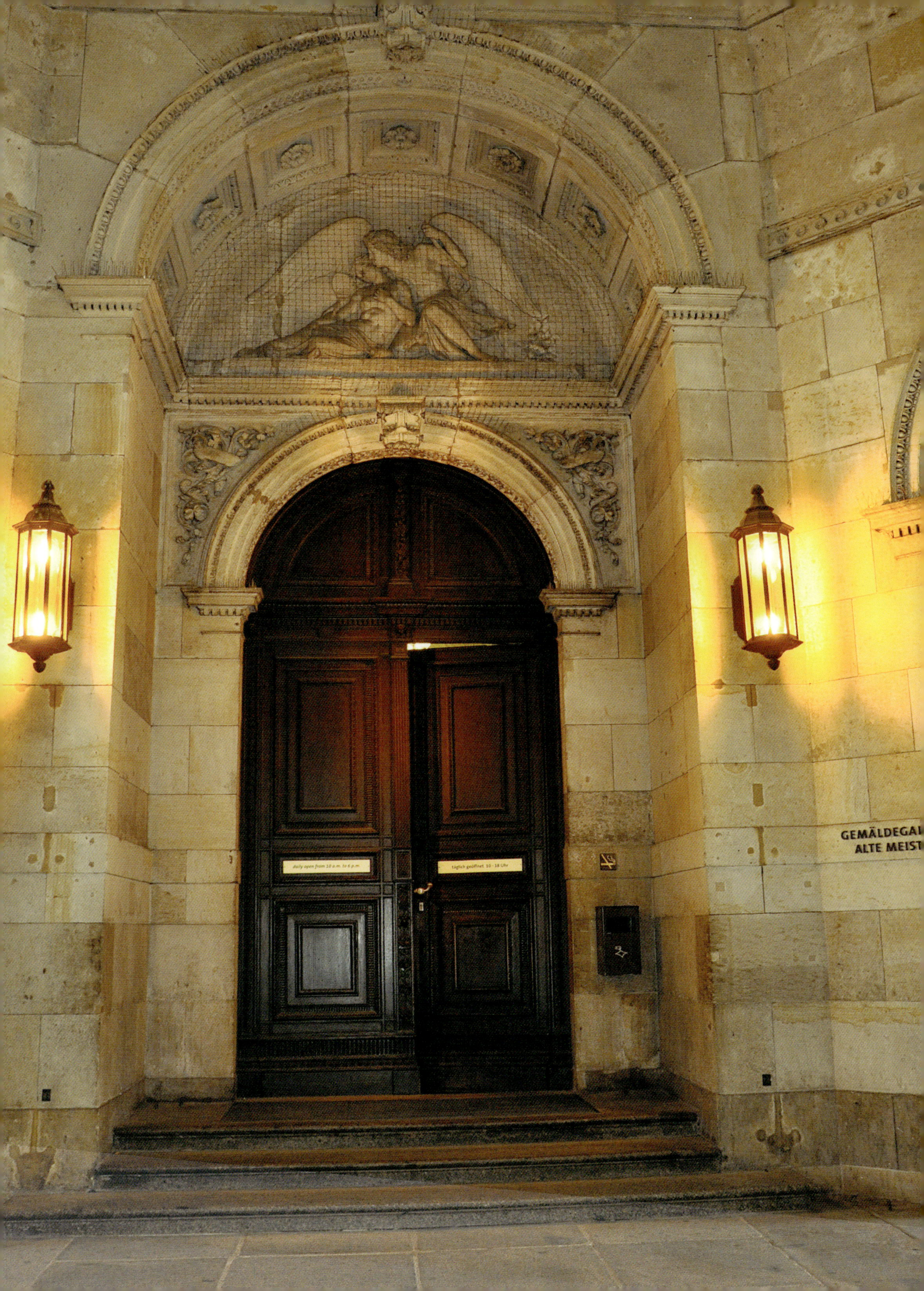
GEMÄLDEGAL
ALTE MEIST

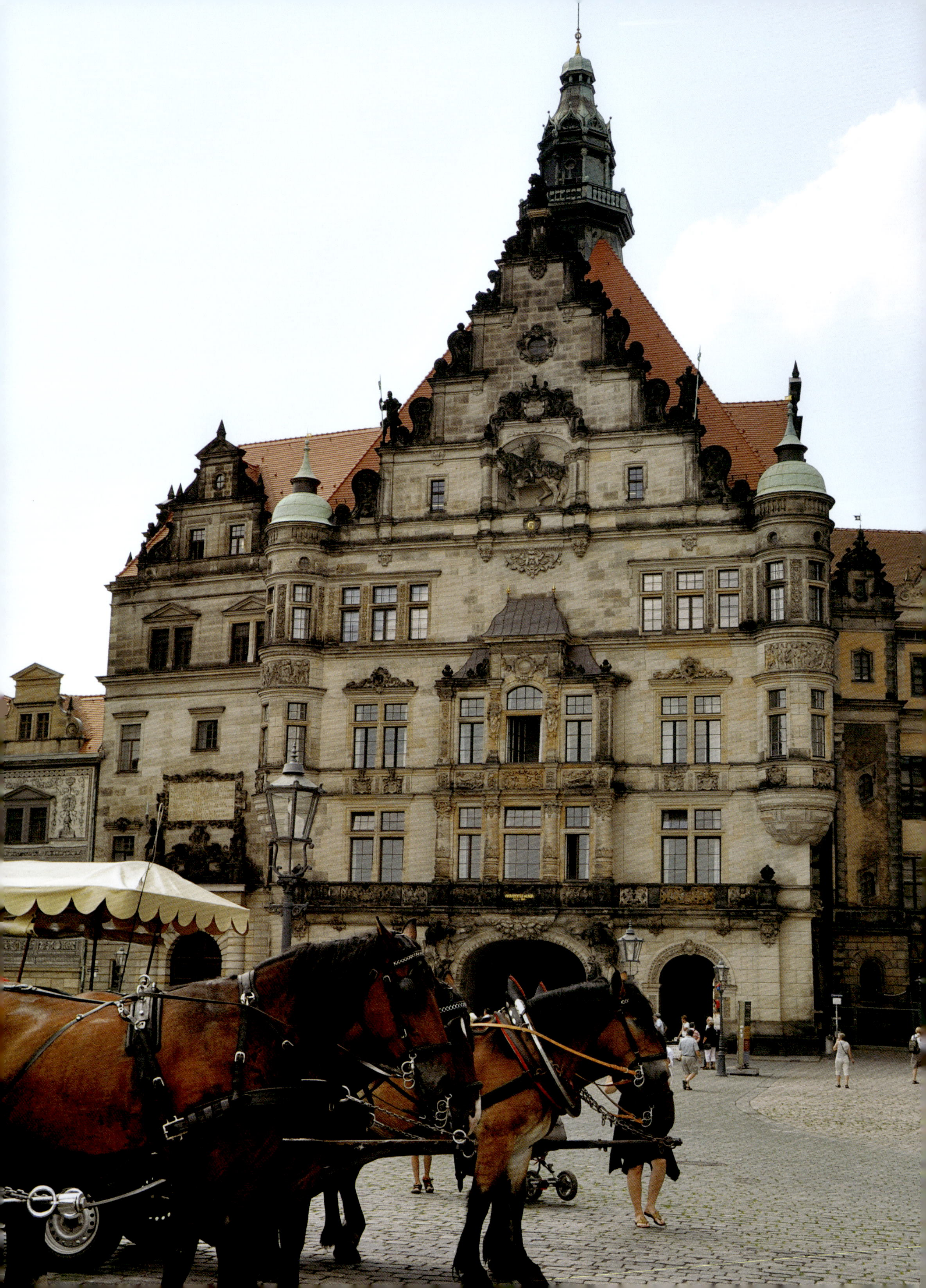

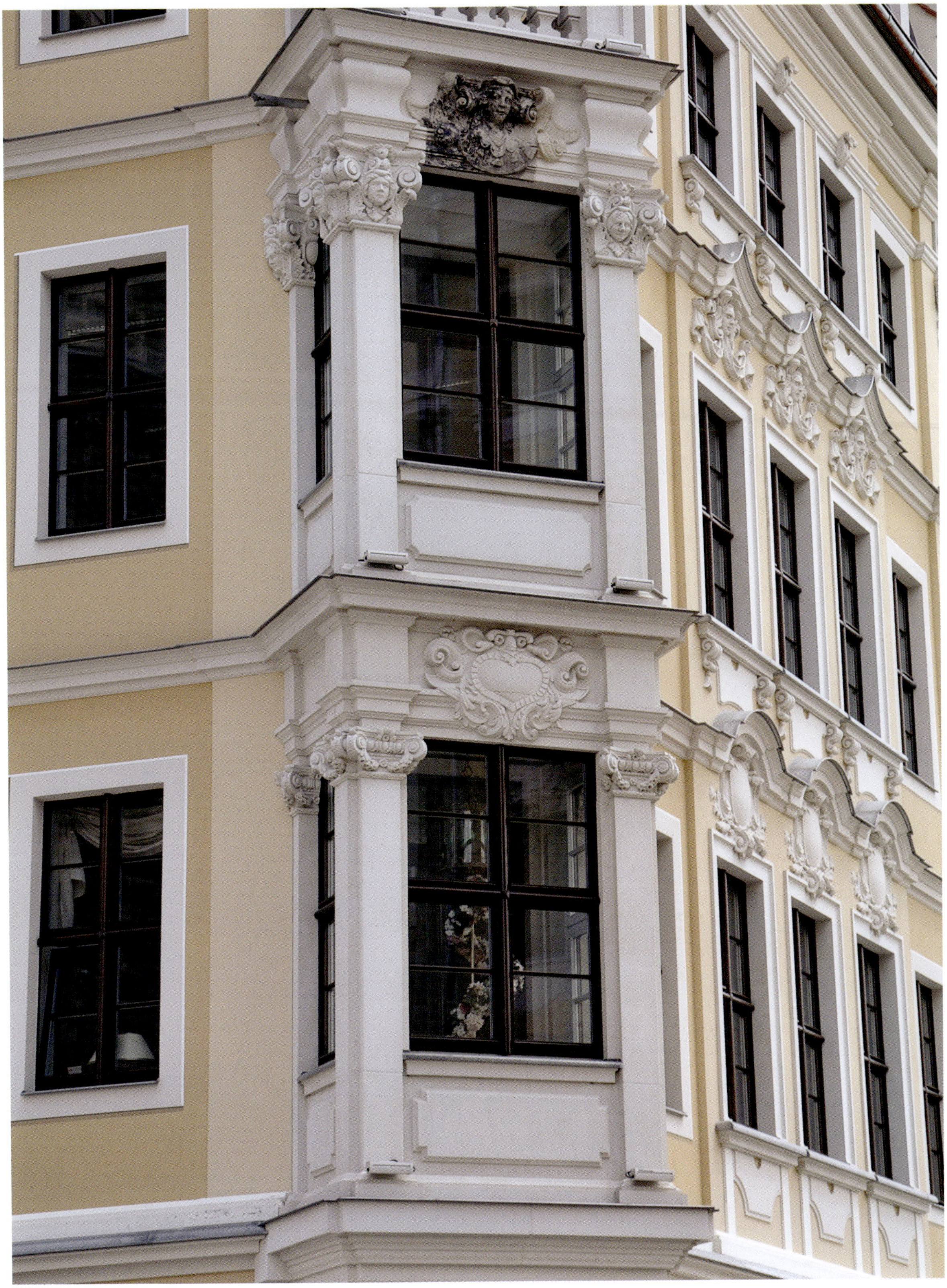

Dresden
The Rampischerstrasse, where the Wodzińskis were lodged during the summer of 1835, and where Chopin was a frequent visitor, lies just off the square of the Frauenkirche.

← The Town Hall stands on the banks of the River Elbe, near the Cathedral.

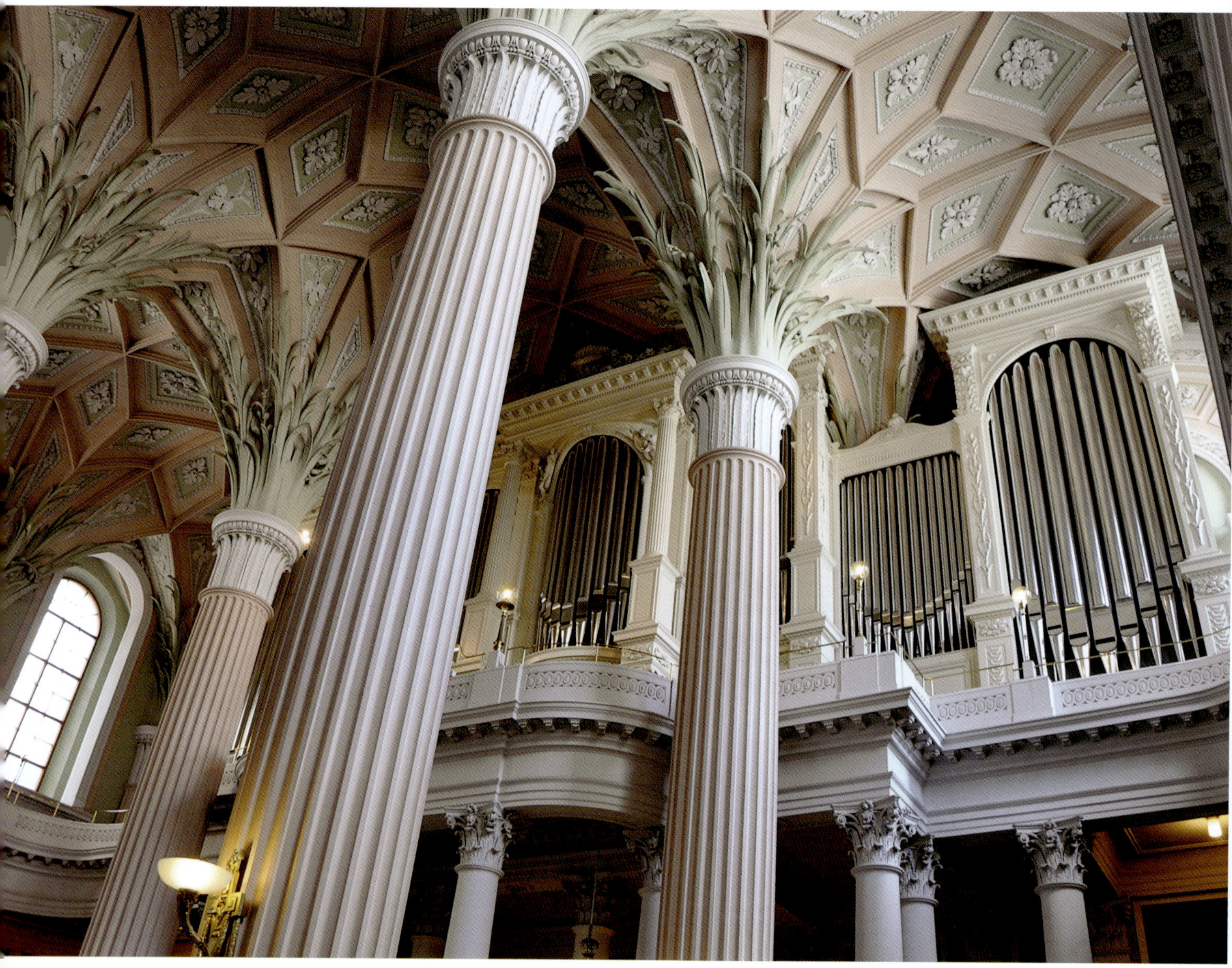

Leipzig

St. Nicholas' Church is one of the two most important churches in central Leipzig. It was built around 1165 when the city was founded. It has been a Protestant seat since 1539 after the Reformation. The church saw the first performance of the Johannes Passion of Johann Sebastian Bach on Good Friday 1724. It also rose to national fame with the anti-communist demonstrations in 1989 when it became the centre of the revolution.

→ The Memorial to Johann Sebastian Bach stands just outside the St. Thomas Church where the great composer worked as a cantor and where he is buried. He was choir director here from 1723 until his death in 1750. Chopin was a great admirer of Bach and would surely have come to pay his respects.

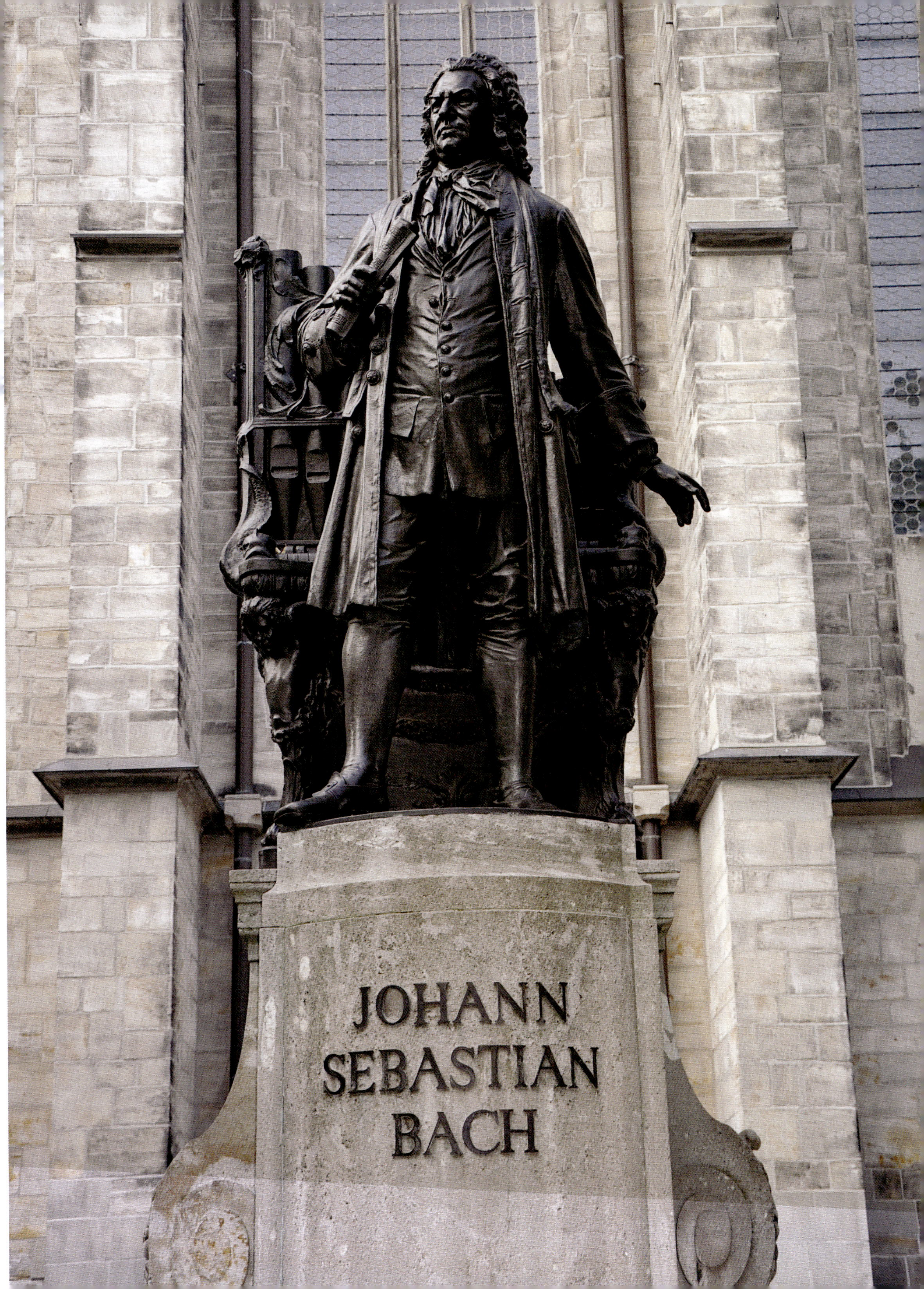
JOHANN
SEBASTIAN
BACH

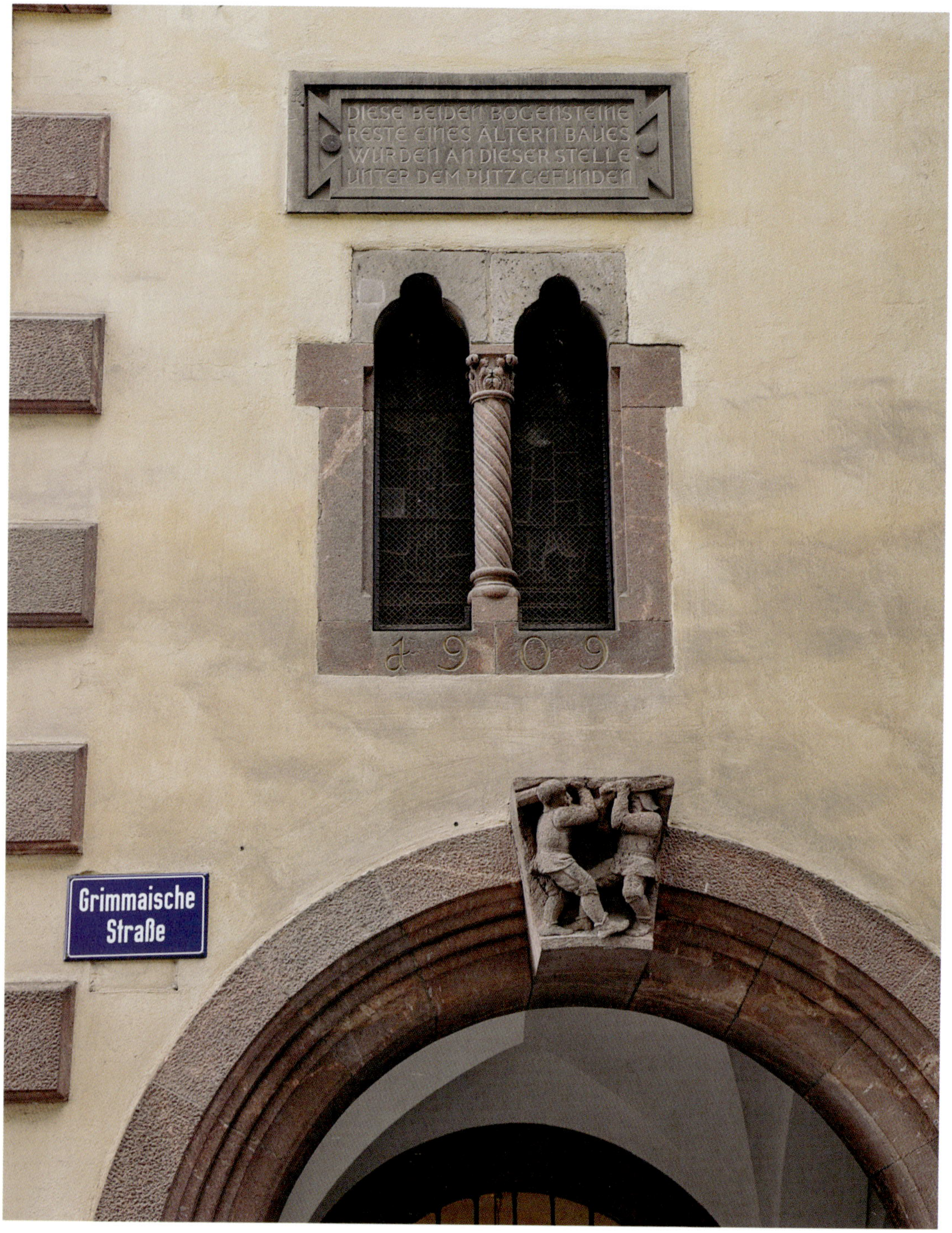

Leipzig

The Grimmaische Strasse sign on side of Town Hall. In 1835 Chopin came to visit the sixteen-year-old Clara Wieck at No. 36, where he also met her future husband Robert Schumann.

→ The old sign above Auerbachs Cellar Leipzig's famous restaurant described in Goethe's *Faust* as the first place to which Mephistopheles takesthe hero on their travels. It is located below the Mädlerpassage a shopping arcade at Grimmaische Strasse 2 in Leipzig's historical district near the market.

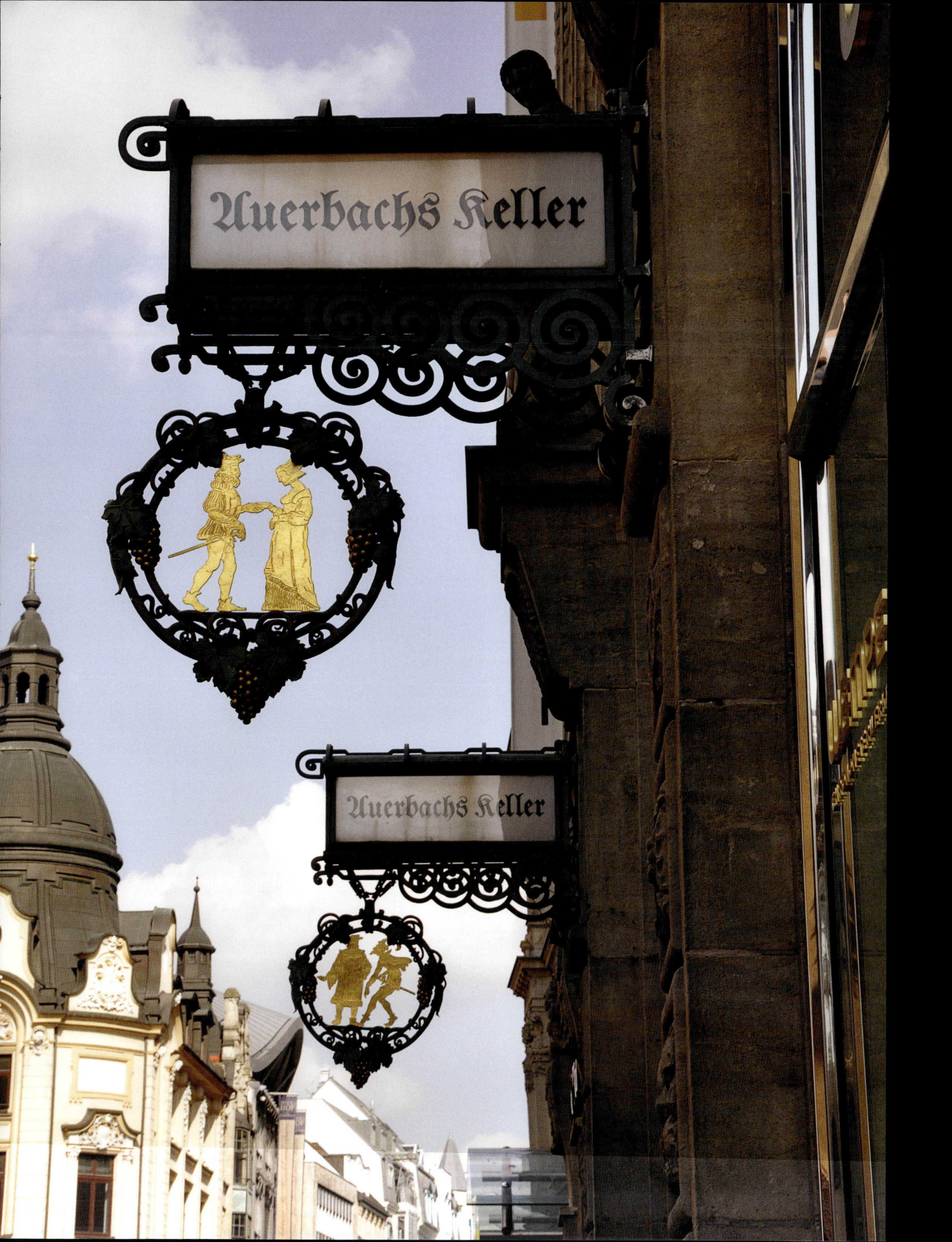
Auerbachs Keller
Auerbachs Keller

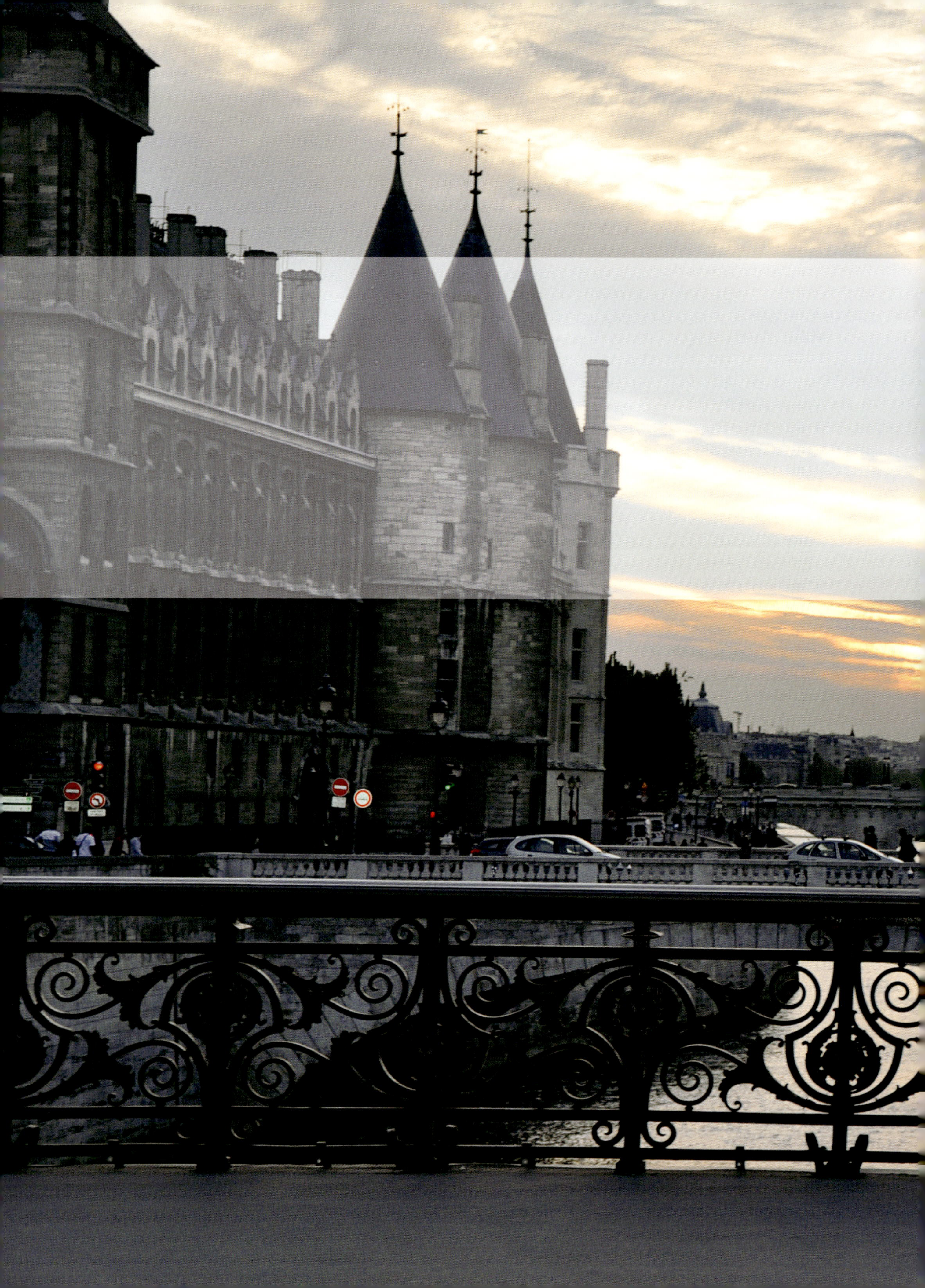

The Paris Years

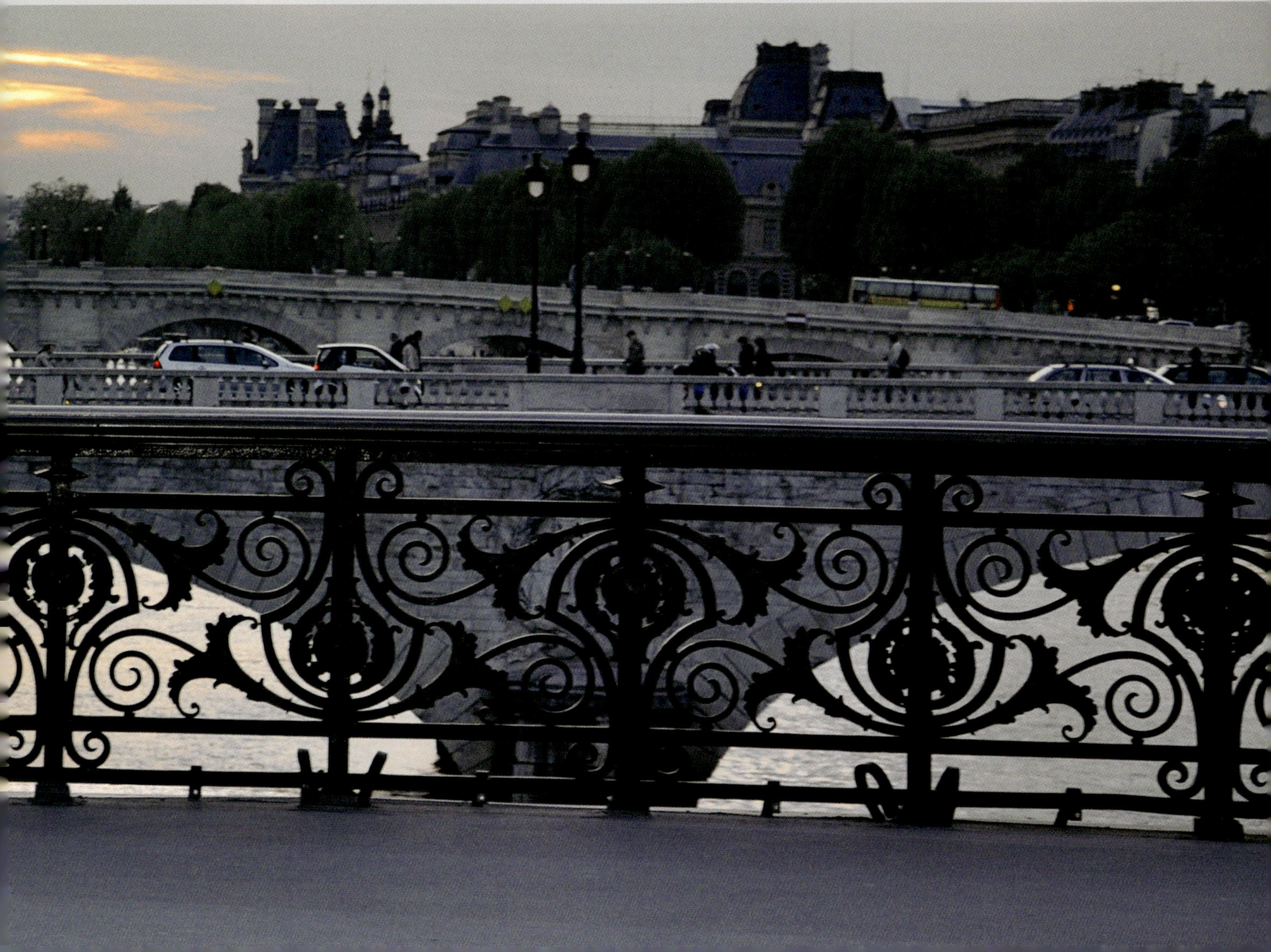

The years 1830-31, and 1848 were marked by widespread pan-European revolutions and unrest. The Polish November Uprising was finally and brutally suppressed in 1831 with the fall of Warsaw to Russia's General Pashkievitch, while in France the Bourbon King Charles X was violently replaced by the Orléanist King Louis-Philippe. Seventeen years later, Europe was again in the throes of violent revolt, in which Louis-Phillippe was in his turn ousted, and sought asylum in Queen Victoria's England. Those seventeen years were the years of Chopin's Paris, as well as those of Liszt, Alkan, Kalkbrenner, Thalberg and Berlioz.

Chopin arrived in Paris in September 1831, and took rooms on the fourth floor at 27 Boulevard Poissonnière, from the balcony of which he could observe the city, with its milling pedestrian throngs and horse-drawn carriages, passing by. This was to be his new world, which he viewed with a mixture of hopes and regrets: hopes for the fame and fortune that had evaded him in Warsaw and Vienna, and regrets for his family in his devastated homeland, now under ruthless Russian rule.

Here you have the greatest luxury, the greatest squalor, the greatest virtue and the greatest vice, you simply cannot imagine the shouting, the commotion, the bustle and the dirt; one could positively lose oneself in this anthill, and the nice thing is that nobody cares what anyone else does.

Chopin to Norbert Kumelski (Paris, 18 November 1831)

He found the city was now home to numerous Polish refugees, among them his own close boyhood friends, including Kazimierz Wodziński and Julian Fontana, as well as high-profile figures such as the Potockis, the Platers and Adam Mickiewicz. Their epicenter was the Hôtel Lambert on the Ile Saint-Louis on the River Seine, which was the seat of Adam Czartoryski and his Polish Government-in-exile – a traditional feature of Polish fate dating back to the Final Partitions of the Polish-Lithuanian Commonwealth some four decades previously.

Chopin soon became assimilated into this Polish émigré scene.

You will not believe how many Poles there are here!

Chopin to Norbert Kumelski (Paris, 18 November 1831)

Chopin was fastidious, and the friendships he developed were often based more on mutual regard than personal characteristics. He liked Berlioz, but not his music, and Liszt admired Chopin more than the other way round, although

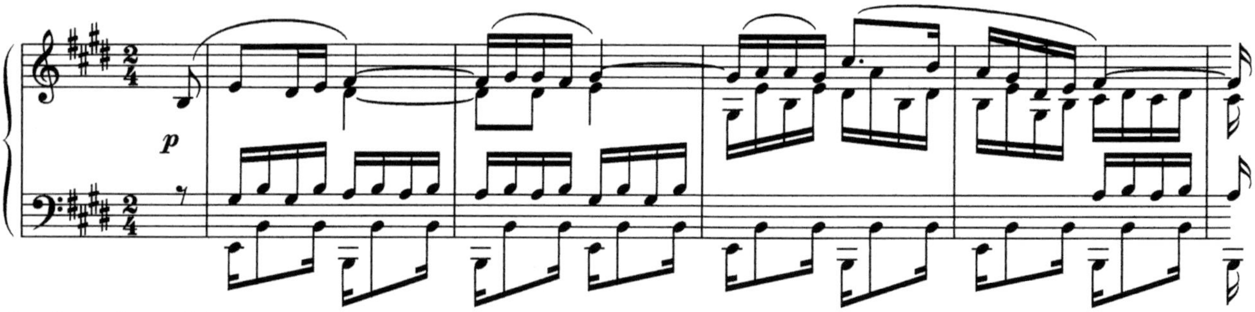

Chopin dedicated his Etude in E Op. 10 No 3, known to his displeasure as Tristesse, to Liszt.

The Cathedral of Notre Dame

A more unusual view, taken from the south-east, of the Cathedral of Notre Dame, with the River Seine in the foreground. The Cathedral has become, together with the Eiffel Tower, an iconic symbol of *la ville lumière.*

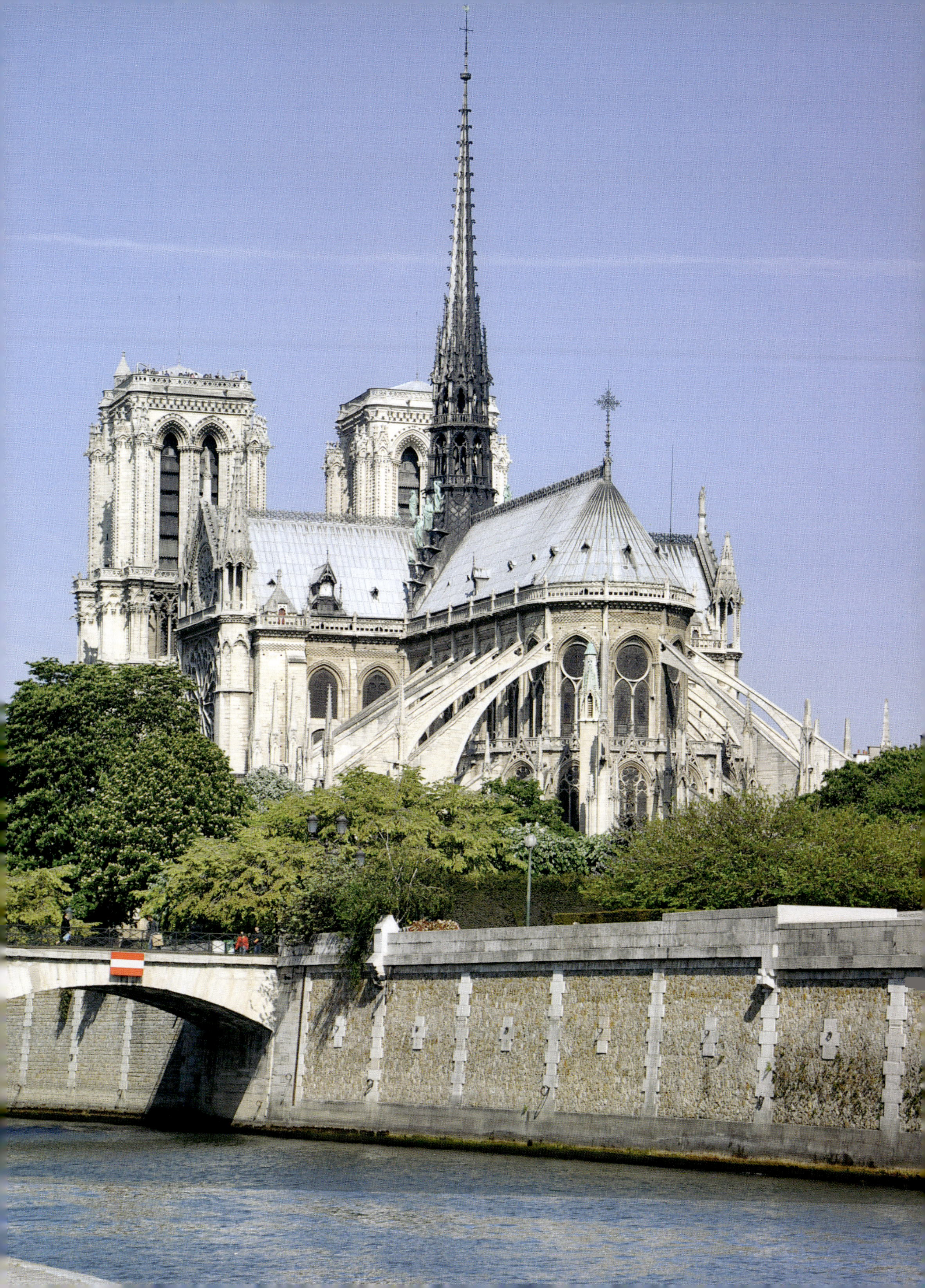

Chopin had a great admiration for Liszt's art. Their relationship later suffered a serious setback when Liszt used Chopin's apartment, in the latter's absence, for a tryst with Pleyel's wife Marie. Among his first significant contacts were pianists Ferdinand Hiller, with whom he developed a deep friendship, Friedrich Kalkbrenner, whose playing he admired enormously and came close to taking lessons from, and piano manufacturer Camille Pleyel, who had a salon at 9 rue Cadet. It was there that Chopin gave his first Paris concert on 26 February 1832. Among those taking part were a string quintet organized by violinist Pierre Baillot and viola player Chrétien Urhan, who played Beethoven's Op. 29 Quintet in C, and sopranos Toméoni and Isambert. Chopin himself played a solo version of his own F minor Piano Concerto as well as his *Là ci darem la mano* Variations. As a special item – of a genre fashionable at the time but of questionable taste – was Kalkbrenner's Grand Polonaise with Introduction and March for six pianists and twelve hands, those of the composer, Chopin, Hiller, George Osborne, Camille Stamaty and Wojciech Sowiński. Mendelssohn, who was visiting Paris, and Liszt were both in the audience and were most impressed with the newcomer in their midst. Chopin's debut was a resounding success.

His second concert, with orchestra, a charity event on 20 May organized by Princess Moskowa, was not as successful. It took place in the hall of the Conservatoire, and "all Paris" was there. Chopin again played the first movement of his F minor Concerto, but his delicate "chamber" touch could not compete with the size of the hall and the orchestra, so his playing was largely lost on the audience. The same happened three years later, on 4 April 1835, when his E minor Concerto failed to impress a restless audience at the Théâre Italien. The final realization of this "touch" factor affected the remainder of his career, and it was not until 3 March 1838, that he played in a two-piano eight-hands arrangement of Beethoven's *Seventh Symphony* at Alkan's concert.

I am not fit to give concerts. The crowd intimidates me and I feel asphyxiated by its eager breath, paralysed by its inquisitive stare, silenced by its alien faces.

Chopin later speaking to Liszt

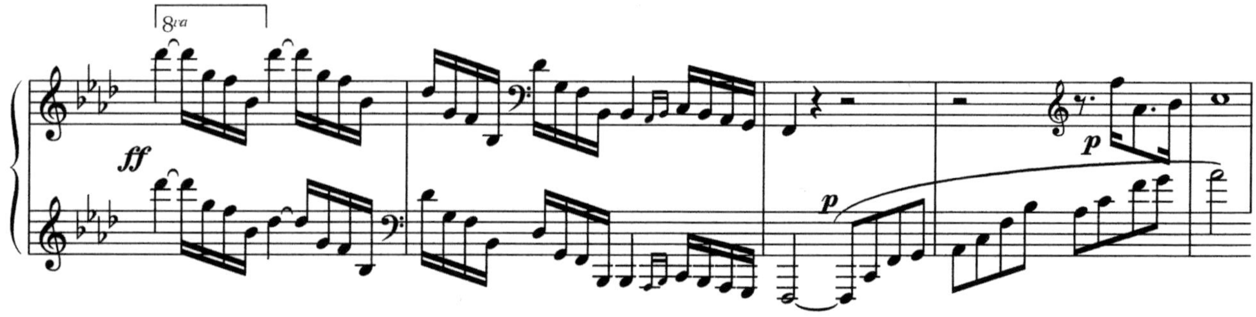

Chopin's Piano Concerto No 2 in F minor was in fact his first. It was dedicated to Countess Delfina Potocka.

Cité Bergère

Chopin lived at 4, Cité Bergère from February 1832 to June 1833, before moving first to no 5, and then later to no 38, chausée d'Antin. Both these buildings were pulled down in the course of Hausmann's redevelopment of central Paris in the second half of the 19th century. The Cité Bergère building, which has remained unchanged, is now an hotel.

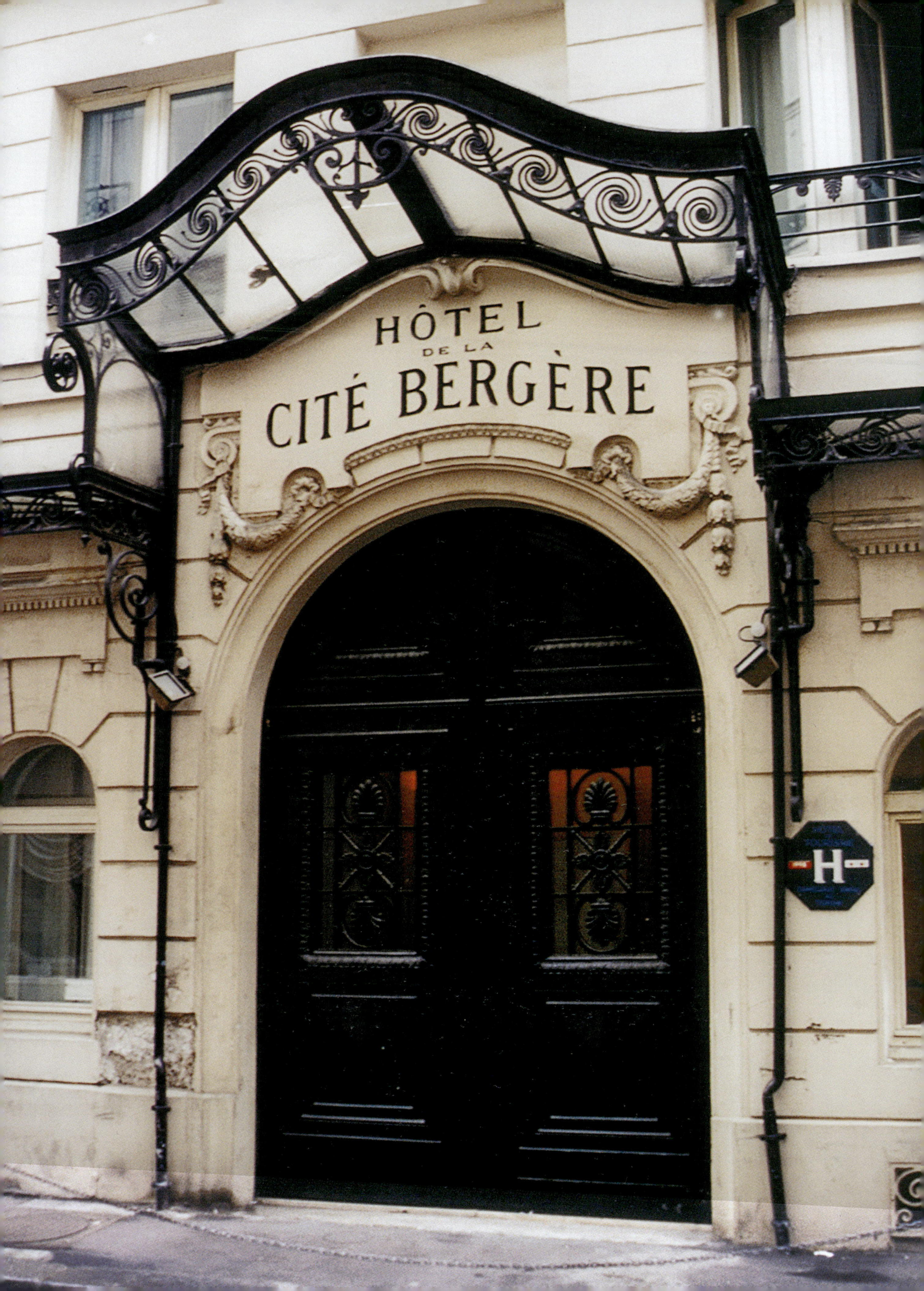
HÔTEL
DE LA
CITÉ BERGÈRE
H

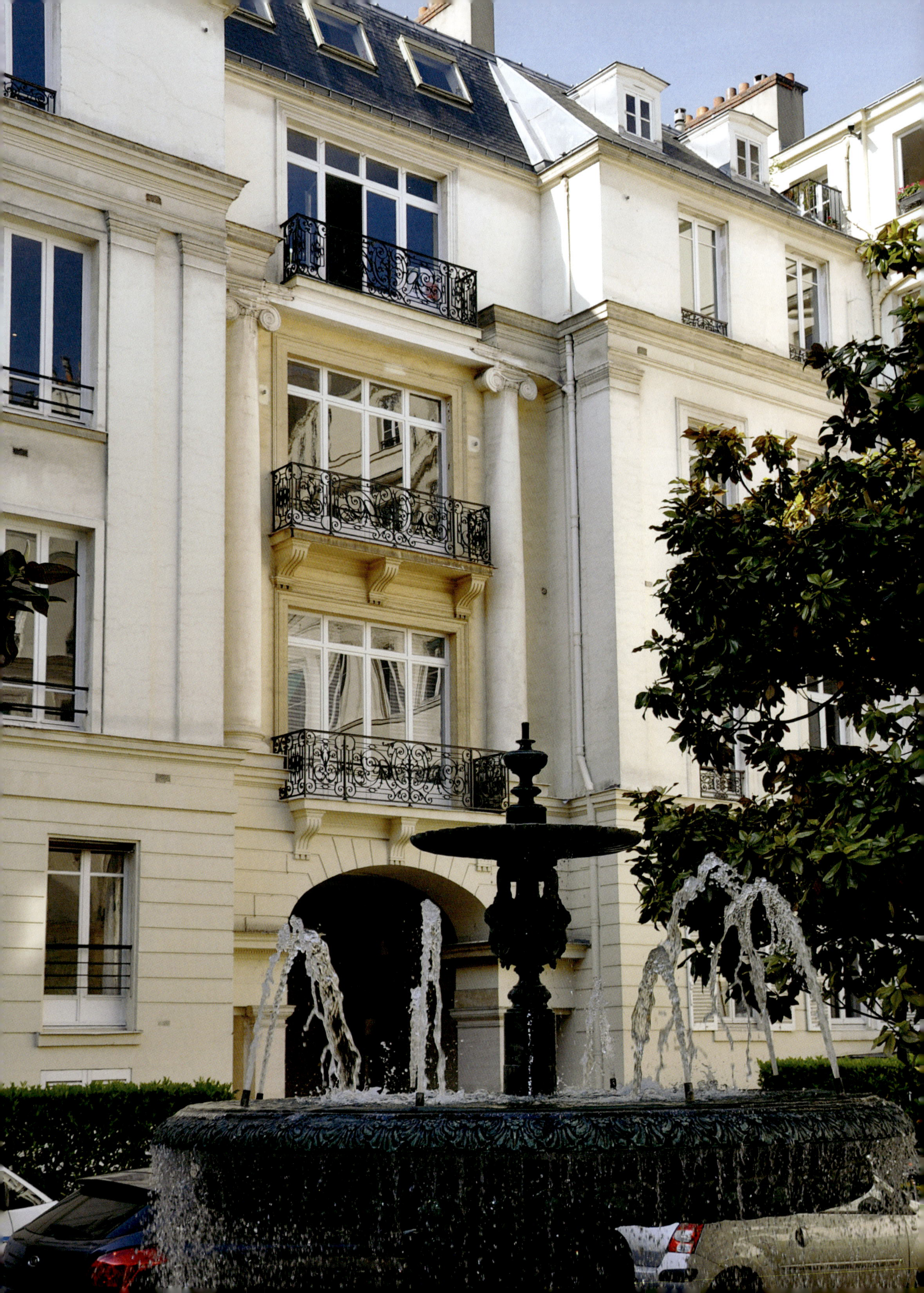

His despondency after the Princess Moskowa event, however, was soon dissipated when he was introduced to the rich and powerful Rothschilds, who recognized Chopin's rare and highly individual talent, and hailed it abroad. Thenceforth his fortunes changed. He gained access to the cream of French society, wealthy and thirsty for the culture of the new Romanticism gripping the city which had replaced Vienna as the world's music capital. Piano lessons were his for the taking, he was a frequent visitor and performer at intimate soirées centred around the Faubourgs of Saint-Germain and Saint-Honoré, which were more suited not only to his "salon" music style, but also to his sense of fashion.

I have got into the highest society; I sit with ambassadors, princes, ministers; and even don't know how it came about, because I did not try for it... At once you have a bigger talent if you have been heard at the English or Austrian Embassy... I have five lessons to give today; you think I am making a fortune? Carriages and gloves cost more, and without them one would not be in good taste

Chopin to Dominik Dziewanowski (Paris, 1833)

What was more, international publishers were beginning to vie for his works, notably Probst-Kistner of Leipzig, Messrs. Wessel of London and Maurice Schlesinger of Paris – in addition to Haslinger of Vienna, who had already published his works.

Soon he was able to move first to the Cité Bergère, then to the smart chaussée d'Antin. He could even afford a manservant. In addition, Chopin had become one of the most loved and respected of all artists among his peers, and their homage was plain to see.

Though this is only my first year among the artists here, I have their friendship and respect. One proof of respect is that even people with huge reputations dedicate their compositions to me before I do so to them; Pixis has inscribed to me his last Variations for military band; also people compose variations on my themes. Kalkbrenner has used my mazurka in this way; the pupils of the Conservatoire, Moscheles' pupils, those of Herz and Kalkbrenner... take lessons from me and couple my name with that of Field.

Chopin to Dominik Dziewanowski (Paris, 1833)

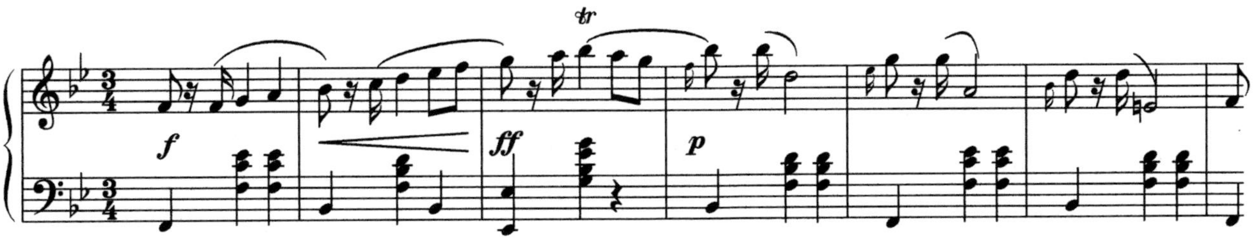

Chopin's Mazurka in B flat Op. 7 No 1, among his most popular, was published by Schlesinger in 1833.

Square d'Orléans

In September 1842 Chopin moved to 9, square d'Orléans, a quiet little enclave off 80, rue Taitbout, which he maintained until June 1849, after his return from Great Britain. Here he lived next door to the composer Alkan, and across the square from George Sand and her son Maurice, who were at no 5. There is a commemorative plaque outside the entrance of no 9, just under the arch.

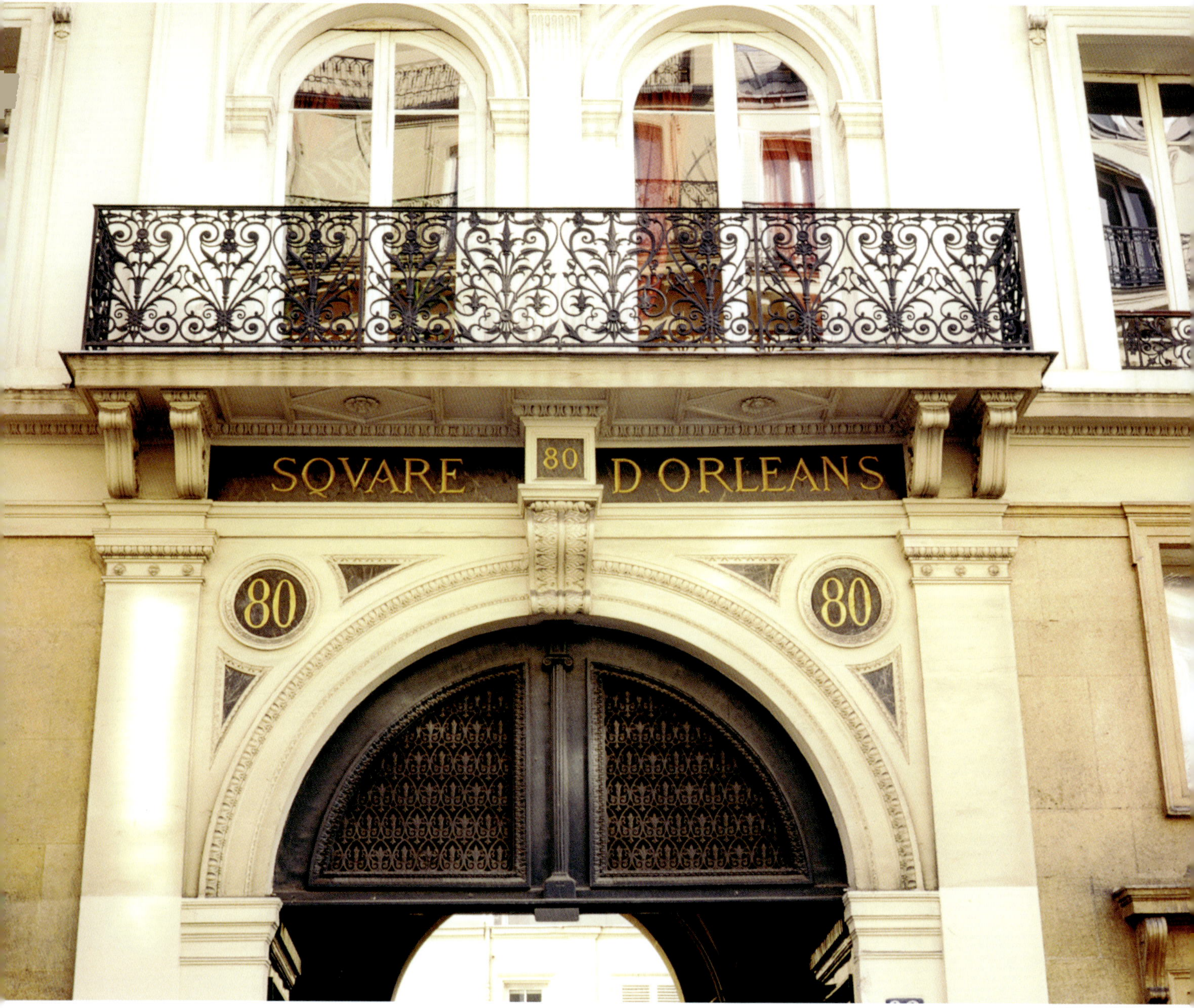

Rue Taitbout

The main doorway of 80 rue Taitbout which leads into the elegant and quiet square d'Orléans, Chopin's home for 7 years. It was from here that he left for his last abode at place Vendôme in September 1849, just a few weeks before his death.

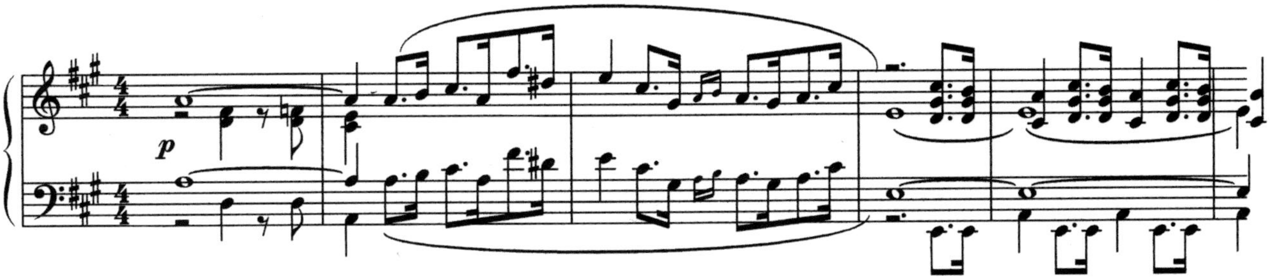

Chopin's Allegro de Concert Op. 46 was originally intended as the first movement of a third Piano Concerto.

Chopin's teacher in Poland, Józef Elsner, had always seen his pupil as a future composer of operas, so it was only natural that Chopin should have befriended Vincenzo Bellini, composer of *Norma* and *I Puritani*, whom he met in 1833. In the event, Elsner was wrong, although the languorous, soaring melody of Italian opera was certainly in evidence in much of Chopin's work, especially in his Allegro de Concert Op. 46, and the later Nocturnes.

At the end of 1832 the inventor of the latter form, John Field, had arrived in Paris to give two concerts. Chopin went to hear him, but was deeply disappointed. Field was by this time sick, a shadow of his former self, and had proved to be a great disappointment.

Chopin was not one to stay in Paris without leaving it at least once a year. In the summer of 1833 he joined one of his closest friends, the cellist Auguste Franchômme, at Coteau, the house at Azay-sur-Cher, just to the east of Tours, which belonged to the lawyer Jules Forest. The Forests were very close friends of Franchômme, who regarded them as a second family, and their only daughter Adèle had also been a pupil of Chopin. The two musicians thoroughly enjoyed their stay, especially as Chopin had a particular love of the cello. Their musical bonding on this occasion resulted in a joint composition, the *Grand Duo Concertante* on themes from Giacomo Meyerbeer's *Robert le Diable*, which was dedicated to Adèle.

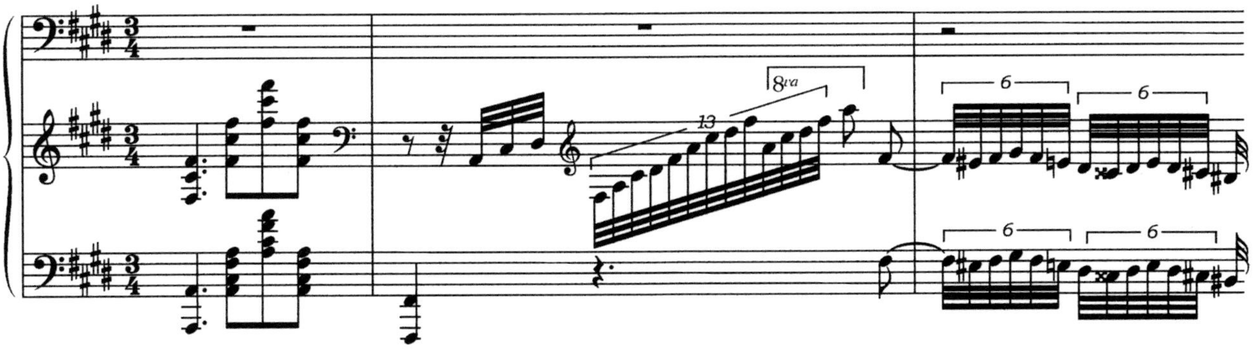

The dramatic opening piano introduction to Chopin's *Grand Duo Concertante* on themes from Giacomo Meyerbeer's *Robert le Diable*, for cello and piano, composed in collaboration with Auguste Franchômme.

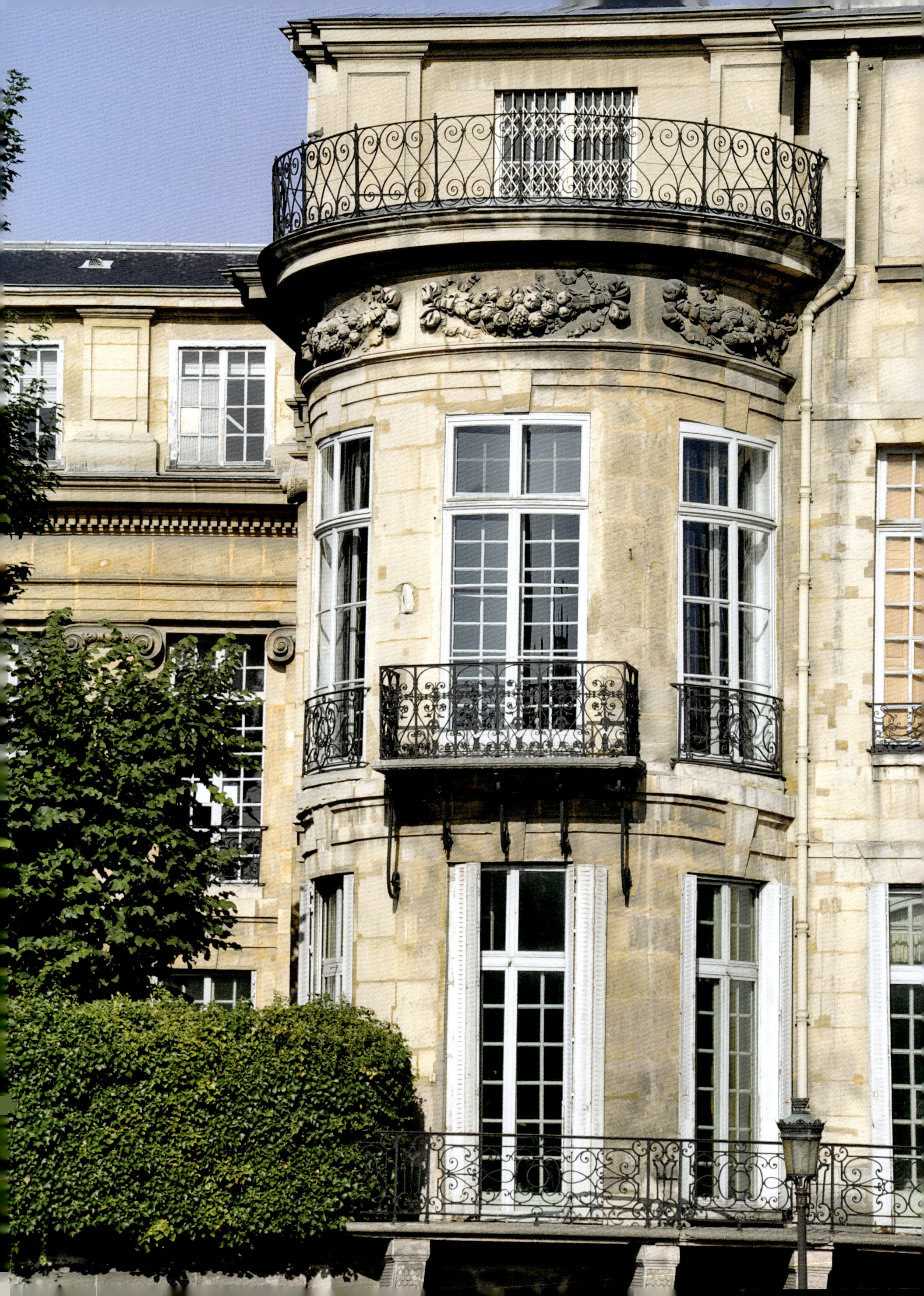

In May 1834, Hiller persuaded Chopin to join him in Aachen for the Lower Rhineland Music Festival, where they met up with Mendelssohn. This took place at the Stadttheater. It was the only time that Chopin ever attended a Festival of this kind. The three pianists returned home by way of Düsseldorf, where Mendelssohn, who was General Music Director there, took them to meet Wilhelm Schadow, the head of the Academy of Art. They continued on down the Rhine to Cologne, where, in addition to the still unfinished Cathedral, they visited the Apostles' Church in the Neumarkt, with its famous statues of the Twelve Apostles. It was here that Mendelssohn left Chopin and Hiller, who continued on their way down the Rhine by steamer to Koblenz, thence by road back to Paris.

At Easter 1835 Chopin visited Enghien-les-Bains, a popular watering place just to the north of Paris. On the other side of the beautiful lake, in the village of Saint-Gratien, stood the fine residence of the Marquis de Custine, who often entertained the cream of Paris society and the artistic set there. It was also there that Delfina Potocka, with whom Chopin had had an affair during his early years in Paris, also had a house. Thus did the area have a sentimental association for Chopin.

The next two years were a series of turning points in Chopin's personal life. It began with an invitation by the Wodzińskis to stay with them in Geneva, where they had moved after the Polish Uprising. Antoni, Kazimierz and Feliks Wodziński had been his school friends in Warsaw, and he had given piano lessons to their little sister Maria. Unable initially to accept the invitation, he did meet up with them several months later, under different circumstances, when, in early August 1835, he boarded the carriage for the first leg of his journey to meet with his parents in the Bohemian spa town of Karlsbad, and, while he was in the region, to take the opportunity to meet up with the Wodzińskis in Dresden. Little did he suspect that little Maria Wodzińska was now not a little girl any more...

When Chopin returned to Paris in the Autumn of 1836 he met, through Liszt, the notorious authoress Aurore Dudevant, better known by her pen name of George Sand. She lived at 19 quai Malaquais, overlooking the River Seine. At the time the love-struck Chopin had eyes only for the image of Maria Wodzińska in his mind, although ultimately, as his engagement to her faded into fantasy, time turned out to be a great healer. The mutual attraction between Chopin and George Sand was very slow off the mark, but by the following year their relationship was sparked into life, and had begun to grow stronger and stronger, until Maria Wodzińska became only a beautiful memory for Chopin and was consigned to the past. At the same time, Chopin's career continued to flourish, even though his health, an important factor in the Maria Wodzińska affair, was increasingly giving serious concern.

Chopin... is turning the heads of all the ladies and making their husbands jealous. He is in fashion. Soon we shall all be wearing gloves à la Chopin.
Antoni Orłowski to his family (29 November 1832)

In the Summer of 1837 he paid his first, and very brief visit to London with Camille Pleyel.

Hôtel Lambert
The Hôtel Lambert, at 1, quai d'Anjou on the Ile Saint-Louis, was the home of the Czartoryski family. It was the main centre of Polish culture and activity, as well as the seat of Poland's provisional government-in-exile following the 1830-31 November Uprising. Chopin, a very good friend of the family, was a frequent visitor, and attended a ball there with George Sand.

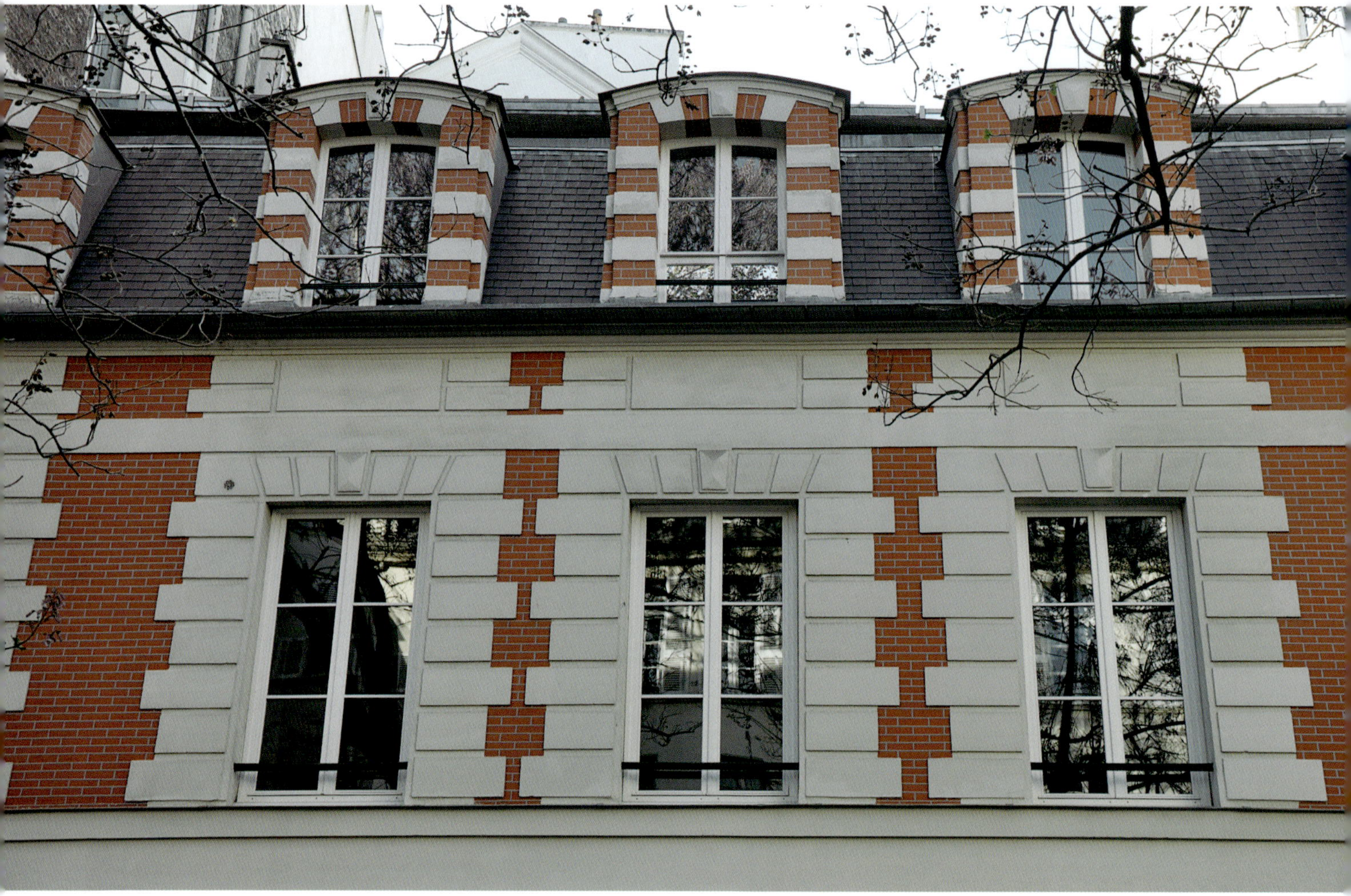

Delacroix Museum & Studio

The building situated at place Fürstenberg, is the former studio of painter Eugène Delacroix, who was a close friend of Chopin and George Sand.

He painted the famous double portrait of Chopin and Sand, which was later cut into two and separated: the Sand to the Ordrupgaard Museum in Copenhagen, and the Chopin to the Louvre.

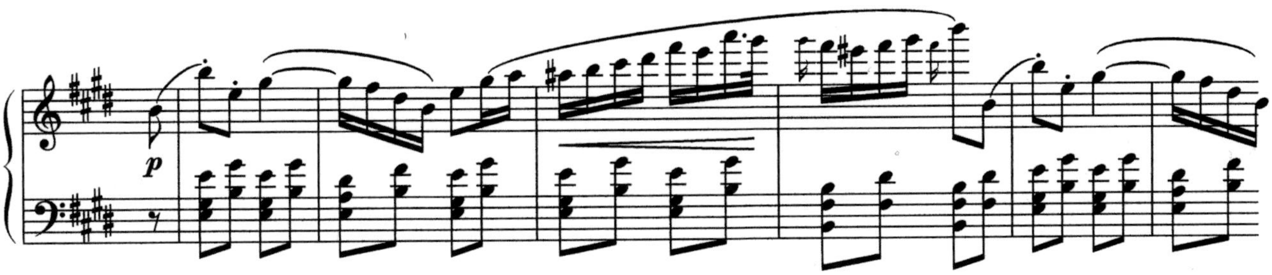

The last movement of Chopin's Piano Concerto in E minor is in the rhythm of a krakowiak.

On his return, he continued teaching and giving occasional performances, always eschewing all larger venues at which his chamber style would be lost. One notable exception was a brief visit to Rouen at the end of March 1838, when he scored a great success with his E minor Concerto at a concert given by his compatriot, violinist and composer Antoni Orłowski.

By October of that year Chopin and George Sand had become lovers, a situation that had to be kept under control for appearances' sake. Living together would have constituted a socially and professionally unacceptable scandal that Chopin, unlike the intellectually anarchic Sand herself, would have been unable to handle. So the couple – with her two children Maurice and Solange – made plans to be together on a more permanent basis, starting with a winter in Majorca, followed by their first summer together at Sand's country house of Nohant, in the Berry region of central France...

The Nohant summer of 1839 drew to a close, and autumn saw Chopin and George Sand back in Paris. For the sake of appearances, Sand took rooms at 16 rue Pigalle, while Chopin found an apartment at 5 rue Tronchet, and resumed his lessons and social life without arousing any suspicions about the true nature of his relationship with George Sand. However, he surreptitiously moved in with her, yet occupying his own quarters, where he could openly receive his pupils without fear of censure.

Like all lovers, they visited various places of interest together, and one of these was Saint-Germain-en-Laye, with its Royal Castle.

Among Chopin's first visitors was Moscheles, whom he had missed during his London visit the previous year. The two pianists exchanged disciplines, played together at a few soirées, and, on October 29, gave a joint performance at court for King Louis-Philippe and his family at Saint-Cloud.

Chopin and George Sand did not go to Nohant again until the summer of 1841. For the next five years their pattern never changed: winter and spring were spent in Paris, summer and autumn at Nohant. It was for Chopin a period of supreme creativity, during which, in the relaxed atmosphere of the Berry countryside, he composed some of his greatest masterpieces.

In Paris he continued to teach, for which he had a formidable talent. He was never short of pupils, who included later performers Marcelina Czartoryska and Karol Mikuli. He also gave two exclusive performances at Pleyel's salon, on 26 April 1841 and 21 February 1842. In the autumn of that year, Chopin and George Sand moved to adjacent up-market apartments, at Nos 5 & 9 square d'Orléans.

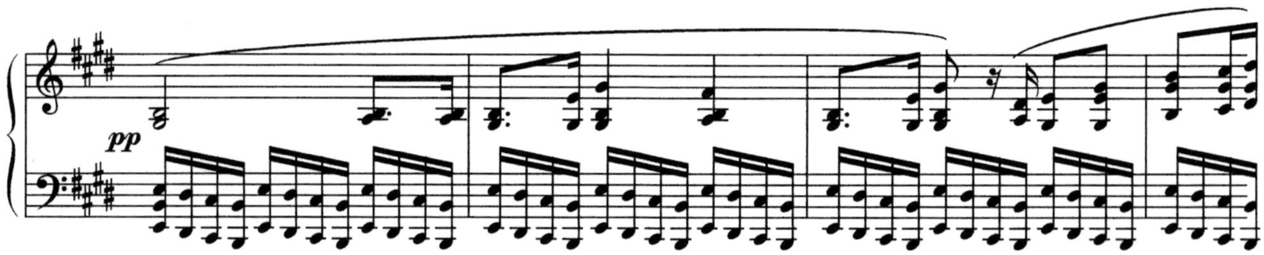

The distinctive galloping Trio section of Chopin's Polonaise in A flat Op. 53 was a contributing factor to its enormous popularity.

Among their numerous friends outside the world of music were artists Eugène Delacroix and Ary Scheffer. The latter had a studio behind his apartment in rue Captal. Chopin visited him there frequently, and on 16 April 1847 sat for his famous portrait.

I have had my cross to carry… Eight years of any settled arrangement was too much… But perhaps, after all, those are the conditions of her life, of her literary talent, of her happiness? Don't let it worry you, for it's all long over. Time is a great physician. I have not managed to get over it yet.

Chopin to Ludwika Jędrzejewiczowa
(Paris, 10 February 1848)

On 11 November 1846, Chopin returned to Paris, his long-term affair with George Sand over. He was, by now, an emotionally broken man, who was never to return to Nohant. The final, agonising nail into the coffin of his relationship with his Angel was driven home during an acrimonious confrontation on the steps of Countess Charlotte Marliani's house on 4 March 1848. By this time his creativity was all but extinguished, and his health had deteriorated into an appalling state.
In addition, the Paris that he knew and loved was no more. King Louis-Philippe had been ousted, and his era of elegance, taste and culture had been replaced by revolution and a new brutalism. Kalkbrenner, Liszt, Berlioz, Thalberg, as well as Chopin's own pupils, among them Thomas Tellefsen, Marcelina Czartoryska and Karol Mikuli, had all gone to seek their fortunes elsewhere, the preferred immediate destination, including that of the ex-King, being London.

Chopin had an additional reason for making plans to do likewise – his wealthy Scottish piano pupil Jane Stirling, who invited him to Scotland to stay with her numerous relatives, an invitation that the deeply depressed Chopin gladly accepted.

On the Wednesday of Holy Week, 1848, an apprehensive Chopin, accompanied by his Italian manservant, boarded the boat train for Calais for the first leg of his second visit to the British Isles.

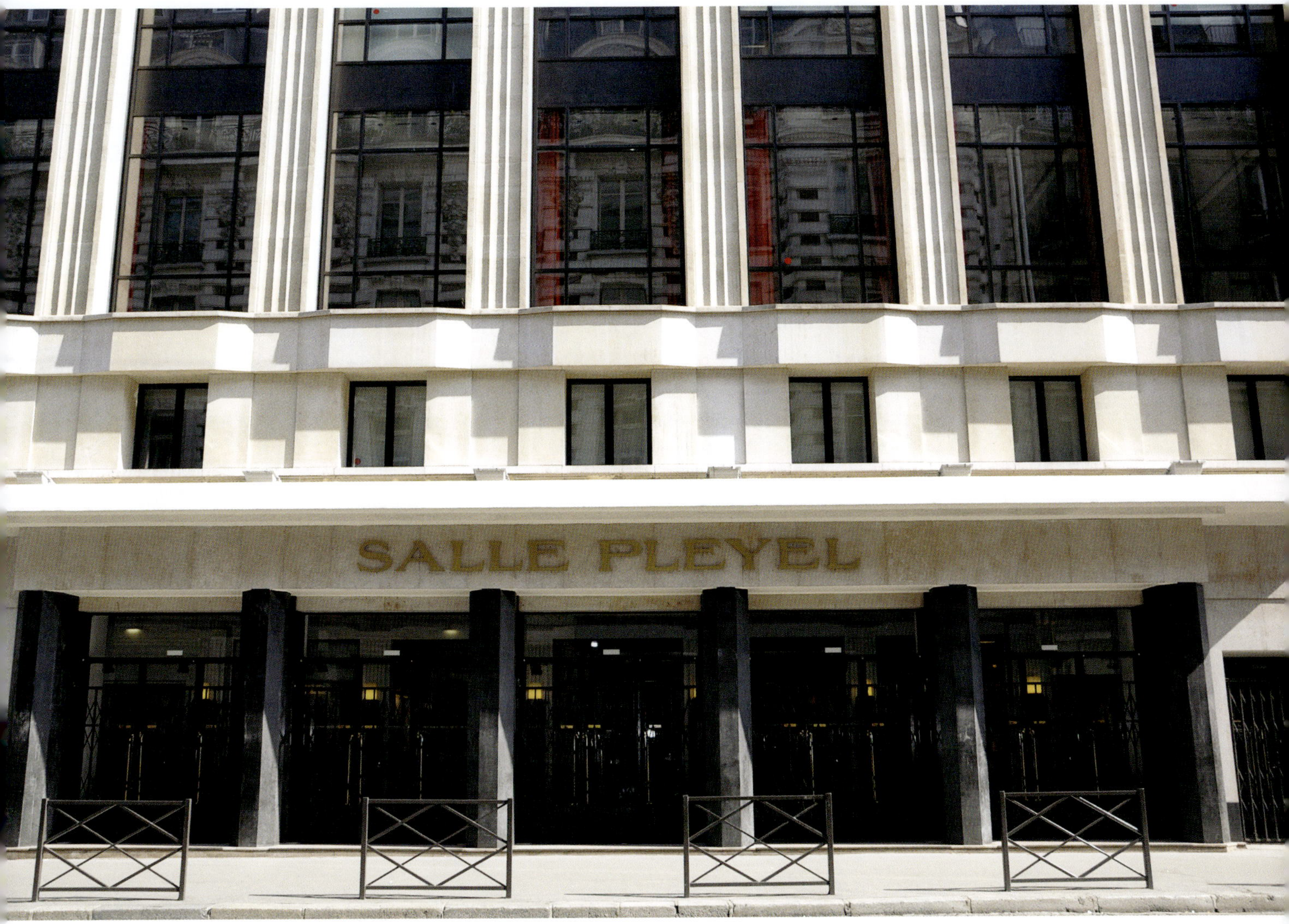

The Salle Pleyel

Today the Salle Pleyel is one of France's premier concert venues. Piano manufacturer Camille Pleyel was one of Chopin's closest friends and sponsors, and supplied all his pianos while in France. He also shipped one to Majorca during Chopin's stay there in 1838 with George Sand. Pleyel accompanied Chopin on his first brief visit to London in the summer of 1837.

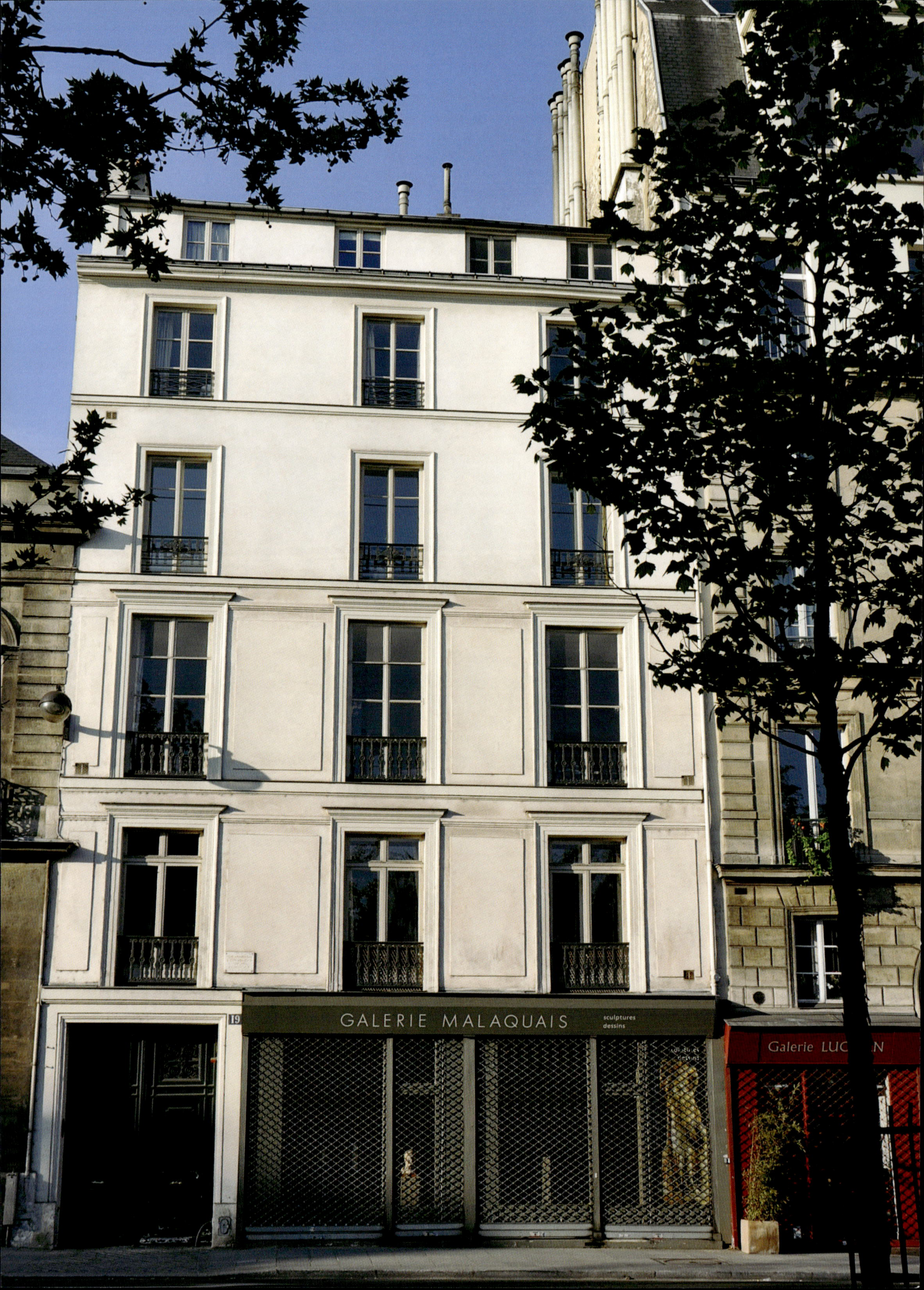
GALERIE MALAQUAIS
sculptures
dessins
19
Galerie

As most of the buildings in Paris connected with Chopin are still standing, the sites are there in some form, allowing for redevelopment and alterations over the decades. 27 Boulevard Poissonnière, which bears a commemorative plaque, is much reduced, and the fourth floor, where Chopin lived, no longer exists. The sites at Cité Bergère, rue Tronchet, rue Pigalle and square d'Orléans are still there much as they were in Chopin's day. Of the concert venues only the Salons Erard in the rue du Mail, and the Théâtre Italien are still there, although the Hotel de Ville has been rebuilt. The Tuileries Palace was destroyed by fire, although the Gardens are still there. Other significant sites are the Hôtel Lambert at 1 quai d'Anjou, on the Ile Saint-Louis, and Sand's apartment in the quai Malaquais. Ary Scheffer's house is now the Ary Scheffer Museum at 16 rue Captal, which contains several Chopin mementoes, and the Delacroix Atelier is in place Fürstenberg. There are statues of the composer in the Jardins de Luxembourg and Monceau.
Outside Paris, the Royal Palace at Saint-Cloud where Chopin played for King Louis-Philippe was destroyed in the Franco-Prussian War in 1871. The residence of the Marquis de Custine at Saint-Gratien, was pulled down in 1860, and the site at today's 67 rue Soeur Angèle is taken up by a modern block of flats.

In Rouen, the house in which Chopin played is still there, in the rue du Gros Horloge, next to the clock in question. The Château at Coteau in Touraine passed into the possession of a descendant of the Franchômmes, Gaston de Lauverjat, through his marriage to Adèle Forest's grand-daughter many years later. It was pulled down and replaced with a new building in 1860-65.
The outhouse, however, is still there, and has now been re-developed into an hotel.

Chopin's excursions from Paris also included a trip to Germany with Hiller and Mendelssohn. In Aachen the Stadttheater has been twice rebuilt, in 1900 and 1945. In Düsseldorf the Academy of Art was rebuilt after its destruction in World War 2. In Cologne, the Church of St. Aposteln is still there, having been restored after World War 2. It is now used as a concert venue.

Quai Malaquais
19, quai Malaquais was the home of George Sand between 1832 and 1836, before she moved out to live with Liszt and Marie d'Agoult, on a temporary basis, to the Hôtel de France at 23, rue Lafitte. It was there that she first met Chopin at a soirée at which he played on 5 November 1836.
The rue Lafitte site is now an underground garage.

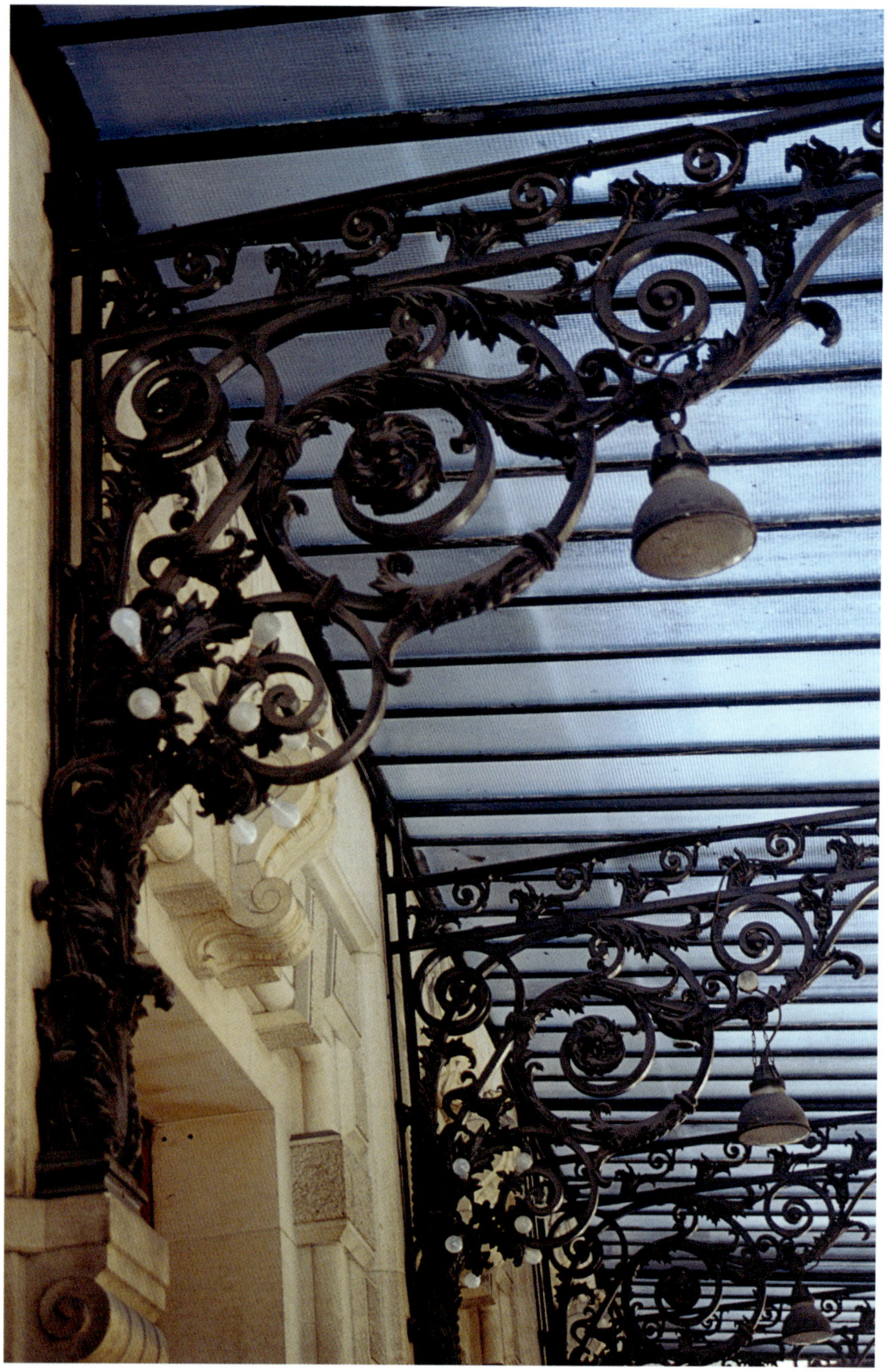

Opéra-Comique

Chopin played at the Théâtre Italien (now Opéra-Comique) with Liszt on 2 April 1833, and again on 4 April 1835, when he performed his E minor Piano Concerto with the orchestra conducted by François Antoine Habenek. This venue, in rue Favard, in the place Boïeldieu, is among the capital's finest venues, and remains unchanged since Chopin's time.

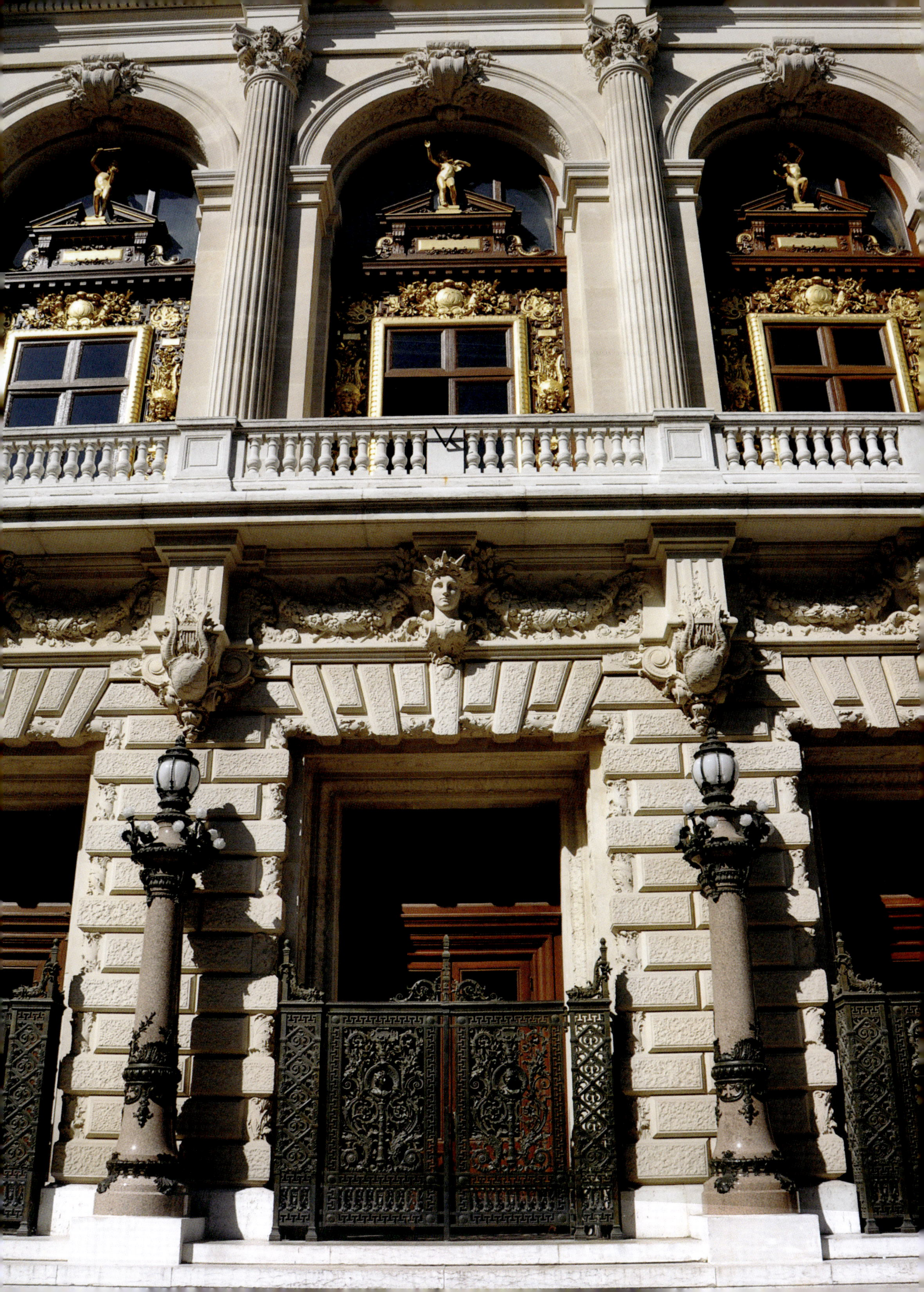

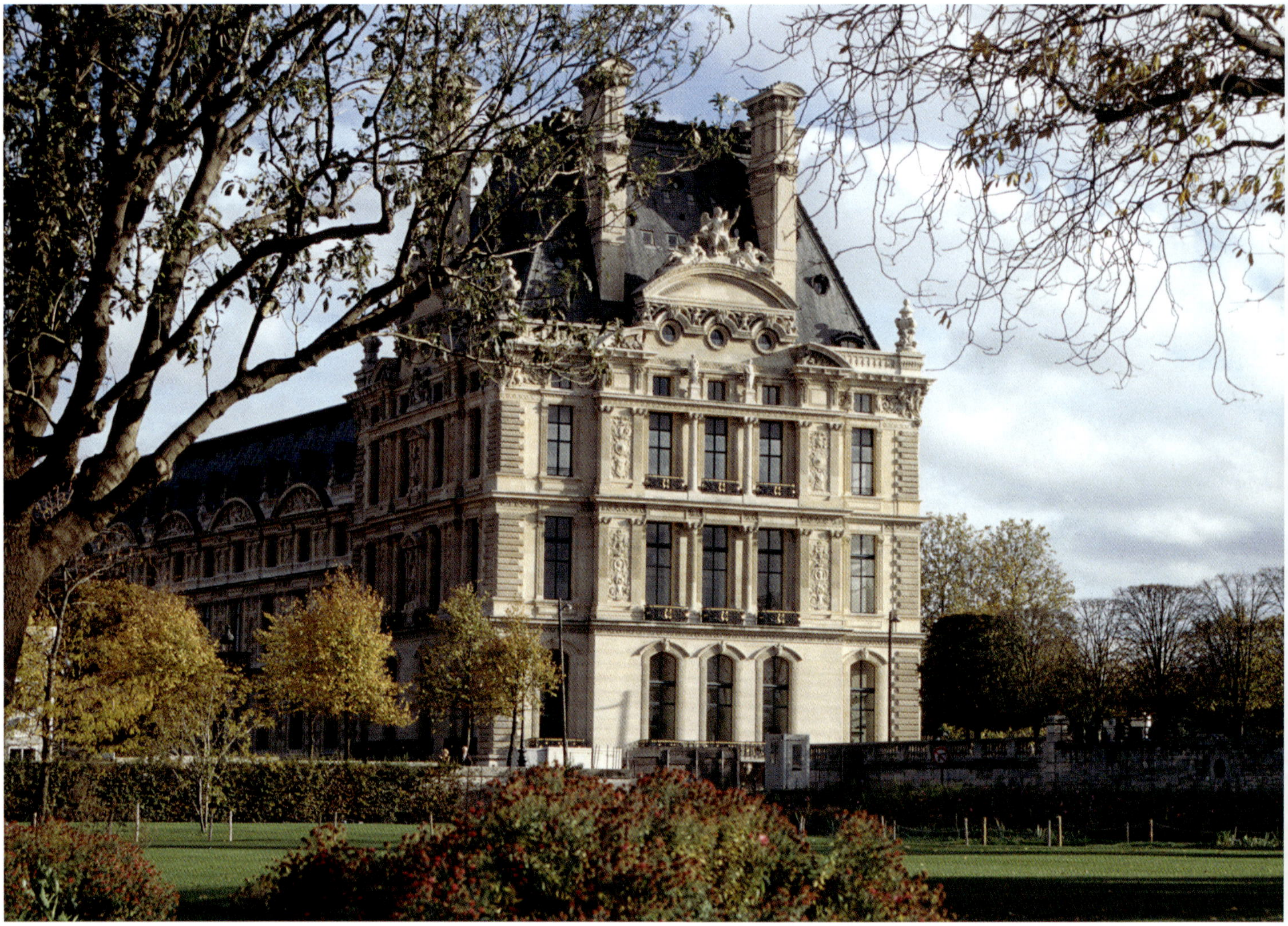

Musée du Louvre

The Musée du Louvre is the largest national museum of France, the most visited museum in the world, and a historic monument. It is a central landmark of Paris. The Louvre Palace began as a fortress built in the late 12th century under Philip II. Remnants of the fortress are still visible. The building was extended many times over the centuries to form the present Louvre Palace and was opened as a museum in 1793.

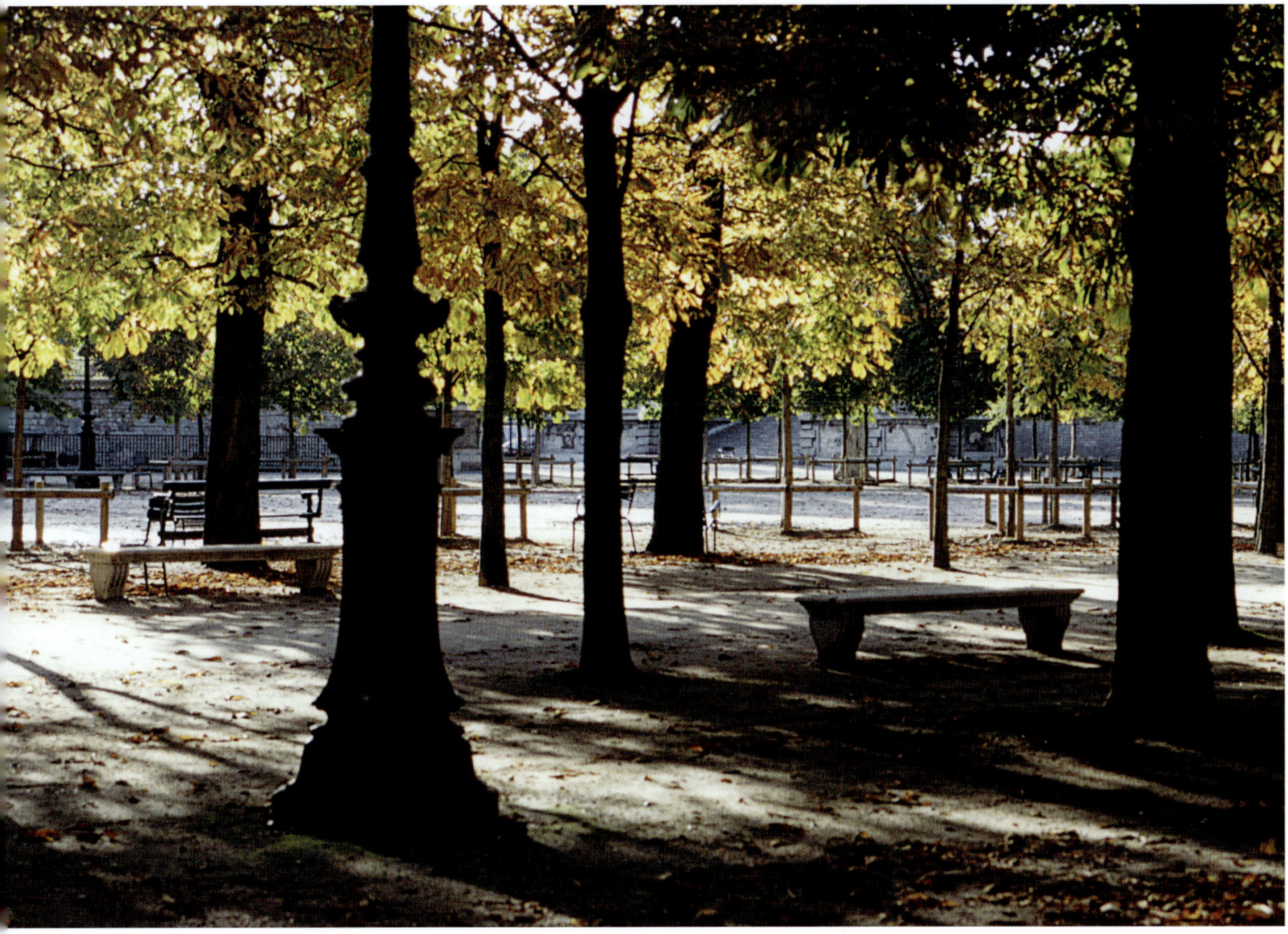

Jardin des Tuileries

On 16 February 1838 Chopin played in front of King Louis Philippe and his family at the Palais des Tuileries, after which he was presented with a silver tea service. The Palace was destroyed by fire in 1891, and today only the Gardens remain. Extending from the Louvre to the place de la Concorde, they are among Paris' favourite parks.

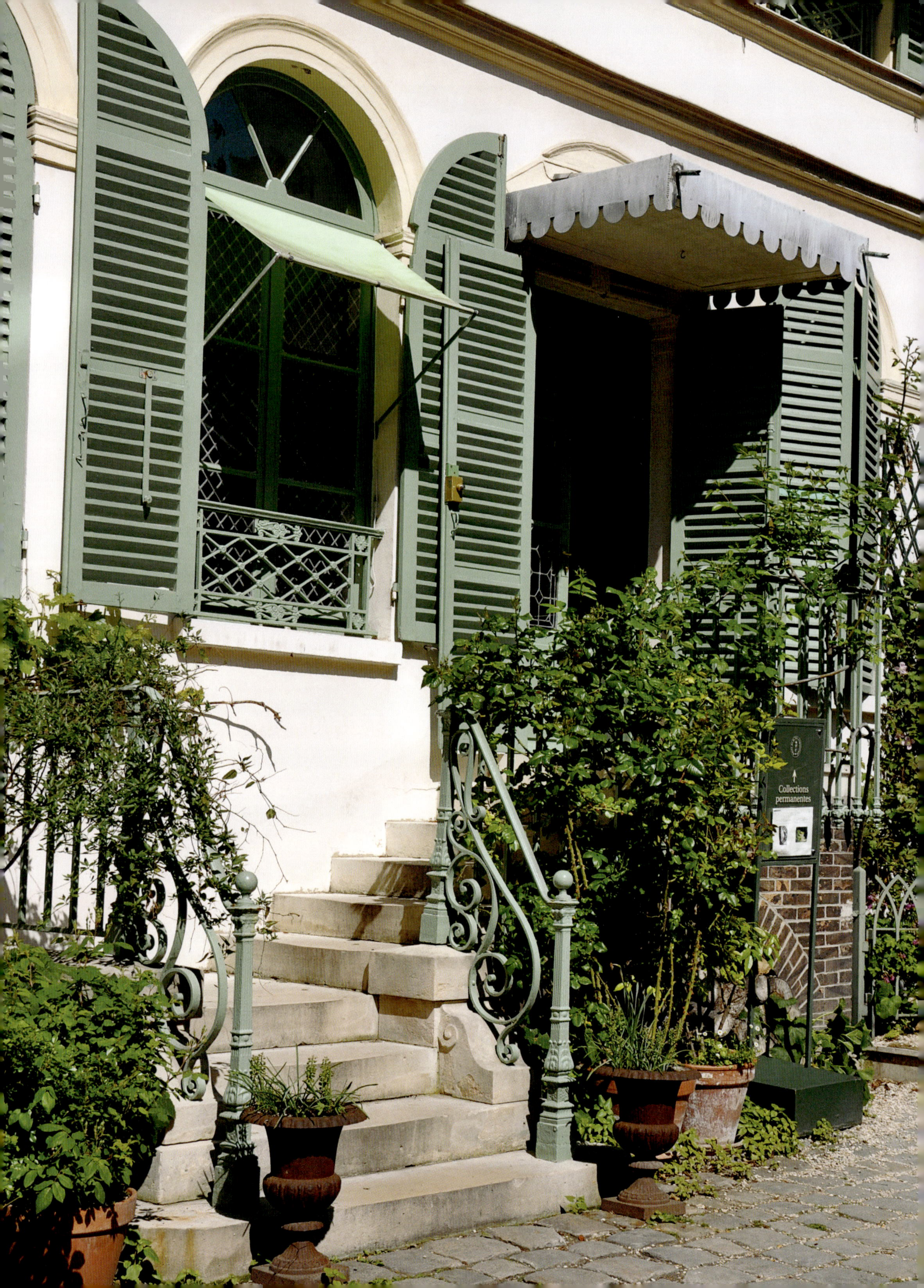
Collections
permanentes

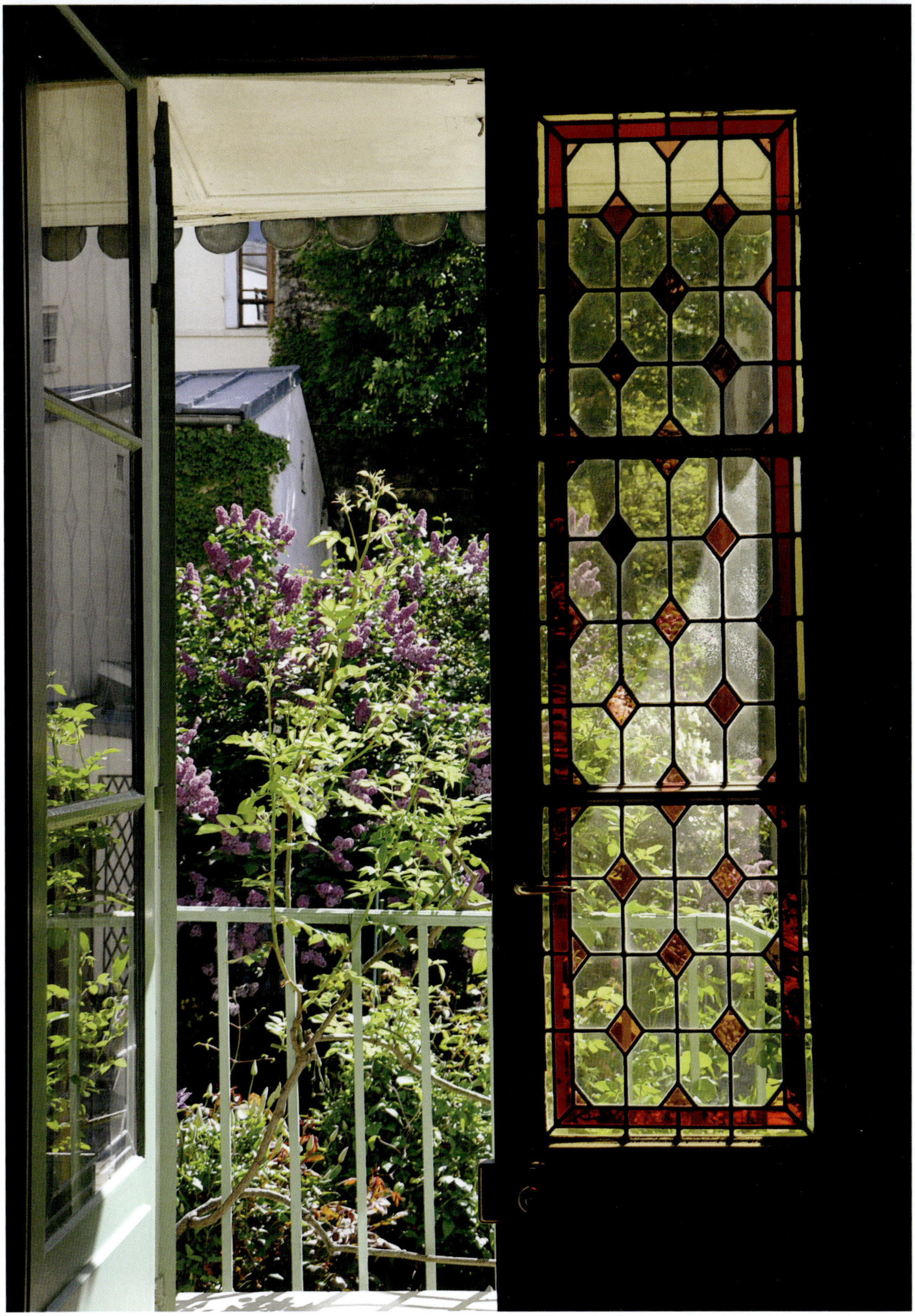

Ary Scheffer Museum

Although the Ary Scheffer Museum, at 16 rue Captal, is mainly dedicated to George Sand, there are a few Chopin mementos housed here as well. Chopin was a good friend of the painter Ary Scheffer, and sat on 16 April 1846 at his studios for the famous painting of the composer. His studios, which Chopin frequently visited, were situated behind the Museum.

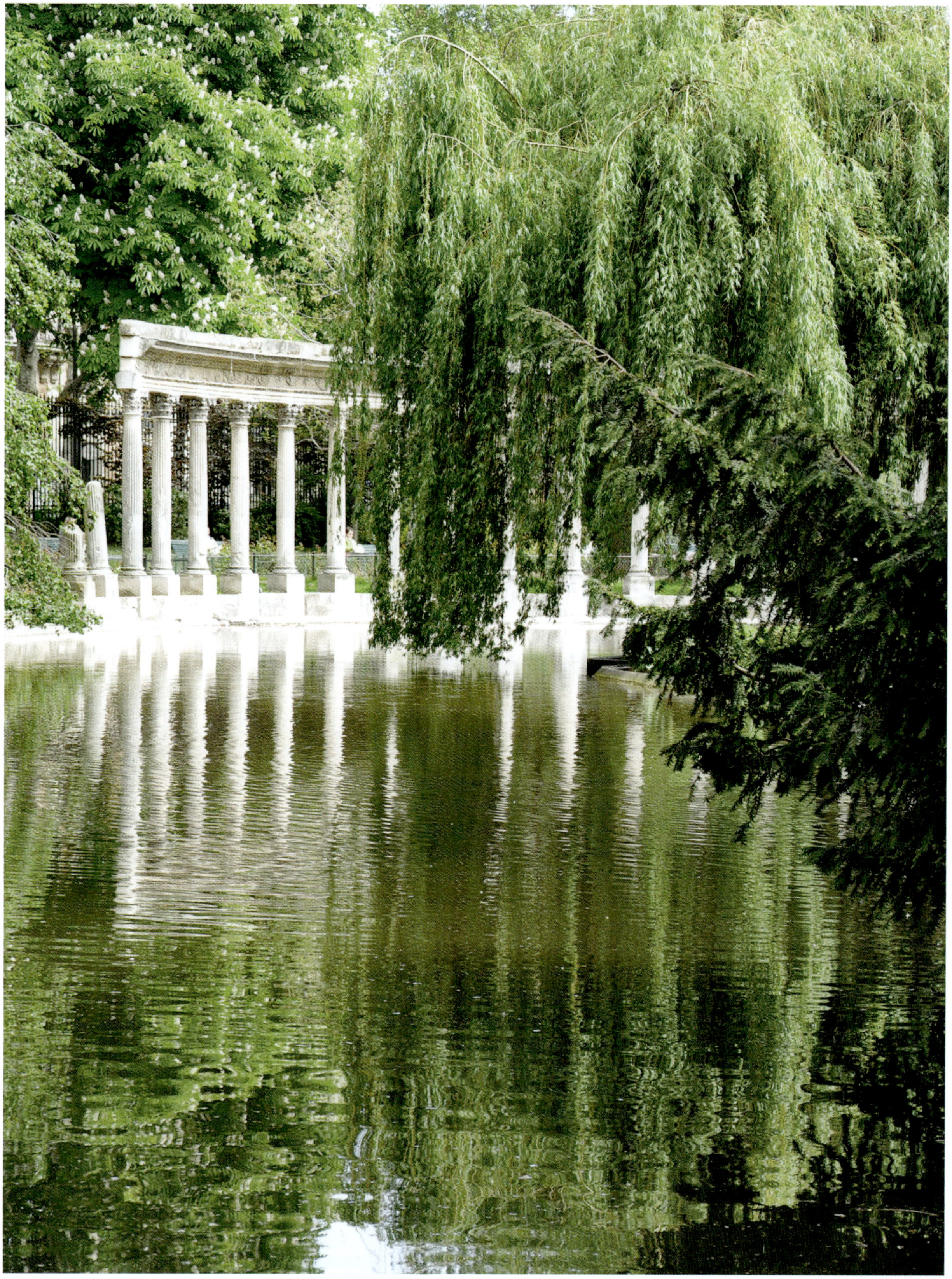

Parc Monceau

The Parc Monceau, just off the Boulevard des Malesherbes, might well have reminded Chopin of the Łazienki Park in the Warsaw of his youth.

→ The main gate of the Parc Monceau.

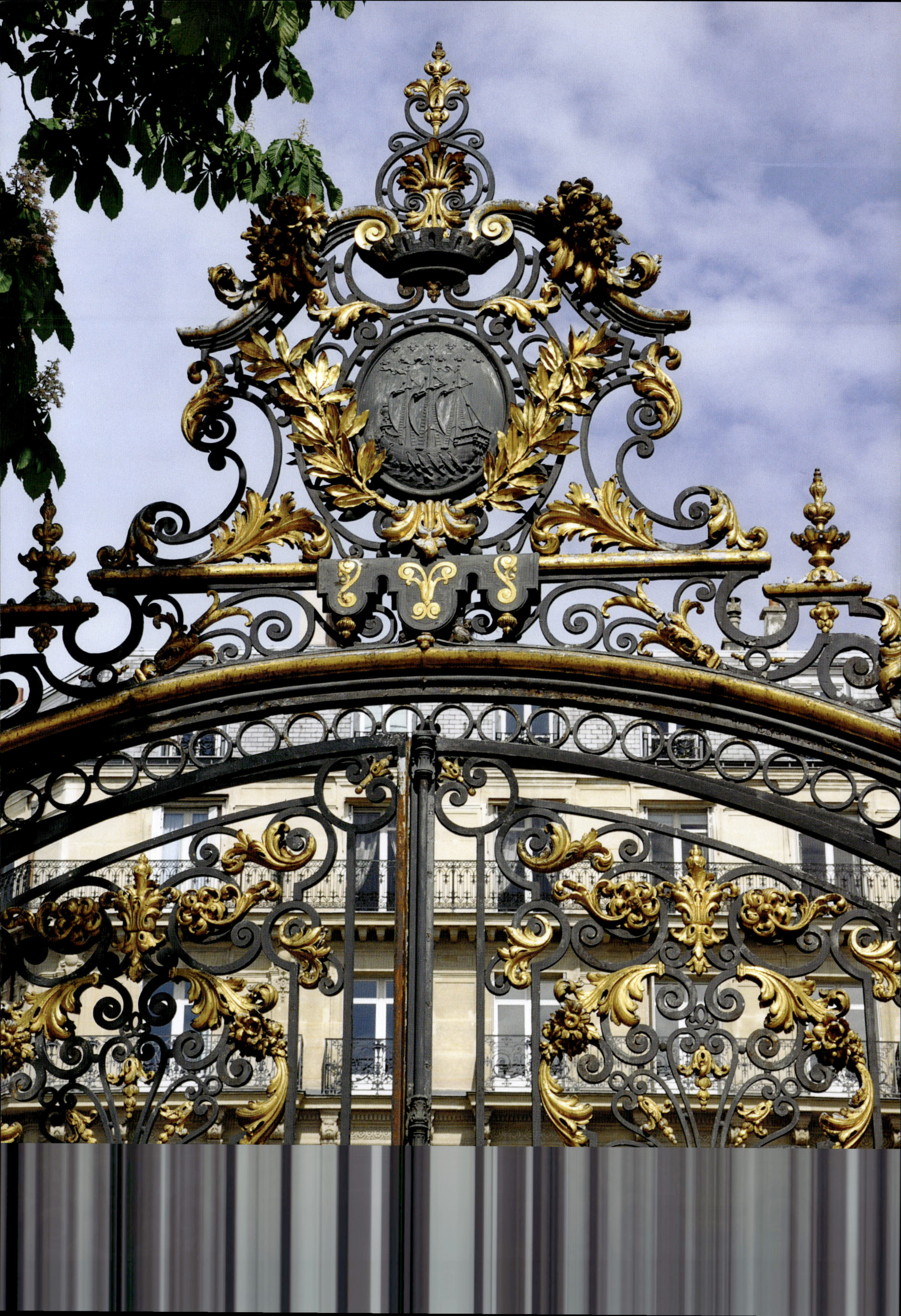

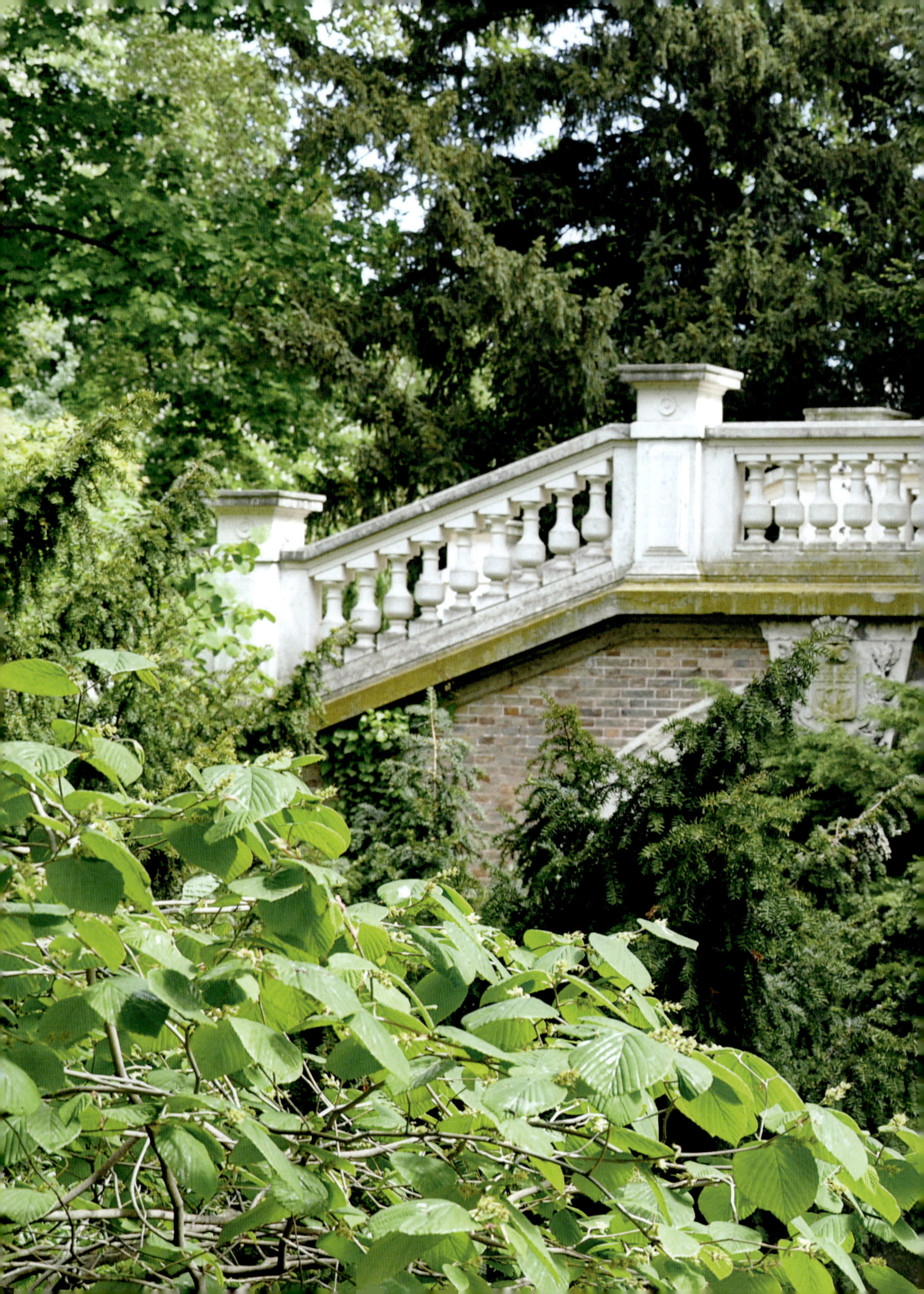

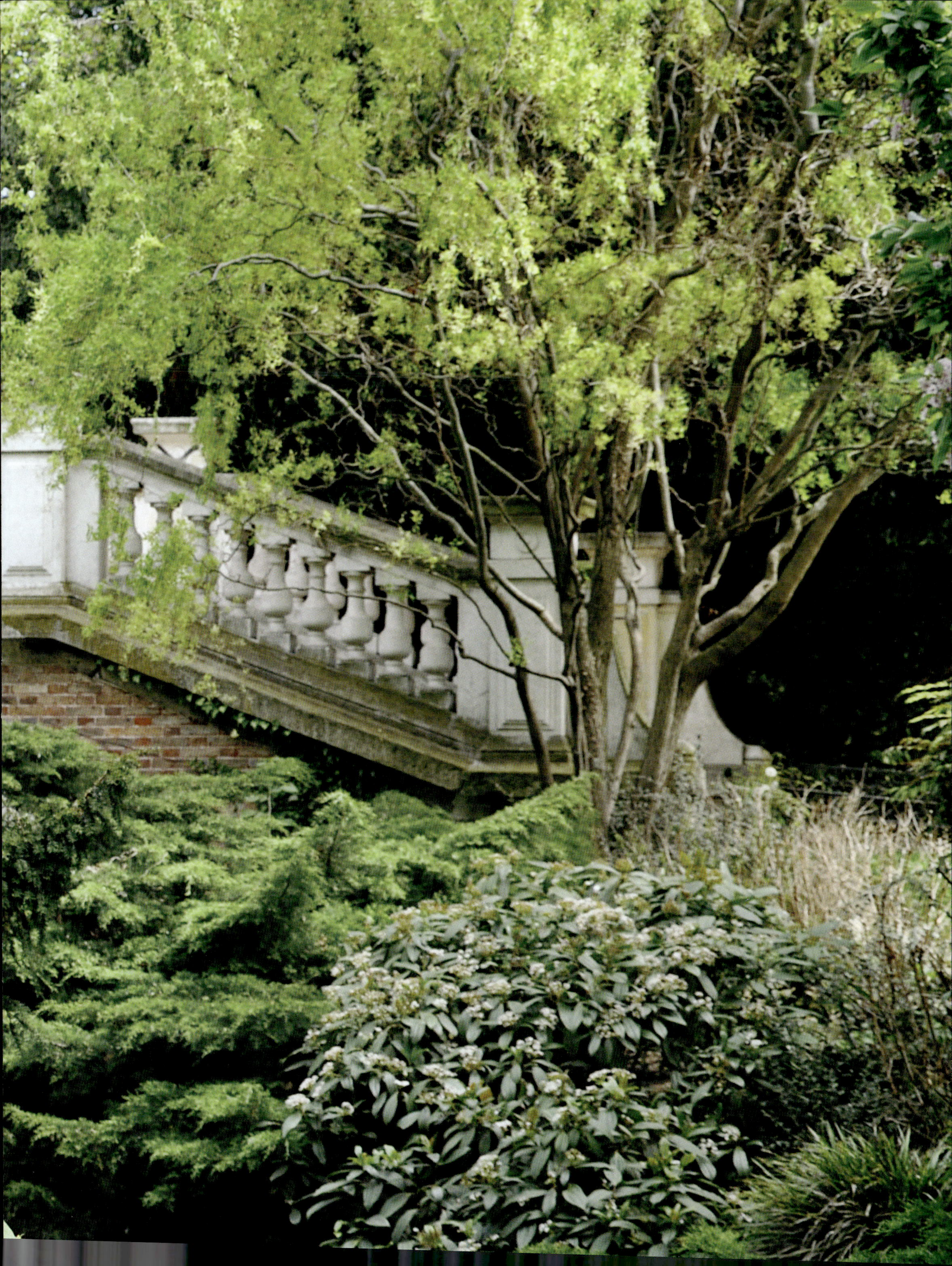

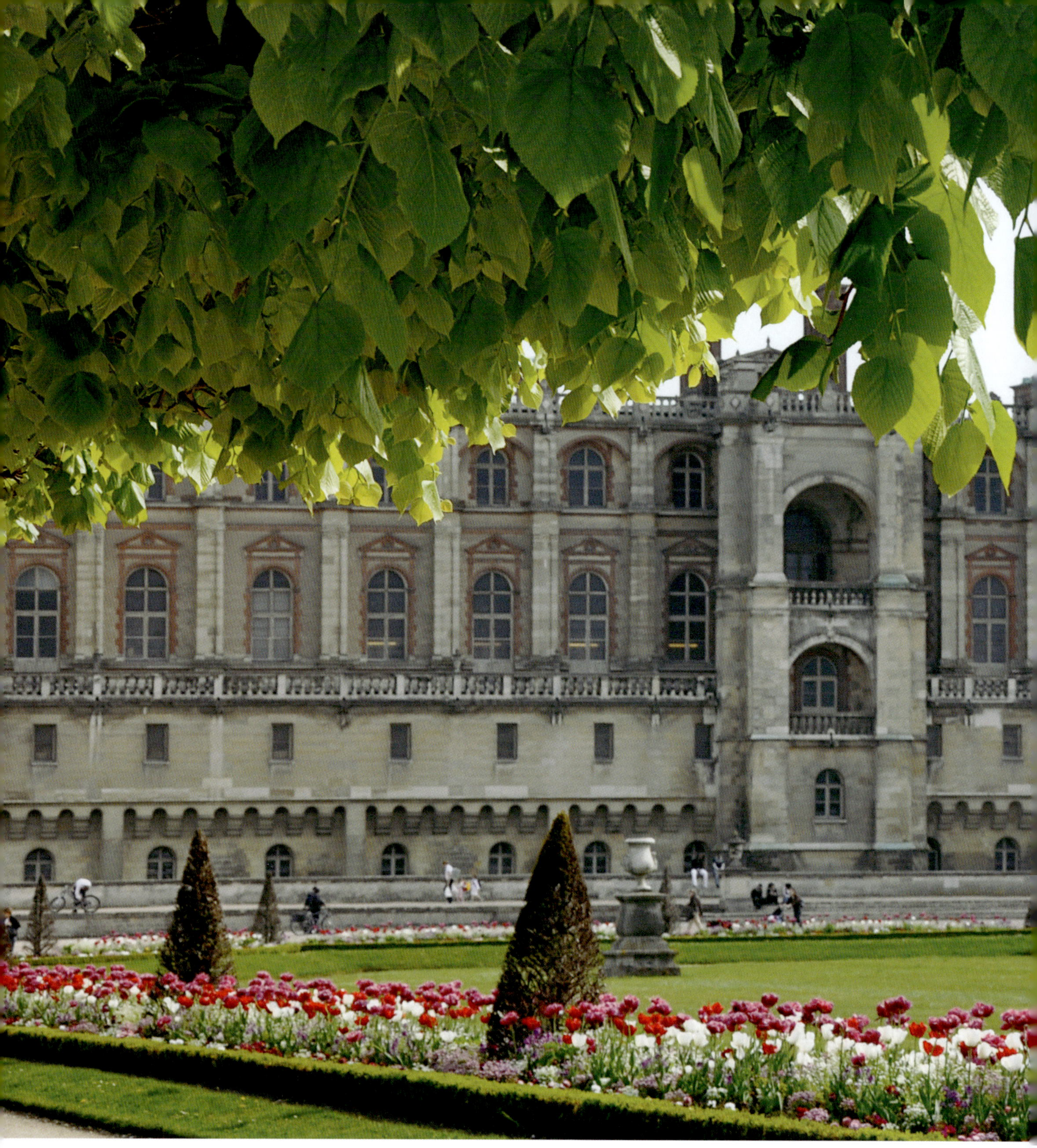

Saint-Germain-en-Laye
Chopin and George Sand came to Saint-Germain en Laye, 20 kilometres west of Paris, as tourists on 11 June 1840. They visited the Royal Castle, which was then open to the public.

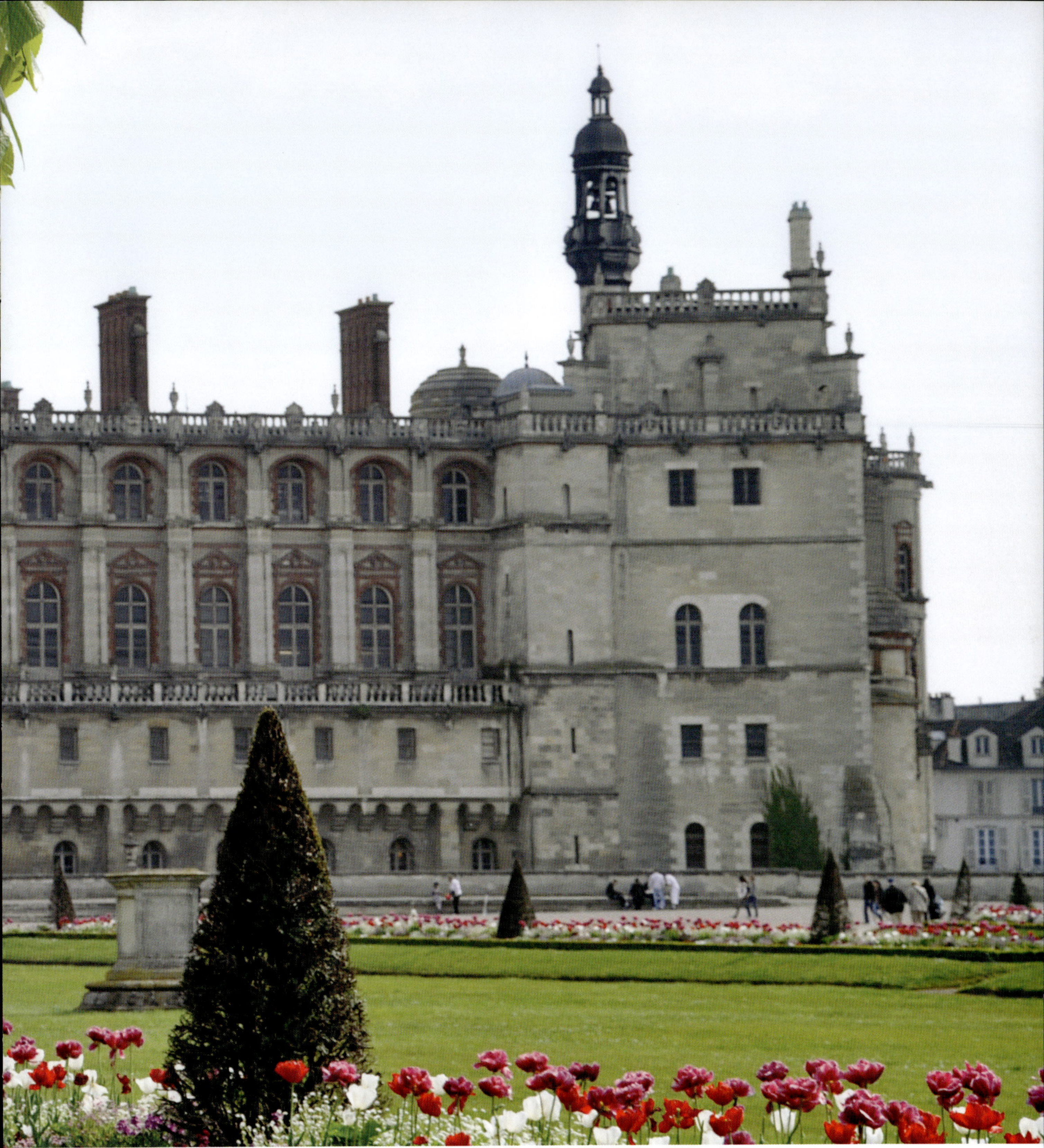

The town was founded in 1020 when King Robert the Pious founded a convent on the site of the present Church of Saint Germain. The present Castle, built on an older one in the reign of Francis I, was a royal town and the Château had been the residence of numerous French monarchs up to time of French Revolution. Louis XIV was born here, and turned the castle over to King James II of England, after his exile following the Revolt of 1688. He is buried in the church of Saint-Germain.

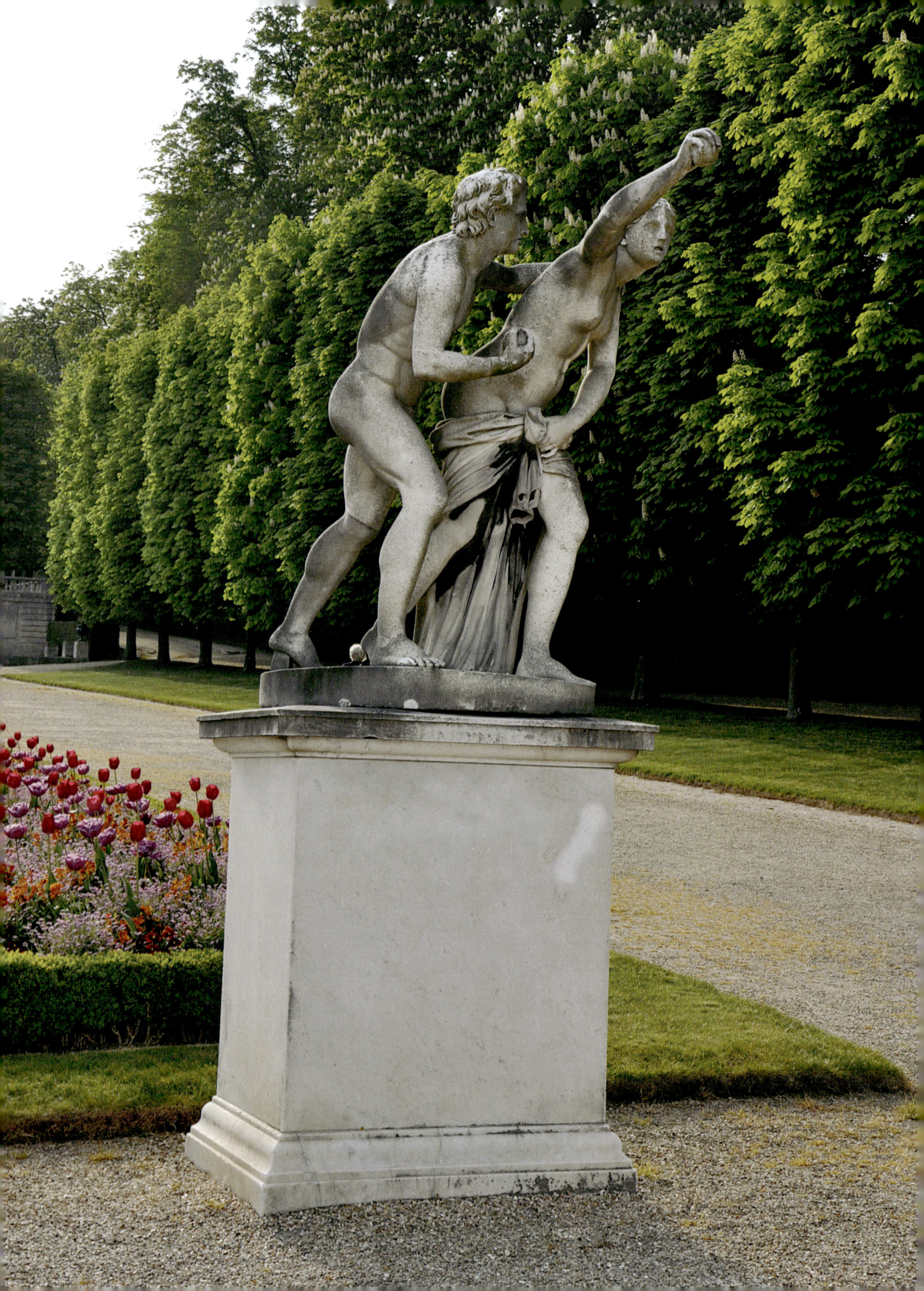

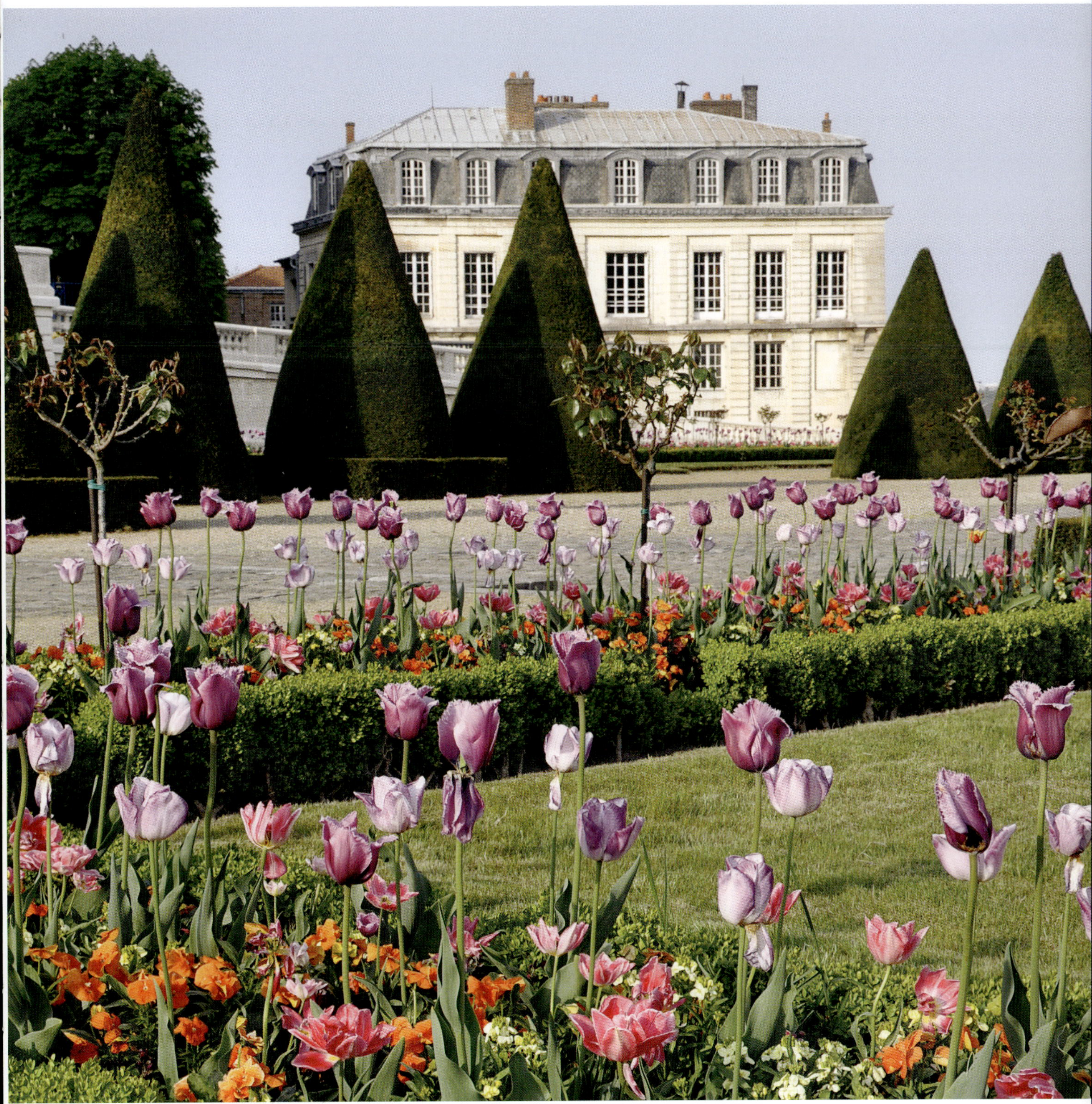

Saint-Cloud

Chopin, together with his friend Moscheles, played at Saint-Cloud, about 7 kilometres to the south west of Paris, in front of King Louis Philippe and his family on 29 October 1839. The Castle was destroyed in 1871 during the Franco-Prussian war, but the gardens and the views onto Paris remain the same as at the time of Chopin. The former Palace was also the site of Napoleon's coup d'état that overthrew the French Directory in 1799.

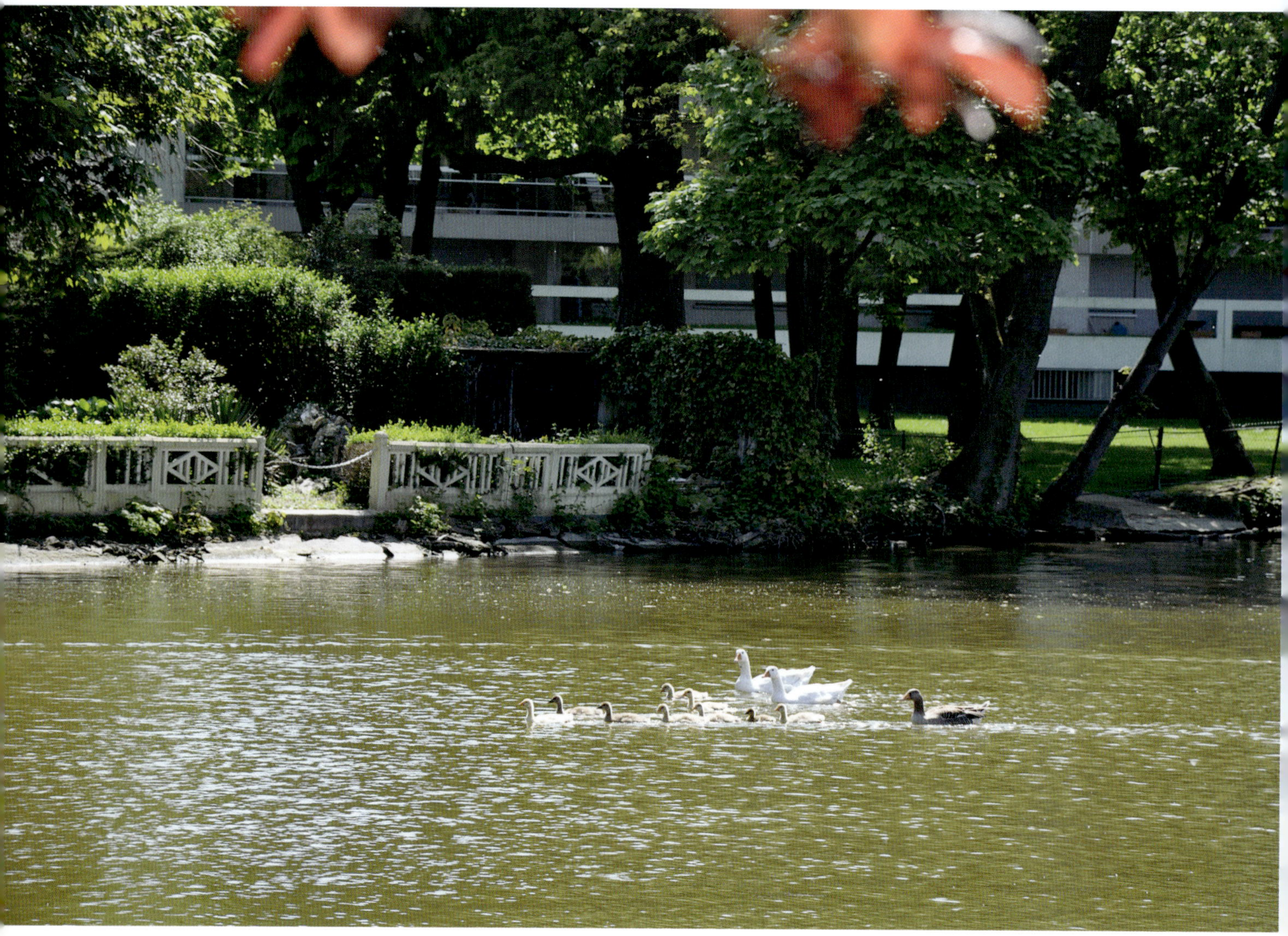

Saint-Gratien

At Easter 1835 Chopin came to Enghien-les-Bains, a popular spa about 25 kilometres to the north of Paris, to visit his friend the Marquis de Custine, who had built a lakeside castle three years previously in Saint-Gratien. Chopin returned on several occasions with George Sand, and met many famous artists and literati of the period such as Lamartine, Hugo, Balzac, Delacroix, Alfred de Musset and Châteaubriand. The castle was destroyed by his heirs in the 1860s.

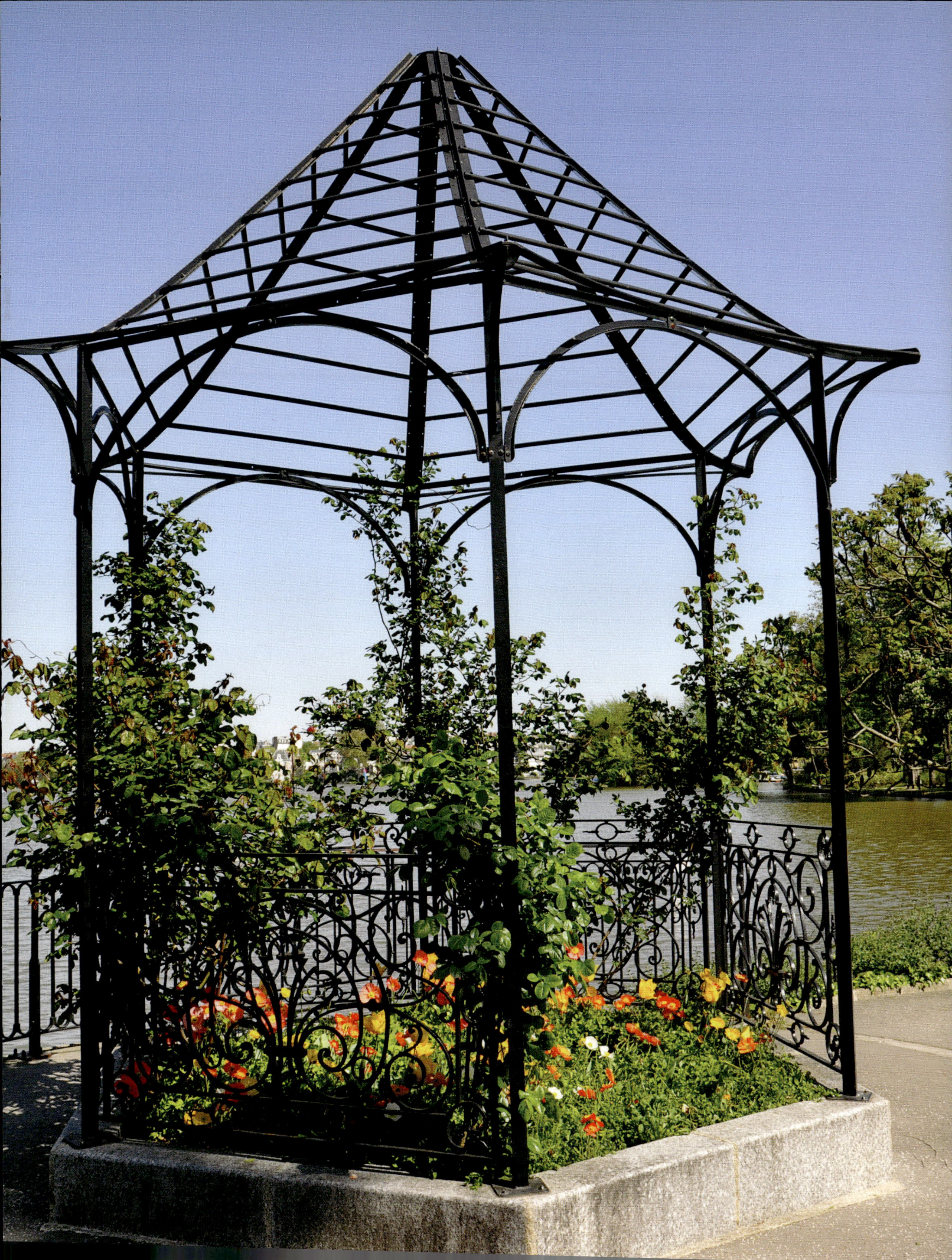

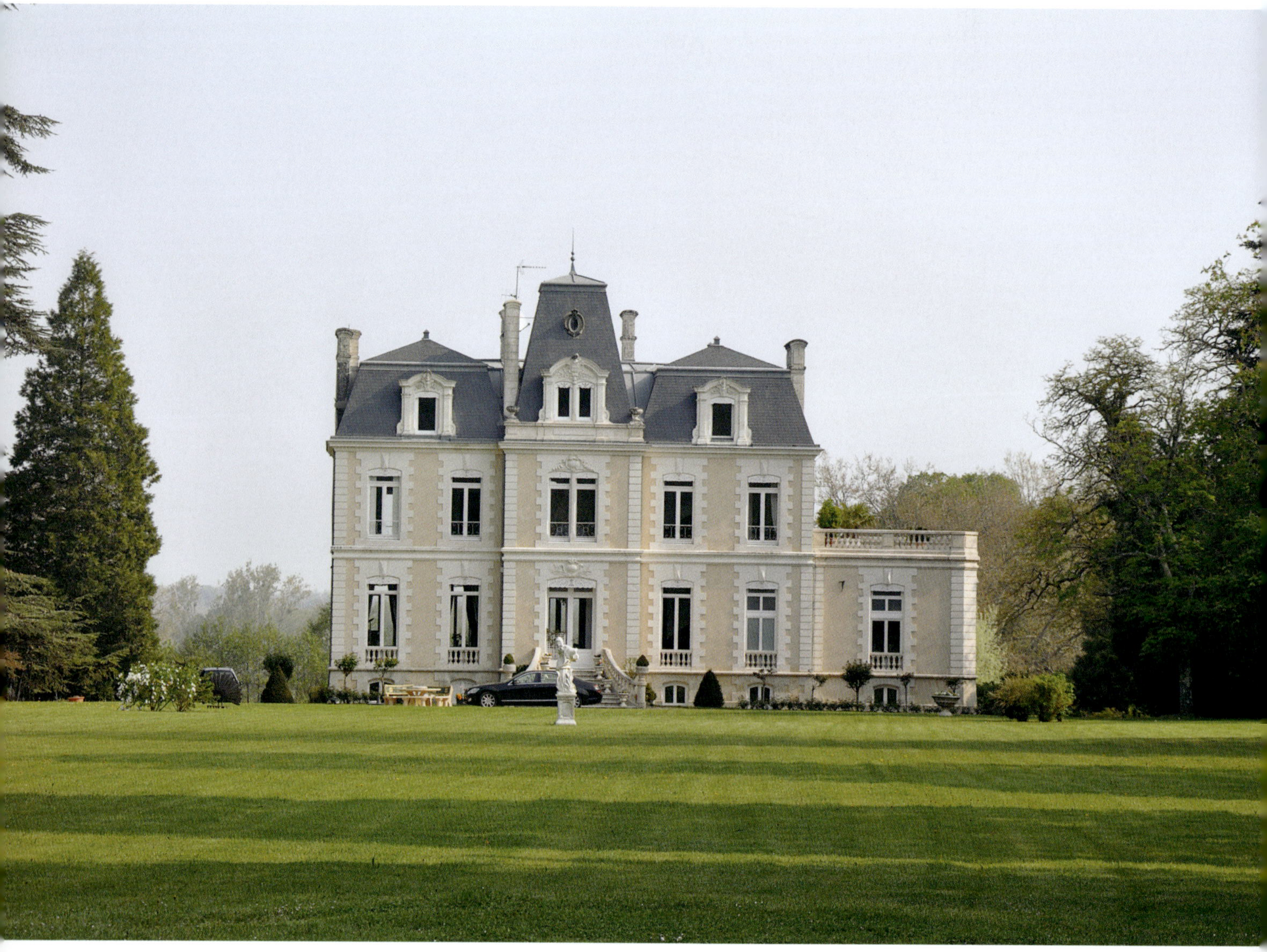

Château de Coteau

Chopin came to the Château de Coteau at Azay-sur-Cher, about 12 kilometres to the east of Tours, for a holiday in 1833 – and possibly also in 1846, with one of his closest friends, composer and cellist Auguste Franchômme. The Château belonged to Franchômme's friend, lawyer Jules Forest, whose daughter Adèle had also been Chopin's pupil.

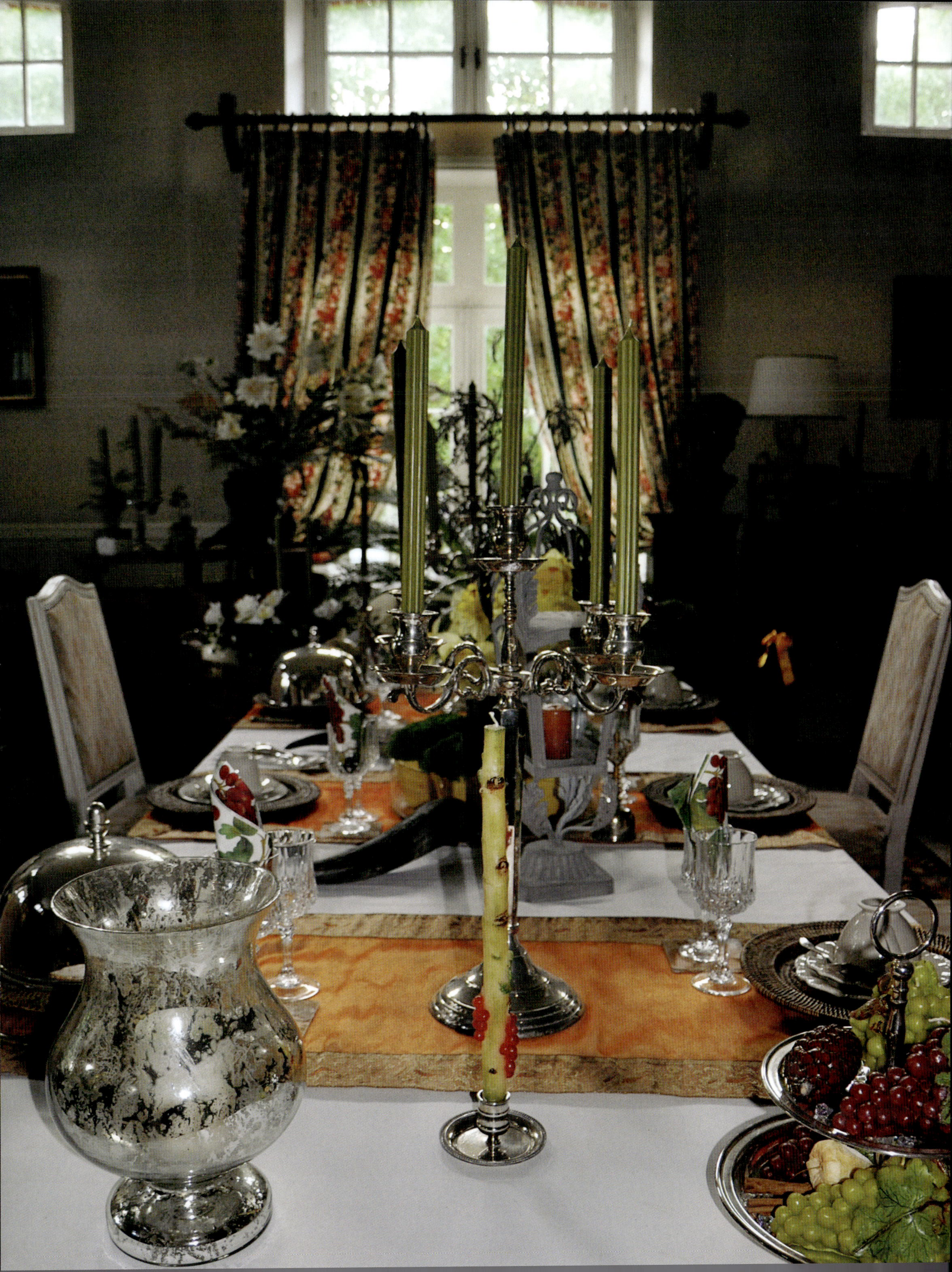

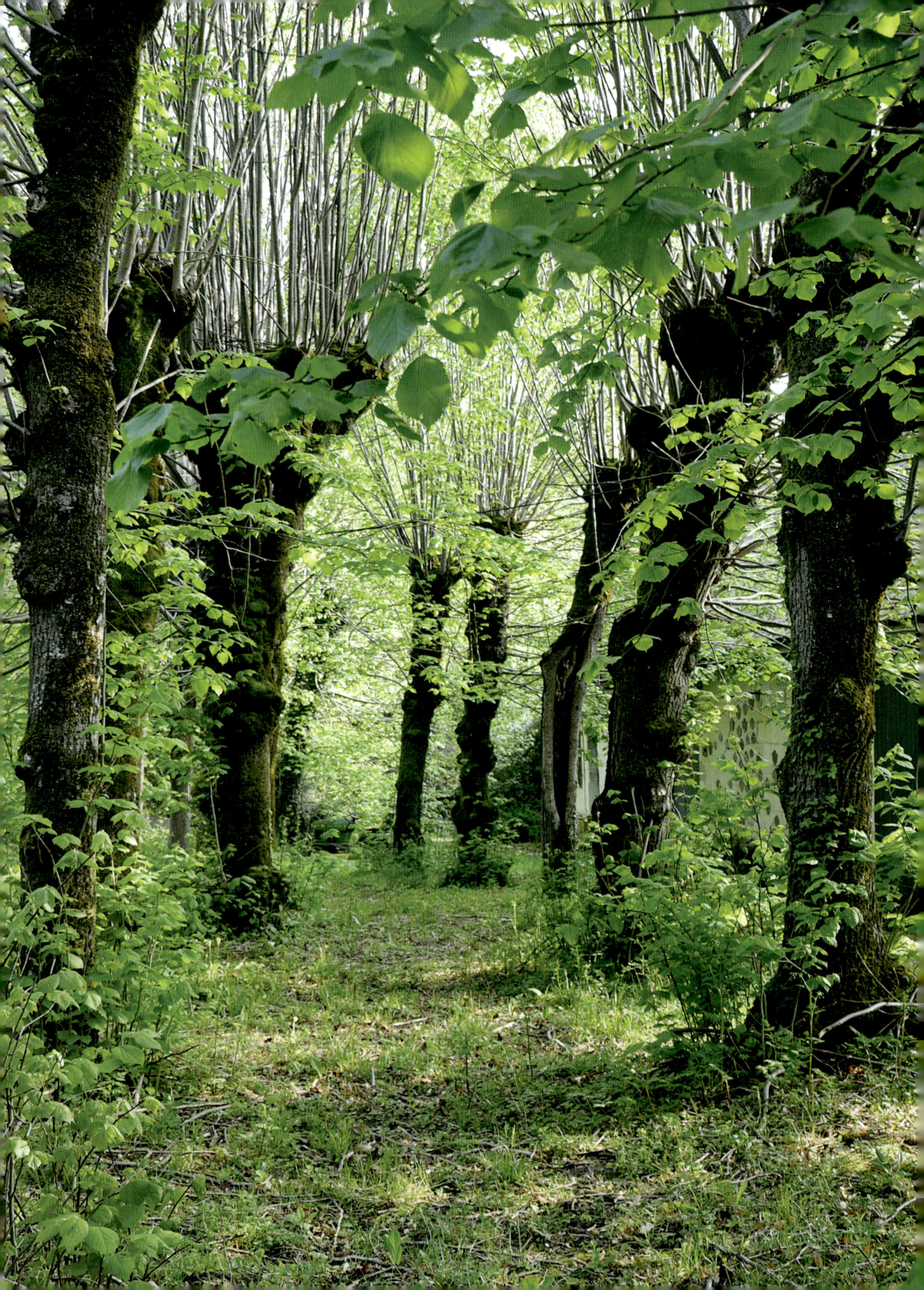

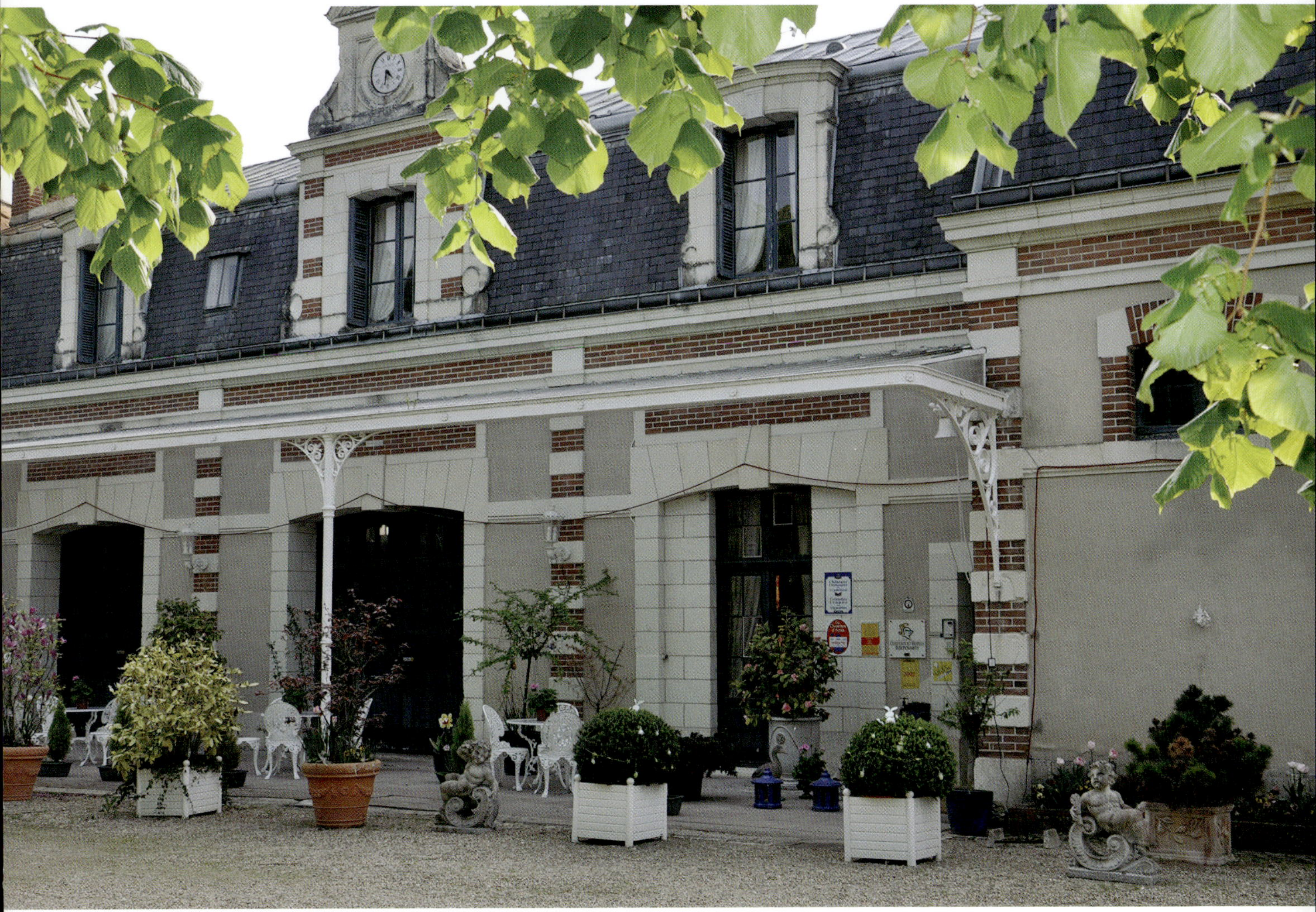

Château de Coteau

The Château de Coteau was destroyed and rebuilt in the 1860s. The outhouse is all that is left of Jules Forest's property, and is largely the original building that Chopin would have known. Today it is an hotel.

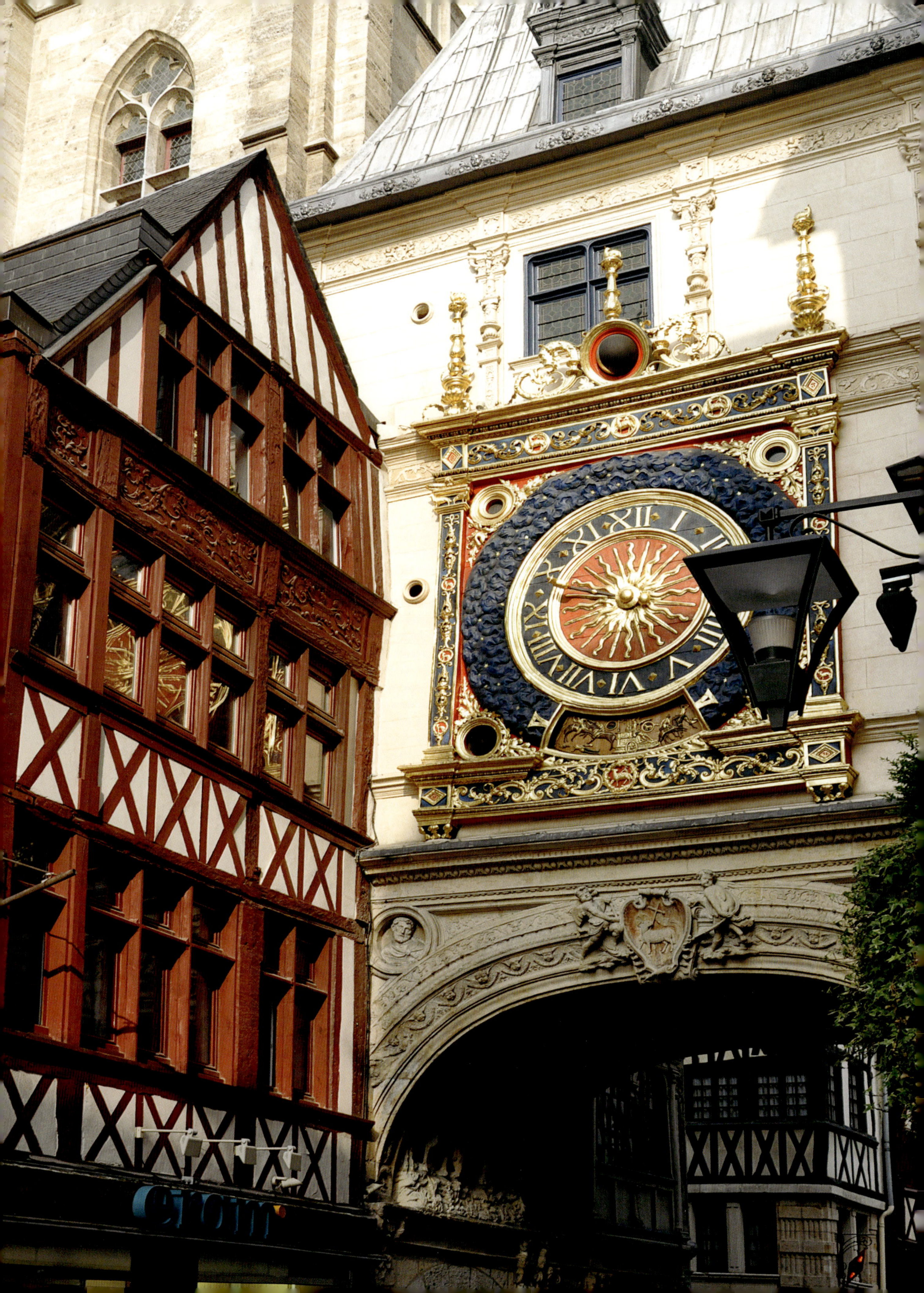

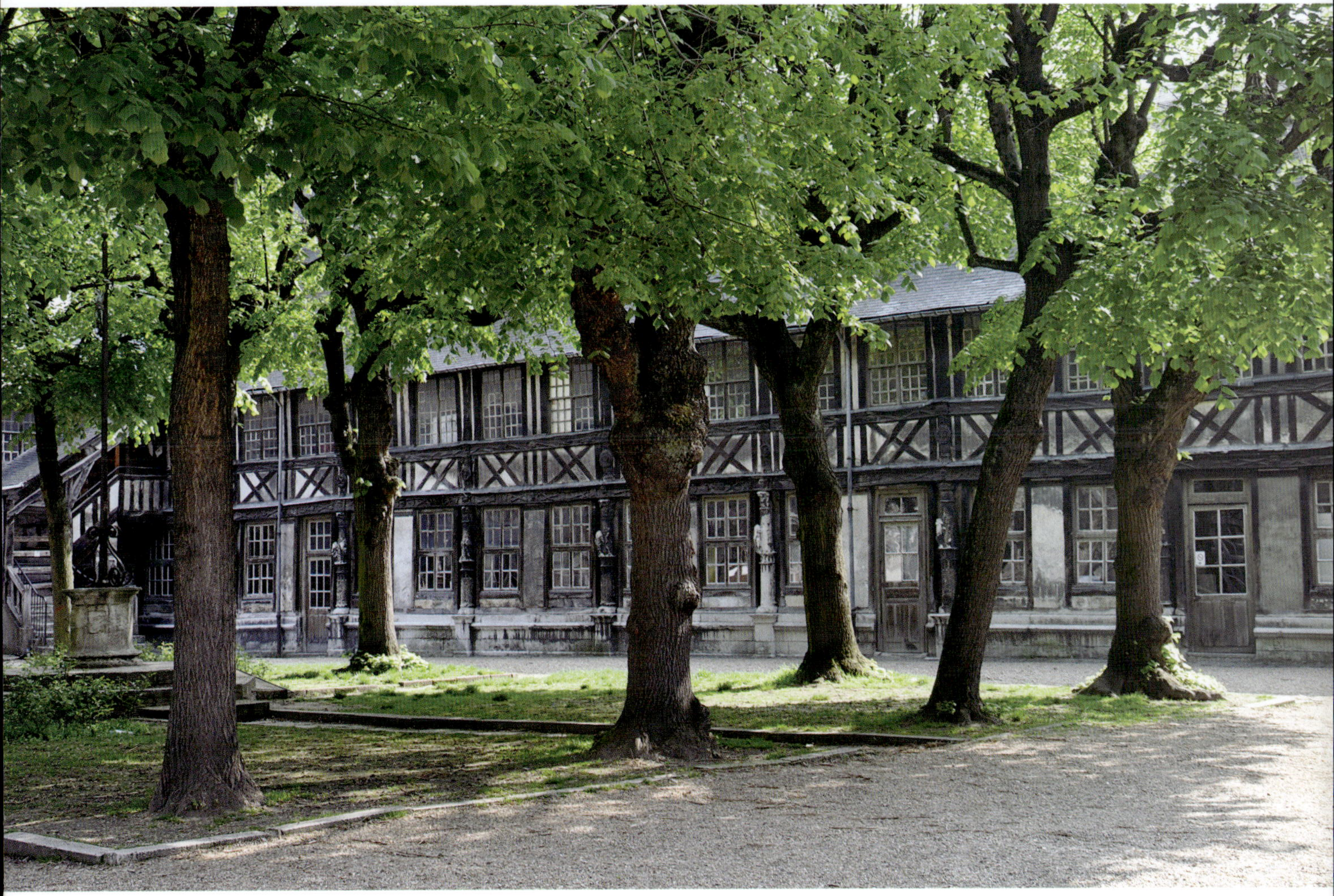

Rouen

Aître Saint-Maclou. This strange site owes its origins to the Black Death of 1348. The authorities, unable to handle the thousands of deaths, were forced to open new cemeteries, and one of these was le Grand Aître Saint-Maclou, where the corpses were buried in communal graves. The galleries around the cemetery were built between 1526 and 1533 to serve as bone deposits. The décor on the wood work appealed to the morbid "gothic" Early Romantic predilection for all things macabre and diabolical that prevailed in Chopin's France.

← The house where Chopin performed in 1838 is still there today, beside the Great Clock.

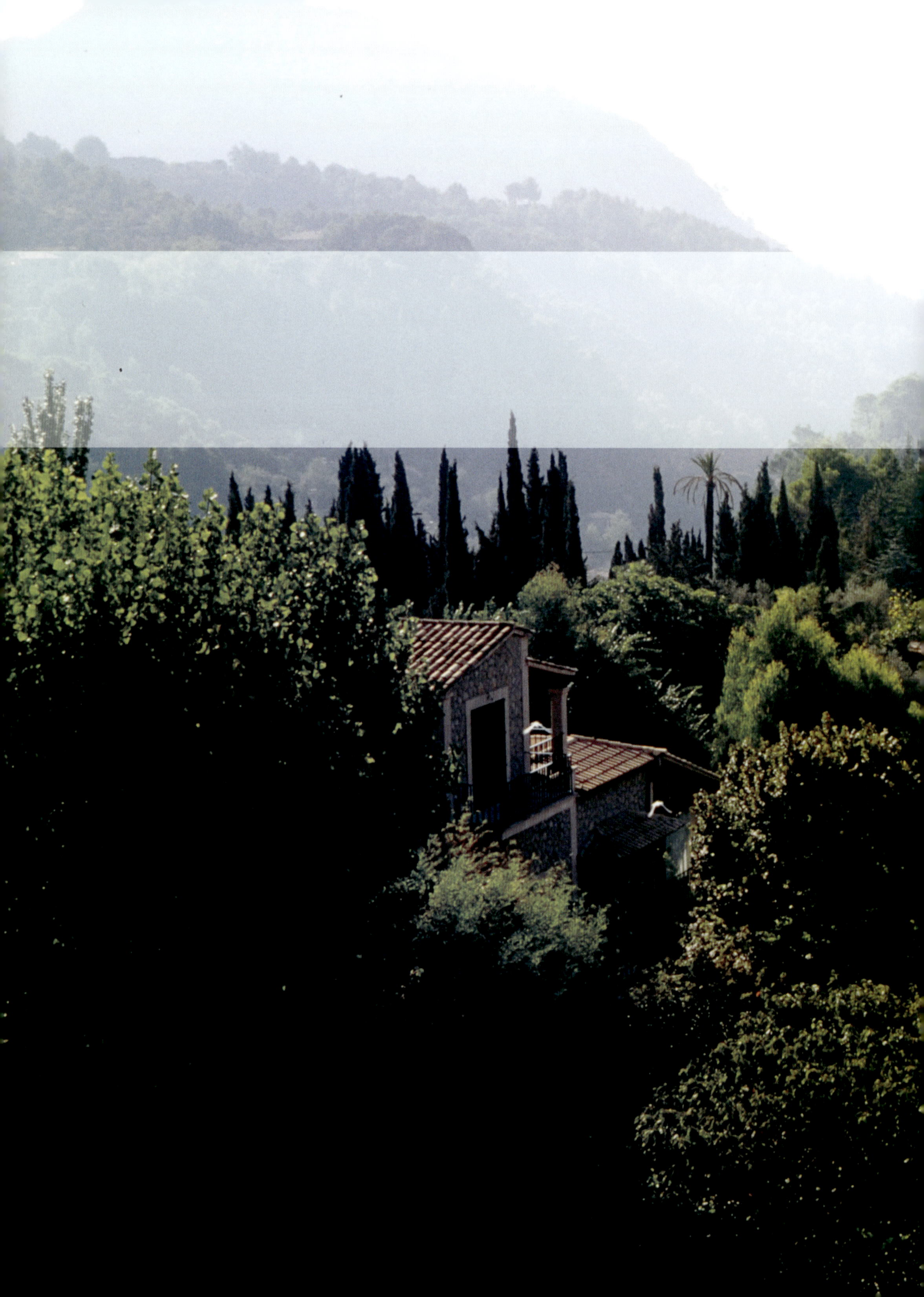

Majorca

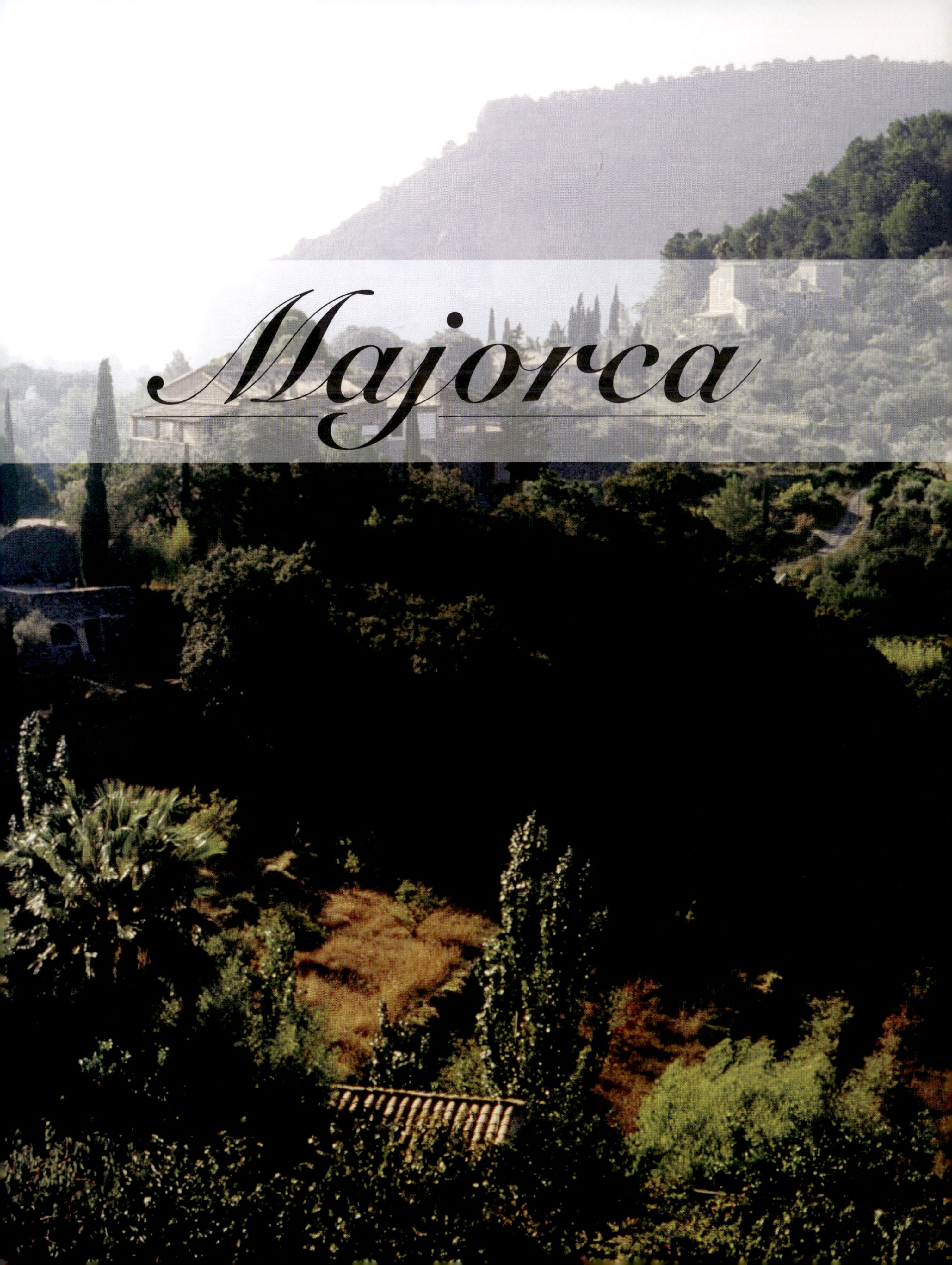

On 27 October 1838 Fryderyk Chopin set off into the autumnal French heartlands for his assignation in Perpignan with George Sand and her children – Solange and Maurice. The coach journey, in the company of the Spanish ambassador, the Juan de Mendizabal, who was returning to Spain, took four days. From Perpignan it was a short drive to Port Vendres, where the Pyrenees met the Mediterranean Sea along the Côte Vermeille. On 1 November the party boarded the ferry *le Phénicien* to Barcelona. Chopin, George and the children stayed for six days at the Hotel *Cuatro Naciones* before boarding the steamboat *el Mallorquin* on 7 November for the day-long voyage to Palma, the capital of Majorca. There they found two small, sparsely-furnished rooms near the harbour gate.

I am in Palma, surrounded by palm-trees, orange-trees, lemon-trees, aloes, fig-trees and pomegranates, etc. A turquoise sky, emerald mountains, and the air from paradise. The sun shines all day long...

Chopin to Julian Fontana
(Palma, 15 November 1838)

They stayed in Palma for a week, sightseeing among the narrow streets, and walking along the seafront to admire the Cathedral. They presented themselves to the French consul, Pierre-Hippolyte Flury.

The music of the bolero reverberates in the loneliest places and on the darkest of nights. There is no peasant who does not have a guitar and who does not take it with him at any hour.

George Sand, *A Winter in Majorca*

On 15 November they rented out villa "Son Vent", in the village of Establiments, some 10 kilometres to the north of Palma, from a Señor Gomez. Son Vent – which means House of the Wind in the Catalan dialect that was the language of Majorca – was a fine but run-down summer residence perched on a hill overlooking the valley of the Torrent sa Riera, at that time only a dry, rock-strewn ditch. The house was starkly furnished, but afforded a breathtaking view of the Majorcan countryside towards the Serra de Cans on the other side of the valley. It was a warm and idyllic three week stay, during which the four went for long walks exploring the dry river bed, with its rocks covered in moss and little bridges half hidden by overhanging willows and poplars.

The weather was enchanting; the lemon trees and the myrtles were still in flower, and once, in early December, I stayed out on the terrace until five o'clock in the morning, enjoying the delightful warm air.

George Sand, *A Winter in Majorca*

On the first day George, an avid walker, organised an expedition along mountain paths to

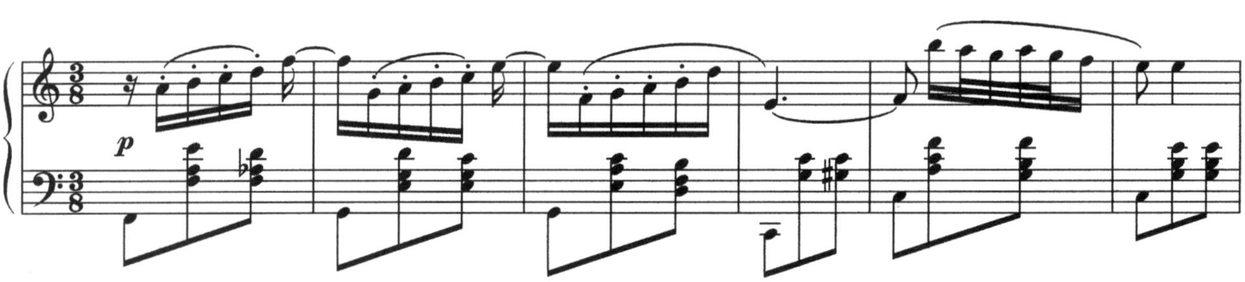

Chopin may well have heard the strains of the authentic bolero on its home ground for the first time on the Spanish mainland, but only drew attention to it in Majorca. His own Bolero in C Op. 19 dates from 1833.

← The spectacular view that Chopin had from cell no 4 at the Monastery of Valldemosa onto the Majorcan countryside… when the sun shone!

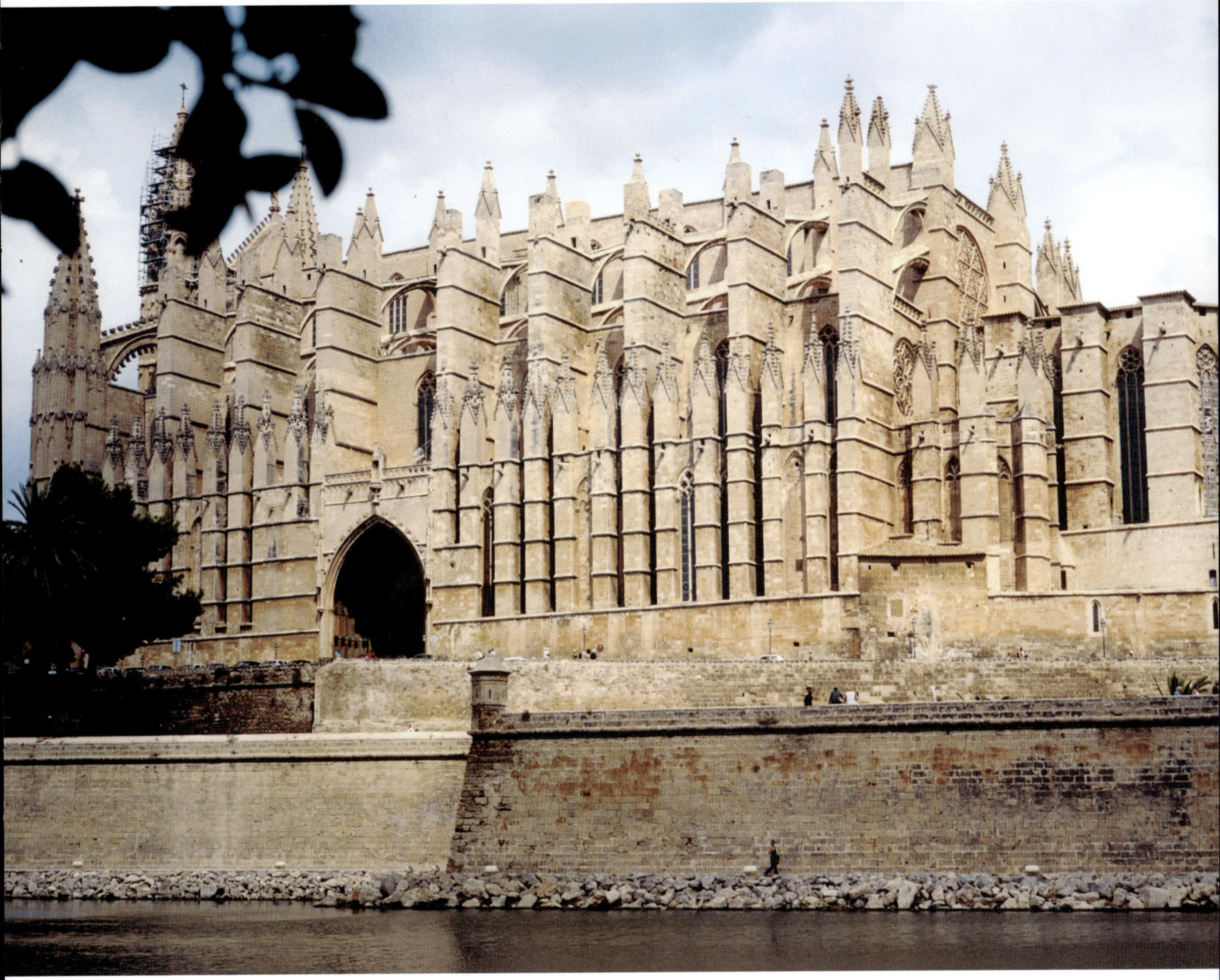

The Cathedral of Palma

Founded by King James I of Aragon in 1229, but only finished in 1601, the Cathedral of Palma di Majorca, known as La Seu, was originally built on the remains of an Arab mosque. It was conceived in the Spanish levantino style with influences of North European Gothic. The Catalan architect Antonio Gaudi was involved in its restoration after 1901.

the Hermitage of the Holy Trinity, perched on a remote crag on the northern coast. The Hermitage consisted of a small chapel with a bell-tower and a house surrounding a courtyard leading through an arch to a terrace for meditation, giving stunning views of the sea below. It was run by a small band of uneducated, rough hermits of no fixed denomination, who had dropped out of society to live a simple, isolated life tending their vegetable gardens in total tranquillity. After that, the walkers continued down the mountain back towards Palma, and stopped at the former Carthusian monastery at Valldemosa. The monastery had been dissolved by the authorities during the upheavals of 1835; with the monks expelled, the government took over the sprawling buildings and rented out the cells, fully furnished. In one of these they met a political refugee on the run from the Spanish authorities, who said that he would shortly be vacating his cell, and was looking for someone to take it over. Having agreed in principle to take the cell over at a later date, the intrepid quartet continued down the mountains back to the sa Riera valley, and to Son Vent. But the long and arduous walk had been too much for Chopin, whose lungs suffered a serious setback, and doctors had to be summoned.

The one sat sniffing what I had spat out, the second listening to whence I spat, while the third one sat and listened to my spitting. The first one told me I should die, the second one, that I was dying, and the third that I was dead already!

Chopin to Julian Fontana (Palma, 3 December 1838)

The idyllic weather came to an end in early December. The rains came with a vengeance, and the temperature dropped abruptly. The rocky river bed became the torrent of its name, tumbling from the western reaches of the Serra de Tramuntana to empty into the Bay of Palma. The dampness seeped through the lime-washed walls of the house, causing them to swell and bubble. The charcoal braziers filled the house with smoke, and wrought havoc with Chopin's already weakened lungs. His coughing became so bad that doctors were summoned again. The word spread among the locals that there was a highly contagious tuberculosis sufferer in their midst, which caused near panic. George received a letter from Señor Gomez giving immediate notice. Fortunately, the refugee's cell in Valldemosa was about to become available. On 10 December Mr. Flury, the French consul, offered them temporary hospitality until they could make the arrangements for the move.

Tomorrow I go to that wonderful monastery of Valldemosa, to write in the cell of some old monk, who perhaps had more fire in his soul than I... I think I shall soon send you my Preludes and a Ballade.

Chopin to Julian Fontana (Palma, 14 December 1838)

Villa "Son Vent" in Establiments

On 15 November 1838 George Sand rented out the villa "Son Vent", in the Village of Establiments, about 10 kilometres to the north of Palma, for herself, her children Solange and Maurice, and Chopin. The name means "House of Wind" in the Catalan dialect. The villa was identified from a sketch made by Maurice when they stayed there. It was a fine but somewhat run-down summer residence, but afforded a breathtaking view of the Majorcan countryside.

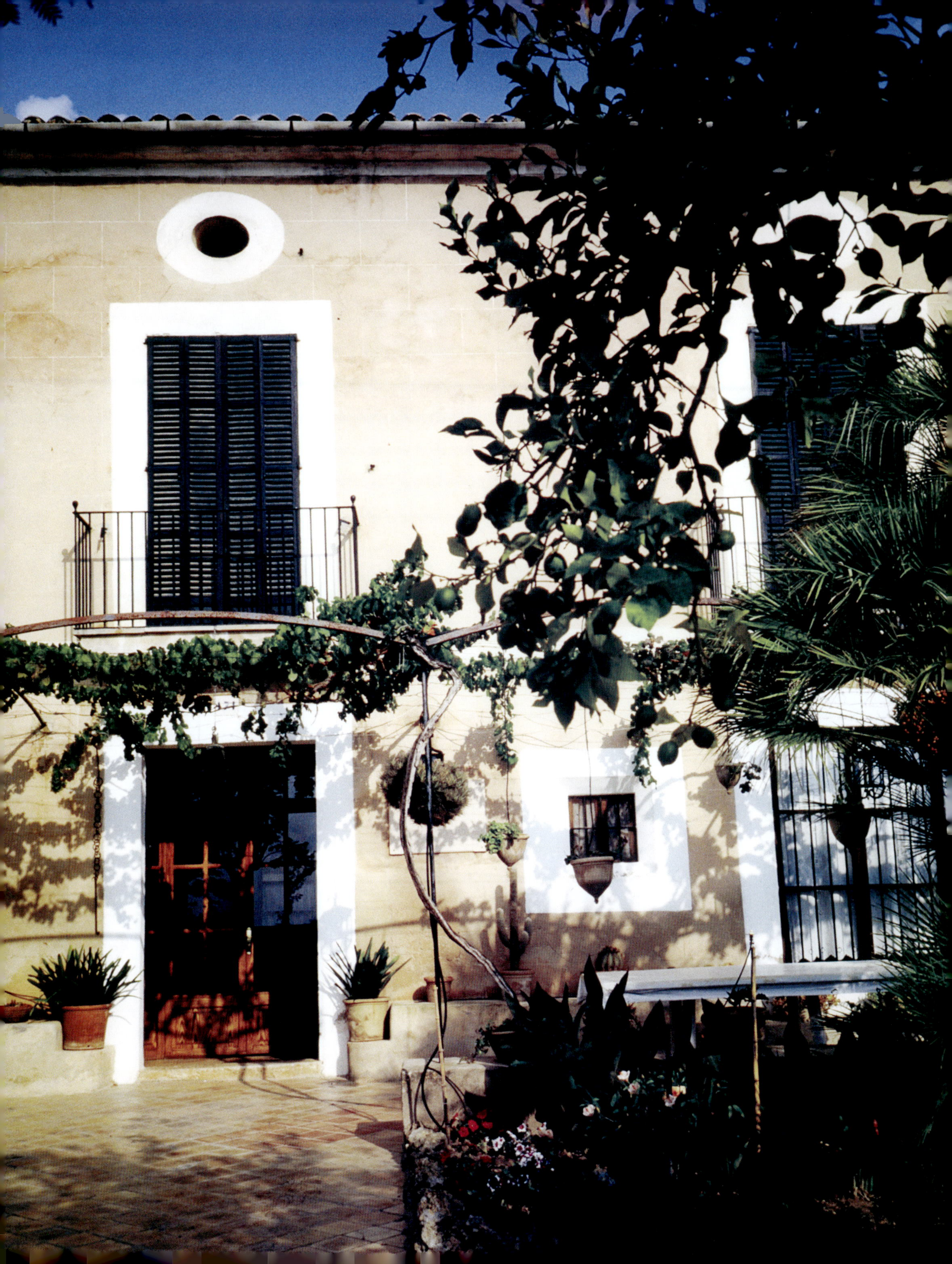

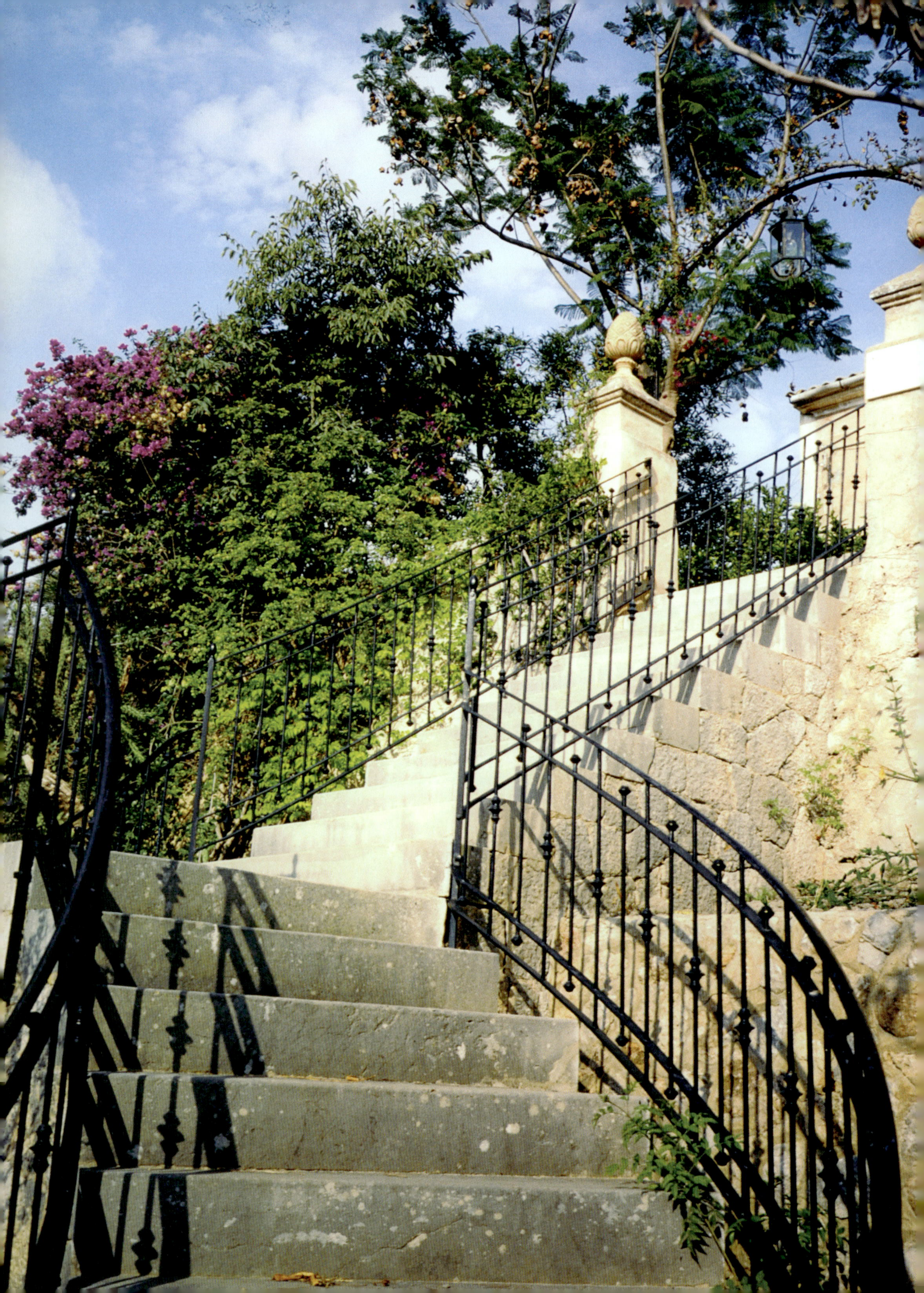

On 15 December, George, Chopin, Solange and Maurice set off in the pouring rain in two carts, bound for the mountains. There was no route as such at the time, although the stretch of track into Valldemosa branched off to the left of today's road, and led down into the valley before climbing again towards the Monastery through the town's ancient gateposts, bearing the coat-of-arms of the House of Aragon. The torrent, now truly worthy of the name, was their constant companion as it tumbled noisily along the rocky bed to join sa Riera further downstream. The Monastery was a sprawling complex of buildings, including the Gothic church that dominated the square before it. The cells, each with its own small terraced garden, were situated in a long cloister overlooking the monastery orchards and vegetable gardens, beyond which the valley stretched down into the misty distance towards Palma. Remnants of centuries of religious ritual and monastic life still lingered three years after the ransacking; ornaments, half-burned candles, vases of long dead flowers and damaged altar-pieces still lay where they fell.

Nature is benevolent here, but the people are thieves, because they never see strangers, and so don't know how much to demand. Oranges can be had for nothing, but a trouser button costs a fabulous sum. But all that is just a grain of sand, when one has this sky, this poetry that everything breathes here, this colouring of the most exquisite places, colour not yet faded by men's eyes. No one has yet scared away the eagles that soar every day above our heads!

Chopin to Julian Fontana (Palma, 28 December 1838)

It was Chopin's intention to spend the winter in composition. He had ordered a new piano to be delivered to Majorca from his friend, piano maker Camille Pleyel, which had not yet arrived, having been constantly delayed by customs bureaucracy. Fortunately, the cell already contained a battered old Pleyel piano in one of the four sparsely furnished rooms that comprised the cell, so Chopin was grateful for small mercies, while he waited for the new one. Unable to brave the elements of the cold and blustery Majorcan winter of 1838-39, he spent most of his time resting or composing in the cell, which was heated only with a foul-smelling smoky stove. The monastery's pharmacy, situated below, still functioned, and he was able to buy incense and balsam to neutralise the smell.

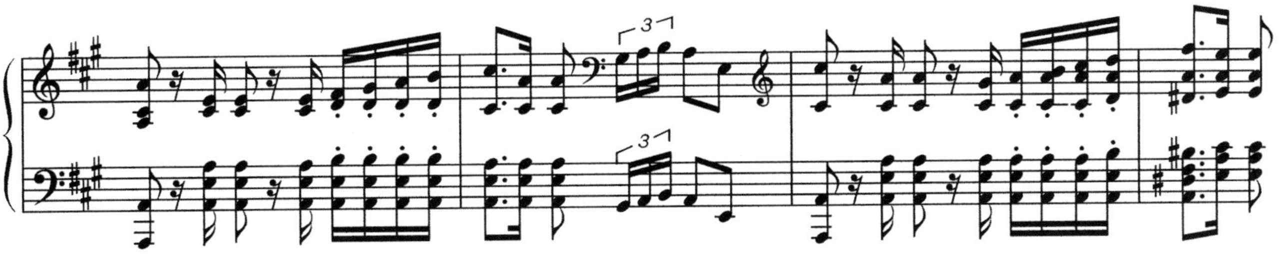

There was nothing remotely military or Polish about Chopin's sojourn in Majorca, but the Polonaise Militaire, perhaps his best-known polonaise, might well have been inspired by the military parades that he watched as a boy in Warsaw.

Villa "Son Vent" in Establiments

Detail of stairs leading up to the villa.

The two Polonaises Op. 40, the so-called "Military" in A, and the brooding C minor, were written in Valldemosa, as was the Scherzo in C sharp minor Op. 39. The chorale-like trio section, interspersed with cascading figures in the treble, were inspired by the echoes of monastic life still pervading the air. The emotionally-charged Ballade in F Op. 38 was also written during these dark, damp days.

Most important was the completion of the set of 24 Preludes Op. 28, modelled on those of Bach, one in each key, which he had started in Paris. Of these No 15 in D flat has passed into legend for its Majorcan association. One day George and Maurice went to Palma to check on the progress of the new Pleyel piano. On their return they were overcome by a particularly heavy storm, and they returned, cold, wet and bedraggled, late that evening, looking like ghosts. *I knew it*, said Chopin, whose sense of humour always helped him through sickness, *I knew that you were dead!* He had been working that day on the Prelude in D flat. When George heard it, with its throbbing repetitive note, she compared it to the sound of raindrops on the tiles of the monastery. It thus assumed the nickname, which Chopin loathed, of "Raindrop" Prelude.

On 12 January 1839, Chopin sent the complete set of Preludes to Julian Fontana in Paris, who was acting as his publishers' agent.

A week later, the new Pleyel piano finally reached Valldemosa, but it only served Chopin for three weeks. By 12 February, with Chopin's health in serious decline, the party left Valldemosa, and spent the night in Palma with Mr. Flury. The next day they boarded *el Mallorquin* once more for Barcelona, where they again put up at the Hotel *Cuatro Naciones*. In an attempt to find warmth, peace and relaxation for her invalid lover, George arranged a few days in the fishing village of Arenys de Mar, a short distance up the coast from the Catalan capital. On 24 February the quartet arrived in Marseilles on the warship, *le Méléagre*. Chopin, for whom the voyage, although the conditions were clean and comfortable, was an added torment, was immediately taken, close to death, to a Dr François Cauvières at 71 rue de Rome, where he lodged for two days. After that, the immediate

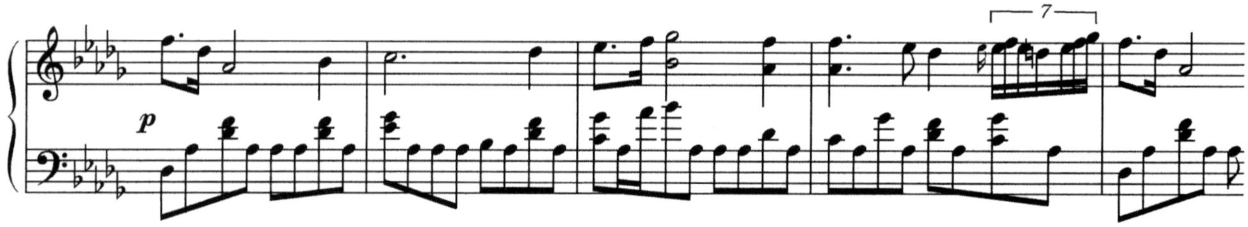

The Prelude in D flat, the so-called "Raindrop" Prelude, is indelibly associated with Chopin's Majorcan experience.

The Hermitage of the Holy Trinity

A short distance to the north of Valldemosa, perched on a remote crag on the north coast of the island, with stunning views of the sea below, is the Hermitage of the Holy Trinity. It consists of a small chapel with a bell tower and a house surrounding a courtyard leading through an arch to a terrace for meditation. Chopin, George Sand and children came here on a visit on 16 November 1838.

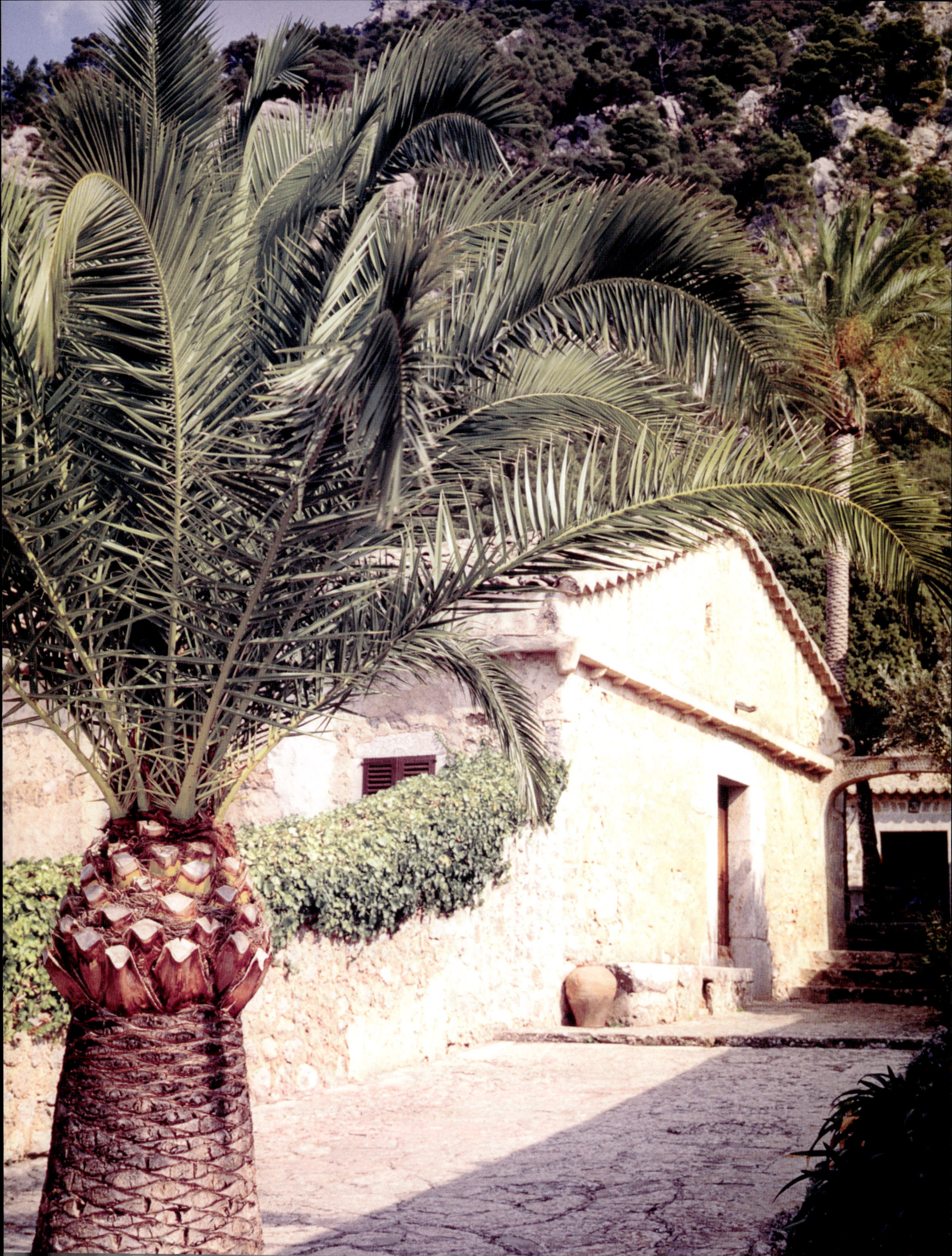

danger over, Chopin rejoined George and the children at the Hotel *de la Darse*, where George dedicated herself to nursing Chopin, who was still extremely ill. Her endless patience, care and diligence brought success, and on 1 April, with the Mediterranean spring in the air, Chopin was well enough for the group to move to the Hotel *Beauvau*.

My Angel is finishing a new novel: Gabriel. Today she is writing in bed all day. You know, you would love her even more if you knew her as I know her today.

Chopin to Wojciech Grzymała (Marseilles, 12 April 1839)

On 24 April Chopin played the organ at a funeral mass for Adolphe Nourrit, one of the most famous tenors of the day. On 8 March, in a fit of depression, he had hurled himself to his death from the top floor of Naples' Hotel *Barbaia*, and his body was being taken by his widow through Marseilles to Paris for burial. The service took place at the Church of Notre-Dame du Mont, where crowds came to hear Chopin play.

About my playing for Nourrit. His body was escorted and is on its way to Paris. There was a funeral mass, and the family asked me to play, so I played during the elevation.

Chopin to Julian Fontana (Marseilles, 25 April 1839)

On 3 May the quartet went for a stay in Genoa. On 22 May, they were back in Marseilles, where they caught a riverboat which took them to the mouth of the Grande Rhone, and thence upstream through the Camargue as far as Arles. There they were met by the coachman with the carriage that George had sent for, to take them on the last stage of their journey, through Avignon, Saint-Etienne, Montbrison, Clermont-Ferrand – to George Sand's manor in Nohant, which they reached at the end of May after a week on the road.

For George the Majorca trip was, apart from a romantic experience, a prolific time, during which she completed three novels, *Lélia*, *Spiridion* and *Gabriel*.

For Maurice it was, in his own words, one of the highlights of his youth, during which his talent for art and drawing came very much to the fore. He drew and sketched at every opportunity, and the Maurice Dudevant collection is like a souvenir album of the whole trip.

For Chopin the trip, although extremely productive, was a disaster which might even have ended in his death, had it not been for the deep affection and tireless care shown to him by his new companion in love.

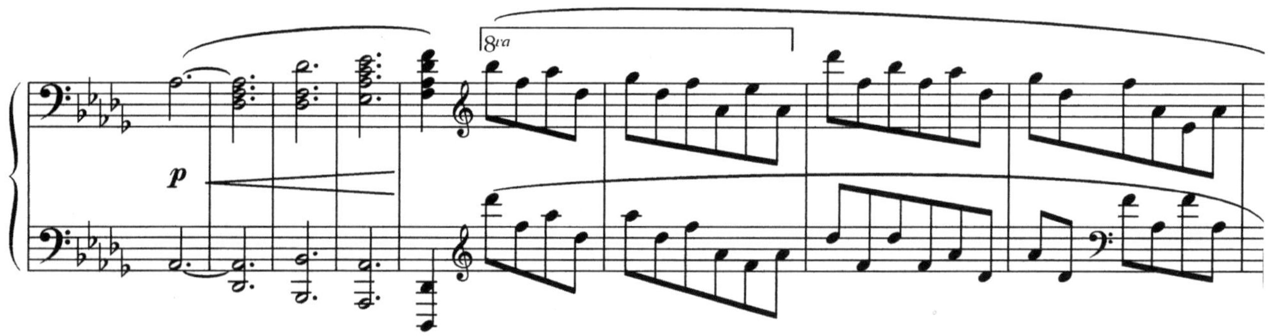

The chorale-like trio of the Scherzo in C sharp minor may have been inspired by the monastic atmosphere of Chopin's cell at Valldemosa.

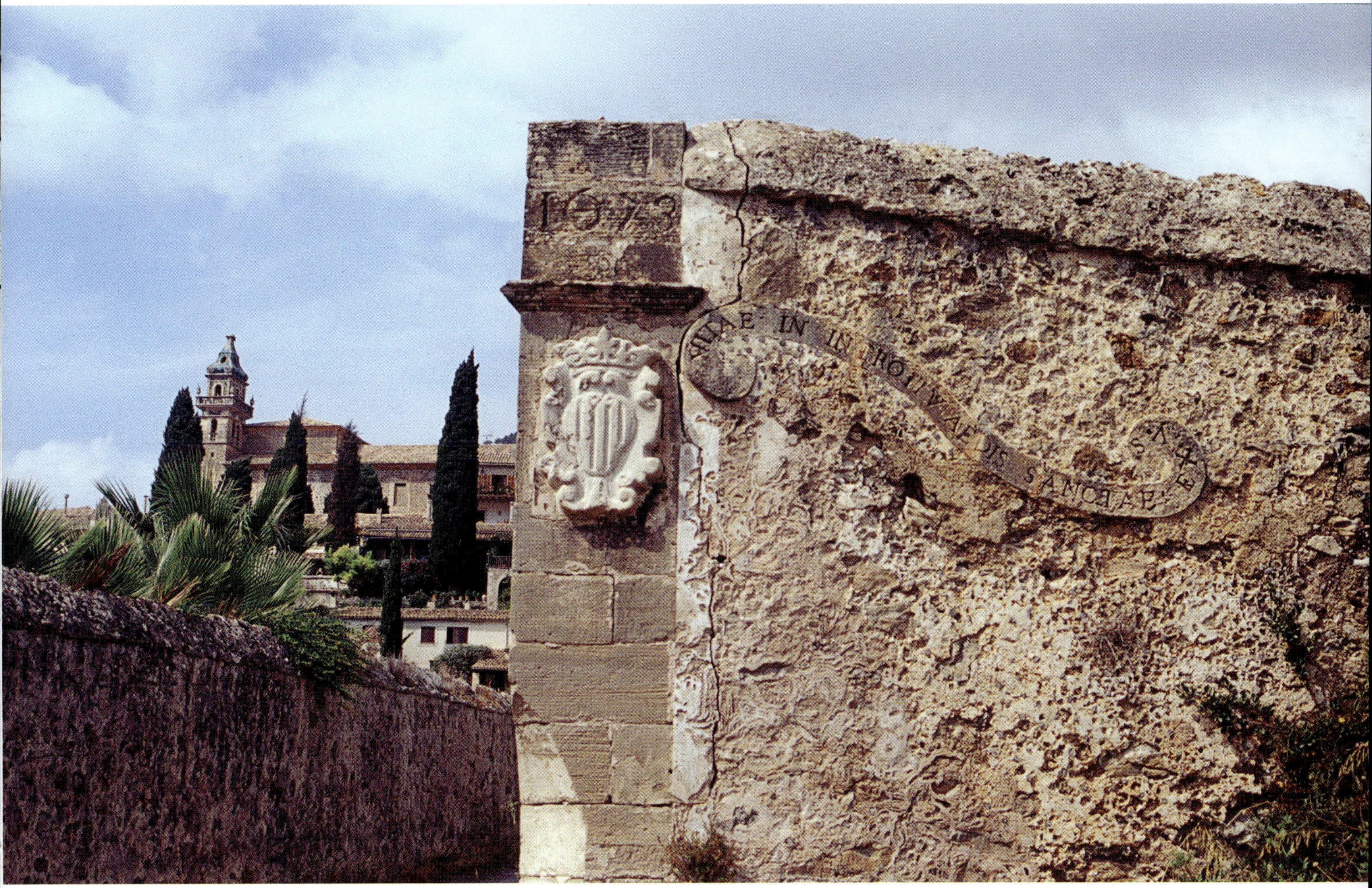

Monastery of Valldemosa

The only approach to Valldemosa from Palma, before today's road was built, was along an old mule track further down the valley, that led through the town's ancient gateposts bearing the coat-of-arms of the House of Aragon.

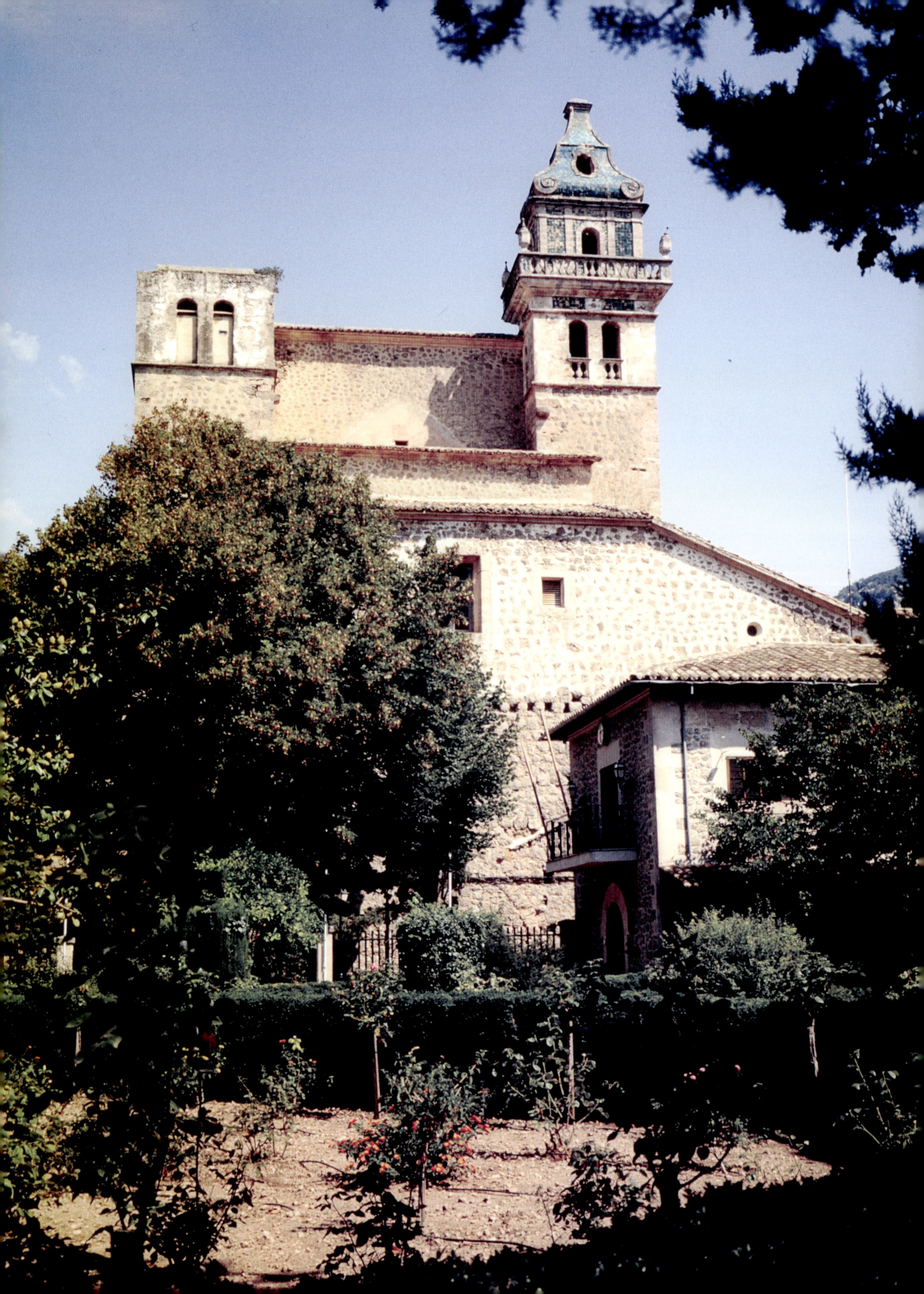

The villa, "Son Vent" is still there, on the road between Establiments and Puigpunyant. The monastery of Valldemosa is largely unchanged, as are the cells. The old piano on which Chopin composed his Majorca works is now in Cell No 2, while the belatedly arrived new Pleyel, which was eventually purchased by a certain Mr. Ernest Canut of Palma, is housed in No 4. Both cells have long and controversially been claimed as the correct Chopin-Sand sites. It is thanks to Maurice's eye for detail that the correct one – No 4 – has finally been verified as such from his sketches. The Hermitage of the Holy Trinity is still there, some 6 km to the north of Valldemosa. The waterfront house where Chopin stayed in Palma and the French Consulate no longer exist. None of the Chopin sites in Barcelona or Genoa exist today, and in Marseilles only the rue de Rome is still there as are remnants of the old Church of Notre-Dame du Mont, beside the new Cathedral.

Monastery of Valldemosa

The monastery was a sprawling complex of buildings that included the Gothic church and cloister, where, between 15 December 1838 and 12 February of the following year, Chopin, George Sand and the children occupied cells Nos. 2 and 4, each with its own small terraced garden.

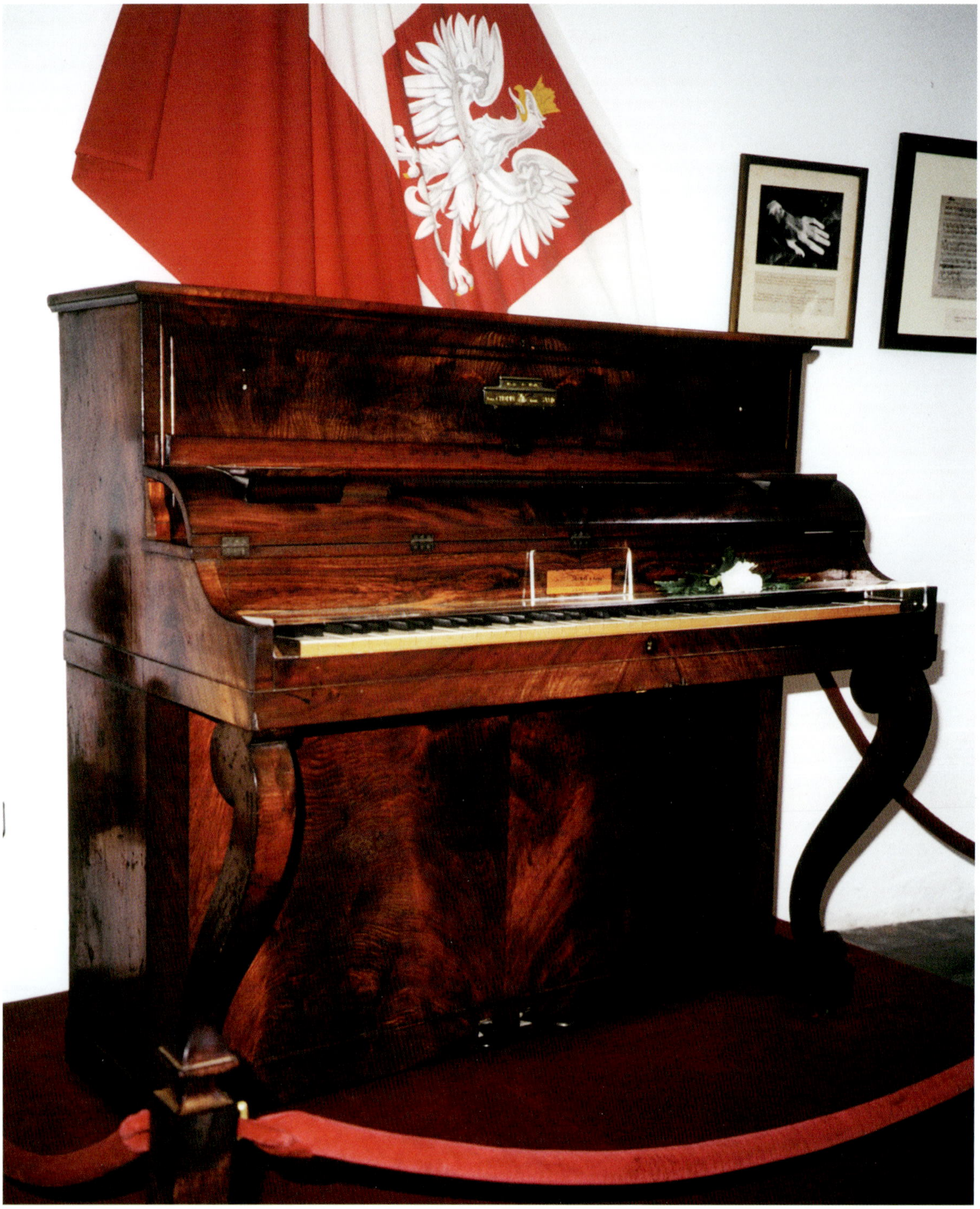

Monastery of Valldemosa

The piano on which Chopin played and composed for most of the time during his stay in Valldemosa, stands in cell No 2. It was on this instrument that many of Chopin's most important works, including the so-called "Raindrop" Prelude, and the "Military" Polonaise, were first heard. The Pleyel piano that he had ordered, and which had only arrived a few days before his departure, now stands in cell No 4.

→ The view from Chopin's cell gave onto his little terraced garden and the valley below.

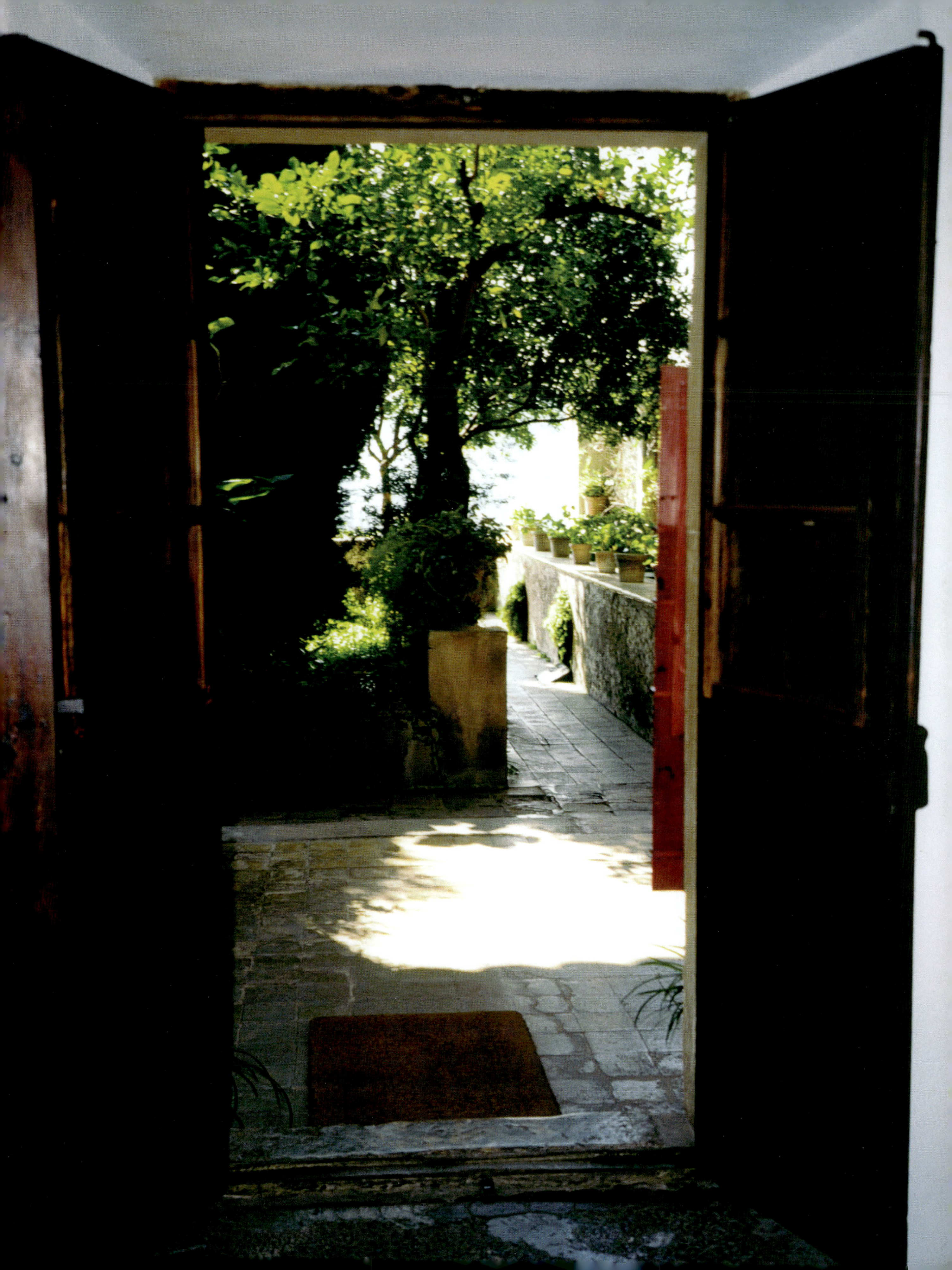

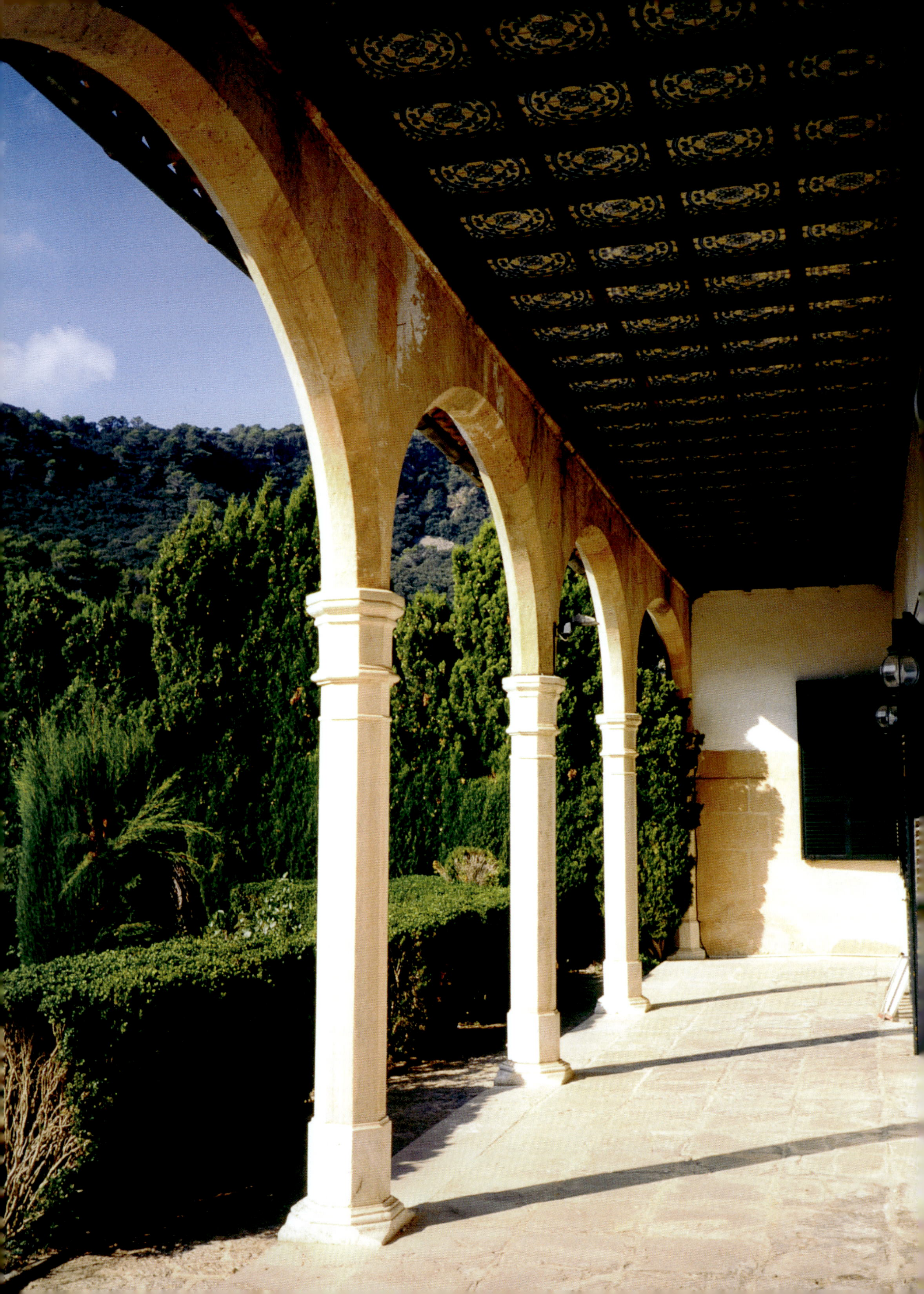

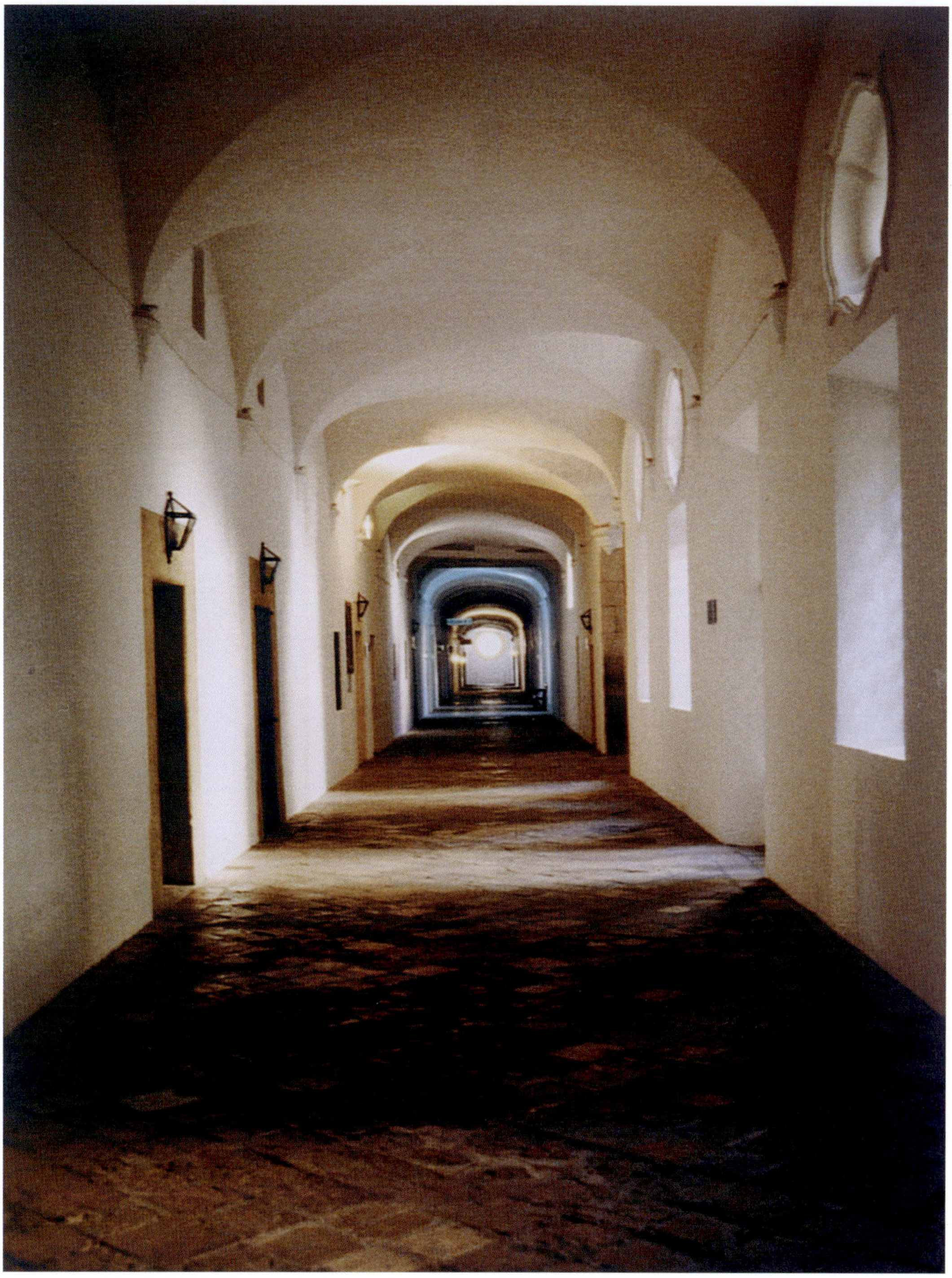

Monastery of Valldemosa

The cells of the monastery all gave onto the cloister.

← The monastery gardens had some very fine features, including arches and other architectural details.

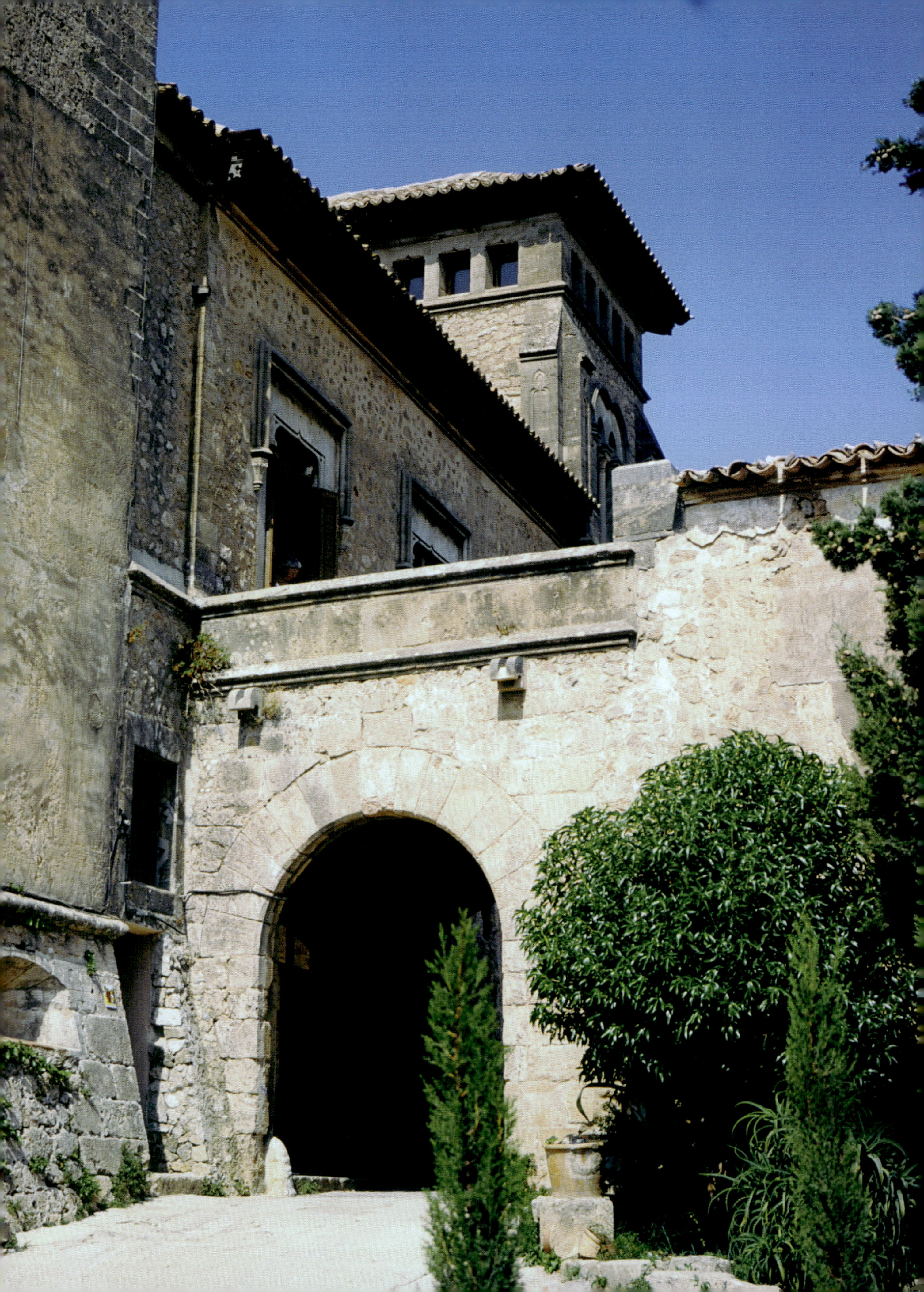

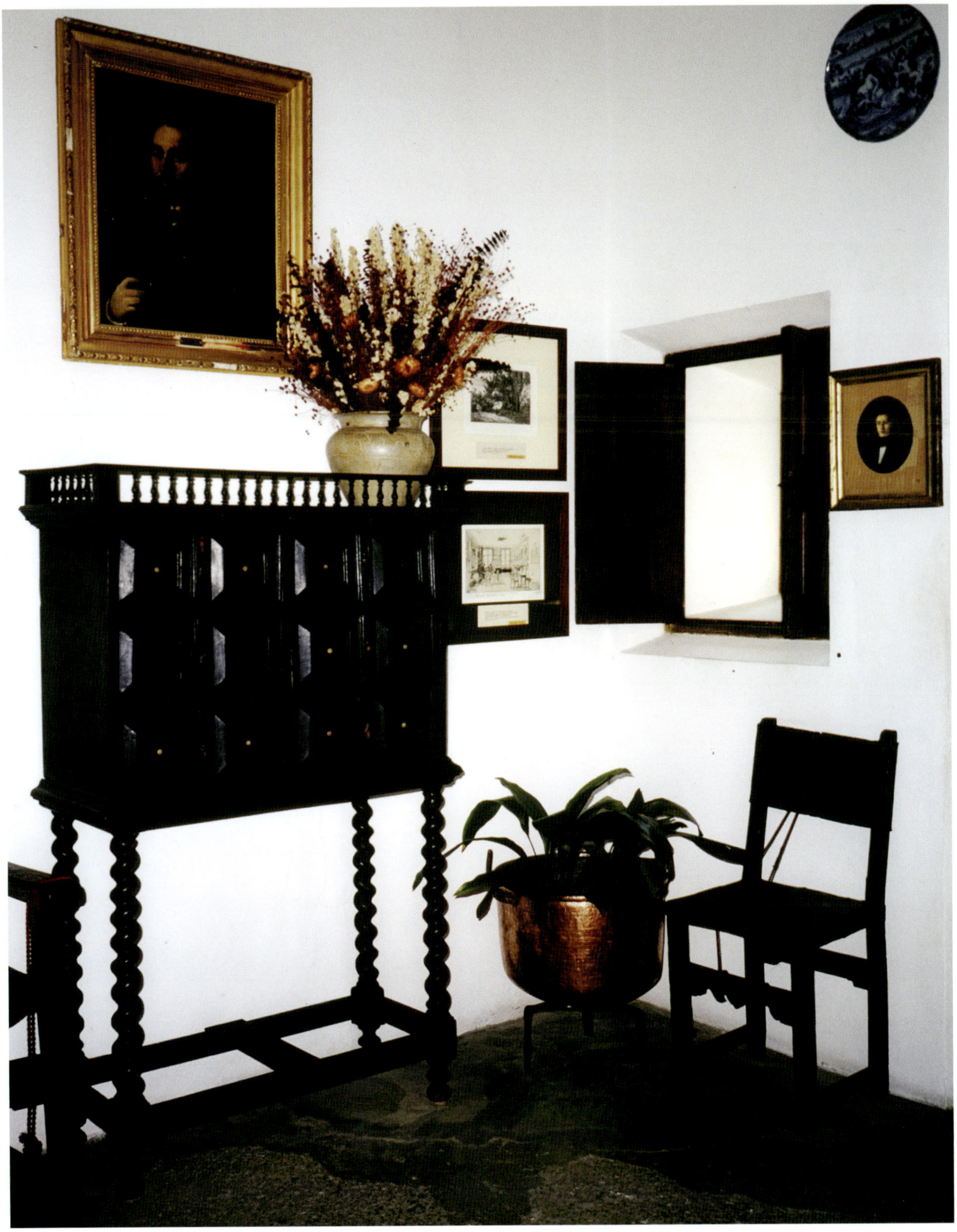

Monastery of Valldemosa
Partial view of the interior of Chopin's cell.

← King Sancho's Palace used to be the nucleus of the old monastery, nowadays it is converted into a luxurious mansion with royally furnished rooms.

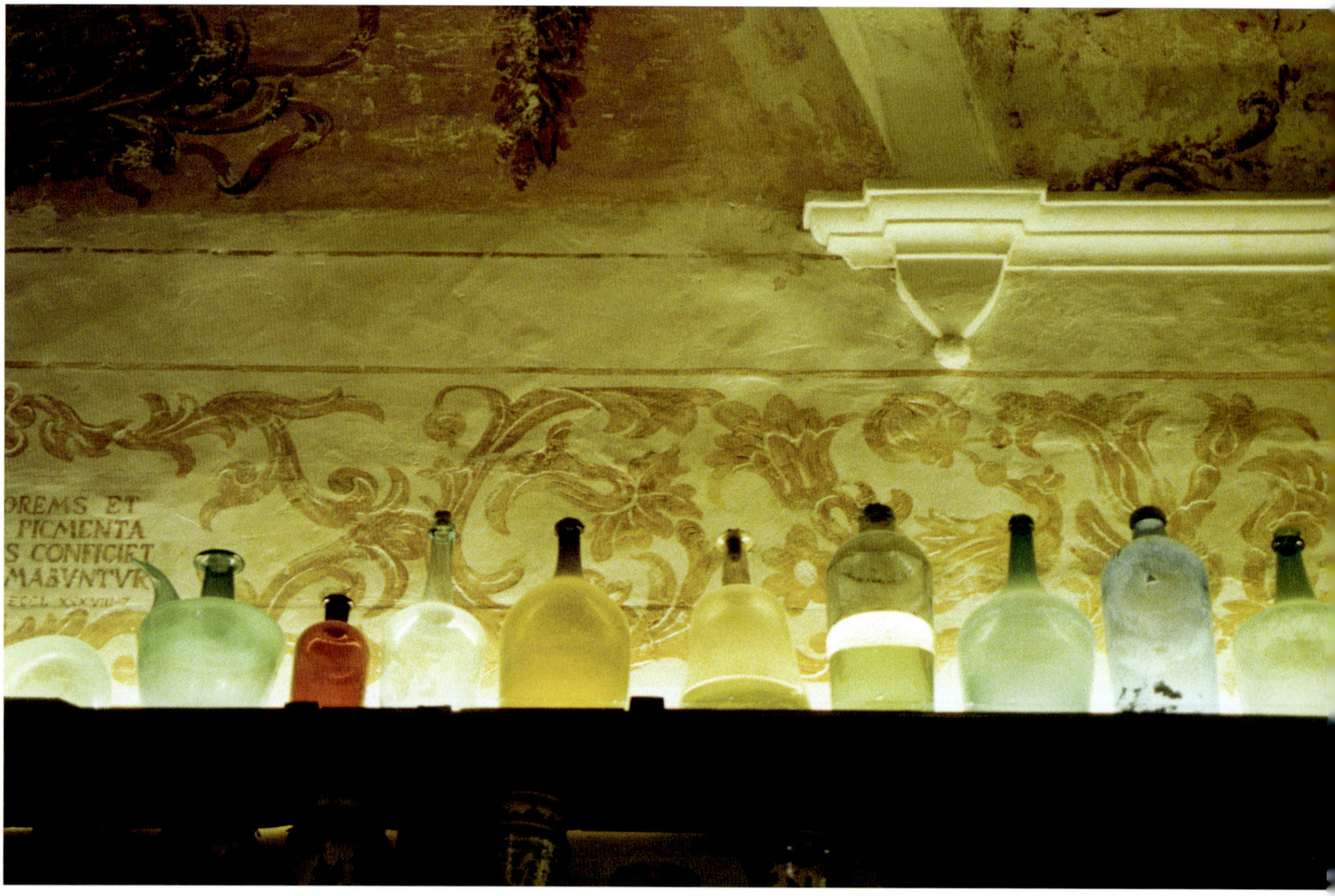

Monastery of Valldemosa

The monastery had a well-equipped Pharamacy, which was already in use during the time of Chopin's stay, a facility which he found useful.

→ The old well in the monastery was at that time the only source of water.

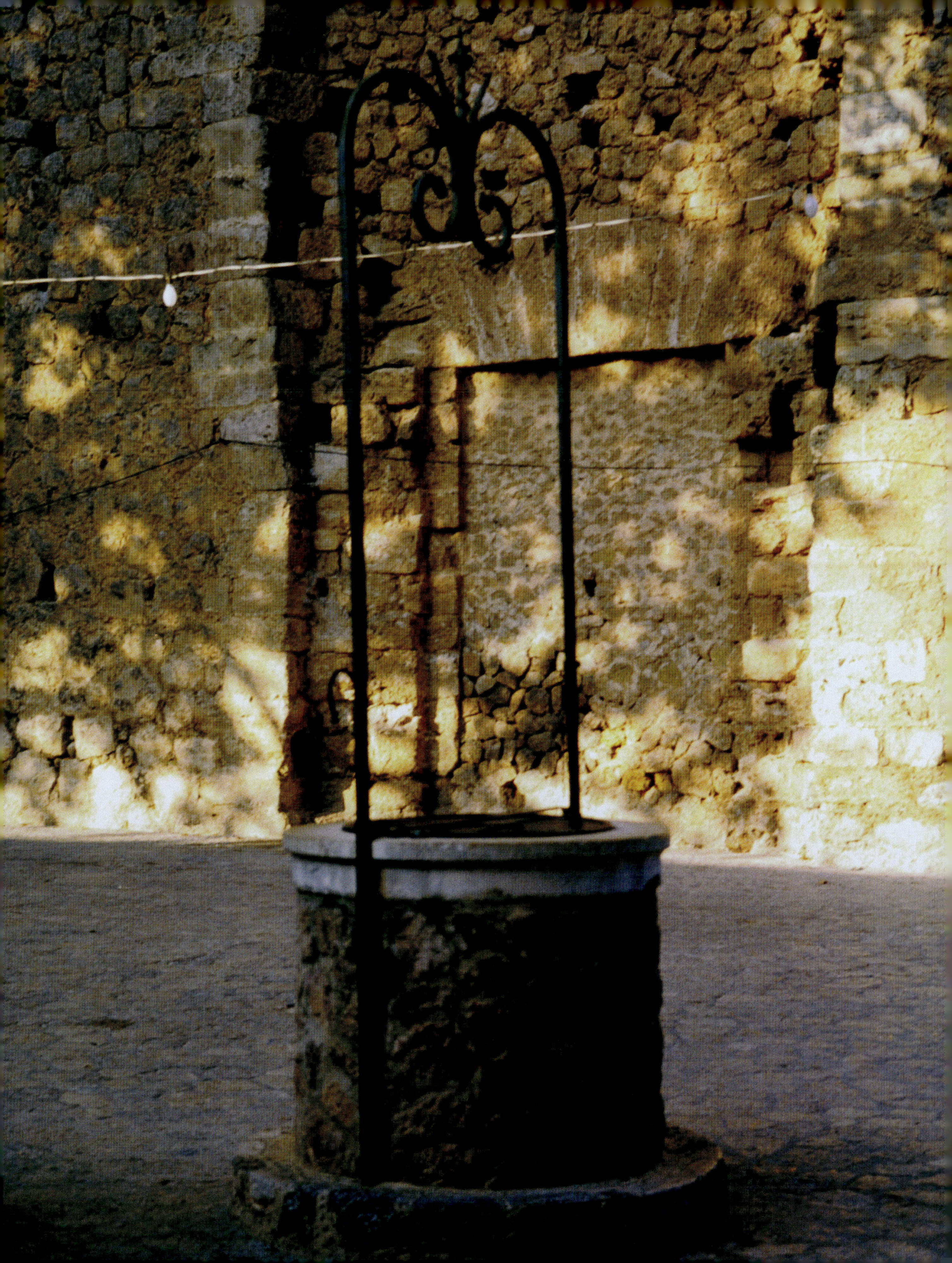

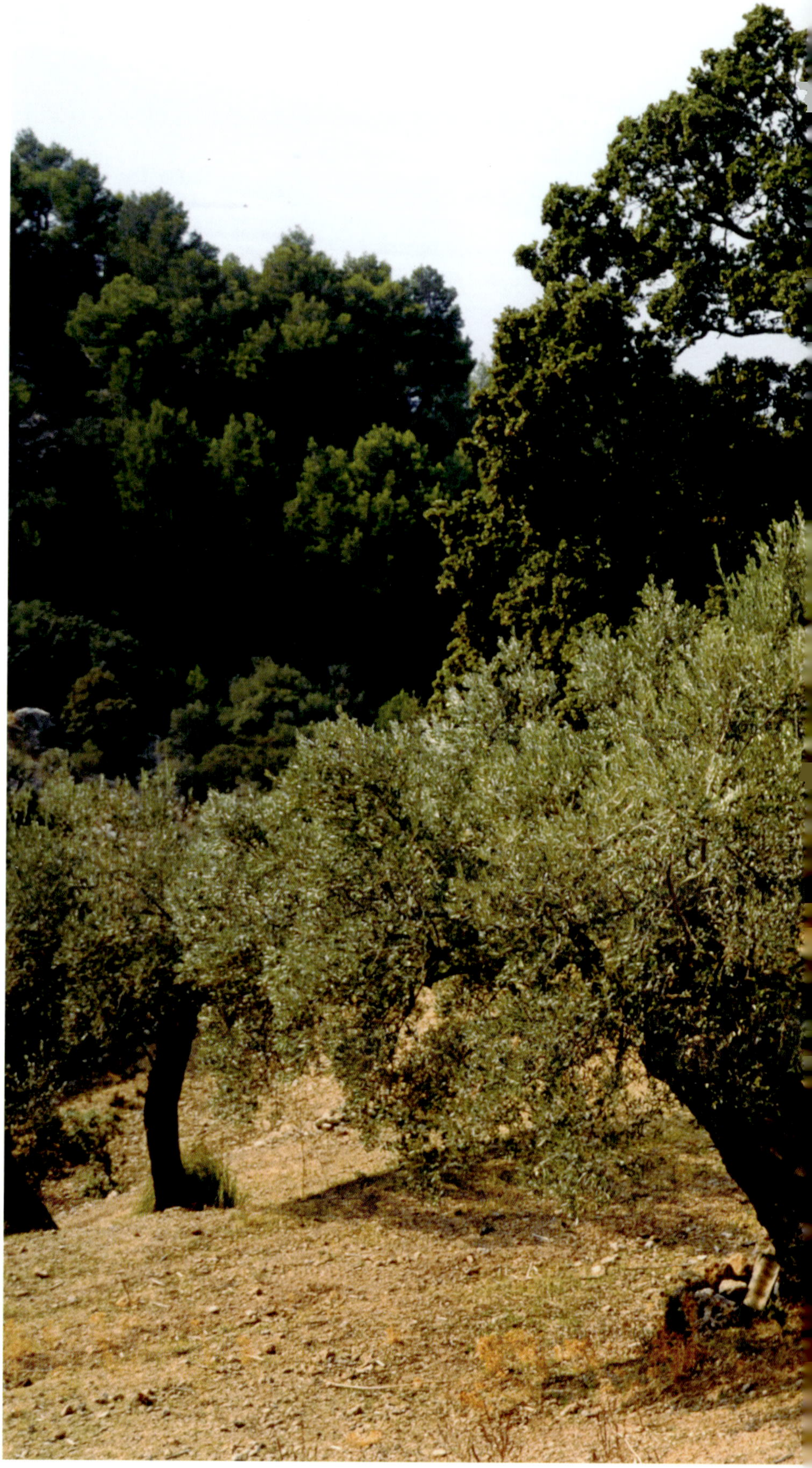

Majorcan landscape
A little olive grove with the sea in the distance.

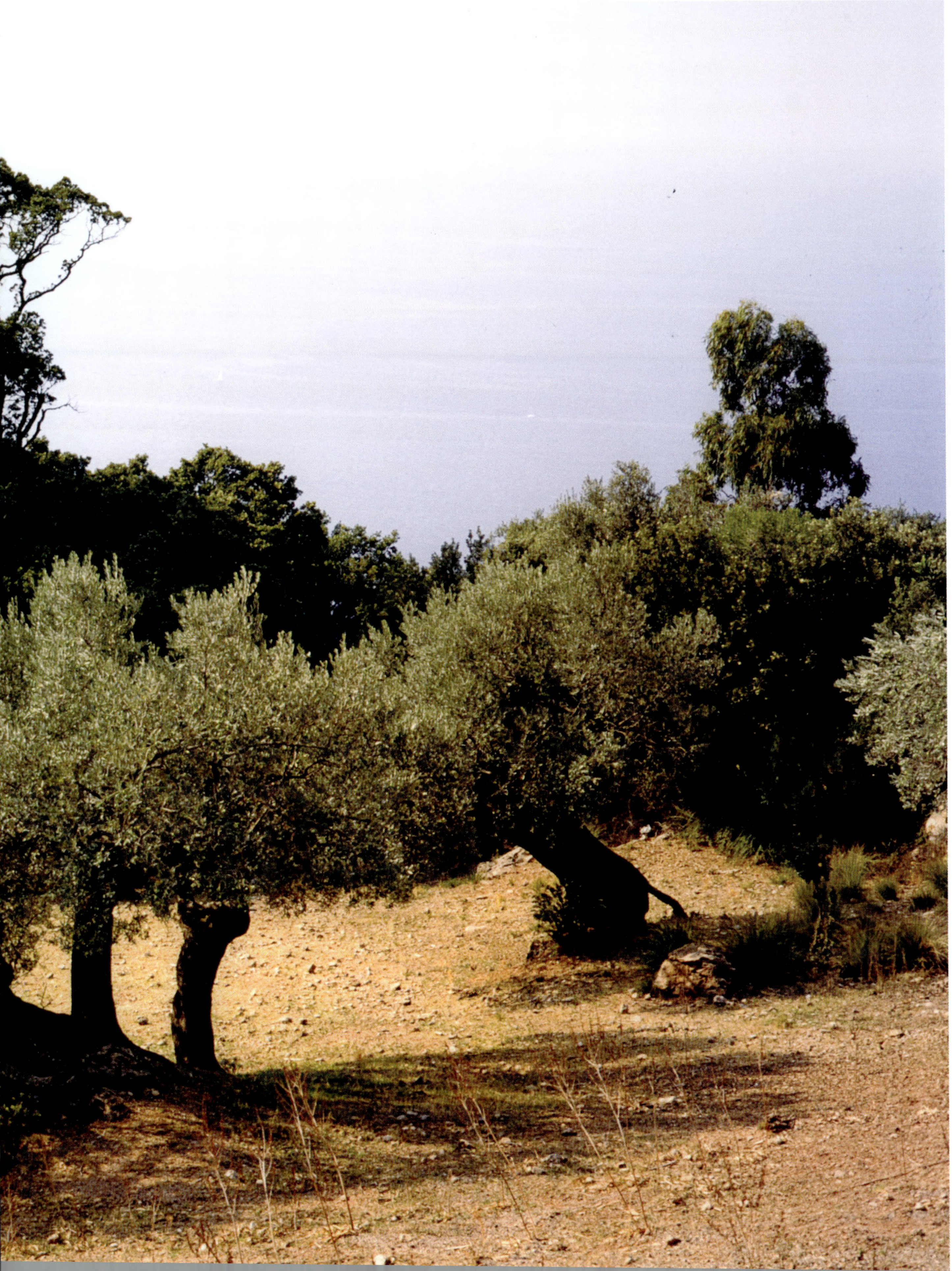

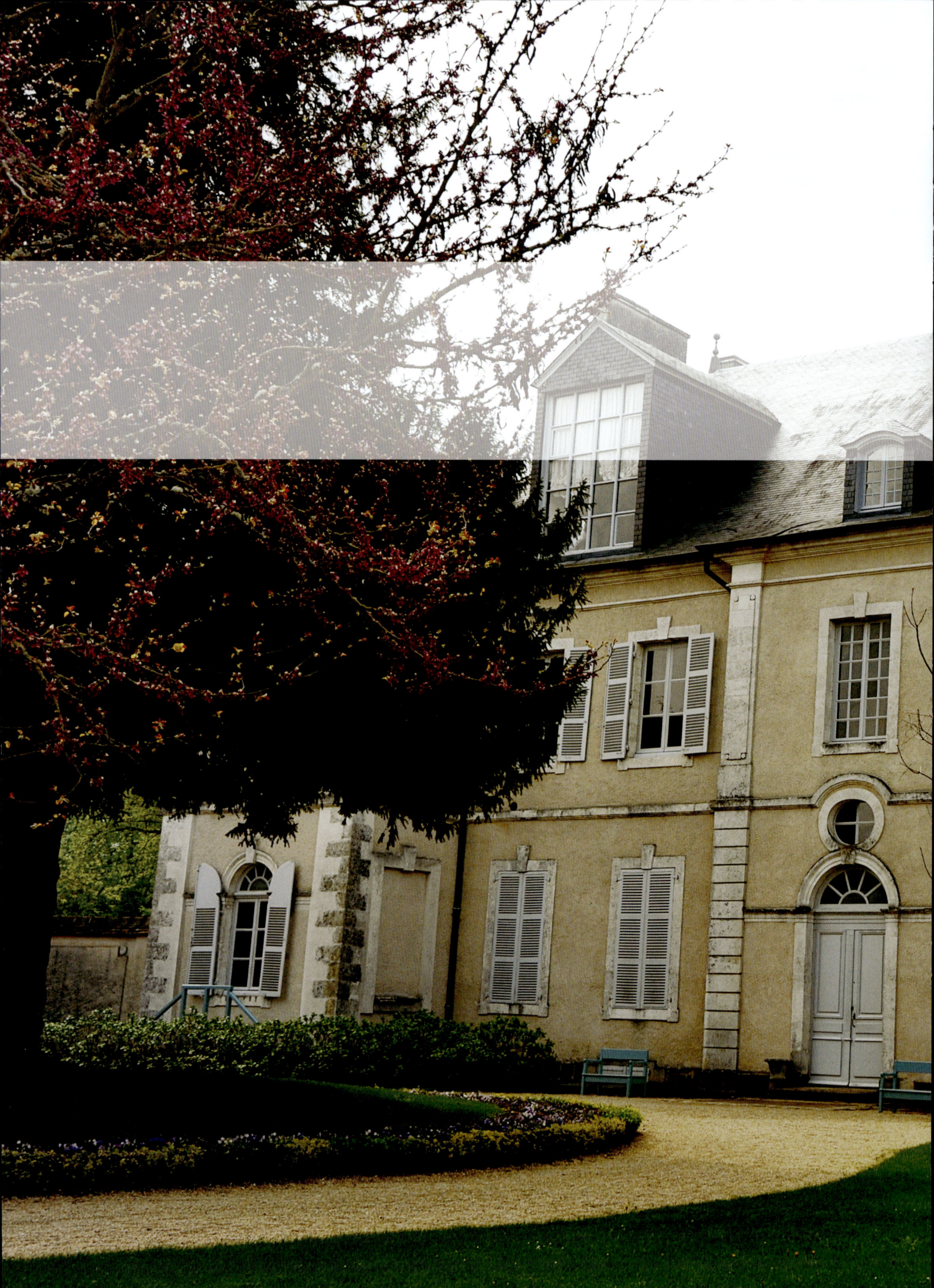

Nohant

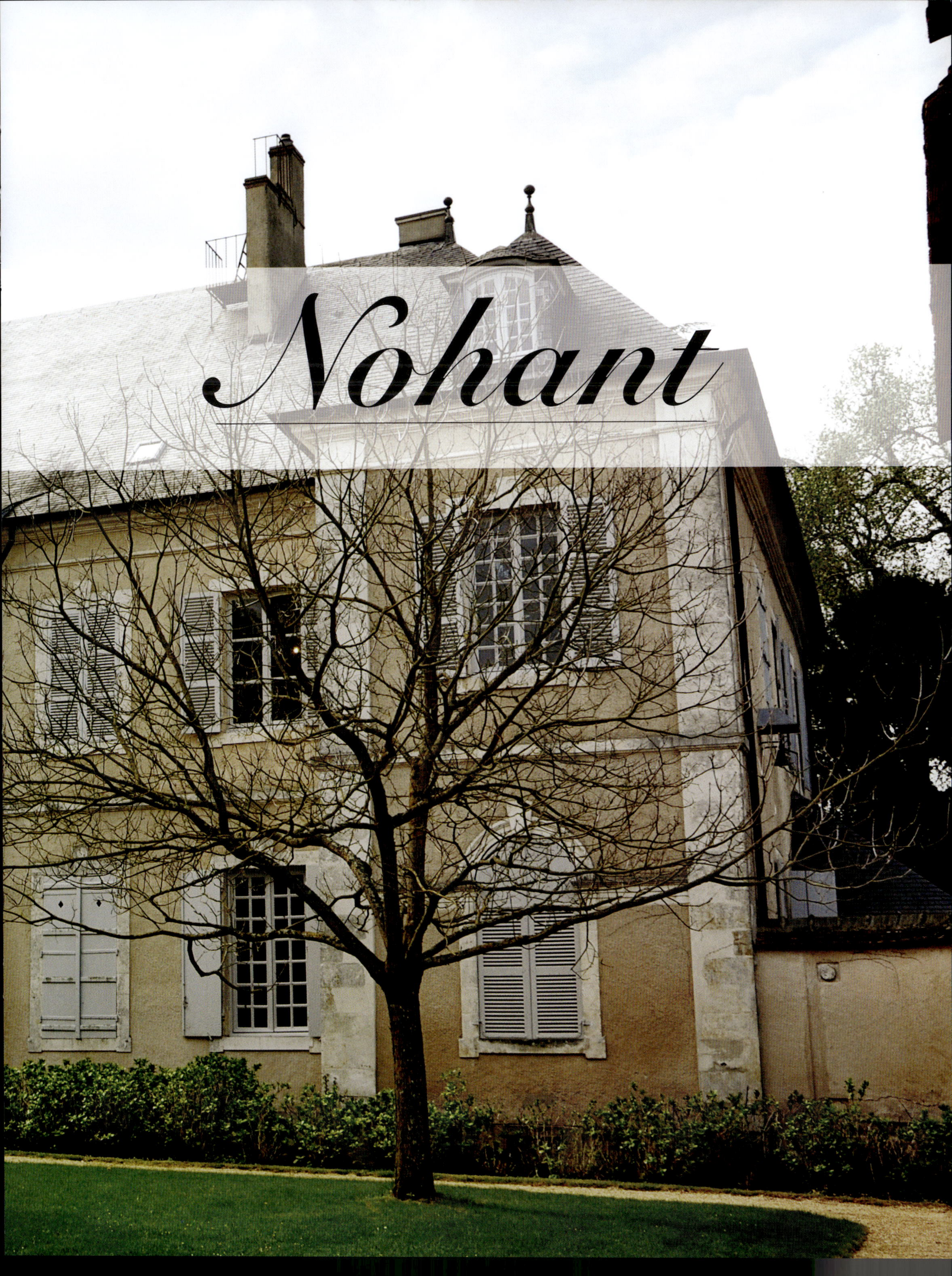

Fryderyk Chopin's first glimpse, in May 1839, of Nohant, which was to become his second home for the next seven years, filled his heart with wonder and joy. Spring, so welcome after the cold, damp months of Majorca, was now giving way to the promise of a long, hot summer, and he was looking forward to rest and recuperation in the sun with his beloved Angel, as he frequently referred to George Sand. The manor was a large, sturdy, four-square, two-storey house situated in the village of Nohant. It was set in its own fruit orchards and garden, in which Sand had planted two fir trees, which she named Maurice and Solange, after her children.

Sand had acquired Nohant, in the heart of the central French region of Berry, at great personal cost. Her grandmother, Marie-Aurore Dupin, had bought the manor in 1793, and it was there that Sand was brought up. In 1821, her grandmother died, leaving her the manor, and a small fortune. When her marriage to Casimir Dudevant broke down, Sand was forced to move out of her beloved Nohant and stay with her half-brother, Hippolyte Chatiron, at the Château de Montgivray close by. After five years of bitter legal acrimony, Sand finally regained possession of Nohant and her fortune from her husband.

Here we are, after a week's travelling. We arrived very comfortably. The countryside is beautiful, with nightingales and skylarks...

Fryderyk Chopin to Wojciech Grzymała
(Nohant, 2 June 1839)

In this remote and rural outback of central France Chopin and Sand could abandon all pretence, and openly lived together with the children as a family – something that would have been impossible in scandal-conscious Paris. Chopin and Sand occupied two large, adjacent upstairs rooms overlooking the garden at the back. For the next seven years they generally spent the winter and spring months in Paris, and the rest of the year they lived at Nohant. Solange and Maurice grew up, gipsy-fashion, as real children of Nature, as their mother largely let them run wild and free.

Our life at Nohant is the same as always, monotonous, quiet and agreeable. We eat outside, friends come to see us, we smoke, we chat, and in the evening, when they are gone, Chopin plays to me at twilight.

George Sand to a friend (Nohant, 15 June 1839)

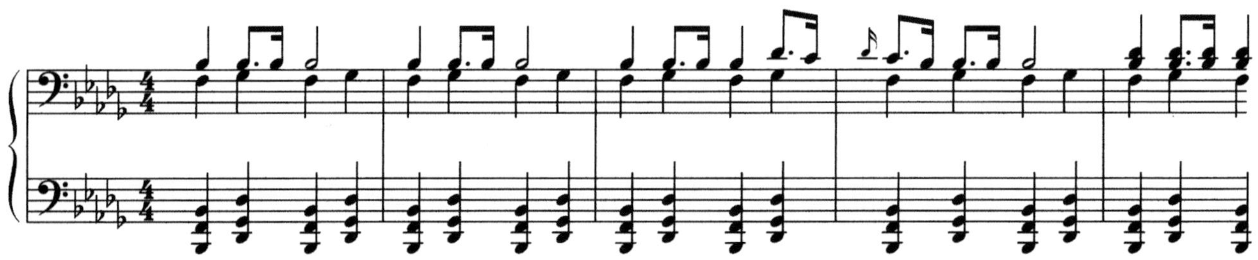

The Funeral March from Chopin's Sonata in B flat minor Op. 35 was written shortly after his arrival in Nohant.

← Nohant manor

Apart from Chopin, George Sand received many illustrious guests in her country house, including Liszt, Marie d'Agoult, Balzac and Flaubert, to mention just a few. The large window on the 2nd floor was in fact an artists' studio used by George Sand's painter friends such as Delacroix and later also by her son, Maurice.

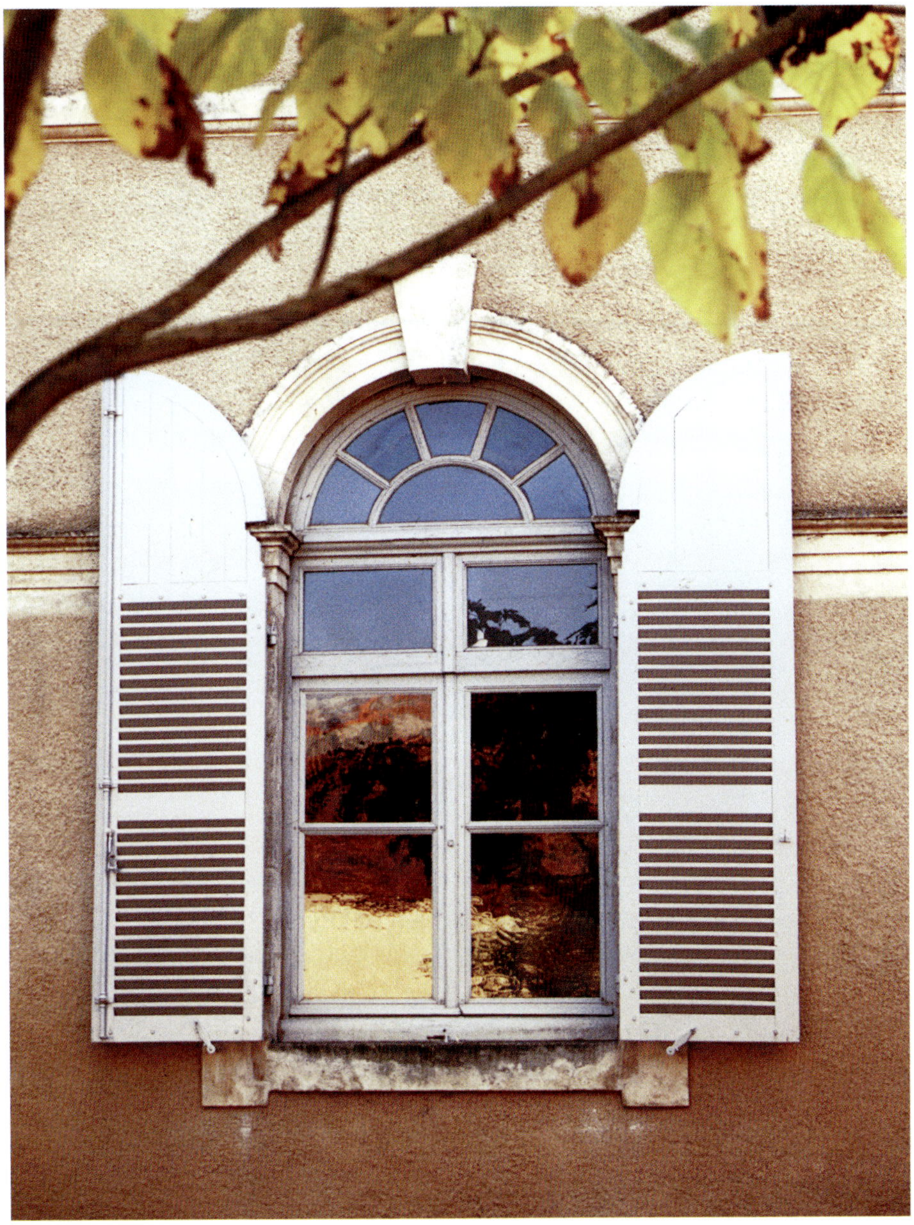

Nohant manor

A ground floor window reflecting the poetic charm of Nohant manor.

To Chopin and Sand the tranquillity of Nohant was an antidote to the bustle of Paris and its heady social and artistic scene. But as Chopin never fully recovered from his Majorcan winter, his continuing ill-health remained a constant source of anxiety for them both. It made Chopin restless, moody, and at times difficult to live with; when in Paris he longed for the quiet of the country, and while in Nohant he longed for the city and its society. Likewise, his creativity veered between periods of concentrated composition and bouts of indolence.

The leaves have not all fallen, only turned yellow, and the weather has been fine for a week; the Lady of the house takes advantage of this by planting and landscaping that courtyard in which, you will remember, there was dancing. There is to be a big lawn and flower beds.

Chopin to his sister Ludwika Jędrzejewiczowa (Nohant, 31 October 1844)

Life in Nohant was easy-going. The days were spent in creativity or in country pursuits, such as walking, going on river trips on the Indre and the Creuse, or – a ritual pastime for Sand every autumn without fail – the making of plum jam. At 5 o'clock a bell was rung summoning everyone, including such house guests as may have been staying, to dinner – which was often served outdoors. Among friends and family who came to stay were artist Eugène Delacroix, singer Pauline Viardot, and, in the summer of 1844, Chopin's sister, Ludwika, and her husband, Kalasanty Jędrzejewicz. They arrived at Nohant, at George Sand's instigation, in the wake of the death of Chopin's father in Warsaw, having first gone to stay at her apartment at 16 rue Pigalle which she had placed at their disposal. Their visit was a breath of fresh air to the very despondent Chopin.

Sometimes, through the window which opens onto the garden, strands of melody waft upwards from Chopin, and mingle with the songs of nightingales and the fragrance of roses. He never stops working.

Eugène Delacroix to a friend (Nohant, 7 June 1842)

Evenings were spent playing billiards or charades, the latter an activity in which Chopin excelled. He was a very gifted and amusing mimic: as a teenager in Poland he used to take part in amateur theatricals to hilarious effect. He also involved himself wholeheartedly in the puppet shows in the miniature theatre that Maurice had established. For these he improvised music on the piano, initially a Pleyel which Sand had originally bought for the benefit of Franz Liszt, who was there in 1837. Chopin later ordered his own, once again from Pleyel, which arrived on 9 August 1841.

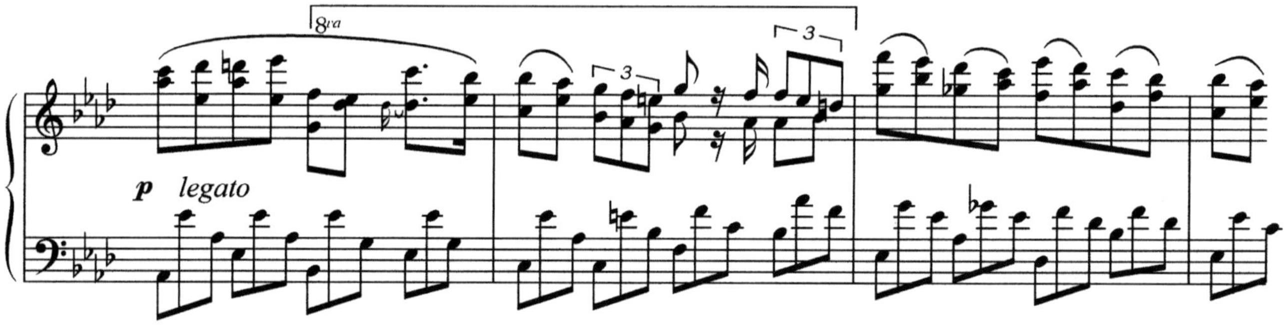

The main theme of Chopin's expansive Fantaisie in F minor Op. 49, dates from Nohant 1841.

Nohant manor

A rear view of the manor with steps leading down from the dining room into the gardens where George Sand and her family and Chopin often ate dinner al fresco on balmy summer evenings.

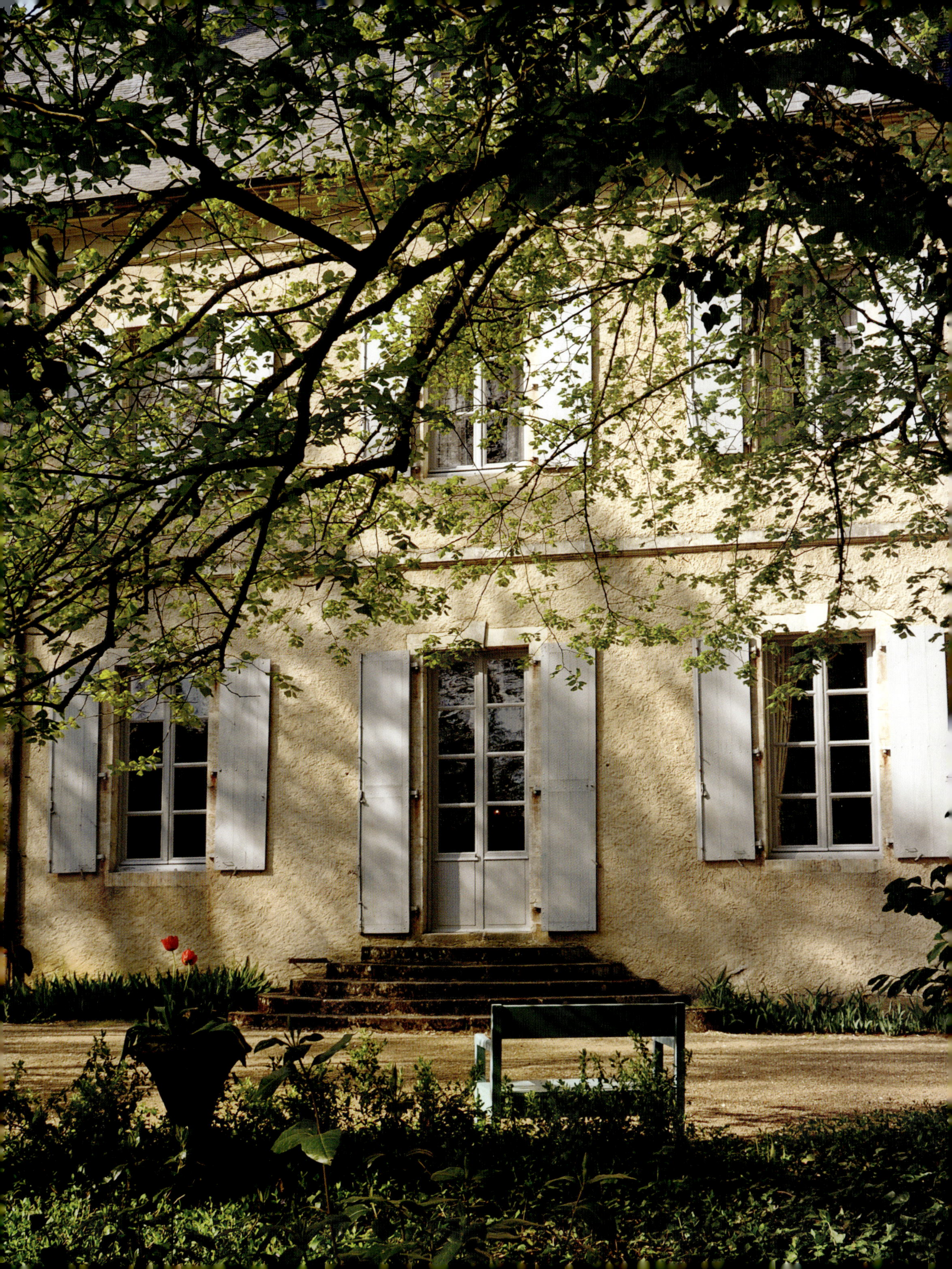

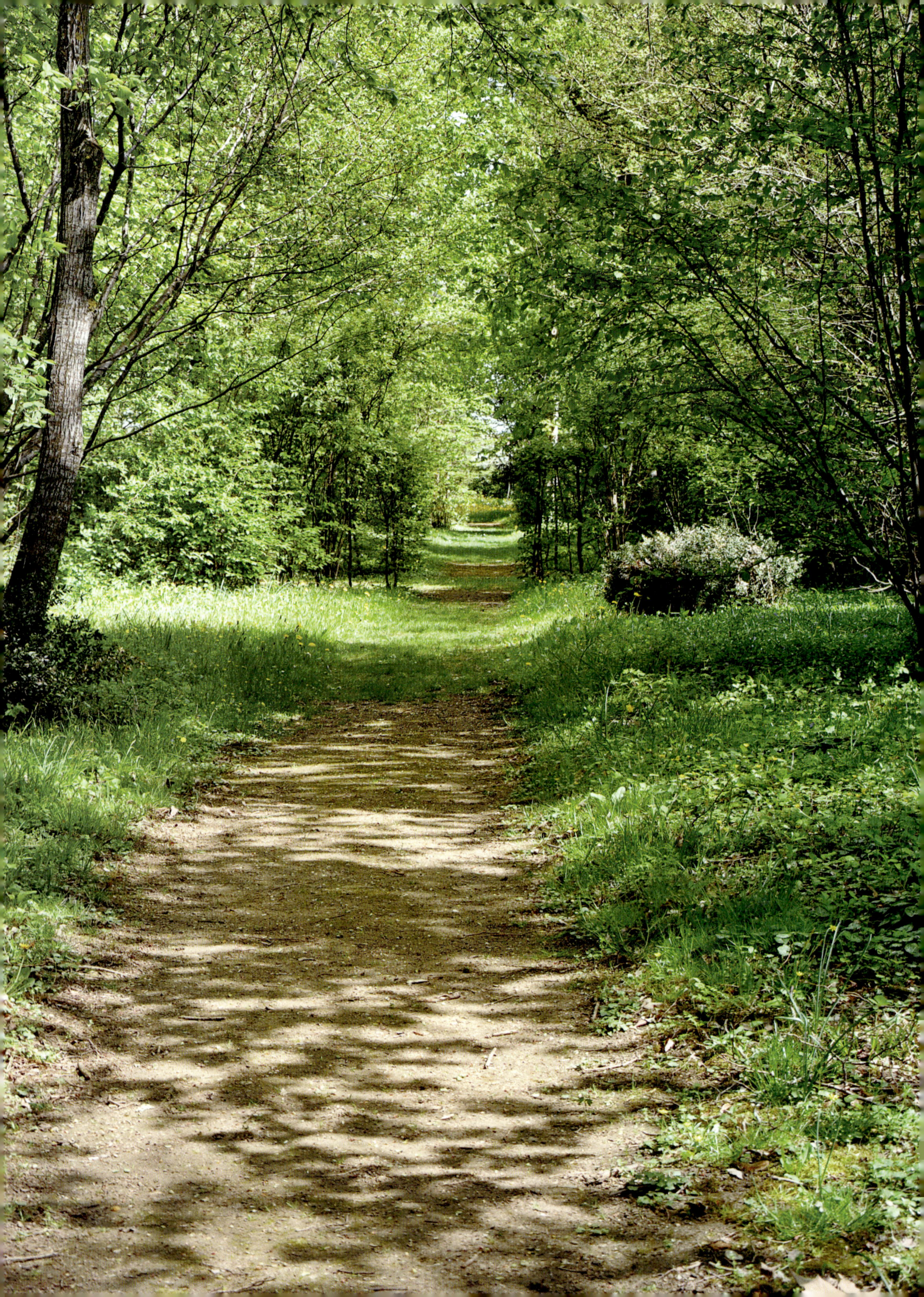

Walking was one of Sand's greatest passions. She would sometimes set off at 3 o'clock in the morning for a long ramble through the Berry countryside, leaving Chopin to wake up to his piano and manuscript paper. The idyllic setting provided him with inspiration for his creative genius – despite bouts of depression and self-doubt. He often joined Sand on such shorter excursions as would not tax his strength too much, notably to Sand's half-brother Hyppolite Chatiron at Montgivray, an hour's walk away, and the small market town of La Châtre was only seven kilometres from Nohant. Sometimes they walked further afield to Sarzay, a village with an imposing mediaeval keep of five round towers, where traditional country fêtes, replete with bagpipe bands, folk dancing and local produce, were a regular attraction.

As more ambitious excursions, Sand organised carriage-drives to more distant beauty spots or places of interest. Of these the most spectacular was undoubtedly the gorge of the young Creuse at Crozant, where Maurice, who never went anywhere without his pencils and sketch pad, found himself in his element. Further south, beyond Bussac, were the ancient monolithic Pierres Jâumatres, perched on top of a mountain commanding breathtaking views of Berry to the north, and the Limousin to the south. Chopin, not up to this particular challenge, resorted to the use of a donkey for the climb to the top.

Several days ago we made an excursion in this neighbourhood to see the banks of the Creuse; the lad did drawings of the views. It was a very successful trip, with friends who are neighbours.

Fryderyk Chopin to Wojciech Grzymała
(Nohant, October 1843)

To the west of Nohant were the ruins of Fontgombault Abbey, situated on the banks of a more mature, luxuriant Creuse near Le Blanc, another favourite destination. To the north, Châteauroux was the region's commercial hub, and the main source of essential supplies at Nohant.

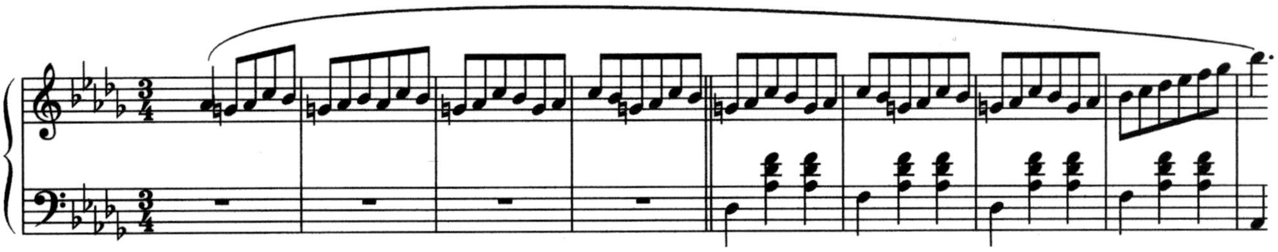

Chopin's Waltz in D flat Op. 64 No 1, the so-called Minute Waltz, was said to have been inspired by a dog chasing its tail.

The park in Nohant manor

A quiet tree-lined path, ideal for a leisurely stroll by George Sand and Chopin.

During those heady years, Sand wrote over 20 literary works, including novels, novelettes, plays and her account of the Majorcan experience, *A Winter in Majorca*. Chopin played the piano and composed some of his greatest and most mature works. These included the towering second and third Sonatas, the grandiose Fantaisie in F minor, the flowing Barcarolle and the wispy and elusive Berceuse. The peace and tranquillity of the Berry nights gave rise to 7 Nocturnes; with his 15 Mazurkas, 2 Polonaises and the introspective Polonaise-Fantaisie in A flat Op. 61, he explored the deepest recesses of his essential Polishness.

By 1845 the idyll was becoming tarnished. Chopin's health deteriorated and Sand was beginning to tire of her consumptive genius. Maurice, now 22 and anxious to assert his own authority on the house, had begun to resent Chopin, who, meanwhile, had become close to Solange. She confided in him as though he were her father, something which Sand resented. Solange had embarked on an affair with the sculptor Auguste Clésinger, a liaison that her mother considered unsuitable, but which nevertheless led to marriage. Chopin sided with Solange in the dispute, which effectively caused the long-term relationship to come to an acrimonious end.

I feel strange here this year; often in the morning I go to the next room, but there's no one there. Sometimes I seem to fill the place of an acquaintance who comes for a few days.

Fryderyk Chopin to his sister Ludwika Jędrzejewiczowa
(Nohant, 20 July 1845)

On 11 November 1846 Chopin returned to Paris from Nohant, never to return.

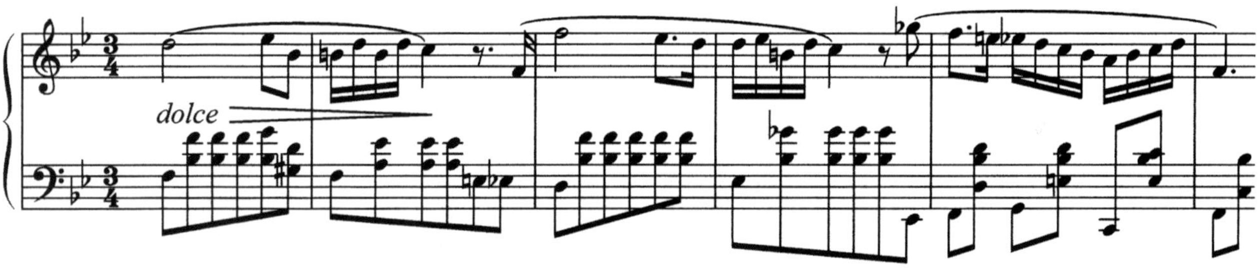

Chopin's rhapsodic Polonaise-Fantaisie in A flat Op. 61 was his last major work.

All the Chopin sites associated with Nohant and its environs exist to this day. The Abbey of Fontgombault has been restored, and is now the home of a Benedictine order, and Nohant itself, its room layout slightly altered, is now France's premier George Sand Museum.

Entrance to the gardens at Nohant manor

Today the manor is open to the public. Visiting the gardens and park during most of the year is free. However, there are no traces of Chopin, as Sand eliminated these after their separation in 1846.

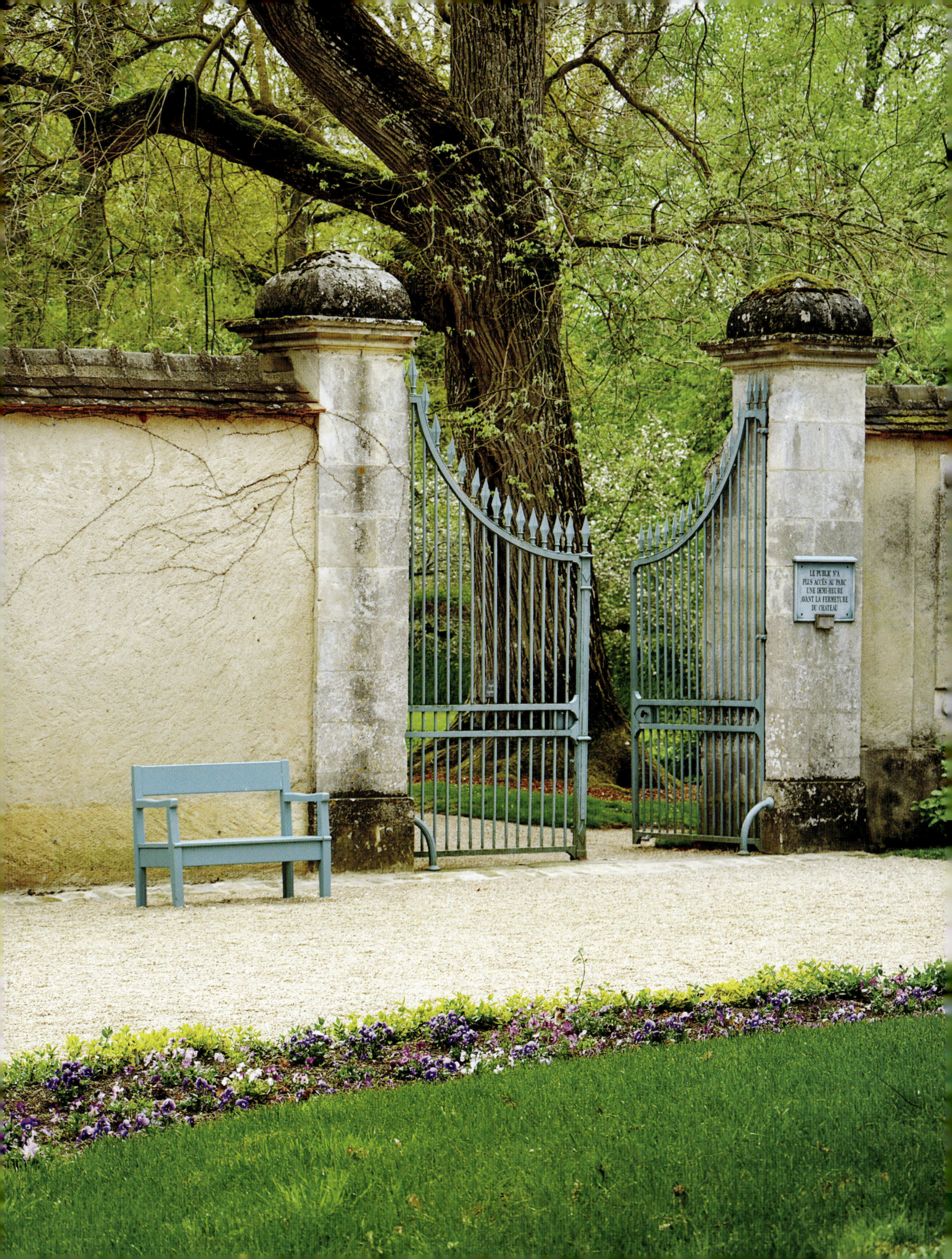
LE PUBLIC N'A
PLUS ACCÈS AU PARC
UNE DEMI-HEURE
AVANT LA FERMETURE
DU CHATEAU

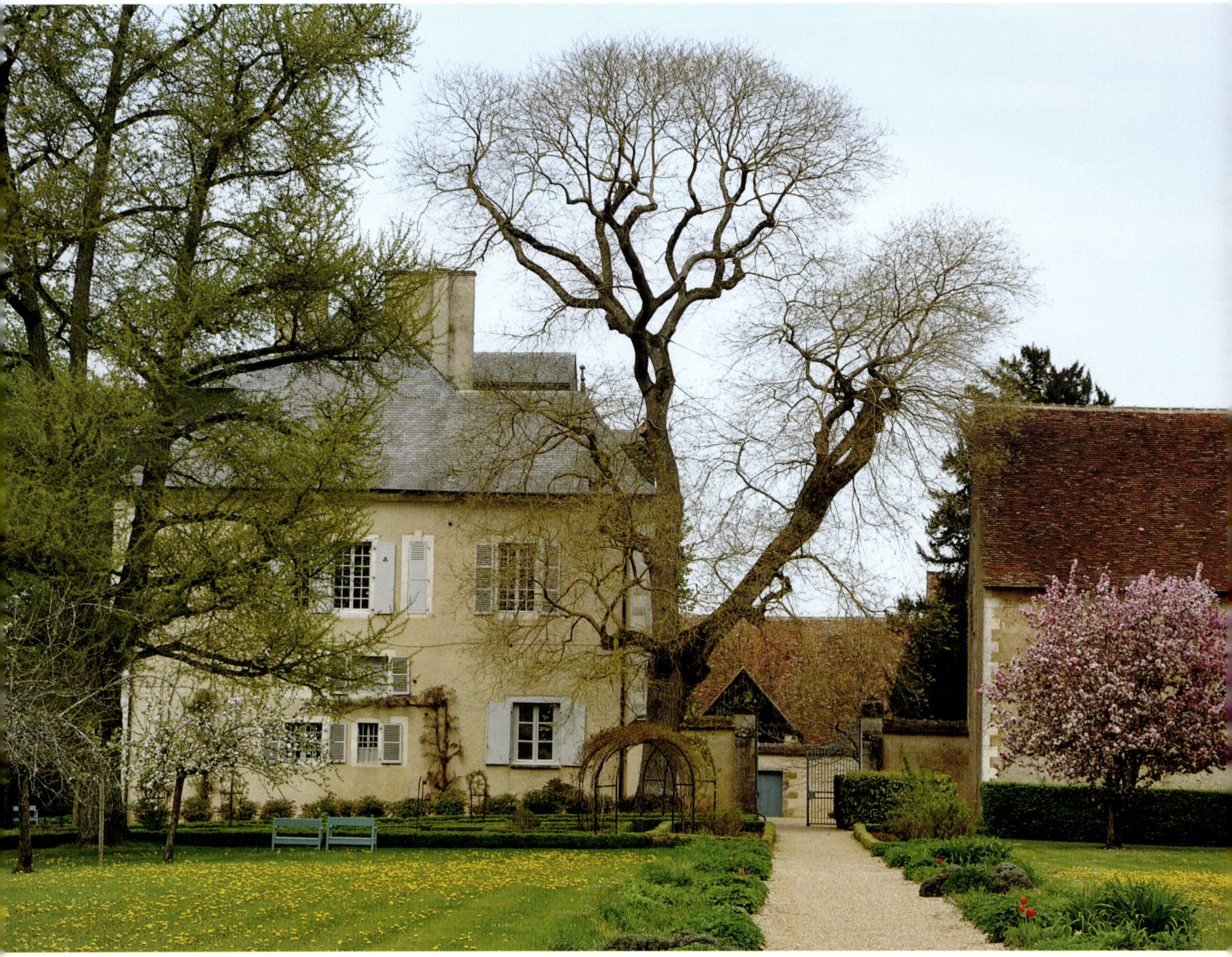

The east side of Nohant manor

This overlooks the garden and orchard where centuries-old trees stand guard over the romantic setting.

→ The gardens at Nohant manor

A detail of the gardens in the spring evokes an air of romance.

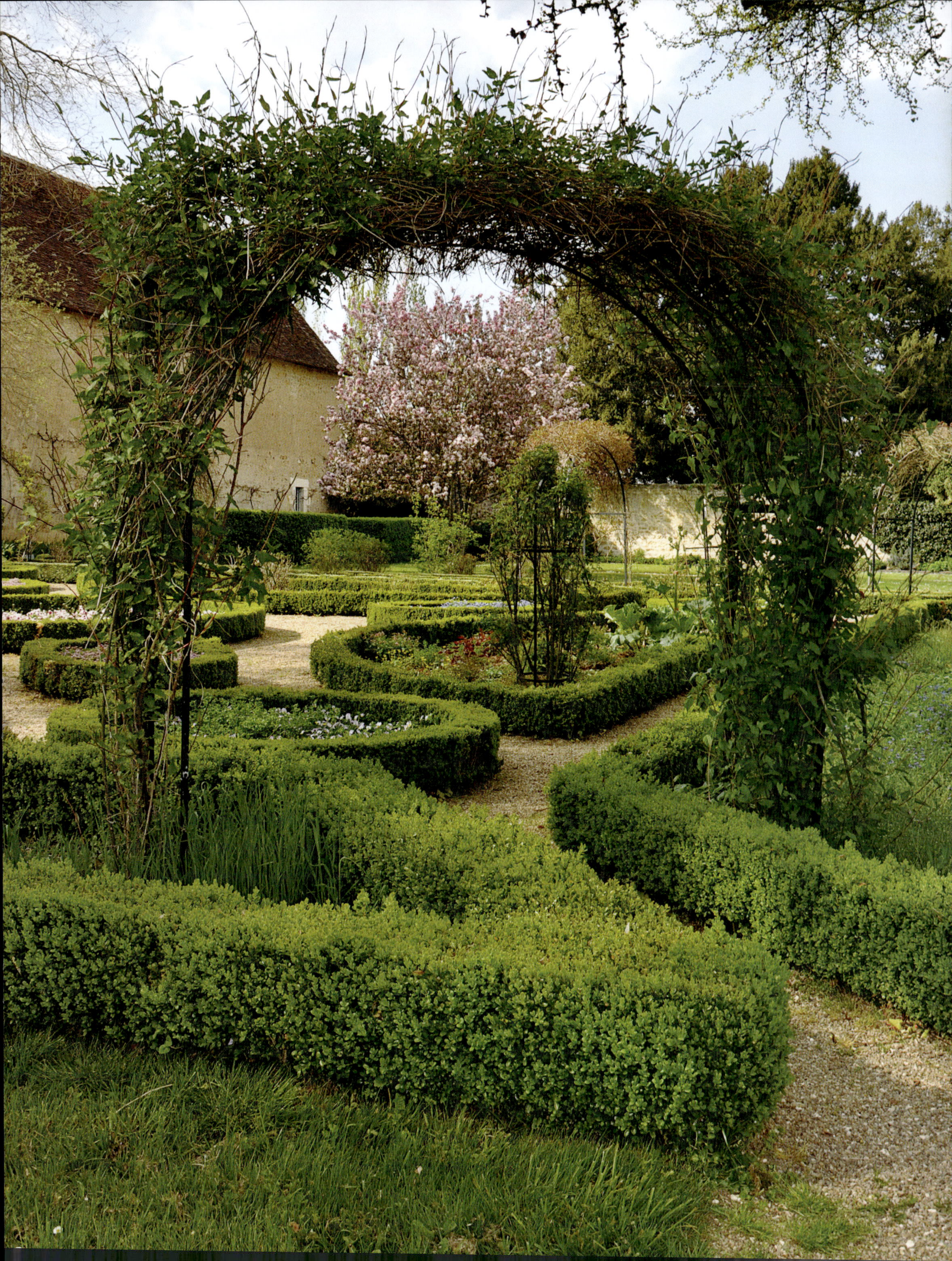

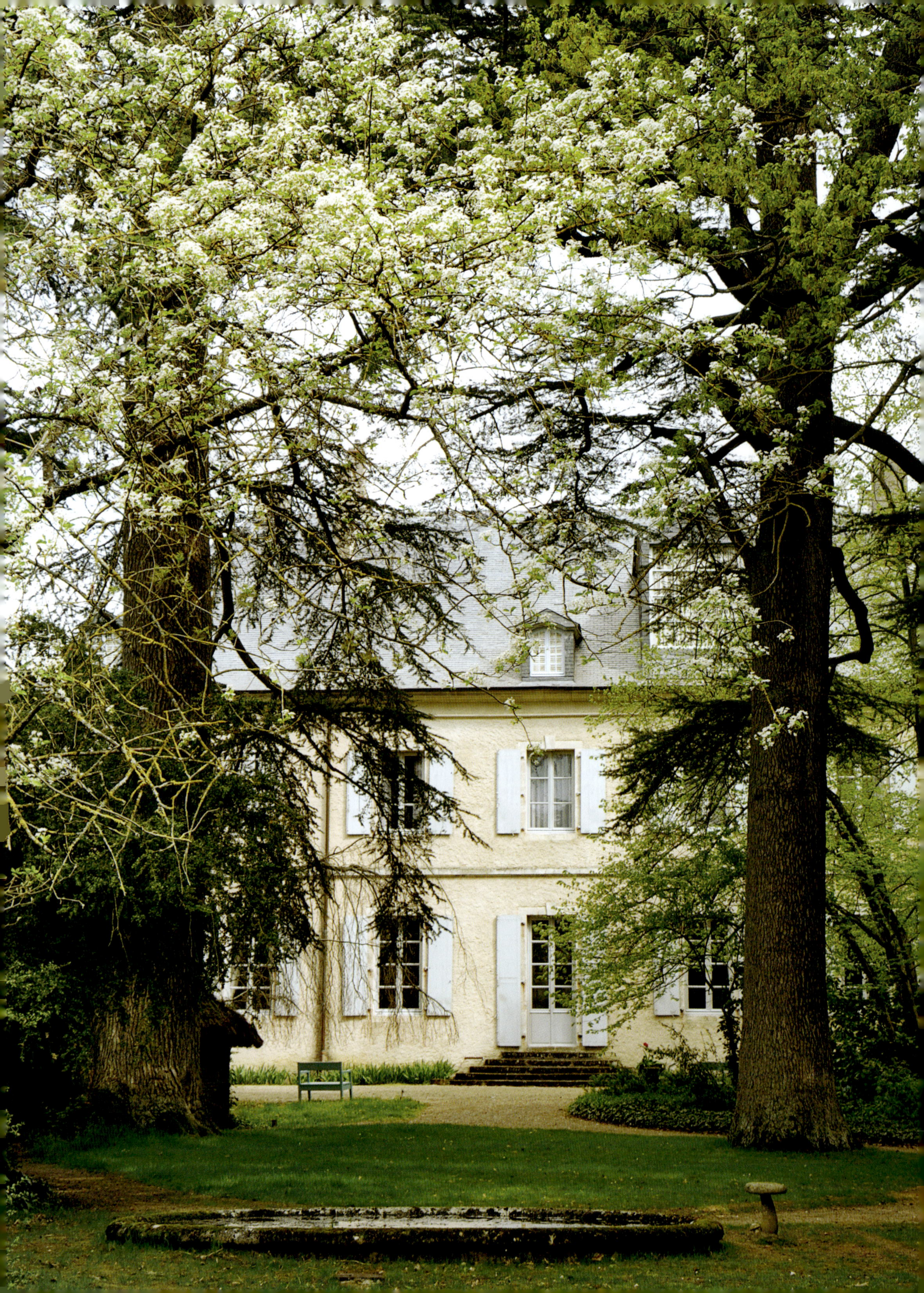

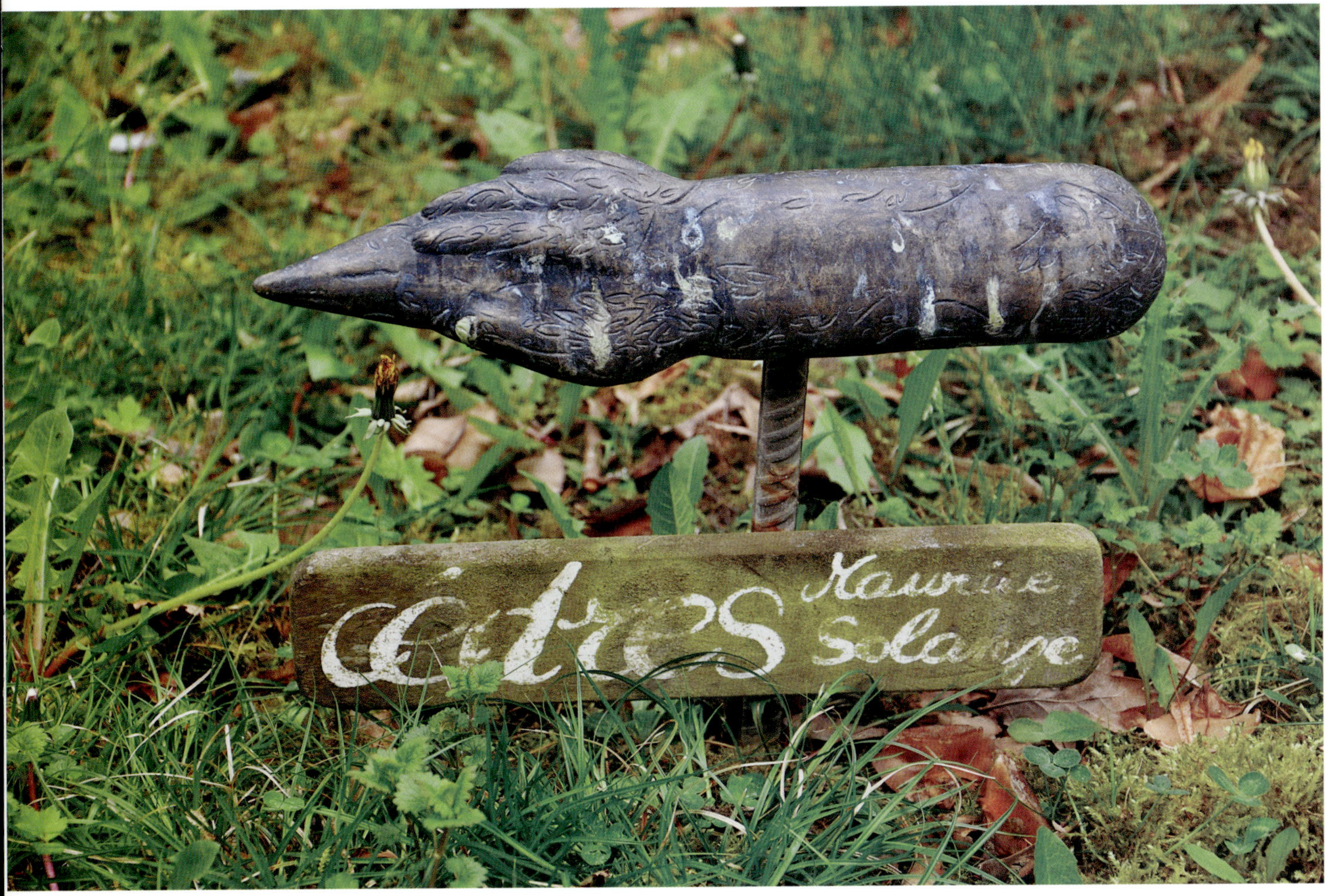

The garden at Nohant manor

A sign points to the two cedars, now well over 160 years old, which were planted by George Sand, who named them Maurice and Solange, after her children.

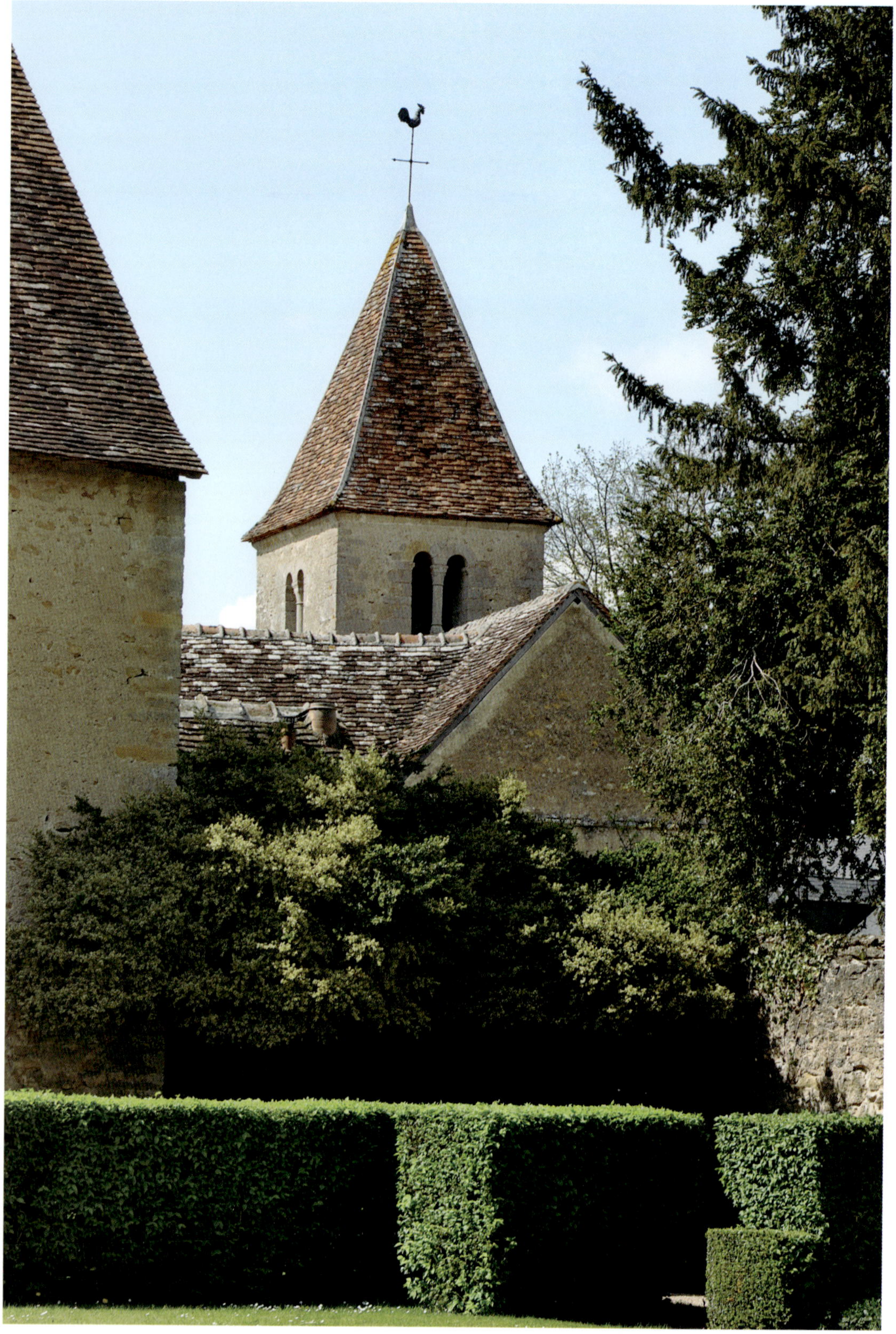

The church of Ste. Anne

The small romanesque church is situated just outside the main entrance to the Nohant manor and can be seen from the gardens.

→ An old cross and a covered entrance are special features of this little gem as well as the stark interior.

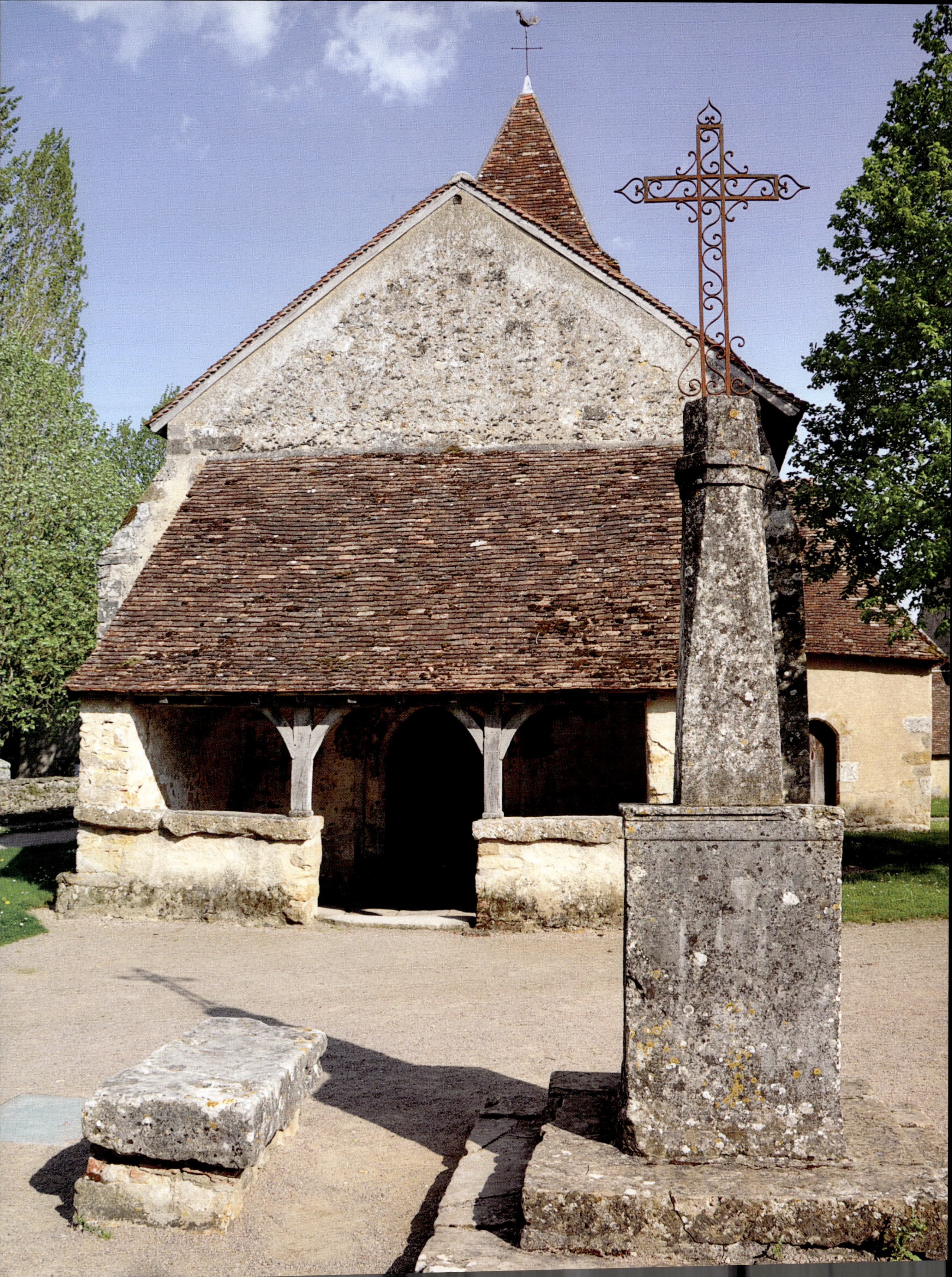

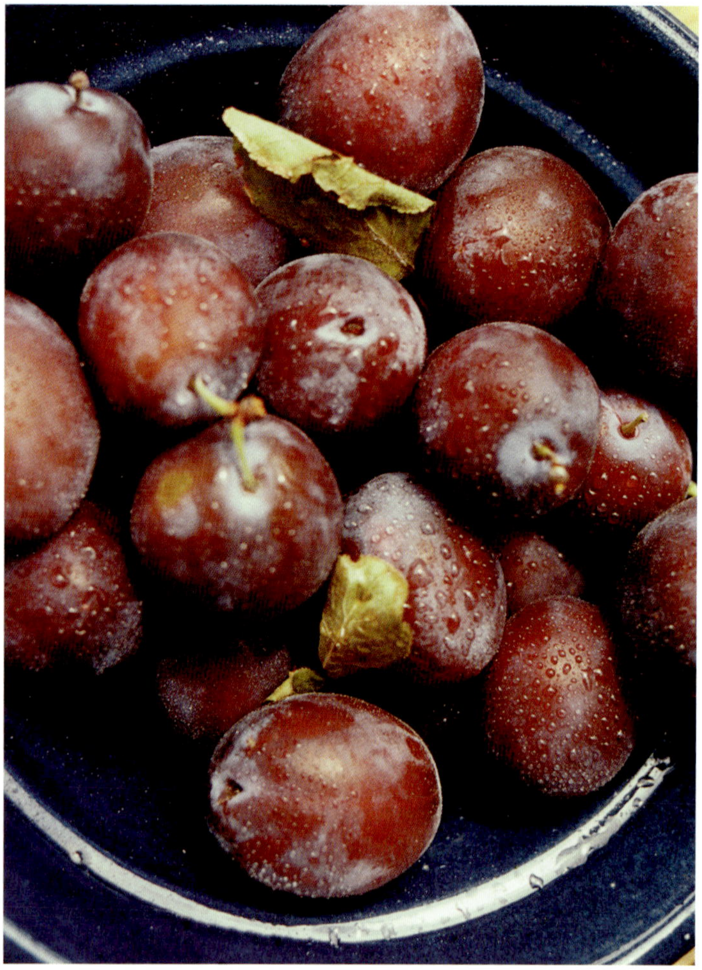

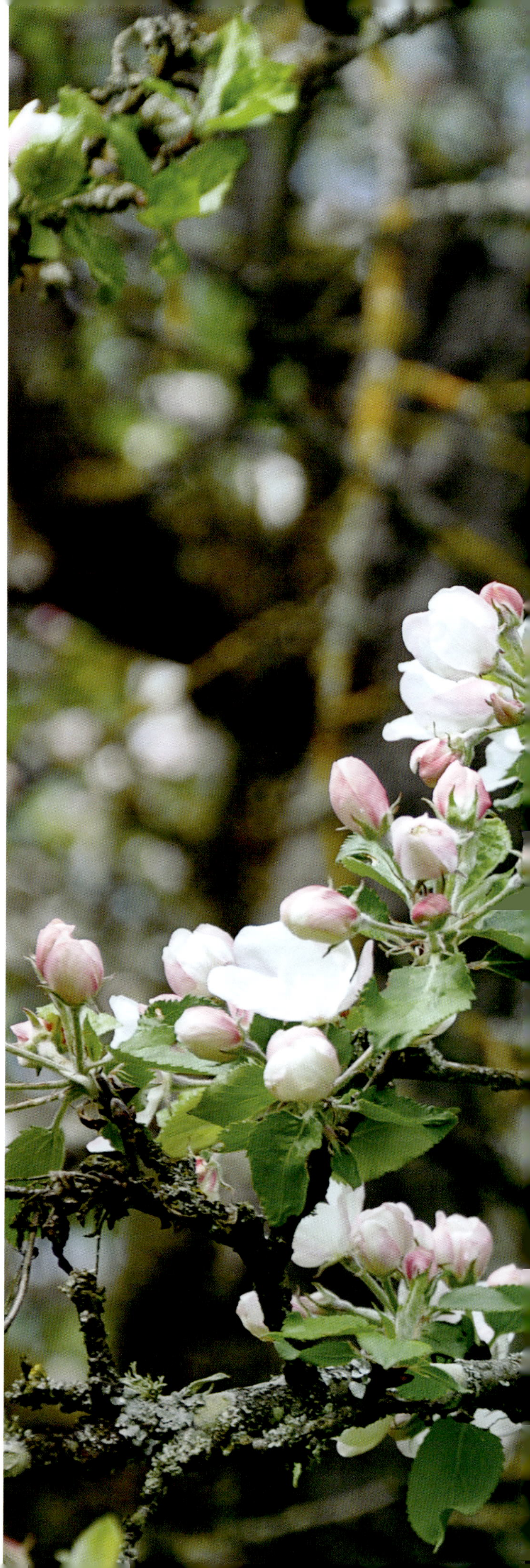

The garden at Nohant manor
Orchard with plum trees in full bloom.
It was George Sand's unwarering ritual to make plum jam every autumn.

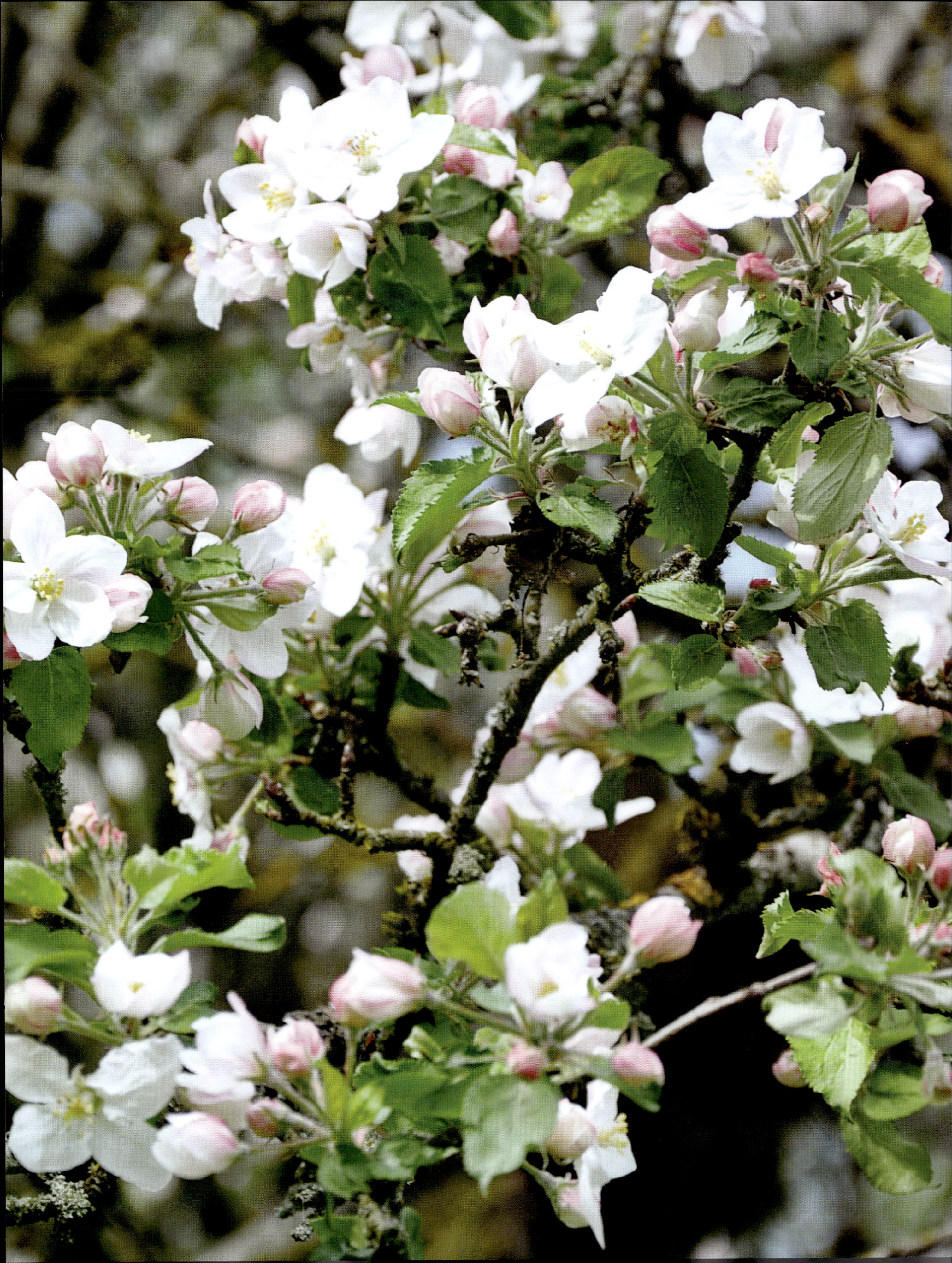

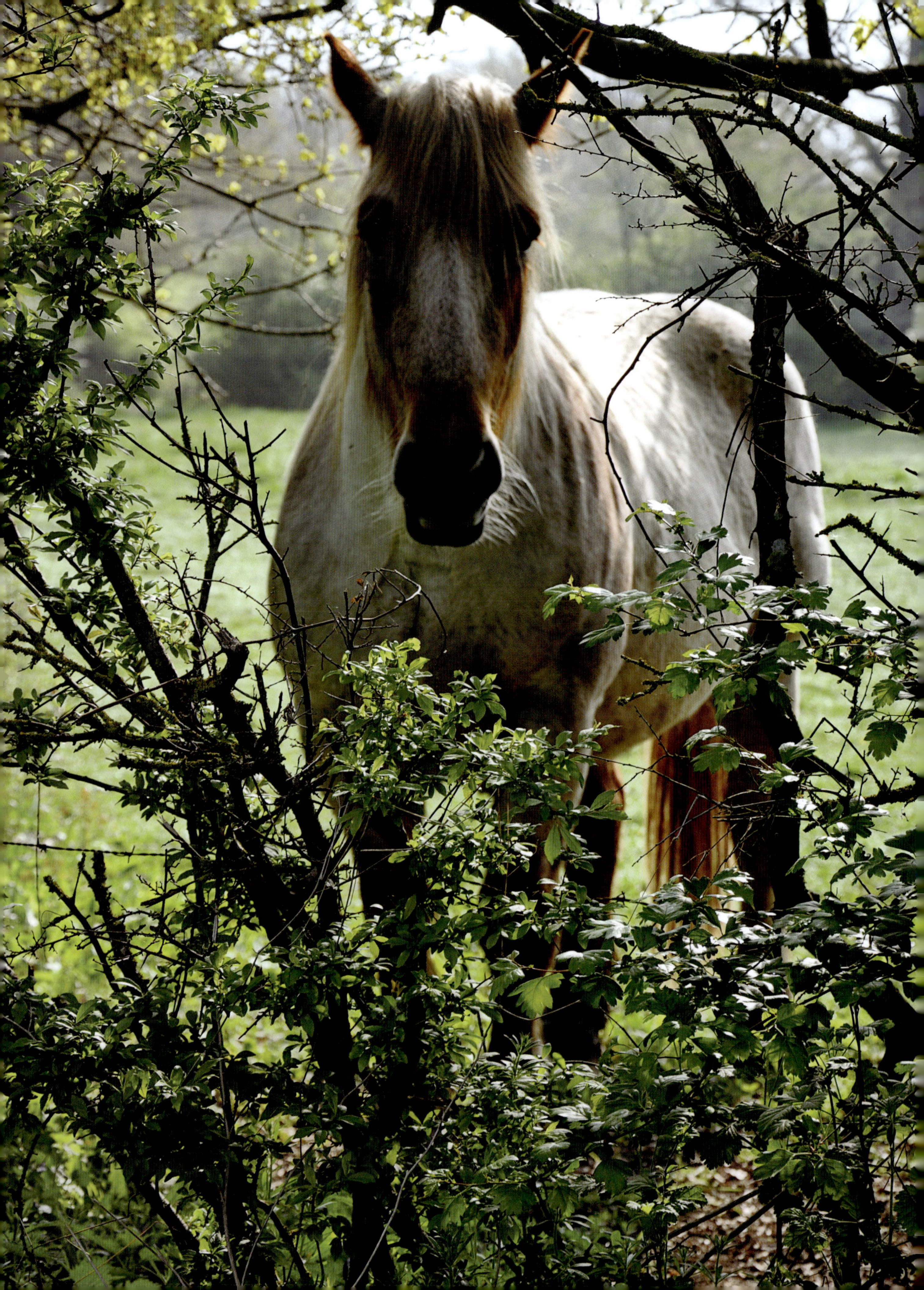

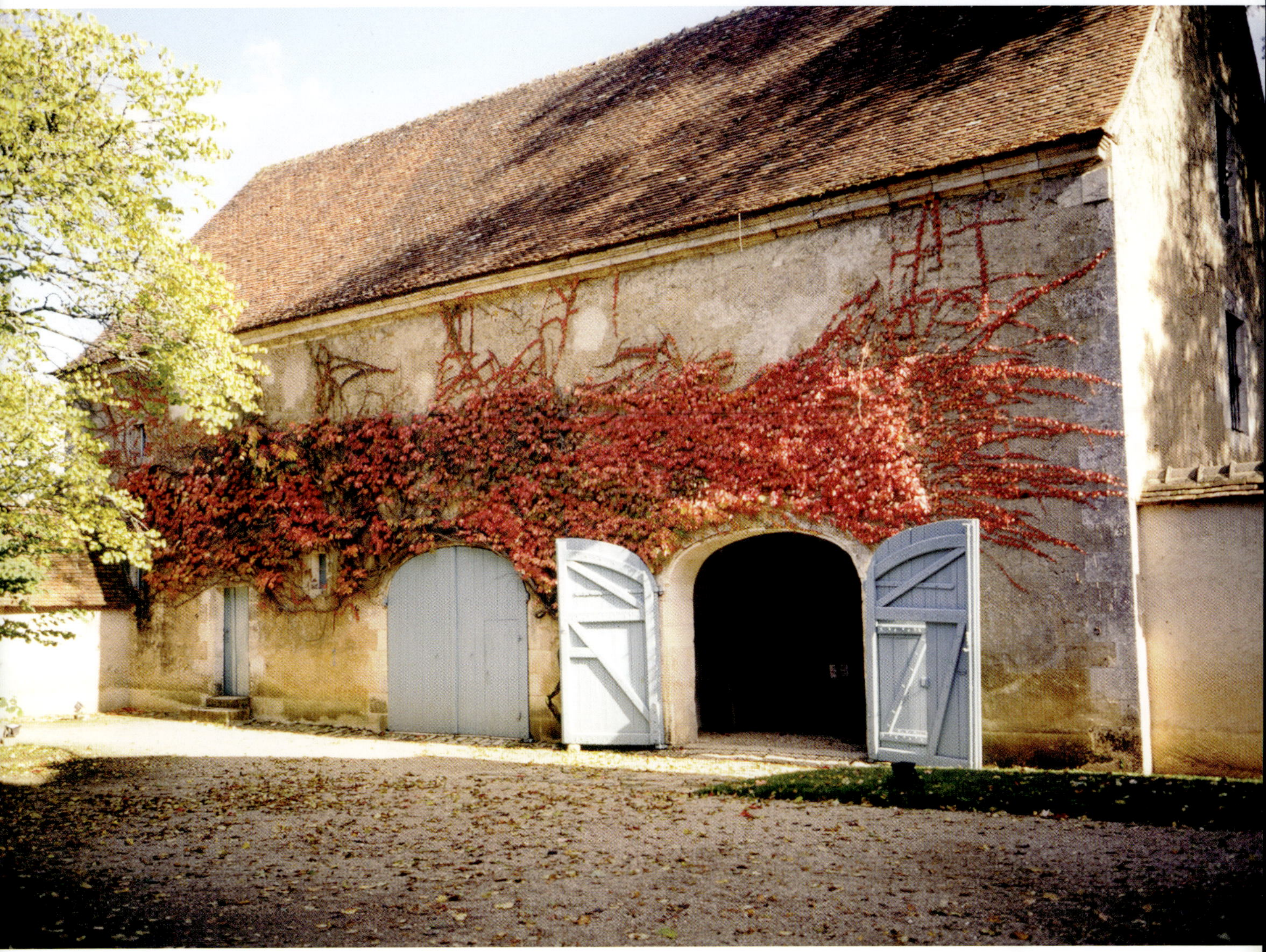

Nohant manor

The former coach house and stables, now the museum shop.

→ **Nohant Area**

An ancient tree-lined road in Berry.

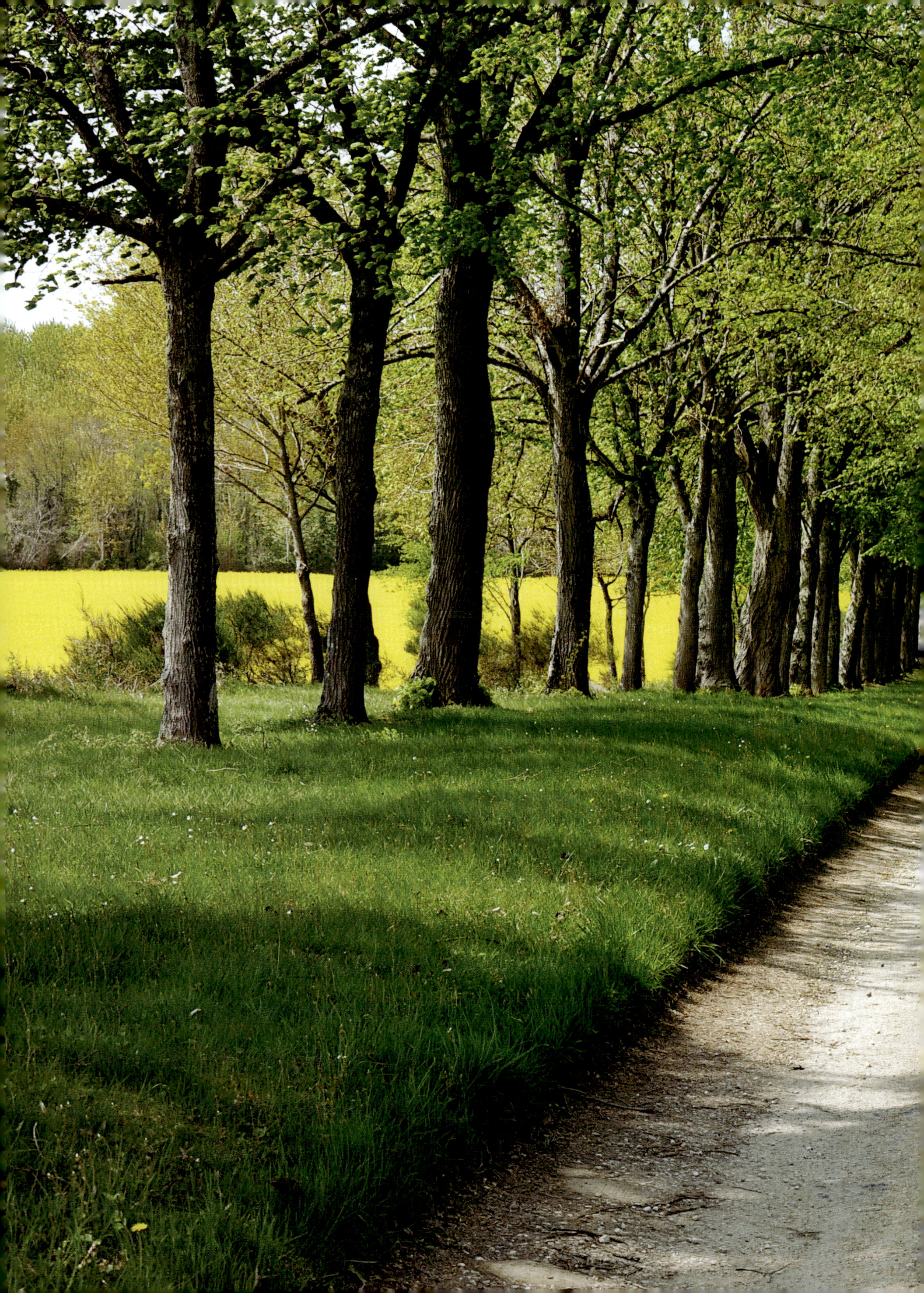

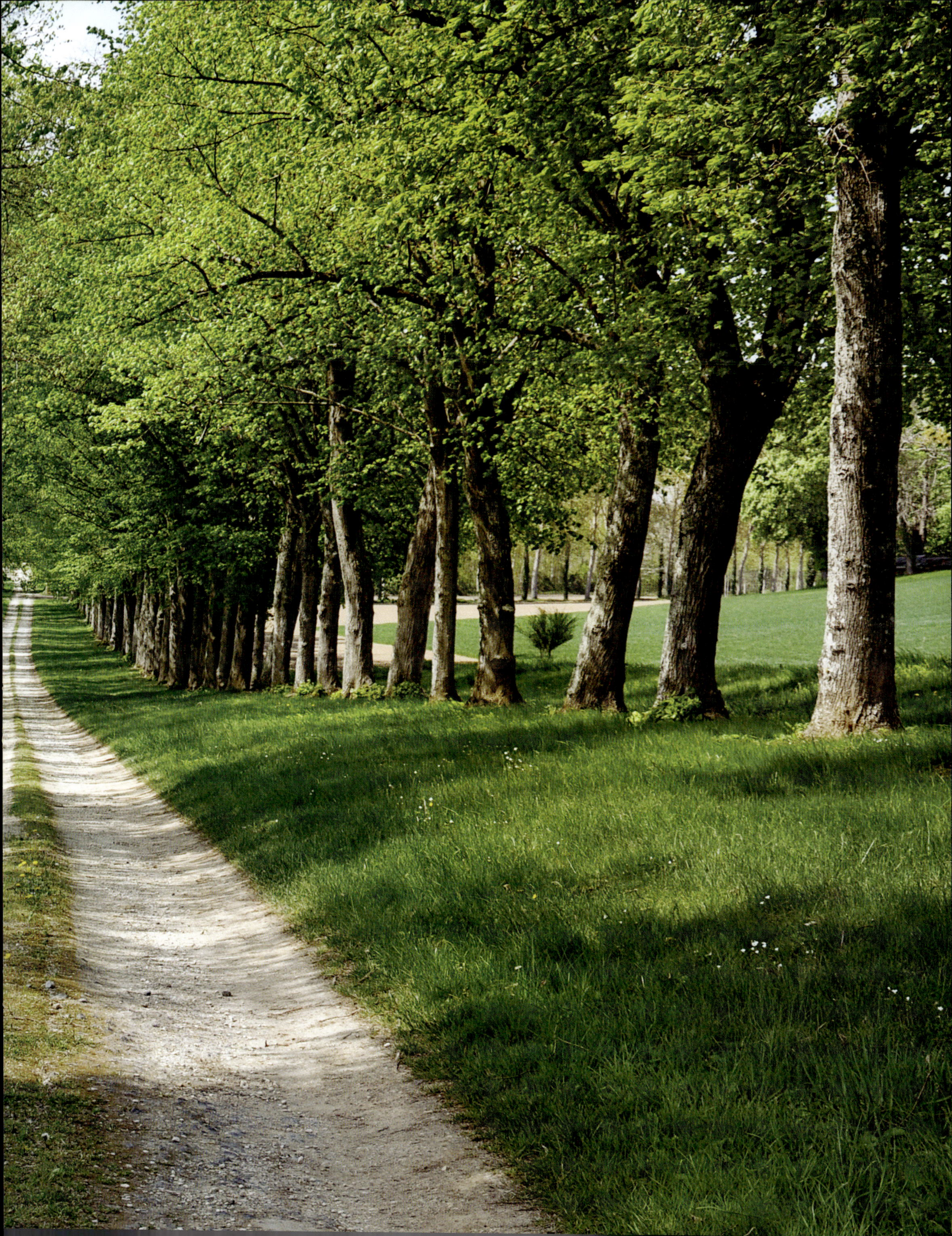

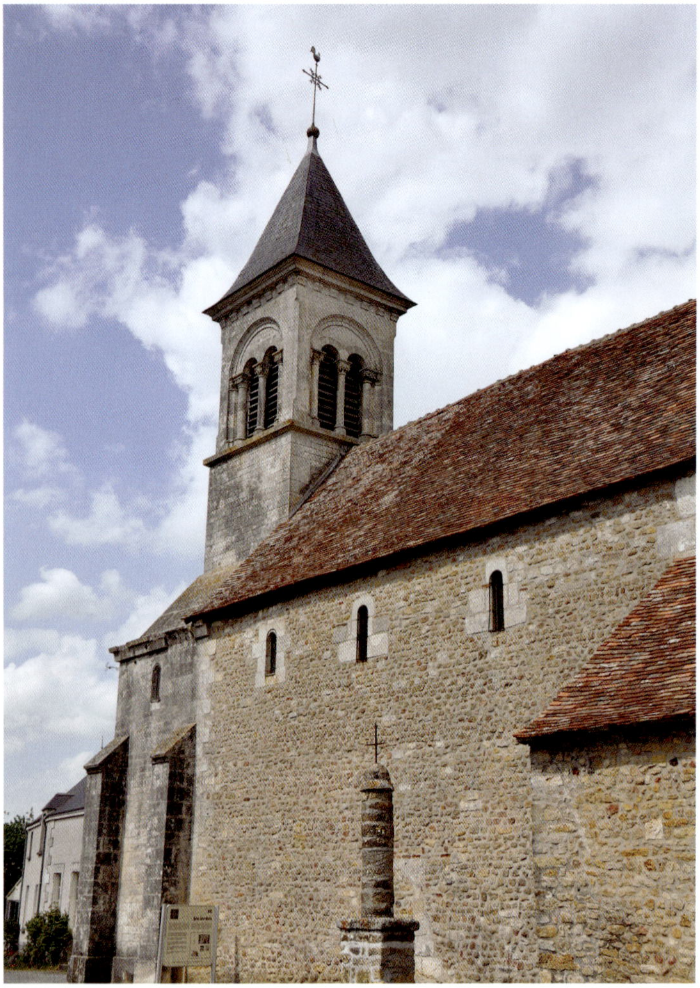

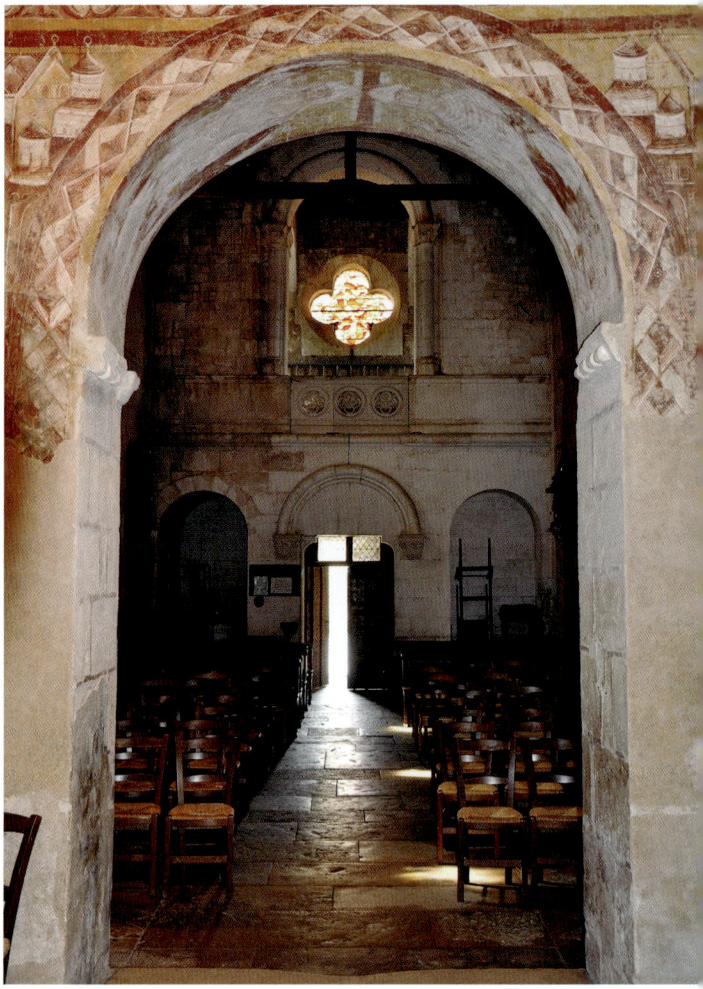

Nohant Vic (Indre)

The village of Nohant Vic is less than a kilometre from Nohan manor. The Church of Saint-Martin de Vic, which dates back to the eleventh century, has some remarkable frescoes from the twelfth century. These were only discovered by chance in 1849 by the Abbé Perigaud, who, with the help of George Sand and her connections, was consequently able to have get the church officially classified as a "monument historique."

→ Château de Culan (Cher)

The Château de Culan, situated some 15 kilometres from Nohant, is one of the oldest French medieval castles still inhabited to this day. The present château dates from the twelfth to the fifteenth centuries, with added Renaissance embellishments. Among the famous people who have stayed here are Joan of Arc, King Louis XI, Madame de Sévigné, as well as George Sand and Chopin, most likely in the summer of 1843.

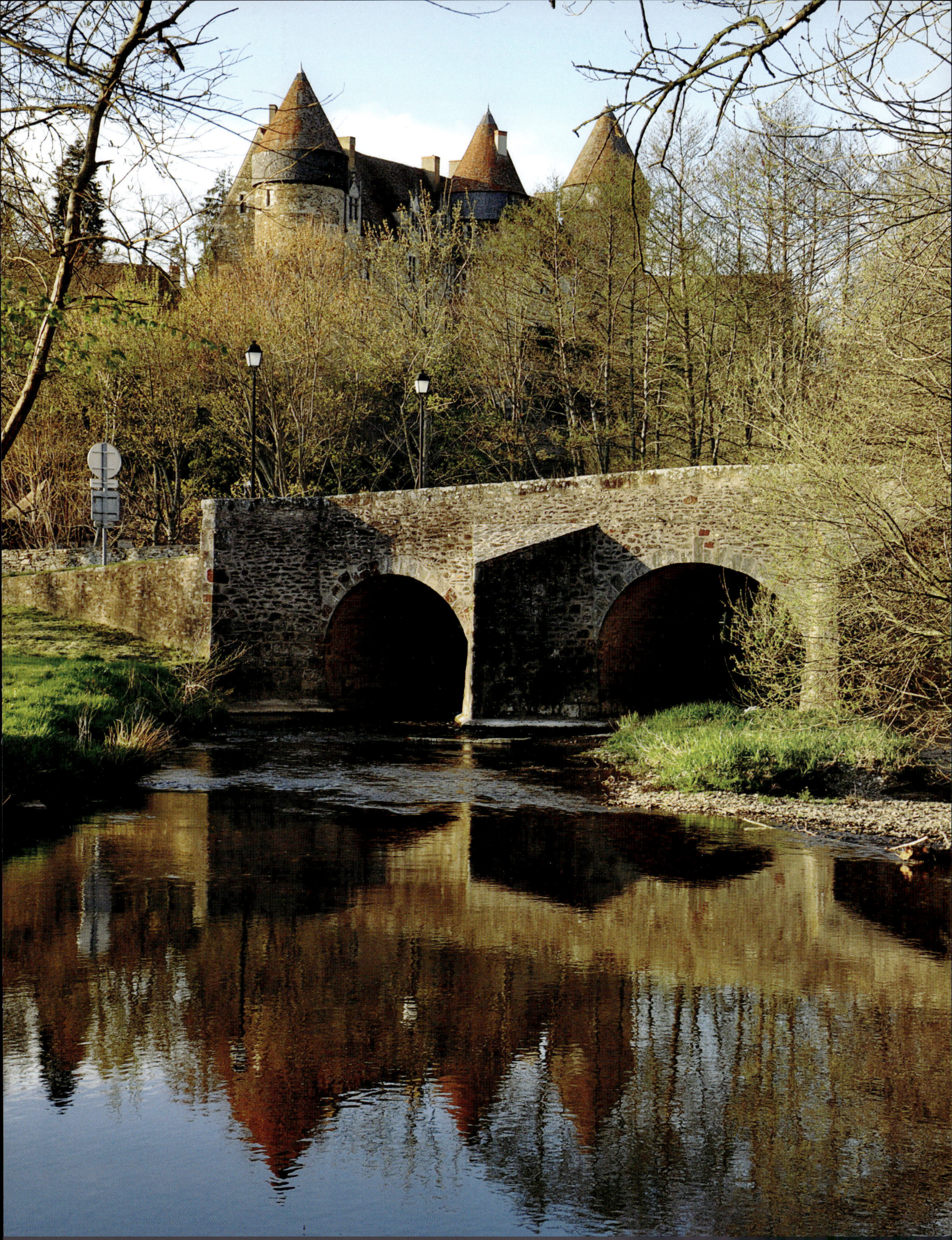

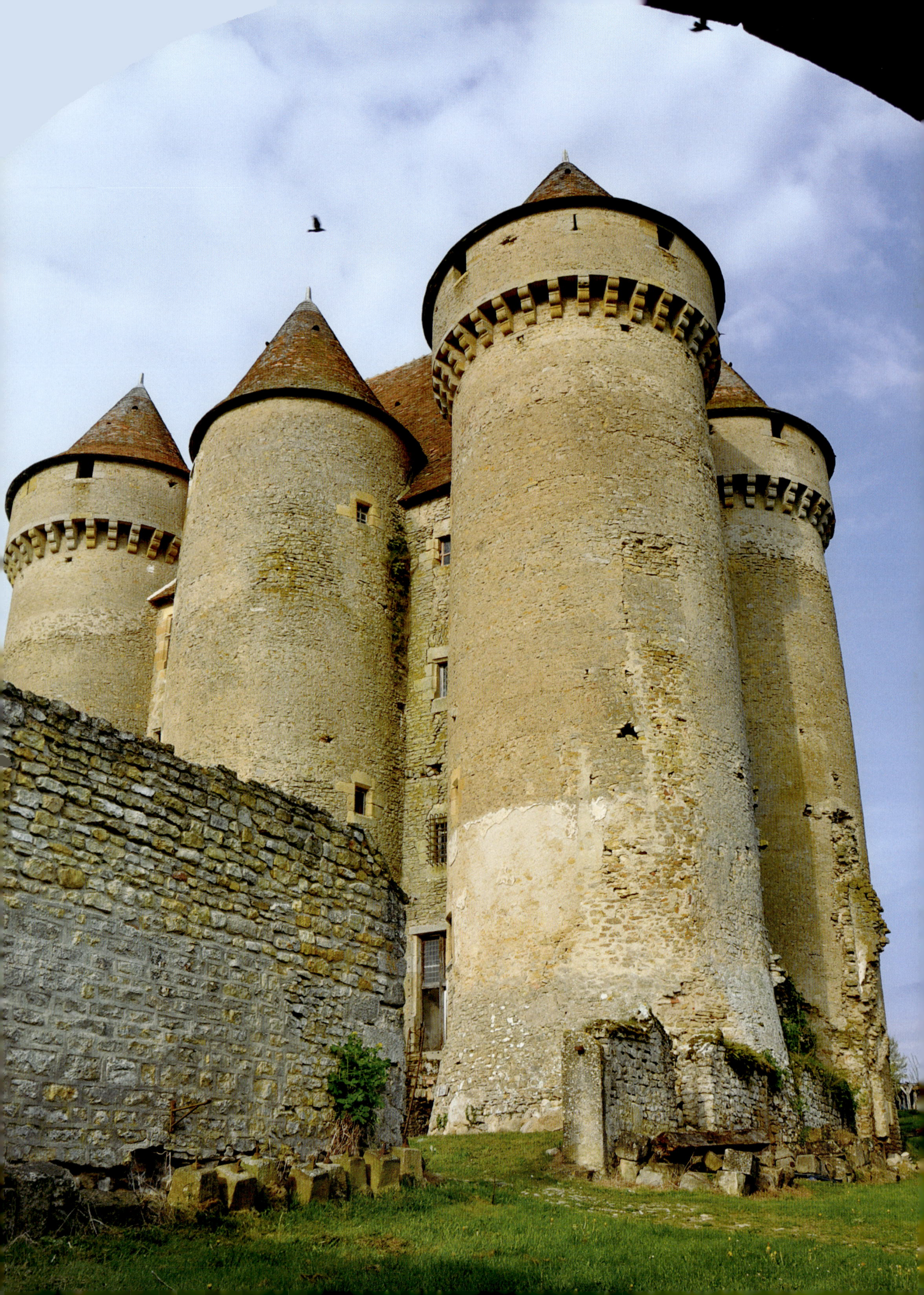

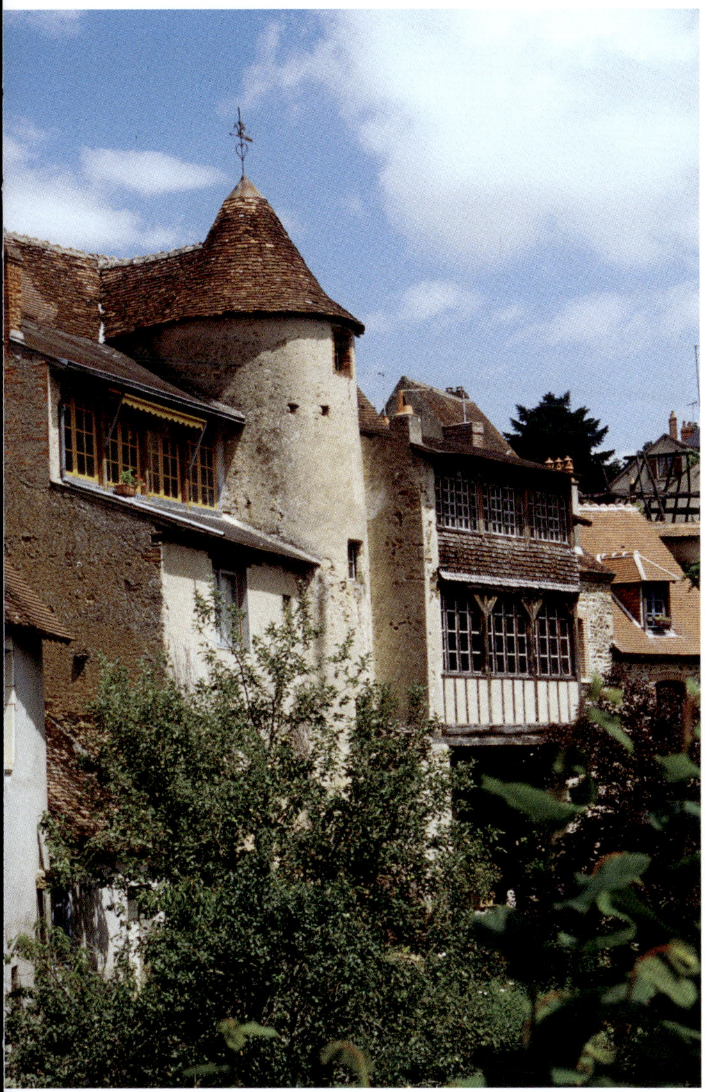

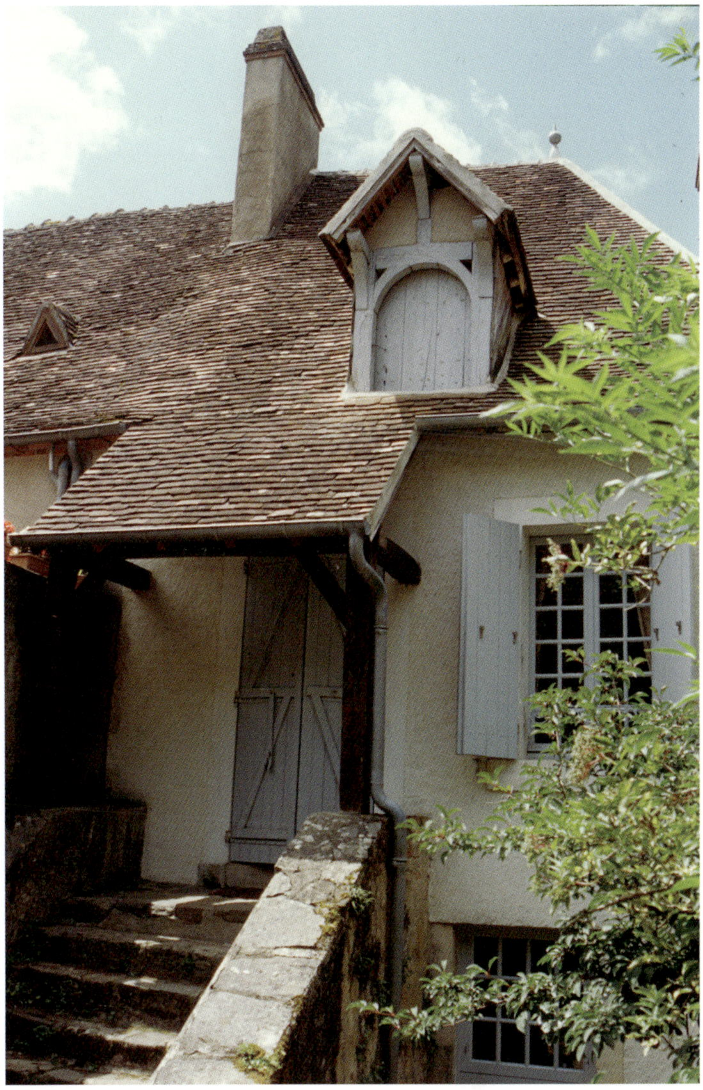

Gargilesse-Dampierre (Indre)

One of Sand's favourite excursions was to Gargilesse-Dampierre, on the River Creuse about 40 kilometres to the south west of Nohant. It entailed an overnight stop in the house pictured in the photo on the right and identified thanks to a painting by J. Veron.

← Château de Sarzay (Indre)

The Château de Sarzay, about 5 kilometres from Nohant, is an imposing medieval fortress comprising originally 38 round towers and 3 drawbridges, built in the fourteenth century. It served as one of the main defences against the English invaders between 1337 and 1453, and is today among France's most important monuments. It was one of Sand's and Chopin's favourite outings, where traditional fêtes, with folk dancing and bagpipes were a ... Sand's novel *Le Meunier d'Angibault* was inspired by the Château de ... correspondence.

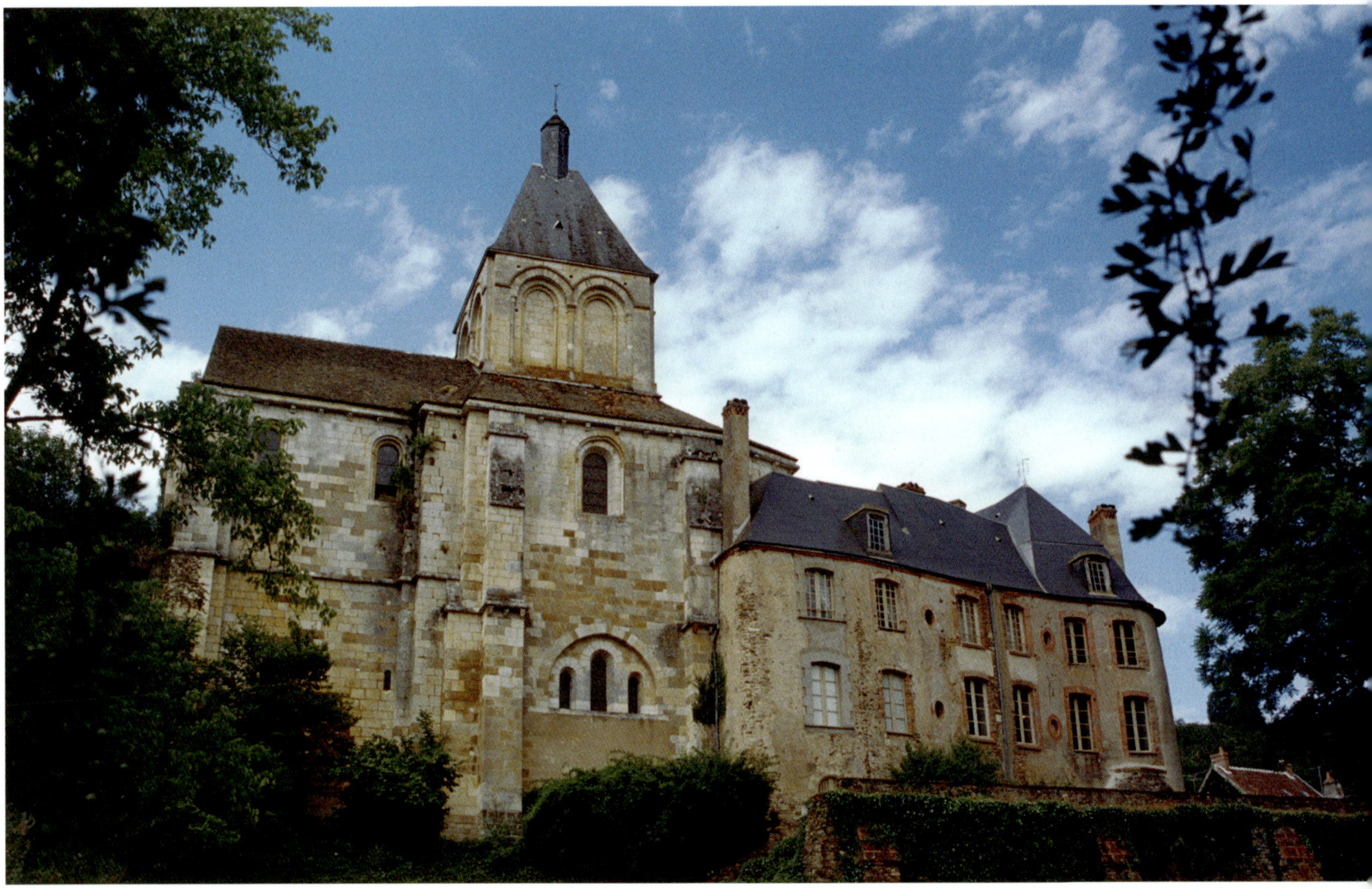

Gargilesse-Dampierre (Indre)

The original château was built as a fortress in the eighth century and has had a long and exciting history. Today the main hall serves as an art gallery.

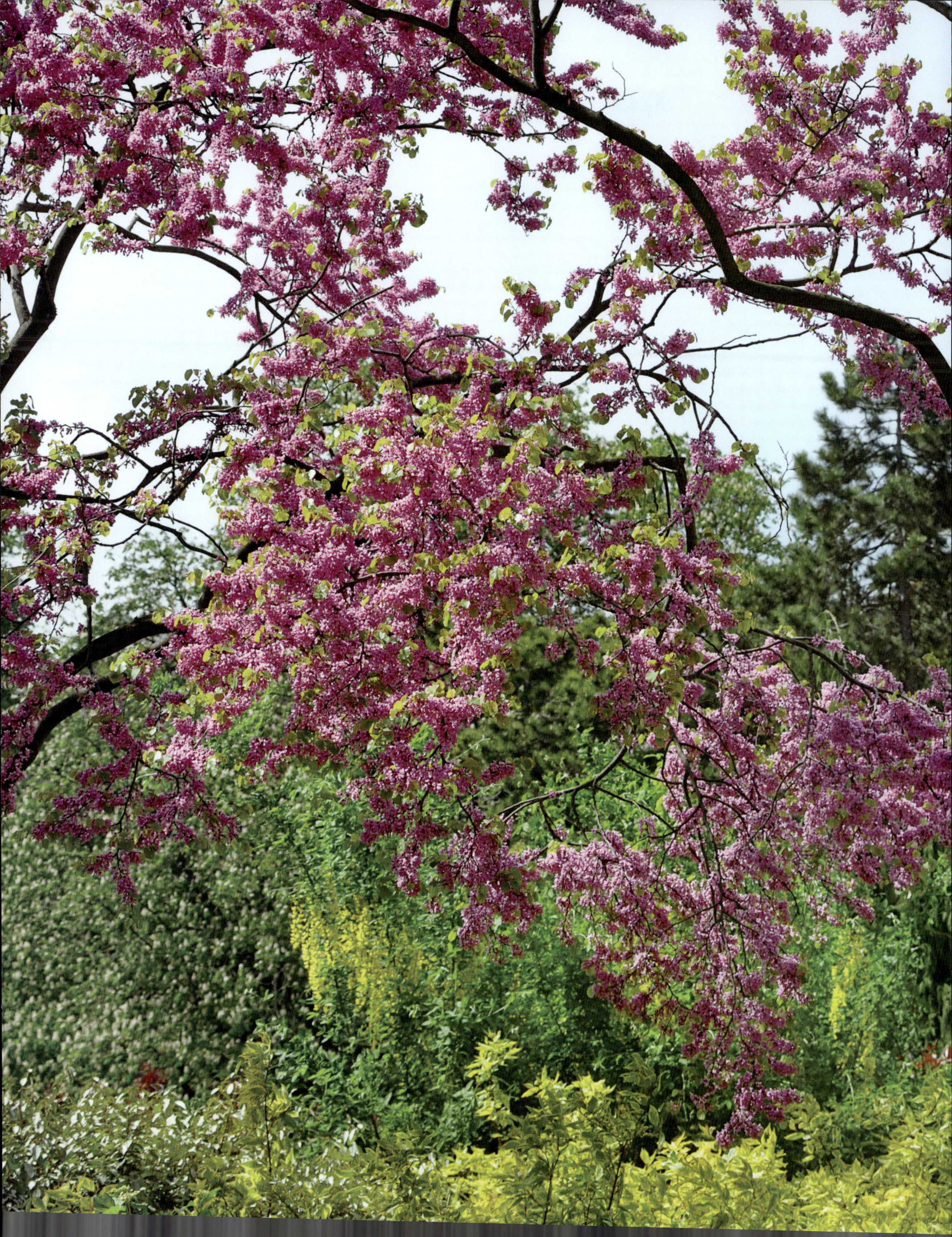

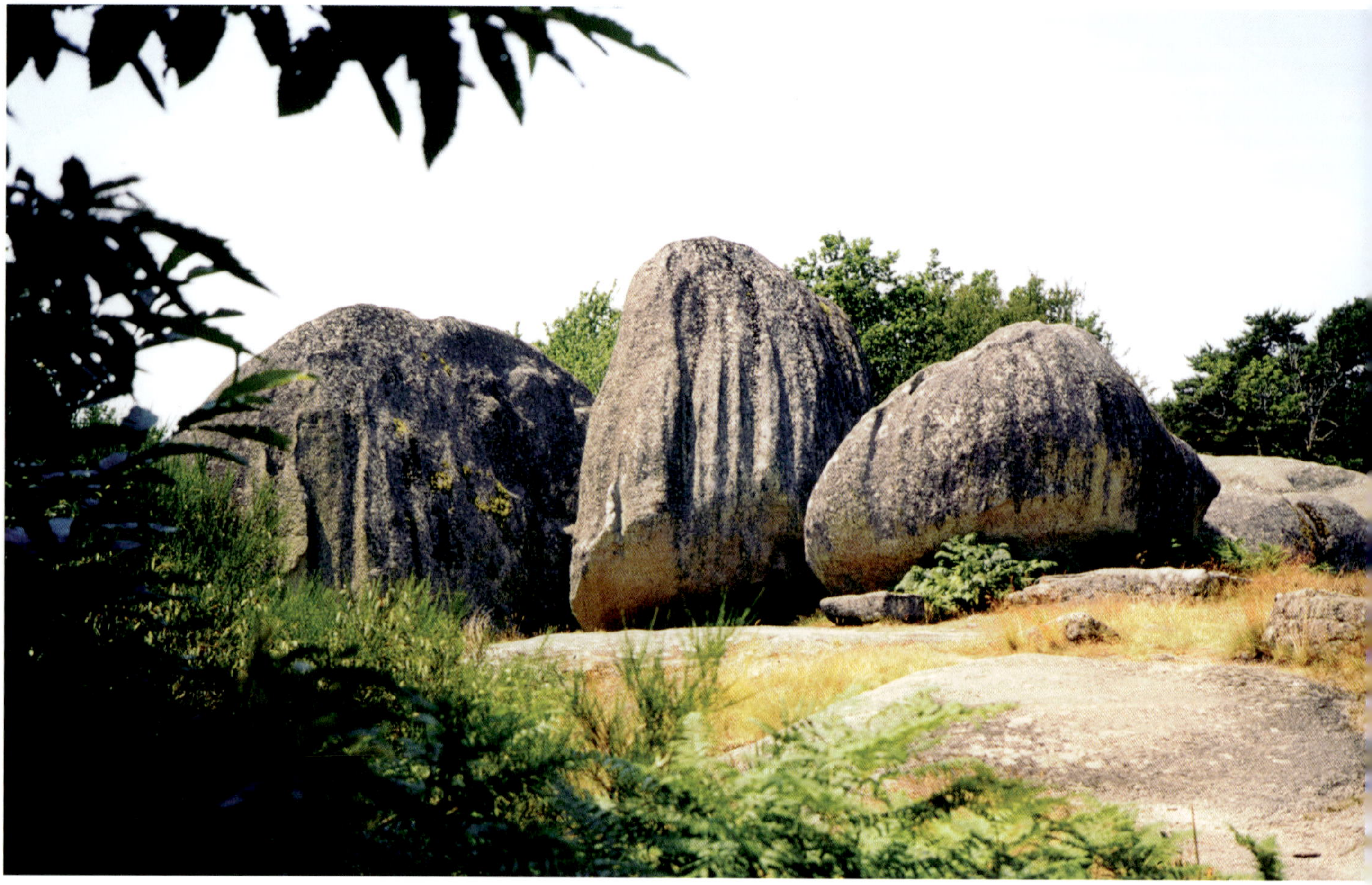

Pierres Jaumâtres (Creuse)

Another outing with carriages organised by Sand was to the Pierres Jaumâtres, monolithic ice age granite rocks perched on top of Mont Barlot, and commanding spectacular views of the Berry region to the north and the Limousin to the south. Chopin resorted to reaching them on the back of a donkey. George Sand set her novel *Jeanne* in this area.

→ Château de Montgivray (Indre)

The Château de Montgivray, about 3 kilometres from Nohant, belonged to George Sand's half-brother Hippolyte Chatiron. When Sand's earlier marriage to Casimir Dudevant broke down, she was forced to leave her beloved Nohant, and stayed for 5 years with Hippolyte. In the summers between 1839 and 1846 Sand and Chopin often visited him at his residence, which today serves as the local town hall.

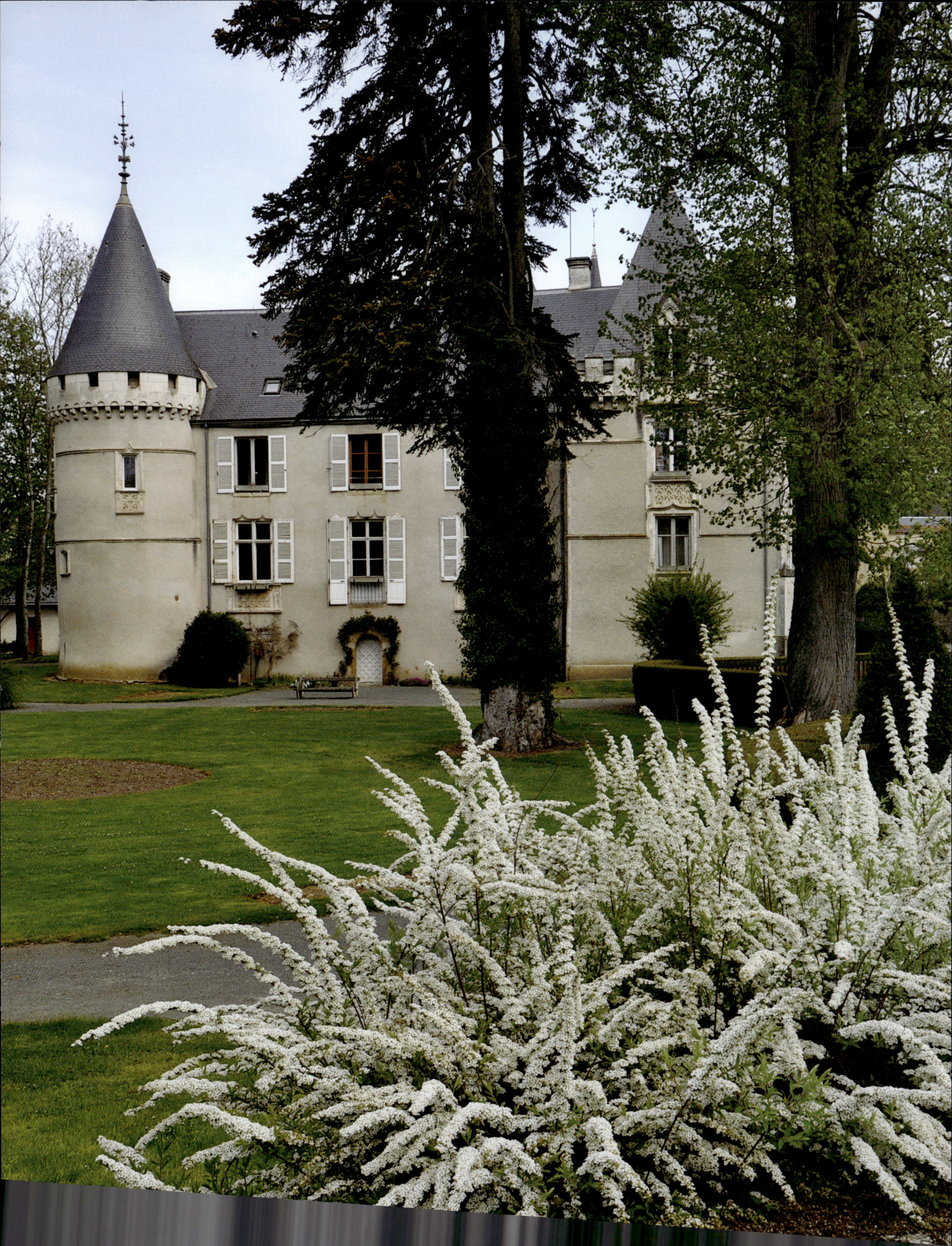

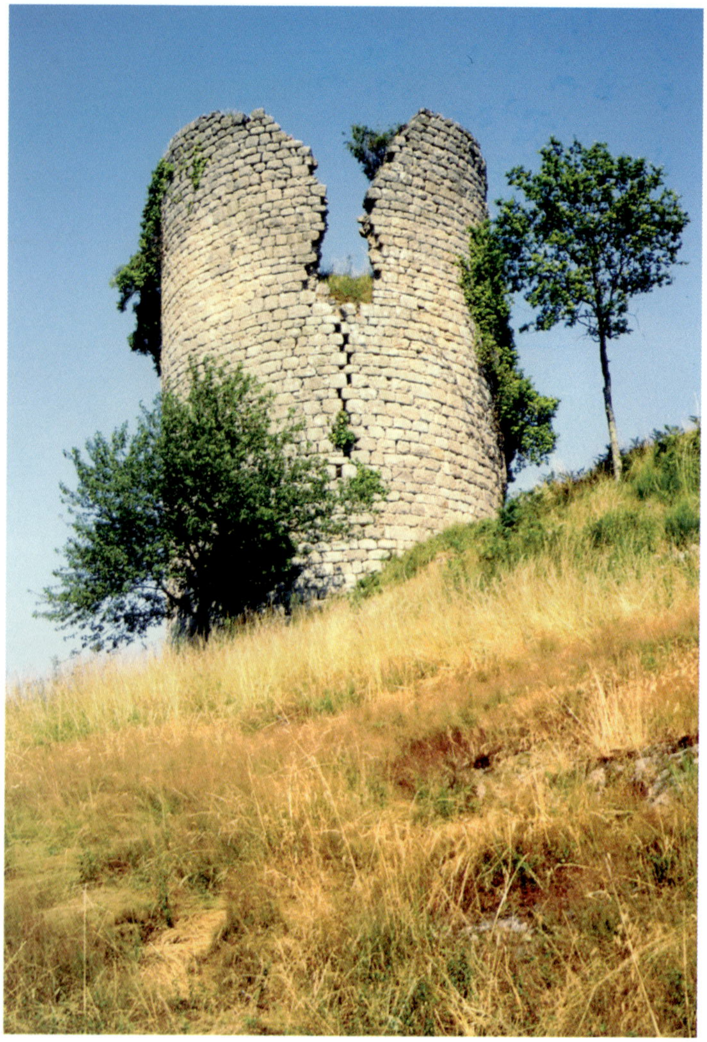

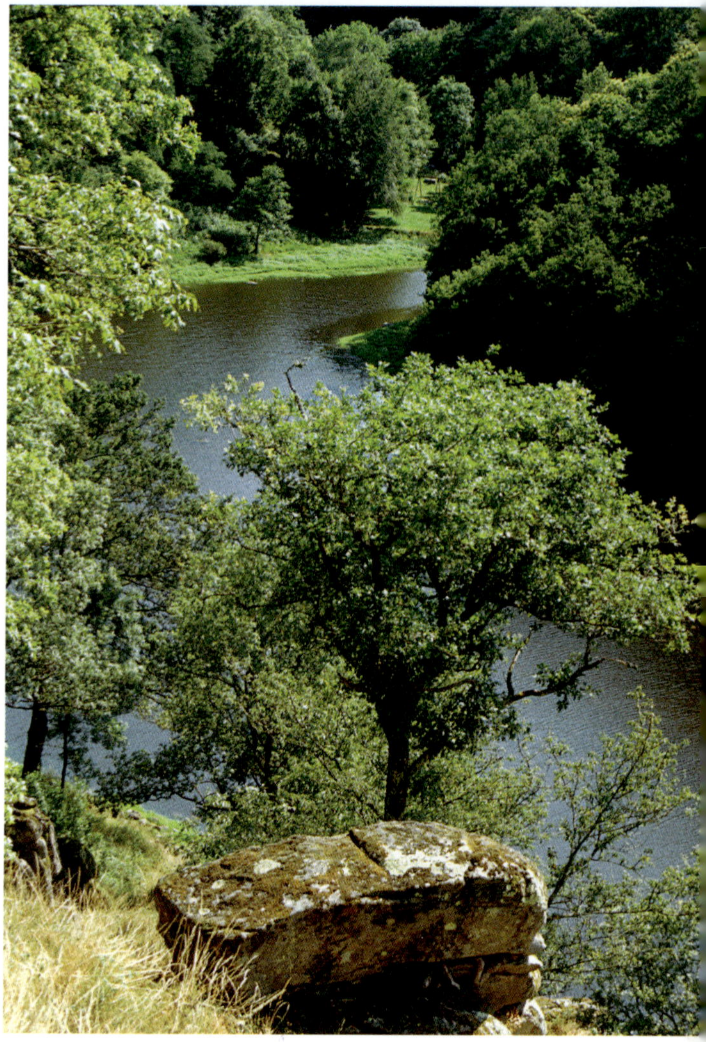

Crozant (Creuse)

The spectacular gorge of the young River Creuse at Crozant was another favourite Sand destination, where the young Maurice, who was never without a sketch pad and pencil, found himself in his element. What little is left of the original thirteenth century château consists of the tower, which bears the name of Isabella of Angoulême, widow of King John I of England, and subsequently the wife of Hugues de Lusignan. After 1606 the château remains served as building material for the local people. A major reconstruction of the whole site is currently in progress.

→ Abbey of Notre Dame de Fontgombault (Indre)

The Abbey of Notre Dame de Fontgombault, another favourite destination of Sand and Chopin, has a very chequered history. It was founded in 1091 on the banks of the River Creuse 10 kilometres from le Blanc as a Cistercian monastery. In the twelfth and thirteenth centuries it witnessed a period of great expansion, with the founding of over 20 priories. It was ravaged by the Protestants in 1569 during the French Religious Wars, and restored late in the seventeenth century. At the beginning of the twentieth century it was bought by a certain Louis Bonjean who established a button factory there, and during World War I it served as a military hospital. Today it is a Benedictine abbey of the Solesmes congregation.

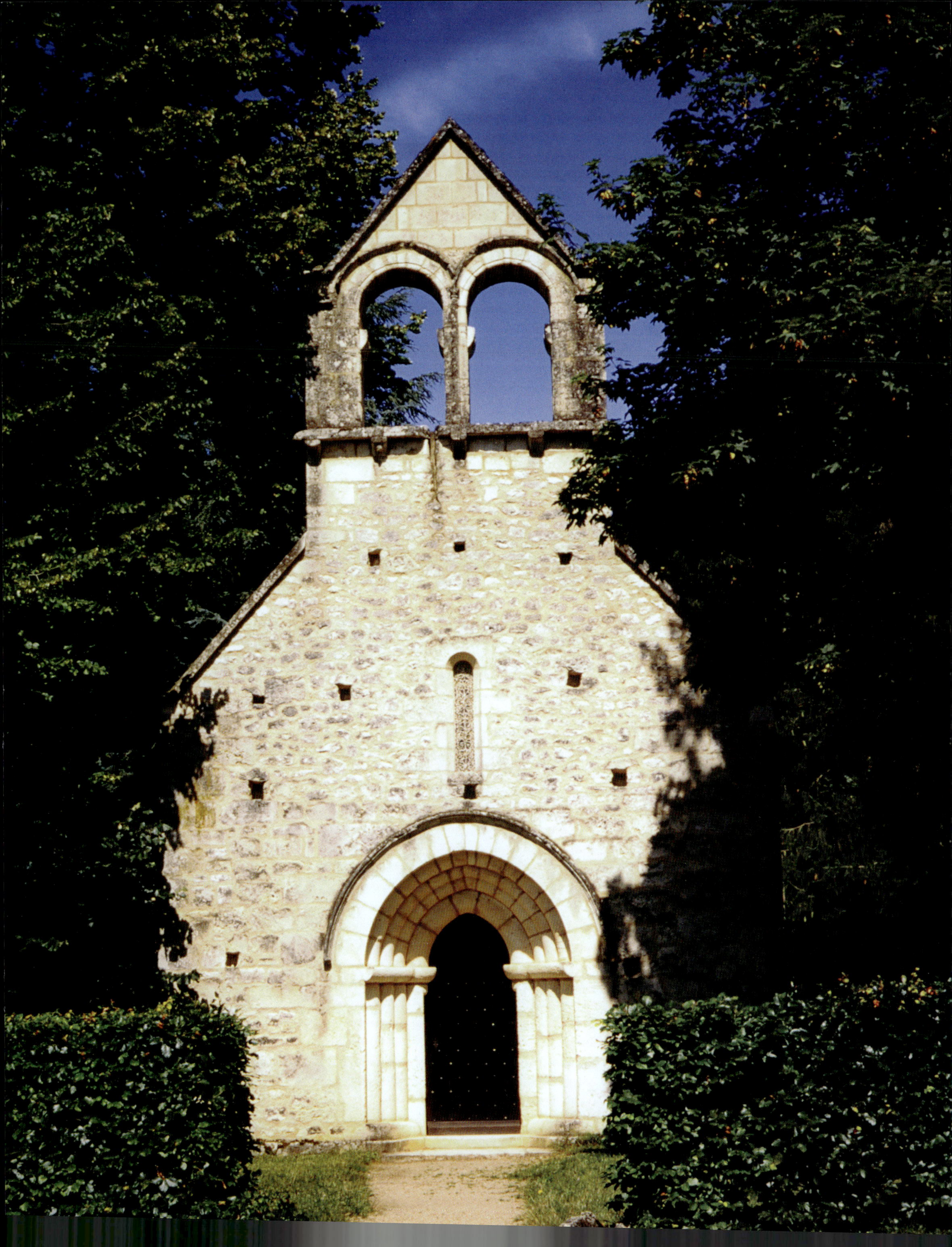

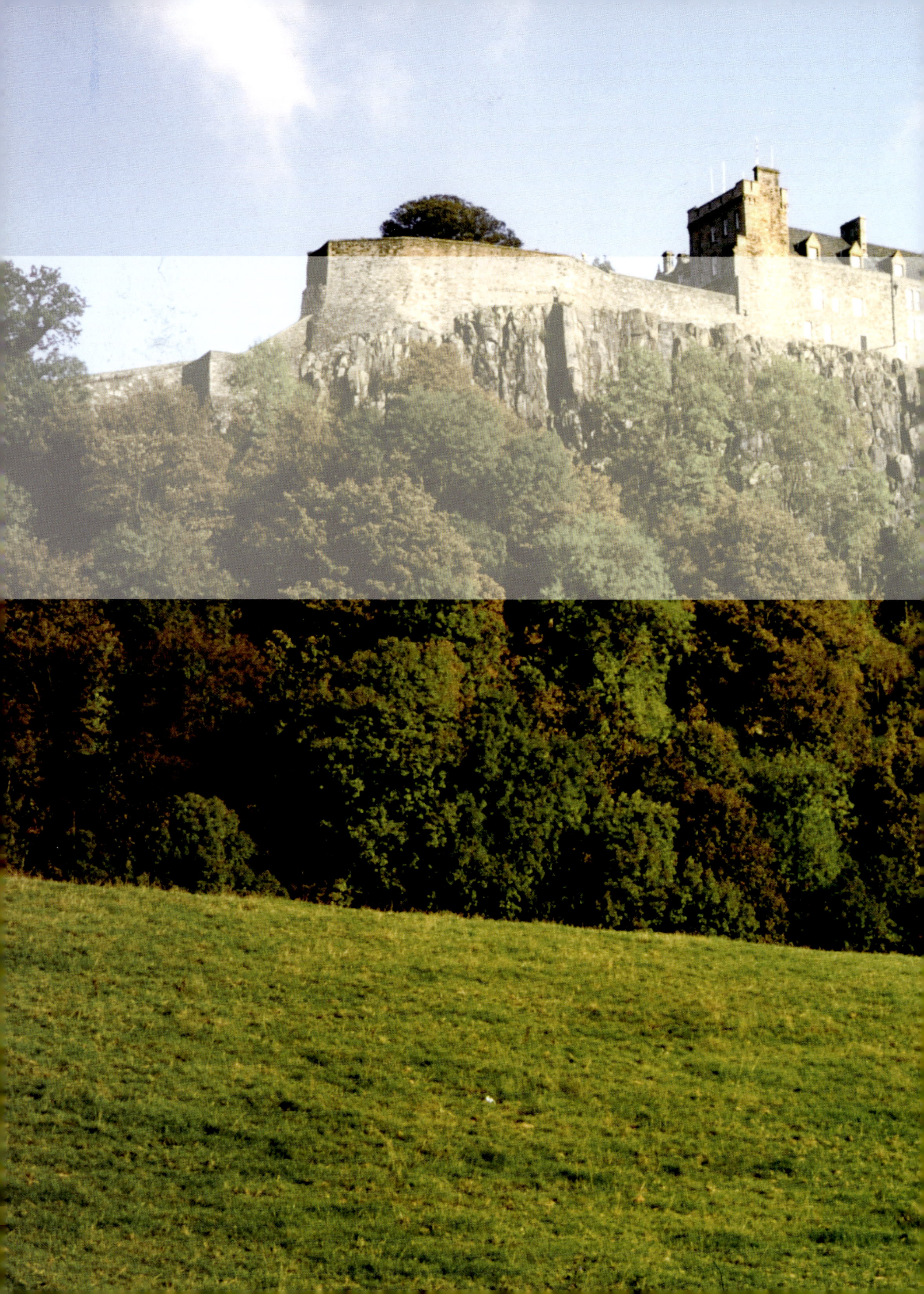

Great Britain

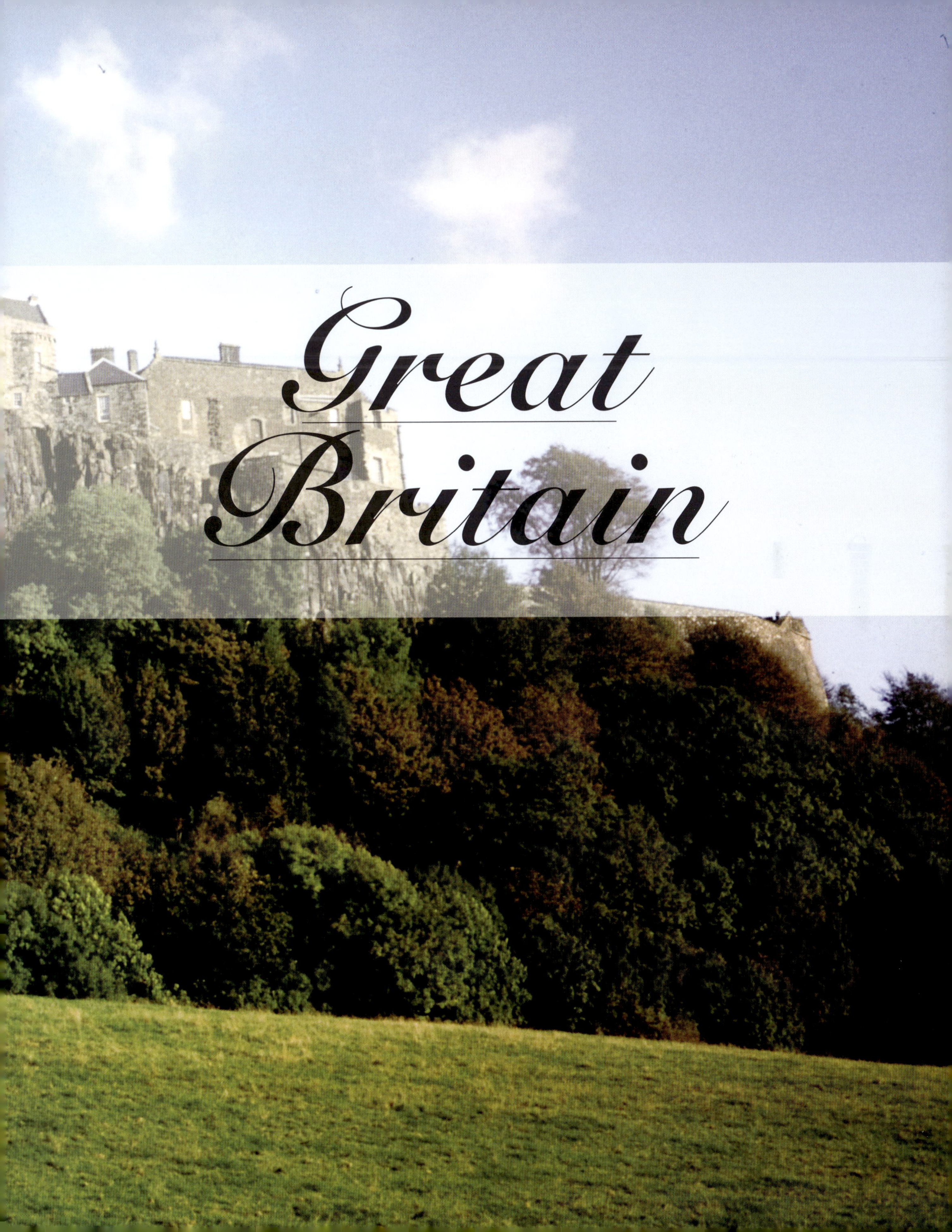

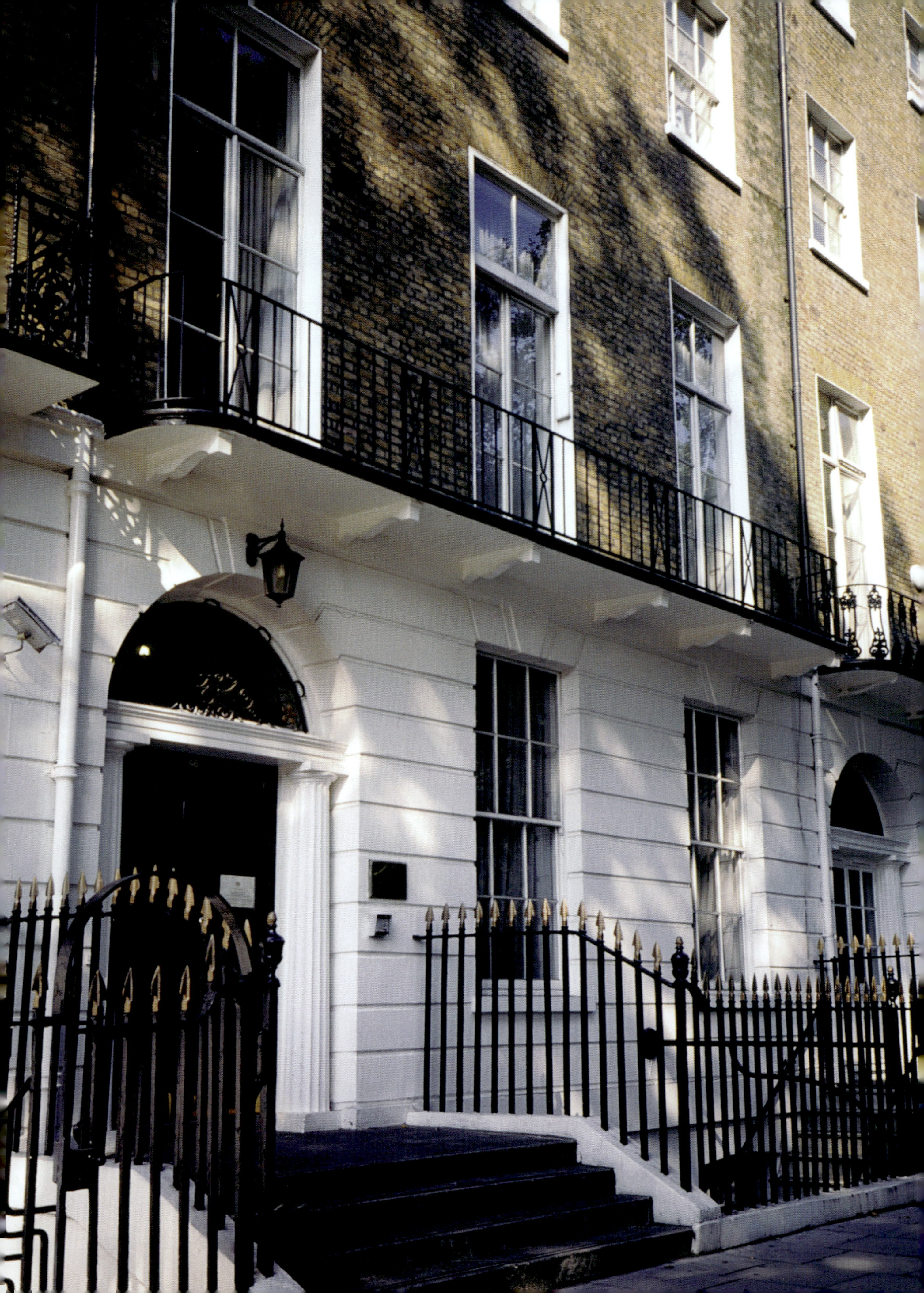

Chopin's first visit to London, in which he chose to travel incognito, was instigated by his friend, piano manufacturer Camille Pleyel, in the summer of 1837. It was largely as an antidote to the composer's depression in the wake of the Maria Wodzińska affair. When they arrived on 7 July, not three weeks after the Coronation of eighteen-year-old Queen Victoria, they found not the "Italian sky" as promised by Chopin's friend Julian Fontana, but a grey and sooty one which duly wrought havoc with his lungs. For all that, Chopin loved London, which at the time was almost as full of displaced Poles as Paris.

The English women, the horses, the palaces, the carriages, the wealth, the luxury, the space, the trees, everything, from the soap to the razors – everything is wonderful – everything ordered, everything educated, everything well-scrubbed.

Chopin to Unknown addressee in Paris (London, July 1837)

Chopin and Pleyel stayed at the Sablonnière, one of London's best hotels, situated on the corner of Cranbourne Street and Leicester Square. There they were met by Stanisław Koźmian, who took the tourists under his wing and showed them the sights. In a hired carriage, the trio also travelled out of town to Hampton Court; Richmond, with its park, Blackwall, a renowned paradise for fish gourmets; Chichester; Royal Windsor, which they visited by riverboat; and Arundel, where they attended a parliamentary election with candidate Lord Dudley Stuart, a politician heavily involved in the "Polish question".

Evenings were spent at the opera, and at a Beethoven memorial concert where Ignaz Moscheles played, although Chopin chose not to visit him in case his anonymity was breached.

Pleyel and Chopin were invited to a soirée at the house of London piano manufacturer James Broadwood in Bryanston Square. Chopin was introduced as Monsieur Fritz from Paris. The ruse worked until Mr. Fritz was asked to play, whereupon his style was instantly recognized, and the whisper went round: "Chopin!".

Thus began a very fruitful relationship between Chopin and the House of Broadwood.

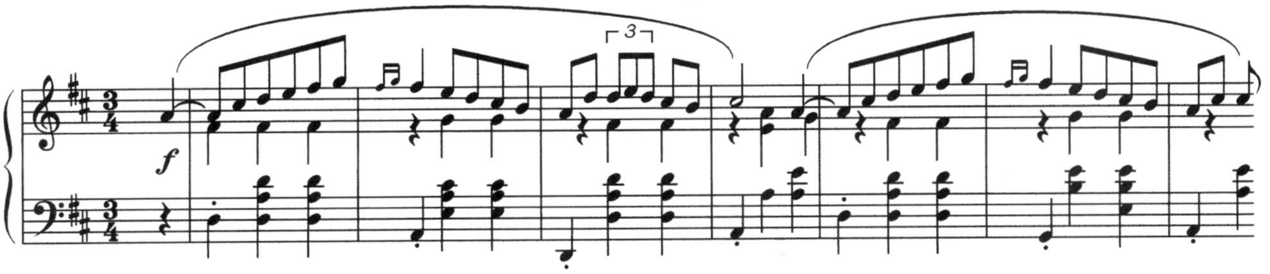

Chopin's Mazurka in D Op. 33 No 2, one of his most popular, was written at around the time of his first visit to London.

London

On his first visit to London in 1837, Chopin and Camille Pleyel were invited to a soirée at the house of London piano manufacturer James Broadwood at 46 Bryanston Square. Chopin, wishing to remain incognito, was introduced as "Monsieur Fritz" from Paris.

← Stirling Castle

Chopin had a spectacular view of Stirling Castle from his window at Keir House – on those rare occasions when the mist lifted...

After three action-packed weeks of high spending, Pleyel and Chopin returned to Paris. Koźmian saw them as far as Brighton, where they stopped to admire King George IV's Pavilion, then only a decade old.

Chopin was in London again just over ten years later, under completely different circumstances. He arrived at London Bridge station by train, with his Italian manservant, on Maundy Thursday, 21 April 1848. He took a cab straight to 10 Bentinck Street, just off Cavendish Square, where Jane Stirling had found him a luxurious apartment. In the event, it was too expensive for Chopin, and, with the help of Karol Szulczewski, who acted as the London agent for Prince Adam Czartoryski's Paris-based Polish Government-in-exile, he soon found cheaper rooms at 48 Dover Street. There he found no less than three pianos waiting for him: an Erard lent by its manufacturer, his favourite Pleyel which he had had brought over from Paris, and a Broadwood, compliments of the London piano manufacturer Henry Broadwood, who had taken over from his father James, who had retired. Henry was to become a good friend and support to the sick composer during his stay in Great Britain. Before moving in, however, he went to Kingston-upon-Thames to visit various friends who had come over from France in the wake of the deposed King Louis-Philippe, and had congregated in the area. Chopin's many friends and former pupils immediately rallied round, and his days were filled with visits and socializing.

My Italian, who is concerned with himself and his accounts, wastes my time in the morning… Add a good servant who would look after me and not waste money and things… I have sent away the stupid Italian… I have a better servant.

Chopin to Wojciech Grzymała
(London, 13 May, 2 June & 8 July 1848)

He dismissed his corrupt and incompetent Italian servant and engaged an Irishman by the name of Daniel. In Chopin's eyes Daniel was the perfect gentleman's gentleman, and proved to be a devoted and tireless tower of strength throughout Chopin's stay in Great Britain.

He then had to think about making a living, so pupils, publications and appearances were a priority. By June he had at least five pupils, each of whom paid him a guinea per lesson, and he sold his two Waltzes, Op. 64, to publishers Cramer, Beale & Co.

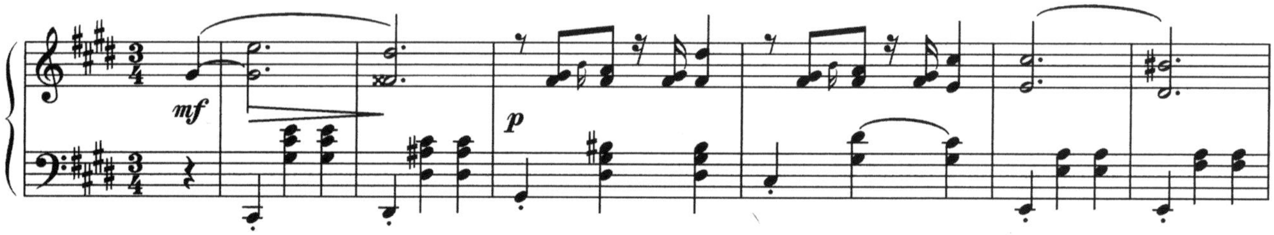

This Waltz, one of a set of two from Op. 64, was dedicated to Baroness Rothschild. Chopin featured both frequently during his stay in Great Britain.

London

Chopin's first London apartment upon his arrival on 21 April 1848, found for him by Jane Stirling, was at 10 Bentinck Street, just off Cavendish Square. Being very luxurious, it proved too expensive. Through his Polish contacts he found cheaper rooms at 48 Dover Street, where there were three pianos waiting for him when he moved in.

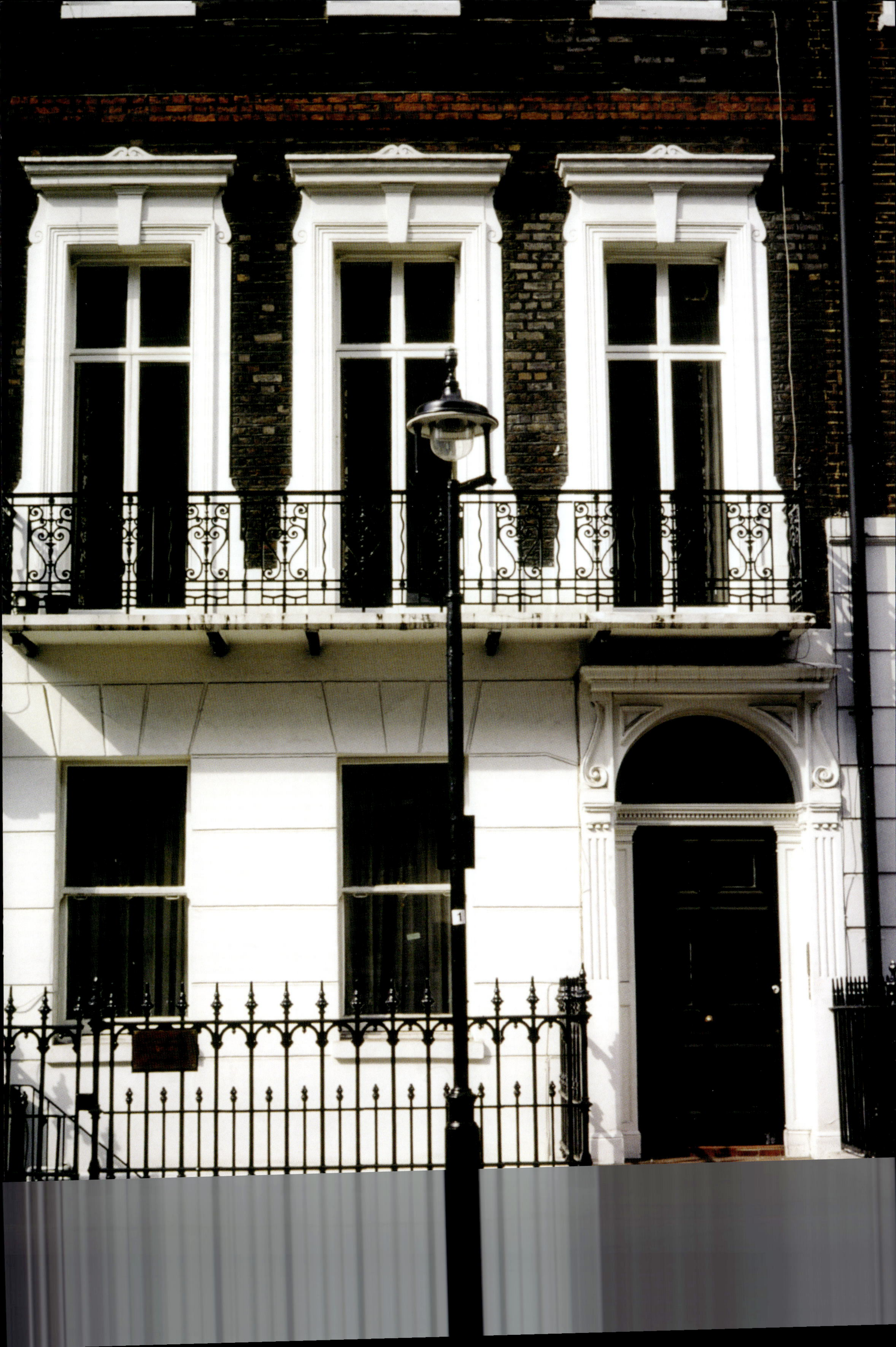

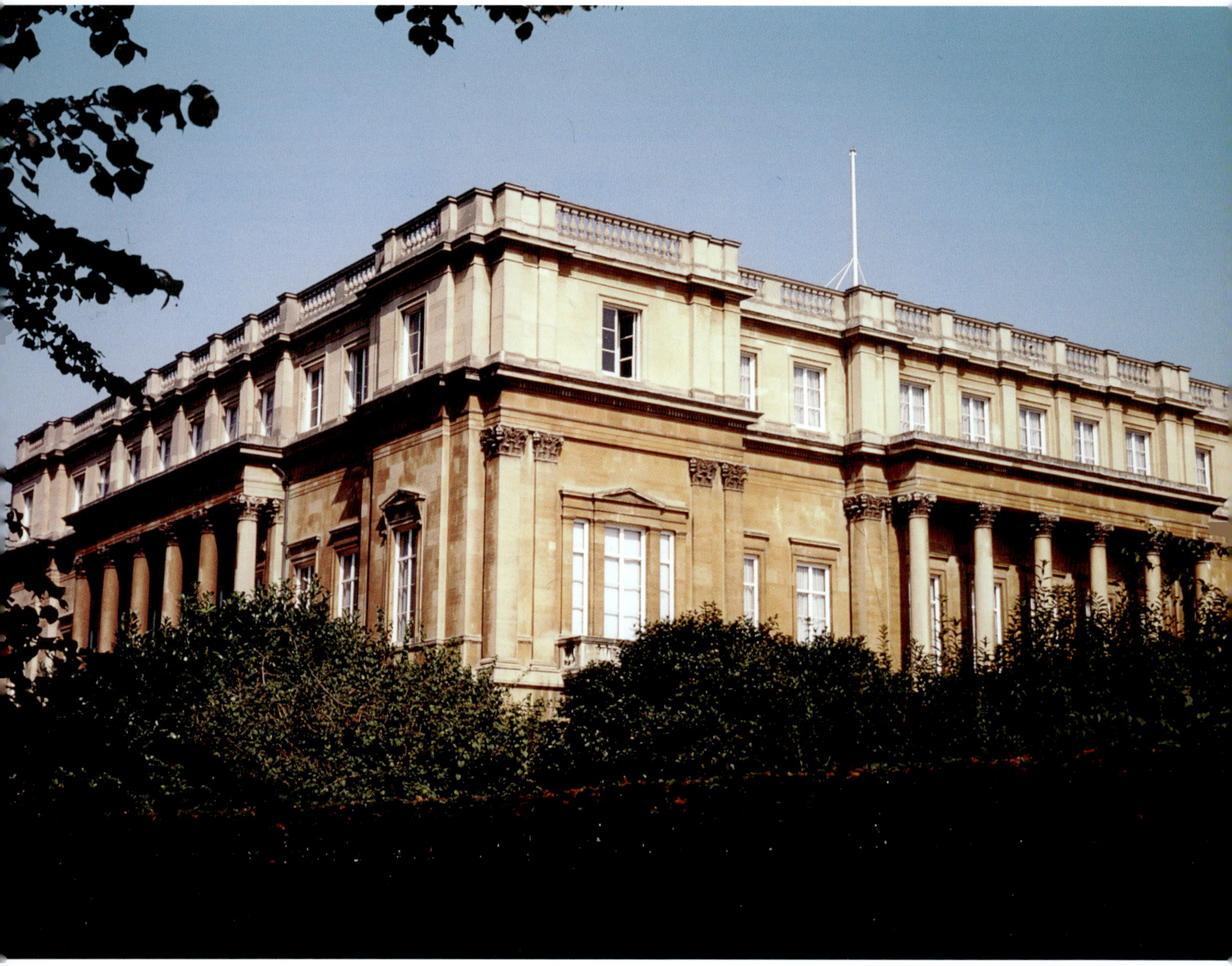

London

Stafford House, in the Mall, was the residence of the Duchess of Sutherland. On 15 May 1848 she gave a soirée at which Chopin played before Queen Victoria and the Duke of Wellington, among other celebrities. Apart from his own mazurkas and waltzes, he played Mozart's *Variations in G minor* for two pianos with Julius Benedict. Today Stafford House is known as Lancaster House.

His first engagement was on 15 May at Stafford House, today Lancaster House in the Mall – but then the residence of the Duchess of Sutherland. Among the guests were Queen Victoria and Prince Albert.

I had several grand evenings directly after I arrived… The Duchess of Sutherland had the Queen to dinner one day, and in the evening only 80 persons belonging to the most exclusive London society. Besides the Prince of Prussia… and the royal family, there were only such persons as old Wellington, and so on… The Duchess presented me to the Queen, who was amiable and talked to me twice. Prince Albert came up to the pianoforte. Everyone told me that both these things are rare.

Chopin to his family (Edinburgh, 19 August 1848)

This was followed by two private matinées, arranged by Henry Broadwood, for which he was paid £300: the first, on 23 June, was at 99 Eaton Place, the Belgravia home of singer Mrs Adelaide Sartoris, and the second on 7 July, at the home of Lord Falmouth at 2 St. James' Square, at which Pauline Viardot also sang.

It is the exquisite delicacy, with the liquid mellowness of his tone, and the pearly roundness of his passages of rapid articulation which are the peculiar features of his execution, while the music is characterized by freedom of thought, varied expression and a kind of romantic melancholy which seems the natural mood of the artist's mind.

George Hogarth, on Chopin's style, writing in the Daily News 10 July 1848

At the end of July the Queen left London for Osborne House, and London emptied, as Society headed for the fresh air of country estate and Scottish grouse moor. The exodus included Jane Stirling and Katherine Erskine, who made for Scotland to prepare for the arrival there of Chopin, as guest of their numerous relatives. Chopin, who found the London air heavy and oppressive to his lungs, looked forward to their promised warm Scottish welcome – not to mention clean air.

Henry Broadwood, ever solicitous of Chopin's well-being, booked three first class seats on the recently opened West Coast line to Edinburgh, by way of Birmingham and Carlisle: one for Chopin, one for Daniel – and one for Chopin's feet. Also on the train, at Broadwood's instigation, was John Muir Wood, the son of Edinburgh music publisher Andrew Wood, and now director of the firm's new Glasgow branch – a useful contact.

The train left London's Euston Station at 9 on the morning of Saturday 5 August, and arrived at Edinburgh's Lothian Road Station exactly 12 hours later. Among those meeting the train was Dr Adam Łyszczyński, who had studied medicine and settled in the Scottish capital after the Polish Uprising of 1830-31. Broadwood had arranged rooms for Chopin at the Douglas Hotel in St. Andrew's Square, into which Daniel had to physically carry his master, who was utterly exhausted by the gruelling train journey.

I made the railway journey from London to Edinburgh by the Express train, 407 miles in twelve hours, and it may have been a little too much for me.

Chopin to Wojciech Grzymała
(Calder House, 19 August 1848)

The following day Chopin stayed in bed all morning, recovering from the journey. By noon, he felt well enough to go sight-seeing with Mrs Łyszczyński – Dr Adam's Scottish-born wife. Driving in a carriage along Prince's Street, Chopin took in the Castle, the Royal Mile, and the new Walter Scott Memorial (he was a passionate admirer of the author) although he was not up to climbing the 287 steps to the top to admire the recently developed Georgian New Town.

The next morning he took a walk, with Daniel in attendance, to Muir Wood's music shop at 12 Waterloo Place. There he heard the sound of one of his mazurkas being played by a blind pianist – a piece of theatre put on for his benefit by Muir Wood, which was much appreciated.

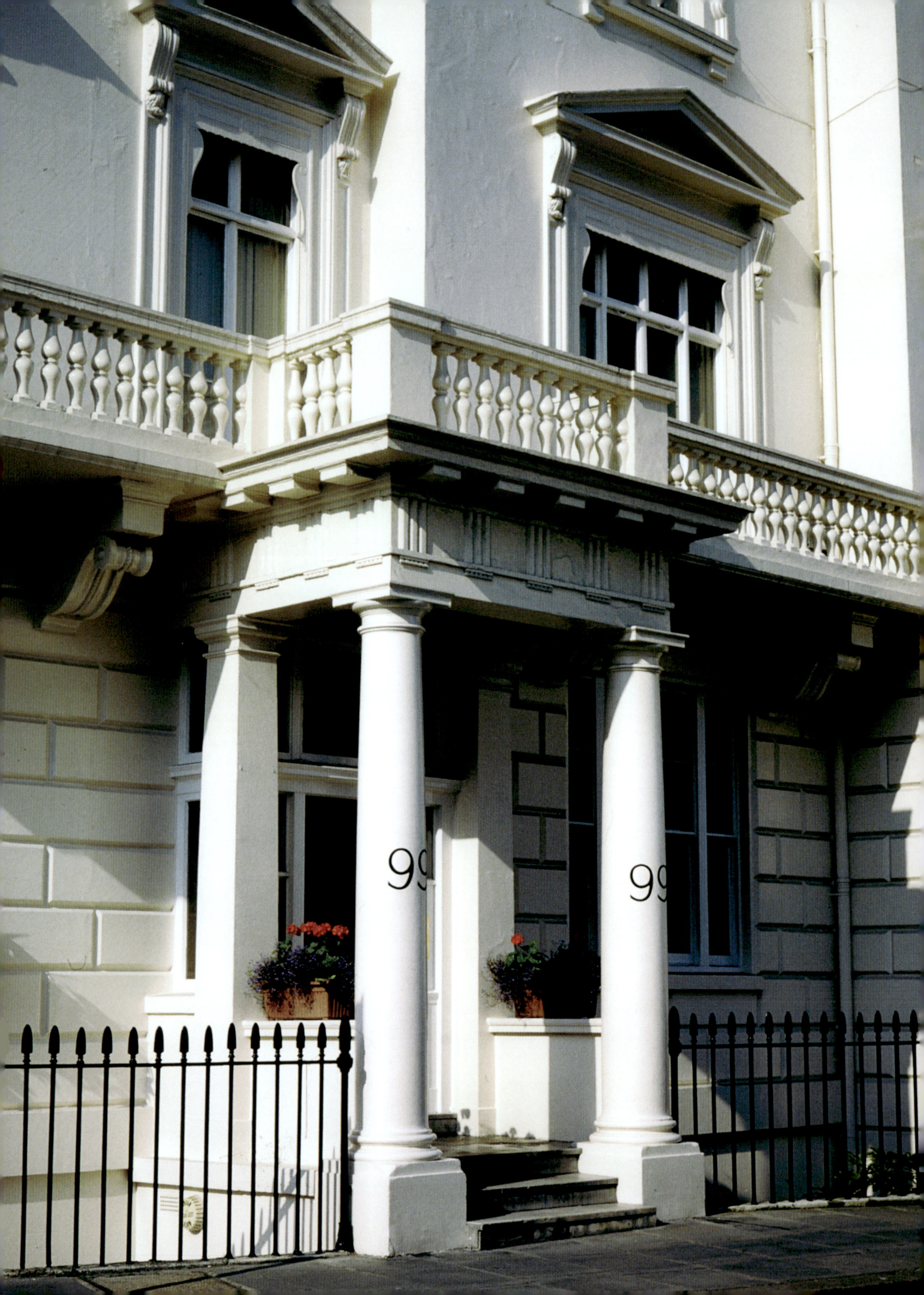
99
99

That afternoon, a carriage arrived to take him to Calder House, the residence of Lord and Lady Torphichen. Among those waiting to welcome him with true Scottish hospitality were Jane Stirling and Katherine Erskine: Lady Margaret Torphichen was their older sister.

The only drawback were the long drawn-out dinners, at which Chopin was forced to sit, breathing in the cigar smoke and unable to converse for lack of English, he was sick and bored. Among the visitors at that time were Norwegian pianist Thomas Tellefsen and Dr & Mrs Łyszczyński.

I am fit for nothing now… everything strains me, and I gasp that way till dinner time. Afterwards one has to sit two hours at a table with the men, look at them talking and listen to them drinking. I am bored to death.

Chopin to Wojciech Grzymała
(Keir House, 1 October 1848)

After three weeks Chopin was back in Edinburgh as guest of the Łyszczyńskis at their house at 10 Warriston Crescent. Mrs Łyszczyński was musical and sang a little, and they had a small Broadwood piano in the drawing room, of which Chopin took advantage. He was by now very ill, had difficulty in breathing, and had to be carried up to his bedroom by the ever faithful Daniel.

My present valet is excellent, and a good fellow, so life is easier for me.

Chopin to Wojciech Grzymała (Calder House, 19 August 1848)

However, under the Doctor's care, he recovered enough, on Friday 25 August, to undertake the 8-hour train journey to Manchester to take part in a concert, which had been arranged for him by Henry Broadwood.

Chopin stayed with his friend, wealthy manufacturer, music lover and patron of the arts Salis Schwabe, at his mansion, Crumpsall House, situated well outside the polluted atmosphere of the heavily industrialized city. The concert, which included Irish pianist George Osborne and several local singers, took place at Manchester's Gentlemen's Concert Hall before 1,200 people – the greatest number Chopin had ever played before. His performance was, as he had expected, largely lost on such a large audience. The ordeal had taken its toll, and Chopin needed a few days of rest at Crumpsall House before returning to the Łyszczyńskis of Warriston Crescent, in preparation for the next stage of his tour of the Stirling family, Johnstone Castle.

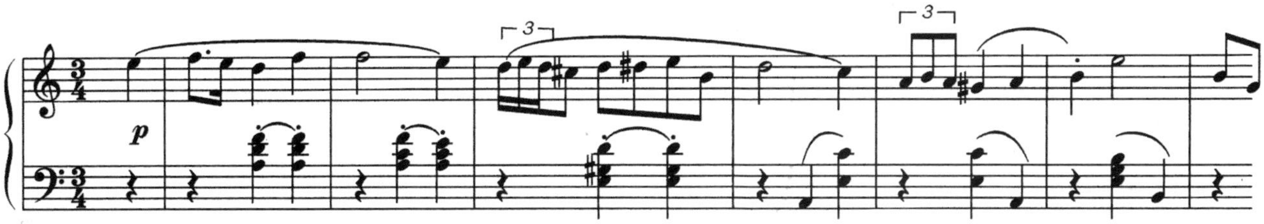

Chopin featured his set of five Mazurkas Op. 7, of which this is No 2 in A minor, during his concerts and soirées in Great Britain.

London

On 23 June 1848 Chopin gaves a concert for 150 people at 99 Eaton Place, the home of singer Adelaide Sartoris. His programme included mazurkas, waltzes and the *Berceuse*.

Johnstone Castle, just outside Glasgow, was the home of Ludovic Houston, the husband of another of Jane and Katherine's elder sisters, Anne. It was an ideal base at which to prepare for a concert in Glasgow that Muir Wood had organized for the end of September. The Castle also served as a springboard for other visits. One of these was to Milliken House, the residence of Sir William Napier, who was married to yet another Stirling girl, Elizabeth. The present building, the White House, was rebuilt from the original stones. Nearby was also Glentyan House, the home of Jane's brother, Captain James Stirling.

Chopin also spent a week at Strachur House, on Loch Fyne, with Lord and Lady Murray, who had been renting the property from the Campbells of Strachur. Sixty-year-old Lady Murray had been Chopin's first pupil in London. Not a first rate pianist, and an even worse concertina-player, she was nevertheless a leading patroness of music in Scotland. At Strachur Chopin enjoyed fresh herring from the loch, salmon from the rivers and venison from the hills, as well as the finest French wines: Lady Murray loved all things French.

I visit one lord after another. Everywhere I meet, together with the heartiest goodwill and boundless hospitality, superb pianofortes, magnificent paintings, famous collections of books; there are also hunting, dogs, dinners without end, cellars, for which I have less use. It is difficult to conceive of the refinement of luxury and comfort that one meets in English [sic] castles.

Chopin to Adolf Gutmann
(Calder House, 16 October 1848)

Meanwhile, another of Chopin's pupils, Princess Marcelina Czartoryska, who was married to Alexander, nephew of Polish Head of Government-in-Exile Prince Adam Czartoryski,

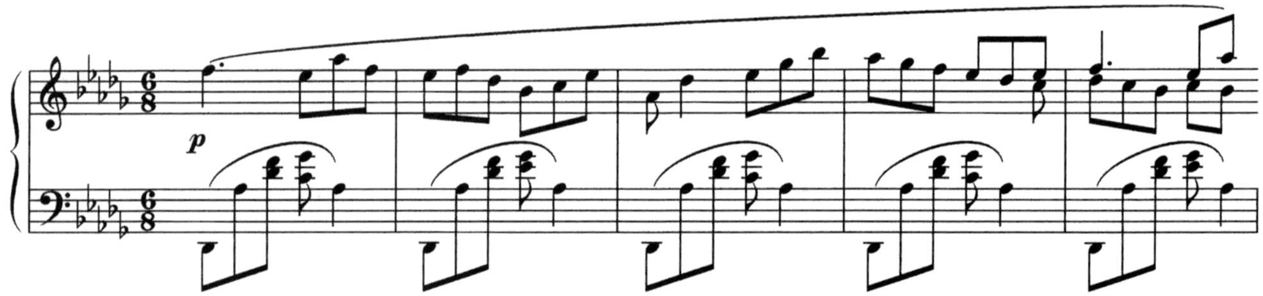

The Glasgow Herald described Chopin's performance of his *Berceuse* at his Glasgow concert: *He took for a theme a few notes which were little else than the common notes of the scale. This simple theme ran through the whole piece, and he heaped on it the strangest series of harmonies, discords and modulations that can well be imagined.*

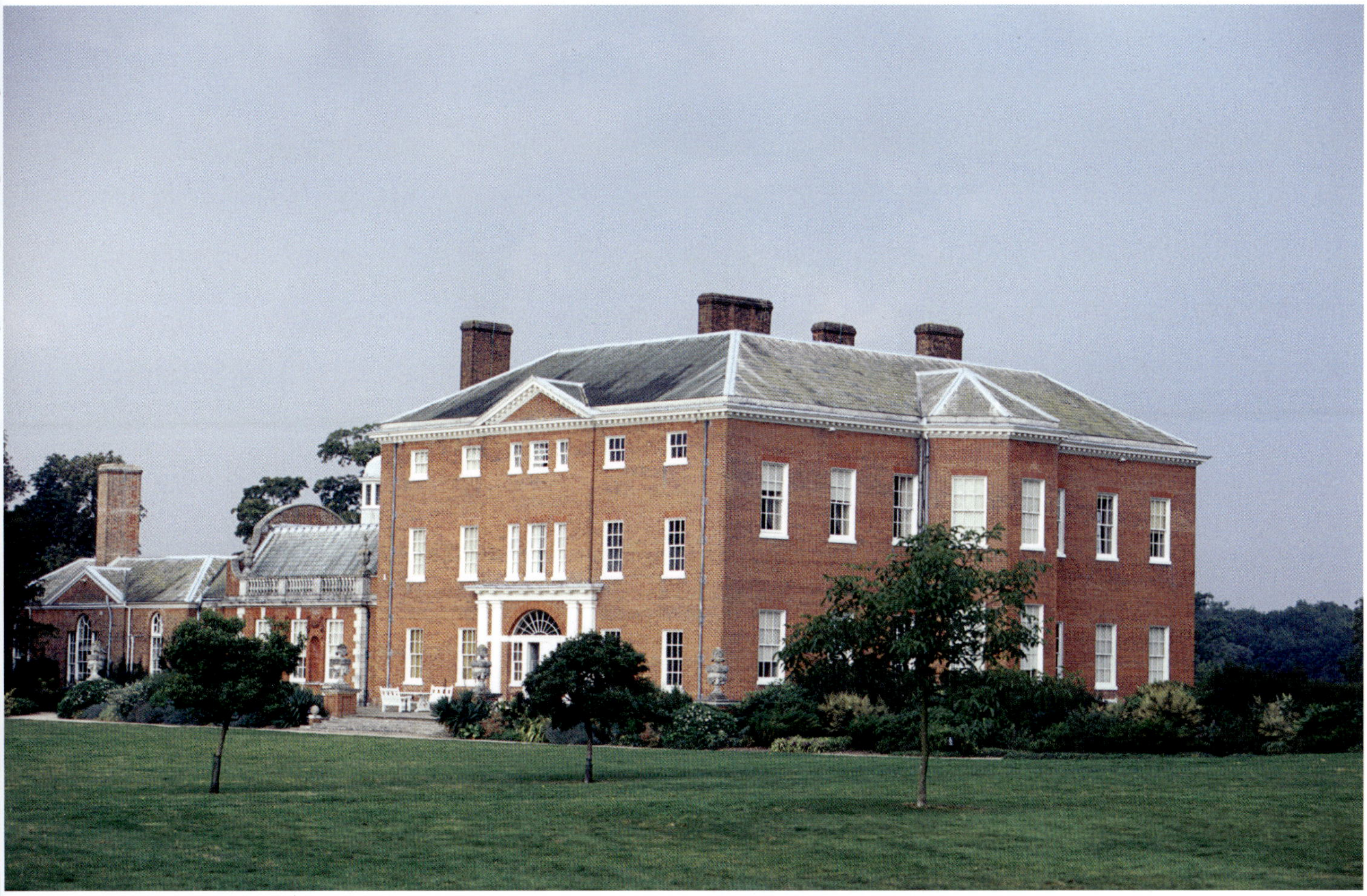

The Keyboard Museum at Hatchlands House, situated about halfway between Guildford and Leatherhead, houses the "Cobbe Collection", which includes the piano on which Chopin played all his concerts while in London during 1848.

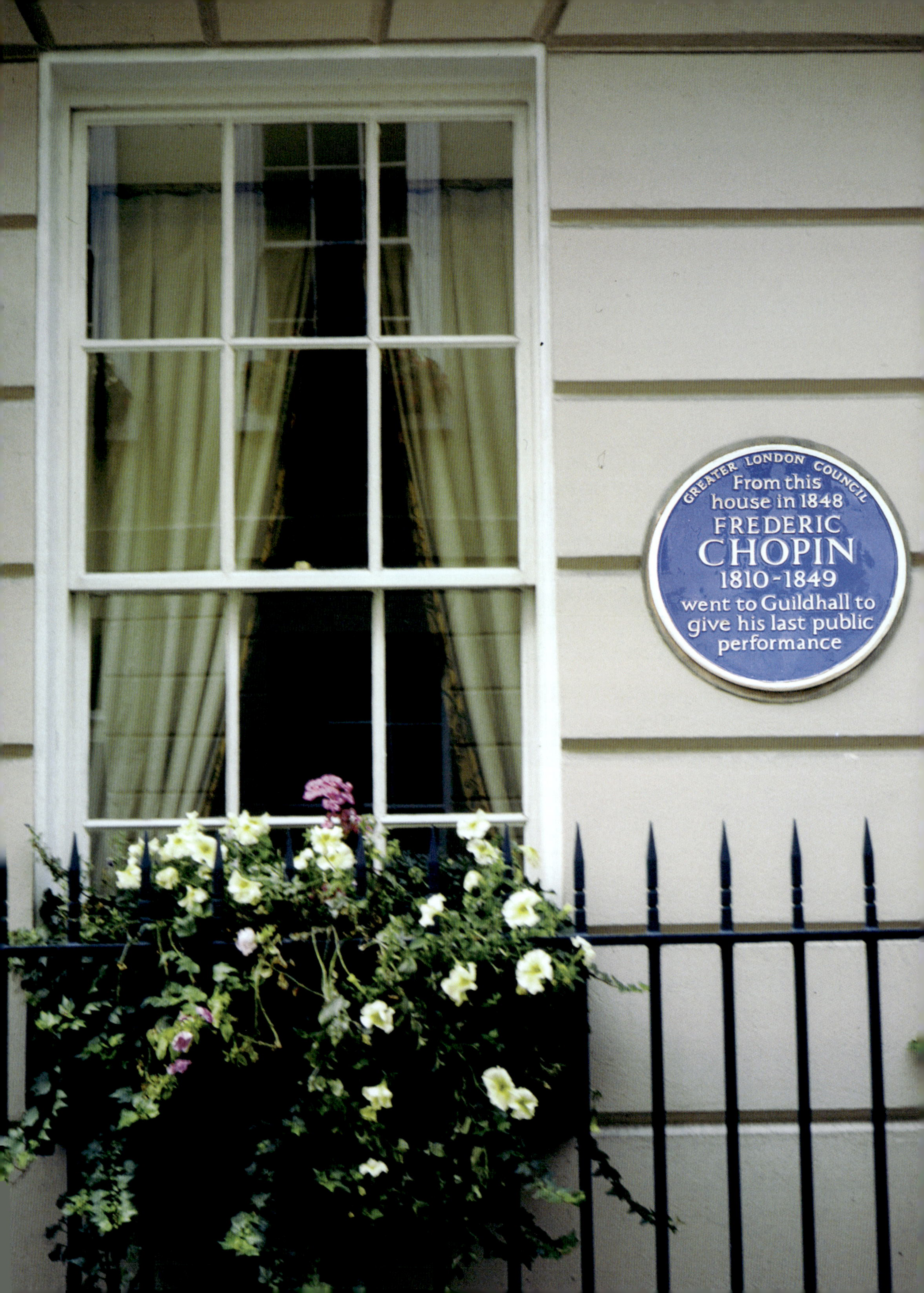
GREATER LONDON COUNCIL
From this
house in 1848
FREDERIC
CHOPIN
1810-1849
went to Guildhall to
give his last public
performance

arrived in Edinburgh on a visit. On hearing the news, Chopin, very anxious to see one of his most successful pupils, immediately took the train back to Edinburgh, and to the Łyszczyński house, to see her.

Princess Marcelina is the same angel of kindness as last year. I revived somewhat under their Polish ambience.

Chopin to Wojciech Grzymała (Keir House, 1 October 1848)

A few days later Chopin returned to Johnstone Castle to prepare for the concert, which took place on the afternoon of 27 September, at the Merchants' Hall in Hutcheson Street. The Hall was packed with the aristocracy and friends who came from all over Scotland to support him. Chopin shared the concert with singer Giulietta Adelasio de Marguerittes, who contributed songs by Guglielmo and Niedermeyer. Among Chopin's pieces singled out for comment were the so-called "Raindrop" Prelude, whose monotonous pulse fascinated many listeners, the *Berceuse*, with its soaring embellishments over a repetitive left hand figure, and the two Nocturnes Op. 55 dedicated to Jane. The concert was, despite Chopin's obvious physical weakness, a great success, and was celebrated with a banquet at Johnstone Castle later that evening.

A chilly autumn was already well advanced when Chopin arrived at Keir House, just outside Dunblane, the residence of author and art connoisseur Sir William Stirling, Jane's uncle and head of the Clan. He had invited Chopin to stay, and his welcome was decidedly warmer than the increasingly inclement weather. Chopin did not go to nearby Kippenross House, Jane's birthplace, as he was unwell on the day of the planned visit. Among the other guests, who had also attended Chopin's Glasgow concert, was Lady Belhaven. She invited Chopin to stay at her residence, Wishaw House, near Motherwell. Only one thing marred an otherwise delightful stay at Keir House: the Scottish Sabbath, totally devoid of all activity, bored Chopin.

No mail, no railway, no carriage, even for a drive, no boat, not even a dog to whistle to… There's a fog, and though from the window at which I am writing, there is the most beautiful view: Sterling Castel [sic]… and mountains, and the lake, and an exquisite park – in short, one of the famous beautiful views of Scotland – all the same, I can't see a bit of it, only every now and then, when the fog is pleased to give way to a few minutes of sunshine that can't fight it much here.

Chopin to Wojciech Grzymała (Keir House, 1 October 1848)

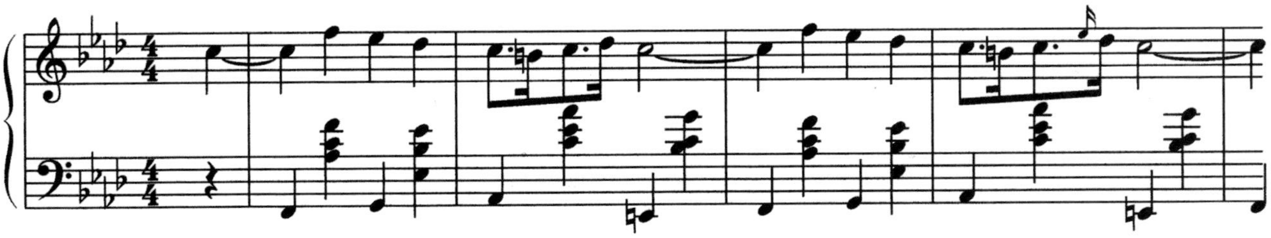

The F minor "Jane Stirling" Nocturne was, as would be expected, one of the mainstays of Chopin's Scottish concert programmes.

London

After his gruelling trip in Scotland Chopin returned to London a very sick man. Henry Broadwood arranged for him not only lodgings at 4 St. James' Place, but also the services of Dr. Mallan, homeopathic physician to Queen Victoria. A commemorative plaque marks Chopin's last London address at 4 St. James Place.

Among Chopin's visits was one to Gargunnock House, to the west of Stirling, the residence of Jane's late brother, Charles Stirling, who had died a decade previously, leaving a widow and several children. The Broadwood piano on which Chopin played as a brand new instrument, is still there.

By 4 October Chopin was back in Edinburgh, again a guest of Dr & Mrs Łyszczyński, to give a concert at the Hopetoun Hall in Queen Street. Again, the reviews stressed what Chopin knew well – that he was more suited to the salon than a concert hall:

His execution was the most finished we have ever heard... As a chamber pianist he stands unrivalled.

Edinburgh Evening Courant 5 October 1848

After the concert Chopin spent one night at the Łyszczyńskis' before going back to Calder House to stay with Lord and Lady Torphichen – and Jane. By this time, he was becoming irritated with Jane's constant attentions and organization of virtually every aspect of his life. So he accepted Lady Belhaven's invitation to stay with her for a few days at Wishaw House – if only to escape from Jane's attentions for a while.

I am writing at Lord Torphichen's. In this castle, just underneath the room in which I write, J. Knox, the Scottish reformer, administered the first communion. Everything here speaks to the imagination: the park with secular trees, the precipices, the ruins of ancient keeps, endless corridors with countless likenesses of ancestors: they even speak of a certain red-capped ghost, which walks about the corridors at midnight.

Chopin to Adolf Gutmann (Calder House, 16 October 1848)

On 17 October Chopin arrived at Wishaw House, a turreted, crenellated, asymmetrical castle standing in its own park. However, he was ill for most of his stay. Then, on 21 October, he was at Hamilton Palace, staying with the Duke and Duchess of Hamilton. Among the house guests there were the expatriate Prince and Princess of Parma, good friends of Chopin's. Their cheery disposition and sense of humour perked Chopin up considerably, and he found himself laughing and making jokes, something that Chopin the mimic and witty raconteur had not done for a long while.

My Scottish ladies are kind. I have not seen them for two or three weeks, but they are coming today. They would have me stay and knock about the Scottish palaces, here, there and everywhere, as I'm invited. They are kind, and so boring, the Lord preserve them... Wherever I go they follow me if they can.

Chopin to Wojciech Grzymała
(Edinburgh, 30 October 1848)

Chopin returned to Edinburgh, where he again stayed with the Łyszczyńskis. He had become not only very ill, but also very difficult and cantankerous – a feature of the effects of tuberculosis in its progressive stages. He finally left Edinburgh for London on 31 October, with Jane and Katherine following soon after. Henry Broadwood had arranged for him not only lodgings at 4 St. James' Place, but also the services of Dr. Mallan, homeopathic physician to Queen Victoria.

London

Guildhall. On 16 November 1848 Chopin played at Guildhall, in the City of London, at a function in aid of the veterans of the Polish November Uprising, at the request of Lord Dudley Stuart, Chairman of the Society for the friends of Poland. It was Chopin's last public performance.

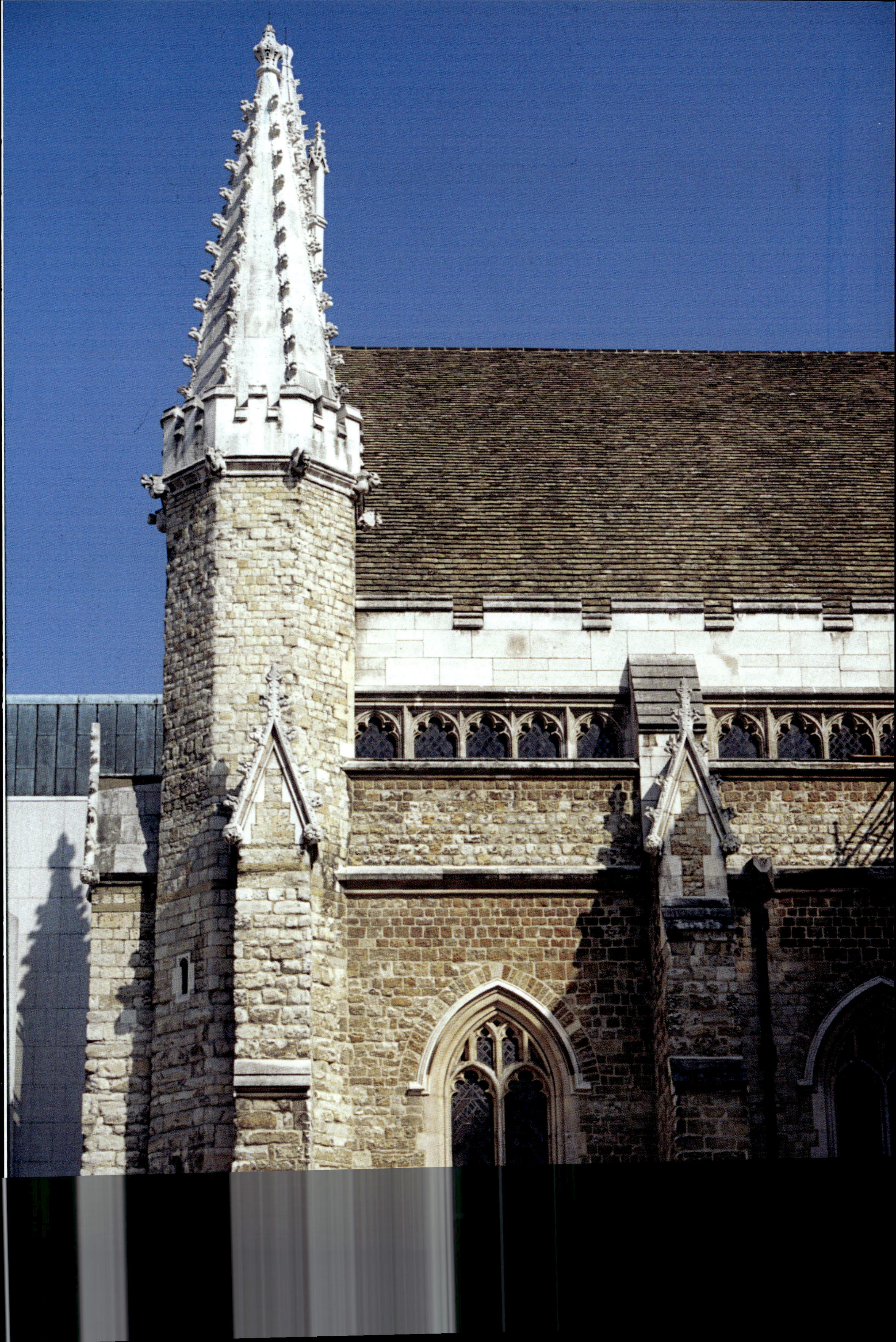

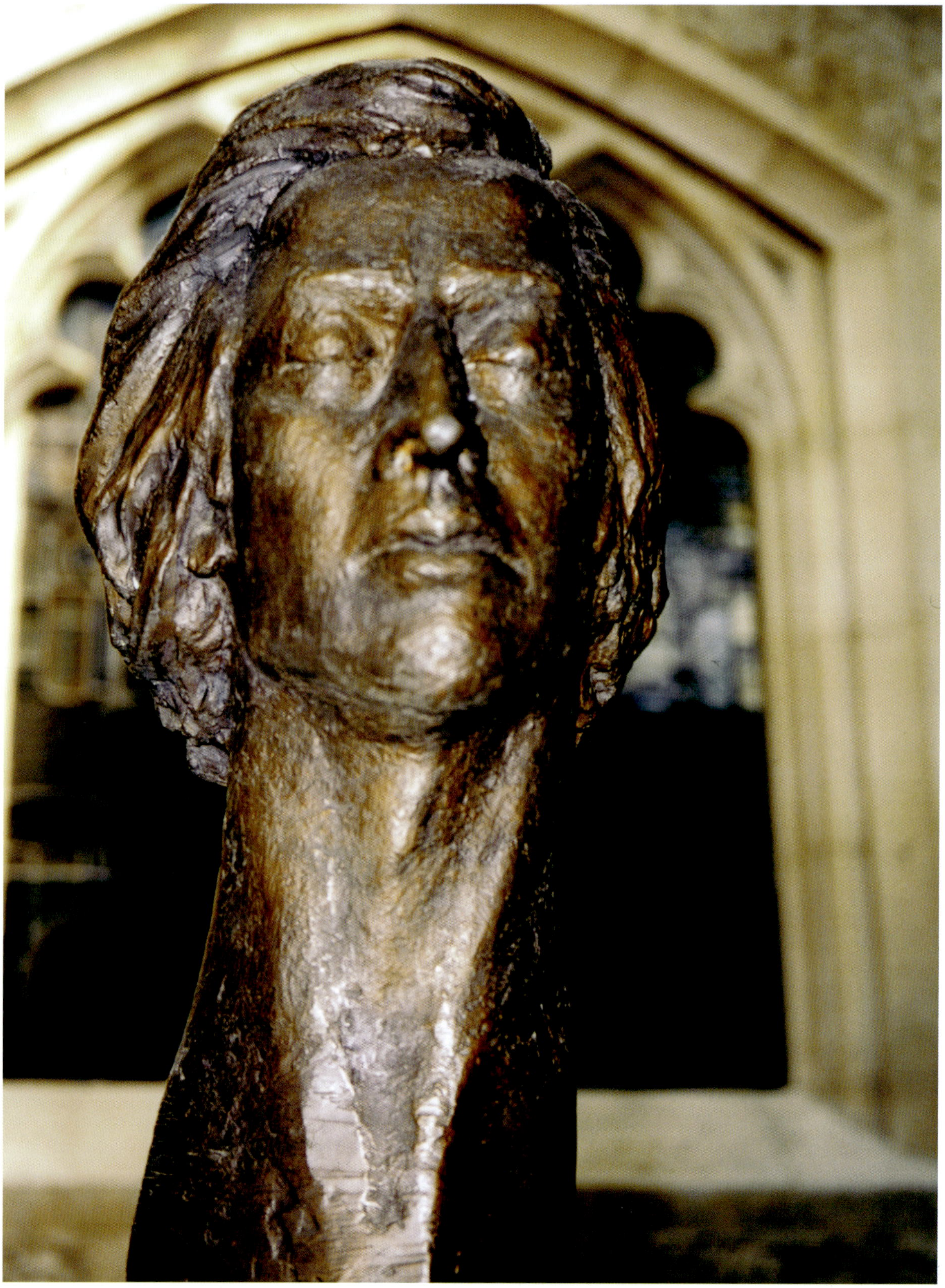

London

A bust of Chopin stands in the entrance of Guildhall.

I have been ill the last 18 days, ever since I reached London. I have not left the house at all, I have had such a cold and such headaches, short breath and all my bad symptoms. The doctor visits me every day; Dr Mallan... stiffened me up so that I could play at that Polish concert and ball.

Chopin to Wojciech Grzymała
(London, 17 November 1848)

Under Dr Mallan's care, Chopin, now barely recognizable after his gruelling Scottish ordeal, became fit enough to give his last concert in Great Britain. This charity event, organised by Member of Parliament, Lord Dudley Stuart, was billed as the "Annual Grand Dress and Fancy Ball and Concert in aid of the Funds of the Literary Association of the Friends of Poland". It took place at London's Guildhall on 16 November. The highlight was the Ball, at which it was *de rigueur* to be seen. Among those present were the Czartoryskis, Karol Szulczewski, Henry Broadwood as well as Jane and Katherine, in addition to the cream of London Society. Dancing was to Mr Adam's Dance Band, and there was also music by an orchestra conducted by Lindsay Soper, a former pupil of Chopin's, and now a successful London professional musician.

Chopin's own contribution was a concert in the Council Chamber of his Etudes, Waltzes and Mazurkas – his least strenuous compositions, yet featuring his characteristic fingerwork which had lost none of those delicate nuances for which it was renowned. Unfortunately, these nuances were largely lost on the talkative crowd bent on an evening of fun. For all that, the many Poles present gave Chopin a rousing ovation, and the event was deemed a great success. Chopin himself was pleased with his performance, after which he immediately returned to his apartment, sick with a raging headache.

M. Chopin played a series of Etudes upon the pianoforte, with all his graceful skill and exquisite refinement of style. We should, however, have listened to him with more satisfaction in the retirement of the drawing room than amid such a disturbed and unreflecting multitude as this. The qualities which gave him his special charm are too delicate and intellectual to challenge the favour of a crowd bent chiefly on physical enjoyment.

"The Sun", 17 November 1848

Chopin never performed in public again. A week later, he returned to Paris.

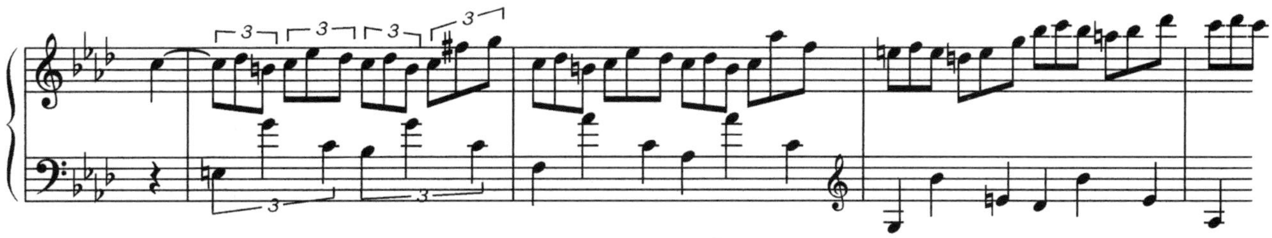

The subtle cross-rhythms of this ethereal and delicate Etude in F minor Op. 25 No 2 made an enormous impression on Chopin's British audiences.

The London addresses of Bentinck Street, St. James' Street, Great Pulteney Street and Dover Street are still there, as is the City of London's Guildhall. Stafford House, where Chopin played to Queen Victoria and Prince Albert, is today Lancaster House in the Mall. 10 Warriston Crescent in Edinburgh bears a plaque commemorating Chopin's sojourn, and is a private residence, and the Hopetoun Rooms, where Chopin's Edinburgh concert took place, is now Erskine House, a commercial building in Queen Street. The Douglas Hotel was situated at today's 34/35 St. Andrew's Square, and Waterloo Place, where Muir Wood's Music shop was situated, is also still there. Calder House, Strachur House, Gargunnock, Keir House and Kippenross House, Jane Stirling's residence are also there, although Milliken House has been rebuilt out of the original materials a short distance from its original site, and only a tower remains of Johnstone Castle at the centre of a modern housing estate, and has recently been converted into a private residence. Wishaw House and Hamilton Palace have been demolished, although the Hamilton Mausoleum is still a prominent landmark in the Strathclyde Country Park, visible from the M74 motorway. The Merchants' Hall in Hutcheson Street, where Chopin's Glasgow concert took place, is no longer there, as the whole street has been extensively redeveloped, and the actual site is now a small shopping and business complex facing the other side of the block to Hutcheston Street. A housing estate now occupies the site of Crumpsall House in Manchester.

Edinburgh

Edinburgh Castle dominates the sky-line of Scotland's capital from its position atop the volcanic Castle Rock. Human habitation of the site dates back as far as the ninth century BC, although the nature of early settlement is unclear. It also features as the backdrop to the annual Edinburgh Military Tattoo, and has become a recognisable iconic symbol of the city and of Scotland itself.

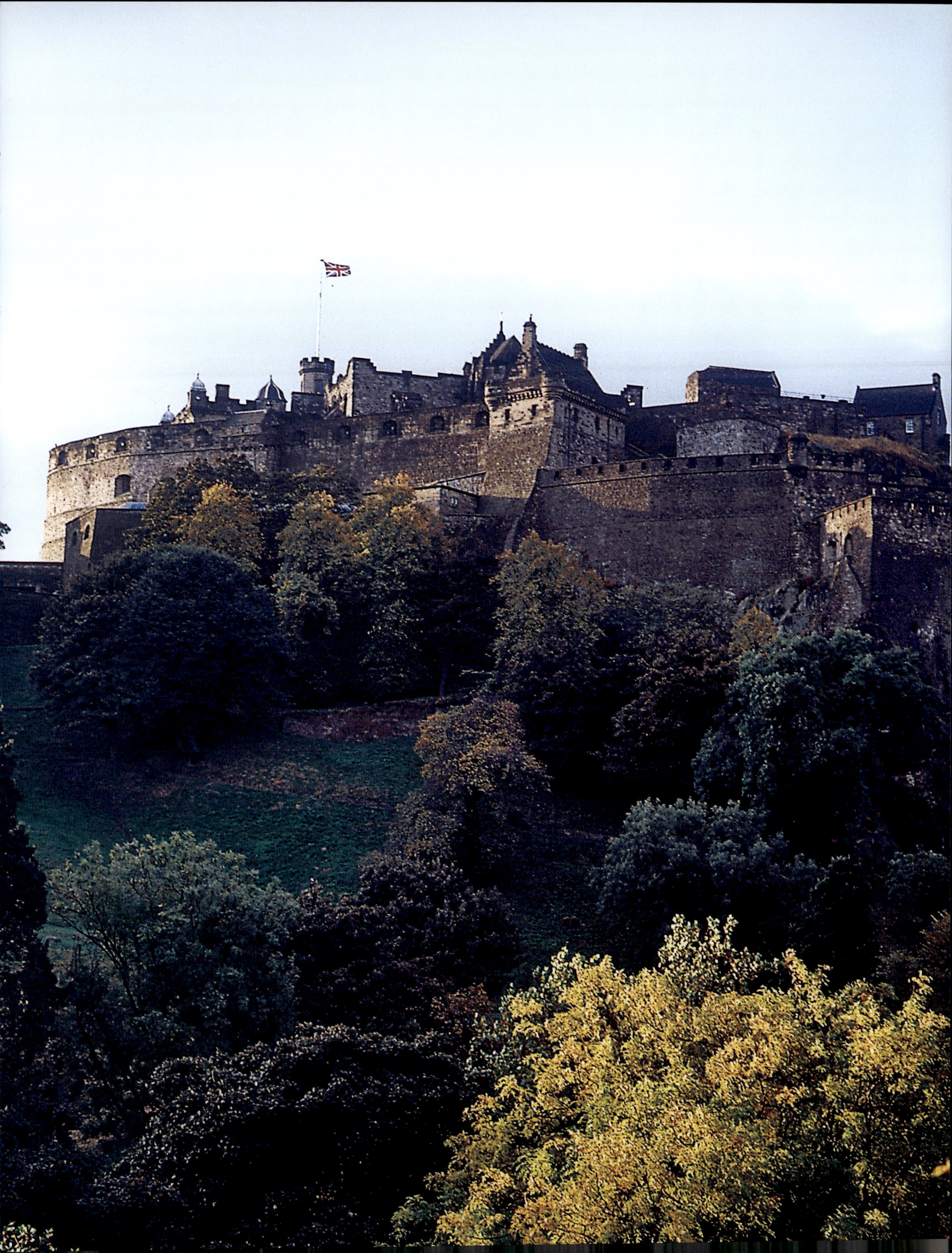

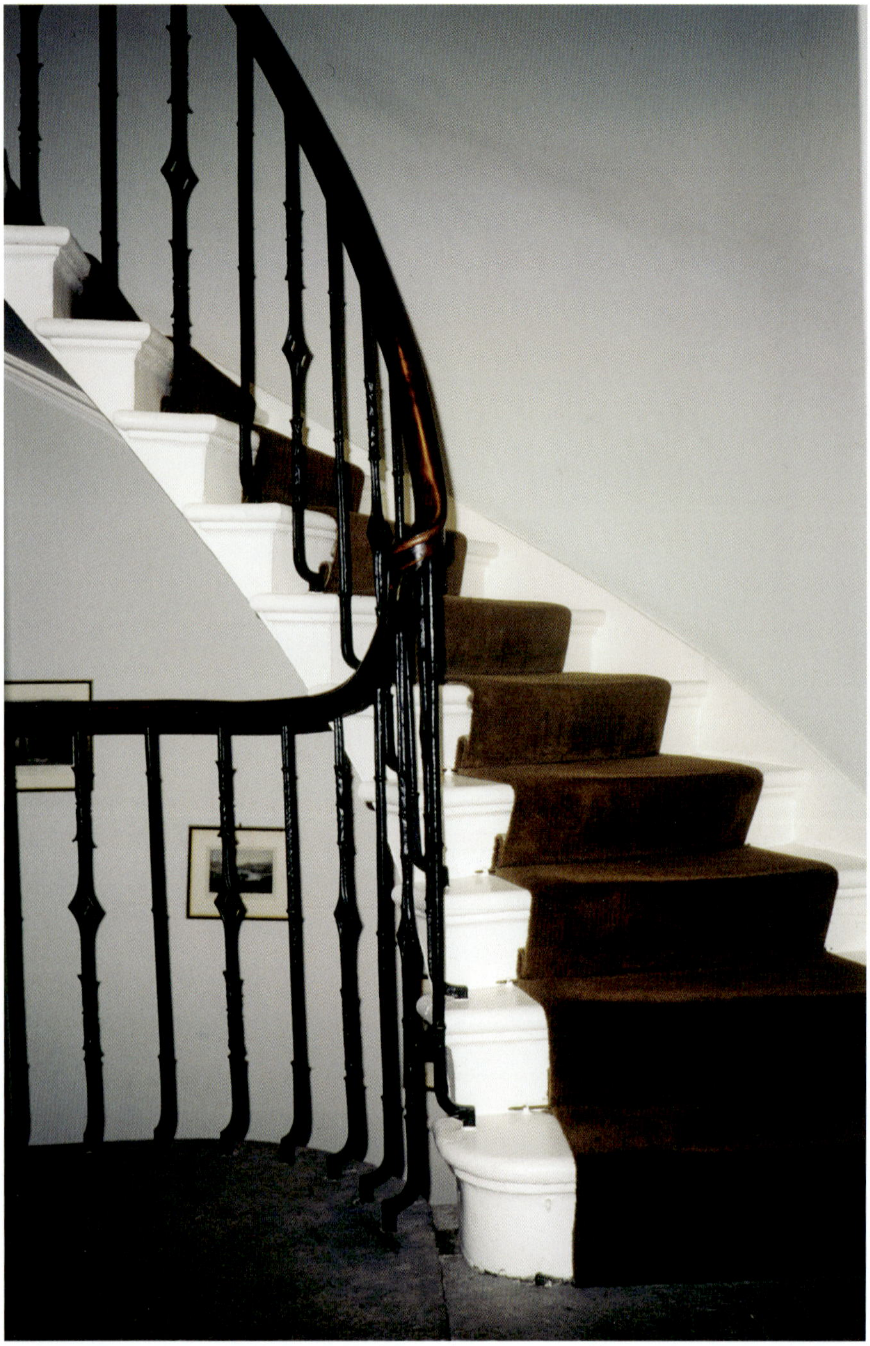

Edinburgh

When in Edinburgh Chopin usually stayed at 10 Warriston Crescent, the home of Dr Adam Łyszczyński, a refugee from the Polish Uprising of 1830-31, who had settled in the Scottish capital and graduated from the Edinburgh School of Medicine. In between his various trips around Scotland, Chopin returned to Warriston Crescent for homeopathic treatment by the Doctor. Chopin's manservant, Daniel, used to carry the enfeebled composer up and down the staircase at 10 Warriston Crescent.

→ In Chopin's day Warriston Crescent was a new development, and a sewer system ran throughout the area now occupied by the gardens.

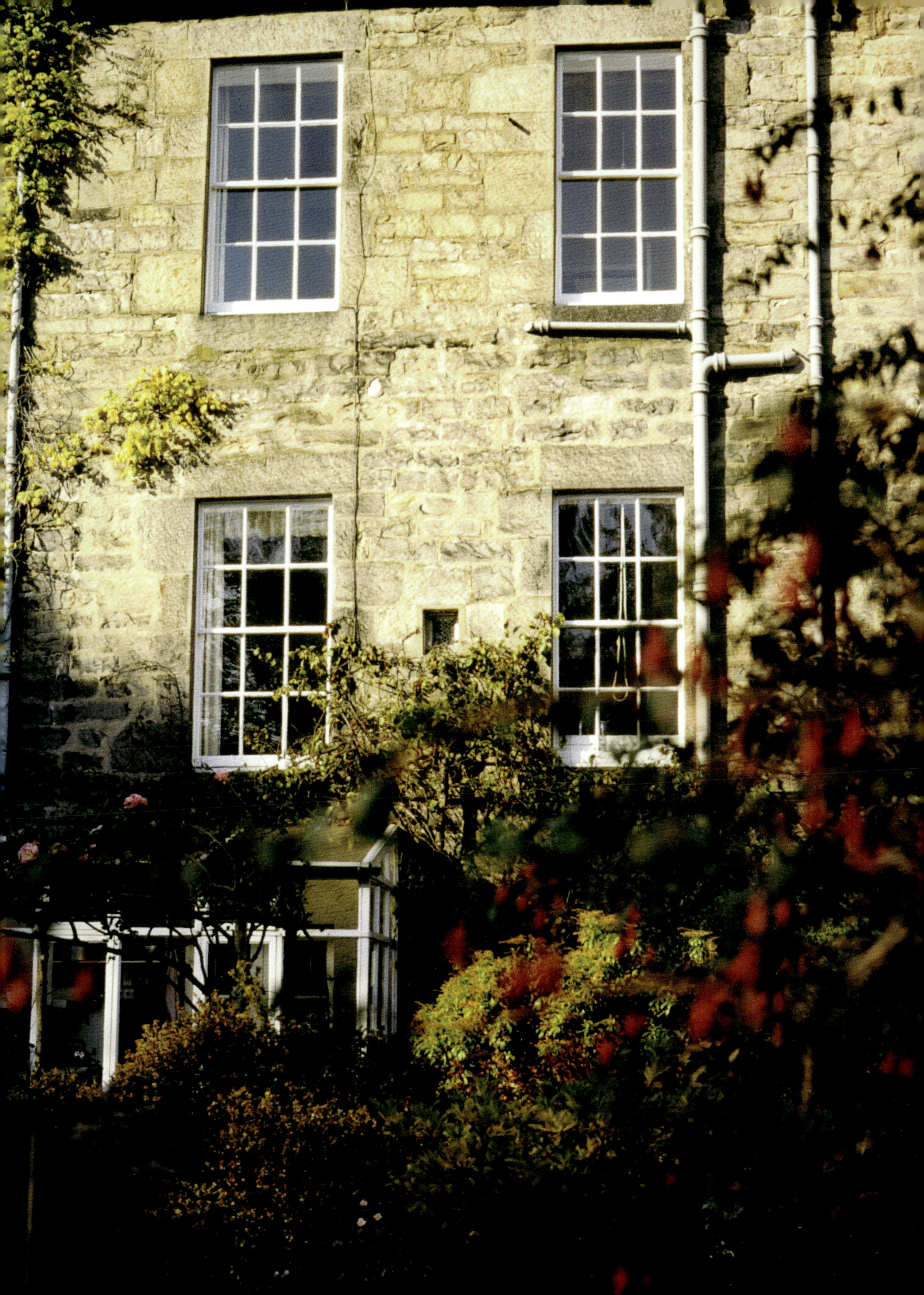

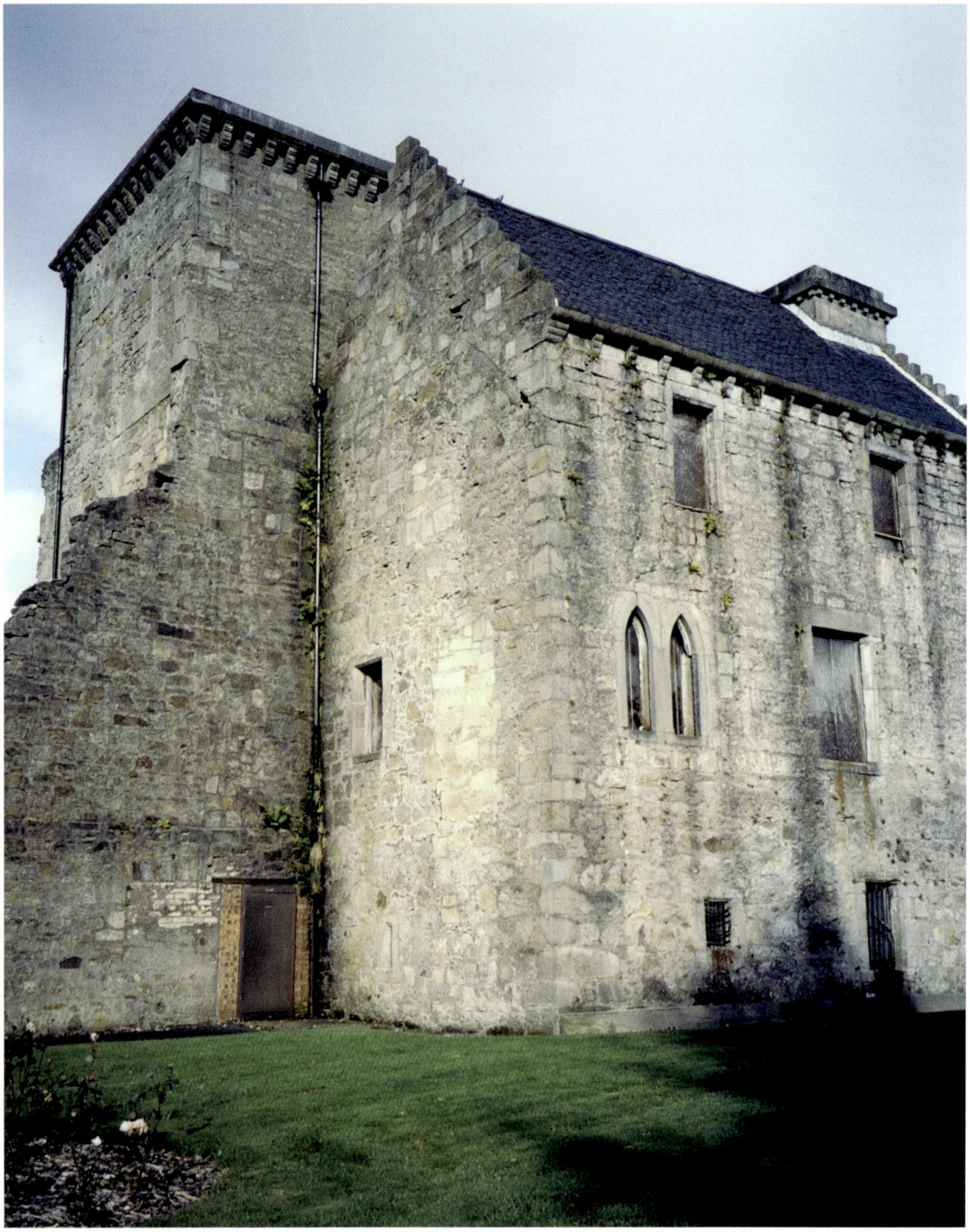

Johnston Castle

Chopin stayed at Johnstone Castle, the home of Ludovik Houston, the husband of Jane Stirling's eldest sister Anne. It was an ideal base at which to prepare for the concert in Glasgow that Muir Wood had organised for him at the end of September 1848. All that remains today of the Castle is one tower, which has been converted into a private residence in the middle of a modern residential area.

→ Calder House

Lord and Lady Torphichen invited Chopin to stay at their residence, Calder House, a short distance out of Edinburgh, and arranged for a carriage to bring him. Among those waiting to welcome him with true Scottish hospitality were Jane Stirling and Katherine Erskine. Lady Margaret Torphichen was their older sister. Chopin stayed at Calder House twice during his stay in Scotland.

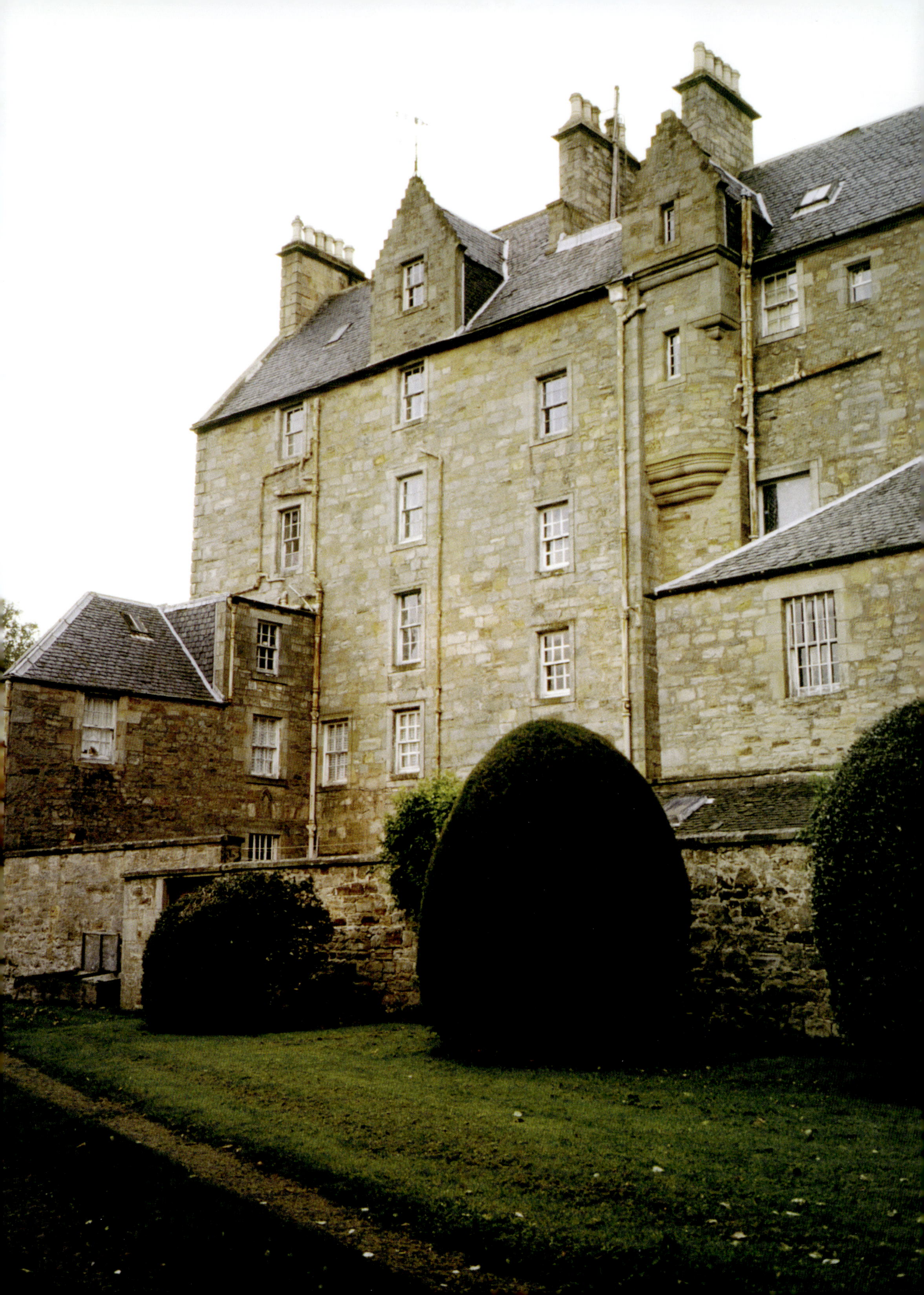

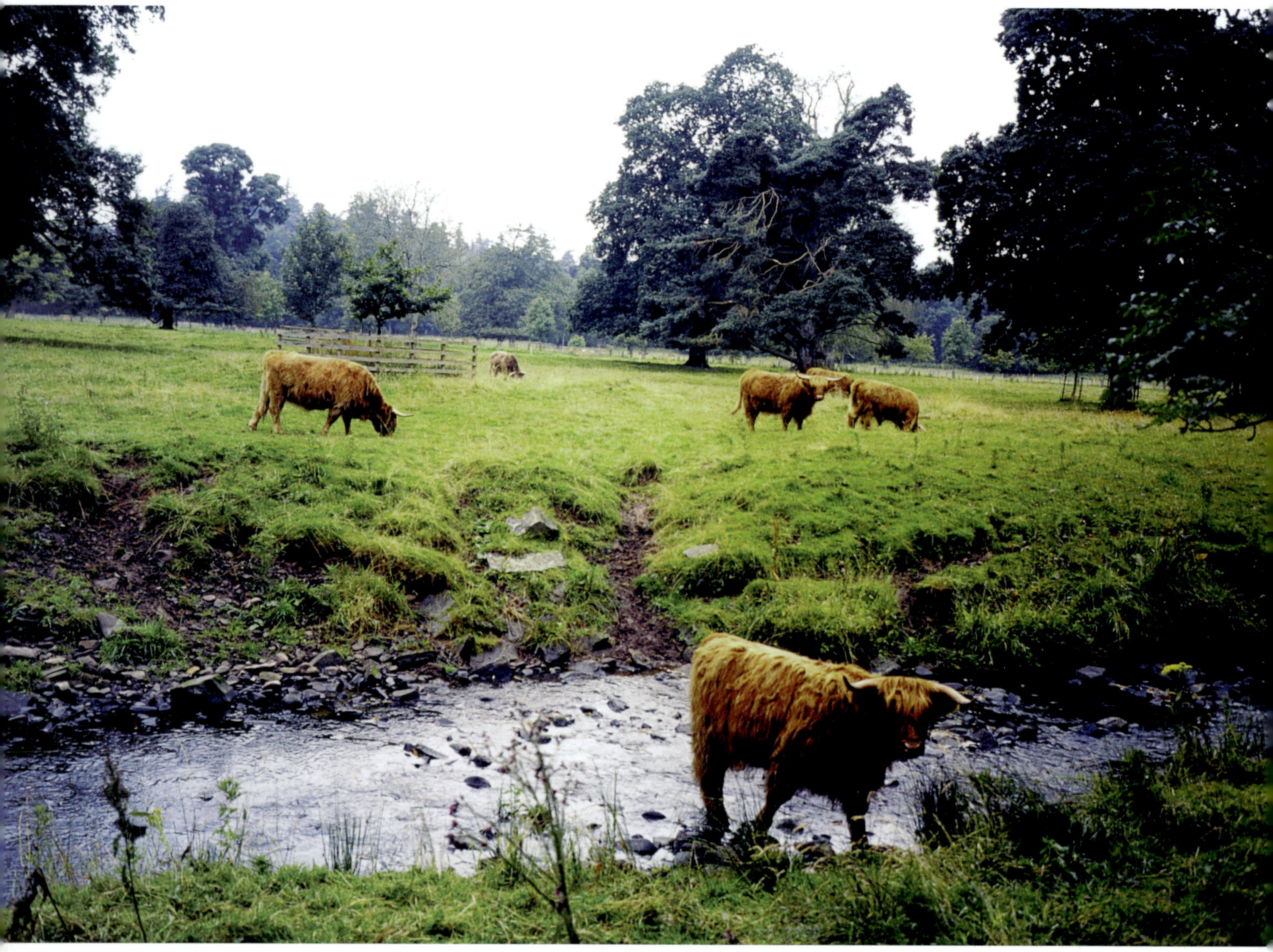

Chopin was most amused by Scottish cattle, and described their fierce appearance to his family.

→ Strachur House

Chopin spent a week at Strachur House, on the banks of Loch Fyne, as a guest of Lord and Lady Murray, who had been renting the property from the Campbells of Strachur. Sixty-year-old Lady Murray had been Chopin's first pupil in London, and was a leading patroness of music in Scotland. Chopin had a good rest here, herrings from the loch, salmon from the rivers and venison from the hills, as well as the finest French wines, as his hosts were devotees of all things French.

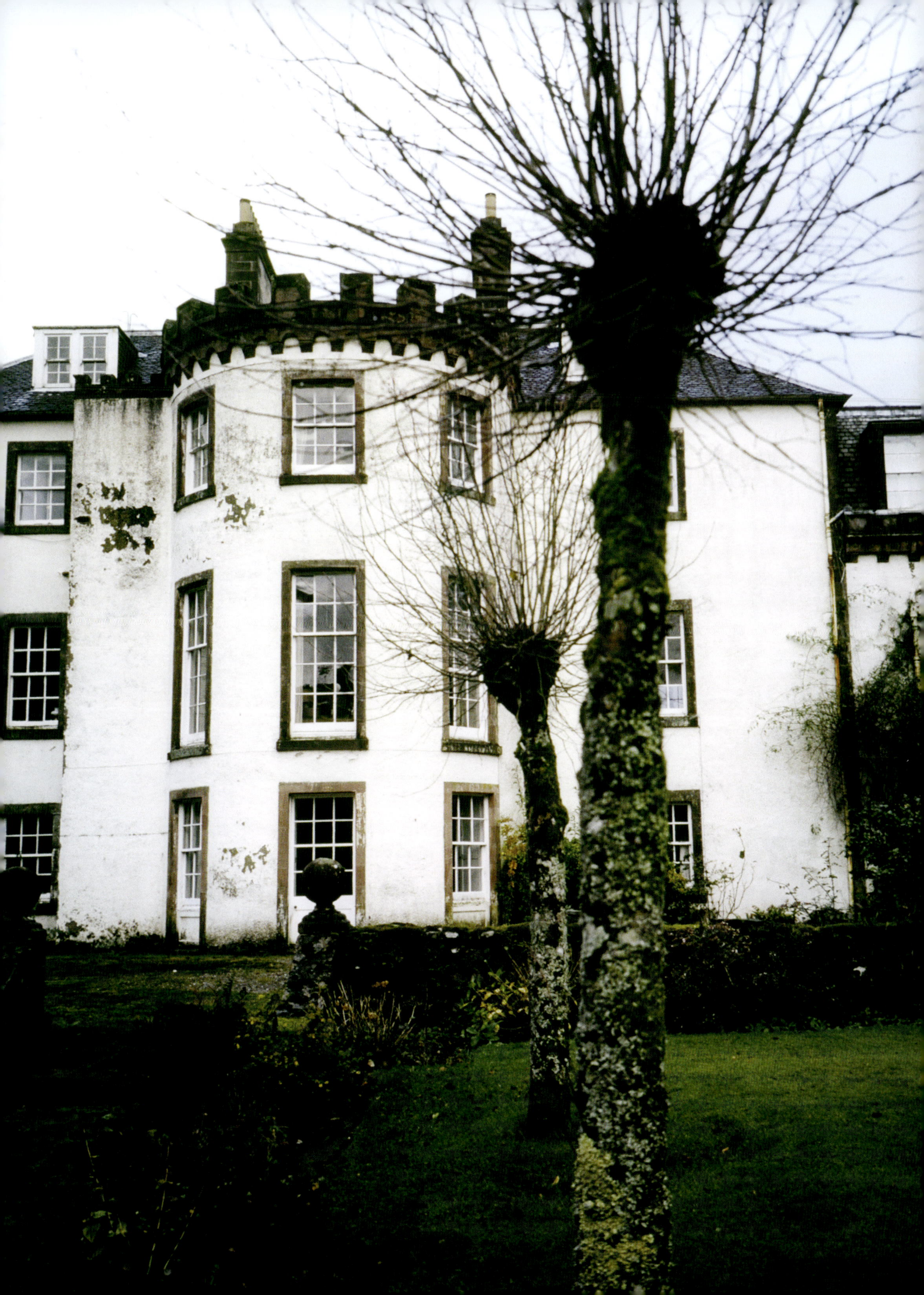

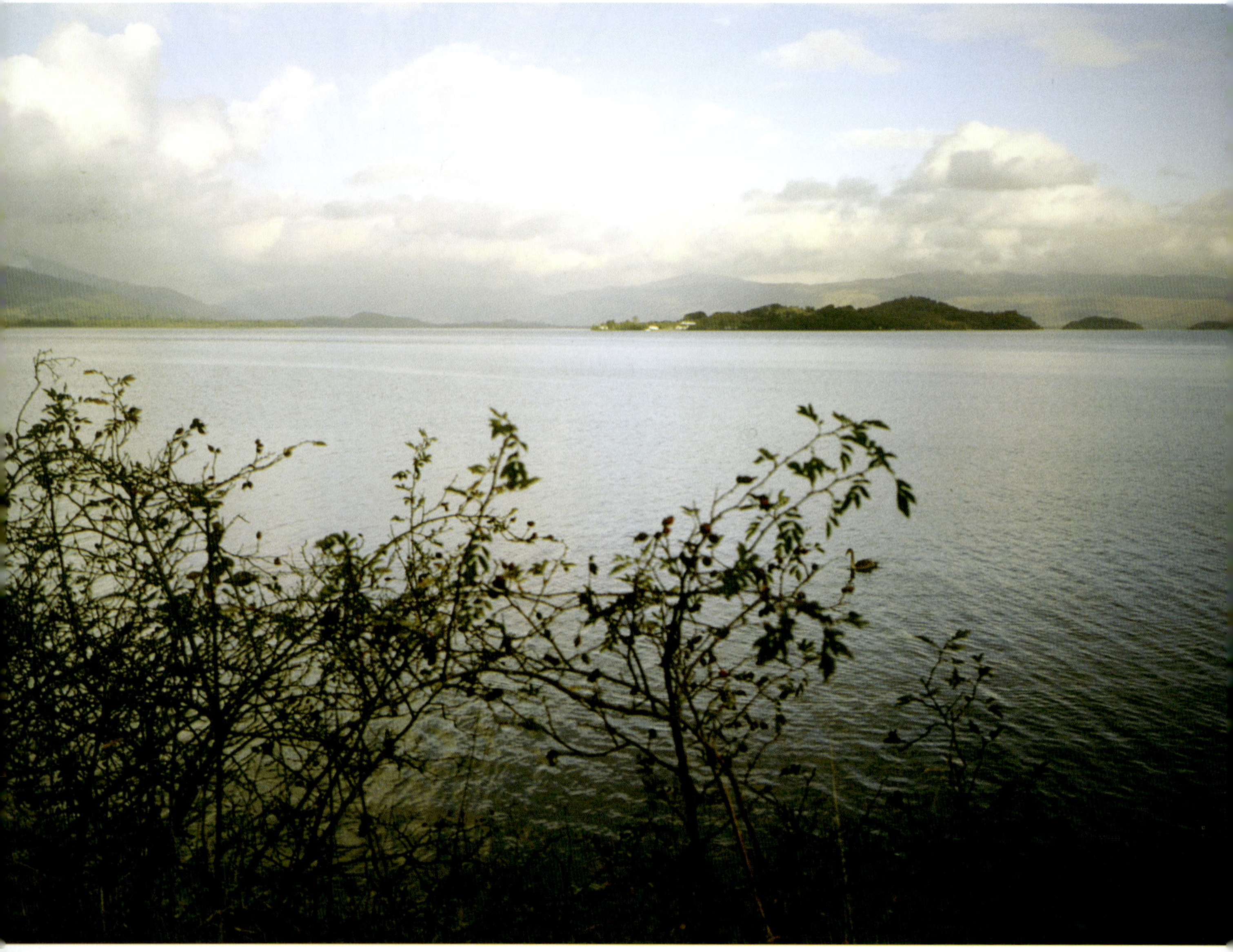

Strachur House

Loch Fyne, on Scotland's west coast, extends 65 kilometres (40 miles) inland from the Sound of Bute, making it the longest of the sea lochs. Chopin claimed that his week at Strachur House, which looks onto this loch, was the happiest moment of his trip to Great Britain in 1848.

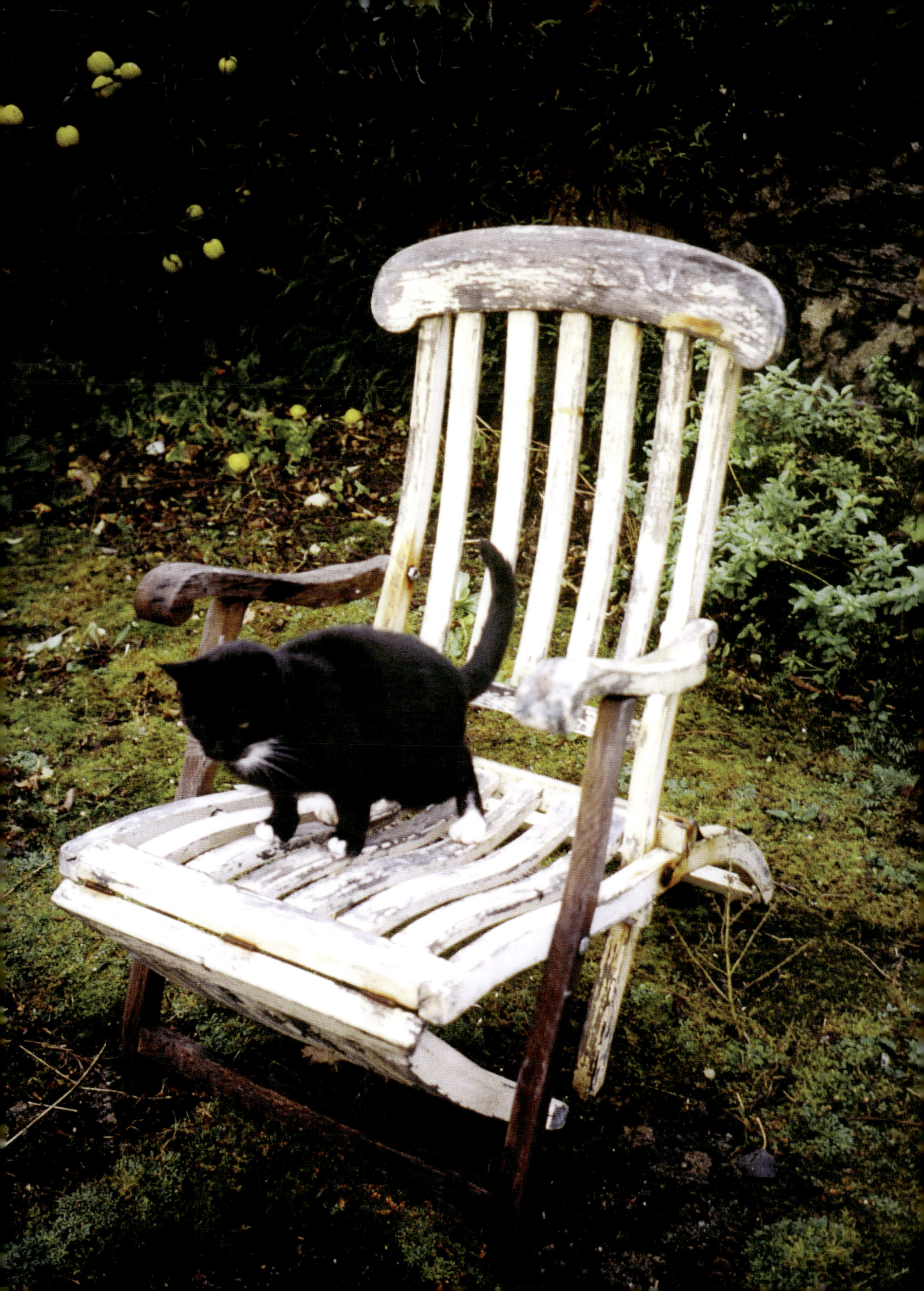

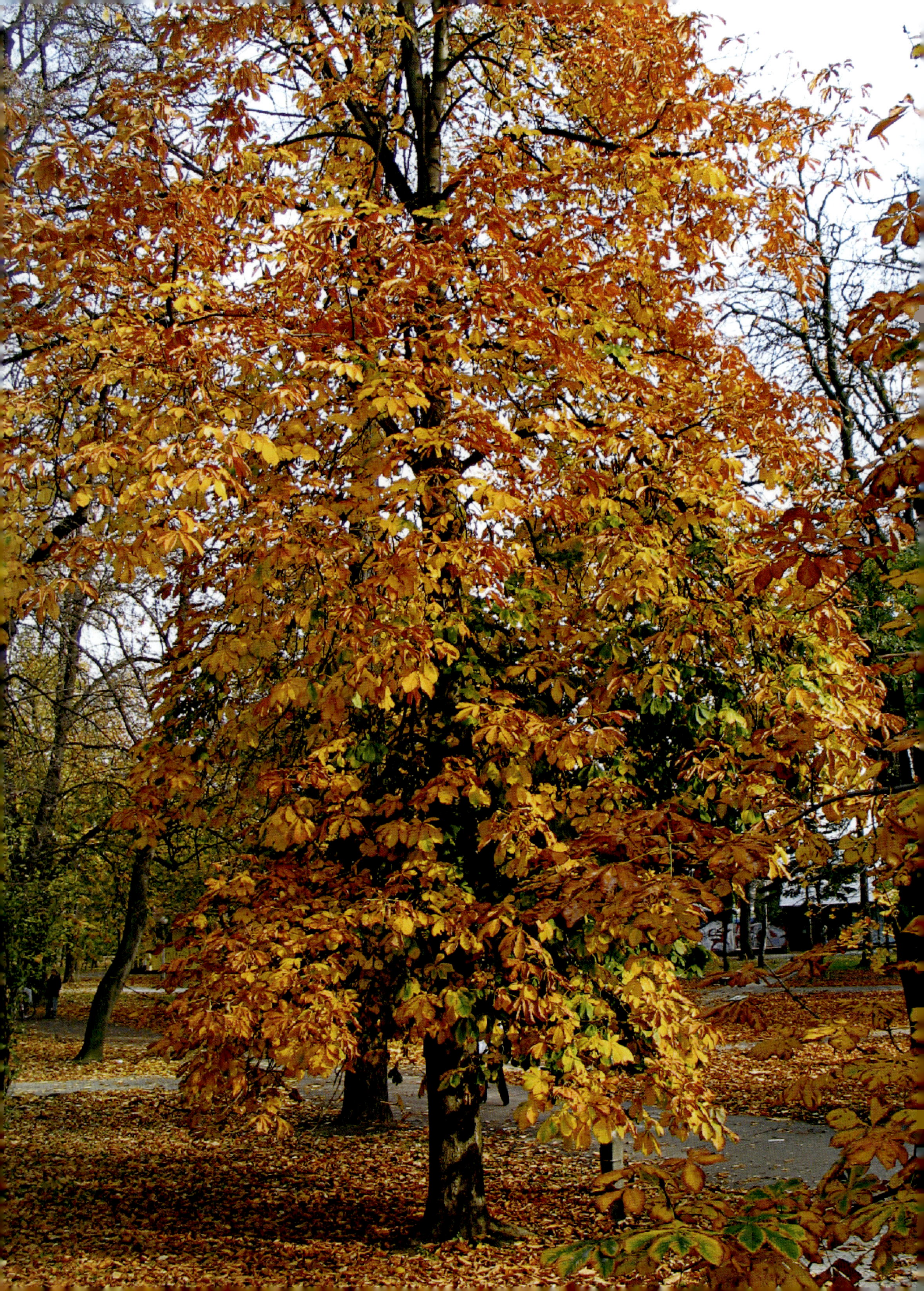

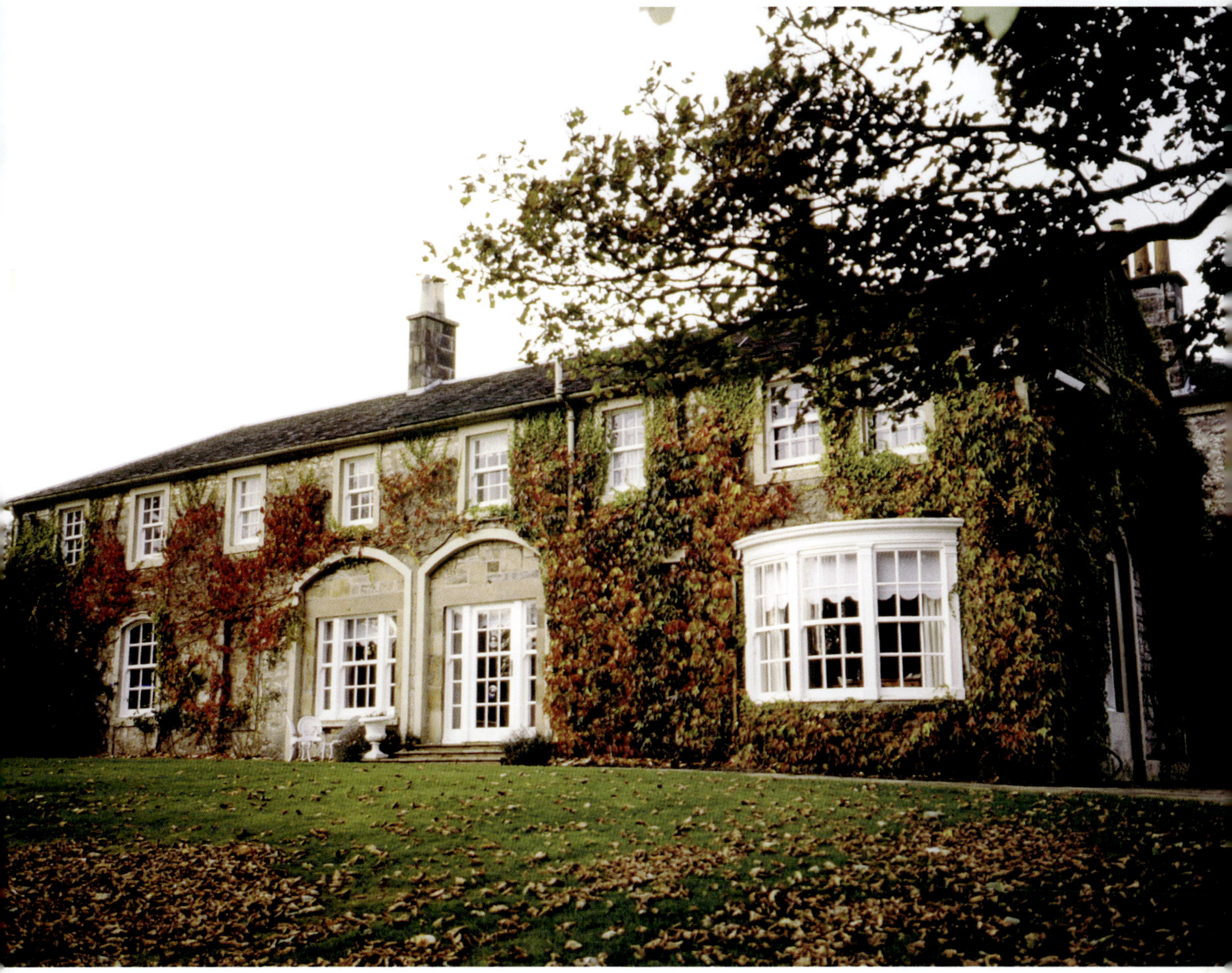

Milliken House

Chopin paid a short visit to Milliken House, near Glasgow, as guest of Sir William Napier, who was married to Jane Stirling's sister Elisabeth. The present building, known as the White House, was rebuilt from the original stones.

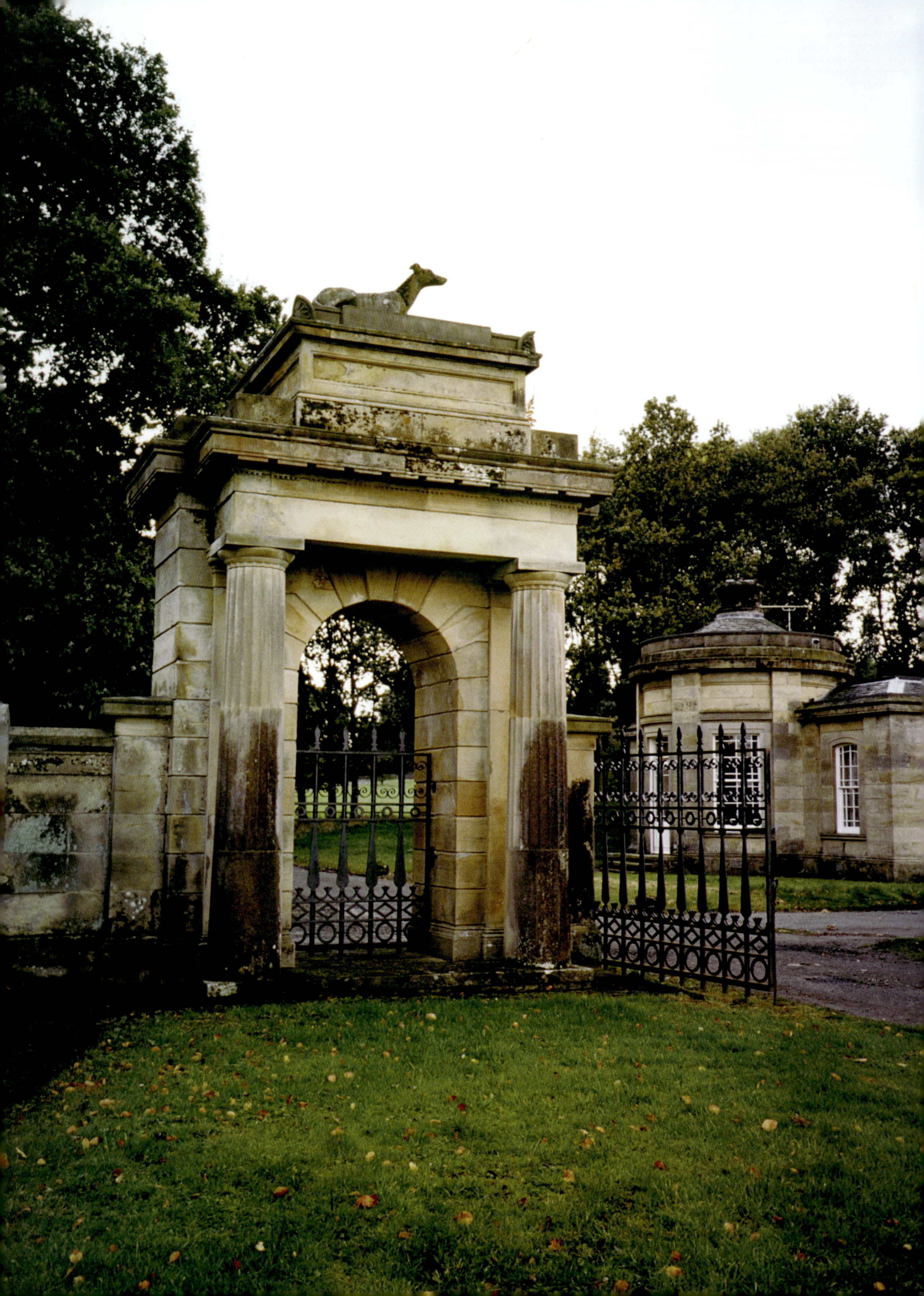

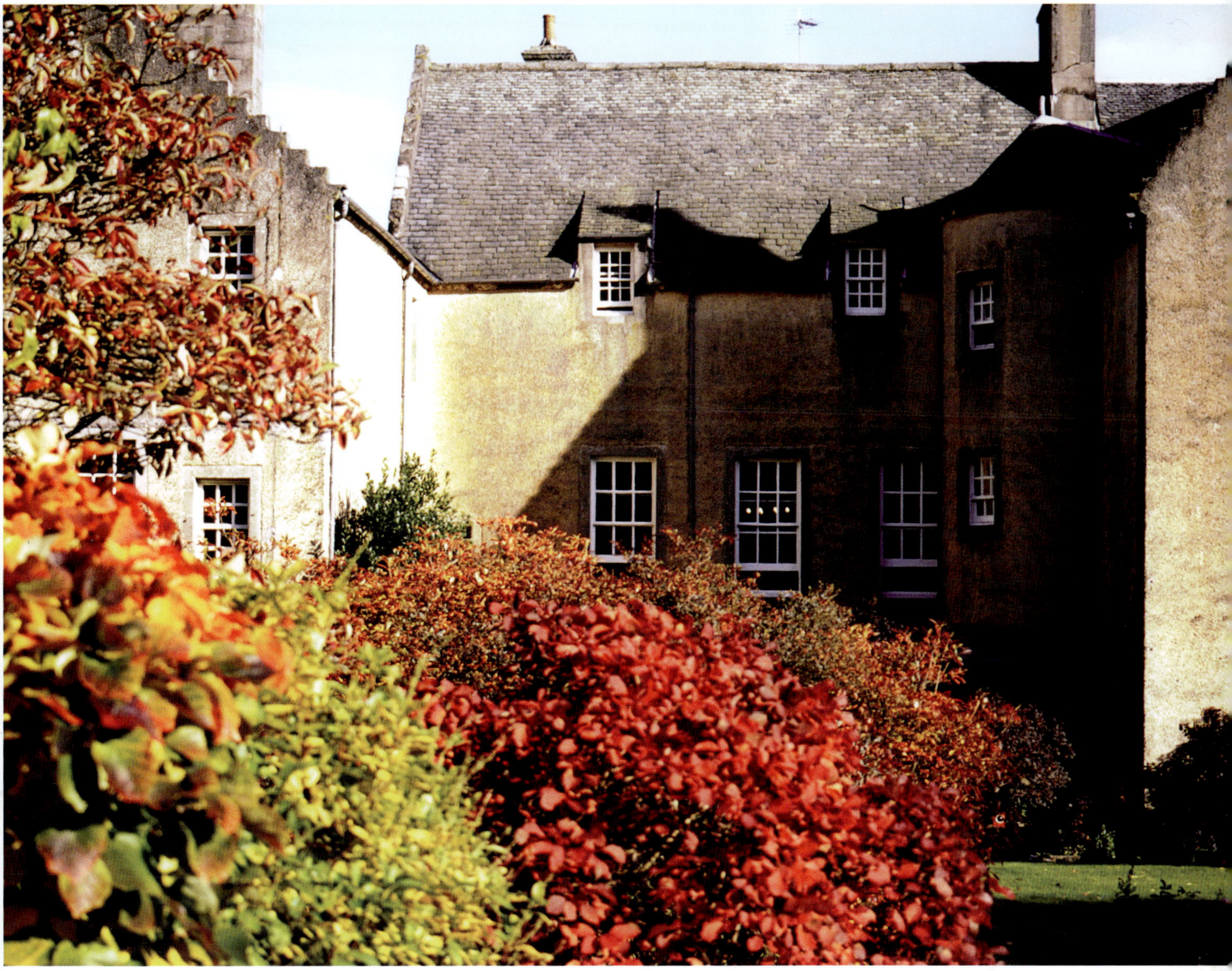

Gargunnock House

Chopin paid a short visit to Gargunnock House – the residence of Jane's brother, Charles Stirling who had died a decade previously, leaving a widow and several children. The Broadwood piano still in the house is reputed to be the one on which Chopin played as a brand new instrument at the time of his visit.

← Keir House

Chopin enjoyed an extended visit to Keir House, situated just outside Dunblane, the home of author and art connoisseur Sir William Stirling, Jane's uncle and head of the Stirling clan. The only thing that marred Chopin's otherwise delightful stay there was the severe Scottish Sabbath, totally devoid of all activity, which bored Chopin.

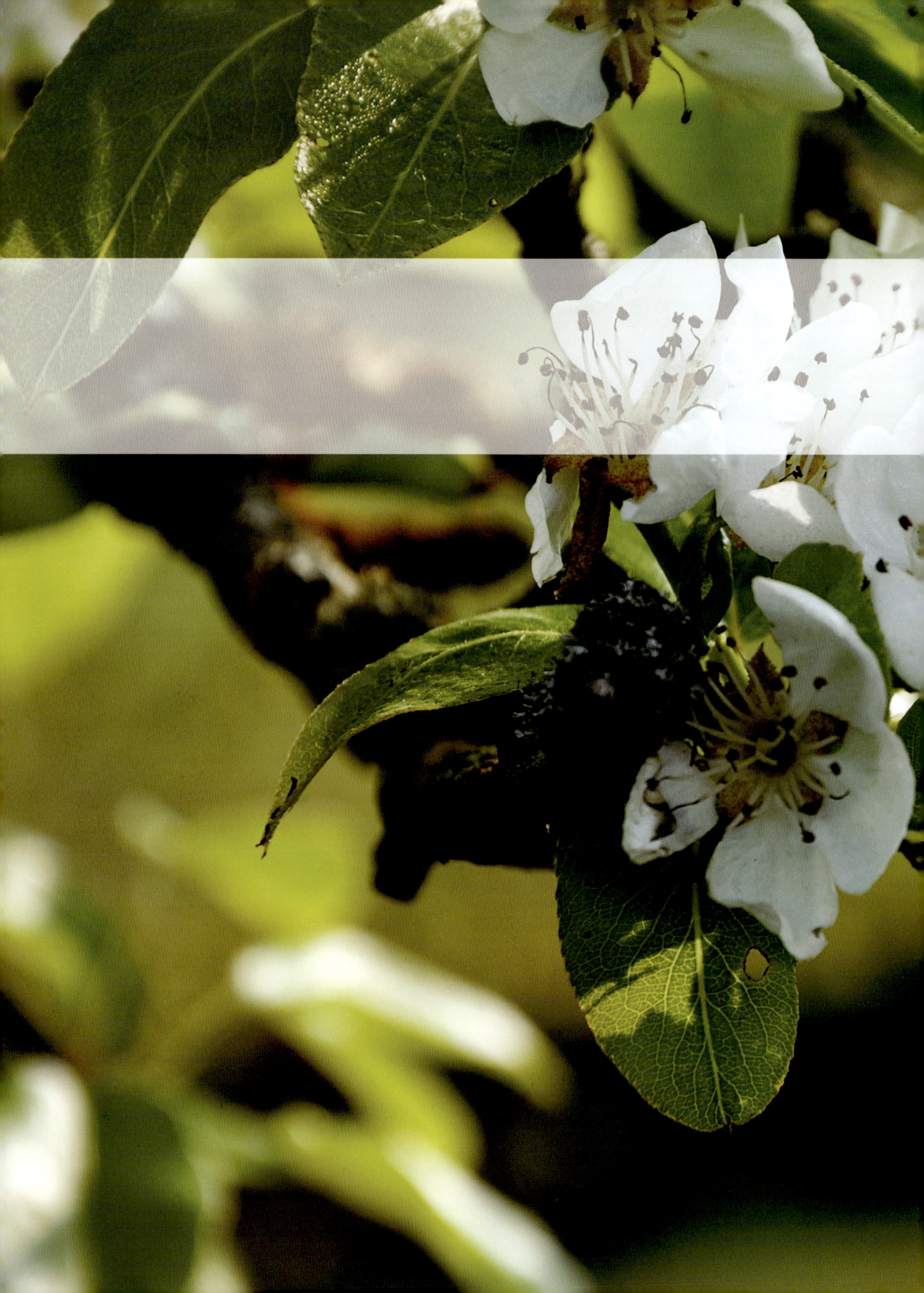

Epilogue

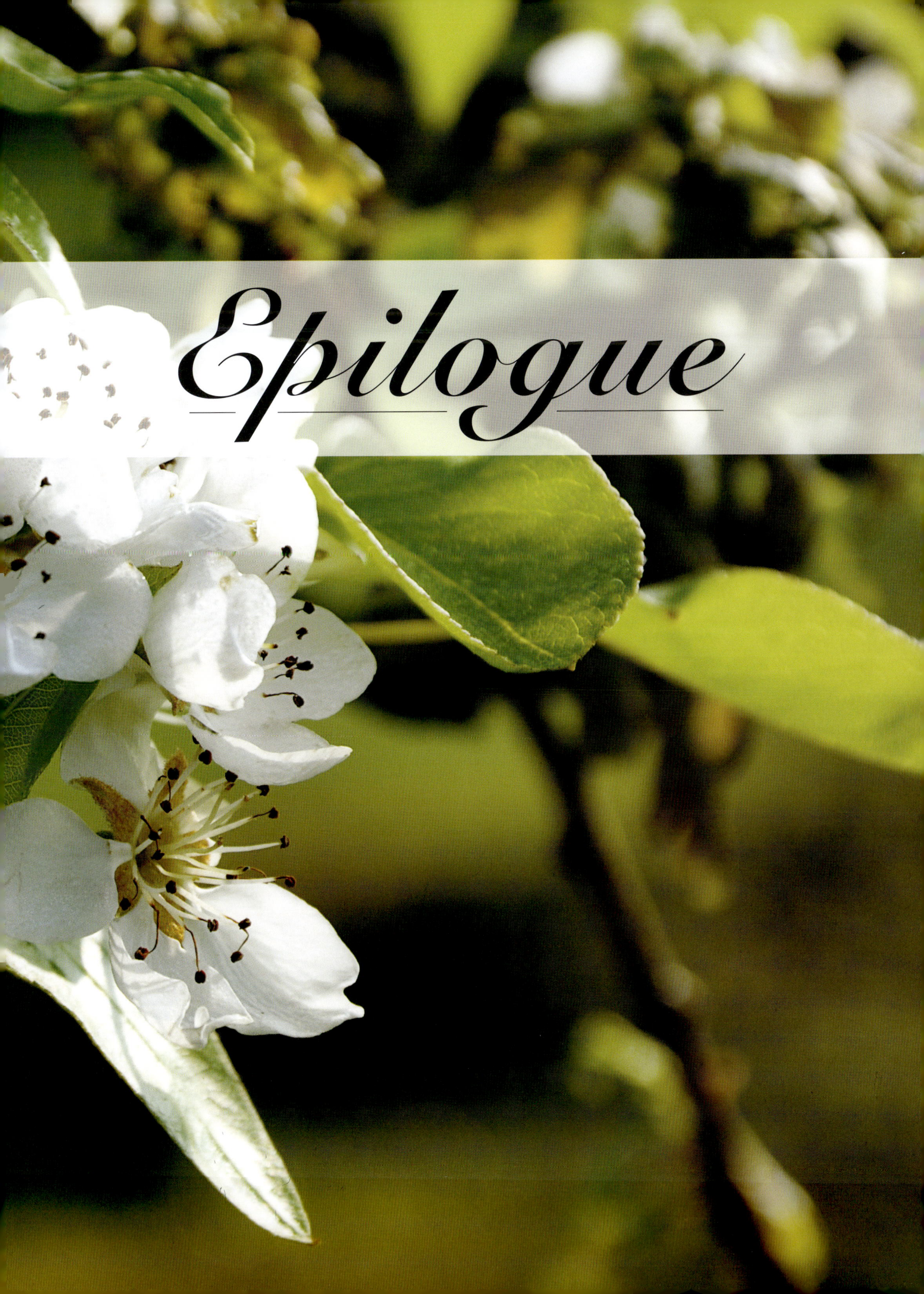

On Friday 24 November 1848 Fryderyk Chopin returned to his Paris apartment in the square d'Orléans after his exhausting trip to London and Scotland. The desperately sick composer spent the ensuing weeks making only a limited recovery. Dr Jean-Jacques Molins, the homeopathic physician who had been treating Chopin in Paris with some success before his departure across the Channel, had died, and he was followed by a succession of other doctors, whose fees gradually ate up all the money that Chopin had earned in Great Britain. As he was now in no fit state either to perform or to earn money by teaching, his prospects were beginning to look grim.

His friends and former pupils rallied round, both to give him moral support, and – surreptitiously – to contribute funds. These included, among very many others, Wojciech Grzymała, Eugène Delacroix, and his former pupils, Adolf Gutmann, Princess Marcelina Czartoryska, Countess Maria Kalergis and Jane Stirling herself. George Sand's daughter Solange Clésinger remained a close friend despite her mother's messy break-up with the composer. Cellist Auguste Franchômme took control of Chopin's finances, and plotted with others, behind Chopin's back, to ensure that there was enough in the kitty for expenses.

I hope that the spring sunshine will be my best doctor.

Chopin to Solange Clésinger (Paris, 13 April 1849)

As the cold Paris winter led into 1849 Chopin rallied somewhat, and was even able to get out on occasions to visit friends and go to the opera. In April these sorties came to an end and he again took to his bed. His condition became critical, he was permanently exhausted, and he began to suffer no illusions as to the eventual outcome of his illness. He directed that in the event of anything happening to him, all his unfinished manuscripts and jottings were to be burned. He also asked for his sister Ludwika Jędrzejewicz to come to Paris from Poland with her husband Kalasanty, and daughter, also called Ludwika. This was seen as a serious move, since he had always made a point of keeping his illness from his family.

If you can, do come. I am ill, and no doctor will help me as much as some of you. My friends and well-wishers think that the best medicine for me will be Ludwika's presence here… so try for a passport.

Chopin to Ludwika Jędrzejewiczowa (Paris, 25 June 1849)

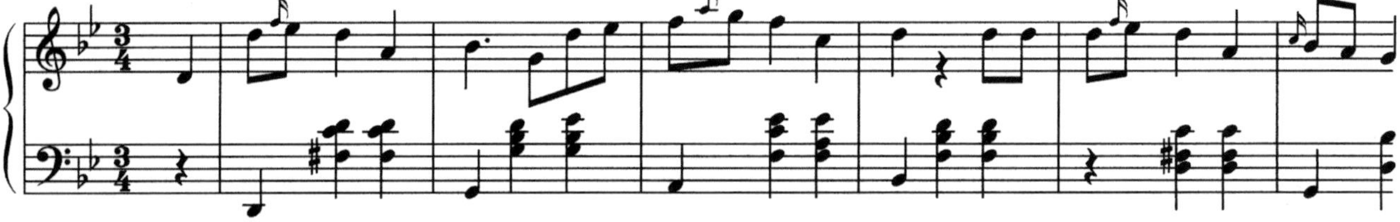

Despite his failing health, Chopin still managed to compose.
Among his works written in 1849 was this Mazurka in G minor Op. 67 No 2.

Paris, Place Vendôme

Bust of Chopin in the room set aside to his memory by the Jewellers Chaumet in the Place Vandôme.

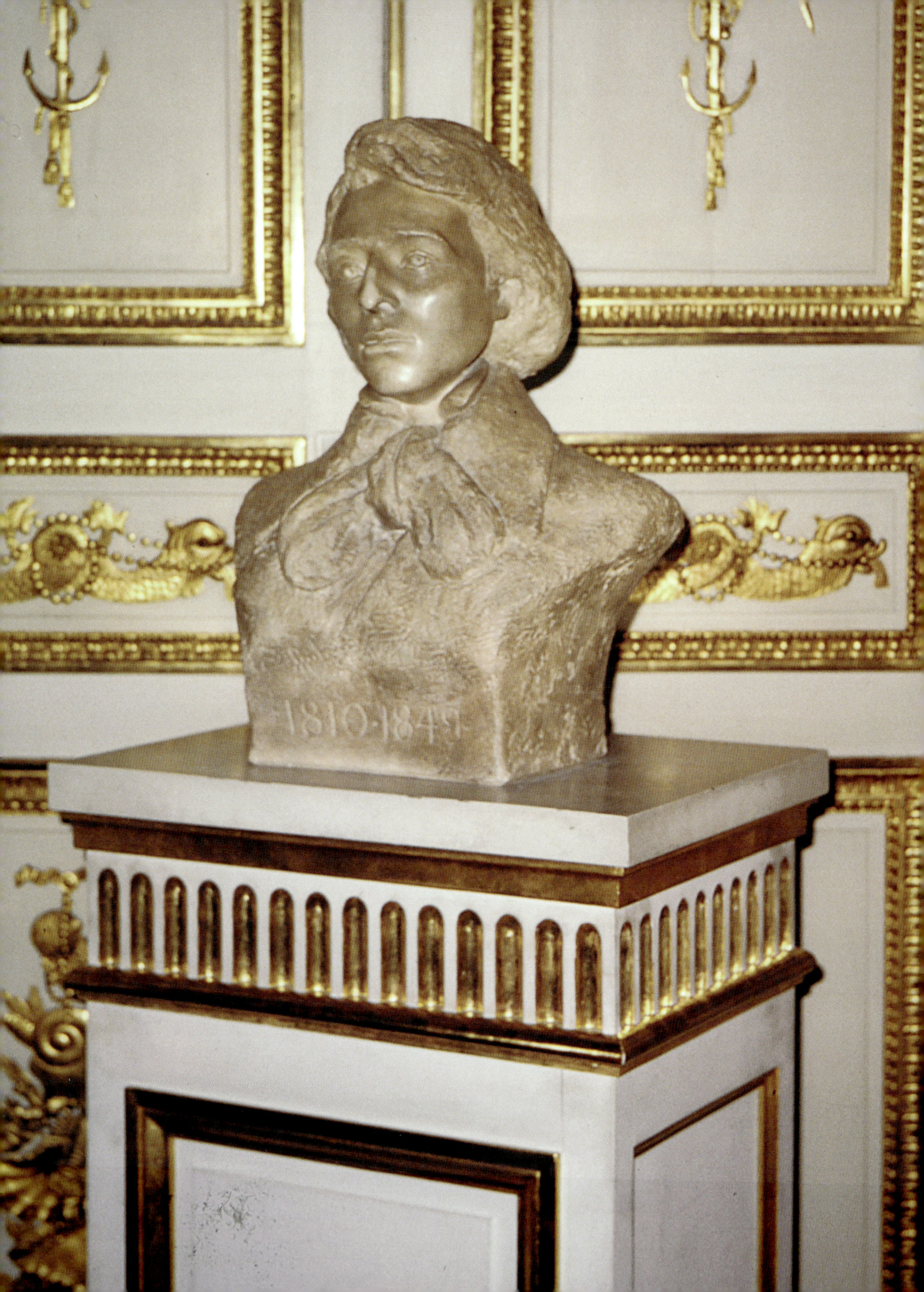
1810-1849

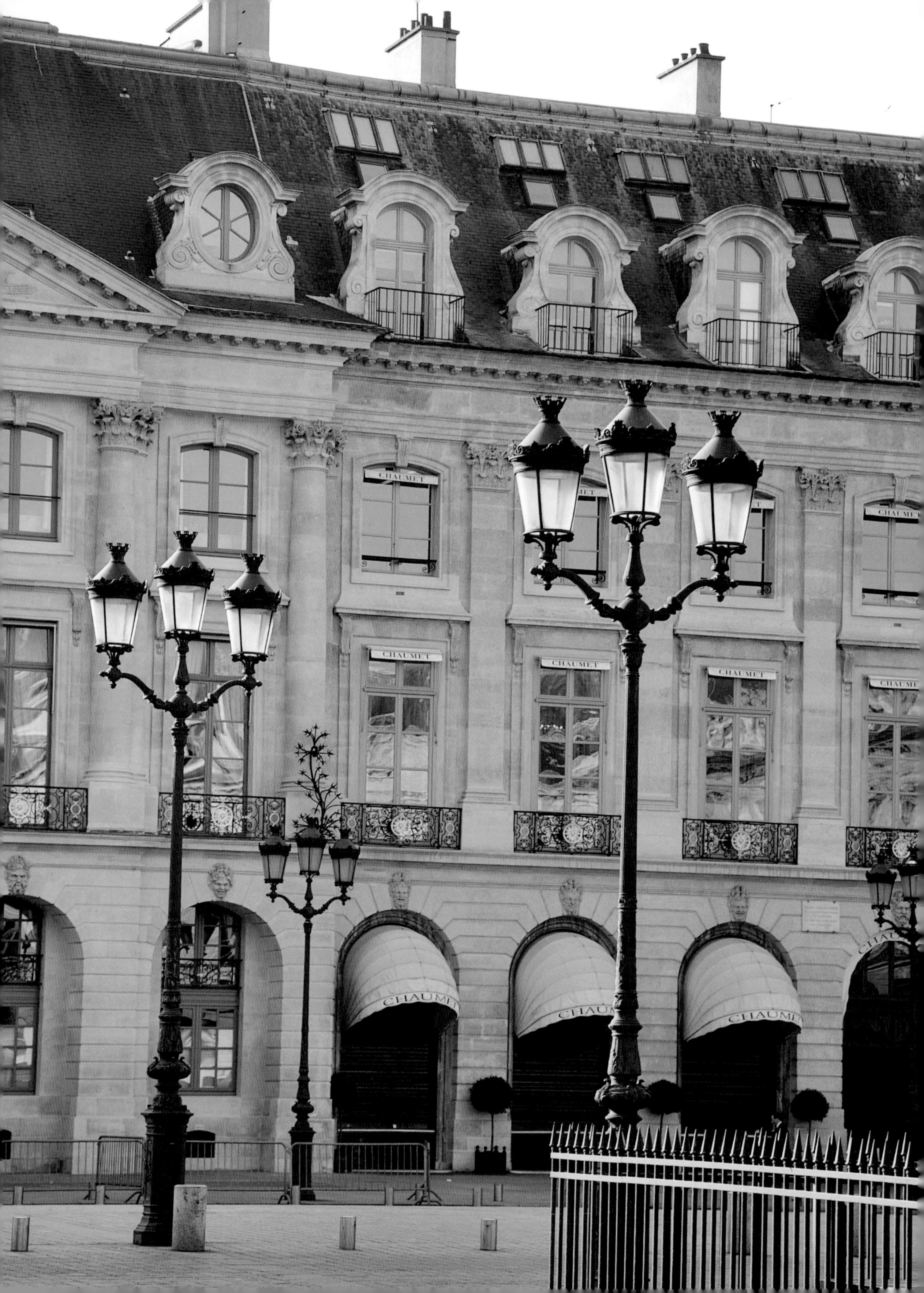
CHAUMET
CHAUMET
CHAUMET
CHAUMET
CHAUMET
CHAUMET
CHAUMET

In May Paris became very hot and stuffy, and the doctors advised Chopin to move out of town. In addition, a cholera epidemic had broken out and was claiming many lives, so he was moved to a quiet apartment in Chaillot, a short distance to the north west of the city, where he continued to be visited regularly by his friends. The spacious second floor apartment at 74 rue Chaillot commanded a spectacular view of Paris and the Seine. He was attended at all times by the faithful Daniel and, in addition, the Czartoryskis had engaged for him a Polish night nurse, a certain Mrs Matuszewska.

Mrs Matuszewska… (whom Princess Anna sent to me so that I should not be alone at night) says that The Lord Jesus will put it right, you know; and perhaps a plaster with honey and starch might help.

Chopin to Wojciech Grzymała (Paris, 2 July 1849)

Even more friends visited the ailing composer, including Berlioz, Jenny Lind, Polish poet Cyprian Norwid, the young bookseller Charles Gavard, Chopin's former object of desire, pianist and singer Delfina Potocka, and Chopin's old school friend, Aleksander Jełowicki, who had become a priest.

Many of Chopin's Catholic friends had expressed their anxiety at Chopin's lapse of faith, and that he had done nothing to prepare himself spiritually for death. Chopin and Fr. Jełowicki spoke often about God, the nature of faith and the Church. Chopin admitted that he was not really a believer, but went along with the priest – perhaps more for friendship's sake than for spiritual reasons, and listened attentively to his lectures and advice.

I have had two haemorrhages during the last night. But I have done nothing about it. I just spit blood, but already much less.

Chopin to Wojciech Grzymała (Paris, 22 June 1849)

On Thursday 21 June Chopin suffered two haemorrhages in quick succession, and coughed up quantities of blood. He put it down to his overall condition, and decided not to make a fuss of it, but Mrs Matuszewska reported the matter and as a result Dr Jean Cruveilhier, a physician of some considerable repute, was called to attend to him. Dr Cruveilhier recognised the final stages of consumption, and prescribed only rest and such alleviation of suffering as could be effected in the given circumstances.

I am very weak. I have some sort of diarrhoea. Yesterday I consulted Cruveille [sic] who advises me to take almost nothing, and just keep still. He said that if homeopathy had done me good in Molin's time, that was because it did not overload me with medicaments and left much to nature. But I see that he also regards me as consumptive.

Chopin to Wojciech Grzymała (Paris, 10 July 1849)

Paris, Place Vendôme

Thanks to his banker friend Thomas Albrecht, Chopin, already a very sick man, moved to 12 place Vendôme in September 1849. His sister Ludwika Jędrzejewiczowa, Marcelina Czartoryska, Solange Clésinger, Adolf Gutmann, Thomas Albrecht and Fr. Jełowicki were all present when he died there on 17 October of that year, aged 39. The apartment was situated at the back of the building looking onto the inner courtyard. His body was laid in state in a room on the first floor overlooking the place Vendôme, which today serves as a miniature Chopin museum with a bust of the composer. The apartment is now the showroom of the Jewellers Chaumet.

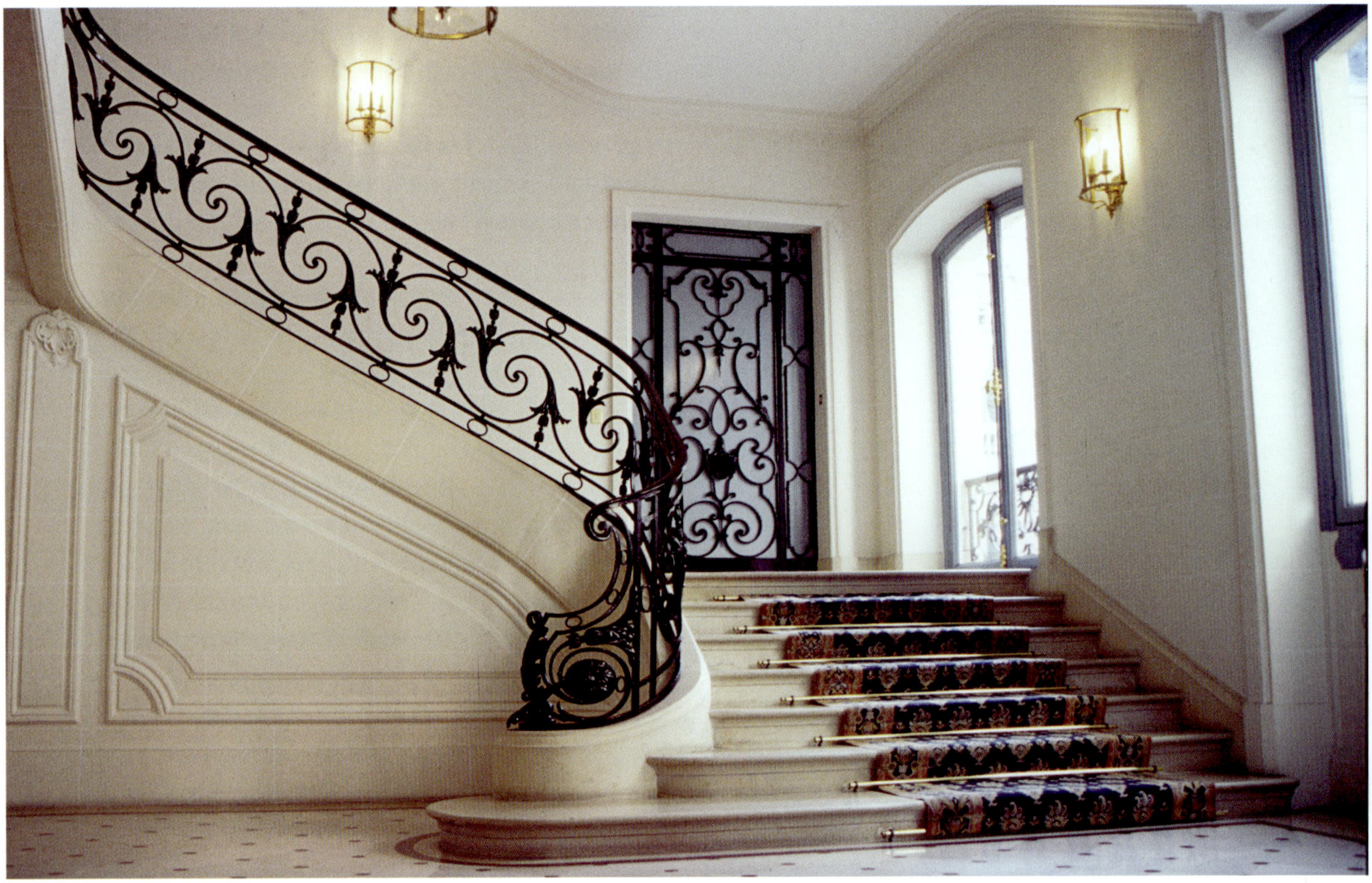

Paris, place Vendôme

The very ornate staicase leading up to Chopin's apartment on the first floor *(by courtesy of the Jewellers Chaumet)*.

All the while Chopin was worried that there was still no sign of his sister Ludwika. The fallout after the pan-European revolutions of the previous year meant that passports and travel permits were subject to bureaucratic hassle, and it was not until Thursday 9 August that the Jędrzejewiczs finally managed to get to Paris. Ludwika was appalled at her brother's condition, finding him very tired and suffering from insomnia and constant coughing fits.

George Sand, who had been receiving conflicting reports about Chopin's health, heard of Ludwika's arrival, and contacted her. Calling on their previous friendship, Sand reckoned that she would get the true picture from Chopin's sister, adding that:

[...] memory of me has evidently been besmirched in your heart, but I think I deserve a word after all that I have suffered.

Ludwika, whose memory of Sand was indeed besmirched, chose not to reply.

In the middle of August Chopin moved back to his apartment in the square d'Orléans, where his condition worsened. A very concerned Dr Cruveilhier summoned two colleagues, Dr Blache and Dr Louis for consultation, further advice and opinions. The idea of Chopin travelling to a warmer climate was dismissed as out of the question. Finding a warmer, sunnier and more comfortable apartment was suggested as the most suitable course of action. Chopin's friend, banker Thomas Albrecht, had an office in the place Vendôme, a prestigious address in one of the French capital's smartest squares. Through him Chopin secured the tenancy of No 12, situated in the same building, of a spacious, seven-room, first floor apartment overlooking the elegant square, dominated by the imposing Grande Armée column and the statue of Napoleon. The prospect of living in this splendid place filled Chopin with hope, and he began making plans for the purchase of furniture, carpets and curtains.

On Sunday 7 October, as he was being examined by a doctor, Chopin muttered that he was in extreme agony, adding, uncharacteristically, that God shows man a rare favour when he reveals to him the actual approach of death. He then asked the doctor to leave him alone. This latest development caused even more visits, some of which were prolonged watches in the adjoining rooms. Moscheles called, as did the devoutly Catholic poet Bohdan Zaleski, one of those anxious about Chopin's lapsed faith. In fact Chopin began asking his friends to pray for him, and listened attentively to their recitations of litanies.

By Friday 12 October Chopin's legs and belly were beginning to swell. Dr Cruveilhier arrived and was so alarmed at Chopin's difficulty in breathing, that he thought death was only a matter of hours away. On Saturday October 13 Fr. Jełowicki again called, and begged him for his soul. This time Chopin conceded. *Take it*, he said. It was then that Chopin received the Last Sacrament with every sign of devotion and sincerity.

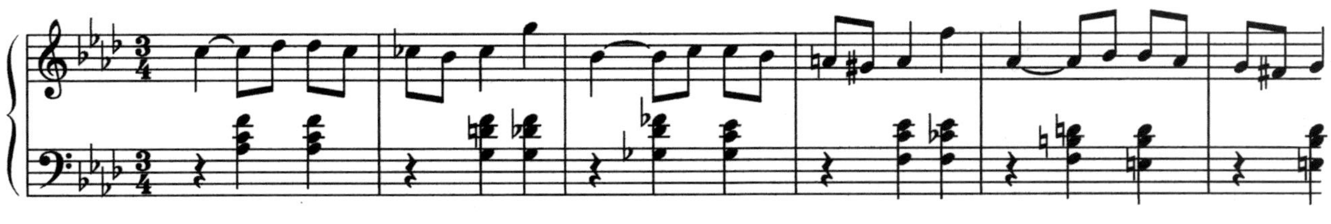

The impressionistic, descending harmonic chord pattern of his Mazurka in F minor Op. 68 No 4 suggests Chopin may have been aware that it was to be his final composition.

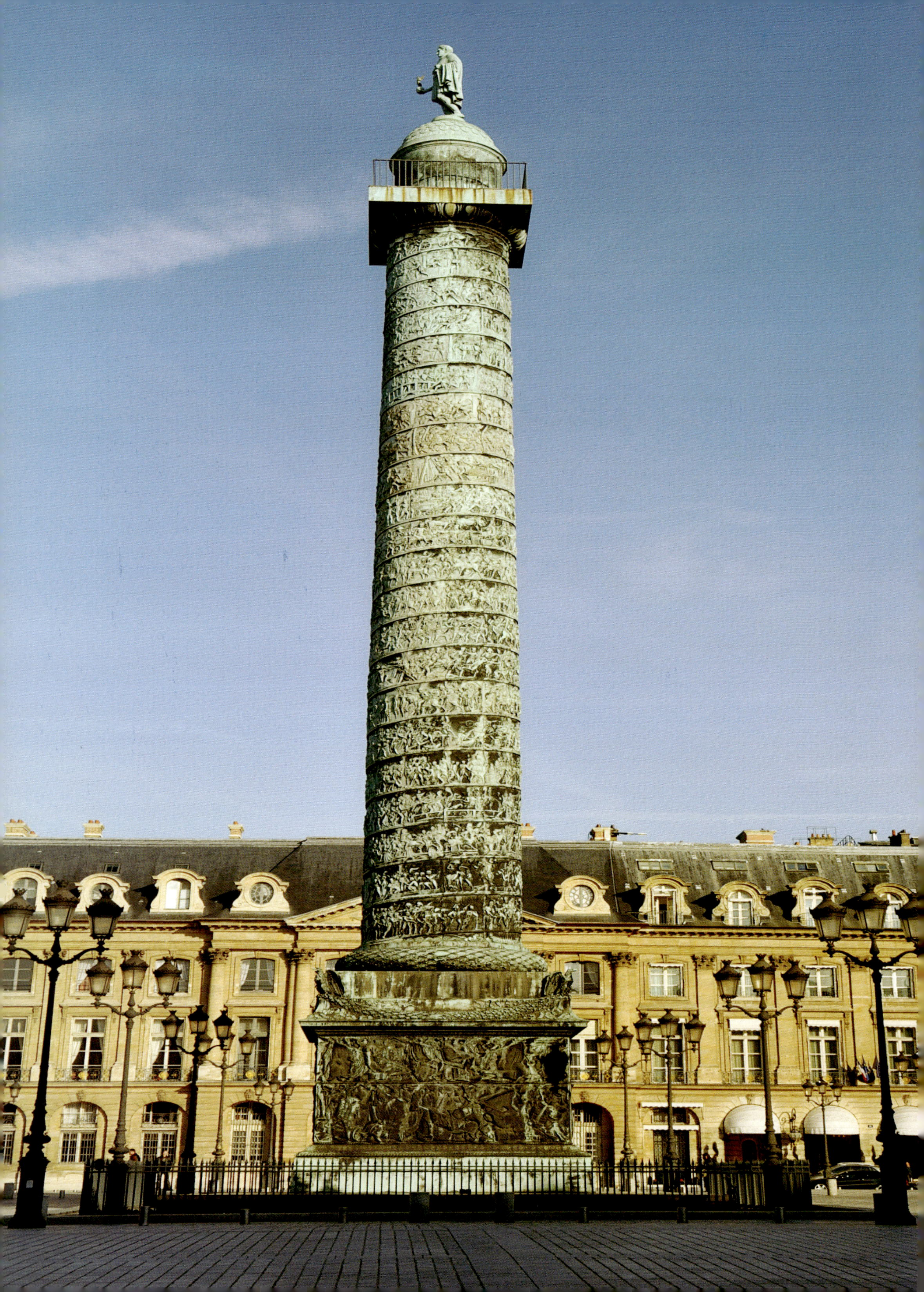

On Monday 15 October, Delfina Potocka arrived in Paris from Nice, and rushed to Chopin's bedside. Chopin was delighted to see her, saying that God had delayed so long in calling him because He wished him still the pleasure of seeing her. He then asked her to sing for him. Gavard, who was there, helped move the piano in the next room to the doorway, and thus Delfina, through her barely controlled sobs, managed to sing to the dying man, accompanying herself on the piano. Her second song was interrupted by Chopin's fit of coughing and what sounded like a death rattle. Marcelina and Franchômme also played him his own Cello Sonata, but that, too, had to be aborted when Chopin broke into a violent coughing fit.

By now Chopin was unable to speak, and could only scribble messages on a piece of paper.

On Tuesday 16 October there was much coming and going at 12 place Vendôme. Friends congregated at Chopin's bedside, or in the other rooms. Chopin was conscious and lucid for most of the day, and asked that after his death his heart should be removed from his body and taken to Warsaw. He also requested that Mozart's Requiem be played at his funeral. The watch continued throughout the evening. About two hours into Wednesday 17 October Fryderyk Chopin died, aged 39, in the presence of Ludwika Jędrzejewiczowa, Marcelina Czartoryska, Solange Clésinger, Adolf Gutmann, Thomas Albrecht and Fr. Jełowicki.

On Tuesday 30 October Paris ground to a standstill as three thousand people attended Chopin's funeral at the Madeleine. Pauline Viardot and Luigi Lablache were the soloists in a performance of Mozart's *Requiem*. As the coffin was being borne out of the crypt, the orchestra played the Funeral March from Chopin's Sonata in B flat minor.

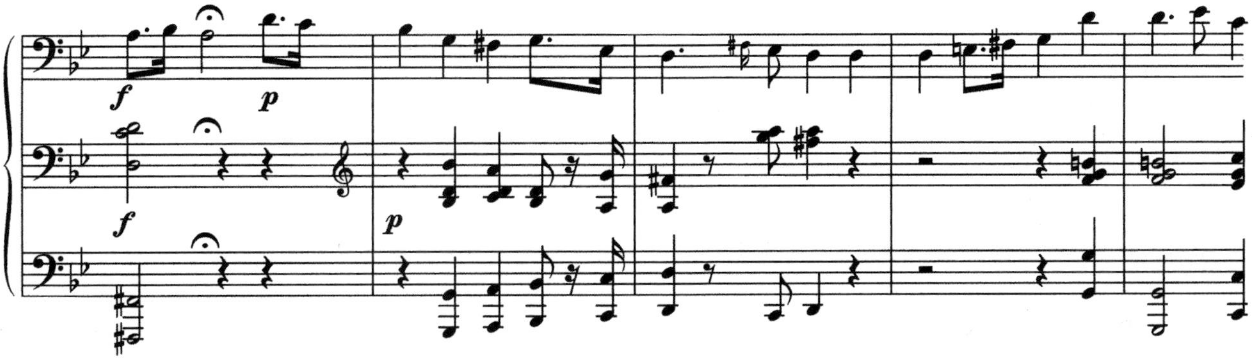

Chopin's Cello Sonata, which Auguste Franchômme and Marcelina Czartoryska played at the composer's death bed.

Paris, Grande Armée Column

This imposing landmark, modeled on Trajan's column, was erected by Napoleon to commemorate the battle of Austerlitz. A statue of Napoleon, bare-headed, crowned with laurels and holding a sword in his right hand and a globe surmounted with a statue of Victory in his left hand, was placed on the top. The square itself, formerly the site of the Hôtel de César, duc de Vendôme, the illegitimate son of Henri IV and his mistress Gabrielle d'Estriées, was laid out in 1702 as a monument to the glory of the armies of Louis XIV.

Fryderyk Chopin was laid to rest in the Père Lachaise Cemetery on the eastern outskirts of Paris. Ludwika later smuggled his heart, preserved in a glass vessel filled with alcohol, first back to her home in Warsaw, then to the Church of the Holy Cross, in the Krakowskie Przedmieście, where it was stored in the catacombs. In 1880 the casket containing Chopin's heart was set into the wall of the church, where it remained until 1944, when German soldiers knocked down the wall and removed the casket with the urn. They took the relic to Commander-in-Chief General von dem Bach, who chose to return it to Archbishop Antoni Szlagowski. The heart was then concealed in various hiding places in Milanówek, and on 17 October 1945, exactly 96 years after Chopin's death, it was handed over to the Chopin Society. After a spell at Żelazowa Wola, Chopin's heart was finally returned to its rightful resting place at the Church of the Holy Cross.

No trace remains of 74 rue Chaillot, but No 12 place Vendôme now houses the Chaumet showroom, and the little room where Chopin lay in state at the front of the building is now a Chopin mini-museum. The Madeleine thrives today as one of Paris' great landmarks, as is Chopin's grave at the Père Lachaise Cemetery.

The most valuable mementoes connected with Chopin and his era are now housed at the Polish Library at 6 quai d'Orléans in Paris, and also in the newly restored Fryderyk Chopin Museum at the Ostrogski Castle in Warsaw.

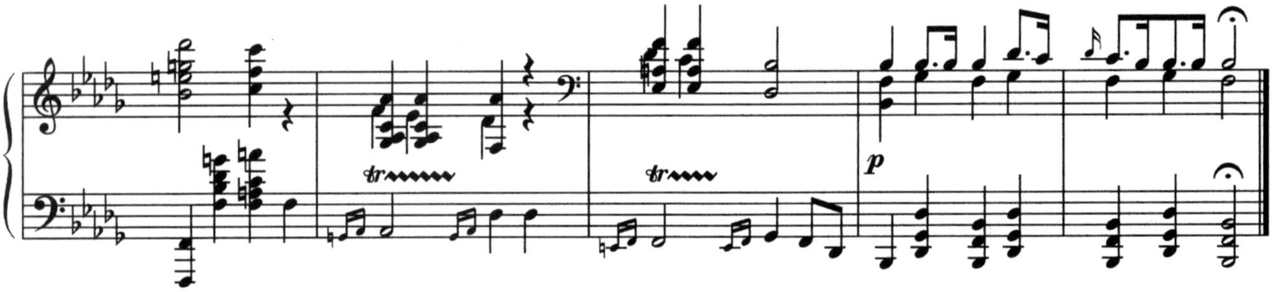

The closing bars of the Funeral March from his Piano Sonata in B flat minor was played at Chopin's funeral at the Madeleine.

Paris, the Madeleine Church

Chopin's Funeral took place at the Church of the Madeleine on Tuesday 30 October 1849. The event was attended by 3000 invited mourners. The front of the church, which had only been completed a few years earlier, was draped in black velvet and embroidered with the initials F.C. The service began with Chopin's own Funeral March from his Sonata in B flat minor, as his coffin was carried to the altar. Mozart's *Requiem* was then performed during the Mass by the chorus and orchestra of the Paris Conservatoire.

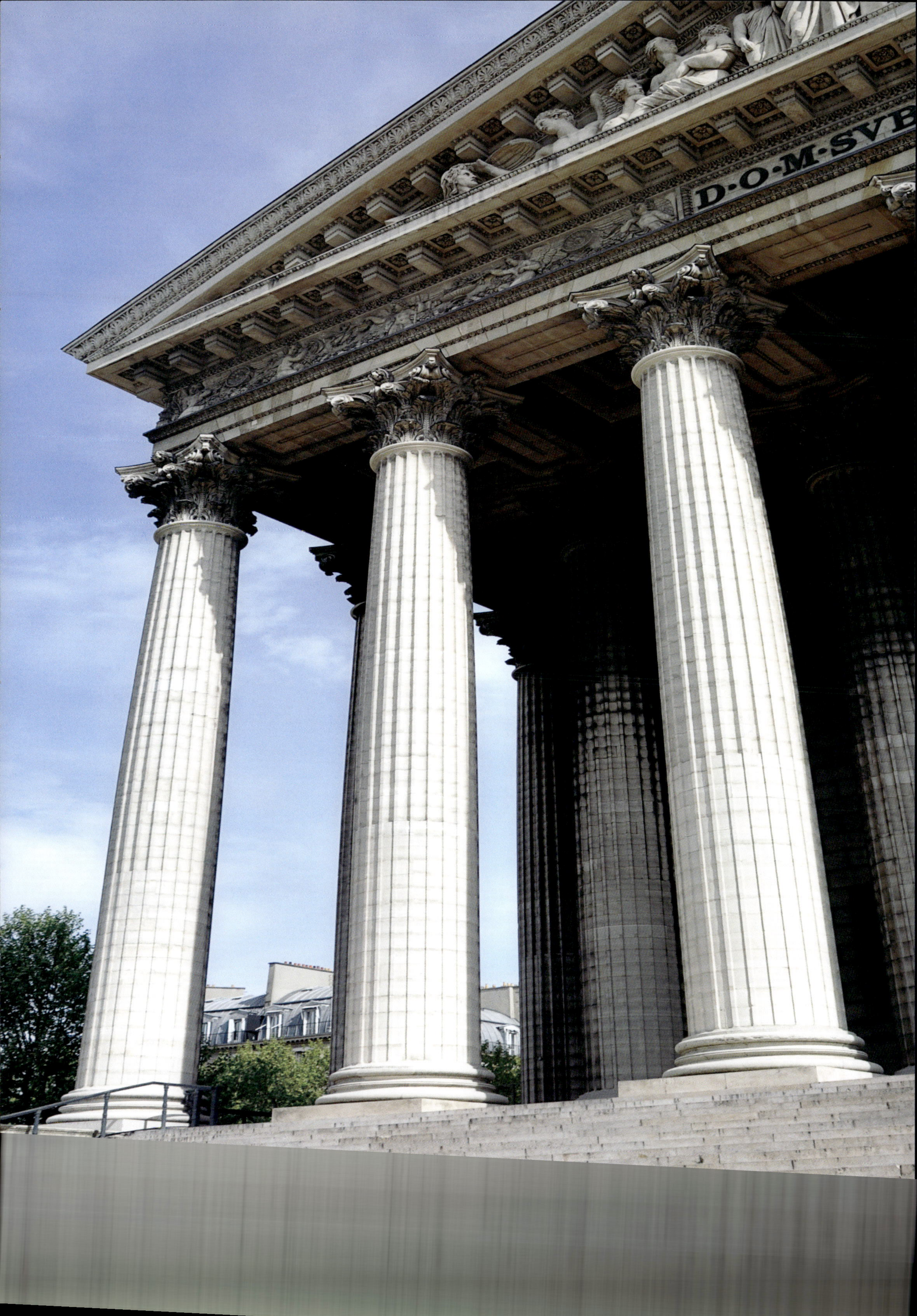
D·O·M·SVB

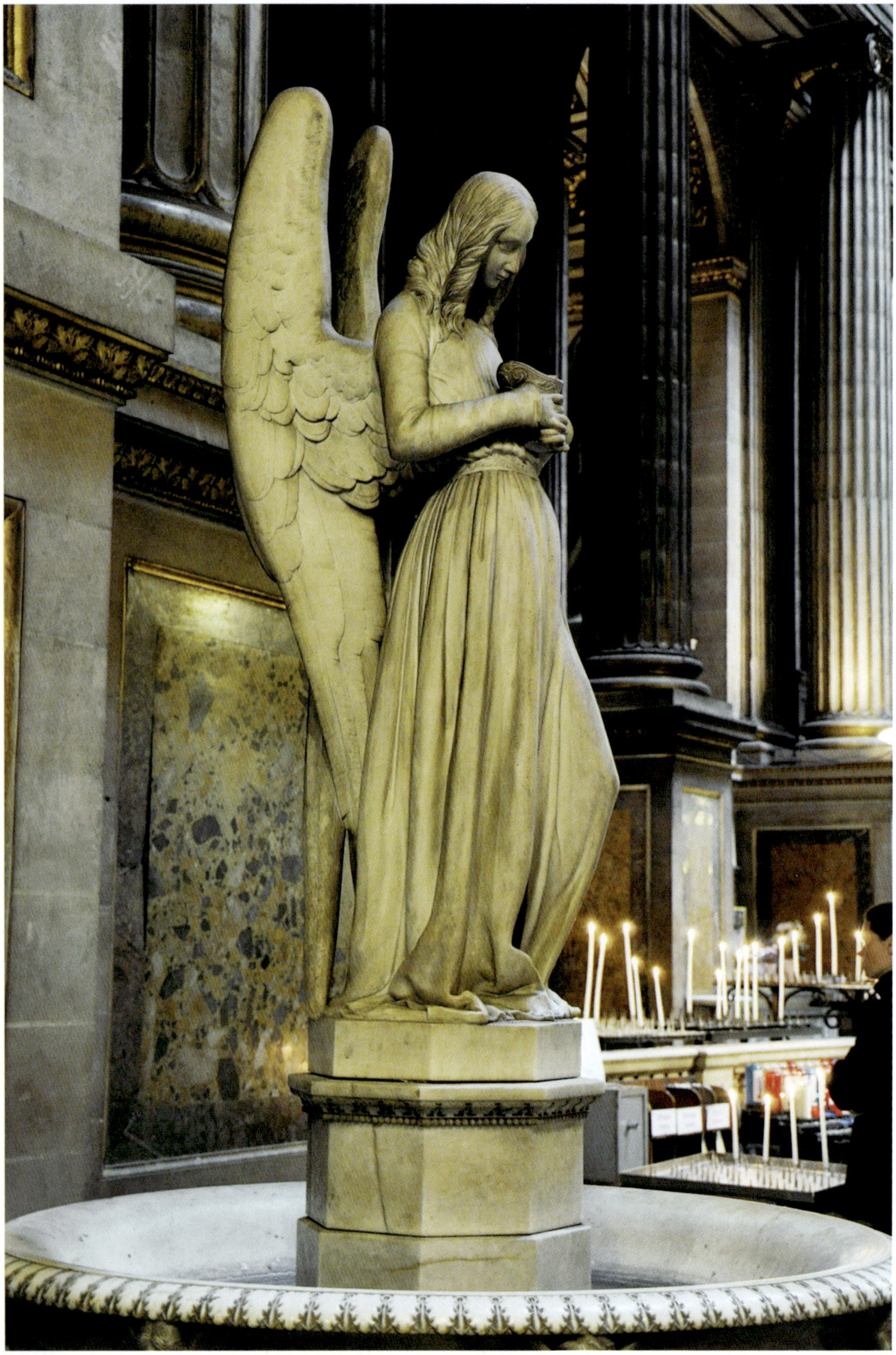

Paris, the Madeleine Church

At the end of the service Chopin's coffin was borne out of the church by pallbearers: Prince Adam Czartoryski, Meyerbeer, Delacroix, Pleyel and Gutmann. Then the whole procession walked to the Père Lachaise cemetery behind a horse drawn hearse. Many thousands followed on foot all the way.

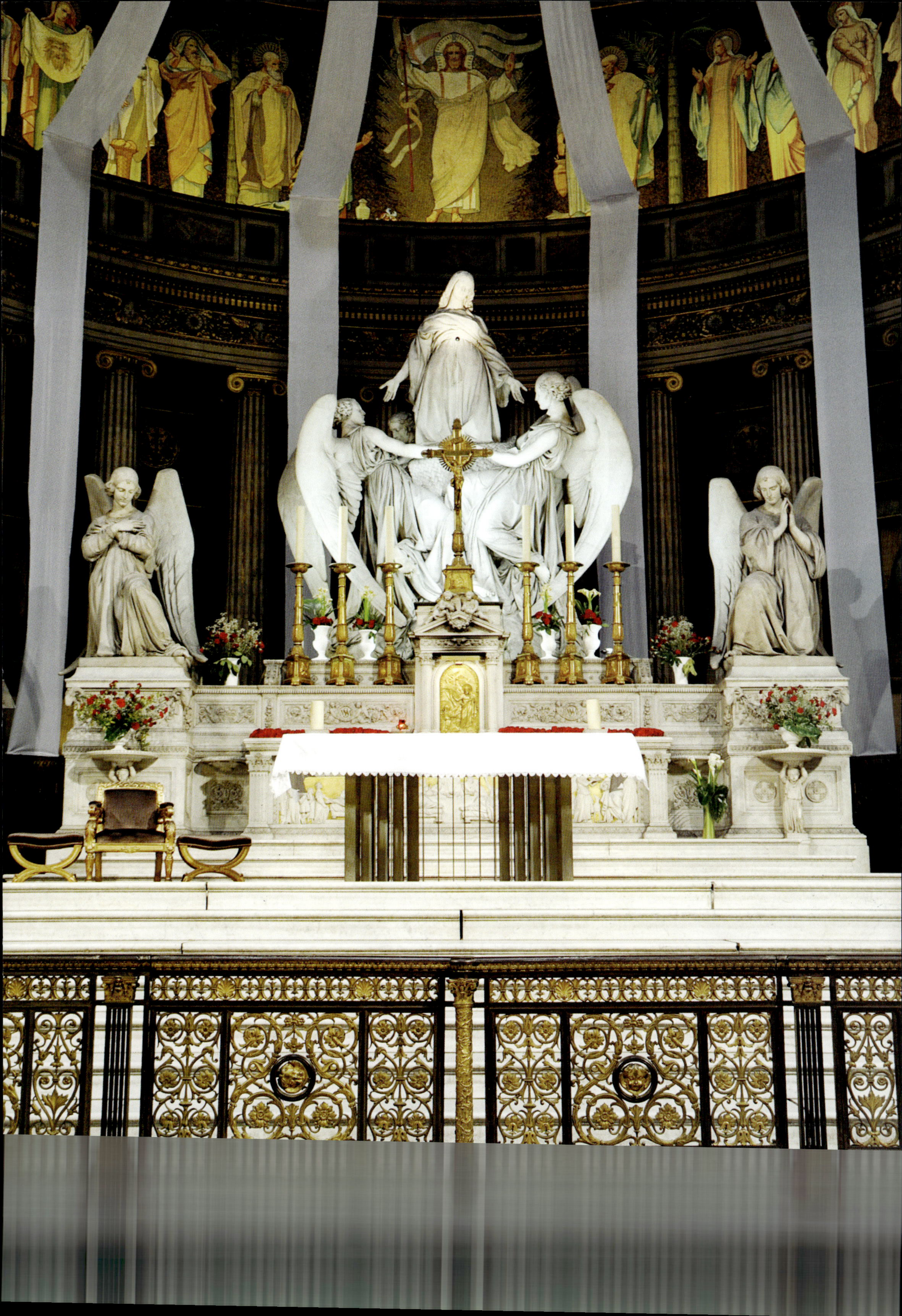

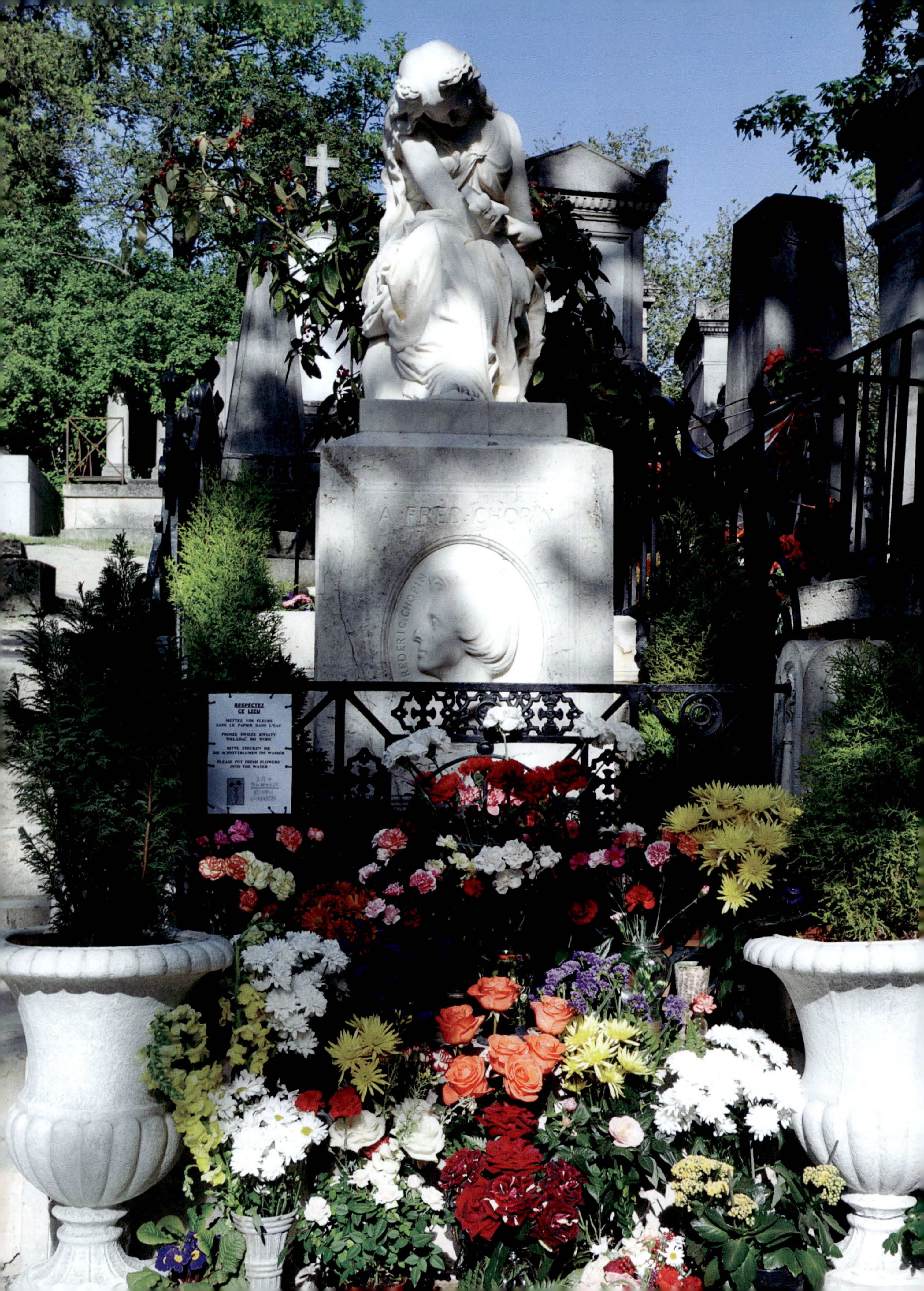
A FRED. CHOPIN
REDERIC CHOPIN
RESPECTEZ
CE LIEU
METTEZ VOS FLEURS
SANS LE PAPIER DANS L'EAU
PROSZĘ ŚWIEŻE KWIATY
WKŁADAĆ DO WODY
BITTE STECKEN SIE
DIE SCHNITTBLUMEN INS WASSER
PLEASE PUT FRESH FLOWERS
INTO THE WATER

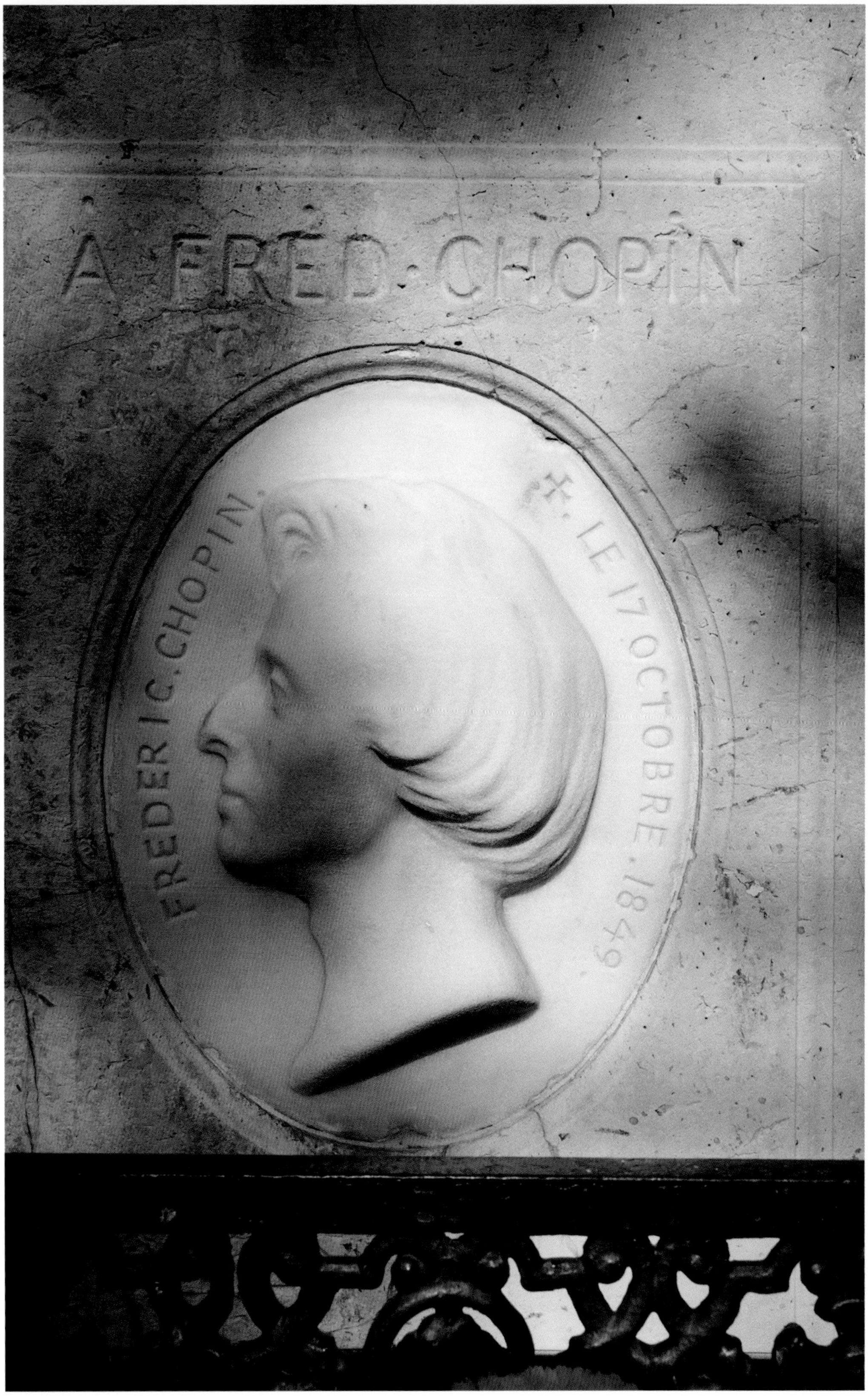

Paris, the Père Lachaise Cemetery

The monument, which still marks Chopin's grave, was sculpted by Solange's husband Auguste Clésinger, and erected there the following year, together with a casket of Polish earth, a bunch of violets and a rose petal from Scotland.

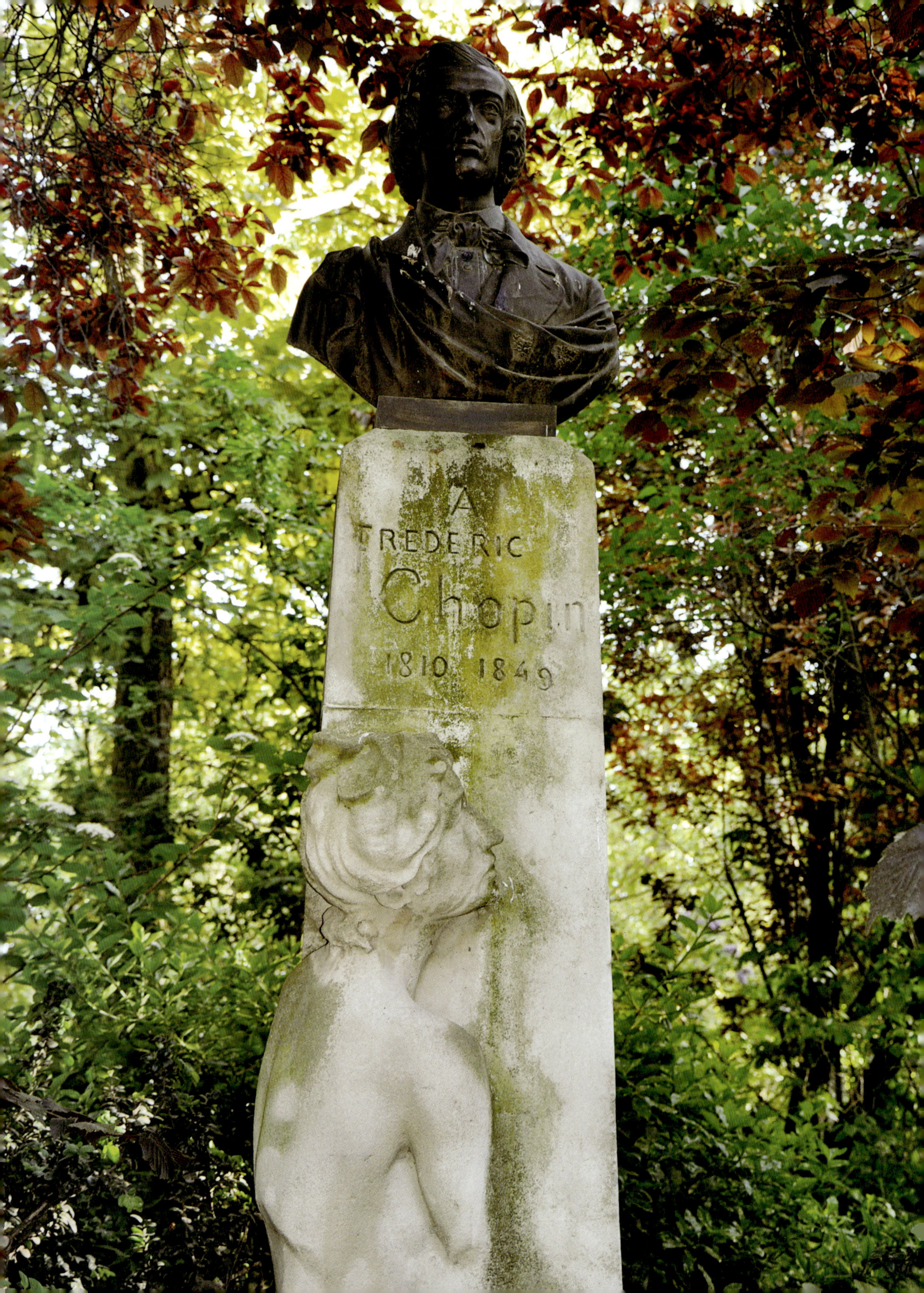
A
FREDERIC
Chopin
1810 1849

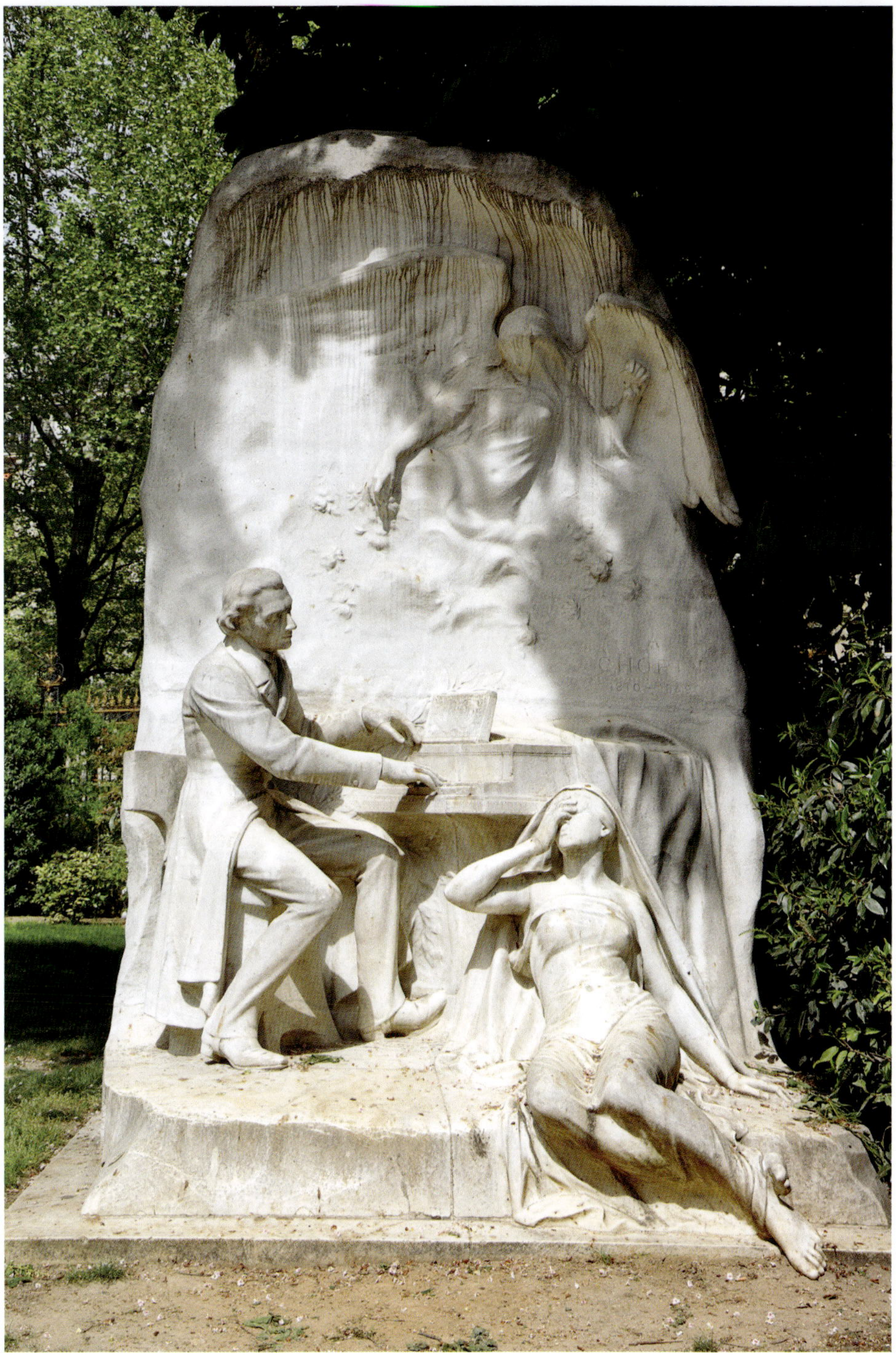

Paris, Parc Monceau

The marble sculpture of Chopin, by Jacques Froment-Meurice (1864–1948), in the Parc Monceau.

← Paris, Jardins de Luxembourg

These Gardens, off rue Guynemer, are the biggest public park in Paris. They contain over 100 busts and monuments to many figures of mythology, royalty, literature and music. Most were commissioned by King Louis Philippe in the 1840s.

... placed on a high pedestal, was only added

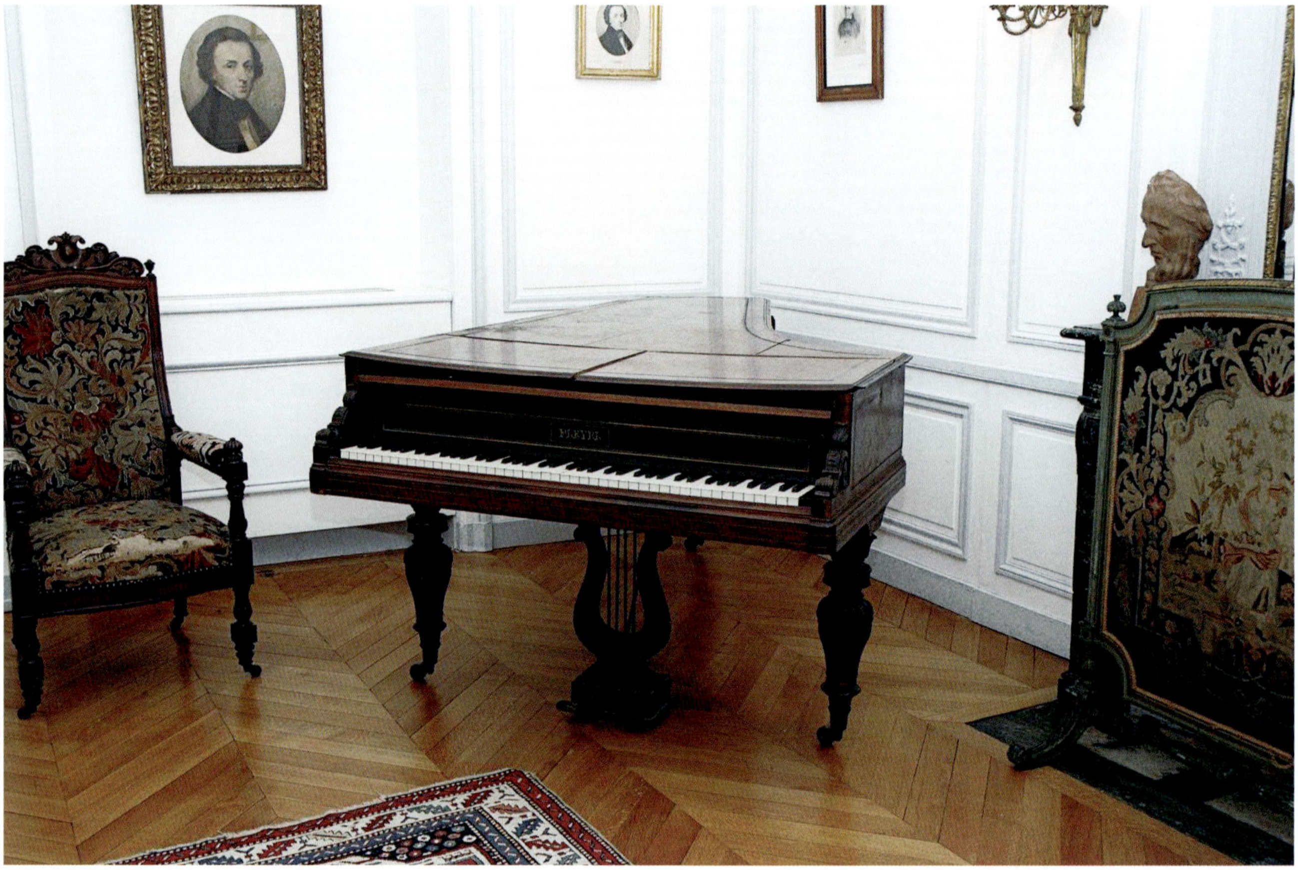

Paris, the Polish Library

The Polish Library in Paris at 6, quai d'Orléans, on the île Saint Louis founded in 1838 is today one of the biggest institutions in the whole world devoted to the Polish culture. One room is set aside in memory of Fryderyk Chopin and in fact is the only Chopin museum in France where you can find many interesting mementos of the 18 years of his life spent in Paris including Chopin's Pleyel piano of 1845. According to tradition Chopin would have played on this Pleyel "demi-queue" piano of 1845 while living in square d'Orléans. A contemporary drawing of Chopin's apartment shows an identical piano, but whether this was the actual model is not known. The piano was donated in 2006 to the Polish Library in Paris by Madame Catherine Migaux, daughter of the composer Pierre Migaux and Madame Christine Migaux, professor of music at the Conservatoire Maurice Ravel in Pontoise
(by courtesy of the Polish Library).

→ Partial view of the Chopin room with photos and mementos including the famous daquerotype, lock of hair and plaster cast of his hand
(by courtesy of the Polish Library).

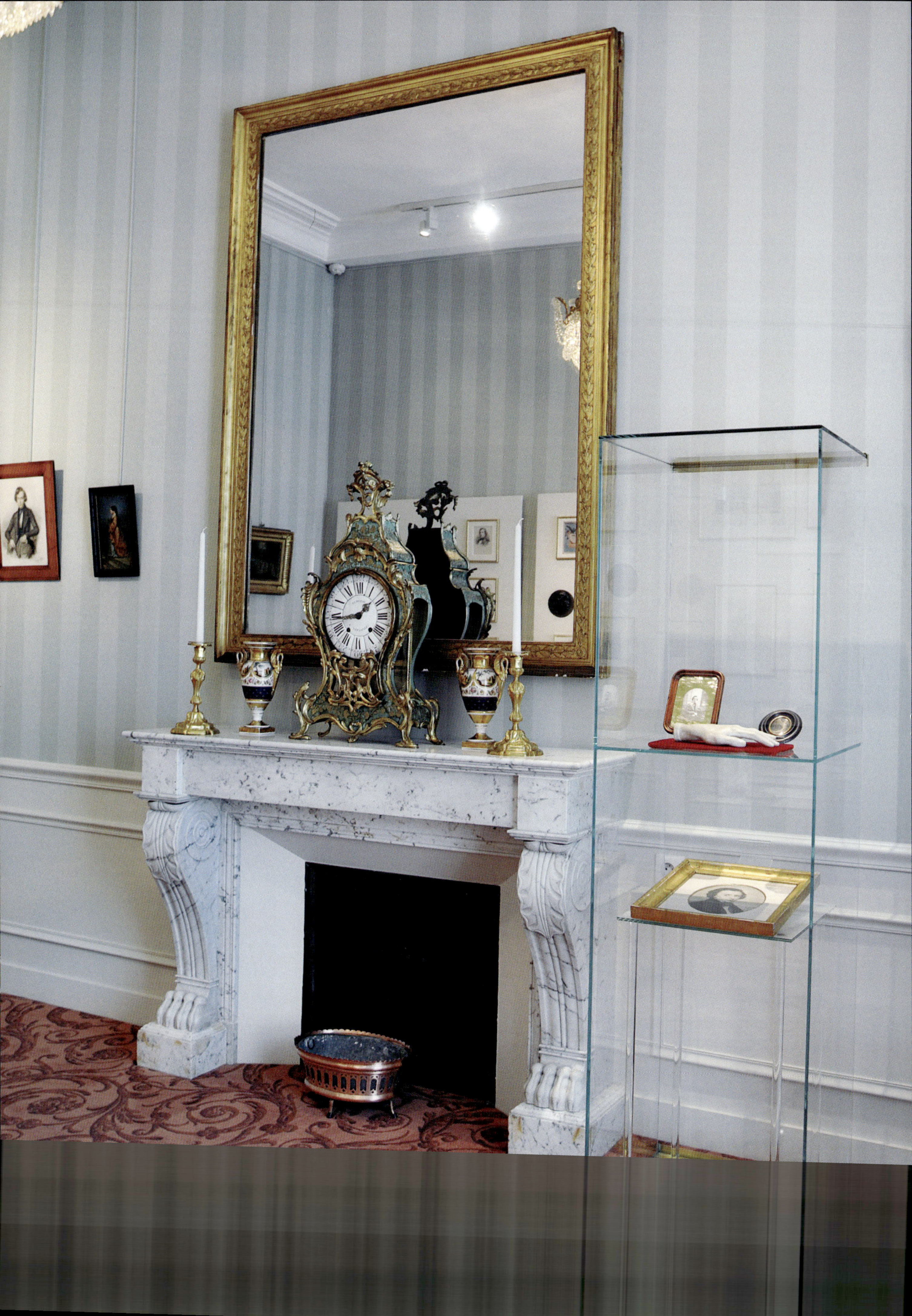

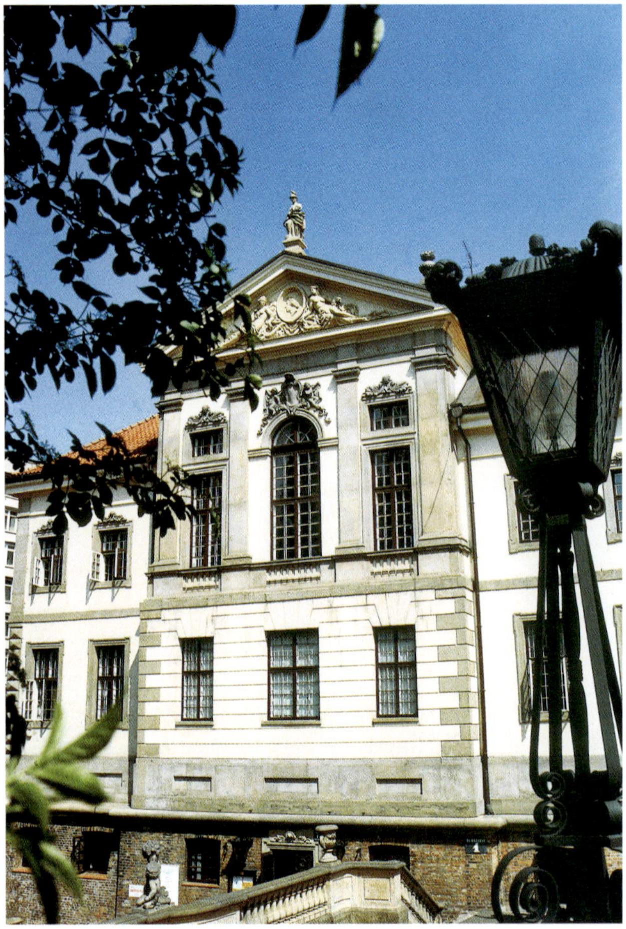

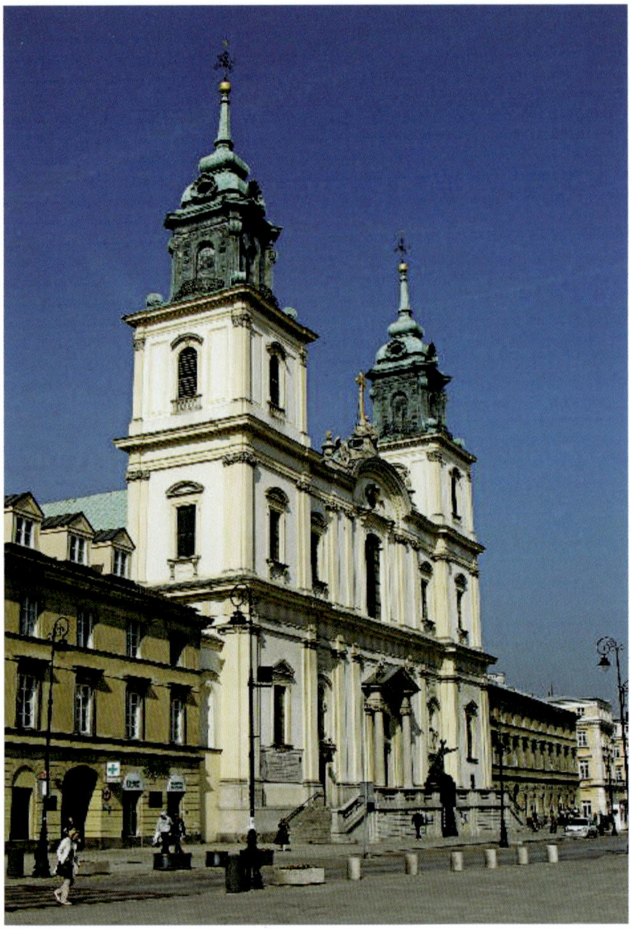

Warsaw, the Ostrogski Castle

This castle, which was a fortified castle at the beginning of the 17th century but was later reconstructed as a baroque palace to a design by Tylman of Gameren. From the 19th century until World War 2 the Musical Conservatoire was located here. It now houses the Fryderyk Chopin Museum.

Warsaw, Church of Holy Cross

The urn containing Chopin's heart, which was smuggled back to Warsaw by his sister Ludwika, was embedded in a column of this church as requested by the composer.

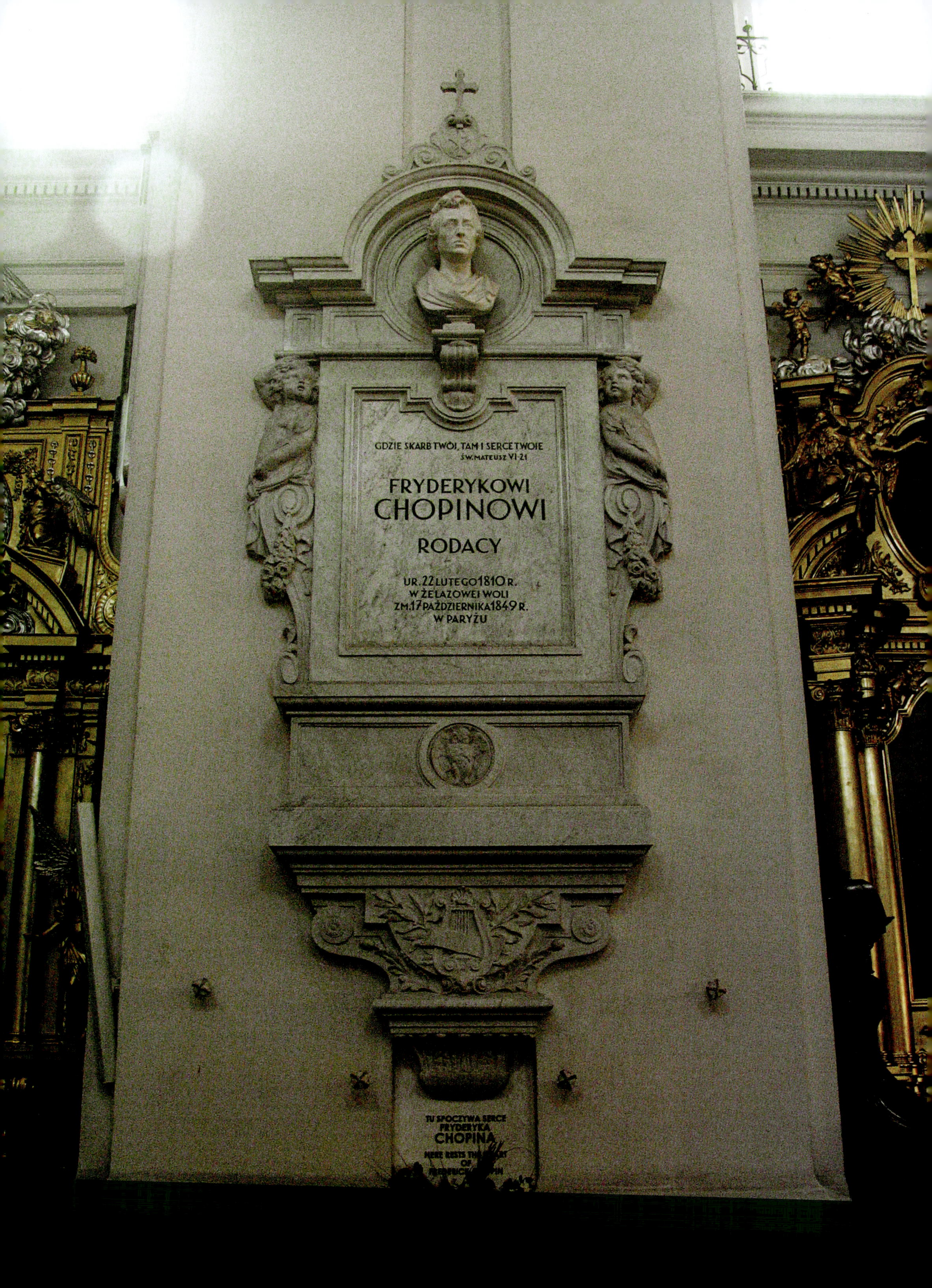
GDZIE SKARB TWÓJ, TAM I SERCE TWOJE
ŚW. MATEUSZ VI-21
FRYDERYKOWI
CHOPINOWI
RODACY
UR. 22 LUTEGO 1810 R.
W ŻELAZOWEJ WOLI
ZM. 17 PAŹDZIERNIKA 1849 R.
W PARYŻU
TU SPOCZYWA SERCE
FRYDERYKA
CHOPINA
OF

The book printed on paper
Arctic Silk+ 130 g/m²

Arctic
BY ARCTIC PAPER

www.arcticpaper.com

Sport i Turystyka – MUZA SA
ul. Marszałkowska 8
00-590 Warszawa
ph. +48 (22) 6297624, 6296524
e-mail:info@muza.com.pl

Order: +48 (22) 6286360, 6293201
Online store: www.muza.com.pl

Warsaw 2010
First Edition

Printing preparation: Jacek Jutrzenka
Printing and binding: DRUK-INTRO S.A., Inowrocław